Case Studies in Jewish Business Ethics

THE LIBRARY OF JEWISH LAW AND ETHICS
VOLUME XXII
Edited by Norman Lamm

Jakob and Erna Michael Professor of Jewish Philosophy
Yeshiva University

Case Studies in Jewish Business Ethics

by

Aaron Levine

KTAV PUBLISHING HOUSE, INC.
HOBOKEN

YESHIVA UNIVERSITY PRESS
NEW YORK

Copyright © 2000 Aaron Levine
Library of Congress Cataloging-in-Publication Data

Levine, Aaron.
    Case studies in Jewish business ethics / by Aaron Levine
        p. cm.-- (Library of Jewish law and ethics ; v. 22)
    Includes bibliographical references and indexes.
    ISBN 0-88125-673-0 (hard cover) -- ISBN 0-88125-664-1 (paper)
        1. Business ethics--Case studies. 2. Ethics, Jewish--Case studies. 3.
    Business--Religious aspects--Judaism--Case studies. I. Title. II. Series.

HF5387.L48 1999 2000
174'.4'089924--dc21   99-049964

        Manufactured in the United States of America
        Distributed by KTAV Publishing House, Inc.
    900 Jefferson Street, Hoboken, New Jersey 07030

For Sarah

My beloved wife and life companion,
my wisest and best friend.

Table of Contents

Foreword

The Library of Jewish Law and Ethics is proud to present yet another impressive work from the pen of Professor Aaron Levine whose specialty is the interface between Halakha (Jewish law) and ethics on one side, and economics—both in theory and in practice—on the other.

What makes this volume very special, and different from the author's previous excellent contributions to the field, is the direction of his instruction; it is from the bottom up, not from the top down. In the latter, he followed a logistical course—from basic principles to specific instances in the world of economics. In the present volume, the direction is reversed—from the particulars of real-life situations to the broader general theories that govern the marketplace from the point of view of classical Jewish law.

If nothing else, this case-study methodology ensures sustained interest by the reader whose main concern is the practical application of Judaic teachings to his/her encounters as an economic person. This inductive, as opposed to deductive, method allows the discussion to appear more related and relevant to the business of business.

The reader should be sensitive to an interesting facet of this study, and that is the relationship between Jewish law and Jewish ethics. There is a plethora of learned articles and books dealing with this issue in a general philosophical fashion. In Judaism, the lines are more blurred, more resistant to clear distinctions and clean lines of demarcation. Indeed, there are those who hold that in Judaism it is of stylistic and not substantive significance. I urge the reader to take note of how our author deals with the law-ethics relationship without necessarily tackling the subject directly. In other words, read the book in a case-study mode... It will prove edifying as well as fascinating.

Norman Lamm, Editor
The Library of Jewish Law and Ethics

Acknowledgments

The preparation and publication of this volume were made possible in part by a grant from the Memorial Foundation for Jewish Culture.

The final stage in the technical preparation of the work was aided by a grant from Yeshiva University. I gratefully acknowledge Dr. William Schwartz, University Professor of Law and former academic vice president, for securing this grant for me, and for his warm encouragement.

Several of the case studies in this volume draw upon earlier articles: "The Firing of Claudia Weinstock" is adapted from my article, "Performance Appraisal and Halakha," in *Hazon Nahum*, eds. Yaakov Elman and Jeffrey S. Gurock (New York: Michael Scharf Publication Trust of Yeshiva University Press, 1997), pp. 598–626; "Toys for Guns" was adapted from my article "Aspects of the Ideology of Capitalism and Judaism," in *Tikun Olam*, eds. David Shatz, Chaim I. Waxman, and Nathan J. Diament (Northvale, N.J.: Jason Aronson, 1997), pp. 265–308.

The case studies "Protecting the Reasonable Man Against Deception in Advertising," "Trading on Superior and Insider Information," and "Insider Trading and Public Policy" draw upon my volume *Economic Public Policy and Jewish Law* (Hoboken, N.J.: Ktav, 1993). The materials have been reworked and expanded.

The case studies "AT&T's Specialty Directory," "Dr. Eric Delbarko and Medical Information Bias," and "Ethical Investment: The Case of Rawley Tobacco" are based on materials I presented at the Eighth Orthodox Forum of Yeshiva University. Under the editorship of my colleague, Dr. Moses L. Pava, and myself, the Proceedings of the Eighth Orthodox Forum will be published by Jason Aronson.

One of my objectives in writing this book was to provide a halakhic analogue to the philosophical approaches that underlie secular business ethics theory today. Toward this end, I have adapted for use in this volume a number of case studies that appear in the secular business ethics literature: "Rubie Indigo's Adventures into Veiled Misconduct" is based, in part, on Paul Blumberg's *The Predatory Society: Deceptions in the American Marketplace* (New York: Oxford

University Press, 1989); "The Encyclopedia Salesman" is based, in part, on a case study that appeared in John B. Mathews, Kenneth E. Goodpaster, and Laura L. Nash, *Policies and Persons: A Case Book in Business Ethics* (New York: McGraw-Hill, 1985), pp. 9–22; "Make the Customer Like You: The Limits of Flattery" is based, in part, on James W. Pickens, *The Art of Closing Any Deal* (New York: Warner Books, 1989); "The Pricing of Pharmaceuticals" draws from a case study appearing in N. Craig Smith and John A. Quelch, *Ethics in Marketing* (Homewood, Ill.: Irwin, 1993); "Lay-offs at Rechev" is based, in part, on a case study by Harold Oaklander in *Case Studies in Business Ethics*, ed. Thomas Donaldson and Al Gini, 3rd ed. (Englewood Cliffs, N.J.: Prentice-Hall, 1993), pp. 153–63.

A note of thanks to members of my family who contributed to this project. My son-in-law and daughter, Drs. Lyle and Bat-Sheva Mitzner, provided insightful comments on material relating to the medical profession. My daughter Aliza made a number of incisive comments and valuable editorial suggestions. In addition, my debt of gratitude to her for inputting on a disk numerous rounds of eleventh-hour addenda to the manuscript. In the experiences of certain of the characters that appear in the case studies, my children discovered autobiographical tidbits of their father's life. I agree. But enough fiction was spliced in to blur or even transmogrify actual events.

My dear friend, Leon M. Metzger, provided a critical reading of this work. His insightful comments, probing questions, uncanny ability to spot ambiguities, and his editorial suggestions made for an improved final product. I am grateful to him for his contribution to this work.

I benefited from the insights and/or assistance of the following: Rabbi Dr. J. David Bleich, Professor Leonard Brandwein, Rabbi Shalom Carmy, Rabbi Irwin I. Haut, Rabbi Dr. Jerry Hochbaum, Rabbi Dr. Israel M. Kirzner, Yaakov Kornreich, Rabbi Dr. Joshua Krausz, Nathan Lewin, Esq., Professor Moses L. Pava, Rabbi Daniel Rapp, Professor Steven H. Resnicoff, Rabbi Hershel Schachter, Dr. Shmuel Shilo, Dr. Norman Rosenfeld, Dr. Hayim Tawil, Dr. Clarence Walton, and Rabbi Mordechai Willig.

The manuscript of this work was typed by Harriet Nachmann. My gratitude to her for her proficiency, alacrity, and incredible reliability. She has an uncanny knack for making order out of chaos.

This volume is the fourth work that I have been privileged to have included in the Library of Jewish Law and Ethics. To the editor, Rabbi Dr. Norman Lamm, president of Yeshiva University, my heartfelt appreciation for his warm encouragement and for the many kindnesses he has extended to me over these many years.

On the occasion of the publication of this volume, I would like to express my appreciation to my academic deans, Dr. Norman Adler of Yeshiva College, Dr. Karen Bacon of Stern College, and Rabbi Dr. Michael D. Shmidman, Dean of the undergraduate programs of Jewish studies of Yeshiva College. My debt of gratitude to them for their outstanding academic leadership. My heartfelt appreciation for their enthusiastic encouragement, and for the personal interest they have taken in my scholarship.

My heartfelt appreciation to Rabbi Dr. Michael Hecht, Rebbe MBHS, professor and associate dean, Yeshiva College. An exemplary model of *Torah u-madda*, his warm friendship and abiding interest in my work have been for me a constant source of encouragement.

For the past eighteen years, I have offered a course in Jewish business ethics at both Stern College and Yeshiva College. Much of the material in this volume has been woven into its curriculum. The course proved to be a vehicle for getting students involved in the current project.

Elisha Graff devoted himself to the project in a truly unforgettable manner. My gratitude to him for his research assistance and for his meticulous work in validating a substantial number of the sources cited in this work.

Yohanan Donath compiled the name index and provided very valuable computer and technical assistance in preparing the manuscript for publication. My gratitude to him for his enthusiasm and single-minded devotion.

My gratitude to Dror Barber for his meticulous work in validating sources and for his technical and computer assistance.

My sincere thanks to Mordecai Gluck and David Mintz for their technical and computer assistance.

I am delighted that this work will make its debut as a textbook in my course, *Economics and Ethical Issues.* The course will be offered in the honors program at Yeshiva College. My thanks to Dean Norman Adler for arranging a stipend from this program to support the preparation of the name and subject indices of this volume.

To the publisher of this work, Mr. Bernard Scharfstein of Ktav, my sincere thanks for his prodding to do this project, and for the enthusiasm and encouragement he has offered.

Dr. Yaakov Elman, associate editor at Ktav and distinguished colleague at Yeshiva University, scrupulously read the entire manuscript and made many valuable suggestions, both substantive and editorial. My debt of gratitude to him.

To Mr. Robert J. Milch, copy editor for Ktav Publishing House, my sincere thanks for his meticulous and resourceful work on my manuscript.

Throughout this project my research was aided by the professionalism and the many amenities extended to me by the library staff of Yeshiva University. In particular, I would like to thank Zalman Alpert, Zvi Erenyi, Chaya Gordon, Rabbi Theodore Lasdun, Rabbi Berish Mandelbaum, Rabbi Yaakov Schulman of the Mendel Gottesman Library; David Crugnola, Avrohom Krohn, and John Moryl of the Pollack Library; and Professor Edith Lubetski (head), Barbara Axelrod, Shulamit Cohn, Sarah Leah Gross, Hindishe Lee, and Vivian Moskovitz of the Hedi Steinberg Library.

New York
Aaron Levine
15 Menahem Av 5759

Introduction

An ancient parable is told of a king who imprisoned a sharp-witted, pious young man by the name of Nosson ha-Harif (lit. the sharp one). One day, the king visited Nosson in the dungeon and told him that he was giving him a chance to gain his freedom:

"This dungeon has two doors. One leads to your freedom, but the other opens into a den of lions. You must choose which door you want to go through. To help you decide, I'm placing two parrots in the dungeon; one is red, and the other is blue. Both parrots know which door will lead to freedom. One parrot always tells the truth, the other parrot always lies. You can pose one question to either of the two parrots. If you're really close to God, you should be able to discover the truth regarding the doors."

It took but a few moments for the anxious look on Nosson's face to turn into a serene smile. An inspiration had overcome him. The "sharp one" was sure he knew how to find out the truth about the doors.

"I'll ask one of the parrots—it doesn't matter which one—to tell me which door the *other* parrot claims will lead to my freedom, and then I'll ask to be led out the *other* door."

An astonished king eagerly waited for the explanation. Ha-Harif continued:

"Suppose I ask red to tell me which door blue claims will lead to my freedom. Now, if red is the truth-teller, he will *faithfully* report to me which door blue claims will lead to my freedom. But since I am presuming blue to be the liar in this scenario, I will select the other door.

"On the other hand, suppose red is the liar, and blue is the truth-teller. In this scenario, red will *falsely* report which door blue claims will lead to my freedom. Again, I am forced to reject red's recommendation and select the other door."

How should the modern world of business relate to Nosson ha-Harif? Is he a hero or role model of some sort, or someone we should, for the most part, regard as irrelevant? The answer to this question is crucial. It will supply us with the keynote theme for this volume, *Case Studies in Jewish Business Ethics*.

Why not identify with Nosson ha-Harif? Because there is something surreal about him. His nimble-mindedness defeats parrots. But in the marketplace, one's opposite number is a person, not a parrot. The challenge we face is not only to defeat evil but also to resist the temptation to inflict evil upon others.

Indeed, we would not be justified in making Nosson ha-Harif the hero and model for the modern marketplace unless we subscribed to Albert Z. Carr's brand of business ethics. In Carr's conceptualization, business is a game of strategy. The duty of the businessman is no more than to comply with the *letter* of the law. In the sphere of business, morality commonly operates on a lower level than the norms prescribed by religion.[1] In this world, the secret to success is to become Nosson ha-Harif and devise the best strategy regardless of whether our opposite number is a liar or a truth-teller. Moreover, for the one who perceives the marketplace in terms of a game of poker,[2] the use of an occasional bluff or lie should be an easy matter. Why the moral qualms? Initiating deceptive conduct amounts to no more than a preemptive attack against someone who was planning the same or worse against you.

From the perspective of Halakhah (Jewish law), Carr's approach to business ethics must be totally repudiated. For one thing, it is not acceptable for morality to operate in compartmentalized spheres. Rather, ethical norms are meant to permeate every aspect and dimension of the life experience: "In all your ways know Him, and He will straighten your paths" (Proverbs 3:6).[3]

Moreover, man's duty is not summed up as an obligation to comply with the law. Instead, man must apply the law to contexts not explicitly covered by legislation.[4] For contexts where his duty is defined by law, man must show a responsibility and a generosity of spirit *lifnim mi-shurat ha-din* (i.e., beyond the letter of the law).[5] Relatedly, for Halakhah, the ideal is for the individual to conduct himself in a manner that will make his integrity objectively evident. This calls for behavior according to objectively verifiable standards and for commitments formulated in precise and unequivocal terms.[6]

Finally, it behooves us to recognize that Carr's genre of business ethics does not develop in a vacuum. What gives it impetus is a legal system that stresses rights over duties. When an individual operates in a milieu where he expects to find rights, it is an easy matter for him to judge that his rights are threatened and to launch a preemptive attack against those who are bent on depriving him of his due.

In sharp contrast, Halakhah emphasizes duties over rights.[7] Justice Moshe Silberg (Israel, 1900–1975) elaborates on this theme. One example that he gives is how the Bet Din (Jewish court) treats a debt. Satisfaction of a debt is actionable, not primarily as enforcement of the creditor's right, but as a means of compelling the debtor to fulfill his religious duty to pay off his debt. How the

Bet Din handles a debt is the prototype of Judaism's whole system of legal obligations.[8] Within the framework of a system that stresses duties over rights, it should come as no surprise that Halakhah allows a market participant little discretion to decide on his own that his particular duties do not apply to the situation at hand.[9]

The upshot of the above analysis is that Nosson ha-Harif is essentially irrelevant as a model for the market participant. How can we relate to a person who defeats evil with sheer brilliance when our primary concern in the marketplace is to educate ourselves with respect to our duties and resist the temptation to inflict evil upon others?

To be sure, Nosson ha-Harif is not totally irrelevant. In situations where bluffing is a permissible tactic, the ideal is still to extricate ourselves from the circumstances through sagacity rather than connivery.[10]

The Plan of This Work

By means of the case study method, this work will explicate the halakhic principles that govern the marketplace in a variety of interactions.

In the opening two vignettes we make the case for moral education. The work then proceeds to present ethical norms relating to advertising, salesmanship, marketing, pricing policies, labor relations, insider trading, and consumer and social ethics in the marketplace.

Inter-Jewish transactions are regulated by the prohibition against paying and receiving *ribbit* (interest). Many of the nuances of this prohibition in the context of commercial transactions are dealt with in this volume. The treatment of *ribbit* includes a discussion of *hetter iska*, a halakhic mechanism that ameliorates the prohibition.

The norms described in *Case Studies in Business Ethics* are transcendent duties prescribed for all market participants in a *nondiscriminatory manner*. The "reasonable man" criterion, for instance, informs the disclosure obligation for both the buyer and the seller. Similarly, the prohibition against engaging in pressure tactics equally constrains the conduct of both buyer and seller. When a commercial transaction entails *ribbit*, both buyer and seller infringe the prohibition. To provide but one more example, the prohibition against causing someone needless mental anguish enjoins the seller against the use of bait-and-switch tactics no less than it enjoins the consumer against insincere comparison shopping.

What Halakhah has to say for the marketplace *defines the very rules of economic participation* and is designed to promote harmonious social relations and generosity of spirit.

While our focus is on Halakhah, comparative analyses in respect to both American law and secular business ethics are also a feature of this work. Yet another concern is the role Halakhah assigns government in fostering business ethics and the approach it urges government to take in respect to specific issues. Both economic theory and economic analysis will be used to clarify and elucidate the issues involved.

In writing this book, I was faced with a stylistic dilemma. On the one hand, business ethics is a very serious subject matter and there seems to be little room for humor. On the other hand, long experience as both rabbi and professor has taught me that humor is a powerful pedagogical device. I wish I had more of it at my disposal! I resolved this dilemma by deciding to make my major thrust at humor not in the text itself but rather in the footnotes of this volume. If the reader fails to discover any humor embedded in the footnotes, I will have at least succeeded in arousing the reader's curiosity to examine my notes more carefully than otherwise. Should the reader, perchance, find more humor in the text than in the footnotes, know well that this was entirely unintended on my part.

1. Albert Z. Carr, "Is Business Bluffing Ethical?" *Harvard Business Review* 46, no. 1 (January–February 1968): 143–53. For a critique of Carr in the secular literature on business ethics, see Daryle Korn, "Business and Game Playing: The False Analogy," *Journal of Business Ethics* 16, nos. 12–13 (September 1997): 1447–52; and Peter Heckman, "Business and Games," *Journal of Business Ethics* 11 (1992): 933–38.

2. Carr, "Is Business Bluffing Ethical?" p. 145.

3. See Berakhot 63a.

4. Nahmanides (Spain, 1194–1270), Ramban, at Deuteronomy 6:18. For an analysis of Nahmanides, see Aharon Lichtenstein, "Does Jewish Law Recognize an Ethic Independent of Halakhah?" in *Modern Jewish Ethics; Theory and Practice*, ed. Marvin Fox (Ohio State University Press, 1975), pp. 62–88. See also Walter Wurzburger, *The Ethics of Responsibility* (Philadelphia: Jewish Publication Society, 1994), esp. chaps. 1 and 2. For a discussion of how Nahmanides' insight might apply to various aspects of the modern business scene, see Moses L. Pava, *Business Ethics: A Jewish Perspective* (Hoboken, N.J.: Ktav, 1997), pp. 150–57.

5. For a discussion of the *lifnim mi-shurat ha-din* concept, see below, pp. 257–62, 358–59, and 362–63.

6. Please turn to pp. 24–7 of this volume.

7. "There was this [man] who walked along, saying: `One who leaves a court having had his coat removed [i.e., the court ruled against him, removing his coat as payment to his opponent] should sing a song as he goes on his way'" (Sanhedrin 7a). That is, "he should be happy that wrongly acquired property was removed from his possession." R. Solomon b. Isaac (France, 1040–1105), Rashi, ad loc.

8. Moshe Silberg, "Law and Morals in Jewish Jurisprudence," *Harvard Law Review* 75 (1961–62): 306–31. For further elaboration of this theme, see Aaron Kirschenbaum, *Equity in Jewish Law Beyond Equity: Halakhic Asperationism in Jewish Civil Law* (Hoboken, N.J.: Ktav, 1991), pp. 1–58.

9. For examples of the operation of this principle, please turn to pp. 358–64 of this volume.

10. See R. Hayyim Mordecai Margoliot (Poland, 1779–1820), *Sha'arei Teshuvah*, at Rabbi Joseph Caro (Israel, 1488–1575) *Shulhan Arukh*, Orah Hayyim 448, n. 8. For the ethics of bluffing, please turn to pp. 223-24, 268-9, 274, and 329-30 of this volume.

1. Moral Education

Rubie Indigo's Adventures into Veiled Misconduct

Rubie Indigo's ethos is succinctly captured by his very name. He craves to stand out and glitter like a ruby among his friends and in society at large. This need for recognition and status makes it important for Rubie to always appear honest, charitable, generous, and gracious. At core, Rubie is, however, the opposite of what he appears to be. Instead of being honest and generous, he is crooked, self-centered, and greedy. No law or ethical principle is sacred in the face of an opportunity for self-aggrandizement, provided, of course, that Rubie feels confident that he can cover up his misdeeds without detection. Rubie is therefore a colossal fraud. His surname, Indigo, best describes his essence. In halakhic discourse, indigo (*kla ilan*) is a word used to describe religious fraud. Indigo is a cheap blue vegetable dye. Outwardly, it resembles *teheilet*, which is identified with the blood of an obscure mollusk. If someone attaches to his garment threads dyed with indigo, he gives the impression that he is fulfilling the mitzvah of *teheilet* when, in fact, he is a fraud.[1]

Rubie's indoctrination into the world of veiled misconduct got an early start when his older brother, Cyrus, ten years his senior, entered the workforce. While working at the local delicatessen, Cyrus boasted to Rubie how his boss would short-weight all but the most discerning customers. He would accomplish this by neglecting to subtract the weight of the wrapping material from the total weight recorded on the scale. What captivated Rubie most was Cyrus' pantomimic reenactment of how his boss would remove the large and jumbo-size paper cups from the uncleared tables, bring them into the kitchen for a rinsing, then return with the cups wrapped neatly in cellophane and place them at the soda fountain for recycling—all with a straight face.

As Cyrus changed jobs, the number of tales of veiled misconduct grew. When Cyrus, for instance, was working in a drugstore, he claimed that the clerks routinely made personal use of the cologne and deodorant and then sold the bottles and cans they had tapped as new. Who would notice that a few sprinkles and sprays were missing?

Rubie at first reacted to Cyrus' tales with disbelief, even accusing him of fabricating the stories for entertainment purposes. Cyrus remained firm, however, reinforcing his credibility by citing chapter and verse from Paul Blumberg's *Predatory Society*. In this book, Blumberg documents widespread deception in the American marketplace.[2] One of Cyrus' favorites was the practice of some retailers to engage in markup/markdown sales. What's entailed here is that shortly before a "sale," a store will mark its prices up, then mark them down to create the illusion of substantial savings.[3] Another one of Cyrus' favorites was the practice of some caterers to promise customers premium liquor, but in actuality provide them with cheap liquor. The deception is accomplished by pouring the cheap liquor into empty bottles of premium liquor.[4]

Without being consciously aware of it, Rubie was being schooled from early youth to take veiled misconduct in stride and even to regard its practice as a challenging game of sorts. By the time Rubie entered the workforce himself, his morals were so shaky that he needed little encouragement to become a real-life villain straight out of the pages of Blumberg's *Predatory Society*.[5]

Raised in a poor home, Rubie had to work to finance his college education. He spent several summers as a mechanic in an auto repair shop. After one month of intensive training, Rubie felt certain that he knew more about cars than the great majority of his customers. Because he felt that his relationship with a typical customer fit perfectly into the *asymmetrical information* model he had studied in Economics 1011, Rubie began exploiting the technical ignorance of his customers and charged them for repairs not done. In one instance, a customer complained that his car would not start. A quick diagnosis revealed that the battery was weak and could be fixed by a simple charging. Instead of informing the customer that the problem was minor and entailed only a small expense, Rubie told the customer that he needed a new starter motor. Ignorant of the workings of an engine, the customer permitted Rubie to install a new starter. Instead of installing a new starter, however, Rubie took out the old starter and painted it. As soon as the paint dried, Rubie put it back in and charged the customer a hefty bill for a rebuilt starter.

In another instance, a customer complained that the car's generator would not start. A quick diagnosis revealed that the problem was a broken fan belt. Instead of informing the customer that the problem was very minor and inexpensive to repair, Rubie exploited the customer's ignorance and informed her that the car's generator was defective. Rubie accomplished the repair by fixing the fan belt and spray painting the old generator. He then charged the customer for a new generator. *Rubie's best tool was his paint can!*

Another summer, Rubie worked as an airport cabby. Exploiting the ignorance of tourists regarding local conditions and customs, Rubie abused his fares in various ways. Routinely, he took the longer and hence more expensive route to the passenger's destination. Rubie's favorite ploy was to charge extra fees for everything. Depending upon how he sized up the naïveté of his customer, Rubie, at one time or another, requested the following surcharges: a dollar for every suitcase the customer brought into the cab; a surcharge for going over the 59th Street bridge; an extra charge for the use of Queens Boulevard; an extra charge for sitting in the front on the grounds that there were already three sitting in the back.

In one instance, a tourist, using barely understandable sign language, seemed to ask Rubie to open the back-seat windows. As the cab raced along the *scenic* route in the *general* direction of the passenger's destination, Rubie was tempted to say, "Lady, the air is extra."

Rubie's excellent grades combined with his varied work experience, including a stint as a management intern at a major bank, propelled him into a prestigious business school. Graduation from business school launched Rubie's career as an investment banker with the prestigious Wall Street firm of Oriole Bros., Inc.

In his professional life at Oriole Bros., Rubie gained access to highly confidential information that could be turned into huge trading profits. But insider trading was illegal, and to trade on the confidential information of one's own firm was the most risky form of this illicit activity. Rubie began looking for an investment banker in a different firm with whom he could exchange insider information. The break Rubie was waiting for came when he met E. Bradford Key, an investment banker with a rival Wall Street firm, Eagle Associates, Inc. He and Key made a gentleman's agreement to exchange confidential information. Each agreed to trade only on the confidential information of the rival firm and not to trade on the confidential information of his own firm.

To ensure secrecy for his trading, Indigo set up a shell corporation in the Bahamas, naming it Yahalom. Indigo then opened a brokerage account for Yahalom at a branch of a Swiss bank located in the Bahamas. Swiss bank secrecy laws prohibited the bank from revealing to anyone the owner(s) of any of its accounts. In fact, only a single scrap of paper in the bank's possession linked Indigo to the Yahalom account. To further protect his anonymity, Indigo instructed the Bahamian bankers to execute his stock orders through several different brokers, so as not to attract attention. Key set up the same mechanism for himself in the Canary Islands.

Indigo and Key felt no sense of guilt or shame whatsoever in setting up their scheme. Insider trading, they reasoned, was rampant on Wall Street, and therefore it was okay for them to play the game too. The objective of this game is to win; and to win big by setting up a foolproof scheme.

The principal issue raised by the preceding vignette pertains to how veiled misconduct can be reduced and prevented. It will be our thesis that from the perspective of Judaism, reducing the incidence of veiled misconduct is fundamentally a matter of character building through effective moral education. Government intervention in the marketplace can work to reinforce the effectiveness of moral education.

Moral Education

The case for moral education begins with the recognition that invisible misconduct manifests a failure on the part of the perpetrator to meet the standard of *yirat shamayyim* (fear of heaven) that the Torah expects from him. This can be seen from the Torah's selective use of the phrase "And you shall fear your God" in connection with its admonitions relating to interpersonal conduct.[6] Use of this phrase is reserved for instances where the target of the admonition may convince himself that he can violate the norm without detection and hence avoid loss of social standing.[7]

Similarly, the Torah's puzzling reference to the Exodus in connection with certain of its precepts is taken by the sages to amount to a warning from God to the smug practitioner of veiled misconduct: "Don't imagine that you will escape punishment just because your misdeeds go undetected by your fellow man. No! Remember that it was I who distinguished in Egypt between the firstborn and those who were not firstborn." Not surprisingly, one of these precepts is the prohibition against false weights and measures;[8] a type of misconduct that appears in the opening vignette.

Admonishing veiled misconduct with the phrase "And you shall fear your God" conveys the notion that overcoming a test of piety is a matter of strengthening one's *yirat shamayyim*. But *yirat shamayyim* cannot be fostered in a vacuum: "A boor cannot be fearful of sin" (Avot 2:6). To be an effective deterrent against veiled misconduct, *yirat shamayyim* must be cultivated in an individual from early childhood. The duty to impart youth with religious instruction and training (*hinnukh*) is a task the sages assigned to parents[9] and the institutions of religious education.[10] There can be no doubt that one aspect of this mission is moral education.

> R. Zeira further ruled: One should not promise to give a child something and then not give it to him, because one will thereby teach him lying, as it is said: *They have taught their tongues to speak lies* (Jeremiah 9:4).[11]

In the thinking of R. Isaiah ha-Levi Horowitz (Poland, 1565–1630), training in truth-telling is the centerpiece of the moral education of youngsters. The ideal is for the father to spare no effort in emphasizing to his child the importance of truth-telling. Toward this end, a father should magnify the punishment for those who lie and glorify the reward for those who speak truthfully. If the child is caught lying, the father should admonish him harshly, instilling great trepidation in him. This approach will guarantee that the child will always go on the straight path, even when not under the father's supervision. Because the child will feel compelled to always tell the truth, he will always depart from evil and do good.[12]

Further insight into the connection between truth-telling and the ability to resist the temptation of veiled misconduct can be obtained from the connection the sages make between truth-telling and belief in God:

> He who speaks truth harbors belief (*emunah*) in God. [In contrast] chronic liars harbor idolatrous fancies (Midrash Pinhas).

> R. Eleazer also said: Whoever dissembles his speech is as though he had engaged in idolatry: Here it is written, *And I shall seem to him as a deceiver* (Genesis 27:12); and elsewhere it is said, *they are vanity, and the work of deceivers* (Jeremiah 10:15).[13]

The key to understanding the connection between deceptive speech and idolatry, according to R. Judah Loew b. Bezalel (Bohemia, ca. 1525–1609), is that the seal of the Almighty is truth. He who possesses the attribute of truthfulness, therefore, *clings to the Almighty*. To engage in deceptive speech, however, amounts to embracing something that has no existence at all. What idolatry and deceptive speech share is that both are vanities; that is, they have no real existence. Hence, whoever dissembles his speech is as though he engaged in idolatry.[14]

Judaism's standard for truth-telling makes it a sin to lie even when the fabrication causes no harm or damage to others. Two varieties of harmless lies are identified: the lie that brings some advantage or benefit, and the lie that brings no discernible benefit. Both varieties are prohibited by dint of Torah law. The latter variety is more egregious and warrants greater punishment[15] because it reflects a love of falsehood for its own sake.[16]

Selfishness and the Ability to Perceive Truth

Hinnukh efforts directed at truth-telling face a formidable barrier in the form of man's natural inclination to selfishness, greed, and self-aggrandizement. These tendencies distort our ability to perceive truth and to act with integrity. The power of greed to distort even the ability of the spiritual elite[17] to perceive truth can be seen from an examination of Halakhah's judicial code of conduct.

Jewish law safeguards the integrity of the judicial decision-making process by means of both preventive measures and corrective action.

Preventive measures take the form of prohibiting the judge in a lawsuit from submitting to any influence that might taint his integrity and calling for him to disqualify himself on the basis of bias.

By force of the verse "You shall not distort justice" (Deuteronomy 16:19), the judge in a lawsuit is forbidden to accept a payment to acquit the guilty or to condemn the innocent. What constitutes a corrupting payment is considerably broadened by force of the verse "You shall take no gift" (Exodus 23:8). Exegetical interpretation of this verse prohibits the judge from accepting payment from one of the opposing litigants even if the payer tells him to acquit the innocent or to condemn the guilty.[18] Rava's (d. 352) rationalization of the latter point of stringency is very telling: "What is the reason for [the prohibition against taking] a gift? Because as soon as a man receives a gift from another he becomes so well disposed toward him that he becomes like his own person, and no man sees himself in the wrong. What [is the meaning of] shohad? Shehu had—'he is one with you.'"[19]

Fully recognizing that bias may be created by means other than the acceptance of money, Jewish law prohibits the judge from submitting to a bribe of words (shohad devarim).[20] Illustrating shohad devarim is the following talmudic incident: Amemar was once engaged in the trial of an action when a bird flew down upon his head and a man approached and removed it. "What is your business here?" [Amemar asked him.] "I have a lawsuit," the other replied. "I," Amemar said, "am disqualified from acting as your judge."[21]

The stringency of shohad devarim applies even to words of greeting. Accordingly, in the event A did not make it a practice to anticipate judge B's greeting with his own greeting, initiating this practice just prior to the time his lawsuit will come up in B's docket amounts to shohad devarim. Since B is regarded as being biased toward A on account of the latter's newfound friendliness toward him, B is disqualified from serving as judge in his lawsuit.[22]

A close friendship or enmity with one of the litigants similarly disqualifies an individual from serving as judge in his lawsuit.[23]

Because greed blinds man's perception of truth and what constitutes integrity, successful moral training in the attribute of truth (emet) perforce must include training against selfish conduct.

Moral training against selfishness begins with the notion that denying one's fellow a benefit when it costs one nothing constitutes obnoxious conduct. The sages identified such conduct with the sin of Sodom.[24] If we can do no more than muster lip service for the sages' condemnation against Sodomitic conduct, then our moral training against selfishness stands on a weak foundation. To make advanced inroads against the attribute of greed, one must both *believe* on an intellectual level and *feel* on an emotional level that Sodomitic conduct is obnoxious.

It would therefore be a mistake to begin moral training of youth with notions of generosity, while skipping as unnecessary a condemnation of Sodomitic conduct. Such an approach places the child's moral education on a shaky foundation because it takes society's condemnation of Sodomitic conduct for granted. As a means of illustrating that society's notions against Sodomitic conduct require considerable reinforcement, I offer the following scenario:

A meets his neighbor B at an affair many miles from their respective homes. A drove to the function in his car. B arrived by means of a car service. The encounter is unexpected by both parties. Upon exchanging pleasantries, A becomes aware that B arrived at the affair by means of a car service and offers him a ride home. Notwithstanding that the gesture allows B to save the cost of a car service on his return trip, it is unethical for A to ask B to pay tolls on the drive home. Since A would bear the expense of tolls in any case, and B does nothing to increase A's expense, it is Sodomitic to request B to make this payment.

In scenarios of this kind it has become almost common practice for the passenger (P) to offer to pay the tolls. In everyday practice, the driver (D) sometimes accepts the offer and sometimes does not. Now, if D really regarded *asking* his passenger to pay the tolls as *obnoxious*, then, he would never take up P's offer to pay the tolls!

Moreover, is it proper for P to offer to pay the tolls? Making the gesture expresses an attitude on his part that while not legally required to make the payment, it is *the gentlemanly or even the expected thing to do and would amount to conducting oneself above the letter of the law*. Now, if it becomes common practice for P to offer to pay the toll, then dropping a hint to P to do so may well no longer be regarded as obnoxious, but instead as merely ungracious and unsociable conduct. What, then, of an outright demand to P to pay the toll? Provided the demand is made in a charming and incidental manner, it may well not be regarded as conduct worthy of condemnation, but as a tolerable irritant of everyday life. P's gesture to pay the toll, therefore, may work in a subtle way to undermine the harsh attitude the sages desired to foster against Sodomitic conduct.

Moral Training and Controlling Envy

To be sure, man's inclination to greed distorts his perception of truth and what constitutes integrity. But envy fuels greed and intensifies it considerably. Effective moral training in the attribute of truth (*emet*), therefore, requires training against envy.

But the sages did not view envy as a totally evil trait. Witness the talmudic aphorism that "jealousy between scholars increases wisdom" (*kinat soferim tarbeh hokhmah*).[25] The objective is not to suppress jealousy entirely but to sublimate it into healthy channels.

Supportive of the notion that controlling envy assumes a central role in moral training is an analysis of the socioeconomic life of the Jewish people in biblical times during the forty-year period of the Wilderness (*dor ha-midbar*). One feature of the economic life of that time was the manna, which descended from heaven on a daily basis.

The society of manna was not a historical curiosity. Its didactic role for all posterity is clearly indicated by the following instruction Moses gave to Aaron: "... take one jar and put a full omer of manna into it; place it before the Eternal for a *safekeeping* for your generations" (Exodus 16:13). In what manner did the manna serve as a safekeeping? Perhaps the answer lies in the control this society exerted over the expression of envy in the daily lives of the people. Let us investigate the role envy played in this society. We begin with the material dimension.

Notwithstanding that no one in the society of manna had to engage in a profession or trade to earn a livelihood, deriving sustenance from the manna is termed by the Torah an *affliction*: "Who fed you in the wilderness with manna, which your fathers knew not; that he might *afflict* you ..." (Deuteronomy 8:16). Commenting on why deriving sustenance from the manna is regarded as an affliction, the Talmud, at Yoma 74b, offers the following rationale:

> R. Ammi and R. Assi [were disputing]. One said: you cannot compare one who has bread in his basket with one who has none. The other said: You cannot compare one who sees what he eats with one who does not see what he is eating. R. Joseph said: This is an allusion to [the reason] why blind people eat without becoming satisfied.

The view that regards the manna as a form of affliction because of its unchanging appearance requires further elucidation. As a preliminary, we take note that underlying this view is the dictum that the manna, with few exceptions,[26] imparted the taste of whatever food the consumer conjured up as he partook of it.[27] Now, since one's imagination could cause the manna to produce practically any food taste, the manna's failure to assume the actual form of the food experienced was a matter of frustration, generating a feeling of deprivation. Adding to this feeling of deprivation was the presumed failure of the manna to emit the aroma of the food being experienced.[28] But why was this deprivation effect necessary?

Addressing himself to this issue, R. Menahem Mendel of Rimanov (Poland, 1745–1815) posits that God limited the amenities of the experience of consuming the manna in order to reduce feelings of jealousy. As long as A's consumable manna was *outwardly* the same as B's consumable manna, invidious comparisons could not be made. But if A's manna had taken on a specific form and color and emitted an aroma, then B, even though he could duplicate A's consumption experience, would imagine that A was deriving greater pleasure from it than he was. Outward differences in manna would inevitably have produced invidious comparisons.[29]

Manna's limitations as a real food produced a *net benefit* for Jewish society. On the one hand, the limitations were felt as detracting from the potential *utility* of the consumption experience. But at the same time, this circumstance weakened the force of envy and therefore worked to foster a level of spiritual growth that would otherwise not have been possible.

To be sure, envy was not absent in the society of manna. Consider that the necessary exertion and time spent in gathering the manna as well as in preparing it varied widely. Time spent and effort exerted here were inversely proportional to one's spiritual status. No laid-back existence was everyday life in the society of manna. People were *graded* on a daily basis on their level of spiritual status. Invidious comparisons were surely made. Instead of playing out in the material realm, these jealousies played out in the spiritual realm.

What the above analysis points up is that manna is a *safekeep* because it presented for posterity a model of how envy should be dealt with. In the material realm, concerted efforts should be made to reduce envy; but in the spiritual realm jealousy should be viewed not just as a tolerable evil but as a *positive good*. We must recognize that envy is a human trait and cannot be eliminated from human society. If envy is suppressed in one realm, it surely will seek expression elsewhere. To successfully reduce envy in the material realm, a proper incentive-disincentive system must be set up to foster competition in the spiritual realm. The exact form this competition should take will, of course, be a matter of debate. But one thing is certain, new directions leading away from current attitudes and practices are needed. To cite one example: the current attitude in many circles is that testing post–high school students in Torah-study programs is in conflict with, or at least detracts from, the ideal of studying

Torah for its own sake.[30] Injecting competitive pressures into the Torah educational enterprise at all levels should, however, provide a solid example of how jealousy can be directed into a healthy outlet.

Hakkarat ha-tov and the Moral Personality

Another key to the moral personality is the character trait of *hakkarat ha-tov* (gratitude). In developing this point, let us examine the biblical narrative of Joseph's struggle in overcoming the wiles of Lady Potiphar, together with the talmudic account of this incident.[31]

> *He adamantly refused. He reasoned with his master's wife.* "My master does not even know what I do in the house. He has entrusted me with everything he owns. No one in this house has more power than I have. He has not kept back anything at all from me, except for you, his wife. How could I do such a great wrong? It would be a sin before God!" (Genesis 39:8–9).
>
> *The woman grabbed him by his cloak.* "Sleep with me!" *she pleaded. He ran away from her, leaving his cloak in her hand, and fled outside* (Genesis 39:12). At that moment, his father's image appeared to him through the window and said, "Joseph, your brothers will have their names inscribed upon the stones of the ephod [the sash of the high priest's robe], and yours among theirs. Is it your wish to have your name expunged from among theirs and be called an associate of harlots?" Immediately *his bow abode in strength* (Genesis 49:24). R. Yohanan said in the name of R. Meir: [This means] that his passion was subdued.[32]

What emerges from the preceding descriptions of Joseph's struggle against sin is the equation of moral turpitude with betrayal. Joseph made this equation on several levels.

On one level, proceeding from the biblical narrative itself, Joseph equated succumbing to Lady Potiphar with *betraying* the trust of her husband, who was his master. Logic does not compel that a test of piety be interpreted as a test of loyalty to Potiphar. Clearly, it was Joseph's revulsion at being an ingrate that pushed this equation on him. In other words, Joseph's deep sense of *hakkarat ha-tov* (gratitude) to Potiphar *personalized* his dilemma, tearing him between lust and loyalty.

By force of the talmudic account, Joseph's moral dilemma is *personalized* on a different level as well. Recall that Joseph invokes his loyalty to God as a means of resisting Lady Potiphar's wiles (Genesis 39:9). But, in the moment of truth, this is apparently not enough to deter him from sin. What provided the extra push for Joseph was the image of his father both admonishing him against sin and reminding him of his destined greatness. In the final analysis, Joseph is deterred from sin by equating succumbing to sin with betraying both his father's moral teachings and his high hopes for him. Now, if Joseph merely gave lip service to Jacob's teachings, what influence could they have had on him once he was no longer under his father's control? What influence could these teachings have had at the moment Joseph faced the seductive powers of lust and at the same time was convinced that his father thought he was either dead or hopelessly missing? Overcoming a sin of passion by conjuring up an image of his father could only be efficacious on the assumption that Joseph cherished his father's moral teachings and harbored a deep sense of gratitude for them. Hence, for Joseph, *hakarrat ha-tov* was the link that transformed moral training into virtuous conduct.

Fostering *Hakkarat ha-Tov*

The previous section identified *hakkarat ha-tov* as a vital factor in achieving effective moral education. Its essential role is to make an individual equate failing a test of piety with letting down (betraying) his parents and/or moral educators. The challenge is therefore to put the family and the school system on a solid footing so that these institutions can maximize their impact on the moral climate of society.

For parents to realize their full moral educational potential, their child-rearing and moral-educational roles must be fully integrated. Such integration makes moral training permeate every aspect of the life experience. In addition, it makes the gratitude parenthood compels inseparable from the gratitude their moral training elicits. This, in turn, works to *personalize* the moral dilemma. As the converse of this proposition, the more compartmentalized moral education is, the less it will elicit ethical conduct.

The selfsame assertion can be made in respect to education. Specifically, to be effective, moral education must permeate the entire curriculum, and character building must comprise a central goal of the educational enterprise. Assigning moral education this role catapults it from the periphery to being an integral part of the educational process. This, in turn, fosters a bonding between students and educators, which, in turn, works to *personalize* the moral dilemma.

Government Subsidization of the Family and School System

In Jewish society, religious education is compulsory[33] and the religious education of the poor is subsidized.[34] Consider that one aspect of religious education is moral training, which is the mission both of parents and of the religious-educational enterprise. Part of the aid given to the poor should be targeted to equip and encourage the family and the school to carry out their moral-educational function.

The Cost Disease of the Service Sector

In assessing the adequacy of the level of support provided, we must consider what Baumol and Blinder call the *cost disease of the service sector*. We will begin with a brief description of this phenomenon and its relevancy to the issue at hand.

The cost disease of the service sector refers to the phenomenon that the prices of services consistently rise faster than the general inflation rate. Consider these facts: From 1948 to 1995, the consumer price index (CPI) in the United States increased at an average rate of about 4 percent per year compounded annually. Over this same period, the corresponding rate of increase of the cost of hospital care, education per pupil, and a visit to a physician was, respectively, 8.6 percent, 7.5 percent, and 5.5 percent. This disparity arises because productivity gains in manufacturing outpace productivity gains in the service sector. Productivity gains lag in the service sector because services, by their very nature, require direct contact between those who consume the service and those who provide it. Doctors, teachers, and librarians are all engaged in activities that require direct person-to-person contact. Moreover, because the quality of services will deteriorate if less time is provided per user, it is difficult to introduce labor-saving techniques in the service sector.

Notwithstanding its lagging productivity gains, the competitive marketplace will force the service sector to raise wages at more or less the same rate as the manufacturing sector. If this were not so, the service sector would lose its labor force. Since costs are increasing faster in the service sector relative to the manufacturing sector, the profit motive will drive the service sector to cut corners in its employment of labor to maintain its profit margins. Hence, if the marketplace is left to its own devices, the quality of the output of the service sector is likely to deteriorate over time.

The cost disease of the service sector does not make deterioration of the quality of its output inevitable. To see why, we need only point out that the source of the problem is not declining productivity in the service sector, but rather, rising productivity in the manufacturing sector relative to the service sector.

Increasing productivity can never make a nation poor. We have a choice. More and better services over time can be obtained, but at some sacrifice in the rate of growth of manufacturing. Government can influence the mix of output between services and manufacturing. Many vital services, such as education and health care, are subsidized by the public sector. To ensure that the quality of these services does not erode over time, the public must be committed to increase its support level per annum above the inflation rate.[35]

The Cost Disease of Moral Training

Let us now relate the cost disease of the service sector to the moral-educational sector. At once, it must be recognized that moral training is essentially a cottage industry. Its effectiveness is predicated upon *quality time,* i.e., personal contact between parents and children, and between teachers and students. Without this quality time, the moral dilemma will not be personalized. Thus, moral training is subject to a cost disease.

What the cost disease of moral training implies for government subsidization of the schooling system is clear-cut. If the quality time (i.e., the personal contact between teachers and students) is not to deteriorate over time, the government must be prepared to increase its support level per annum over the inflation rate. Moreover, since moral education will be effective only if it is integrated into the entire curriculum, this subsidy must increase for the entire educational program.

As far as the parental institution is concerned, it is a vital service sector that operates outside the marketplace, and this fact must be recognized. Given the economic pressures to earn a livelihood and the tantalizing rewards of the marketplace, parents must be provided with appropriate incentives to take their parenting and moral-educational roles seriously. With the aim of putting the family on a sound economic footing, government subsidization of the basic needs of the family is required. Such programs as subsidized health care and generous tax deductions for dependents indexed to the CPI are indicated.

Government and Veiled Misconduct

Another aspect of Halakhah's approach to combating veiled misconduct is the role it assigns government. The government's role is to ferret out veiled misconduct. Its duty is also to improve the informational channels of the marketplace to prevent this misconduct from happening. Let us take up, in turn, each of these elements.

Ferreting Out Veiled Misconduct

The responsibility of government to ferret out veiled misconduct can be seen from an analysis of the following talmudic text:

The secret things belong unto the Lord our God, but the things that are revealed belong unto us and to our children forever (Deuteronomy 29:28). Why are the words *lanu ulebanenu* [unto us and to our children] and the *ayin* of the word *ad* [forever] dotted? To teach that God did not punish for transgressions committed in secret until the Israelites had crossed the Jordan. This is the view of R. Judah. Said R. Nehemiah to him: Did God ever punish [all Israel] for crimes committed in secret; does not Scripture say *forever*? But just as God did not punish [all Israel] for secret transgressions [at that time], so too did He not punish them [corporately] for open transgressions until they had crossed the Jordan.[36]

R. Menahem b. Solomon Meiri (France, 1249–1316) regards R. Judah's view as normative. The practical implication of this view, according to Meiri, is that society's judges, sages, and leaders must do more than simply deal with issues brought to them. Rather, they must search out and deal with the hidden wrongdoing of society and take measures to remedy the misconduct they discover. Failure to search out hidden wrongs makes the entire community vulnerable to punishment for the sins of evildoers.[37]

The responsibility for government to ferret out hidden misconduct is also evident from Halakhah's call for the appointment of commissioners to supervise the honesty and accuracy in the use of weights and measures.[38]

Carrying out its role to ferret out misconduct requires the government, in the opinion of this writer, to conduct sting operations to discover wrongdoing in industries that are particularly prone to veiled misconduct. The auto repair and taxi cab industries appear to be good candidates here.

Improving the Information Channels in the Marketplace

Another approach for government to reduce instances of veiled misconduct is to legislate tougher disclosure obligations for sellers of products and services. Evidencing Halakhah's support for this approach is an analysis of the role price commissioners played in the ancient talmudic foodstuffs ordinance.

Out of concern for the subsistence needs of the masses, the sages enacted a 20 percent profit-rate constraint for vendors dealing in commodities essential to human life (*hayyei nefesh*). This ordinance was directed at individual vendors and should not be identified with a price-fixing function for the Jewish court. Its practical significance was merely to prohibit sellers from collusively restricting supply for the purpose of raising their profit margin above the 20 percent level.

One aspect of the foodstuffs ordinance was the appointment of market commissioners to monitor the regulated sector. Now, if the ordinance was never intended to countermand market conditions, then the role of market officials, it appears, must merely have been to enforce the competitive norm. Without this monitoring, ignorance of market conditions could have resulted in transactions concluded in divergence from the competitive norm.

To be sure, judicial redress is often open to victims of price divergence of this sort in the form of a claim of *ona'ah* (price fraud). But the *ona'ah* claim is at best an *ex post facto* remedy. Legal technicalities often make it difficult for a complainant to recover losses on account of *ona'ah*. Moreover, many instances of *ona'ah* go undetected by the victim. Out of concern for the subsistence needs of the masses, the sages added another layer of protection in the foodstuffs sector. Price commissioners were assigned for the purpose of enforcing market price and preventing instances of *ona'ah*.[39]

The implication of the above analysis for the modern marketplace is that government should take action to improve the information channels of the marketplace. Resources should be concentrated in industries dealing with the subsistence needs of the masses and characterized by the problem of asymmetrical information.

In 1969, Congress passed the Consumer Protection Act. This act requires all lenders, not just banks, to provide information to consumers about the cost of borrowing, including a standardized interest rate (called the annual percentage rate or APR) and the total finance charges on the loan. The Fair Credit Billing Act of 1974 requires creditors, especially credit card issuers, to provide information on the method of assessing finance charges and requires that billing complaints be handled quickly.[40] Halakhah would applaud these laws.

In New York City, the Consumer Affairs Department requires vendors of prepared food to prominently display in their stores per-unit price information for the items they sell. This approach could easily be extended to reduce many instances of fraud rooted in the asymmetrical-information problem. To cite but one examples, the law could require vendors of food to prominently display for their customers a sign saying that customers may not be charged for the wrapping material of their orders. Or, as another example, the public's general ignorance regarding which items sold in a drugstore are taxable could be cleared up by requiring drugstores to prominently display this information for their customers.

Increased government monitoring and efforts to improve the information channels in the marketplace can significantly reduce the kind of fraud that thrives because of the problem of asymmetrical information. But it must be recognized that the root cause of veiled misconduct is the failure of the home and the school system to achieve effective moral training. Government efforts aimed at increased deterrence must therefore be understood as a secondary line of defense against veiled misconduct. Without a vigorous commitment to moral training, increased government deterrence efforts may, ironically, work only to spur wrongdoers to more sophisticated means of avoiding detection and/or shift veiled misconduct to industries where government monitoring is less aggressive.

1. See Bava Mezia 61b.

2. Paul Blumberg, *The Predatory Society: Deceptions in the American Marketplace* (New York: Oxford University Press, 1989). To be sure, the deceptions Cyrus ascribed to his boss are also cited in Blumberg, pp. 30–31, 145, 151. Since Cyrus' revelations are recorded in Blumberg's book, there's no telling whether he actually witnessed the conduct, as he claims, or simply fabricated the stories for the purpose of providing entertainment for his younger brother, Rubie.

3. Ibid., pp. 33–37.

4. Ibid., p. 151.

5. In his summer jobs, Rubie had actually *copied* the villainy described in Blumberg, pp. 63–71 and pp. 49–52.

6. The Torah makes use of the phrase "And you shall fear God" in connection with the following moral imperatives: the prohibition against offering ill-suited advice (Leviticus 19:14); the duty to bestow honor to a talmudic scholar (Leviticus 19:32); the injunction against causing someone needless mental anguish (Leviticus 15:17); the interdict against charging interest (Leviticus 25:36); and the prohibition against working an Israelite bondsman oppressively (Leviticus 25:43).

7. Kiddushin 32b and R. Solomon b. Isaac (France, 1040–1105), Rashi, s.v. *davar ha-masur la-lev*.

8. Bava Mezia 61b.

9. The father's moral-educational role proceeds most directly from the mitzvah of *hinnukh*. This rabbinically mandated mitzvah requires the father to train his children in the performance of mitzvot which they will be subject to when they reach adulthood (Hagigah 4a). Relatedly, this mitzvah assigns the father an interventionist role whenever he observes his children engaged in wrongdoing, with the additional duty to remonstrate them for their misconduct. Cf. Joseph Caro (Israel, 1488–1575), *Shulhan Arukh*, Orah Hayyim 343:1. The father's role of remonstrator continues, of course, even after his children reach adulthood by dint of the pentateuchal mitzvah of *tokhahah* (reproof; Leviticus 19:17).

The *hinnukh* a son receives in normative conduct is potentially reinforced by dint of the father's pentateuchal obligation to teach him Torah (Kiddushin 29a). This obligation requires the father to teach his son the entire *Torah she-biktav* (Written law; cf. *Sh.Ar.*, Yoreh De'ah 246:6 and comments ad loc. of *Turei Zahav*, n. 2, and *Siftei Kohen*, n. 5.

For a glimpse at how the moral-educational role of the father worked itself out in practice, see Israel Ibn Al-Nakawa (Spain, 14th cent.), *Menorat ha-Maor*, ed. H. G. Enelow, vol. 4 (New York: Bloch, 1932), p. 145.

For the mother's role as enabler in connection with the mitzvah of *Talmud Torah*, see Berakhot 17a. For the mother's obligation to transmit the experience of Sinai to her children, see Aaron Soloveichik, "The Fire of Sinai," in *Building Jewish Ethical Character*, ed. Joseph Kaminetsky and Murray I. Friedman (New York, Fryer Foundation, 1975), p. 12.

Authorities dispute whether the sages imposed the mitzvah of *hinnukh* on the mother. For opposing views, see R. Abraham Abele b. Hayyim ha-Levi Gombiner (Poland, ca. 1637–1683), *Magen Avraham* to *Sh.Ar.*, Orah Hayyim 343, no. 1, and R. Samuel b. Nathan ha-Levi Kolin (Bohemia, 1720–1806), *Mahazit ha-Shekel* to *Sh.Ar.*, Orah Hayyim 343, n. 1. In any case, Halakhah assigns a vital role to the mother as a moral educator of her children. One manifestation of this role is the mother's responsibility to remonstrate with her children for wrongdoing. In this regard many authorities assign greater responsibility to the mother than the father. Cf. R. Isaiah ha-Levi Horowitz (Poland, 1565–1630), Shelah, *Sh'ar ha-Otiot*, ot *Derekh erez*.

For a description of the vital role mothers historically assume in the moral education of their daughters, see R. Moses b. Hanoch, *Sefer Brontshpiegel*, quoted and translated by Solomon Schimmel, "Ethical Dimensions of Traditional Jewish Education," in *Studies in Jewish Education*, ed. Barry Chazen, vol. 1 (Jerusalem: Magnes Press, 1983), pp. 94–95.

10. Bava Batra 21a.

11. Sukkah 46b.

12. R. Isaiah ha-Levi Horowitz, *Shnei Luhot ha-Berit*, Sha'ar ha-Otiot 4.

13. Sanhedrin 92a.

14. R. Judah Loew b. Bezalel, *Hiddushei Aggadot*, Sanhedrin 92a.

15. R. Jonah b. Abraham Gerondi (Spain, ca. 1200–1264), *Sha'arei Teshuvah*, sha'ar 3:186; R. Israel Meir ha-Kohen Kagan (Poland, 1838–1933), *Sefat Tamim* 6; R. Baer b. Jacob (Poland, 18th cent.), *Yad ha-Ketannah*, De'ot 10, n. 9; R. Eliezer Judah Waldenberg, *Responsa Ziz Eliezer* 15:12. A minority position in this matter is advanced by R. Eliezer b. Samuel of Metz (Alsace, ca. 1175). In his view, a falsehood that generates no harm or damages to someone else does not violate Torah law (Yere'im 235). In R. Waldenberg's opinion (*Ziz Eliezer*, ad loc.), Yere'im would be in agreement that such a falsehood is nevertheless *prohibited* by dint of rabbinical decree.

16. *Sefat Tamim*, loc. cit.

17. To qualify for appointment to the position of judge, an individual must meet stringent moral standards, see Maimonides (Egypt, 1135–1204), *Yad*, Sanhedrin 2:7.

18. Ketubbot 105b; *Yad*, op. cit. 23:1; R. Jacob b. Asher (Germany, 1270–1343), *Tur*, Hoshen Mishpat 9:1; *Sh.Ar.*, Hoshen Mishpat 9:1; R. Jehiel Michel Epstein (Belarus, 1829–1908), *Arukh ha-Shulhan*, Hoshen Mishpat, 9:1.

19. Ketubbot 105a; *Yad*, loc. cit.; *Tur*, loc. cit.; *Sh.Ar.*, loc. cit.; *Ar.haSh.*, loc. cit.

20. Ketubbot 105b.

21. Ketubbot 105b; *Yad*, op. cit. 23:3; *Tur*, op. cit. 9:4; *Sh.Ar.*, op. cit. 9:1; *Ar.haSh.*, op. cit. 9:1.

22. R. Joshua ha-Kohen Falk (Poland, 1555-1614), Sma, *Sh.Ar.*, op. cit 9, n.4; *Ar.haSh.*, loc. cit.

23. Sanhedrin 29a; R. Isaac b. Jacob Alfasi (Algeria, 1012–1103), Rif, ad loc.; *Yad*, op. cit. 23:6; R. Asher b. Jehiel (Germany, 1250–1327), Rosh, Sanhedrin, 3:23; *Tur*, op. cit. 7:8, 10; *Sh.Ar.*, 7:7; *Ar.haSh.*, op. cit. 7:9-10.

Judicial disqualification proceeds as a definite matter, according to majority opinion, only when the judge is either a *close* friend or a presumed enemy of one of the litigants. Here, the judge must, as a matter of strict law, remove himself from the case. Should he preside over the case, his verdict would be rendered null and void. An association of a more superficial nature with one of the litigants requires the judge only as a matter of propriety to remove himself from the case. Should he preside over the case, his verdict would not be rendered void. Maimonides, according to the interpretation of R. Joel Sirkes (Bah, *Tur*, op. cit. 7:11) equates the superficial and the close relationship cases. In both instances, presiding over the case does not render the verdict null and void, despite the impropriety committed.

24. Cf. Ketubbot 103a. For an excellent survey and analysis of the *kofin* principle in the talmudic and responsa literature, see Dr. Shmuel Shilo, "*Kofin al Midot Sedom:* Jewish Law's Concept of Abuse of Rights," *Israel Law Review* 15, no. 1 (1980): 49–78.

25. Bava Batra 22a.

26. One amoraic opinion recorded at Yoma 75a; Pesikta Zutrata B-ha'alotkha. The exceptions were the taste of cucumbers, melons, leeks, onions, and garlic. The manna did not produce these tastes because these foods do not agree with women in pregnancy.

27. Yoma 75a; Tosefta Sotah 4:1; Exodus Rabbah 25:3.

28. *The Torah Discourses of the Holy Tzaddik Reb Menachem Mendel of Rimanov* (1745–1815), translated by Dov Levine (Hoboken, N.J.: Ktav, 1996), p. 543.

29. Ibid., pp. 543–47.

30. R. Herbert W. Bomzer, *The Kolel in America* (New York: Shengold, 1985), p. 24. For R. Bomzer's suggestions for improving evaluation and accountability in the *Kolel*, see ibid., pp. 141–42.

31. This section draws from my *Economic Public Policy and Jewish Law* (Hoboken, N.J., Ktav, 1993), pp. 95–113.

32. Sotah 36b.

33. Bava Batra 21a; *Yad*, Talmud Torah 11:1; *Tur*, Yoreh De'ah 245:1; *Sh.Ar.*, Yoreh De'ah 245:7; *Ar.haSh.*, Yoreh De'ah 245:9.

34. *Ar.haSh.*, op. cit. 245:9, 27.

35. William J. Baumol and Alan S. Blinder, *Economic Principles and Policies*, 6th ed. (New York, Harcourt Brace Jovanovich, 1996), pp. 326–29.

36. Sanhedrin 43b.

37. R. Menahem b. Solomon Meiri, *Beit ha-Behirah*, Sanhedrin 44a.

38. Rami b. Hamma, reporting in the name of R. Isaac, Bava Batra 89a; Rif ad loc.; *Yad*, Genevah 8:20; Rosh, Bava Batra 5:22; *Tur*, Hoshen Mishpat 231:2; *Sh.Ar.*, Hoshen Mishpat 231:2; *Ar.haSh.*, Hoshen Mishpat 231:3.

39. Aaron Levine, *Economic Public Policy and Jewish Law*, (Hoboken, NJ., Ktav, 1993), pp. 24, 28–32.

40. Frederick S. Mishkin, *The Economics of Money, Banking and Financial Markets* (New York: Addison-Wesley, 1997), p. 307.

Kushta and Moral Education

The central importance truth-telling plays in the *hinnukh* (religious train-ing) experience is reminiscent of the talmudic account of how the people of Kushta were devoted to truth-telling:

> Rava said: At first I used to say that there is no truth in the world. But then one of the rabbis said to me, and R. Tavut was his name, and some say that Rav Tavyomei was his name, that even if they gave him all the rich-es in the world, he would not lie. He related the following story to me: He once visited a certain town by the name of Kushta [whose inhabitants] would not tell a lie and none of the people from there died before his time. He married a woman from among them, and he had two sons by her.
>
> One day, his wife was sitting and washing her hair. Her neighbor came and knocked on the door, asking to speak to her. Thinking that it would not be proper to tell the neighbor that his wife was washing her hair, he said to [the neighbor]: "She is not here." Subsequently, his two sons died. The people of the town came to him and asked: "What is the reason for this?" He told them what had happened. They said to him: "We beg you, leave our town and do not incite death against these people."[1]

Inculcating habits of truth-telling in children requires the development of a concrete program. Extrapolating the lifestyle of the people of Kushta should therefore prove fruitful in identifying the contours of such a program.

What is immediately striking is that Kushta is a place of incredibly stern justice. R. Tavut (Tavyomei) suffers the loss of his two children and expulsion from the town all because he spoke a harmless untruth. The punishment appears to far exceed the severity of the sin committed. Moreover, R. Tavut's conduct would certainly be regarded as permissible in ordinary society. A very similar case involving an unexpected caller was dealt with by R. Shelomoh Zalman Auerbach (Israel, 1910–1995). In his treatment of this question, R. Auerbach posited that an individual is under no obligation to see someone against his will. Accordingly, if K knocks on D's door without an appointment, D is under no obligation to see him. Moreover, D's right to privacy puts him under no duty to inform K what he is doing at that time and/or why he does not wish to see him. Informing K, through a member of the household, that he is unavailable, however, runs the risk of insulting K. If K was important enough, D would surely interrupt whatever he is doing and give K an audience. With the aim of avoiding friction with K, D should therefore inform K, through a mem-ber of the household, that he is *not home*. Since the latter response avoids a strained relationship, it constitutes a permissible lie and is therefore an applica-tion of the principle of *darkhei shalom* (fostering harmony and goodwill).[2]

Perhaps the key to understanding R. Tavut's expulsion is that his conduct should be evaluated not only in terms of its inherent worthiness but also in terms of the impact it exerted on the moral climate of Kushta.

There can be no doubt that R. Tavut's conduct undermined the moral climate of Kushta. The Talmud describes R. Tavut as a man who would give up all the treasures of the world so as not to tell a lie.[3] But the people of Kushta went beyond this standard. They would not utter even a *permissible lie* because they were committed to promote truth as a positive value and were prepared to suffer any pain necessary to accomplish this.

Kushta was upset with R. Tavut not because his conduct was egregious. No! It certainly was not. Rather, they asked him to leave because the incident proved that he was not one of them; it proved that he was not committed to the lifestyle necessary to promote truth as a positive value in life. From the perspective of a Kushtanite, the main disappointment with R. Tavut was that the incident occurred altogether. A Kushtanite would regard it as a worthwhile enterprise to think through the possibility, remote as it may be, that an unexpected caller might come just at the moment one was engaging in a private activity. One who is committed to upholding truth as a positive value is desperately concerned not to be caught in a situation where the use of a permissible lie is the only way out to avoid embarrassment and/or a strain in relations. A Kushtanite would therefore schedule a private activity only at a time that enjoyed an almost zero probability that a caller would come by, notwithstanding any inconvenience the odd scheduling would entail.

Understanding R. Tavut's expulsion in this light allows us to view the death of his children in terms other than as a manifestation of divine retribution against him. Quite to the contrary, R. Tavut committed no misdeed. In fact, his standard of integrity was exemplary, but it fell short of Kushta's standard. Since the Kushtanites were conferred with the divine grace of being insulated from natural debilitating and destructive forces, they lived incredibly long lives. Without this special divine protection, natural forces bombard man and continually threaten him with death and injury. Because R. Tavut was not protected by this special divine shield, his family's physical well-being was subject to the vicissitudes of natural forces. The death of his children, therefore, should be viewed as the result of the removal of the special divine shield rather than as a manifestation of divine retribution.

The human costs involved in maintaining a Kushtanite life style are manifold. Let us begin with the economic sphere. There can be no doubt that the people of Kushta worked very hard to earn their livelihood and were, in all probability, not wealthy. To see why, one can extrapolate how Kushta conducted its commercial transactions compared to ordinary society.

In ordinary society, commercial gain can be made by exploiting someone's ignorance. But capitalizing on an informational advantage is not always immoral. Consider that Halakhah's *disclosure* obligation is geared not to the expectations of one's *actual* opposite number but to the expectations of a *hypothetical reasonable man* in that position.[4] What constitutes reasonable expectations will, in turn, depend upon the type of transaction with which one is dealing. Consider the sale of a consumer good. Here, the buyer's reasonable expectations require the seller to disclose any defect in the product at hand.[5] The seller's reasonable expectations, however, work to limit the extent of his disclosure obligation. Accordingly, if the transaction was face-to-face, the seller is not responsible to point out to the buyer the visibly obvious defects in the product. The reasonable expectation here is that the buyer readily picks up the flaws without the seller having to specifically point them out to him. Hence, voiding or adjusting the terms of the concluded transaction on the basis of these visibly obvious flaws is not entertained by the Jewish court.[6]

What constitutes reasonable expectation changes radically when one moves from the sale of a consumer good to the sale of a speculative asset. Here, the reasonable expectation is that the entire transaction is made possible only because the seller (S) and the buyer (B) harbor variant and possibly even opposite expectations: B buys because he is convinced that the price of the asset will rise. S sells because he believes the price will fall. Alternatively, S may basically agree with B but nonetheless is convinced that other assets will rise more. Given the variant and even opposite beliefs that underlie a trade in a speculative asset, entry into this marketplace is accompanied by *a warning to the reasonable man that he should research all the publicly accessible information on which his trade will be made.* If he ignores this warning in whole or in part, he is at his own risk.

The reasonable-man standard puts into sharp relief the difference between the person who is looking for every opportunity to make a statement that integrity is his life force and the one who is just concerned with not violating the law of deception. The latter (A) will look at his opposite number and see not a real person but only a *hypothetical* person who represents the *reasonable man.* Accordingly, A's disclosure will be measured, based on the expectations of the statistical man. If it turns out that the expectations of A's actual opposite number were dashed, A will not be concerned, provided his disclosure satisfied the expectation of the hypothetical reasonable man. In sharp contrast, the man (B) who is looking for every opportunity to make a statement that integrity is his life force will never regard his opposite number as an abstraction and a statistic. Because each transaction is another opportunity to make a positive statement about integrity, B is concerned that he should not dash the expectations of the actual, real person with whom he is dealing. For B, the actual person with whom he is dealing is, for the purpose of the trade at hand, the entire universe. Concern not to dash the expectations of the actual person one is dealing with leads to an obsessive need to *share* information with that person.

The following story, told by R. Elya ha-Kohen Dushnitzer, *mashgiah* (supervisor) of the Lomzer Yeshiva in Petah Tikvah, Israel, illustrates this principle: R. Elya was anxious to sell a *pardes* (orchard) he owned in Ir Shalom, outside Tel Aviv. An opportunity to do so came about when a former student, Michel Rosenblitz, connected with an American who was interested in buying it. Michel arranged a bus trip for the three of them to travel from Jerusalem to Ir Shalom to see the *pardes*.

As the three were sitting in the bus from Jerusalem the conversation naturally turned towards the *pardes*. "You know," R. Elya said to the American, "the Talmud (Bava Metzia 29b) states that if someone wishes to lose his money, he should hire workers and not watch over them. If you expect to live in America and won't be here to oversee your workers, I don't recommend that you buy the *pardes*. It would be what the Talmud (Kesubos 107b) calls putting money on *keren ha-tzvi* (the horns of a running deer); you would lose it very quickly."

Michel looked at R. Elya in disbelief. He knew very well that the American wouldn't be coming to Israel often and so he might just listen to R. Elya's sound advice and the whole deal would fall through. The American, however, just listened, nodded his head and didn't say anything.

R. Elya continued: "I think you should know," he said to the American, "there are quite a few trees in the orchard which bear no fruit at all. They are mostly in the northwest corner. I just wanted you to know that."

Michel was beside himself, and yet at the same time marveled at his rabbi's honesty. He began to understand why the *pardes* hadn't been sold for so many years. He listened with relief as the American said, "Rebbe, it's no problem. I want to buy the orchard anyway."

"But that's only because you don't know its faults," R. Elya retorted. A little while later, R. Elya said, "There is also a small section of the trees surrounded by rocks and stones that have stunted the growth of the oranges." Michel was afraid that the American would surely get off at the next stop and return to Jerusalem. But he didn't say a word. He just listened and nodded his head.

Finally, they came to Ir Shalom and made their way to the *pardes*. "Here," said R. Elya, taking the man by the hand, "let me show you where those bad trees are. The Mekhilta says you cannot compare seeing something to merely hearing about it." And they began walking through the *pardes*.

Suddenly the American looked at his watch, stopped, took out a small bottle of pills from his pocket, took one and swallowed it. "What's that?" asked R. Eyla curiously. "Is everything all right?"

"Oh, its nothing, nothing," said the American, brushing away the question. "Nothing to worry about."

"No, tell me," insisted R. Elya. "What did you take from that little bottle?"

"It's nothing," repeated the American. "I have a minor heart problem and my doctor in America gave me these pills that I have to take every few hours. It's really all right."

"*Oy!*" exclaimed R. Elya. "*Zolst du zein gezunt* (May you be well). *Der Aibishter zoll dir helfen* (May God help you)." Then R. Elya shook his head and said, "I'm afraid that this *pardes* will be too much of a strain on you. With your condition, I certainly would not recommend that you buy it. For one thing, you certainly won't be able to travel to Israel too often to oversee it, and besides I know how much aggravation this *pardes* can be. There is simply no way I can sell it to you. With your delicate heart, you would be throwing out your money and hurting your health at the same time." Taking the American's hand in both of his, he said most fervently, "*Zolst du zein gezunt* (May you be well)."

Despite the American's protests, R. Elya refused to sell him the *pardes*. Instead, he wished him a *refuah shelaimah* (complete recovery), thanked him for his interest, and that was the end of their association.[7]

The above incident took place in the middle of the twentieth century, but just as easily could have been retrieved from the archives of Kushta.

One who is constantly looking to make his life experiences a positive statement regarding integrity is eager to share information in the marketplace with his opposite number. The sharing goes to the point of not regarding one's opposite number as an *adversary*. Indeed, the only way to be sure that we are not dashing the expectations of our opposite number is to imagine that we have exchanged places with that person in the trade at hand.

Sharing information with one's opposite number in a commercial transaction eliminates the possibility of earning profits on the basis of asymmetrical information. Kushtanites were therefore, in all probability, very hard-working and not wealthy; and they probably never realized a windfall economic gain in their lives.

Let us now turn to the social realm. In ordinary society, the use of innocent lies often works wonders to prevent strain and diffuse tension and even hatred in human relations. Altering the truth even for the purpose of enhancing human relations is, however, not legitimate in Kushta.

In the hands of parents, educators, and employers, the use of praise is a powerful motivational device. In Kushta, the use of false praise even to motivate worthy endeavor and noble achievement is prohibited.

In ordinary society, one can achieve popularity by sporting a good sense of humor and by the clever use of flattery. In Kushta flattery is an intolerable trait. Relatedly, humor, as we know it today, was probably nonexistent in Kushta. This is so because much of humor entails ridicule or aspects of falsehood in the form of misstatement, overstatement, and/or understatement.[8]

In ordinary society, the self-image and confidence of the misfortunate can be built up by offering false praise and false hope. In Kushta, misery may not be relieved in this manner.

Does the description of life in Kushta lead to the proposition that Kushta was a drab place, devoid of warm human relations. No! "Love your neighbor as yourself" (Leviticus 19:18), as R. Akiva put it, is a great principle of the Torah.[9] Since Kushta was a righteous place, this principle must have achieved the highest level of fulfillment there. Now, if Kushtanites could not resort to conventional humor, flattery, and clever lies as a means of meeting their responsibilities toward their fellow man, *other means to fulfill these obligations had to be found.* What Kushtanites could not accomplish by means of false and insincere words, they had to compensate for with the expenditure of their time and resources, and even in adjustments to their lifestyle.

The upshot of our thesis is that R. Tavut's commitment to truth and integrity *was very close to, yet so far from* Kushta's living reality of these concepts. The difference between R. Tavut and Kushta manifested itself in lifestyle. Because the human cost of the Kushtanite lifestyle was so enormous, the danger that its people would emulate R. Tavut's lifestyle was very real. By means of the slippery slope, R. Tavut's presence was a threat to Kushta's life. Indeed, *good, not evil, may be the biggest enemy of greatness.*

The Patriarch Jacob and the Kushta Standard

In Jewish tradition, the patriarch Jacob is regarded as the paragon of truth and integrity.[10] One period of Jacob's life for which the Torah provides us with much detail is the twenty years he was in the employ of his father-in-law, Laban. Our purpose here will be to demonstrate that in this relationship Jacob displayed a virtue that was objectively evident. The affinity between Jacob's conduct and the standard we extrapolated to be the norm in Kushta will be readily apparent.

Tending Laban's flock, Jacob exerts himself to the utmost for him and never idles on his time.[11] When a mishap occurs, Jacob never shifts the blame, but

instead makes good the loss even when he is not legally required to do so.[12]
After fourteen years in his employ, Jacob decides to take leave of Laban, leading
to the following dialogue between them (Genesis 30:27–30):

> Laban said to him: "If I have found favor with you, stay. I have noted the
> omens and seen that the Lord has blessed me for your sake. Fix your own
> wage, and I will pay it." Jacob answered: "You know well how I have served
> you, and how your livestock fared under my care. Before I came, you had
> little indeed, but now it has increased greatly; the Lord has blessed you
> wherever I have turned. But when am I to provide for my own house-
> hold?"

By ascribing his good fortune to Jacob's piety rather than to his diligence,
Laban, notes R. Samson R. Hirsch (Germany, 1808–1888), fails to recognize
Jacob's integrity.[13]

R. Hirsch's insight provides us with an understanding of why Jacob decides
to remain in Laban's employ despite his exploited status until now. Jacob considered it his mission to perfect in himself the character trait of integrity. His
failure to make an *impact* on Laban proved to Jacob that he had not yet achieved
the highest level of integrity. Jacob therefore redoubled his efforts to display a
level of honesty that would make his integrity *objectively evident*. Toward this
end, he proposes a plan for compensation in which he deliberately exposes himself to an objectively verifiable standard: All the spotted and mottled lambs will
be removed from Laban's flock, leaving in his (Jacob's) care only the single-colored lambs. Jacob's wage will consist of the mottled and spotted goats born
from the single-colored herd.[14] Jacob proclaims: "Thus my honesty will tell,
when you come to look into my wages with you: Any goat in my lot that is
not speckled and spotted, any sheep that is not dark, you may consider to have
been stolen" (Genesis 30:33).

Paradoxically, Jacob's grand display of honesty fails to make an impact on
Laban. The personification of duplicity,[15] Laban reads ambiguity into even the
most objectively precise terms of agreement. Accordingly, the exact definition
of Jacob's wage is unilaterally changed by Laban no less than ten times in five
years.[16] Jacob's miraculous success, with the aid of the striped rods, in producing spotted animals from the herd of single-colored ones is nevertheless taken
by Laban's coterie as outright theft.[17]

However, persistence in displaying his honesty in an objectively evident
manner does finally bring success to Jacob. His integrity makes its impact on
Laban at their encounter at the mountain of Gilead. Jacob and his family had
stealthily fled from Laban. When Laban overtakes them at Gilead, he is full of
accusations and complaints. He says to Jacob (Genesis 31:26–30):

What have you done? You have deceived me and carried off my daughters as though they were captives taken in war. Why did you slip away secretly without telling me? I would have sent you off with rejoicing and song, with music and tambourines and harps. You did not even let me kiss my daughters and grandchildren; you have acted foolishly. It is in my power to do you harm; but last night the God of your father said to me, "Beware of saying anything to Jacob, either good or bad." If you had to leave because you longed so much for your father's home, why did you steal my gods?

In his reaction to Laban's outcry, Jacob once again adheres to an objective standard of honesty: "I was afraid, for I thought you would take away your daughters from me by force. If you find your gods in anyone's possession, he shall not live. In the presence of our kinsmen, identify whatever of yours I may have, and take it" (Genesis 31:31–32).

When Laban's search for his idols turns up nothing (Genesis 31:33), Jacob unleashes a tirade against him. Jacob contrasts his own integrity with Laban's perfidy during their entire twenty-year relationship (Genesis 31:36–42). Only at this point is Laban moved to propose a covenant of peace between himself and Jacob (Genesis 31:44). Jacob's integrity has finally made its impact on Laban.

The encounter between Jacob and Laban at Gilead brings into sharp relief the contrast between authentic and false integrity. While Jacob adheres to an objectively verifiable standard of honesty, Laban's claims are not subject to verification. Masquerading as a doting father, Laban berates Jacob for depriving him of the opportunity to embrace his daughters and grandchildren before they took leave of him (Genesis 31:38). Laban's protest that he would have sent off Jacob amidst musical accompaniment amounts to nothing more than an unsubstantiated claim, bordering on mockery in the light of their previous relationship (Genesis 31:27). Finally, Laban's assertion that God commanded him to do Jacob neither good nor evil amounts to another unverifiable claim (Genesis 31:29).

The Gilead episode demonstrates that championing the cause of integrity often requires polemics with both attackers and evildoers. If integrity is to elevate the moral climate of society, its exponent must choose his battles carefully. The temptation to disprove the charges of an attacker must be resisted if such polemics would divert society's attention from one's own honesty. Jacob resists the temptation to explode Laban's masquerade as a doting father. To do this, Jacob would only have to relate to Laban Rachel and Leah's reaction when Jacob asked them to flee with him. "Rachel and Leah answered him, saying: `Have we any share or heritage left in our father's house? Are we not regarded as strangers by him? He has sold us, and then used up our money'" (Genesis 31:14–15).

A lesser man surely would have seized the moment for sweet revenge by *setting the record straight.* Jacob, however, knows that his prime concern must be to establish his own integrity. The true feelings of Leah and Rachel toward their father are secondary. To avoid diverting attention from the central issue, his own integrity, Jacob allows Laban's self-serving pretense as a doting father to go undisputed. Jacob, who epitomizes integrity, chooses his battles carefully and is not obsessed with a need to set the record straight as regards his opponent's wrongdoing.

All this demonstrates that Jacob subjected himself to objectively verifiable standards and formulated his commitments in precise and unequivocal terms. The affinity between Jacob's conduct and the standard we extrapolated as the norm in Kushta is readily apparent.

Moral Education and Kushta

Because inculcating habits of truth-telling is the centerpiece of moral education, the world of *hinnukh* naturally connects to Kushta. This connection becomes firmer with the following dictum of R. Zeira: "One should not promise to give a child something and then not give it to him, because one will thereby teach him lying, as it is said: *they have taught their tongues to speak lies* (Jeremiah 9:4)."[18]

Analysis of R. Zeira's dictum will demonstrate that it echoes the philosophy of Kushta. Let us begin by discussing some of the ethical norms governing the making and breaking of a promise.

The most fundamental concern is that one should never make a commitment unless one fully intends to carry it out. Verbalizing a commitment without an accompanying resolve of the heart to carry it out is a commitment made in bad faith and constitutes unethical conduct.

> A person is forbidden to act in a smooth-tongued and luring manner.
> He should not speak one thing outwardly and think otherwise in his heart.
> Rather, his inner self should be like the self which he shows to the world.
> What he feels in his heart should be the same as the words on his lips.[19]

Someone who retracts a verbal commitment is called untrustworthy;[20] and the Jewish court will admonish and publicly reprove the offender for this misconduct.[21] Nevertheless, breaking a promise is permissible in certain circumstances. Consider the following two scenarios:

1. A verbally commits himself to confer B with a largess. Subsequently, A has second thoughts and wishes to retract his commitment. Provided A made his commitment in good faith, his subsequent retraction is not unethical. Given

the considerable expense involved, B presumably never relied on the promise, and hence A's retraction did not dash B's expectations.[22]

2. A promises to give B a certain item as a gift for, say, his birthday. Before the date arrives, the price of the item rises sharply. B wishes to retract.

A similar case involving a sales transaction is dealt with by talmudic authorities: Buyer B and seller S commit themselves to a sales transaction. Before the transaction proceeds further, to the point either of B's making a deposit or of the parties becoming legally bound, the market price of the item rises. On account of the price rise, S wishes to retract. Authorities dispute whether S's retraction should be regarded as unethical.[23] In this matter, R. Jehiel Michel Epstein (Belarus, 1829–1908) holds that S's retraction would not brand him as untrustworthy.[24] Presumably, R. Epstein would rule the same in the birthday gift case.

Given that the breaking of a promise is sometimes permissible, why does R. Zeira state his dictum in absolute terms without qualification. What must be inferred is that one *may never break a promise to a child*. Given the child's immaturity, he (she) will not appreciate and fully understand the rationale for why the retraction is morally acceptable. Relatedly, the boundaries between morally acceptable and morally unacceptable retraction will be blurred as far as a child is concerned.

Since it is morally unacceptable to break a promise to a child, prudence demands that an adult should avoid, as much as possible, making promises and threats to children.

Recall R. Auerbach's ruling that one may instruct a member of his household to inform an unexpected caller that he is not home. Addressing himself to this issue, R. Nahum Yavrov (Israel, contemp.) posits that this instruction should not be given in the presence of a child, and certainly one should not use a child to deliver the untruth to the unexpected stranger. To be sure, the untruth is a permissible lie, but any involvement of a child here will habituate him (her) to lie. R. Yavrov bases his ruling on R. Zeira's dictum.[25]

What proceeds from the above analysis of R. Zeira's dictum is that *hinnukh* demands a standard of honesty higher than the standard acceptable for the adult world. Further support for the this thesis can be drawn from Yevamot 63a:

> Rav was constantly tormented by his wife. If he told her, "Prepare me lentils," she would prepare him small peas; [and if he asked for] small peas, she prepared him lentils. When his son Hiyya grew up, he gave her [his father's instructions] in reverse. "Your mother," Rav remarked to him, "has improved!" "It was I," the other replied, "who reversed [your orders] to her." "This is what people say," the first said to him, "'Thine own offspring teaches thee reason'; however, you must not continue to do so, for it is said,

They have taught their tongue to speak lies, they weary themselves, etc. (Jeremiah 9:4).

Why Rav objected to Hiyya's conduct requires explanation. Insofar as Hiyya made use of lies to promote domestic harmony between his parents, his conduct should have been regarded as a praiseworthy application of the principle of *darkhei shalom*. Commentators have advanced various explanations.[26] One explanation that has much relevancy for the *hinnukh* obligation is offered by R. Solomon Luria (Poland, 1510–1573). In his view, Rav objected to Hiyya's conduct because it entailed a *habitual lie.* To be successful, Hiyya would have to engage in his ruse for an indefinite period of time. Because habitual lying, even for a permissible purpose, debilitates one's character, Rav objected to Hiyya's conduct.[27]

R. Luria's thesis requires elaboration. If habitual lying, even of the permissible kind, corrupts, then why did Rav approve of Hiyya's conduct for his own use? If the ruse is prohibited for Hiyya, it should also be prohibited for Rav.

The difficulty is removed under the assumption that truth and integrity must be held up to a higher standard in the world of *hinnukh* than in other contexts.

By dint of his own testimony, Rav would have used Hiyya's ruse if only he had thought of the idea himself. Because the ruse serves to counteract spiteful behavior on the part of his wife, there can be no question of its permissibility. But approving Hiyya's conduct would have made Rav remiss in his *hinnukh* obligation. This is so because a father must not only teach his son not to lie, but must go further and teach him to uphold truth as a positive value. Hiyya's efforts to promote domestic harmony were, of course, admirable. But Rav could not commend Hiyya for his efforts because he used lies to achieve his objective.

While truth must operate on a higher plane in the world of *hinnukh* as compared to the adult world, some amount of intersection with the adult standard of honesty must be admissible. This is so because *hinnukh* is religious training not just for an ideal world but for the real world. In the real world an individual will assuredly encounter many instances where the use of some form of untruth will be the only means to end, mitigate, or avoid strife and discord. Recall R. Yavrov's strictures regarding allowing a child even to *witness* the delivery of an untruth to an unexpected caller. But R. Yavrov himself points out variations of the case where the use of a lie by a child would be permissible. A case in point occurs when the father is sleeping and the child assesses that if he tells the unexpected caller the truth, the caller will expect the child to wake up his father. Suppose, however, the child assesses that his father would not want to be awakened to meet the unexpected caller. Here, the only way to avoid strife is for the child to tell the unexpected caller that his father is not home.[28]

Relatedly, in the instance where children are involved in a scuffle, a child is permitted to make use of lies as a means of ending the discord among his play-mates.[29]

The thrust of the preceding discussion leads to the proposition that the use of permissible lies has some place in the world of *hinnukh*. But its main place should be in the theoretical realm. In this regard, parents and teachers should stress that the use of permissible lies is only a *second-best* solution to real world problems.

The flip side of the above proposition is to avoid the pitfall of operating in compartmentalized moral spheres. Specifically, the ideal Kushta sets for the child's everyday routine must be related to the child's study of the Pentateuch. If children are taught to conduct their lives in such a manner that they will always be in a position to make positive statements about truth and integrity, they will experience a sense of dissonance when they learn about an instance where the conduct of a righteous biblical figure falls short of this standard. This dissonance comes to a peak in the figure of the patriarch Jacob. As mentioned earlier, Jacob personifies integrity and truth; yet his conduct in acquiring the birthright from Esau and stealing Isaac's blessings from him appears to fall short of the Kushta standard. Is the Kushta standard the ideal for *all* transactions in the human experience? To succeed, *hinnukh* efforts must exert an *integrative* force on the life of the child. For this reason, Torah educators must address the above issue head-on.[30]

Conscientious efforts to inculcate truth and integrity as positive values work to bring the adult world closer to the pristine world of *hinnukh*. This is so because the task of promoting integrity and truth as a positive value challenges parents and educators to come up with creative solutions to ending strife and discord without the use of lies and deceptions. It also challenges them to avoid circumstances that would be a natural setting for permissible lies and permissible broken promises, even to the extent of changing their lifestyle. The dividend society reaps from this type of *hinnukh* is that each successive generation of youth enters the adult world with a new burst of moral energy, and society moves to a higher and higher standard of integrity.

Problem

R. Nahum Yavrov (Israel, contemp., *Niv Sefatayim*, pp.106-8) presents a number of instances, culled from the rabbinical literature, where legitimacy is given for a teacher of Torah to make use of an "untruth" as a pedagogical device:

(1) With the aim of testing his students on the knowledge they have acquired, it is permissible for a teacher of Torah to make inaccurate statements

to them and see whether they pick up on the inaccuracy (Sh. Ar., *Yoreh De'ah* 246:12)

(2) To drive home the lesson that review is absolutely essential for retention, it is permissible for the teacher to himself feign a lack of recall of the subject matter and tell the students that even a teacher forgets, if he does not review (*Tosefta Oholot 16*).

(3) With the aim of encouraging his students to ask questions to clarify difficulties, even at the expense of being regarded as foolish, the teacher may present ideas to the students that he knows in advance he will have to either correct or modify in response to his students anticipated questions (Nazir 57b).

(4) With the aim of encouraging his students to take on the tractate at hand, the teacher may tell the students that the tractate is easy, when in fact the teacher regards it as difficult(R. Yaakov Reicher, Austria, d.1733, *Iyun Yaakov*, Bava Mezia 23a)

(5) If the teacher sees that the students are not participating, he may misquote a passage of the text he is teaching them in order to arouse them to question him on what he said and get them involved in the subject matter. (Zevahim 62b).

Would the above pedagogical techniques be approved in Kushta?

1. Sanhedrin 97a.

2. R. Shelomoh Zalman Auerbach, quoted by R. Yaakov Yehezkel Fish, *Titan Emet l'Yaakov* 5:24.

3. The text follows R. Judah Loew b. Bezalel (Prague, ca. 1525–1609), Maharal, *Hiddushei Aggadot*, Sanhedrin, ad loc., in understanding the talmudic narrative as conveying that R. Tavut achieved a lofty standard in truth-telling, just below the standard of Kushta, *before* he came in contact with this community. See, however, R. Samuel Eliezer b. Judah ha-Levi Edels (Poland, 1555–1623), Maharsha, Sanhedrin, ad loc.

4. For the development of this thesis, please turn to pp. 35–45 of this volume.

5. R. Joseph Caro (Israel, 1488–1575), *Shulhan Arukh*, Hoshen Mishpat 228:6, 232:6.

6. R. Binyamin Rabinovits-Teomim, *Hukkat Mishpat* 16:1, be'urim 2, n. 2.

7. R. Paysach J. Krohn, *The Maggid Speaks* (New York: Mesorah, 1987), pp. 66–71.

8. There can be no doubt that humor has its place in a Kushta lifestyle as well. Consider that the tanna in Avot (6:5) counts *mi'ut sehok* (limited laughter) as one of the forty-eight qualities necessary for *kinyan Torah* (i.e., making Torah the essence of one's being). Commenting on this attribute, R. Israel b. Gedaliah Lipschutz (Germany, 1782–1860), *Tiferet Yisrael*, ad loc., equates *mi'ut sehok* with *milta d'bedihuta* (humor) and goes on to praise humor, in limited form, as a positive quality in Torah scholarship. In this regard R. Lipschutz makes reference to the practice of the amora Rabbah, who said something humorous to his students before beginning his Torah discourses (Pesahim 117a). See also Ta'anit 22a.

For a discussion of permissible and mitzvah outlets for expressing mockery and ridicule, see R. Shelomoh Zalman Braun (New York, 1911–1995), *Shearim Mezuyanim be-Halakhah* to R. Solomon b. Joseph Ganzfried (Hungary, 1804–1886), *Kizzur Shulhan Arukh* 30, n. 3.

9. Jerusalem Talmud, Nedarim 9:4.

10. Micah 7:20; Makkot 24a; *Tanna debei Eliyahu Rabbah* 6.

11. Genesis 31:6; Midrash Rabbah Genesis 70:20; Bava Mezia 93b; Midrash Tanhuma, Parshat Vayetse; Midrash haGadol, Genesis 30:42; Maimonides (Egypt, 1135–1204), *Yad*, Sekhirut 13:7.

12. Genesis 31:39; Bava Mezia 93B; R. Naphtali Zevi Judah Berlin (Russia, 1817–1893), *Ha-Amek Davar*, Genesis 31:39.

13. R. Samson R. Hirsch's commentary at Genesis 30:27.

14. Genesis 30:32–33 and commentaries ad loc.

15. Genesis Rabbah 75:5.

16. R. Joseph Kimhi, quoted by R. David Kimhi (France, 1160–1236), Radak, Genesis 31:7.

17. Genesis 30:1. Nahmanides (commentary at Genesis 30:37) finds no element of dishonesty in Jacob's use of striped rods. Given that the contract called for offspring of a certain color to belong to him, Jacob had every right to promote his own interest by seeking to ensure such births. Given Laban's ignorance regarding the ramification of the use of the striped rods, it is even possible, avers Nahmanides, that Jacob negotiated with Laban the legitimacy of their use at the outset of the agreement. For other defenses of Jacob's use of the striped rods, see Radak and R. Eliyahu Mizrahi (Turkey, 1440–1525), Mizrahi, ad loc.

18. Sukkot 46b.

19. *Yad*, De'ot 2:6.

20. R. Yohanan, Bava Mezia 49a; R. Isaac b. Abraham Alfasi (Algeria, 1013–1103), Rif, ad loc.; *Yad*, Mekhirah 7:89; R. Asher b. Jehiel (Germany, ca. 1250–1327), Rosh, Bava Mezia 4:12; R. Jacob b. Asher, (Spain, 1270–1340), *Tur*, Hoshen Mishpat 204:11–12; R. Joseph Caro (Israel, 1488–1575), *Sh.Ar.*, Hoshen Mishpat 204:78; R. Jehiel Michel Epstein (Belarus, 1829–1908), *Arukh ha-Shulhan*, Hoshen Mishpat 204:89.

21. See sources quoted in *Hukkat Mishpat*, op. cit. 1:4, Mekorot 9 and be'urim 13.

22. See sources cited in n. 20 above.

23. See R. Moses Isserles (Poland, 1525 or 1530–1572), Rema, *Sh.Ar.*, Hoshen Mishpat 204:11. R. Isserles himself rules stringently in this matter.

24. *Ar.haSh.*, op. cit. 204:8. In this case, R. Epstein opts that not to retract would be a matter of *middat hasidut* (pious conduct). Tosafot (Bava Mezia 24b) rules that *lifnim mi-shurat ha-din* (conduct beyond the letter of the law) pertains only to making a claim on one's toil and effort, but not to the requirement of incurring financial loss. R. Epstein's mention of *middat hasidut* here should, therefore, be understood as saying no more than that not to retract is praiseworthy conduct. A *requirement* not to retract does not, however, obtain here even on a *lifnim mi-shurat ha-din* level.

25. R. Nahum Yavrov, *Niv Sefatayim* 3:32, hiddushim 57–58.

26. Cf. R. Jacob b. Joseph Reicher (Austria, d. 1733), *Iyun Yaakov*, commentary on *Ein Yakov*, Yevamot 63a.

27. R. Solomon Luria, *Yam Shel Shelomoh*, Yevamot 6:46.

28. *Niv Sefatayim* 3:32, hiddushim 58

29. R. Shelomoh Zalman Auerbach and R. Yosef Shalom Elyashiv, quoted by R. Yaakov Yehezkel Fish in *Titan Emet l'Yaakov*, op. cit. 5:10.

30. I am indebted to Leon M. Metzger for bringing up this point.

2. Advertising and Marketing

Protecting the Reasonable Man Against Deception in Advertising

Any message of mass communications will be understood by the members of its target audience in various ways. Some may regard the message as informative and entertaining, while others may find it vague and misleading. The basic issue for government regulation of advertising is which consumer to protect. Should the law protect only reasonable, sensible, and intelligent consumers who conduct themselves carefully in the marketplace? Or must it also protect ignorant consumers who conduct themselves carelessly?

The Issue in American Law

Prior to 1914, misleading advertising claims in the United States were adjudicated by the judicial system under common law. The governing principle for these cases was the reasonable-man standard. Accordingly, an advertiser could not be held liable for misrepresentation unless the court decided that a reasonable man would rely on the false or deceptive message. Under this standard, the person the courts protected was not the average or typical person, but rather an idealized person who always operated in the marketplace without the slightest negligence.

In 1914, the Federal Trade Commission (FTC) was established. This independent governmental agency was given the mandate to investigate unfair and predatory competitive practices, and to declare illegal all "unfair methods of competition and commerce." In 1938, its mandate expanded to include the mission of preventing false and misleading advertising.

The FTC in its early history, as Professor Ivan Preston documents, broke away from common law precedent and adopted the ignorant-man standard in protecting consumers against deceptive advertising. Preston cites several rulings that typify the agency's attitude during its early years.

In 1919, for instance, the FTC ordered a manufacturer to stop advertising that its automobile batteries would "last forever."[1] Since the same ad offered the customer, for the additional charge of 50 cents per month, the right to receive a replacement battery as soon as the purchased one wore out, no reasonable person would put stock in the claim that the battery would last forever. Nonetheless, the FTC viewed the replacement service clause as confirming the deceptiveness of the "last forever" statement. The case indicated that the FTC felt that the law should protect even those consumers who conducted themselves carelessly in the marketplace.

The ignorant-man standard reached an extreme when Clairol was forbidden to say that its dye would "color hair permanently." The FTC deemed that the public would take this as a claim that all the hair a person grew for the rest of her life would emerge in the Clairol color.[2]

Eventually, the standard applied by the FTC in these cases gave way to a narrower view of which consumer the agency should protect. The new attitude was articulated in the case of *Heinz W. Kirchner*.[3]

The case concerned an inflatable device to help a person stay afloat and learn to swim. Called SwimEzy, it was worn under the swimming suit and was advertised as being invisible. It was not invisible, but the FTC found it to be "inconspicuous," and ruled that was all the claim of invisibility would mean to the public. But what about those who might take the claim to mean that the device was wholly invisible or bodiless? The FTC made it clear that it no longer intended to protect people so ignorant.

> True—the Commission's responsibility is to prevent deception of the gullible and credulous, as well as the cautious and knowledgeable. . . . This principle loses its validity, however, if it is applied uncritically or pushed to an absurd extreme. An advertiser cannot be charged with liability in respect to every conceivable misconception, however outlandish, to which his representations might be subject among the foolish or feebleminded. . . . A representation does not become "false or deceptive" merely because it will be unreasonably misunderstood by an insignificant and unrepresentative segment of the class of persons to whom the representation is addressed.[4]

While the decision in *Heinz W. Kirchner* amounted to a repudiation of the ignorant-man standard, it by no means returned us to the reasonable-man standard of common law days. Rather, what emerged from this ruling was a "modified reasonable-man standard." The new standard equated the reasonable person with the typical or average person as actually observed in the marketplace.[5]

The Issue In Jewish Law

Before we discuss this issue, it should be noted that misleading and deceptive advertising is prohibited in Halakhah under the interdict against creating a false impression (*geneivat da'at*).

The biblical source of the *geneivat da'at* interdict is disputed by talmudic decisors. R. Jonah b. Abraham Gerondi (Spain, ca. 1200–1264) places such conduct under the rubric of falsehood (*sheker*).[6] R. Yom Tov Ishbili (Spain, ca. 1250–1330), however, subsumes it under the Torah's admonition against theft (*lo tignovu*, Leviticus 19:11). What *lo tignovu* enjoins is both theft of property and "theft of the mind" by means of deception.[7]

Bearing directly on the issue of deceptive advertising in Halakhah is the disclosure formula the rabbis of the Talmud devised to inform townspeople that the day's supply of meat was not kosher. A public announcement to this effect served a double purpose. Since it made it impossible for Gentile patrons to be duped into believing that the meat they were buying was kosher, it averted the possibility of the proprietors of kosher butcher shops violating the *geneivat da'at* interdict. It also alerted the Jews of the town not to purchase meat from a Gentile supplier on that day.

In respect to the exact formulation of the announcement, the following discussion takes place at Hullin 94a:

> What is the form of the proclamation? R. Isaac b. Joseph said, "Meat for the army has fallen into our hands" (*nafla bisra l'bnei heila*). And why not proclaim, "*Trefa* meat for the army has fallen into our hands" (*nafla trefta l'bnei heila*)? Then they would not buy it. Then are we not deceiving them? No. They are deceiving themselves. As in the following incident: Mar Zutra the son of R. Nahman was once going from Sikara to Mahoza, while Rava and R. Safra were going to Sikara; and they met on the way. Believing that they had come to meet him he said, "Why did the rabbis take the trouble to come so far [to meet me]?" R. Safra replied, "We did not know that the Master was coming; had we known of it, we should have put ourselves out more than this." Rava said to him, "Why did you say that to him? Now you have upset him." He replied, "But we would be deceiving him otherwise." "No. He would be deceiving himself."

The preceding passage presents several difficulties. First, given that an explicit announcement of the presence of non-kosher meat in the butcher shops repels Gentile customers, formulating the announcement in ambiguous terms should amount to a deliberate attempt at deception. Why, then, do we regard the purchase of non-kosher meat by Gentiles on the basis of the ambiguous announcement as constituting only self-deception on their part? Second, how can the Mar Zutra episode serve as support for the permissibility of making a calculated ambiguous announcement when the encounter between the rabbis and Mar Zutra was entirely fortuitous and the rabbis did nothing to create the false impression that they constituted a welcoming party for him?

In offering a solution to these difficulties, we note, to begin with, that the Talmud does not say that the proclamation *nafla bisra l'bnei heila* was implemented only after experience with the *nafla trefta* proclamation resulted in the loss of the Gentile trade. Switching of this sort, because it is calculated to "throw off" the Gentiles and restore the lost business, constitutes a *deliberate* attempt at deception. What the Talmud says is simply that the rabbis *theorized* that an *express* proclamation of *trefa* would repel the Gentile customers. Hence the *nafal trefta* proclamation was never used.

This leads to the proposition that *nafal bisra* entailed no *deliberate* attempt at deception. Since no announcement at all was made when the available supply consisted entirely of kosher meat, *nafal bisra* should clearly communicate the message that the meat for sale is not kosher. Both this proclamation and the *nafal trefta* proclamation communicate the same message, but with different promotional slants. *Nafal trefta* is decidedly negative, openly proclaiming that the meat is unfit for Jewish consumption but available for sale to Gentiles. *Nafal bisra l'bnei heila*, on the other hand, openly conveys only that Gentiles are the desired customer base of the product; the unfitness of the product for Jewish consumption is indicated only by means of reasonable implication.

The proposition that the difference between the two proclamations is merely a matter of promotional slant is supported by the comment of R. Solomon b. Isaac (Rashi; France, 1040–1105) as to why Gentiles are repulsed by the *nafal trefta* proclamation: "It is a disgrace for them, since we do not want to eat it."[8] What makes non-kosher meat obnoxious to the Gentile is not the essentially value-free datum that Jews do not eat it, but rather the formal declaration that they do not *desire* to eat it. The following observation will clarify the point. There are two categories of non-kosher meat. One is meat derived from an animal that was not slaughtered in accordance with Jewish ritual law (*nebelah*). The second is meat derived from an organically defective animal (*trefa*). Since there is no qualitative difference between *nebelah* and kosher meat, the Gentile should rationally be indifferent between the two. Similarly, at fair market value, a Gentile should find no reason to reject *trefa*. Thus, if the Gentile finds non-kosher meat obnoxious, it is not the product itself that repulses him, but the manner in which it is marketed. Expressly representing to him that the meat is *trefa* makes it a disgrace for him to purchase it, as the declaration openly proclaims that it is unfit for Jewish consumption but suitable for Gentiles.

Thus, *nafal bisra* is not deceptive disclosure, but a creative way of marketing a product so that it becomes acceptable to Gentiles, whose sole reason for rejecting it would be the word *trefa* used in its promotion. Since no announcement is made when the butcher shops are selling only kosher meat, *nafal bisra* should convey to a reasonable person that the meat is not kosher.

Recall that the Talmud characterizes those misled by *nafal bisra* as being guilty of self-deception. The result of the analysis in the preceding paragraphs shows that this applies only to the few who mistakenly think that the meat being offered for sale is kosher in the absence of an explicit declaration to the contrary. But for the vast majority of patrons, no misunderstanding whatsoever takes place, for they correctly read into *nafal bisra l'bnei heila* an implicit notification that non-kosher meat is being offered for sale.

Given the role the reasonable-man principle plays in extricating *nafal bisra* from a deceptive characterization, the affinity of this case to the Mar Zutra incident is readily apparent. In the latter case, too, it is the reasonable-man standard that frees the rabbis' conduct from the *geneivat da'at* interdict. If not for the judgment that a reasonable person would regard their encounter with Mar Zutra as clearly fortuitous, they would be obliged to correct Mar Zutra's mistaken belief that they constituted a welcoming party for him.

Further support for this thesis can be derived by comparing the text at hand with a point in *geneivat da'at* law expounded in the Jerusalem Talmud at Makkot 2:6. The case entails the following elements: A is well versed in one tractate of the Talmud, but the townspeople mistakenly think he is proficient in two tractates and accord him the honor due someone who is proficient in two tractates. The Jerusalem Talmud rules that A is obligated to disabuse the townspeople of their mistaken impression of him. This ruling apparently contradicts the rule, elucidated at Hullin 94a, that an individual is exempt from correcting a mistaken impression that is rooted in self-deception. Ready reconciliation of the two texts follows, however, from the reasonable-man hypothesis. An individual need only be concerned about a mistaken impression held by a reasonable person. Since the various tractates of the Talmud, especially those in the same order,[9] are interconnected, complement each other, and overlap somewhat, proficiency in one tractate can easily be mistaken for proficiency in two tractates. Accordingly, a talmudic scholar must disabuse the townspeople of their inaccurate assessment of him. In sharp contrast, since a reasonable person would interpret Mar Zutra's encounter with Rava and R. Safra as nothing more than fortuitous, no corrective obligation devolved upon the rabbis to disabuse Mar Zutra of his error. In a similar vein, a reasonable person will take *nafal bisra* as constituting an implicit declaration that the meat at hand is not kosher. Accordingly, use of this formulation does not constitute deliberate deception.

In sum, claims of deception against a seller are evaluated on the basis of the reasonable-man standard.

The Average or Idealized Man

It remains necessary to clarify whether Halakhah regards the reasonable person as an average person or an idealized person. Several cases relating to the law of debt bear directly on this issue.

Under certain conditions, if B acknowledges a debt to L, but does so outside a Bet Din (court of law),[10] the acknowledgment is not binding. Consider, for instance, the following case: L confronts B with a claim that he is due a sum of money. B acknowledges the debt in the presence of onlookers, but subsequently refuses to pay. The case moves on to a Bet Din, where B insists that his earlier acknowledgment of a debt obligation to L was merely a jest. It was his way of responding in kind to what he regarded as a ridiculous claim (*mashteh ani bakh*, "I was just jesting with you.").

B's *mashteh ani bakh* defense will be accepted by the Bet Din.[11] Moreover, even when B does not make this defense explicitly, but merely denies that he ever admitted owing the money, the court will assume that something equivalent took place, since a person is not expected to remember words thrown out in a jocular way (*milta d'kedi lo dekhirei inshei*).[12]

However, where B enters a plea of *mashteh ani bakh*, whether explicit or implicit, the Bet Din will require him to affirm his defense by means of an oath (*shevuat hesset*).[13]

Mashteh ani bakh averts a court judgment against B only if he offers this defense himself. If B remains silent, the Bet Din will not deny L's claim by suggesting that the acknowledgment was made in jest and then turn to B for his confirmation.[14] Nevertheless, if B dies before the court proceeding begins, and L's claim is against B's estate, the Bet Din will entertain the possibility that the acknowledgment was made in jest and will require of B's heirs only that they take an oath that they did not receive instructions from B to make payment to L.[15]

The *mashteh ani bakh* defense has no standing when B not only acknowledged the debt but told the onlookers to serve as witnesses in the matter. *Attem edai* ("you are my witnesses") makes B's acknowledgment of the debt objectively evident. A's subsequent plea that it should not be taken seriously is rejected outright. Moreover, if B remains silent, L's charge of *attem edai* to the onlookers may also work to vitiate B's *mashteh ani bakh* defense. This obtains when B initially acknowledges the debt in the face of L's claim, and L then goes ahead and charges the onlookers with *attem edai*. However, if B was silent all along, his *mashteh ani bakh* defense remains intact.[17]

Another scenario involves the following elements: B volunteers to C in the presence of onlookers that he owes L, say, $1,000. B then asks the onlookers to serve as witnesses in the matter. On the basis of this admission, L enters a claim of $1,000 against B. Despite the fact that all the elements of an objectively evident admission of a debt of obligation are in place here, B may still have grounds to claim that the admission was not made in a serious vein. This occurs when B insists that he made the admission only so that the public would not hold him to be a wealthy man.[18] This explanation is accepted even when B was known at the time to be poor.[19] In the latter instance, B's motive would have been to make it appear that he was even poorer than people assumed.[20] According to many authorities, the Bet Din is required to suggest this line of defense to B if he does not himself bring it up.[21]

When the proceeding is against B's estate rather than against B, the court will entertain the possibility that the admission was bogus on the grounds discussed above. Accordingly, it will require that B's heirs only take an oath that B did not instruct them to make a payment to L.[22]

Underlying B's slippery defense is an implicit admission that he fell short of the highest ethical standards in his dealings with L. An ethically sensitive person is straightforward and does not employ ambiguity to further his cause. Confronted with an unfounded claim, he will not first acknowledge it and then say that he only meant to mock it; instead, he will respond to a baseless claim with a simple denial. Less ethical still is the practice of admitting to fictional debts so as not to be regarded as wealthy. If the intent is to create a false impression of poverty rather than to disabuse a false impression of wealth, the practice is clearly immoral. In the final analysis, B's explanation of his conduct is accepted because it comports well with the conduct of ordinary people,[23] and the court will not evaluate B's conduct as though he were a highly ethical person. Moreover, when L's claim is made against B's estate, the court itself will bring up the less than highly ethical defense of *mashteh ani bakh* because the conduct of the ordinary person must serve as the model in evaluating B's actions.

The court's attitude toward B's slippery defense translates into a guidepost telling L how to interpret B's actions. For the given circumstances, L should not have taken seriously B's admission or acknowledgment that he owed him money. Doing so would have been reasonable only if B were a highly ethical person. More realistically, L should decide what meaning to attach to B's actions on the basis of the behavior to be expected of the average person.

Thus, Halakhah identifies the reasonable man as the man in the street rather than as a member of an idealized ethical elite.

The Rationale for the Reasonable-Man Standard

Our discussion of the reasonable-man standard indicates that when applied to mass media advertising, it serves to limit the disclosure and disabusing responsibility of the seller vis-à-vis his target audience. Provided that the message will not mislead a reasonable person, the seller need not be concerned about the likelihood that some people will be deceived by the ad. This point of leniency in *geneivat da'at* law may be derived from the judgment the rabbis made when they authorized the *nafal bisra* proclamation even though they realized that it would mislead some people. Because a reasonable person would take the declaration as an implicit announcement that the meat was not kosher, any erroneous impression on the part of the ignorant could be written off as self-deception.

Why the predictable deception of the ignorant is not regarded as deliberately deceptive conduct on the part of the seller is explained by the buyer's responsibility, imposed on him by the Halakhah, to educate himself in respect to market conditions. The following examples demonstrate this point.

1. Without explicitly informing customers of the practice, a grain distributor may mix together the grain he buys from the various farmers in the area.[24] Since it is generally understood in the marketplace that this is done, the distributor need not be concerned that a particular customer is unaware of the practice.[25]

2. Because it gives meat a deceptively fatty and succulent appearance, a butcher is prohibited from soaking meat in water.[26] Nevertheless, if this practice is common among butchers in a certain place, the prohibition is suspended, as local customers are expected to be aware of it and not be misled.[27]

3. The ethics of the price terms of a transaction concluded within the framework of a competitive norm is governed in Halakhah by the law of *ona'ah* (overreaching). Depending on how widely the price of the subject transaction departs from the competitive norm, the injured party may have recourse to void or adjust the transaction. Elsewhere in this volume we demonstrate that *ona'ah* is the right of a market participant to trade the commodity at hand on the basis of its competitive norm. Nonetheless, Halakhah does not protect mindless conduct in the marketplace. Accordingly, if the price discrepancy involved goes beyond the margin of error, no remedy whatsoever will be called for. Because Halakhah expects market participants to have an approximate notion of the competitive norm, the only plausible explanation for explaining the outrageous price terms is that the intention of the parties was not to trade the commodity at hand but merely to use it as a *vehicle* to effect a voluntary gift transfer.[28]

Thus, information gathering is the buyer's responsibility to the same degree that providing information is the seller's responsibility. The seller is obligated to ensure that a reasonable person will not be misled by his representations. But the onus is on the buyer to educate himself to function in the marketplace as a reasonable person. If the buyer fails to operate in the marketplace as a reasonable person, and suffers some detriment on account of his misunderstandings, confusions, and misperceptions, the seller is not responsible.

Transparently False Claims and the Reasonable Man

The reasonable-man standard should not be taken as validating a patently false claim on the grounds that the average man in the street is *not misled* by the message. From the standpoint of Halakhah, general recognition in the marketplace that a seller's explicit claim is false does not transform the representation into a truthful message. It remains false, albeit transparently false. Transparent falsity will not deceive a reasonable person, but it will dupe the ignorant and the credulous. Making a representation involving an explicitly false claim, even if the falsity is obvious to a reasonable person, is an act of deception perpetrated against the ignorant. The fact that the great majority of people exposed to the representation are not duped by it does not excuse the active deception perpetrated against the ignorant and credulous. In sharp contrast, when the seller's claim is rendered misleading only because ignorant people read an eccentric meaning into it, the claim retains its non-deceptive character, and those who misread it are deceiving themselves. Elsewhere we have elaborated on this theme.[29]

Moving Toward a Quantitative Measure for the Reasonable Man

As demonstrated above, the standard called for in Halakhah to protect society against deception in a mass communications message is in conformity with the reasonable-man standard enunciated in *Heinz W. Kirchner.*

In applying the *Heinz W. Kirchner* criterion to specific cases, the courts have ruled that an advertising message can be deceptive even if it misleads only a minority of the targeted audience. In this regard, the courts have adopted a 15 percent benchmark. Let us examine two of these cases.

1. In a 1964 decision, the FTC held Benrus Watch Company guilty of a misleading pricing policy. It was the practice of the company to pre-ticket each watch that left its plant. This practice created the impression that the pre-ticketed price was the usual retail price of a Benrus watch. In fact, Benrus watches regularly and usually sold at a price considerably below the so-called list price. Thus, consumers who were induced to buy the watch by being offered a con-

siderable discount below list were duped into a false sense of bargain. Moreover, Benrus always referred to the list price in advertisements that offered consumers trade-in deals. Because the list price was fictitious, the savings the consumer was supposed to realize from the trade-in offer were grossly exaggerated.

In defense of its practice, the company presented a market research study which indicated that a full 86 percent of consumers surveyed understood Benrus' list price as a rough guide to the value of the product or as a ceiling price. This overwhelming majority were not misled into thinking that the list price was in fact the regular or prevailing price actually paid in the market for the pre-ticketed product.

The FTC ruled against Benrus. In rejecting the survey evidence, the FTC felt that the 14 percent of the public that were misled constituted a substantial segment of the market and was entitled to protection against deception.[30]

Benrus appealed the FTC decision. But in 1965, the United States Court of Appeals, Eighth Circuit, affirmed the FTC's decision against the company.[31]

2. In a 1970 case, the FTC found the Firestone Tire and Rubber Company guilty of unfair and deceptive advertising. The following text was used by the company in its advertising campaign:

> When you buy a Firestone tire—no matter how much or how little you pay—you get a safe tire. Firestone tires are custom-built one by one. By skilled craftsmen. And they're personally inspected for an extra margin of safety. If these tires don't pass all of the exacting Firestone inspections, they don't get out.
>
> Every new Firestone design goes through rugged tests of safety and strength far exceeding any driving condition you'll ever encounter. We prove them in our test lab. On our test track. And in rigorous day-to-day driving conditions. All Firestone tires meet or exceed the new Federal Government testing requirements. (They have for some time.)
>
> Firestone—The Safe Tire. At 60,000 Firestone Safe Tire Centers. At no more cost than ordinary tires.

In its review of the ad, the FTC felt that the company should have qualified its representation by stating that the safety of any tire is affected by conditions of use, such as inflation pressure, vehicle weight, and wear.

In defense of its ad, Firestone averred that its intention was not to give a guarantee of absolute safety but only an assurance to consumers that "Firestone did everything humanly and technically possible to sell tires free of defects." To buttress this defense, Firestone cited its own consumer survey, which showed that only 15.3 percent of a scientifically selected sample of tire purchasers thought the "Safe Tire" ad meant that "Every Firestone tire is absolutely safe no matter how it is used and regardless of the tire inflation pressure and load of the car"; or that "Every single Firestone tire will be absolutely free from any defects."

The FTC ruled against Firestone. On appeal, the court referred to the consumer survey the company had conducted but felt that 15.3 percent of tire users—and for that matter even 10 percent of users—constituted a substantial group that deserved protection against deception.[32]

Under the Lanham Trademark Act, a competitor can sue his rival in federal court for false and misleading advertising. If a competitor takes this route, he must, however, bear the cost of litigation. An alternative procedure is to seek action from the FTC, which protects competitors as well as consumers. Nonetheless, competitors frequently take the federal court route, at their own expense, because they are not certain that the FTC will pursue the precise action they desire.

In his survey, Preston offers the generalization that the minimum required benchmarks to establish the presence of deception is the range of 20 to 25 percent in FTC cases and as low as 15 percent in Lanham cases.[33]

At this juncture, let us consider the quantitative measure of deception for the Jewish firm that targets its advertising message at a Jewish audience. Given the halakhic agreement with the reasonable-man standard, would Halakhah go along with the quantitative benchmark secular society has crafted for this criterion? Resolution of this issue revolves around the scope of the rule that for disputes between Jews in matters of civil law "the law of the land is law" (*dina d'malkhuta dina*). Four views on this issue can be identified.

1. Taking the most narrow view on the scope of *dina d'malkhuta dina* is R. Joseph Caro (Israel, 1488–1575). In his view, Halakhah recognizes *dina d'malkhuta* only in respect to matters the government has a financial stake in, such as taxes and currency regulation.[34]

2. Adopting a much wider scope for *dina d'malkhuta* is R. Mosheh Isserles (Poland, 1525 or 1530–1572). In his view, it applies to civil law generally. Conflict between Halakhah and *dina d'malkhuta*, in his view, is generally decided in favor of *dina d'malkhuta*.[35] There are, however, exceptions to this rule. It does not hold in relation to the law of inheritance;[36] nor does it give Jews the option of taking their dispute to secular courts,[37] or to have the secular court's evidentiary procedure imposed on them.[38] Moreover, *dina d'malkhuta* is recognized only when the law involved either benefits the government or was enacted for the benefit of the people of the land.[39]

3. Disputing R. Isserles, R. Shabbetai b. Meir ha-Kohen (Lithuania, 1621–1662) avers that in litigation between Jews, the law of the land finds its

validity only when the non-Jewish law does not contradict Halakhah, or in a case where the practical application of Halakhah is not clear.[40]

4. Following R. Shabbetai b. Meir ha-Kohen's line, R. Abraham Isaiah Karelitz (Israel, 1878–1953) sharply disputes the notion that there are any lacunae in Halakhah. A halakhic position can be extrapolated for every issue. If *dina d'malkhuta* contradicts Halakhah, even if the Halakhah was derived by means of extrapolation, the law of the land must be set aside.[41]

Many decisors regard R. Isserles' position as normative.[42] If we adopt his view, there should be no doubt that Halakhah would go along with the secular court's 15 percent benchmark for the reasonable-man standard. This conclusion follows also if we follow R. Shabbetai b. Meir's position, as the 15 percent benchmark contradicts no *explicit* halakhic rule.

Finally, let us consider the possibility that the secular benchmark is consistent with R. Karelitz's position as well. To begin, we take note of the *mi'ut hamazui* (small but significant percentage) rule. This rule states that Halakhah regards a condition as prevailing even though it is not based on observed fact but only on a small but significant statistical probability.[43] To illustrate: The rule is that the majority of those who engage in ritual slaughter are presumed to be competent and certified. Nonetheless a small but significant minority of ritual slaughterers are not competent and are not certified. Because the number of those not certified constitutes *mi'ut hamazui*, we may not rely on the majority rule when the would-be ritual slaughterer stands in front of us. Here, we may not allow him to proceed without first investigating his credentials.[44]

Applying the *mi'ut hamazui* rule to the case at hand tells us that we may not dismiss a complaint that a mass communication message is deceptive unless we are sure that only a *small and insignificant* percentage of the targeted group agrees with this assessment.

How is *mi'ut hamazui* translated in quantitative terms? Addressing himself to this issue, R. Jacob b. Aaron (Lithuania, d. 1844) regards *mi'ut hamazui* as generally translating into a 10 percent benchmark.[45] Disputing R. Jacob b. Aaron, R. Yosef Shalom Elyashiv (Israel, contemp.) feels that *mi'ut hamazui* translates into a 15–20 percent range. The specific issue R. Elyashiv dealt with is the prohibition on eating fruits and vegetables without first being sure that the produce is free of worms. If 15–20 percent of a particular species is known to contain worms, it is prohibited to eat the species without first ascertaining that the fruit or vegetable at hand is free of worms.[46]

As the preceding discussion indicates, adopting the 15 percent benchmark as the quantitative measure of deception stands on solid halakhic ground.

One final caveat. When the issue is danger to life rather than just the violation of a prohibition, Halakhah takes a more protective stance.[47] The Firestone

Tire and Benrus Watch cases should therefore not be equated. If a 15 percent benchmark is adopted as the test for deception when the issue is a monetary matter, a lower benchmark should be adopted when the consequence of deception puts the consumer's health or physical safety at risk.

Problem 1

Modern advertising messages often couch their claims in vague and indefinite terms. Adams and Maine cite a number of examples and offer the following commentary:

> "Four out of five doctors recommend" this remedy. But who are the doctors? What are they doctors of? How many of them were asked about the product? Without answers to these obvious questions, the recommendation is pretty empty.
>
> "No preservative added" says the wrapping on a loaf of bread. None added since when? Since the baker finished putting them in? No preservative added to what? The ones that were already there? The statement may be true, but this claim is also empty, as it actually says nothing about the nature or quantity of preservatives in your bread.
>
> One famous hamburger chain asserts that its burgers are "made with 100 percent pure beef." This claim is meant to suggest that the burger itself is all beef. But, of course, it doesn't say that—it only says that 100 percent pure beef is *an ingredient* from which the burger has been made: It is merely the beef, not the burger, that is pure. Such cleverly worded ads might fool some, but what they say is technically true.[48]

How would Halakhah treat these ads?

Problem 2

In 1991, the FTC accused Kraft General Foods of false advertising in the promotion of its Kraft Singles product. Kraft Singles are individually wrapped slices of process cheese food. The company's ads claimed that Singles slices were made from five ounces of milk compared with "hardly any" for the imitators. The ads emphasized the calcium provided by the milk. These claims were false because not all the milk used in cheesemaking gets into the cheese. As much as 30 percent of the milk is lost in the cheesemaking process. Thus not all the calcium from the original five ounces got into the cheese.

In responding to the FTC charges, Kraft effectively conceded that the ads conveyed a false impression. The company , however, claimed that it could not be prosecuted because its false representations were not material, that is, the false claims did not affect consumers' purchasing decisions.

To bolster its assertion of *nonmateriality,* Kraft presented survey evidence to the FTC. Kraft's survey showed people ranking calcium only seventh among nine factors that might affect whether they would buy Singles. This showed that calcium was not material, the company said.

Moreover, the Kraft surveyor informed people that each slice of Singles contained only 70 percent of the calcium in five ounces of milk. Equipped with this knowledge, 96 percent of those surveyed maintained that they would continue to buy Singles.

The FTC rejected Kraft's survey evidence and ruled that Kraft's false claims met the materiality test.[49]

Critically evaluate Kraft's survey evidence in respect to the materiality issue. What position would Halakhah take in this case?

Problem 3

With the aim of eliciting a few laughs, the Pittsburgh Brewing Company produces its Iron City Beer under a special label during the holiday season. The beer's name changes to Olde Frothingslosh, and the label proclaims that Olde Frothingslosh is the "only beer in which the foam is on the bottom."

A customer bought some Olde Frothingslosh to amuse friends at a party and was disturbed to find that the claim was nothing but a *big lie:* The foam was right up there on top where it always is! She wanted her money back from the beer distributor.[50]

How would Halakhah treat the disappointed customer's complaint? What position would Halakhah take regarding the Old Frothingslosh advertising campaign?

1. *FTC v. Universal Battery,* 2 FTC 95 (1919).

2. *Gelb v. FTC,* 144 F.2d 580 (2d Cir. 1944), following Gelb, 33 FTC 1450 (1941).

3. *Heinz v. Kirchner,* 63 FTC 1282 (1963).

4. Ibid. at 1290.

5. Ivan L. Preston, *The Great American Blowup: Puffery in Advertising and Selling* (Madison: University of Wisconsin Press, 1975), pp. 162–74.

6. R. Jonah b. Abraham Gerondi, *Sha'arei Teshuvah,* sha'ar 3, ot 184.

7. R. Yom Tov Ishbili, Ritva, at Hullin 94a.

8. R. Solomon b. Isaac, Rashi, at Hullin 94b.

9. The Mishnah is divided into six orders (*sedarim*): (1) Zera'im ("seeds"), (2) Mo'ed ("festivals") , (3) Nashim ("women"), (4) Nezikin ("damages"), (5) Kodashim ("holy things"), and (6) Toharot ("purities"). The various tractates of the Babylonian Talmud fit into these orders, but two of them, Kodashim and Toharot, are not found in the Jerusalem Talmud.

10. R. Jehiel Michel Epstein (Belarus, 1829–1908), *Arukh ha-Shulhan,* Hoshen Mishpat

81:10.

11. Sanhedrin 29a; R. Isaac b. Jacob Alfasi (Algeria, 1013–1103), ad loc.; Maimonides (Egypt, 1135–1204), *Yad*, To'en ve'Nitan 6:6–7; R. Asher b. Jehiel, (Germany 1250–1327), Rosh, Sanhedrin 3:25; R. Jacob b. Asher (Germany, 1270–1343), *Tur*, Hoshen Mishpat 81:1; R. Joseph Caro (Israel, 1488–1575), *Shulhan Arukh*, Hoshen Mishpat 81:1; *Ar.haSh.*, op. cit. 81:1.

12. Sanhedrin 29b; R. Isaac b. Jacob Alfasi (Algeria, 1013–1104), Rif, ad loc., *Yad*, op. cit. 6:6; Rosh, loc. cit.; *Tur*, loc. cit., *Sh.Ar.*, loc. cit.; *Ar.haSh.*, loc. cit.

13. R. Saadiah Gaon (Egypt, 882–942), quoted by Rosh, loc. cit.; *Tur*, loc. cit., *Sh.Ar.*, loc. cit.; *Ar.haSh.*, loc. cit.

14. Rif, loc. cit., *Yad*, loc. cit. 6:8; Rosh, loc. cit.; *Tur*, loc. cit. ; *Sh.Ar.*, op. cit. 81:3; *Ar.haSh.*, loc. cit.

15. *Tur*, loc. cit.; *Sh.Ar.*, loc. cit.; *Ar.haSh.*, loc. cit.

16. Sanhedrin 29a; Rif, ad loc.; *Yad*, op. cit. 6:6; Rosh, loc. cit.; *Tur*, loc. cit.; *Sh.Ar.*, loc..cit. 81:6; *Ar.haSh.*, loc. cit.

17. *Tur*, loc. cit.; *Sh.Ar.*, op. cit. 81:7; *Ar.haSh.*, loc. cit.

18. Sanhedrin 29a; Rif, ad.loc.; *Yad*, op. cit. 7:1, Rosh, loc. cit.; *Tur*, loc. cit.; *Sh.Ar.*, op. cit. 81:3.

19. R. Mosheh Isserles (Rema, Poland, 1525 or 1530–1572), *Sh.Ar.*, op. cit. 81:14; *Ar.haSh.*, op. cit. 81:3.

20. R. Joshua ha-Kohen Falk (Poland, 1565–1614), Sma to *Sh.Ar.*, Hoshen Mishpat 81, n. 31; *Ar.haSh.*, op. cit. 81:3.

21. Rosh, loc. cit., Rema, op. cit. 81:14; *Ar.haSh.*, op. cit. 81:5. For a contrary view see, *Yad*, op. cit. 6:8; R. Joseph Habiba (Spain, early 15th cent.), *Nimmukei Yosef* at Rif, Sanhedrin 29b; R. Shabbetai b. Meir ha Kohen (Poland, 1621–1662), Siftei Kohen to *Sh.Ar.*, op. cit. 81, n. 39.

22. *Ar.haSh.*, op. cit. 81:5.

23. R. Joseph Habiba (at Rif, Sanhedrin 29b) finds the practice rooted in the desire to distance oneself from the evil eye.

24. Mishnah, Bava Mezia 4:12; Rif, ad loc.; *Yad*, Mekhirah 18:7; Rosh, Bava Mezia 4:24; *Tur*, op. cit. 228:16, *Sh.Ar.*, op. cit. 228:16. *Ar.haSh.*, op. cit. 228:12.

25. Rashi to Mishnah, Bava Mezia 4:12; *Tur*, loc. cit.; *Sh.Ar.*, loc. cit.; *Ar.haSh.*, loc. cit.

26. Baraita, Bava Mezia 60b; Rif ad loc., *Yad.*, Mekhirah 18:3; Rosh, Bava Mezia 4:24; *Tur*, op cit. 228:9; *Sh.Ar.*, op. cit. 228:9; *Ar.haSh.*, op. cit. 228:5.

27. Sma to *Sh.Ar.*, op. cit. 228, n. 16; *Ar.haSh.*, loc. cit.

28. Please turn to pp. 127–31, 194, and 234 of this volume.

29. See Aaron Levine, *Economic Public Policy and Jewish Law* (Hoboken, N.J.: Ktav, 1993), pp. 88–92.

30. 64 FTC 1018 (1964).

31. 352 F.2d 3l3 (1965).

32. 481 F.2d 246 (1973).

33. Ivan Preston, "The Elements of Deceptiveness Law," in *Business Ethics for the 21st Century*, ed. David M. Adams and Edward W. Maine (Mountain View, Calif.: Mayfield, 1998), pp. 365–70.

34. *Sh.Ar.*, Hoshen Mishpat 369:6–11.

35. R. Mosheh Isserles, Rema, *Sh.Ar.*, op. cit. 369:11.

36. Ibid.

37. Rema, op. cit. 26:1.

38. Rema on the understanding of R. Mordecai b. Abraham Jaffe (Prague, ca. 1535–1612), *Ir Shushan*, Hoshen Mishpat 369.

39. Rema, op. cit. 369:11.

40. Siftei Kohen, *Sh.Ar.*, Hoshen Mishpat 73, n. 39. In litigation between Jew and non-Jew, *dina d'malkhuta* is operative (Siftei Kohen, ad loc.).

41. R. Abraham Isaiah Karelitz, *Hazon Ish*, Hoshen Mishpat, Likutim 16, alef.

42. R. Mosheh Feinstein (New York, 1895–1986), *Iggerot Mosheh*, Hoshen Mishpat 2:62; R. Yosef Eliyahu Henkin (New York, 1880–1973), *Teshuvot Ivra*, vol. 2, p. 176. See also the list of authorities cited by Professor Shmuel Shilo, *Dina D'malkhuta Dina* (Jerusalem: Hebrew University Press, 1974), p. 157, n. 26.

43. For a comprehensive treatment of *mi'ut hamazui*, see R. Shmuel ha-Levi Wosner (Israel, contemp.), *Responsa Shevat ha-Levi* 4, Yoreh De'ah 81.

44. Hullin 12a and R. Nissim b. Reuben Gerondi (Spain, ca. 1290–ca. 1375), on Rif, Hullin 12a.

45. R. Jacob b. Aaron, *Mishkenot Ya'akov*, Yoreh De'ah 17.

46. Ruling of R. Yosef Shalom Elyashiv as reported by R. Joseph I. Efrati in a letter to R. A. Panet, dated 1995. I am indebted to R. Yosef Eisen of the Orthodox Union for making available this letter to me.

47. Hullin 10a.

48. Business Ethics For The 21st Century, op. cit., p. 357.

49. Ivan L. Preston, The Tangled Web They Weave: Truth, Falsity, And Advertisers (Madison, Wis.: The University of Wisconsin Press, 1994), pp. 47–51.

50. Preston, *Great American Blowup*, p. 163.

The Glatt Boat Affair

Glatt Boat offers a three-hour cruise along the Florida keys. The cruise features music and an elegant glatt kosher dinner under the supervision of a nationally recognized kashrut organization.

From the beginning of its operations, Glatt Boat was embroiled in controversy over the issue of social dancing. When couples made their way to the dance floor, the supervising rabbi would ask them to stop dancing. If they refused, the rabbi would have the music stop playing in order to get his way. Eventually, at the insistence of the kashrut organization, a no-social-dancing clause was inserted into its contract with Glatt Boat.

Neither in its publicity brochure nor at its ticket sales booth did Glatt Boat publicize the no-dance rule. Instead, Glatt Boat sprung the no-dance rule on a captive clientele.

For some patrons, Glatt Boat's failure to announce the no-social-dancing rule beforehand meant that it forfeited the right to *impose* this policy on a captive clientele. Indeed, some customers fully expected an opportunity to engage in social dancing during the cruise. In its publicity brochure, Glatt Boat let it be known that it leased its vessels from World Class Boats. World Class Boats routinely features social dancing during its cruises. While Glatt Boat made no explicit claim that its intent was to mimic the cruise service offered by World Class Boats, forming this impression from the brochure was certainly possible.

Other customers took the opposite tack, insisting that it was management's *duty to impose* the no-dance rule. The halakhic validity of Glatt Boat as a business venture demanded this, because social dancing is prohibited in Jewish law.[1] If management failed to impose a no-dance rule, it would be taking on the role of facilitator of a prohibited act, and hence be in violation of the *lifnei iver* interdict.[2] Moreover, there was no need to promulgate the no-dance rule in advance, because the word "glatt" in the name of the cruise adequately signaled it. For these patrons, the name of the cruise, Glatt Boat, communicated not only a meticulous kashrut standard but also that the *ambiance* of the cruise would be comfortable for the most scrupulously observant.

Glatt Boat and *Lifnei Iver*

In adjudicating the conflicting claims, the most fundamental issue is whether the halakhic validity of Glatt Boat as a business venture hinges on its adopting a no-dance rule.

An analogous case is treated in the responsa of R. Mosheh Feinstein (New York, 1895–1986): A London-based caterer (A) inquired whether it was permissible for him to rent his hall and provide food for a wedding feast when it was certain that social dancing would take place at the affair. Offering two different rationales for his ruling, R. Feinstein allowed the caterer to take the job.

In his first rationale, the pivotal consideration was that *lifnei iver* on a biblical level is not violated when the transgressor can obtain the prohibited object without the assistance of the facilitator. Since many caterers would be happy to take up the social dancing affair if A refused the job, violation of *lifnei iver* on a biblical level was not at issue here. But accepting the job amounts to "abetting transgressors" (*mesayye'a lidei overei averah*) and should therefore violate the rabbinical extension of the *lifnei iver* interdict. Extenuation in the above case can, however, be found in R. Shabbetai b. Meir ha-Kohen's (Poland, 1621–1662) ruling that *mesayye'a lidei overei averah* does not apply when the transgression involved is committed deliberately.[3] To be sure, this leniency is disputed by R. Abraham Abele b. Hayyim Gombiner (Poland, ca. 1637–1683).[4] But consideration of another extenuating factor makes the lenient ruling compelling even according to the later view. This is the circumstance that if A refuses the catering job, the customer might turn to a caterer whose kashrut is not reliable. A's acceptance of the job may well have the effect of *reducing* the sum total of sinful behavior at the affair.[5]

In his second rationale, R. Feinstein opines that making an object available to an individual cannot be regarded as abetting a transgression unless the article involved is used primarily for prohibited purposes. Should this not be the case, subsequent use of the article by the recipient for a prohibited purpose does not brand the one who made it available an abettor of a transgressor. Accordingly, since the catering hall is primarily rented for permissible purposes, i.e., the wedding ceremony and banquet, its rental should not be regarded as abetting transgressors. If the above line of reasoning is not accepted, argues R. Feinstein, it would be forbidden to sell pots and pans to Sabbath desecrators because they will certainly use those utensils for cooking on the Sabbath. The circumstance that the hall is rented primarily for permissible purposes is, for R. Feinstein, the most critical element of the case; so much so that he regards this *factor alone* as sufficient to remove the *lifnei iver* interdict *entirely*, on both the biblical and rabbinical levels.[6] Accordingly, the rental is permissible even if other caterers are not available to take the job.[7]

The similarity between Glatt Boat and the catering case is readily apparent. Let us take a closer look at the comparison.

In R. Feinstein's first rationale the critical factor, as will be recalled, is the accessibility of the prohibited item to the customer from a source other than the present supplier. In both cases the interest of the customer is not in social dancing per se, but rather in a whole bundle of amenities that take the form of a wedding hall and a cruise, respectively. Given the multifaceted nature of the customer's interest, no two suppliers can be expected to supply a bundle of amenities that the customer would regard as perfectly substitutable. One could argue, however, that the cruise market is far more differentiated than the wedding catering hall market. This is so because the range of wedding halls a typical customer considers will vary in a narrow range in respect to location, quality, and price. But the guests and the ceremony will essentially be the same, regardless of where the wedding is held. In sharp contrast, the kosher meal served aboard Glatt Boat is a *unique* feature. In addition, the glatt kosher dinner feature will attract a customer base far different than would be attracted to competing cruises. The more differentiation involved, the less reliable the judgment that the customer would, in any case, have been engaged in the same prohibited activity had it not been facilitated by the present supplier. If the accessibility argument is invalid, the *lifnei iver* interdict remains intact, notwithstanding that the prohibition is violated deliberately.

In respect to R. Feinstein's second rationale, the identity between the two cases is compelling. What Glatt Boat is selling is a cruise that features a glatt kosher dinner. Hence the company hands over to its customers a permissible item. If customers choose to use their access to the vessel to engage in social dancing, the owners would then be technically disassociated from the activity and therefore would not be regarded as abetting transgressors.

Customers' Expectations and the Disclosure Obligation

As demonstrated above, Halakhah does not compel Glatt Boat to adopt a no-dance policy. Suppose, however, that Glatt Boat desires to adopt such a policy, but is concerned that announcing the no-dance rule in advance would send a signal to the public implying that the cruise is only for the ultra-Orthodox. Many potential customers would be repelled, believing that the ambiance aboard the cruise would make them self-conscious or otherwise uncomfortable. Given this business interest, is it unethical for Glatt Boat not to promulgate the no-dance rule in advance, and, instead, spring the rule on a captive clientele?

In addressing this issue, one consideration is that Glatt Boat never represented, either explicitly or implicitly, that its cruise would feature the opportunity to engage in social dancing. Dismissing a customer's complaint on the basis of this reasoning, however, is invalid in Halakhah. This is so because silence is not an adequate disabusing mechanism in respect to customer expectations. Rather, it is the other way around: customer expectations determine the nature of the disclosure obligation.[8]

Let us not, however, lose sight of the fact that Glatt Boat promulgates its message via a brochure that reaches a large target audience. In a mass communication message, the deception of an insignificant minority of the targeted audience need not concern the advertiser. What counts is whether the reasonable man is deceived. Quantitatively this translates, as discussed in the preceding chapter, into the assertion that unless 15 percent of the targeted audience is deceived, the ad is acceptable.[9]

Can Glatt Boat rely on its own self-assessment that its representations regarding the cruise will not deceive the reasonable man? No. The judgment of a seller will be biased by the profit motive, which renders his self-assessment unreliable.

Supporting this contention is Halakhah's call for the appointment of pubic inspectors to ensure the honesty of commercial weights and measures.[10] R. Jehiel Michel Epstein (Belarus, 1829–1908) explains that voluntary self compliance is not relied upon to ensure the integrity of commercial weights and measures because of the unconscious distorting effect that the profit motive exerts on vendors. R. Epstein employs the same rationale to explain the ruling by Maimonides (Egypt, 1135–1204)[11] that in matters of kashrut one may only patronize a vendor who is known to be reliable.[12]

Another source for extrapolating the halakhic view on the reliability of self-assessment is the wine barrel–hospitality case discussed at Hullin 94a. Here we are told that a host (H) should not delude his guest (G) into believing that he has acted toward him with magnanimous hospitality when in fact he has not done so. Opening a barrel of wine in honor of someone usually constitutes a gesture of magnanimous hospitality, as the wine remaining in the barrel may deteriorate as a result of its exposure to air. The magnanimity of the gesture is considerably reduced, however, when H happened to have sold the barrel of wine to a retailer just prior to the arrival of G (a price adjustment with the retailer will, of course, be made). In the latter case, H bears the responsibility to disabuse G of his false impression. In this connection, the Talmud relates a hospitality incident involving R. Judah and Ulla. R. Judah opened a barrel of wine in honor of Ulla. The barrel had been sold before Ulla arrived. Two versions of the incident are recorded. In one, R. Judah told his guest about the sale. In the other, no such disclosure took place. The second version is defended by the Talmud on the grounds that Ulla was very dear to R. Judah, and consequently he would have treated him hospitably even if it entailed considerable expense.[13]

Curiously, the point of leniency in *geneivat da'at* law that emerges from the R. Judah–Ulla incident is conspicuously omitted by Maimonides and R. Jacob b. Asher (Germany, 1270–1343) in their discussions of the wine barrel–hospitality case. Noting the omission, R. Aryeh Judah b. Akiba (Poland, 1759–1819) posits that the aforementioned codifiers regard the talmudic incident as lacking general applicability. Only a host like R. Judah, i.e., someone of exceptional moral character, is free of the obligation to correct his guest's false impression that he had been treated with magnanimous hospitality. In the instance of someone like R. Judah, the host's self-assessment that he would confer generous hospitality on his guest even if it entailed a considerable expense is completely reliable. Such a self-assessment would not, however, free an individual of ordinary moral character from his obligation to make the disclosure. For an ordinary person, such a self-assessment amounts to self-delusion. Confronted with an actual opportunity to confer generous hospitality on a friend only at a considerable expense, the average person would find many convenient excuses not to do so. Since the point of leniency in *geneivat da'at* law that emerges from the R. Judah–Ulla incident does not have general applicability, Maimonides and R. Jacob b. Asher do not mention it.[14]

R. Aryeh Judah b. Akiba's conclusion regarding the unreliability of self-assessment apparently places him at odds with the responsa literature in respect to an issue dealing with the counteracting of unwarranted bias in the labor market. The specific issue involves the question of whether an individual is permitted to dye his beard to make himself look younger so as to enhance his chances of securing employment. Addressing this question, R. Mosheh Mordecai Epstein (Israel, 1866–1922) permits the conduct provided the employer's expectations with respect to performance will be met. Realizing that productivity could decline sharply with advancing age, R. Epstein points out that in the final analysis, the conduct's legitimacy rests on the honesty of the job seeker's self-assessment.[15] Advancing a similar analysis, R. Eliezer Meir Preil (New Jersey, 1881-1934) arrives at the same conclusion.[16] R. Mosheh Feinstein concurs with these rulings.[17]

If we distinguish between self-assessment cases relating to routine circumstances and those relating to extraordinary hypothetical situations, we approach a reconciliation of the opinions. Self-assessment may very well be reliable when it relates to ordinary, predictable life situations. Even though productivity may drop off with advancing age, honest self-appraisal can indicate to the senior job seeker whether he can meet the employer's performance standards. The reliability of self-assessment in the realm of the hypothetical is another matter. Individuals of ordinary moral character cannot extrapolate with any degree of accuracy how they would react to a hypothetical situation requiring extraordinary effort on their part.

In the final analysis, the job seeker's self-assessment of his ability is reliable because he knows that it will be subject to objective verification. This is supported by the talmudic text at Hullin 94a, referred to earlier in this volume.[18]

Recall that Mar Zutra jumped to the conclusion that Rava and R. Safra, whom he met on his way to Mahoza, were a welcoming party in his honor. Rava felt that Mar Zutra was guilty of self-deception, and thus that there was no need to disabuse him of his error. Rava's confidence that his judgment was correct was rooted, as it appears to this writer, in the knowledge that Mar Zutra himself would soon come to the same conclusion. After all, Rava and R. Safra were traveling in the opposite direction of Mar Zutra. As soon as the three men parted company and went their separate ways, Mar Zutra would realize that Rava and R. Safra had not come as a welcoming party for him. The certainty that Mar Zutra's hindsight judgment would confirm his own *a priori* judgment gave Rava the confidence that his assessment was correct.

The selfsame feature of objective verifiability is what gave the rabbis in the same reference text at Hullin 94a the confidence that the marketplace would understand *nafal bisra* as an implicit declaration of *trefa*. If the rabbis were wrong, then the *nafal bisra* proclamation would greatly unsettle the marketplace. Sellers would think that they were representing their meat as non-kosher, but the Gentile clientele would take the representation to mean that the meat was kosher. This misunderstanding would manifest itself in a significant number of complaints of deception against the Jewish butchers. Any unsettling of the marketplace as a result of the proclamation of *nafal bisra* informs the rabbis that they erred in expecting the marketplace to read the meaning they intended into *nafal bisra*. This, in turn, will necessitate its replacement with a *nafal trefta* announcement.

What this implies for modern advertising is that a seller's judgment that his advertising copy will not deceive a reasonable person is generally unreliable. This leads to the proposition that advertising copy must be pilot-tested before it is released. A scientifically designed pilot test can ascertain the impressions the advertising message will have on the target group, as well as the inferences this group will draw from it. Should the results fail to conform to actuality, revision of the ad would be in order.

Relaxation of the pilot-testing requirement would apply under certain conditions, as when the advertising claim is subject to independent verification by the consumer.[19]

Given the unreliability of self-assessment, Glatt Boat must operate under the assumption that its ad will lead the reasonable person to believe that social dancing will be an option abroad the cruise. Without first conducting a survey to validate its contention that the reasonable person expects no such option, the company has no right to spring a no-social-dancing rule on its patrons. Such a policy makes the company's advertising guilty of creating a false impression and violates *geneivat da'at*.[20]

One aspect of the company's *geneivat da'at* violation is in relation to those who make up their minds to take the cruise on the basis of the assumption that it will afford them the opportunity for social dancing. To be sure, the number of duped customers falling into this category will probably be very small. But a *sustained* policy of springing a no-dance rule on a captive clientele will inevitably result in duped customers of this variety.

By and large the duped customers will be people whose decision to take the cruise *did not hinge* on the assumption that it would afford the opportunity for social dancing. *Geneivat da'at* is violated in relation to this group as well. What is objectionable here is the unwarranted goodwill Glatt Boat secures by means of its promotional technique. Believing their tickets entitle them to a larger bundle of amenities than Glatt Boat is in actuality prepared to deliver, the customers attach an erroneous element of bargain to the cruise. To be sure, this illusion of bargain will be short-lived, dissipating at the moment the no-dance rule is sprung on them. Hence the illusion of bargain will not eventuate in any unwarranted *future gain* for Glatt Boat. But the above consideration does not work to remove the *geneivat da'at* interdict. This is so because the essence of the interdict, as R. Joseph David Epstein points out, is not the unwarranted gain but rather the unwarranted favorable attitude secured.[21] Accordingly, the promotion violates *geneivat da'at* law, notwithstanding that the illusion it creates is both short-lived and will not eventuate in an unwarranted gain for the company.

The No-Dance Rule and *Ona'at Devarim*

A no-dance policy that is not promulgated in advance will inevitably produce dashed expectations. If the expectations of social dancing are reasonable, Glatt Boat is responsible for the disappointment. Causing someone needless mental anguish violates the *ona'at devarim* interdict.[22]

Disclosing the no-dance rule only at the ticket booth but leaving the publicity brochure intact does not suffice to remove the *ona'at devarim* interdict. Such a policy creates the setting for a bait-and-switch scenario. Consider the following sequence: Responding to the brochure and believing that the cruise will afford the opportunity for social dancing, a couple arrives at the ticket booth to make a purchase. When they are informed of the no-dance rule, their expectations are dashed, but because they have already arrived at the pier and are not willing to spontaneously change their plans, they decide to purchase the tickets anyway. The only way this bait-and-switch scenario can be avoided is for Glatt Boat to put the no-social-dancing rule into its publicity brochure.

Tokhahah and the No-Dance Rule

The objection we raised against a no-social-dancing rule that is sprung on the captive passengers is reinforced in consideration that the rule relates to the enforcement of a religious code of conduct. Interference with the dancing is not just a matter of enforcing an unannounced rule but amounts to *admonishing* the couples involved for violating a religious norm. Remonstrating with and/or dissuading a fellow Jew from violating a religious tenet, to be sure, is a positive duty.[23] But this duty has its limits. The duty does not apply when the admonition or dissuasion subjects the would-be violator to public embarrassment.[24] This is the case here, because in the absence of an advance and explicit no-social-dance rule, social dancing will begin spontaneously in full view of the dining crowd. Any attempt to break up the dancing would therefore be fraught with the danger that the couples involved will be publicly embarrassed, especially if resistance to the request to stop the dancing is met by stopping the music. Moreover, an essential factor in making the case for the halakhic validity of Glatt Boat as a business venture, despite the predictability that social dancing will take place during the cruise, is the presumption that the infraction involved will be violated deliberately. This in turn, however, creates the presumption that the admonition will not be effective. Authorities dispute whether the duty to rebuke one's fellow remains operative, at least in some manner, when the admonishment will not be heeded.[25] Nevertheless, when there is reason to believe that the admonition will not only not be heeded but will prove counterproductive, all disputants agree that the admonition should not be attempted.[26] This is the case here. One consideration leading to this assessment is the embarrassment factor, discussed above. Another consideration is that absent an explicit no-dancing rule stated in advance, patrons who choose to engage in social dancing during the cruise may very well feel that their tickets *entitle* them to this option. These considerations make a *prima facie* case against interference, as such action would, in all probability, engender hatred and distrust among Jews.

The possibility that interference with the social dancing would engender resentment by the couples on the dance floor is of no concern when an official no-dance rule is promulgated in advance of the ticket sales. Here, Glatt Boat's authority to interfere with the social dancing derives from contract law rather than from the law of rebuke.

Pilot-Testing and the No-Dance Rule

Pilot-testing represents a means by which Glatt Boat can halakhically validate its desired policy of operating the cruise with a no-dance rule but not promulgating this rule beforehand. Mechanically, prior to its maiden commercial voyage, Glatt Boat should expose its publicity brochure to a sampling of its targeted market. The objective of the survey would be to determine whether social dancing is a reasonable expectation. By exposing the target market to the brochure, the net impression of the somewhat-conflicting signals sent by Glatt Boat and World Class Boats can be assessed. In this survey the only opinions that count are those of persons who have a definite interest in taking the cruise. One could not honestly include himself in this group unless the three-hour cruise at the $65 asking price was a preferred item in his budget.

Suppose the pilot test reveals that less than 15 percent of the targeted audience believes that social dancing will be an option aboard the cruise. This finding halakhically validates Glatt Boat's desire to operate its cruise with a no-dance rule without promulgating the rule beforehand. Operating its business in this fashion will undoubtedly dupe some people into taking the cruise in the belief that social dancing will be an option. But since only an *insignificant* minority are left disappointed by the no-dancing rule that is sprung on them, the company is not guilty of deception. Rather, the duped patrons are guilty of self-deception.

The flip side of the coin is that a pilot-testing finding that more than 85 percent expect a no-dancing rule imposes a duty on Glatt Boat to *impose such a rule*, even though it did not announce the no-dancing rule in advance. Failure to do so makes the company responsible for the dashed expectations of the reasonable man.

An initial empirical finding that the expectation for social dancing was unreasonable does not validate Glatt Boat's no-dancing policy on a permanent basis. We must take into account the possibility that Glatt Boat's customer base may shift over time. Accordingly, the firm must continuously monitor its customers' attitudes by administering an exit questionnaire at the conclusion of each cruise. This alone will alert the firm as to when a switch to an explicit advance no-dance policy is indicated.

1. For the source and analysis of this prohibition, see R. Mosheh Feinstein (New York, 1895–1986), *Responsa Iggerot Mosheh*, Even ha-Ezer 2:13.

2. *Torat Kohanim*, Leviticus 19:14; Maimonides (Egypt, 1135–1204), *Yad*, Rozeah 12:14.

3. R. Shabbetai b. Meir ha-Kohen, Siftei Kohen, *Sh.Ar.*, Yoreh De'ah 151, n. 6, on the understanding of R. Ezekiel b. Judah Landau (Prague, 1713–1793), *Dagul me-Revavah*, ad loc.

4. R. Abraham Abele b. Hayyim Gombiner, *Magen Avraham, Sh.Ar.*, Orah Hayyim, 347, n. 4.

5. Underlying this rationale are several halakhic positions which are points of contention in the rabbinic literature. One keystone is the contention that availability to the violator of the prohibited item from an alternative source of *purchase* frees the facilitator of the *lifnei iver* interdict. Suspending the interdict on this basis requires, however, an elastic reading of the standard case of *lifnei iver* discussed in the Talmud. This case deals with the prohibition of

offering a cup of wine to a *nazir*. If the wine is physically accessible to the *nazir* without the assistance of a facilitator, as would be the case when both parties are on the same side of the river (*had ivar denahara*) then *lifnei iver*, at least on a biblical level, is not violated (Avodah Zarah 6b). Adopting an elastic reading of this text, R. Mordecai b. Hillel ha-Kohen (Germany, 1240–1298) suspends the interdict even when the alternative means available to the violator consist not of physical access to the item, but only in the ability to *buy* it from a source other than the facilitator. Accordingly, R. Mordecai permitted a Jew to sell a heathen an item that will be offered in worship of an idol, provided the same item can be purchased elsewhere. R. Mosheh Isserles (Poland, 1525 or 1530), Rema, *Sh.Ar.*, Yoreh De'ah 151:2, adopts this view. Other decisors adopting R. Mordecai b. Hillel's view include R. Mordecai b. Moses Schwadron (Poland, 1835–1911), Maharsham 2:184, 6:11; and R. Abraham b. Ze'ev Nahum Bornstein (Poland, 1839–1910), *Responsa Avnei Nezer*, Yoreh De'ah 126.

Another school of thought adopts a strict-construction view of Avodah Zarah 6b. Availability to the violator of the prohibited item from an alternative source is not a mitigating factor for the facilitator unless the item is *physically accessible* to the violator without the need to buy it from another source. This is the view of R. Elijah b. Solomon Zalman (Lithuania, 1720–1797), *Bi'ur ha-Gra, Sh.Ar.*, Yoreh De'ah 151:8.

Another keystone for R. Feinstein's first rationale is the halakhic position that availability of the prohibited item to the violator from another source is a mitigating factor even when the other source is also a Jew and in consequence the *lifnei iver* interdict is in any case violated. Another school of thought, however, takes the view that the *lifnei iver* interdict for the facilitator remains intact unless the alternative source of supply is a non-Jew. This position is espoused by R. Judah Rosanes (Turkey, 1657–1727), *Mishneh le-Melekh*, Yad, *Malveh* 4:2. R. Abraham Danzig (Prague, 1748–1820), *Hohkmat Adam* 130:2, rules in accordance with R. Rosanes. R. Hayyim Hezekiah Medini (Russia, 1832–1904), *Sedei Hemed* 2:30–34, cites a number of authorities who follow R. Rosanes' view.

6. In a different responsum (Orah Hayyim 2:62), R. Feinstein expresses hesitation as to whether his second rationale in the catering case can be relied upon when the issue at hand is *lifnei iver* on a pentateuchal level of violation.

Addressing this issue, Rabbi J. David Bleich avers that a number of authorities dispute the validity of the second rationale R. Feinstein offers in the catering case. In the opinion of these authorities, the sale of an article whose primary use is permissible is not sanctioned when the vendor is *certain* that the article will be used by the buyer for a forbidden purpose. See J. David Bleich, *Contemporary Halakhic Problems*, vol. 4 (New York: Ktav, 1995), pp. 92–104.

7. R. Mosheh Feinstein, *Iggerot Mosheh*, Yoreh De'ah 1:72.

8. For sources and discussion of this point, see pp. 118–21.

9. For development of this point, see pp. 41–45.

10. Bava Batra 89a; R. Isaac b. Jacob Alfasi (Algeria, 1013–1103), Rif, ad loc.; *Yad*, Genevah 8:20; Rosh, Bava Batra 5:22; R. Jacob b. Asher (Germany, 1270–1343), *Tur*, op. cit. 231:2; R. Joseph Caro (Israel, 1488–1575), *Sh.Ar.*, op. cit. 231:2; R. Jehiel Michel Epstein (Belarus, 1829–1908), *Arukh ha-Shulhan*, op. cit. 231:3.

11. *Yad*, Ma'akhalot Asurot 11:25.

12. *Ar.haSh.*, Yoreh De'ah 119:2.

13. Hullin 94a.

14. R. Aryeh Judah b. Akiba, *Lev Aryeh*, Hullin 94a.

15. R. Mosheh Mordecai Epstein, *Responsa Levush Mordecai* 24.

16. R. Eliezer Meir Preil, *HaMe'or* 1:26–27.

17. *Iggerot Mosheh*, Yoreh De'ah 2:6.

18. Please turn to p. 35 of this volume.

19. For elaboration of this point, see Aaron Levine, *Economic Public Policy and Jewish Law* (Hoboken, N.J.: Ktav, 1993), pp. 82–88.

20. Hullin 94a; Rif, ad loc.; *Yad*, De'ot 2:6; *Mekhirah* 18:1; R. Asher b. Jehiel (Germany, 1250–1327), Rosh, Hullin 7:28; *Tur*, Hoshen Mishpat 228:6; *Sh.Ar.*, Hoshen Mishpat 228:6; *Ar.haSh.*, Hoshen Mishpat 228:3.

21. R. Joseph David Epstein, *Mizvat ha-Shalom* (New York: Torat ha-Adam), p. 243.

22. Leviticus 25:17.

23. Leviticus 19:17; *Yad*, De'ot 6:7–13.

24. Sotah 10b and Tosafot ad loc. Maimonides (*Yad*, De'ot 6:8) allows for the possibility of public rebuke in the sphere of law pertaining to the obligation between man and God (*bein adam l'Makom*). But this only after private rebuke fails.

25. Espousing the view that the *tokhahah* obligation is suspended when it is certain that the admonishment will not be heeded are R. Eleazer b. R. Shimon and R. Abba at Yevamot 65b. Ruling in accordance with this position is R. Isaac b. Jacob Alfasi (Rif, ad loc.) and Tosafot, Bava Batra 60b. R. Mosheh Isserles (Rema, *Sh.Ar.*, Orah Hayyim 608:2), however, regards the *tokhahah* duty as remaining intact even when it will not be heeded. In public, a single protest will suffice. But in private the admonisher must persist until the transgressor begins either to curse or to assault him.

26. R. Yehudah Amital, "Rebuking a Fellow Jew: Theory and Practice," in *Jewish Tradition and the Nontraditional Jew*, ed. Jacob J. Schacter (Northvale, N.J., Jason Aronson, 1992), p. 121.

Negative Puffery: The Case of Baby Oragel

Comparative advertising has enjoyed legitimacy in the United States since 1972, when the FTC began advocating this form of marketing. This stratagem entails advertising in which a named competitor's product is unfavorably compared to the speaker's product. A particularly irksome variety of this tactic, called negative puffery, occurs when the disparagement takes the form of half-truths or misleading opinion about a competitor's product.

Currently, the only recourse open to a target of comparative advertising is to sue under the common-law tort action of injurious falsehood. But the law of injurious falsehood, as Professor Paul T. Hayden points out, is an inadequate theory to combat disparagement in modern comparative advertising. This is so for two reasons. First, in bringing action in such cases the plaintiff must prove that the disparaging representation is false. Many courts, however, have concluded that only *factual* misrepresentation meets this test. The second difficulty is the requirement for the plaintiff in tort law to prove special damages in the form of pecuniary loss in order to obtain relief.

With the only defense against comparative advertising being the law of injurious falsehood, it is no surprise that negative puffery flourishes virtually unchecked by common law as a legally accepted means of marketing.

Hayden cites a Baby Orajel ad as an example of the type of negative puffery that is legally acceptable today:

> Tears in his eyes, a crying baby screams at you from the left half of the page as the same infant, now joyful and contented, laughs at you from the right. "Teething baby. Up to 30 minutes after Children's Tylenol," reads the caption under the miserable child. And beneath the happy baby: "Teething baby. Within 1 minute after Baby Orajel." The text of this nationally distributed magazine advertisement cautions, "If you're giving your baby Children's Tylenol, your baby could wind up suffering up to thirty minutes longer than necessary," and advises, "But don't take our word for it. Just ask the baby on the right."[1]

In his critique of the present legal treatment of comparative advertising, Hayden argues that negative puffery should be regulated as a possible violation of both deceptive advertising and unfair competition. If the representation is "likely to deceive or mislead" a significant number of prospective purchasers, it should be disallowed.

Moreover, in bringing suit against the negative advertisement of a competitor, the plaintiff should not be burdened to prove special damages. Rather, demonstration of "likely commercial detriment" should suffice. This entails no more than a demonstration that the negative ad would likely influence the conduct of prospective buyers and in consequence result in harm for the plaintiff, either in the form of customer loss or in reputational damage. Indeed, the above-mentioned elements constitute the standard embodied in the new Restatement of Unfair Competition.

On the basis of the above criterion, Hayden objects to the Baby Orajel ad. What this ad conveniently conceals is that *Orajel wears off more quickly than Tylenol.* Given Tylenol's offsetting advantage, Baby Orajel's representation is both selective and unbalanced. It could just as easily been said that "the child given Orajel will be crying in thirty minutes while the child given Tylenol will be smiling gleefully." The ad is misleading.

The ad is also disparaging because it implies that Tylenol is ineffective in combating teething pain.

In Hayden's judgment, Baby Orajel's ad should be regarded as deceptive and therefore disallowed.[2]

Baby Orajel and *Geneivat Da'at*

In evaluating the ethics of Baby Orajel's ad from the perspective of Halakhah, Hayden's analysis of why the ad is misleading is most relevant. By both concealing Tylenol's offsetting advantage and associating Tylenol with a shrieking, miserable infant, Baby Orajel manages to generate for itself a more favorable impression of its product than is warranted. The ad hence clearly violates the *geneivat da'at* interdict.[3]

Baby Orajel and *Lifnei Iver*

Another problem with the negative ad is that its formulation amounts to the proffering of advice. Its use of the comparative-merit stratagem transforms the message from a mere representation to a superiority claim. To be sure, there is nothing inherently unethical about making a superiority claim. If a company really believes that its product beats the competition, advancing a superiority claim does not make the company guilty of proffering ill-suited advice. But Orajel's ad goes beyond making a superiority claim. By associating Tylenol with a shrieking baby, Orajel *shames* the public into not searching further for teething medication. Because Orajel's ad amounts to *active dissuasion* to become informed on the merits of Tylenol, the ad amounts to ill-suited advice and violates the interdict against proffering ill-suited advice (*lifnei iver*).[4]

Let us consider the possibility that the Baby Orajel ad violates *lifnei iver* even in respect to those people who don't rely on the Orajel ad and end up buying Tylenol on the basis of their finding that the latter medication is longer-lasting.

To begin, we note that the *lifnei iver* interdict comes in two varieties: One aspect is the prohibition for A to aid or abet B in the commission of a sin. The second aspect consists of the prohibition for A to give B ill-suited advice.[5] In respect to the first aspect, authorities dispute whether A violates *lifnei iver* when the sin he encourages B to commit is, in actuality, not committed by B.[6] One school of thought, led by R. Malachi b. Jacob ha-Kohen (Italy, d. ca. 1785) takes the view that *lifnei iver* prohibits A from setting up B with an *opportunity* to sin. Whether B ends up committing the sin or not is immaterial as far as A's infraction is concerned.[7] Another school of thought, led by R. Isaac Blaser (Russia, 1837–1907) relieves A of *lifnei iver* violation unless the sin he encourages B to do is actually committed by B.[8] The same dispute should apply to the second aspect of *lifnei iver*, namely, the prohibition to give someone ill-suited advice. Whether the Baby Orajel ad violates *lifnei iver* in respect to the target consumer who does not rely on the ad and ends up not buying the product is, therefore, a matter of halakhic dispute.

Another point to consider is whether Orajel violates *lifnei iver* in respect to consumers who encounter the company's ad only after they have already become informed on the merits of alternative teething medicines. Consider that this group does not take the company's claim as *advice*, even on the level of information that warrants further investigation. Instead, the informed consumer immediately recognizes the company's claim as misleading. In respect to the informed consumer, the company cannot be said to be guilty of proffering ill-suited advice.

While the informed consumer rejects the ad, she is assuredly offended by it. For one, the ad insults her intelligence. Moreover, as a concerned person, the informed consumer should feel a sense of outrage that the ad exploits the ignorance of the uninformed. In respect to the informed consumer, the Orajel ad violates the prohibition of causing someone needless mental anguish (*ona'at devarim*).[9] Supporting this proposition is the comment of R. Solomon b. Isaac (Rashi, France, 1040–1105) on the biblical source of this prohibition: "And you shall not hurt the feelings of one another" (Leviticus 25:17). In relating this verse to the *ona'at devarim* prohibition, Rashi avers that the verse prohibits an individual from giving someone self-serving, ill-suited advice.[10] Reading the prohibition on engaging in this type of conduct into the *ona'at devarim* interdict raises a difficulty in that this conduct is already prohibited by dint of the prohibition of *lifnei iver* at Leviticus 19:14. The difficulty is readily resolved with the proposition that the prohibition against proffering ill-suited advice comes in two varieties. One aspect obtains when the recipient of the advice either relies on it or at least treats it as valuable enough to warrant further investigation. Here, the adviser violates *lifnei iver*. The second aspect obtains when the recipient immediately recognizes the advice as ill-suited. Because the advice mocks the intelligence of the recipient, the adviser violates the *ona'at devarim* interdict.

Baby Orajel and the Interdict on Talebearing

Another moral concern with the Orajel ad is that it may infringe upon the biblical interdict against talebearing.[11]

Talebearing occurs when A makes a damaging, albeit *true*, report about B's misconduct to C. Two varieties of this misconduct have been identified by the sages. If C is merely a third party in respect to a true but damaging report, then A's talebearing is called *lashon ha-ra*. Should C be the victim or intended victim of B's wrongdoing, then A's talebearing is called *rekhilut*. Depending upon the circumstances, talebearing may involve the violation of a total of thirty-one pentateuchal positive commandments and prohibitions.[12]

Included in the interdict against talebearing is the prohibition forbidding a storekeeper to deprecate the merchandise of a competitor.[13] Since Baby Orajel's mass media ad exposes both the general public as well as potential customers to its denigration of Tylenol, both the *lashon ha-ra* and *rekhilut* aspects of the tale-bearing interdict may be infringed upon.

To be sure, if A's motive in making his report is to avert a loss for C, then the talebearing interdict may very well be suspended. But before A may make his report, a number of very restrictive conditions must be met. Elsewhere in this volume we have detailed these conditions.[14] Absent any identifiable loss or harm, the discussion does not even advance to a consideration of whether these restrictive conditions are in place. In the case at hand, what *objective harm* does Tylenol represent to the consumer? Far from being ineffectual, Tylenol is an authentic teething medication, having both advantages and *limitations*. Its advantage consists of its being long-lasting, and its limitation is that it is slow-acting. Moreover, at present there is no teething medication on the marketplace that is both fast-acting and long-lasting. Both Orajel and Tylenol have offsetting advantages and *limitations*. Given that Tylenol's product presents no *objective harm* to the consumer, there is no justification for Orajel to *selectively* disclose information regarding Tylenol in the form of disclosing Tylenol's limitations as a teething medication.

Baby Orajel and *Mitkabbed Biklon Shel Havero*

By use of the comparison technique, Baby Orajel manages to *magnify* the virtue of its product at the expense of Tylenol. This promotional device may run afoul of R. Yose b. Hanina's dictum: "Anyone who elevates himself at the expense of his friend's degradation has no share in the world-to-come" (*mitkabbed biklon havero ein lo helek l'olam ha-ba*).[15] Before relating R. Yose b. Hanina's dictum to the case at hand, consider a number of caveats that apply to this dictum.

1. First, note that the key word in R. Yose b. Hanina's dictum is degradation (*kalon*). Elevating oneself at the expense of someone else is not per se obnoxious. What makes it so is when the elevation is achieved at the expense of someone else's *degradation*.

Relatedly, R. Hayyim Hezekiah Medini (Russia, 1832–1904) ruled that voicing an opinion that A is a greater talmudic scholar than B does not amount to degrading B and is therefore a permissible statement.[16]

Thus, R. Yose b. Hanina's dictum does not lead to a blanket prohibition of comparison advertising. Negative advertising comes into question only when a seller magnifies the attractiveness of his product by pointing out *defects* or *flaws* present in a rival's product. But increasing the desirability of his product by pointing out that it has features that are not offered in rival products does not violate R. Yose's dictum.

2. Another consideration in identifying the parameters of what constitutes *kalon* is the difference in price between the rival products. Suppose the inferior product sells at a lower price. Here, the undesirable feature of the inferior product should be regarded as a limitation rather than as a defect. This is so because consumers, to a certain extent, trade off quality for a price reduction. Accordingly, provided the superior product clearly communicates in its negative comparison ad that the competing product is *cheaper*, pointing out the rival product's defects does not violate *mitkabbed bikalon*. Illustrating this principle is the following negative comparison ad that Vanish Dust Vacuum Cleaner put out against its rival, Spotless Carpet Vacuum:

> Spotless Carpet Vacuum sells for $150. Our model, Vanish Dust Vacuum, sells for $200. Don't imagine for a moment that you'll get a bargain if you buy Spotless Carpet. Keep in mind these facts. When in use, Spotless Carpet registers 90 decibels on the decibel meter. In addition, Spotless Carpet weighs, without attachments, a full 20 lbs. Vanish Dust, on the other hand, registers only 2 decibels on the decibel meter and weighs, without attachments, a scant 2 lbs. Check out the difference. We're confident you'll buy Vanish Dust.

3. Finally, *mitkabbed bikalon* does not apply in the context of defensive advertising. A variation on the previous example will illustrate this point:

Suppose Spotless Carpet sells for $230 and Vanish Dust sells for $200. Spotless Carpet advertises that its model has an expected useful lifetime of six years, whereas Vanish Dust has an expected useful lifetime of only four years. The ad conveniently does not mention that users of Spotless Carpet will have to tolerate bulkiness in weight and an annoying noise level. In addition, the ad makes no mention that Vanish Dust is $30 cheaper than Spotless Carpet. Because Spotless Carpet's ad is misleading, it is morally acceptable for Vanish Dust to defend itself by pointing out the aforementioned defects in the higher-priced Spotless Carpet Model.

Let us now relate R. Yose b. Hanina's dictum to our case study. Consider that Tylenol's inability to deliver quick relief is in the nature of a limitation rather than a defect in its product. Yet Orajel projects this feature of Tylenol's product as a definite defect. It does so by projecting Tylenol with the image of a *shrieking, miserable* baby. Orajel *magnifies* the value of its own product by comparing it not to the *actual* Tylenol product but to a *distorted image* of it. Hence Orajel violates R. Yose b. Hanina's dictum.

Let us change the scenario a bit. Suppose a new company, ASL, arrives on the scene and develops a teething medication that is both fast-acting and long-lasting. In the new state of affairs, an infant suffering from teething pain will clearly benefit more from ASL's product than from any other teething product available in the marketplace. In this new environment, it should not be objectionable for a third party, such as *Consumer Reports*, to report on the capabilities, limitations, and prices of the various teething medications available in the marketplace. Notwithstanding that it will inflict substantial commercial damage on both Orajel and Tylenol, the report averts wasteful expenditures and unnecessary pain for consumers. The report should therefore have no trouble meeting the standards set for suspending the interdict against talebearing. For ASL itself to engage in negative comparative advertising is, however, another matter. Consider the possibility that the new advance in teething medication might very well transform Orajel's short-lasting feature and Tylenol's slow-acting feature into defects rather than just limitations. This is so because Tylenol and Orajel's shortcomings can be regarded as merely limitations only when they offer some offsetting advantage, including price, over ASL. When this is not the case, purchasing either Orajel or Tylenol is clearly an unwise expenditure entailing unnecessary pain for the infant. To avoid violation of the *mitkabbed biklon* interdict, the following approach is suggested for ASL:

> ASL is the best teething medication available. Nothing beats it for its quick action and long-lasting relief. Check it out! You owe it both to your infant and to yourself.

Baby Orajel and *Mozi Shem Ra'*

In its negative ad, Baby Orajel does not content itself with merely stating in words that Tylenol is incapable of delivering fast relief. Instead, it uses the imagery of a shrieking, miserable baby to convey this message. By employing the imagery of a shrieking baby, Orajel may well create the erroneous impression that Tylenol is *so pathetically slow-acting* as to render it *almost useless* as a teething medication. Regardless of its intent, Orajel may thus be guilty of *libel* against Tylenol. Maligning or slandering someone is a violation of the prohibition against *mozi shem ra'* (defaming one's fellow).[17] A saving factor here is that Orajel's ad is a mass communications message. What matters, therefore, is the interpretation of the reasonable man.[18] Accordingly, if 15 percent of Orajel's targeted audience construes the company's ad as asserting that the teething medication of its rival Tylenol is for all intents and purposes *useless*, then Orajel's ad is guilty of *mozi shem ra'*. If less than 15 percent of the targeted audience is left with this impression, Orajel violates *lashon ha-ra'* rather than *mozi shem ra'*.

Reformulating the Baby Orajel Ad

The preceding discussion demonstrates that Baby Orajel's ad is a moral minefield. Reformulation of the ad is imperative. One thing is for sure, the shrieking baby must go! With the aim of drawing attention to its distinctiveness and at the same time avoiding the above infractions, the following approach is suggested:

> Orajel is the fastest-acting teething medication available. True, Tylenol is longer-lasting, but Tylenol takes as much as 30 minutes to kick in.
>
> What's more important here? Minimizing your baby's suffering or minimizing the time you spend staying up with your baby? The makers of Orajel are confident that you will do the right thing.

1. *Parents Magazine*, November 1989, p. 111.

2. Paul T. Hayden, "A Goodly Apple Rotten at the Heart: Commercial Disparagement in Comparative Advertising as Common Law Tortious Unfair Competition," *Iowa Law Review* 76 (1990): 67–102.

3. For the biblical source of the *geneivat da'at* interdict, please turn to p. 35.

4. *Torat Kohanim* at Leviticus 19:14; Maimonides (Egypt, 1135–1204), *Yad*, Rozeah 12:14.

5. Cf. *Yad*, op. cit. 12:12–14.

6. For an extensive discussion on this point, see R. Jeroham Fishel Perla's commentary on *Sefer ha-Mitzvot* of R. Saadiah Gaon, Minyan ha-Lavin 54. He traces the issue to the geonic period.

7. R. Malachi b. Jacob ha-Kohen, *Yad Malakhi* 367.

8. R. Isaac Blaser, *Peri Yizhak* 2:49.

9. Leviticus 25:17; Mishnah, Bava Mezia 4:10; R. Isaac b. Jacob Alfasi (Algeria, 1012–1103), Rif, ad loc.; *Yad*, Genevah 14:12; R. Asher b. Jehiel (Germany, 1250–1327), Rosh, Bava Mezia 4:22; R. Jacob ben Asher (Germany, 1270–1343), *Tur*, Hoshen Mishpat, 228:1; R. Joseph Caro (Israel, 1488–1575), *Shulhan Arukh*, Hoshen Mishpat 228:1; R. Jehiel Michel Epstein (Belarus, 1829–1908), *Arukh ha-Shulhan*, Hoshen Mishpat 228:1.

10. Rashi at Leviticus 25:17.

11. Leviticus 19:16.

12. R. Israel Meir ha-Kohen Kagen (Poland, 1838–1933), Hafez Hayyim, *Lavin* 117, *Essin* 114.

13. Hafez Hayyim, *Hilkhot Issurei Lashon ha-Ra, Be'er Mayim ha-Hayyim* 5:7.

14. Please turn to pp. 283–4 of this volume.

15. Jerusalem Talmud, Hagigah 8a.

16. R. Hayyim Hezekiah Medini (Russia, 1832–1904), *Sedei Hemed* IV, k'lal 86, p. 524.

17. Please turn to p. 302, note 3, of this volume.

18. For development of this point, please turn to pp. 35–45 of this volume.

AT&T's Specialty Directory

In 1991, AT&T published a specialty 800-number directory entitled "Gifts, Catalogs and Celebrations." To decide which households were to receive the special directory, the company searched its electronic phone records for frequent callers of each 800 number category. AT&T was thus able to promise advertisers that the special directory would reach consumers with a guaranteed appetite for gifts and catalog phone services.

AT&T's project was attacked by the Chicago Association of Direct Marketing as an "invasion of privacy." AT&T responded that its special directory posed no threat to privacy. Quite to the contrary, the directory would save money and time for those using it. A company spokesperson compared searching for frequent 800-number callers to other ways that AT&T analyzes customers' calling patterns for marketing purposes. For instance, the company might offer discounts to volume long-distance callers, or a special deal on calls to a particular foreign country.

In the current state of affairs, the laws on phone-record privacy are weak and sometimes contradictory. A few states, including California, generally forbid disclosing phone records without a customer's consent. But the federal law that protects the confidentiality of phone conversations suggests that it is legal for phone companies to divulge their records.

In 1979, the Supreme Court of the United States, in *Smith v. Maryland*, held that "it is too much to believe that telephone subscribers . . . harbor any general expectations that the numbers they dial will remain secret." The court ruled that a suspected robber had "voluntarily conveyed numerical information to the telephone company" and thus "assumed the risk that the information would be divulged" to the police without a warrant.[1]

AT&T's Special Directory and Halakhah

From the standpoint of Halakhah, AT&T's publication of a special directory presents several concerns.

One concern is the privacy issue. In this regard a sharp contrast can be drawn between secular law and Halakhah. In secular law, as mentioned earlier, a communication is not automatically confidential. It becomes so only when it is judged that the parties involved reasonably expected their communication to be confidential. In Halakhah, however, the communication of any personal or proprietary information is *automatically* confidential unless permission to disclose it is explicitly given.

This principle is explicated at Yoma 4b:

Where is it derived that [if] one relates something to one's fellow [the latter is commanded] "thou shall not tell"? For it is said, *and the Lord spoke to him from the tent of meeting, saying* (Leviticus 1:1).

The Hebrew word for "saying," which appears in the text, is vocalized *l'e-mor*. Exegetically, the four letters of the word, i.e., *lamed, alef, mem, resh*, can be arranged to read as two words: *lo emor*, "do not say." Taken together the two readings of the word impart the message that if God had not explicitly instruct-ed Moses to disclose what He had told him to the Jewish people, Moses would not have been permitted to do so, notwithstanding that he had no instruction either explicit or implicit not to disclose what he had been told.

In his treatment of the prohibition "You shall not go as a talebearer among your people" (Leviticus 19:16), Maimonides (Egypt, 1135–1204) writes:

Who is a gossiper? One who collects information and [then] goes from person to person, saying: "This is what so-and-so said"; "This is what I heard about so-and-so." Even if the statements are true, they bring about the destruction of the world.

There is a much more serious sin than [gossip], which is also included in the prohibition: *lashon ha-ra*, i.e., relating deprecating facts about a col-league, even if they are true.[2]

What Maimonides teaches us here is that if A conveys private information about B to C, even though the information is *truthful and not derogatory*, A vio-lates "You shall not go as a talebearer."[3]

Another general principle in Jewish privacy-protection law emerges from an analysis of the edict of Rabbenu Gershom b. Judah Me'Or ha-Golah (France, ca. 960–1040) against reading another person's mail without permission.[4] Standing at the basis of this edict, according to R. Jacob Hagiz (Israel, 1620–1674), is the admonition "You shall not go as a talebearer among your people" (Leviticus 19:16). What the verse prohibits is the bearing of someone's private information, whether it is for self-consumption or for the purpose of revealing it to someone else.[5]

Let us now apply these rules to evaluate the ethics of AT&T's project.

Becoming an AT&T customer entitles a subscriber (A) to conduct private conversations using the company's switching and electronic equipment. Recall that the interdict against talebearing includes the prohibition on uncovering confidential information for self-consumption. Now, since A does not give the company *explicit* permission to examine and/or make use of his phone records, such permission extends only to what must be done for billing purposes.

Developing and analyzing the information to obtain *more detailed personal information* on A is prohibited.

If AT&T wants to offer frequent long-distance callers a discount, analyzing its phone records to determine which customers fit into that category does not entail the *uncovering* of data beyond what it uses for billing purposes. Specifically, determining which customers should be offered a discount does not necessitate an identification of the *actual* people customers call. The customer's privacy is therefore not violated here. But compilation of a special directory for gifts, catalogs, and celebrations entails an *analysis* of records of phone calls that connect customers to 800-number firms dealing in those categories. The success of the venture is predicated upon AT&T's ability to convince advertisers that the phone customers who will be sent the specialty directory will make frequent use of it. AT&T's special-directory project, therefore, violates the privacy of its customers.

In defense of the policy, one could argue that the project results in a benefit for the customers who are selected to receive the special directory. Legitimacy should be given to the project on the basis that it is self-evident that the targeted group give their *implicit* approval of the project in advance. This dictum is referred to in the talmudic literature as *anan sahadei* (lit. we are witnesses [in the matter]).

The principle of *anan sahadei* is illustrated by the following scenario in connection with the mitzvah of restoring lost property (*hashavat avedah*): Suppose two animals, one belonging to A and the other to B, are in danger of drowning. A is on the scene, but B is not. A is willing to rescue B's animal at the expense of losing his own less valuable animal, but he demands compensation for his loss. In the absence of A, a group of three can act on B's behalf and agree to A's stipulation. A's stipulation is binding on B even if the sum demanded equals the replacement cost of the animal. The sentimental attachment B has for his animal creates a presumption that he will end up with a net advantage even if he pays the rescuer the replacement cost of the animal.[6]

The *anan sahadei* principle finds ready application to the case at hand. Requiring AT&T to seek permission from its customers before undertaking the special-directory projects adds significantly to the cost of the project. We take it as a given that these incremental costs make the project less attractive for the company compared to alternative investments. Thus AT&T finds itself in a position to judge for its customers whether the contemplated project is in their best interest. Since the customers who receive the special directory benefit from the company's project, it can be presumed that they approve of the project and waive their privacy rights in the matter.

Before the *anan sahadei* principle can be invoked here, however, it must be recognized that compilation of the special directory requires the company to sift through the phone records of *all* its customers, both those who will receive the directory and those who will not. Conferring a benefit to one group of customers cannot be legitimized if it is at the expense of violating the privacy of another group of customers.

This objection can, however, be dismissed, because there is no violation of the privacy of those who do not receive the directory. Sifting through the phone records is accomplished by means of a computer. Violation of customer privacy does not become an issue until the computer comes up with some list or file which the company has access to. For customers who are not selected, no file or record is maintained. The privacy of these people is not violated. To be sure, a company file is produced and maintained in respect to the customers who will be receiving the special directory. Privacy invasion becomes an issue in respect to this group. But, since receiving the special directory is a clear-cut benefit for the members of the selected group, they presumably waive their privacy rights in this matter.

We should note that *anan sahadei* works only to legitimize the *launching* of AT&T's special-directory project. Should a targeted phone subscriber refuse the special directory, he would be within his rights to insist that his name be removed from any file the company keeps in respect to the project.

In the final analysis, the application of the *anan sahadei* principle to the case at hand is problematic. This is so because any judgment that AT&T's project results in a benefit for those selected for the special directory hinges on the status of privacy-invasion law in the United States. In the current state of affairs, the information AT&T develops regarding its customers, such as a list of frequent 800-number callers, is not subject to any government regulation in respect to disclosure to third parties or required security measures against unauthorized use of the information.[7] Currently, AT&T's internal ethical code forbids disclosing customer information to third parties.[8] Presumably, the company installs an adequate security system to safeguard against unauthorized use of customer information. Since it is only AT&T's official policy and procedures that safeguard the confidentiality of information the company develops regarding its customers, arrival of the specialty directory on the doorstep of some customers may very well be an unwelcome event. For these customers, the directory is, of course, beneficial, but it brings with it the anxiety that their lifestyle is in the *process* of becoming a matter of public knowledge.

Exploiting Customer Assets for Commercial Gain

Another problem AT&T's project raises is that production of the directory may entail exploiting the assets of its customers for commercial gain. Given the prohibition on uncovering confidential information, AT&T's authority to examine phone records extends only to what its billing requirements necessitate. The information AT&T develops regarding the affinity of its customers for gifts, catalogs, and celebrations clearly goes beyond this need. This information is the property of the customers. Commercializing it by producing a special directory amounts to exploiting the assets of the company's customers for commercial gain. The analogue of the above case is R. Yose's dictum, recorded at Mishnah Bava Mezia 3:2:

> [If] one rents a cow from another and lends it to someone else, and it dies naturally, the renter must swear that it died naturally, and the borrower must pay the renter. Said R. Yose: How can that person do business with another's cow? Rather, the cow should be returned to the owner.

In the view of the first opinion expressed, when the animal dies, the renter becomes exempt from paying and acquires the animal. Since the renter is not liable for accidents, he takes the oath merely to placate the owner. Therefore, the borrower, who is responsible for accidents, must pay the renter.[9] R. Yose, however, regards the renter who lends out the deposit as an agent of the owner.[10] Therefore, the payment for the cow should be given to the owner, not the renter.[11]

While talmudic decisors follow R. Yose's line,[12] authorities are in disagreement regarding the conditions necessary to trigger the prohibition on doing business with someone else's property.

The majority position calls for disgorgement whenever A makes commercial use of B's property while having no right to make use of it. The circumstance that B suffers no loss thereby is not a saving factor according to this school of thought.

Exemplifying this point of view are the following two rulings of R. Solomon b. Abraham Adret (Spain, ca. 1235–1310):

A rents B's field to C without having any authority to do so. Given that the property in question has not been up for rental, B suffers no loss thereby. Nonetheless, it would be unconscionable for A to keep the rent, as this would amount to doing business with another's property. R. Adret, however, hedges on a definitive ruling regarding the disposition of the rent B received. It might be appropriate, he points out, to return the rent to C on the grounds that B suffers no loss.[13] In another application of R. Yose's dictum, R. Adret ruled that if A builds up B's ruin and rents it to C, A must surrender the rent to B. Since the ruin is not rentable without A's improvements, this too is a case where A's commercialization of B's property entails no loss for B.[14]

A final example of a ruling which follows the above line is a subletting case that came before R. Joseph Habiba (Spain, late 14th–early 15th cent.). A rents an apartment from B and then sublets it at a higher rent to C. In respect to the disposition of the rent differential, R. Habiba finds the critical factor to be whether A was within his rights to sublet the apartment. If A's subletting was legal, then he bears no responsibility to surrender the differential to B. B's unjust-enrichment claim against A is dismissed on the grounds that A's gain causes B no harm (*zeh neheneh ve-ze lo haser*). The circumstance that B suffers no loss as a result of A's subletting activity, however, is not a saving factor when A did not have permission to sublet the apartment to C, as would be the case when C's household was larger than B's. Here, A must surrender the rent differential to B on the grounds that it is unconscionable to do business with someone else's asset.[15]

A minority interpretation of R. Yose's dictum is expressed by R. Ephraim b. Aaron Navon (Turkey, 1677–1735). Disgorgement, in R. Navon's view, is called for only when the following two conditions obtain: (1) the defendant's commercialization of the plaintiff's property was unauthorized; (2) the plaintiff suffers a loss in conjunction with the unauthorized use of his property. Understanding this to be the position of R. Habiba, R. Navon insists that the subletting case speaks of the instance where A rents an apartment from B below its market value and then goes ahead and sublets it to C at a higher price. Here, A bears a responsibility to surrender the differential to B in the event the subletting was not legal. If A was, however, within his rights in subletting the apartment to C, Halakhah does not compel him to surrender the differential to B, despite the loss B suffers in conjunction with A's commercial activity.[16]

R. Yose's dictum finds ready application in the case at hand. Since the information AT&T develops regarding the affinity of its customers for gifts, catalogs, and celebrations is the property right of its customers, the production of a special directory amounts to exploiting the assets of its customers for commercial gain. Consider also that the production of a special directory entails an invasion of privacy for the targeted group, as discussed earlier. The call for disgorgement should therefore obtain even according to the minority-opinion understanding of R. Yose.

One could argue, however, that disgorgement does not obtain for the case at hand. Consider that for any firm other than the telephone company, ascertaining which households frequently call 800 numbers is either impossible or prohibitively expensive. What imparts value to AT&T's special directory is the company's ability to assemble data regarding the phone habits of a *huge* number of people. Companies are willing to place ads in the special directory *only* because AT&T will send the directory to a huge targeted group. Now since it is AT&T that imparts value to otherwise worthless information, the production of a special directory cannot be said to exploit the assets of its customers for commercial purposes.

Recall, however, that R. Adret applied R. Yose's dictum to the instance where A builds up B's ruin and rents it to C. What can be generalized from this application is that disgorgement applies even when the unauthorized user first enhances the market value of someone's asset before making commercial use of it. There is, however, a distinction between the two cases. A ruin has commercial value, if for only speculative purposes. Building up the ruin does not create value *ex nihilo* but merely enhances existing value. In contrast, the frequency of an individual's calls to 800 numbers and the type of 800 numbers he calls have absolutely no value as isolated pieces of information. Since AT&T's work creates value *ex nihilo*, the special directory cannot be characterized as exploiting the assets of its customers for commercial gain.

The Consumer Data Base Industry

Jewish privacy law puts to question the legitimacy of firms whose business it is to collect information about consumers from public and private sources and produce a data base from this information which they sell to direct marketing companies. To illustrate: some states allow their motor vehicle bureaus to sell driver license information. These files contain information regarding motorists' height, weight, and use of "corrective lenses." Consumer data base firms buy this information. By selecting out the tall people and those whose weight is disproportionate to their height, these firms produce useful data bases for marketers of weight-loss programs and manufacturers of clothing for overweight and tall people.

There can be no doubt that the typical consumer objects to allowing a third party access to information he gives a firm while transacting with it. In a 1991 *Time Magazine* survey, 93 percent of those polled felt that companies that sell information about their customers should be legally required to ask permission from their customers before doing so.[17] Thus, invoking the *anan sahadei* principle as a means of justifying the practice of third-party design of data bases has no validity.

Self-Regulation vs. Government Regulation

Currently, American law protects customer records against disclosure to third parties only on a selective basis. In this regard, the Fair Credit Reporting Act, passed in 1970, allows consumers to correct errors in their credit reports, and a 1982 law limits disclosure to third parties. Under the Electronic Fund Transfer Act of 1980, banks must notify individuals when disclosing records to third parties. Cable and video-rental companies and public libraries may not disclose choices individuals make or other personal information without consent. Finally, the 1986 Electronic Communications Privacy Act prohibits telephone, telegraph, and other communications services from releasing the contents of messages they transmit.[18]

Recognition that disclosure of customer records to third parties violates their customers' privacy has led some firms to introduce internal codes that prohibit the practice. AT&T and Chase-Manhattan's codes, for instance, contain a flat prohibition on the disclosure of customer records to third parties. Warner Amex's code, on the other hand, states that it will disclose information about its subscribers only in aggregate form. The guidelines of the Direct Mailing Association (DMA), the association of firms dealing in direct mail, contains a strong statement regarding its members' responsibility for the security of personal data and the need to take strict measures to guard against unauthorized use and access, alteration, or dissemination, both generally and by its employees specifically.[19]

From the standpoint of Halakhah, reliance on the self-regulation of firms to ensure the privacy of their customers is not an adequate approach. The inadequacy of relying on voluntarism here follows from several considerations.

One concern is that the focus of self-regulation efforts described above is on exhorting firms to safeguard the confidentiality of personal data in their possession. No guidelines, however, are offered in respect to the more fundamental issue of what kind of information a company is allowed to compile and maintain regarding its customers. Halakhah, as will be recalled, addresses the latter issue. It imposes a duty on the firm to guard itself against intruding on the privacy of its customers. Record-keeping beyond what is necessary for billing purposes clearly violates this duty.

Another concern is that Halakhah sees self-regulation as unreliable when the profit motive biases an individual to violate the standard involved. A case in point is Halakhah's call for the appointment of public inspectors to ensure the honesty of commercial weights and measures.[20] Why voluntary self-enforcement is not relied upon to ensure the integrity of commercial weights and measures is explained by R. Jehiel Michel Epstein (Belarus, 1829–1908) as stemming from the unconscious, distorting impact the profit motive exerts on vendors. R. Epstein uses this rational to explain Maimonides' ruling[21] that in matters of kashrut one may only patronize a vendor who is known to be reliable.[22]

The potential the profit motive has to bias firms to violate Halakhah's privacy standard is particularly acute. Consider that much of the information any single firm assembles regarding its customers is typically not threatening to them. But culling bits of information about someone from each of the wide variety of firms he transacts with might reveal much about his personality and spending habits. Would not employers and insurance companies eagerly welcome the opportunity to glance at the dossiers of prospective employees and subscribers describing their health-related purchases, reading habits, leisure industry expenditures, political affiliations, and charitable contributions? The opportunity for abuse here cannot be overstated. Now, if a company regards disclosing information regarding its customers as innocuous, and this information is valuable to a third party, industry ethical codes will not prove much of a deterrent against disclosure. Within the climate of voluntarism, rampant violation of the consumer's privacy can therefore be expected.

Government Regulation Against Invasion of Privacy

Rather than rely on self-regulation, Halakhah would recommend government legislation to protect the privacy of consumers. This legislation would prohibit firms from compiling and maintaining files on their customers beyond what is necessary for billing purposes. The legislation would also prohibit firms from making customer information available to third parties. Appropriate penalties for violating these codes of conduct should be part of this legislation.

Problem

In 1936, the following case came before the Kentucky Court of Appeals (265 Ky. 418, 96 S.W. 2d 1028 (1936):

> Edwards discovered an entrance on his property leading to a cave 300 feet underneath the property of his neighbor Lee. There was absolutely no means to enter the cave from Lee's property. Edwards installed walkways and lights in the cave and gained substantial revenue by charging tourists admission. When Lee discovered Edwards' use of the cave beneath his property, he sought an injunction and an accounting of the profits resulting from the use of this cave. Edwards argued that he should not be held liable because the cave was of no practical use to Lee without an entrance, and, in any case, the property had not been injured or damaged. Moreover,

he argued, Lee should not be entitled to damages because, even if an injunction was granted, Lee would have the cave in the same condition it had always been, handicapped by no greater degree of usefulness than it was before Edwards trespassed on it.

Notwithstanding Edwards' arguments, the court held Lee entitled to an injunction prohibiting Edwards from using the cave beneath Lee's property. Moreover, the court held Edwards obligated to account to Lee the share of profits received from the portion of the cave beneath his property even though it was of no possible use to him.[23]

How would Halakhah rule in this case?

1. Michael W. Miller, "As Phone Technology Swiftly Advances, Fears Grow They'll Have Your Number," *Wall Street Journal*, December 13, 1991, B1.

In *Smith vs. Maryland*, referred to in the *Wall Street Journal* article, Justices Marshall and Brennan issued a dissenting opinion: "Privacy is not a discrete commodity, possessed absolutely or not at all. Those who disclose certain facts to a bank or phone company for limited business purpose need not assume that this information will be released to other persons for other purposes." *Smith v. Maryland*, 442 U.S. 735, 748 (1979) (Marshall, J., dissenting).

In the text we demonstrate that Halakhah would be in agreement with the dissenting opinion of the court in *Smith*.

2. Maimonides, *Yad*, De'ot 7:2

3. R. Joseph Caro (Israel 1488–1575), *Kesef Mishneh* at Yad, loc. cit.

4. R. Moses b. Naphtali Hirsch Rivkes (Lithuania, d. ca. 1671/72), *Be'er ha-Golah*, Sh.Ar., Yoreh De'ah 334, n. 123.

5. R. Jacob Hagiz, *Responsa Halakhot Ketannot* 1:276.

6. Tosafot, Bava Mezia 31b.

7. Miller, "As Phone Technology Swiftly Advances."

8. Mary Gardener Jones, "Privacy: A Significant Marketing Issue for the 1990's," *Journal of Public Policy and Marketing* 10, no. 1 (Spring 1991): 140.

9. *Tanna Kamma*, Mishnah, Bava Mezia 3:2.

10. Rosh, Bava Mezia 3:5.

11. Mishnah, Bava Mezia 3:2.

12. R. Isaac b. Jacob Alfasi (Algeria, 1012–1103), Rif, Bava Mezia 34b; *Yad*, Sekhirut 1:6; R. Asher b. Jehiel (Germany, 1250–1327), Rosh, Bava Mezia 3:5; R. Jacob b. Asher (Germany, 1270–1343), *Tur*, Hoshen Mishpat 307:5; Sh.Ar., Hoshen Mishpat 307:5; R. Jehiel Michel Epstein (Belarus, 1829–1908), *Arukh ha-Shulhan*, Hoshen Mishpat 307:5.

13. Rashba, Bava Kamma 21a.

14. Rashba quoted in *Nimmukei Yosef*, Bava Mezia 8.

15. R. Joseph Habiba, *Nimmukei Yosef*, Bava Kamma 2.

16. R. Ephraim b. Aaron Navon, *Mahaneh Efrayim*, Sekhirut 19.

17. Ellen R. Foxman and Paula Kilcoyne, "Information Technology, Marketing Practice, and Consumer Privacy: Ethical Issues," *Journal of Public Policy and Marketing* 12, no. 1 (Spring 1993): 106.

18. Ibid., p. 112.

19. Jones, "Privacy," p. 140.

20. Rami b. Hamma, reporting in the name of R. Yizhak, Bava Batra 89a; Rif, ad loc.; *Yad*, Genevah 8:20; Rosh, Bava Batra 5:22; *Tur*, Hoshen Mishpat 231:2; *Sh.Ar.*, Hoshen Mishpat 231:2; *Ar.haSh.*, Hoshen Mishpat 232:3.

21. *Yad*, Ma'akholot Asurot 11:15.

22. *Ar.haSh.*, Yoreh De'ah 119:2.

23. The description of the Edwards case is taken verbatim from Irwin H. Haut, "Abuse of Rights and Unjust Enrichment: A Proposed Restatement of Jewish Law," in *National Jewish Law Review* 2 (1987): 55–58. See R. Haut's halakhic analysis of this case (ibid.).

Dr. Eric Delbarko and Medical Information Bias

Dr. Eric Delbarko practices internal medicine in the Rover Hill section of the Lollypop Valley. His office is constantly bombarded with samples, promotional materials, and useful freebie reminders from brand-name pharmaceutical companies. Delbarko derives special satisfaction when the opportunity arises to dispense the samples to indigent patients. Upon receiving the free medications, the surprised patients will invariably beam and thank the doctor lavishly for saving them the expense of filling a prescription.

The same companies sponsor informational lunches. Delbarko is an eager participant of these lunches, regarding them as a welcome respite from his hectic daily routine. If not for this benefit, Delbarko would be forced to comb the medical journals and consult colleagues to keep abreast of the latest advances in prescription drugs. The educational advantage Delbarko derives from the marketing activities of the brand-name pharmaceutical companies is second only to the benefit he derives from Continuing Medical Education as far as his professional growth is concerned.

Some of Delbarko's patients suffer from a high blood pressure condition. The drug Dr. Delbarko prescribes for this condition is the brand-name drug called Calan. One day, Ari Frailey, one of Delbarko's patients on Calan, surprised the doctor by angrily asking why Delbarko did not prescribe a generic drug called Verapamil for his condition. Before getting into the particulars of Frailey's complaint, a few preliminary remarks regarding generic drugs are in order.

Under current conditions, patent law confers a brand-name drug with a monopoly position for seventeen years. Once a drug loses its exclusive patent rights, competition begins in earnest as manufacturers produce generic versions of the original. Because they don't have to shoulder the costs of research and development or marketing, generic companies can sell compounds far more cheaply than the brand-name equivalents. When a product goes off patent, the first generic on the market generally costs at least 30 percent less than the brand-name version. As more generic competitors enter the market, the price drops still further.

Patent law allows drug companies to trademark the specific shape and color of their pills. A generic drug may therefore not look the same as its branded equivalent, but the FDA requires that the active ingredient must be identical. It also requires generics to be formulated so that they are absorbed into the body at essentially the same rate.[1]

Now, for the particulars of Frailey's outburst:

"Doc, my daughter is a first-year resident at one of the Harvard hospitals.

She claims that the hospital's formulary says that the generic drug Verapamil is *therapeutically interchangeable* with the brand-name drug Calan. But, doc, the difference in price is enormous! Calan is costing me $45 per hundred 80-milligram tablets, but Verapamil costs only $7 for the same supply."[2]

Visibly shaken and offended by Frailey's outburst and challenge, Delbarko responded curtly:

"I put in long hours in my practice; to say nothing of the emergencies I respond to. What little time I have left I devote to keeping up with the latest diagnostic techniques and the newest innovative treatment programs. I can't be bothered with the *economic side of medicine*."

The Brand Name–Generic Drug Substitution Issue and Halakhah

Let us begin with a critique of Delbarko's attitude that he bears no responsibility to inform himself regarding the brand name–generic drug substitution issue. Society certainly would take him to task for this. Consider that since the mid-1970s, state legislation has allowed pharmacists to dispense lower-priced generics in place of the prescribed brand-name drugs. Of the state statutes in effect since 1980, as many as one quarter provide for mandatory rather than merely permissive substitution.[3] To be sure, explicit instruction by the physician not to substitute requires the pharmacist to dispense the prescription as given.[4]

By allowing pharmacists, in the absence of a physician override, to dispense brand-name prescriptions in generic form, the law effectively gives notice to the physician that his inattention to the appropriateness of a generic substitution could result in harm to his patient. Thus the law places an onus on the doctor to *educate himself* in respect to the generic substitution issue. Given this responsibility, prescribing a brand-name drug instead of its cheaper generic equivalent provides a setting for the violation of the prohibition against proffering ill-suited advice (*lifnei iver*).[5] Several scenarios present themselves. Let us make use of our case study to illustrate them.

Suppose Delbarko prescribes Calan for Frailey and, in addition, exercises the override option. Delbarko's override ensures that the pharmacist will not substitute the lower-priced generic Verapamil for Calan. Since the doctor's ill-suited advice inevitably results in a financial loss for Frailey, Delbarko violates *lifnei iver*.

Suppose, however, that Delbarko prescribes Calan but does not exercise his override privileges. Here, Delbarko's prescription should not always be deemed ill-suited advice. Consider that in some states mandatory generic substitution is called for. Here, Delbarko's prescription of Calan will inevitably be filled as

Verapamil. Because Delbarko's prescription does not even carry a *potential* for financial loss for Frailey, his prescription should halakhically not be dubbed as ill-suited advice.

The above judgment does not, however, hold for the circumstance where, in the absence of an override, substitution for the generic equivalent is only permissible but not mandatory. Here, Delbarko's prescription for Calan carries with it a potential of loss for Frailey. Reinforcing the probability of loss for Frailey is the empirical finding that in the absence of an override only about 15 percent of prescriptions with a brand name are actually filled with a generic product.[6]

Recall that decisors dispute whether an individual violates *lifnei iver* when his ill-suited advice is not actually taken up by the person he advises.[7] An application of the above dispute obtains here when Delbarko's prescription for Calan is actually filled as Verapamil.

Of all the scenarios discussed so far, the most clear-cut instance of violation of *lifnei iver* obtains when Delbarko prescribes Calan and, in addition, exercises his override privilege. Let us consider the possibility that in this instance Delbarko must make good on Frailey's loss. The case at hand is analogous to the instance where a professional moneychanger errs in his judgment that a certain coin will circulate. If the moneychanger took a fee for his services, he is liable to make good on the client's loss.[8]

Some authorities understand the moneychanger case broadly as referring even to the circumstance where the advisee feels free to ignore the moneychanger's advice.[9] Others understand the case narrowly, as referring only to circumstances where the advisee, for all intents and purposes, feels compelled to accept the moneychanger's judgment.[10] This would be the case, for instance, when the advisee was a vendor who received cash payment for his merchandise and the moneychanger is called upon to resolve a dispute between the buyer and the seller as to whether the currency paid will circulate. Should the advisee be free to ignore the judgment of the moneychanger, no liability obtains for the latter in the event that he makes an erroneous judgment. In the case at hand, the patient is not really free to ignore the doctor's prescription. A prescription always follows a diagnosis. Given the patient's investment in obtaining the doctor's diagnosis, following through with filling the prescription is rational, if not compelling. Since the indicated medication cannot be obtained without a prescription, the patient effectively has no option other than to get the prescription filled.

We take note that all disputants agree that if the advisee makes it clear that he relies on the judgment of the moneychanger, the latter is liable in the event of error.[11] If the advisee pays for the moneychanger's opinion, this has the same effect as stating that he is relying on his opinion in the matter. Since the damage resulted directly from relying on the expert's advice, the expert's action is a form of *garmi*.[12]

All this means that a case can be made to hold a doctor liable for a patient's loss resulting from prescribing a brand-name drug when an equivalent generic drug is available.

Generic Substitution and *Ona'ah*

Another issue the case study raises is whether Calan violates *ona'ah* (price fraud) by charging a higher price than generic Verapamil. Recall that *ona'ah* applies to a differentiated product market.[13]

In evaluating the merit of the *ona'ah* claim against Calan, the differential costs Calan and Verapamil operate under must be considered. Calan's costs of production include substantial outlays for applied research and clinical trials. These outlays can only be recovered over a period of many years. Verapamil, on the other hand, brings its product to the market by simply reproducing Calan's product under a different name, shape, and color. The obvious differences in cost between the competing medications makes the exemption from the prohibition of *ona'ah* called *nose be-emunah* (selling on trust) applicable here.[14]

Nose be-emunah obtains when the vendor divulges to a prospective buyer both his cost price and his proposed profit margin. Should the buyer agree to these terms and consummate the transaction with a *kinyan* (symbolic act), a subsequent finding that the cost price involved *ona'ah* does not allow the plaintiff to modify the original transaction in any manner. By agreeing to allow the vendor a specified profit margin, the buyer demonstrates that he is not concerned with the objective value of the commodity. Since realization of the agreed-upon profit rate required the sale to be concluded at the stipulated price, subsequent claims of *ona'ah* are denied.[15]

Nose be-emunah has limited validity in justifying Calan's pricing policy. Consumers know neither Calan's cost price nor its profit margin. Stretching the *nose be-emunah* exemption to its limits can say no more than that consumers are willing to afford the seller a reasonable profit on the basis of his known cost differential. But in the present state of affairs, consumers certainly don't regard the profits of drug companies as reasonable. In this regard we need only take note of the 1993 report of the Congressional Office of Technological Assessment. This report concluded that during the 1980s pharmaceutical companies, on average, earned roughly 15 to 30 percent *more* profit each year than needed to attract adequate investment capital.[16] The upshot is that without a significant reduction in its profit rate, the price differential the brand-name company earns over its generic rival cannot be defended on the basis of the *nose be-emunah* exemption.

The price differential a brand-name drug maintains over its generic counterpart violates *ona'ah* in a blatant manner when the brand-name company itself produces and sells the generic drug. Here, the price differential amounts to a deceptive selling practice.

Information Bias in the Medical Field and Halakhah

Let us now turn to a consideration of Delbarko's favorable attitude toward the educational benefit he derives from the promotional activities of the brand-name drug companies.

While a company has every right to promote its products, offering a doctor a reward as a means of inducing him to prescribe its products subjects the doctor to a bias and is therefore halakhically objectionable.

How an offer of favor works to taint objectivity can be seen by the standard Halakhah sets for the judicial code of ethics. We describe this code elsewhere in this volume.[17] Note that the judicial code of conduct does not apply only to individuals who adjudicate formal litigations. The residents of a community, according to R. Mosheh Isserles (Poland, 1525 or 1530–1572), must cast their votes in a referendum in accordance with what they perceive the public interest to be.[18] Noting this requirement, R. Mosheh Sofer (Hungary, 1762–1839) invalidated a communal election for the post of rabbi when it was discovered that some of the members of the community had accepted graft to cast their ballots for a particular candidate.[19] What follows, in our view, is the imposition of the judicial code of conduct on anyone who is called upon to make judgments in matters pertaining to the public interest and welfare.

The guideposts for the judicial code of conduct have much relevancy for the issue at hand. Since a patient relies on the medical judgment of his doctor, the doctor's professional role assumes a quasi-judicial character. A drug company's offers of a reward for prescribing its drug work only to distort a doctor's objectivity in serving the best interests of his patients. This distorting influence is at work even in the instance when the doctor dispenses the free samples to an indigent patient. Because the practice saves the patient money, the doctor may convince himself that the free sample is the optimal treatment for the medical condition at hand when, in fact, the medication is only a second-line drug. While the distorting influence is obvious when the gift consists of expensive excursions, this conduct should be objectionable even when it takes on the form of reminders and informational lunches. Maintaining objectivity requires a doctor to obtain his information regarding drugs from the medical literature and from peer recommendations.

Drug Company Sponsorship of Continuing Medical Education

The informational bias drug companies introduce is not confined to the rewards they shower upon doctors to induce them to prescribe their products. In addition, these companies introduce bias by their sponsorship of Continuing Medical Education as well as by their sponsorship of journal supplements.

Continuing Medical Education (CME) is designed to force physicians to stay abreast of new medical technologies. Many state licensing boards require practicing physicians to complete a specific number of credits each year. Sponsorship of CME by drug companies runs the risk that the company's interest in promoting its product will outweigh its concern for educating doctors objectively about new medical developments.[20]

Drug company sponsorship of CME entails the creation of a false impression when it fails to disclose up front its relationship with the lecturers at the seminars. Creating a false impression violates the *geneivat da'at* interdict.[21] Disclosure of the relationship between the lecturer and the drug companies is, however, not sufficient. Since the lecturer is paid an honorarium by the drug company, his presentation will inevitably be skewed in favor of the sponsor's product.

With the aim of promoting objectivity in the presentation of medical information, *Consumer Reports* proposes that the medical profession itself should assume the responsibility to adequately fund CME.[22] Shifting the sponsorship of Continuing Medical Education from the pharmaceutical companies to the medical profession itself is, as indicated above, in line with the halakhic approach in this matter.

Drug Company Sponsorship of Journal Supplements

Doctors consistently name medical journals as one of their main sources of unbiased information. Especially valued are peer-reviewed journals. Drug companies have found an effective way to use these journals' credibility for their own purposes by subsidizing the publication of "supplements." Piggybacked onto regular issues of the journal, supplements use the same sober-looking design and typography as the regular articles. Frequently, the supplements are based on symposia sponsored by the same companies that pay for the publication. Exacerbating the problem, many journals actively market their willingness to publish supplements.[23]

A drug company violates *geneivat da'at* law when it sponsors a journal supplement so designed as to give the impression that it is part of the medical journal it is attached to. To prevent false impressions of this kind, *Consumer Reports* calls for journal editors to design their single-sponsor supplements in a manner that clearly differentiates them from regular edition matter. This can be achieved by means of prominently displayed notices, different typography, and different page layout.[24] Once again, the proposal by *Consumer Reports* is consonant with the halakhic approach in this matter.

1. "Do We Pay Too Much for Prescriptions," *Consumer Reports* 58, no. 10 (October 1993): 675.

2. For the comparison figures quoted in the text, see ibid.

3. Statutes differ in respect to how the physician override becomes operative. In some states it becomes effective when the physician signs the prescription on a line labeled "Do Not Substitute" or "Dispense as Written" (DAW). In other states the override becomes effective only if the doctor *writes out* such an instruction. See James J. Wheaton, "Generic Competition and Pharmaceutical Innovation: The Drug Price Competition and Patent Term Restoration Act of 1984," *Catholic University Law Review* 35 (Winter 1986): 445.

4. Ibid., pp. 437, 447.

5. *Torat Kohanim*, Leviticus 19:14; Maimonides (Egypt, 1135–1204), *Yad*, Rozeah 12:14.

6. Wheaton, "Generic Competition and Pharmaceutical Innovation," p. 446, n. 56.

7. Please turn to pp. 61—2 of this volume.

8. R. Jacob b. Asher (Germany, 1270–1343), *Tur*, Hoshen Mishpat 306:6; R. Joseph Caro (Israel, 1488–1575), *Shulhan Arukh*, Hoshen Mishpat 306:6; R. Jehiel Michel Epstein (Belarus, 1829–1908), *Arukh ha-Shulhan*, Hoshen Mishpat 306:13.

9. Rabbenu Yoel, quoted by R. Israel of Krems (Germany, d. 1375), *Haggahot Asheri*, Bava Kamma 9:16; R. Jonathan Eybeschuetz (Prague, 1695–1764), *Tummim*, Sh.Ar., op. cit. 146, n. 19; R. Mosheh Sofer, Novellae Bava Batra 30b.

10. Rabbenu Efraim, quoted in *Haggahot Asheri*, op. cit.

11. R. Shabbetai b. Meir ha-Kohen (Poland, 1621–1662), *Siftei Kohen*, Sh.Ar., op. cit. 129, n. 7; *Ar.haSh.*, op. cit. 306:13.

12. *Ar.haSh.*, loc. cit.

13. Please turn to p.127 of this volume.

14. Bava Mezia 51b; R. Isaac b. Jacob Alfasi (Algeria, 1012–1103), Rif, ad loc.; *Yad*, Mekhirah 13:5; Rosh, Bava Mezia 4:17; *Tur*, op. cit. 227:35; Sh.Ar., op. cit. 227:27; *Ar.haSh.*, op. cit. 227:28.

15. *Yad*, loc. cit. For a variant view of what constitutes selling on trust, see *Haggahot Asheri*, Bava Mezia 4:17.

16. *Pharmaceutical R & D: Costs, Risks and Rewards* (Washington, D.C.: U.S. Congress, Office of Technology Assessment, 1993), p. 2.

17. Please turn to p. 6 of this volume.

18. Rema, Sh.Ar., Hoshen Mishpat 163:1.

19. R. Mosheh Sofer, *Responsa Hatam Sofer*, Hoshen Mishpat 160.

20. "Pushing Drugs to Doctors," *Consumer Reports*, February 1992, pp. 90–92.

21. Samuel, Hullin 94a; Rif, ad loc.; *Yad*, Genevah 18:3; Rosh, Hullin 7:18; *Tur*, op. cit. 228:6; Sh.Ar., op. cit. 228:6, *Ar.haSh.*, op. cit. 228:3.

22. "Pushing Drugs to Doctors," p. 94.

23. Ibid., pp. 93–94.

24. Ibid., p. 94.

3. Salesmanship

The Encyclopedia Salesman

Henry Blackwell is the chief marketing strategist for Galaxy Educational Enterprises, Inc. (GEE). The company publishes a twenty-volume encyclopedia geared to young teenagers as well as other educational materials. Blackwell believes that money spent to discover good prospects and obtain their goodwill is money well spent. Let us proceed to describe Blackwell's marketing plan and the experiences he had in implementing it.

The plan begins with an ad placed in publications that reach a substantial number of professional households. The ad invites the reader to send away for a free travel brochure designed to make "travel in Europe fun for young teenagers." Blackwell reasons that families whose teenage children go on European vacations either alone or with their parents are good prospects to buy an encyclopedia. The ad promises delivery of the brochure within two weeks.

When Blackwell receives the responses, he uses the information at hand to ascertain the telephone numbers of the persons who requested the free brochure. Let us recount what happened with the Fisher family.

Blackwell called Sam Fisher and told him that he was following up on his request for the free brochure. Blackwell went on to say that GEE had asked him to conduct a neighborhood survey on local attitudes regarding the adequacy of educational resources in the home and the community.

"If you would be so kind to allow yourself and your wife to be interviewed for the survey, I'll be very happy to personally deliver the brochure at the time of the interview. Please be assured that the interview will take no more than ten minutes of your time. And, oh, yes, I insist that you and Mrs. Fisher should be compensated $10 each for your time."

Fisher was agreeable. When Blackwell arrived at the Fisher home, he was immediately ushered into the living room. Blackwell took out a questionnaire and proceeded to ask the couple a number of questions, including inquiries about their professional status, educational level, and the number of children they had in school. Finally, Blackwell asked the couple if they felt that the educational resources at home and at school were adequate. Because the Fishers' answer to this question was less than a very firm yes, Blackwell felt that his cue had arrived to launch a sales pitch for the encyclopedia. Blackwell always uses a couple's answers to the survey questions to determine his negotiating strategy. In the present instance, Blackwell's instinct told him that he was dealing with an almost zero probability of making a sale, even if he offered both a deep discount from the regular price along with an installment plan. The telltale sign for this pessimism was Sam Fisher's continuous reference to the endless educational opportunities surfing the net offered. But there was still hope. Neither Mrs. Fisher nor the children were computer literate. Confident that he could now prove his mettle as a super-salesman, Blackwell proclaimed:

"Mr. and Mrs. Fisher, I have exciting news for you. On the basis of your responses to the educational survey, you qualify for a free encyclopedia set from GEE. It's a $1,200 value, and you're going to get it for *nothing*."

The Fishers appeared to be happy to hear the news and listened intently as Blackwell went on to explain that GEE wanted to promote sales by placing the encyclopedia set in a model home. All the company would require of them was to produce a testimonial letter regarding the tremendous educational benefit the family derived from the set. To facilitate matters, the company would be glad to write the letter, subject, of course, to the couple's approval. In addition Galaxy would like the set to serve as a showcase for other potential customers. Accordingly, should the Fisher's get a request to look over the set, they should graciously allow the potential customer to come into their home and browse through the volumes. All this sounded eminently reasonable to the Fishers until Blackwell got to the part regarding the proper display and maintenance of the encyclopedias. Blackwell explained that it would be reasonable for the company to expect the Fishers to display the set in elegant fashion and protect the volumes from physical abuse. The company would therefore require the Fishers to keep the set in an appropriate bookcase, which it would provide at a cost of $100. As the couple was digesting the bookcase requirement, Blackwell brought up one final item:

"Knowledge, as you will appreciate, becomes rapidly obsolete. To ensure that you maximally benefit from our educational product, please understand, that my company requires you to purchase its annual supplements. Your commitment here need not extend beyond the publication date of our next edition of the encyclopedia, which is planned in six years from now. The annual cost for the supplement is $40. Why, if you like, you can apply your $20 interview fee toward the first payment. Marvelous! Look how painless the payment schedule will be!"

At this juncture, Blackwell felt that all his efforts might have been wasted, for Mr. Fisher raised his voice and said: "I'm sorry, we're just not interested. As I told you, again and again, the kids can surf the net."

Blackwell's instinct told him that the situation called for high-pressure tactics.

"My dear folks! Long experience has taught me that when a family rejects a phenomenal offer to acquire our encyclopedia, it's for one of three reasons: (1) the family is poor; (2) the parents are ignorant and boorish, and therefore don't appreciate the value of the encyclopedia as an educational tool; and (3) the parents are indifferent to the welfare of their children.

"Now, are you going to look me in the eye and tell me that you fit into one of these categories? What's all the hesitation about? . . .I'll tell you what I'll do. If you pay me up front for the six annual supplements, I'll shave off $60 from the price. One hand washes the other! You save us billing costs, and we'll pass on the savings to you. So do we have a deal for $220?"

The Fishers shook hands on the deal. A veritable triumph for Blackwell!

Let us begin the halakhic analysis of Blackwell's conduct with a consideration of the ethics of the approach he uses to gain entry into the Fisher home. Blackwell's primary motive in seeking entry to the Fisher home is to make a sales pitch for the GEE encyclopedia. Instead of informing the Fishers forthrightly of his commercial intent, Blackwell makes use of an *elaborate pretext*. His conduct manifests a conviction that the open approach will fail. People are, after all, reluctant to admit strangers, and especially sales people, into their homes. Something much more inventive is called for. By following up on the couple's request for the free brochure, Blackwell establishes immediate *legitimacy* for himself. He cleverly builds on the initial rapport and maneuvers to get the couple to agree to a ten-minute interview.

Because Blackwell conceals from the Fishers his primary motive for wanting to visit them and instead reveals only his secondary motive, he is guilty of a form of falsehood (*sheker*). This prohibition is derived from an analysis of R. Natan's dictum at Yevamot 65b. Here, R. Natan expounds that it is not only permissible to alter the truth for the sake of peace but a positive duty (mitzvah) to do so. R. Natan derives this from an episode in the life of Samuel the prophet: God charged Samuel to go to Bethlehem and anoint one of Jesse's sons as king of Israel. Whereupon Samuel inquired: "How shall I go? For, if Saul hears, he will kill me" (I Samuel 16:2). In response to Samuel's concern God created a pretext for him: "You shall take a heifer with you, and you shall say, `I have come to slaughter [a sacrifice] to the Lord'" (I Samuel 16:2).

R. Natan's dictum requires some elaboration. In what manner did Samuel alter the truth? After all, true to his word, he offered the sacrifice and invited the elders of Bethlehem to join him in the sacrificial feast (I Samuel 16:15). Addressing himself to this issue, R. Yom Tov Ishbili (Spain, 1270–1342) points out that Samuel's *primary* mission was to anoint one of Jesse's sons king of Israel. Concealing this from the inquisitive elders of Bethlehem and revealing to them only his secondary purpose in coming constituted a form of *sheker*. What allowed Samuel to conduct himself in this fashion was his motive to preserve peace. Since God Himself provided Samuel with the pretext, it can be derived that it is a mitzvah to alter the truth in order to preserve peace.[1]

Given Blackwell's *entirely commercial intent* in using a pretext to gain entry into the Fisher home, his conduct constitutes a form of *sheker*, and is prohibited.

Blackwell's use of this pretext also violates *geneivat da'at* (creating a false impression). The particular nuance of this prohibition that is violated here is dealt with in the Talmud in connection with the account of Absalom's plot to usurp the crown from his father, King David. Absalom's plot entailed the "deceiving of three hearts."[2] His elaborate scheme began by "deceiving the heart of the men of Israel."[3] With the aim of both undermining David's system of justice and ingratiating himself with the masses, Absalom mingled with those who sought adjudication of their disputes in King David's court and proclaimed: ". . . see, your words are good and right; but there is none of the king's [judges] to hear you. . . . Oh, who will appoint me judge in the land, and every man who has a quarrel or suit, will come to me, then I will [surely] do him justice" (II Samuel 15:34). In the first phase of his plan, Absalom succeeds in generating for himself a massive amount of unwarranted goodwill. His objective was to draw upon this goodwill to support his quest for the crown.

In the next phase of his plot, Absalom deceives the heart of his father, King David, as well as the heart of the Sanhedrin (the Jewish high court). The particulars are as follows:

Absalom approaches his father, King David, asking permission to go to Hebron to fulfill a sacrificial vow, and David consents (II Samuel 15:79). Whereupon Absalom maneuvers the king into issuing a royal order for two persons of Absalom's choice to accompany him to Hebron. Absalom shows the royal order to separate groups of two, again and again, and thereby amasses an entourage consisting of two hundred associates of the Sanhedrin.[4]

In the last phase of his plot, Absalom sends spies throughout the tribes of Israel and instructs them: "As soon as you hear the sound of the shofar, then you shall say: `Absalom is king in Hebron'" (II Samuel 15:10).

Absalom's religious journey to Hebron was the event that launched his public quest to usurp his father's crown. Because Absalom hid his true motive in seeking permission to go to Hebron, he was guilty of *sheker*. Absalom's misconduct violated *geneivat da'at* law as well. This is so because his pretext was a duping mechanism to secure what he would never otherwise be given. Had David known Absalom's primary designs, he would not have given him permission to go to Hebron. Absalom's plot would have been still-born.

In a similar vein, Absalom's misuse of the royal order for an entourage violated *geneivat da'at*. Had the individuals he approached known Absalom's primary motive, they presumably would not have joined him. By making repeated use of the royal order, Absalom created the false impression that the Sanhedrin as an institution supported his quest for the crown. Absalom was therefore guilty of deceiving the heart of the Jewish court.

Let us apply the above nuance of *geneivat da'at* law to the issue at hand. Consider that on the basis of Blackwell's explicit representations, the Fishers expect to expend no more than ten minutes of their time with him. But Blackwell uses his entry into the Fisher home as a springboard to launch a sales pitch for the encyclopedia. Instead of spending only ten minutes with Blackwell, the Fishers are tied up for, say, forty minutes with him.

Blackwell's *geneivat da'at* violation is compounded. Consider that GEE advertised a free brochure designed to "make travel in Europe fun for young teenagers." In reality, the brochure is no more than a cut-and-paste job made up of information regarding selected European capitals culled from the encyclopedia. The brochure does not even pass muster as a general tourist information guide, let alone as a travel booklet geared to the interests of young teenagers. Let us assume, for argument's sake, that the ad dashes the expectations of the reasonable man. Does the ad violate *geneivat da'at* law? A saving factor here is that we are not dealing with a sale transaction but rather with a free offer. The view of R. Jacob Tam (France, ca. 1100–1171) is here operative. He held that the donor of a gift is prohibited from misrepresenting its nature to the recipient. Absent *affirmative* misrepresentation, a benefactor need not be concerned that the recipient might take his gift to be more than it actually is.[5]

Following R. Jacob Tam's line, GEE's ad violates *geneivat da'at* law. This is so because the company *explicitly* misrepresents its brochure to the public. Now, if GEE's ad violates *geneivat da'at*, then Blackwell's pretext becomes nothing but a mechanism to dupe the Fishers into allowing him to enter their home. Specifically, had the Fishers only known that the brochure would be of no value to them, they would not have sent away for it, and consequently Blackwell would have no basis to enter the Fisher home. To be sure, Blackwell got the Fishers to agree to a paid interview. But this circumstance does not make his entry into their home legitimate. Why? Consider that if he had not first softened the Fishers' resistance to strangers by following up on their request for the free brochure and offer to personally deliver it, they would never have agreed to the interview. Moreover, the arrangement for the interview is a sham and hence a false pretext. This is so because the educational survey Blackwell purports to conduct is not a survey in the conventional sense, but instead is a device to pry out private information from the Fishers which he later will use to his advantage when negotiating price terms with them. What proceeds from the above is that Blackwell's entry into the Fisher home should be characterized as entry by means of deception and hence in violation of *geneivat da'at.*

Testimonial Letter

GEE's use of the Fishers' testimonial letter in its advertising campaign may entail violation of *geneivat da'at* law. Consider that the value of a benefit can only be properly evaluated in light of the opportunity cost involved in acquiring it. GEE advertises the price of the encyclopedia as $1,200, exclusive of the bookcase and annual supplements option. But the Fishers acquired the set for $220, including the bookcase and the right to six annual supplements. Since the company conceals the special deal it made with the Fishers, the reasonable man may assume that the Fishers paid full price for the set. If the reasonable man does not apply the appropriate discount to the Fishers' testimonial, the company generates more goodwill than is warranted with the letter, thereby violating *geneivat da'at* law.

Installment Plans

Another issue at hand is Blackwell's use of the installment plan as a means of inducing purchase of the encyclopedia set. Several aspects of Blackwell's conduct will be put to question here.

1. Blackwell typically suggests the possibility of an installment plan only in reaction to a client's protest that he cannot afford to purchase the encyclopedia. Blackwell's answer is the installment plan. Since the purchase becomes obtainable only if the customer goes into debt, the purchase may find halakhic disfavor. Halakhah's disapproval of financing living standards by going into debt can be derived from an analysis of the sliding-scale sacrifice.

In the time of the Temple, the offering of sacrifices formed a part of the expiation process for transgressors seeking atonement. The sacrificial requirements in connection with certain classes of offenses allowed the penitent to offer a sliding-scale sacrifice. To illustrate the nature of the sliding-scale sacrifice, we will describe its application in connection with a particular qualifying offense, the false oath of testimony. This offense occurs when A falsely swears to B that he is not privy to information relevant to his case. The sacrificial aspect of A's atonement process requires him to offer a female sheep or goat. Should A's means not suffice, he may substitute two turtledoves or two young pigeons for the animal sacrifice. If his means do not suffice for birds, he offers a tenth of an ephah of fine flour.[6]

The means criterion, according to *Torat Kohanim*, translates into allowing the penitent to move down the sliding scale if bringing the more expensive sacrifice would put him into debt.[7]

Noting the means criterion, R. Aaron ha-Levi (Spain, 1235–1300) advances the opinion that if a poor man offers the rich man's sacrifice, he does not fulfill his obligation. This ruling is rationalized on the grounds that since the Almighty shows compassion to the poor man by allowing him to bring a sacrifice according to his means, it would not be proper for the poor man to reject the gesture by incurring an expense for his sacrifice beyond his means. Sound practical advice regarding living standards should be derived from the sliding-scale sacrifice: An individual should not live beyond his means. Such conduct could lead the individual to unethical aggrandizement as a means of sustaining his habit of high living.[8]

Before *Torat Kohanim*'s criterion can be applied to contemporary society, several caveats are in order. First, we take it as a given that Halakhah has no objection to borrowing in order to achieve the common standard of living. Second, if the concern is that incurring indebtedness results in living beyond one's means, then the stricture should apply only when meeting the installment payments would predictably force the borrower to cut back on his accustomed standard of living. Here, there is real concern that the deprivation effect the indebtedness brings on will lead to aggrandizement as a means of maintaining one's accustomed lifestyle.

Proceeding from these caveats, Halakhah has no objection per se against financing living standards by means of installment debt. Given that householders differ in respect to wealth, income, and budget priorities, a wide variety of circumstances exist where the purchase of a particular item on an installment basis does not entail living beyond one's means. Given these circumstances, a salesperson need not be concerned that the customer cannot afford the item at hand, and thus that offering an installment plan amounts to proffering the customer ill-suited advice. Pushing an installment plan on a customer who has already declared that he cannot afford the purchase either for cash or on an installment basis, however, amounts to proffering ill-suited advice and violates the *lifnei iver* interdict.[9] Recall that some decisors conceptualize the *lifnei iver* interdict to consist of the *mere offering* of ill-suited advice.[10] Whether untoward consequences result or not is immaterial as far as violation of the prohibition is concerned. Following this line, pushing an installment plan on a customer after the customer has declared he cannot afford the purchase either for cash or on a credit basis violates *lifnei iver*, even if the sales pitch proves, in the final analysis, to be unsuccessful.

2. Another problem with Blackwell's installment plan is that it may violate

ribbit law. *Ribbit* is Halakhah's prohibition of both receiving and making interest payments.[11] The prohibition applies only to transactions involving Jews.[12] *Ribbit* is violated on a biblical level, called *ribbit kezuzah*, when the interest stipulation is made in the context of a *loan* transaction.[13] By rabbinical enactment, the *ribbit* interdict is considerably expanded and extended. These extensions are called *avak ribbit* (lit. the dust of *ribbit*). An important component of these extensions is *ribbit* charged in the context of a commercial transaction (*derekh mekah umemkar*).[14]

GEE's use of the installment plan violates *avak ribbit* law. In all its advertisements and promotions, GEE quotes its price as $1,200. Blackwell's offer of an installment plan calling for total payments that exceed the $1,200 cash price amounts to a *premium for tolerating delay in payment*. Thus the plan violates *avak ribbit* law.[15]

GEE can, however, revamp its approach to installment debt and thereby avoid violation of *avak ribbit*. The following permissible scenario described by R. Mosheh Isserles (Poland, 1525 or 1530–1592) provides, in the opinion of this writer, the underpinning of a valid restructuring plan.

S makes B a two-tiered price offer for the merchandise at hand: If B buys on credit, the price will be $12, but if he buys on a cash basis, the price will be only $10. This arrangement violates *avak ribbit* law. But suppose the credit transaction became legally binding before S introduces his cash discount offer. Here, the arrangement is valid.[16] The rationale for this distinction is provided by R. Yaakov Yeshayahu Bloi (Israel, 1929–): In the former case, the introduction of two prices into the negotiating process compels us to view the differential the credit price entails as a *premium* S demands for tolerating delayed payment. In sharp contrast, if the transaction became *legally* binding before the cash discount offer is injected, then only one price was operative in the transaction. This is the credit price. S's stipulation, then, becomes no more than an offer to *assume* B's debt for a price of $10.[17]

By logical extension, GEE should be allowed to advertise that it is selling the encyclopedia set on a monthly installment plan consisting of twelve $110 payments. The ad should go on to say that anyone who *legally binds himself to purchase the encyclopedia on a credit basis* will be offered a reduced price of $1,200 for an immediate cash payment. What the above mechanism does is to make the cash discount into nothing more than an offer to assume the customer's debt to the company for a cash payment of $1,200. *Avak ribbit* is avoided.

Prepayment Discount

Another *avak ribbit* problem with Blackwell's price negotiation stratagem is his offer of a discount if prepayment for the annual supplements is made. Let us discuss the prepayment discount case in general terms and then apply the principles to the case at hand.

Discount sales that call for payment for the merchandise before its delivery violate *avak ribbit* law.[18] Since, by rabbinical enactment, *kesef* (money) does not effect transfer for movable property, payment does not confer the buyer (B) with legal title to the merchandise. B's payment is therefore essentially a loan extended to the seller (S), which is paid back on the delivery date with merchandise having a higher market value than B's transfer.[19]

The prepayment-discount scheme is, however, legitimate when the transferred article is not a standardized product.[20] An appearance of *ribbit* is not evident here, as S may theoretically opt to deliver an article commensurate in value to B's payment on the agreed-upon date.[21] There is one caveat. For the discount to be valid, S may not expressly offer to B a two-tiered price deal.[22]

With the appearance of *ribbit* remaining intact in the standardized-product case, legitimacy is not given to the discount-prepayment scheme unless equivalent merchandise is in S's possession at the time of the sale. This condition is satisfied even if the merchandise is not readily accessible to S at the time of the sale. This requirement is referred to as the *yesh lo* condition.[23]

Why *yesh lo* helps remove the *ribbit* interdict in the standardized-product case is explained by R. Isaac b. Sheset Perfet (Spain, 1325–1408) as stemming from the fact that *kesef* effects transfer of movables by dint of pentateuchal law. Since S has equivalent merchandise in his possession at the time of the sale, B's payment effects for him legal title to the extent that his transfer is not regarded as a loan to S.[24]

These criteria equip us to assess whether Blackwell's prepayment-discount scheme falls within the boundaries of permissibility. Since the copies of the annual supplement for any given year will be identical, the case at hand falls into the standardized-product variant discussed above. By linking the discount to the saving the company will make on annual billings, Blackwell avoids making a *ribbit*-tainted, two-tiered price offer to the Fishers. But the *yesh lo* condition fails here because the annual supplements do not exist now. GEE, therefore, cannot be said to have equivalent merchandise to give the customer at the time the prepayment-discount offer is made.

A saving factor here is that the annual supplements the Fishers agree to buy do not yet exist. The Fishers therefore face considerable uncertainty in regard to what exactly they will be getting for their money. Blackwell, for instance, makes no representations regarding the investment GEE is committed to make in producing the annual supplement. The company's investment here may vary from year to year, with the result that the quality of the annual supplements will vary too. Moreover, suppose GEE goes out of business over the next six years. What then? Given these uncertainties, it is not at all clear that the cash payment the

Fishers are making now should be characterized as a *discount from the fair market value* of the yearly supplements.

An analogous case is recorded at Bava Mezia 64a: S stipulates to B an upfront price of, say, $300, for the entire milk production of his goats for the year. Given that the milk yield of the goats is not known at the time the deal is struck, B's up-front payment of $300 may turn out to be either an overpayment or an underpayment for the *quantity* of milk he actually receives. B's $300 payment, therefore, should not be viewed as a *discount* he receives for paying for the milk before delivery and hence a violation of *avak ribbit* law. Instead, the $300 payment should be viewed as the price S must accept in order to *induce* B to assume the *risk* the transaction entails.[25]

Basing himself on this, R. Yizhak Yaakov Weisz (Israel, 1902–1989) defends the widespread practice among publishers of offering a pre-publication-discount price. The practice does not violate *avak ribbit* because the one who pays up front assumes the loss in the event one or more of the volumes in the multivolume set is either produced in defective form or is not published at all. In sharp contrast, the publisher will not realize the post-publication price he sets unless he *actually* delivers the volume(s) in question in *perfect condition*. Thus the lower pre-publication price should not be viewed as a discount from the post-publication price. Moreover, consider that in the case at hand, the publisher sets the post-publication price of his work *before* the work is actually issued. This price should therefore be regarded as the base or reference price (*yaza ha-sha'ar*) of the work only in respect to transactions that call for the publisher to deliver the work free of any defect. Since, in the case at hand, the one who pays up front agrees to accept the work irrespective of defective workmanship on the part of the publisher, the lower up-front price should not be regarded as a discount from the post-publication price.[26]

The affinity of the preceding case to our scenario involving a prepayment-discount offer for an encyclopedia set with annual supplements is readily apparent.

The *avak ribbit* problem inherent in the installment plan and prepayment-discount cases can be remedied by use of *hetter iska*, a subject that will be taken up in the next chapter..

High-Pressure Tactics

One final matter. Blackwell's use of high-pressure tactics violates the Torah's prohibition of "And thou shalt not lust (*lo tahmod*)."[27]

Violation of *lo tahmod* entails the following elements: B desires to acquire an item S owns. S refuses B's offer. As a means of overcoming S's initial resistance, B increases his bid or pesters S to accept his original offer. Alternatively, B petitions S's friend to induce him to change his mind. Acquiring S's item by means of these pressure tactics violates for B the prohibition against coveting.[28]

A declaration of *rozeh ani* (I am willing) by S at the time he parts with the article removes for B, according to R. Abraham b. David of Posquières (1125–1198), the *lo tahmod* interdict.[29] In his formulation of the interdict, however, Maimonides (Egypt, 1135–1204) offers no such caveat.[30]

B's high-pressure tactics also violate the biblical prohibition of "and thou shall not covet (*lo tit'avveh*)" (Deuteronomy 5:18). The essence of this prohibition consists of "plotting of the heart" to overcome S's initial rejection of the offer.[31] The prohibition is violated even if B's effort to overcome S's rejection does not succeed.[32]

The prohibition against coveting is formulated in the codes in terms of the buyer's behavior. By logical extension, posits R. Yaakov Yeshayahu Bloi, the prohibition should apply to the seller's conduct as well. Accordingly, a seller who uses high-pressure tactics to induce someone to buy an item violates *lo tahmod*.[33]

R. Bloi's line of reasoning apparently leads to the proposition that a seller (S) is prohibited from offering a customer (B) more favorable price terms as a means of overcoming his initial rejection of the offer. But consider that in certain instances B signals in advance that he is interested in S's product or service, provided it is available at the right price. This occurs when B initiates the sales encounter or when B gives S an appointment to make a sales presentation to him. Here, there should be no objection to S offering B more favorable price terms as a means of overcoming B's initial rejection of the offer. Analogously, if S puts up his asset for sale, there should be no objection to B making escalating bids as a means of inducing S to agree to the sale.

Suppose, however, that S barges in on B and makes a sales pitch to him. Here *lo tit'avveh* and *lo tahmod* should prohibit S from offering a more favorable price as a means of overcoming B's initial rejection of the offer. If S wants to continue his sales pitch, he must first secure B's explicit permission to do so.

Let us apply the above analysis to our case study. Consider a variant of the opening vignette: Blackwell gains entry into the Brown home by means of his pretext to personally deliver the travel brochure and to conduct an educational survey. After the conclusion of his educational survey, Blackwell springs an offer to sell GEE's encyclopedia set for $1,200 cash. The Browns reject the offer. Without first securing permission from them to make an installment plan offer, Blackwell is prohibited from continuing his sales pitch. Since Blackwell effectively barged in on the Browns with the encyclopedia offer and never received a signal from them that they were interested in buying the set provided the price was right, overcoming their initial rejection by offering more favorable price terms violates *lo tit'avveh* and *lo tahmod*. Ethical conduct requires Blackwell to seek the Browns' permission before continuing with his sales pitch.

Far more troubling are the high-pressure tactics Blackwell employed in his dealings with the Fishers. Recall that Blackwell shamed the couple into changing their mind about acquiring the encyclopedia set by telling them that only parents who are either poor, stupid, or care nothing about their children reject a fantastic offer to acquire the set. Because Blackwell gained entry into the Fisher home by means of a pretext, the offer of even a price reduction to overcome the couple's rejection of his offer should be prohibited. Blackwell's use of insult and shame to achieve his ends is particularly outrageous, as this form of pressure should be prohibited even if Blackwell makes his sales pitch by invitation. Being invited to make a sales presentation suggests no more than that the couple might be interested in acquiring the set provided the price is right. The invitation does not, however, signal their willingness to change their mind by being shamed or insulted. Blackwell's high-pressure tactics violate both *lo tit'avveh* and *lo tahmod*.

1. R. Yom Tov Ishbili (Spain, 1270–1342), Ritva, Yevamot 65b. For an identical comment, see R. Samuel Eliezer b. Judah ha-Levi (Poland, 1555–1631), Maharsha, Yevamot 65b.

2. ". . . and because he stole three hearts, the heart of his father, the heart of the court of justice, and the heart of Israel. As it is said, *so Absalom stole the hearts of the men of Israel* (II Samuel 15:6). Therefore three darts were thrust through him" (Mishnah, Sotah 1:8).

3. II Samuel 15:6.

4. Jerusalem Talmud, Sotah 1:8.

5. R. Jacob Tam, quoted in Tosafot to Hullin 94b, s.v. *amar*, and by R. Asher b. Jehiel (Germany, 1270–1343), Rosh, Hullin 7:18. R. Shelomoh b. Jehiel Luria (Poland, 1510–1573), *Yam Shel Shelomoh*, Hullin, ad loc., claims that R. Isaac b. Jacob Alfasi (Algeria, 1013–1103), Rif, and R. Mosheh of Coucy (France, early 13th cent.), Semag, agree with R. Tam. See also R. Abraham Joseph Ehrman, *Halikhut Olam*, p. 98.

6. Leviticus 5:11; Keritot 10b; Maimonides (Egypt, 1135–1204), *Yad*, Shegagot 10:14.

7. *Torat Kohanim* 5:7.

8. R. Aaron ha-Levi (Spain, 1235–1300), *Sefer ha-Hinnukh* 123. R. Aaron ha-Levi's position here, according to R. Joseph b. Moses Babad (Poland, 1800–1872), *Minhat Hinnukh*, ad loc., is contradicted by Mishnah Nega'im 14:12.

9. Leviticus 19:14; *Torat Kohanim* 19:14; *Yad*, Rozeah 12:14.

10. Please turn to p. 62 of this volume.

11. Exodus 22:24; Mishnah, Bava Mezia; Rif ad loc.; *Yad*, Malveh 4:2; Rosh, Bava Mezia 5:80; R. Jacob b. Asher (Spain, 1270–1340), *Tur*, Yoreh De'ah 160:2; R. Joseph Caro (Israel, 1488–1575), *Shulhan Arukh*, Yoreh De'ah 160:1; R. Abraham Danzig (Prague, 1748–1820), *Hokhmat Adam* 130:1.

12. *Yad*, op. cit. 5:1; *Tur*, op. cit. 159; *Sh.Ar.*, op. cit. 159:1.

13. Cf. *Hokhmat Adam* 131:13.

14. R. Mosheh Isserles (Poland, 1525 or 1530–1592), Rema, *Sh.Ar.*, op. cit. 161:1.

15. Bava Mezia 65a; Rif, ad loc.; *Yad*, op. cit. 8:1; Rosh, op. cit. 5:21; *Tur*, op. cit. 173:1;

Sh.Ar., op. cit. 173:1; *Hokhmat Adam*, 139:1.

16. Rema, *Sh.Ar.*, op. cit. 173:3.

17. R. Yaakov Yeshayahu Bloi, *Berit Yehudah* 22:10 and nn. 24–25.

18. R. Nahman, Bava Mezia 63b; Rif, ad loc.; *Yad*, op. cit. 9:6; Rosh, op. cit. 5:11; Tur, op. cit. 173:7; *Sh.Ar.*, op. cit. 173:7.

19. *Berit Yehudah*, op. cit. 23:1, n. 2.

20. Rema, *Sh.Ar.*, op. cit. 173:7; *Hokhmat Adam* 139:14. For a variant view, see R. David b. Samuel ha-Levi (Poland, 1586–1667), *Turei Zahav, Sh.Ar.*, loc. cit., n. 12.

21. R. Moses b. Naphtali Hirsch Rivkes (Lithuania, ca. 1671/72), *Be'er ha-Golah, Sh.Ar.*, op. cit. 173, n. 18.

22. Rema, loc. cit.; *Hokhmat Adam*, loc. cit.

23. R. Nahman, Bava Mezia 63b; Rif, ad loc.; *Yad*, loc. cit.; Rosh, loc. cit.; Tur, loc. cit.; *Sh.Ar.*, loc. cit. Some authorities (quoted in Tur, op. cit.) allow S to explicitly offer a two-tier price deal when *yesh lo* is satisfied. R. Mosheh Isserles (Rema, 173:7), however, rejects this leniency. Rema's disallowance of the two-tier price deal, in the opinion of this writer, applies only when S does not couple his offer with some exculpatory explanation for the two-tier price deal. Supporting this restrictive understanding of Rema's stringency is R. Yaakov Yeshayahu Bloi's treatment of subscription discounts for magazines. While offering a two-tier price deal is prohibited, the two-tier price becomes legitimate, according to R. Bloi (*Berit Yehudah* 23:7), if the publisher announces that the lower price for the subscription is for the *commitment* to buy the magazine over a long period of time. If this reason is not explicitly given, the discount must be taken as offered in order to obtain for the publisher advance use of the purchasing price and is therefore prohibited.

24. R. Isaac b. Sheshet Perfet (Spain, 1325–1408), *Responsa Ribash*, quoted by R. Joseph Caro, *Beit Yosef, Tur*, op. cit.

25. Baraita, Bava Mezia 64a; R. Solomon b. Isaac (France, 1040–1105), Rashi, loc. cit., s.v. *mutar*; *Yad*, op. cit. 9:3; Tur, op. cit. 173:9; *Sh.Ar.*, op. cit. 173:9.

26. R. Yizhak Yaakov Weisz, *Minhat Yizhak* 4:99.

27. Exodus 20:14; Deuteronomy 5:18.

28. *Yad*, Gezelah 1:9; Tur, Hoshen Mishpat 359:9; *Sh.Ar.*, Hoshen Mishpat 359:10; R. Jehiel Michel Epstein (Belarus, 1829–1908), *Arukh ha-Shulhan*, Hoshen Mishpat 359:89.

29. R. Abraham b. David of Posquières (France, 1125–1198), Rabad, at *Yad*, loc. cit.

30. *Yad*, loc. cit. The dispute between Maimonides and Rabad is explained by R. Yom Tov Vidal of Tolosa (Spain, 14th cent.), *Maggid Mishneh, Yad*, ad loc., as follows: Maimonides regards the prohibition of *lo tahmod* as consisting of the exertion of effort to overcome B's resistance to part with his article. B's declaration of *rozeh ani* at the end of the process, therefore, does not remove *lo tahmod*. Rabad, however, regards the prohibition as consisting of acquiring B's article when he is unwilling to sell it. B's declaration of *rozeh ani* at the moment of transfer thus removes *lo tahmod*.

31. *Yad*, op. cit. 1:10; Maimonides, *Sefer ha-Mitzvot*, lo ta'aseh 66; Tur, op. cit.; *Sh.Ar.*, op. cit.; *Ar.haSh.*, op. cit. 359:8.

32. See R. Joel Sirkes (Poland, 1561–1650), Bah, at Tur, Hoshen Mishpat 359, n. 9, and R. Joshua b. Alexander ha-Kohen Falk (Poland, 1555–1614) Sma, at *Sh.Ar.*, Hoshen Mishpat 359, n. 16.

33. R. Yaakov Yeshayahu Bloi, *Pithei Hoshen*, Hilkhot Genevah ve-Ona'ah, p. 30, n. 26.

Hetter Iska

Loan transactions involving Jews are regulated by the laws of *ribbit*.[1] *Ribbit* law prohibits both the receiving and the making of interest payments.[2]

The *hetter iska* mechanism, which originated in the sixteenth century, was developed as a means of avoiding violations of *ribbit* law. It is credited to R. Mendel Avigdor of Cracow. The standard *hetter iska* document used today is, however, a variant of R. Avigdor's form. At the end of this section, a standard *hetter iska* form is reproduced along with a second form that incorporates R. Avigdor's original formulation.

The basic objective of *hetter iska* is to restructure as a business partnership what would otherwise be a loan transaction. In the *hetter iska* arrangement, F furnishes capital to MP for the purpose of investing the funds in merchandise or some other business venture for the benefit of both parties. The distinctive feature of *iska* is that F, the financier, is a silent partner, and MP, the recipient, is the managing partner. Because F plays no operational or managerial role in the business enterprise, *avak ribbit* law regulates the *iska* partnership. A description of these regulations follows, along with the features *hetter iska* attaches to the partnership arrangement to make it into an attractive investment for the financier.

Profit-Loss Division Constraint

An *iska* agreement calling for the financier to reap more than 50 percent of the profits but to absorb less than 50 percent of the losses is prohibited. From the standpoint of the financier, such an arrangement, in talmudic terms, is "near to profit and far from loss" and hence violates *avak ribbit* law.[3]

While any *symmetrical* profit-loss division frees the *iska* arrangement from the "near to profit and far from loss" prohibition, transferring capital for *iska* purposes without any stipulation in regard to the profit-loss division confers upon the transfer a half-loan, half-deposit (*hazi milveh, hazi pikkadon*) character. Profits and losses in the non-express case are therefore divided equally between the financier and the managing partner.[4] Conventionally, the *hetter iska* document today calls for the profits and losses to be divided equally between the financier and the managing partner. This form is hence dubbed *hazi milveh, hazi pikkadon*.

Compensation for Labor and/or Managerial Services

Avak ribbit law requires the financier to stipulate compensation for the managing partner in return for his labor and/or managerial services rendered during the *iska* term. The compensation requirement, referred to as the *sekhar tirha* condition, follows from an examination of the legal status of the *iska* transfer. Given that responsibility for accidental loss is what legally differentiates a debtor from a bailee, Halakhah confers a loan-deposit status on the *iska* arrangement. The portion of the capital transfer that the active partner assumes responsibility for takes on the character of a debt, while the remaining portion takes on the character of a deposit. Now, since the agreement calls for MP to invest the funds for the benefit of both himself and F, performing the managerial function gratis amounts to a disguised interest premium as a precondition for receiving the loan.[5]

Providing the stipulation is agreed to before the capital transfer is made, the *sekkar tirha* requirement may be satisfied with a nominal fee. Pre-*iska* term arrangement of *sekkar tirha* allows the nominal fee to suffice even when the *iska* generates an opportunity cost to the managing partner in the form of calling for him to desist from selling his own wares while merchandising the *iska*.[6]

Making *Iska* into an Attractive Investment Vehicle

The innovation of *hetter iska* transformed the basic *iska* partnership into an attractive investment from the standpoint of the financier.

1. To insure his principal, F may attach conditions to the *iska* and stipulate that if they are not met, responsibility for losses devolves entirely on MP. Specifications of the types of investment MP may enter into with the *iska* and the security measures he must adopt for the *iska* income are examples of conditions F might want to attach to the *iska*. Since fulfillment of the conditions is feasible and MP may avert full responsibility for losses by adhering to them, the arrangement is not regarded from F's standpoint as "near to profit and far from loss."[7] What follows is the inadmissibility of setting conditions that are either impossible to fulfill or are not usually undertaken by business people. Such stipulations on the part of F constitute a subterfuge to exact *ribbit* and are therefore forbidden.[8] On similar grounds, R. Abraham Y. Karelitz (Israel, 1878–1953) disallows F from stipulating conditions that do not in any way relate to the *iska* arrangement. Violating the *avak ribbit* interdict on this account, for example, would be a stipulation disallowing MP from eating grapes for the entire term of the *iska* agreement and calling for his assumption of full responsibility for losses should he violate this condition.[9]

Stipulations of the permissible variety, it should be noted, do not impede the managing partner's flexibility to depart from the conditions. Since his intention is to seize upon opportunities for greater profit, his departure from the stipulation is not morally objectionable as long as he faces the consequences of failure.[10]

Another clause that may be inserted in the *iska* agreement for the purpose of securing F's principal is the stipulation that MP's claim for loss will be accepted only if it is corroborated by the testimony of designated witnesses (C and D).[11] Disqualifying the testimony of all witnesses except C and D is permissible, according to R. David b. Samuel ha-Levi (Poland, 1586–1667), as long as these designated individuals are known to be at least slightly conversant with the *iska* affair.[12]

2. To increase the chances of earning a profit on the capital transfer, F may stipulate that MP's claim regarding the amount of profits the *iska* realizes will be accepted only by means of his solemn oath (*shevuah hamurah*). Insofar as MP can always maintain accurate records of the *iska* transactions and take the solemn oath in regard to the profits realized, the solemn oath element of the agreement does not characterize it, from the standpoint of F, as "near to profit and far from loss.[13]

Requiring corroboration of the profit claim by means of designated witnesses violates *avak ribbit* law, however. Why the designated-witness condition is admissible in connection with the loss claim but not here is explained by an examination of the strength of the counterclaim in each case. While F can positively attest to the amount of the *iska* transfer, he cannot with certainty dispute MP's profit report. Given the weak nature of F's counterclaim in the latter case, he may not disqualify all but a few designated witnesses from validating MP's statement. Moreover, assuming the veracity of the statement, the overpayment occasioned by agreement to the designated witness clause could be given to F in the form of a gift. Since the payment in its entirety amounts to no more than the principal, *ribbit* law is not violated. In contrast, any overpayment of profits to F occasioned by the designated witness clause would violate *ribbit* law even if the differential is given as a gift, since the total payment F receives exceeds his principal.[14]

To further increase his chances of earning a profit, F may stipulate that payment of an agreed to sum, referred to as *sekhar hitpashrut*, would relieve MP of both his solemn oath obligation and any further monetary obligation should F's share in the profits exceed this sum. Similarly, the *iska* agreement may call for F to receive a fixed sum as his share in the profits, with the proviso that MP may reduce this payment by any amount by taking a solemn oath that F's share in the profits did not amount to this sum.[15] To increase the probability that F will actually realize the *sekhar hitpashrut*, the *iska* agreement may call for the attachment of all MP's business profits to the *iska* venture.[16] This clause effectively precludes MP from opting for the solemn oath unless F's pro-rated share in the profits that all MP's ventures earned during the *iska* term fell short of the *sekhar hitpashrut* sum.

Limitations of the *Hetter Iska* Arrangement

The discussion to this point has demonstrated that *hetter iska* should in no way be viewed as a subterfuge to overcome *ribbit* law. Rather, it is a device to structure a capital transfer as a business partnership between the financier and the recipient. Indeed, secular courts have recognized *hetter iska* as a document that creates a partnership rather than as a loan instrument; and for this reason have legitimized a return for the financier that exceeded the prevailing usury law limit.[17]

Because *hetter iska* is not, as R. Mosheh Feinstein (New York, 1895–1986) put it, "an incantation or charm" to permit *ribbit*, both parties must fully understand the nature of the partnership they are entering into.[18]

Another aspect of taking *hetter iska* seriously is to understand both its limitations and its risks as an investment vehicle. A discussion of these caveats follows, together with the application of *hetter iska* to the encyclopedia salesman vignette in the previous chapter.

The Definition of *Iska*

In addressing the issue of the limitation of the use of *hetter iska*, the most fundamental concern is how expansively Halakhah defines *investment* as far as the use of *hetter iska* is concerned.

A very broad view of investment transactions is advanced by R. Joseph Saul Nathanson (Ukraine, 1810–1875). Classified as *iska*, in his view, is a capital transfer that makes it possible for the recipient to continue his normal income-generating activities. Accordingly, R. Nathanson ruled that a religious-school teacher may acquire capital by means of *hetter iska* for the purpose of paying off his debts. Without the capital transfer, the teacher would be forced to leave his job and seek a higher-paying one elsewhere. Since the transaction allows him to continue on his job, it is classified as *iska*, with the consequence that it may call for dividends for the financier.

Also qualifying as *iska*, in R. Nathanson's view, is the acquisition of capital by an individual for the purpose of debt reduction to avert the forced sale of his home. Receiving dividends here is legitimized because the profit for the recipient of the transfer consists of both the avoidance of a capital loss and the circumstance that it becomes unnecessary for him to rent an apartment.[19]

Disputing R. Nathanson's view, R. Meir Arak (Poland, ca. 1925) and others conceptualize *iska* profit as earnings realized either from the investment of the original capital or from a capital or merchandise the recipient substitutes for it. Profits in the form of avoidance of liquidation or loss would not, in this view, legitimize the receipt of dividends by the financier.[20]

Despite the narrow application of *hetter iska* proceeding from the view of R. Arak and others, this arrangement can easily accommodate the *businessman* desiring to raise capital for personal needs. Toward this end, the *iska* arrangement would be designed in the following manner: F transfers capital to B for general *iska* purposes, but gives him permission to make immediate use of the funds for personal finance. To legitimize the payment of dividends to F, B transfers to F part-ownership of merchandise in his possession equivalent in value to the original capital transfer. This merchandise substitutes for the original sum and assumes its legal character. Should B not have in his possession substitutable merchandise at the time the *iska* was entered into, he obligates himself to acquire merchandise during the *iska* term and sell it at a profit for the benefit of himself and F.[21]

Misappropriation of *Iska* Funds for Personal Use

Having received capital for the purpose of *iska* (business), the recipient is obligated to invest it in a commercial venture and is prohibited from making personal use of it.

The prohibition on making personal use of the *iska* applies even to its loan portion:

> Now that we say that it is a semi-loan and a semi-trust, if he [the managing partner] wishes to drink beer therewith [i.e., for the loan part] he can do so. Rava said: [No] It is therefore called *iska* [business] because he can say to him, "I gave it to you for trading, not for drinking beer." (Bava Mezia 104b)

Talmudic decisors regard Rava's position as normative.[22] Insofar as no *explicit* restriction was agreed to regarding the disposition of the loan portion of the *iska*, Rava's position requires an explanation. Addressing himself to this issue, R. Solomon b. Isaac (Rashi, France, 1040–1105) regards the restriction as proceeding from the implicit mandate MP is operating under to manage the *iska* in a manner that maximizes F's return on his investment. Since putting the loan portion of the *iska* at risk in the venture effectively drives MP to be more diligent in his management of the enterprise, the *requirement to do so* is self-evident in the agreement.[23]

In a similar vein, Tosafot points out that the consequence of not investing the loan in the venture is to immediately expose F's entire capital to loss, with no additional capital to draw upon if needed. The implicit mandate to operate the *iska* to maximize F's gain requires MP, therefore, to invest the loan portion of the *iska* in the venture.[24]

Let us take note that in respect to the trust portion of the *iska*, a bailor-bailee relationship exists between F and MP. MP's use of the funds in a manner that departs from F's mandate constitutes misappropriation (*shelihut yad*).[25]

MP's misappropriation of the trust portion of *iska* for personal use, according to R. Barukh b. Samuel of Mainz (Germany, 1150–1221), transforms the trust portion of the *iska* into a debt. With the *entire* capital transfer now taking on the legal character of a debt, return of anything more than the principal violates *ribbit* law.[26]

Following the above line of reasoning, R. Shneur Zalman of Liadi (Russia, 1745–1813) posits that even if the *iska* agreement expressly allows MP to make personal use of the capital transfer on a loan basis, appropriation for personal use by MP of any sum in excess of the portion of the capital transfer he took responsibility for disallows F from earning the agreed-upon profit rate on that differential. F's right to receive his profit rate on this differential can be restored, however, by returning the temporary loan to a third party, T. Acting on behalf of F, T repossesses the appropriated sum and returns it to MP for *iska* purposes. This device does not suffice in the misappropriation case. Here, the original character of the *iska* is not restored unless the misappropriated sum is directly returned to F and recycled by him to MP for *iska* purposes.[27]

Limitations on the *Sekhar Hitpashrut* Sum

Since *hetter iska* does not permit interest payments, the *sekhar hitpashrut* sum it calls for, according to R. Mosheh Feinstein (New York, 1895–1986), must reflect no more than the financier's pro-rated anticipated return on the planned *iska* investment. To illustrate, suppose the following: The capital transfer is $100,000; the agreement calls for the profits and losses to be divided equally between the financier and the managing partner; and, finally, the *sekhar hitpashrut* is set at $10,000. Setting the *sekhar hitpashrut* sum at $10,000 implies that the anticipated return on the venture is 20 percent. Now, if the parties involved do not even optimistically anticipate a return on the *iska* of at least 20 percent, there is no justification for setting the *sekhar hitpashrut* at $10,000.[28]

In his treatment of the above matter, R. Yisroel Reisman (New York, contemp.) suggests that the restriction can be overcome by making the *iska* investment open-ended. Given the possibility that some investments may reap extraordinary returns, setting the *sekhar hitpashrut* at a relatively high sum can be defended.[29]

Another way around the restriction would be to structure the capital transfer entirely as a trust. R. Avigdor's original innovation of *hetter iska* incorporated this concept.[30] *Hetter iska* of this variety is dubbed *kullo pikkadon* (lit. wholly a trust). Setting up the *iska* in this fashion frees the capital transfer of any loan character. What *kullo pikkadon* does is to make the active partner's management of the *iska* entirely for the benefit of the financier. In consequence, the financier is entitled to 100 percent of the profit, but he also must sustain 100 percent of the losses. Because in *kullo pikkadon* the financier's share of the profit is identical with the entire profit the venture is expected to earn, this variety of *iska* naturally allows for a higher *sekhar hitpashrut* than would be allowed had the *iska* been structured as part-loan and part-trust.

Drawback of the Solemn Oath Provision

In his analysis of *hetter iska*, R. Shiloh Raphael (Israel, contemp.) feels that the document is a shaky financial vehicle from the standpoint of the financier. Recall that the financier's confidence in his ability to realize the *sekhar hitpashrut* sum is predicated on the *aversion* of a pious person to take an oath even to verify what he knows to be the truth. But an aversion to oath-taking cannot be presumed today. Now, if the managing partner takes an oath that the *iska* earned no profits at all, the financier will have no further recourse.[31]

One approach to R. Raphael's concern is to make the solemn oath requirement more unpalatable and onerous for the managing partner than the requirement set out in the standard *hetter iksa* document. In this regard, R. Mosheh Feinstein allows the *hetter iska* document to call for the managing partner to take the oath in the setting of a public prayer session at the juncture of the Torah reading. In addition, the document can call for the managing partner to accept upon himself a curse in the event his declarations are untruthful.[32]

R. Raphael's own solution to the problem he addresses is more radical. In his view, the solemn oath clause should be dispensed with entirely. Instead of requiring the managing partner to verify the profits by means of an oath, the document should give the financier the right to participate in all managerial decisions relating to the *iska* as well the right to examine the managing partner's financial records. The document can then go on to stipulate that the financier agrees to give up these rights in exchange for a designated sum. This designated sum corresponds to the *sekhar hitpashrut* of the conventional *hetter iska* document.[33]

Another limitation of the solemn oath clause of *hetter iska* occurs when the financier has personal knowledge regarding how the *iska* has performed. Here, the financier may not demand of the investor that he attest to the *iska* results by means of an oath. Demanding an oath under these conditions characterizes the investing partner's oath as an oath taken in vain or for no purpose, and therefore constitutes a forbidden oath.[34] If the financier has no right to demand an oath, then he loses his bargaining chip to obtain the *sekhar hitpashrut.*

Given the pivotal role the solemn oath plays in triggering the *sekhar hit-pashrut* requirement, the financier should design the *hetter iska* agreement in a manner that will ensure that he does not lose the right to demand that the investing party take the oath. R. Mosheh Feinstein advises that the financier should make the *iska* open-ended, leaving the investment vehicle to the discretion of the managing partner. Because the managing partner does not know what form the *iska* investment took, he will be within his rights to demand that the managing party take an oath regarding the performance of the *iska.* If the active partner does not want to take the oath, he can free himself of the oath, according to the agreement, by paying the financier the agreed-to *sekhar hit-pashrut* sum.[35]

Hetter Iska and the Sale of an Encyclopedia

We now turn to the application of *hetter iska* to the encyclopedia case study. Recall that a number of Blackwell's sales pitches entailed an *avak ribbit* problem. These included the pre-delivery payment-discount offer and the installment plan offer. Both of these scenarios lend themselves to the *hetter iska* mechanism. Let us begin with the pre-delivery payment-discount case.

Pre-Delivery Payment Discount

Recall that Blackwell offered the Fishers a bookcase and rights to six future annual supplements for an immediate cash price of $220. Since the goods GEE promises to deliver in the future are more valuable than the $220 outlay the Fishers are asked to make, the transaction entails violation of *avak ribbit.*

To free the transaction of an *avak ribbit* problem, it can be structured in the following manner. Instead of handing over the $220 as *payment* for a good to be delivered in the future, the Fishers should furnish the sum to GEE for the purpose of setting up an *iska* partnership with the company. GEE will be the managing partner, and the Fishers will assume the role of silent partner in the venture. The reporting periods for the performance of the *iska* should be set to coincide with the date the bookcase will be delivered as well as with the publication dates for the six annual supplements. With the publication of the sixth annual supplement, the *iska* arrangement ends. Finally, *sekhar hitpashrut* for each reporting period is set equal to the value of the bookcase and the six annual supplements, respectively.

Installment Plan

With the aim of avoiding violation of *avak ribbit*, an installment plan to purchase GEE's encyclopedia can easily be restructured into a *hetter iska* agreement. Recall that GEE's advertised cash asking price for the encyclopedia is $1,200. Suppose the Browns agree to buy the set for $1,560 on an installment basis stretching out over twelve equal monthly payments. Instead of billing the Browns $130 each month as partial payment for the encyclopedia, GEE should set out to establish an *iska* partnership with them. Toward this end, GEE should furnish the Browns with the encyclopedia and fix its value at $1,200. What should be designated as the *iska*? Perhaps the encyclopedia itself can be regarded as an *iska*? Arguing in favor of viewing the encyclopedia in this fashion is the circumstance that the set imparts *knowledge* and hence builds up human capital for the Brown children. Using the set will enhance the *quality* of the education of the Brown children and will eventually translate into higher lifetime earnings for them.

While there can be no doubt that the encyclopedia takes on the character of an *investment good* of sorts, there is no way of determining what rate of return the Brown family realizes on the encyclopedia over the *iska* term. Moreover, one could argue that the Brown family realizes no *economic* return on the encyclopedia investment until such time as their children enter the job market. Thus, designating the encyclopedia as the *iska* is unacceptable from several standpoints. Because the economic return the Browns realize on the encyclopedia is impossible to ascertain, demanding that the Browns verify the figure they claim by means of an oath amounts to demanding that they take a false oath. Moreover, given the strong probability that the economic return for the relevant time interval is zero, the solemn oath clause serves as a powerful temptation for the Browns to actually take an oath that the return was zero and effectively escape thereby the responsibility to pay a premium for the encyclopedia above its cash price.

What the above analysis indicates is that GEE should insist that the Browns *substitute* some other business asset for the encyclopedia to serve as the *iska* of their joint commercial venture. Given that personal knowledge of exactly what the *iska* is may compromise GEE's ability to demand an oath of the Browns regarding the performance of the *iska*, it should leave to the Browns' discretion the selection of the *iska*.

We are not out of the woods yet. Recall R. Feinstein's caution that *hetter iska* is not a "charm or incantation." Suppose GEE desires a 10 percent premium above its cash price for selling the encyclopedia on an installment basis. But suppose the Browns are people whose assets consists of bank accounts yielding only a 5 percent return. Since the assets already in possession of the Browns cannot possibly yield the *sekhar hitpashrut* sum that the *hetter iska* calls for, the *iska* arrangement will be nothing but a sham unless the Browns *at the very least intend* to invest in a new asset that could conceivably yield the *sekhar hitpashrut* GEE seeks. Given the very significant gap between the return the Browns currently receive on their assets and the rate of return implicit in the *sekhar hitpashrut* sum GEE seeks, use of the *kullo pikkadon* form of *hetter iska* would be very helpful and therefore recommends itself.

Now, suppose that the Browns are risk averters to the extreme and harbor a closed mind regarding entering into a speculative investment. Given that the Browns intend to do *absolutely* nothing in respect to achieving GEE's investment goals, the *hetter iska* agreement is nothing but a subterfuge to arrange a *ribbit* payment.[36]

Let us change the scenario a bit. Suppose the Browns are receptive to making a speculative investment, but end up making no new investment over the *iska* term. Here, given the *good faith* intent of the Browns, the *iska* arrangement is certainly not a sham. But consider that it is a clear-cut matter that the Browns' assets did not earn more than a 5 percent return over the *iska* term. GEE must therefore absorb the risk that the Browns might opt to take an oath that the *iska* earned no more than 5 percent.

Hetter Iska: Hazi Milveh Hazi Pikkadon Form[37]

I, the undersigned, have received the sum of $ _____ from _____ (hereafter referred to as the "Investing Partner"), for investment in an *Iska* partnership, subject to the following terms:

In exchange for the aforementioned sum, the investing partner shall acquire a share (in the value of the funds received) in any investment, real estate or business which I own. In the event that no such investments exist, the investing partner will acquire partnership (in the value of funds received) in any future investment which I shall make. The investing partner hereby appoints me as an agent to execute this investment (or investments), as I deem appropriate, on his behalf. This investment (or investments) shall be owned jointly by the investing partner and myself. Any profits realized or losses sustained shall be shared equally between the investing partner and myself.

Any claim of loss must be verified through the testimony of two qualified witnesses in, and under conditions acceptable to, an Orthodox Jewish court of law. Any claim regarding the amount of profit generated by this investment (or investments) shall be verified under solemn oath, before and under conditions acceptable to, an Orthodox Jewish court of law.

It is agreed that if I return the abovementioned principal to the investing partner, together with an additional _____ as payment for his share of the profits which are generated, then I will not be required to make any further payment nor will I be required to make an oath. I am obligated to make this payment on or before_____. If payment is not made by this time, the terms of this *Iska* shall continue.

I have received one dollar from the investing partner as payment for my services during the term of our partnership.

In the event of any conflict between the terms of this *Iska* agreement and the terms of any other agreement signed by the two parties in regard to these funds, the terms of this agreement shall prevail.

This agreement shall follow the guidelines of *Hetter Iska* as explained in Sefer *Berit Yehudah*.

It is agreed that any dispute which may arise in connection with this agreement shall be submitted before _____. Judgment rendered by the aforesaid authority may be entered in any court having jurisdiction thereof.

Dated _____

Signature of the Recipient _____

Signature of the Investor _____

Hetter Iska: Kullo Pikkadon Form[38]

I, the undersigned, have received the sum of $ _____ from _____(hereafter referred to as the "Investing Partner"), for investment in an *Iska* partnership, subject to the following terms:

In exchange for the aforementioned sum, the investing partner shall acquire a share (in the value of the funds received) in any investment real estate or business which I own. In the event that no such investments exist, the investing partner will acquire partnership (in the value of funds received) in any future investment which I shall make. The investing partner hereby appoints me as an agent to execute these investment(s) as I deem appropriate, on his behalf. These investment(s) shall be owned by the investing partner.

Any profits realized or losses sustained shall be allocated to the investing partner. However, ____ percent of the profits shall be retained by the undersigned for his services during the term of this *Iska*.

Any claim of loss must be verified through the testimony of two qualified witnesses in, and under conditions acceptable to, an Orthodox Jewish court of law.

Any claim regarding the amount of profit generated by this investment (or investments) shall be verified under solemn oath, before and under conditions acceptable to, an Orthodox Jewish court of law.

It is agreed that if I return the abovementioned principal to the investing partner, together with an additional _____ as payment for his share of the profits which are generated, then I will not be required to make any further payment nor will I be required to make an oath. I am obligated to make this payment on or before _____. If payment is not made by this time, the terms of this *Iska* shall continue.

In the event of any conflict between the terms of this *Iska* agreement and the terms of any other agreement signed by the two parties in regard to these funds, the terms of this agreement shall prevail.

This agreement shall follow the guidelines of *Hetter Iska* as explained in Sefer *Berit Yehudah*.

It is agreed that any dispute which may arise in connection with this agreement shall be submitted before _____. Judgment rendered by the aforesaid authority may be entered in any court having jurisdiction thereof.

Dated _____

Signature of the Recipient _____

Signature of the Investor _____

1. Maimonides (Egypt, 1135–1204), *Yad*, Malveh 5:1; R. Jacob b. Asher (Germany, 1270–1340), *Tur*, Yoreh De'ah 159; R. Joseph Caro (Israel, 1488–1575), *Shulhan Arukh*, Yoreh De'ah 159:1.

2. Exodus 22:24; Mishnah, Bava Mezia 5:11; R. Isaac b. Jacob Alfasi (Algeria, 1013–1103), Rif, ad loc.; *Yad*, op. cit. 4:2; R. Asher b. Jehiel (Germany, 1270–1343), Rosh, Bava Mezia 5:80; *Tur*, op. cit. 160:2; *Sh.Ar.*, op. cit. 160:1; R. Abraham Danzig (Prague, 1748–1820), *Hokhmat Adam* 130:1.

3. Bava Mezia 70a; Rif, ad.loc., *Yad*, op. cit. 5:8; Rosh, Bava Mezia 5:50; *Tur*, op. cit. 177:1; *Sh.Ar.*, op. cit. 177:1; *Hokhmat Adam* 131:4, 142:1.

4. Bava Mezia 104b; Rif, ad.loc.; *Yad*, op. cit. 6:2; *Rosh, Bava Mezia* 9:9; *Tur*, op. cit. 177:2; *Sh.Ar.*, op. cit. 177:2; R. Yaakov Yeshayahu Bloi (Israel, 1929–), *Berit Yehudah* 35:23 and n. 3.

5. Bava Mezia 68a; 104b; *Yad*, op. cit. 6:2; Rosh, Bava Mezia 9:9; *Tur*, op. cit. 177:12; *Sh.Ar.*, op. cit. 177:2; *Hokhmat Adam* 142:2.

6. R. David b. Samuel ha-Levi (Poland, 1586–1667); *Turei Zahav*, *Sh.Ar.*, op. cit. 177, n. 5; R. Shabbetai b. Meir ha-Kohen (Poland, 1621–1662), Siftei Kohen, *Sh.Ar.*, op. cit. 177, n. 9: *Hokhmat Adam*, loc. cit.

For the monetary requirements of the nominal fee, see R. Ezra Basri (Israel, contemp.), *Dinei Mamonot*, vol. 1, pp. 14–45.

7. Tosafot, Baba Kamma 102a; R. Barukh b. Shmuel (Germany, 1150–1221), quoted in *Mordecai*, Bava Kamma 9:122; *Tur*, op. cit. 177:14; *Sh.Ar.*, op. cit. 177:5; Rema, op. cit. 177:5

Hokhmat Adam 142:26. Limiting the protective force of the devolvement clause, R. Abraham Y. Karelitz, *Hazon Ish,* Yoreh De'ah 176:1, posits that the *iska* agreement may only call for MP to assume full responsibility for loss when the losses occur as a result of his failure to adhere to F's conditions. Should the realized losses be unrelated to MP's departure from F's conditions, the loss must be divided according to the profitloss stipulation of the *iska* agreement. R. Shneur Zalman of Liadi (Russia, 1745–1813), *Shulhan Arukh of the Rav,* Hilkhot Ribbit, n. 44, however, validates the devolvement clause even for losses not caused by MP's departure from F's conditions.

8. R. Abraham b. Mordecai haLevi (Egypt, late 17th cent.), *Ginnat Veradim,* Yoreh De'ah 6:9.

9. *Hazon Ish,* loc. cit.

10. Rema, loc. cit.; *Hokhmat Adam* 142:6.

11. R. Israel b. Petahiah Isserlein (Germany, 1390–1460), quoted in *Turei Zahav, Sh.Ar.,* 167, n. 1, and in *Siftei Kohen, Sh.Ar.,* op. cit. 167, n. 1; *Hokhmat Adam,* loc. cit.

12. *Turei Zahav,* loc. cit.

13. *Turei Zahav,* loc. cit; *Siftei Kohen,* loc. cit.; *Hokhmat Adam,* loc. cit.

14. *Turei Zahav,* loc. cit.; *Kunteres haSma Arukha,* ot 9; see *Berit Yehudah* 37:9, n. 23.

15. R. Mosheh Isserles, *Responsa Rema,* n. 80; R. Meir b. Gedaliah Lublin (Poland, 1588–1616), *Responsa Maharam Lublin* 135; *Hokhmat Adam* 142:7.

16. R. Mosheh b. Joseph Trani (Israel, 1500–1580), *Responsa Mabit* 43; *Ginnat Veradim,* Yoreh De'ah 6:89; R. Joseph Saul Nathanson (Poland, 1800–1875), *Responsa Sho'el u-Meshiv,* vol. 3, pt. 1, siman 137.

17. *Leibovici v. Rawicki,* 57 Misc.2d 141, 290 N.Y.S.2d 997 (Civ. Ct. 1968).

18. R. Mosheh Feinstein, *Iggerot Mosheh,* Yoreh De'ah 2:62.

19. R. Joseph Saul Nathanson, *Responsa Sho'el u-Meshiv,* vol. 1, pt. 3, siman 160; vol. 3, pt. 1, siman 133. Sharing the above broad definition of *iska* are R. Shalom Mordecai Shwadron (Poland, 1835–1911), *Responsa Maharsham* 2:215, 252, and R. Mordecai Yaakov Breisch (Switzerland, 1895–1977), *Responsa Helkat Yaakov* 3:199, 200.

20. R. Meir Arak, *Imrei Yosher* 1:108. R. Arak's position is articulated in various forms of elaboration in earlier rabbinic literature. Cf. *Ginnat Veradim,* op. cit. 6:4; *Shulhan Arukh of the Rav,* op. cit. seif 42; R. Solomon b. Joseph Ganzfried (Hungary, 1804–1866), *Kizzur Shulhan Arukh* 66:10; R. Solomon Leib Tabak (Hungary 1832–1908), *Erekh Shai* 177:7.

21. See *Imrei Yosher,* loc. cit. According to R. Arak, requiring a third party to take possession of the merchandise on behalf of A when B acquires it is unnecessary. B's resolve, at the time he purchases and transacts with the requisite merchandise, that his actions are on behalf of A suffices to allow A to acquire part-ownership in the merchandise.

For an alternative *hetter iska* arrangement designed to accommodate the businessman desiring capital for personal use, see *Kizzur Shulhan Arukh* 66:20.

22. *Yad,* Sheluhin ve-Shufetin 7:4; *Tur,* op. cit. 177:30, *Sh.Ar.,* op. cit. 177:30.

23. Rashi at Bava Mezia 104b.

24. Tosafot, Bava Mezia 104b.

25. Rema, *Sh.Ar.,* Yoreh De'ah 177:5.

26. R. Barukh b. Shmuel (Germany, 1150–1221), quoted by R. Mordecai b. Hillel (Germany, 1240–1298), Mordecai Bava Kamma 9:122, and by Rema, *Sh.Ar.,* op. cit. 177:5.

27. *Shulhan Arukh of the Rav,* loc. cit., seif 42.

28. *Iggerot Mosheh,* loc. cit.

29. R. Yisroel Reisman, *The Laws of Ribbis* (New York: Mesorah, 1995), p. 399, fn. 53.

30. See R. Samuel b. David Moses ha-Levi (Poland, 1625–1681), *Nahalat Shivah,* no. 40.

31. R. Shiloh Raphael, *Torah she-be-al Peh*, vol. 19 (Jerusalem: Mossad Harav Kook, 1977), pp. 100–105.

32. *Iggerot Mosheh*, loc. cit.

33. Raphael, *Torah she-be-al Peh*, p. 125.

34. *Iggerot Mosheh*, loc. cit. See also the authorities quoted by Rabbi J. David Bleich in *Contemporary Halakhic Problems*, vol. 2 (New York: Ktav, 1983), p. 379, fn. 2.

35. *Iggerot Mosheh*, loc. cit.

36. See R. Avraham Mosheh Lewanoni, *Mishnat Ribbit* 22:18, n. 24.

37. Reisman, *Laws of Ribbis*, p. 421.

38. Ibid., p. 424.

Sheldon Hass' Brand of Limited Paternalism

Sheldon Hass is a salesperson at Alpha Furniture. His knowledge of furniture and his ability to put together ensembles for his customers is second to none. With a sense of mission, Hass is driven to use his expertise to maximize the satisfaction of his customers. Toward this end, if a customer enters the store open-minded, with no specific item in mind, Hass will proceed to elicit the customer's particular needs and tastes, and the amount of money he or she wants to spend on a piece or set of furniture. Once Hass fully understands the customer's objectives and constraints, he sets out to recommend the best buy in the store for the customer.

Because Hass believes that his responsibility is to ensure that the customer makes an *informed* decision, he will offer options even when the customer comes in with something specific in mind. His general approach of eliciting the particular needs, tastes, and constraints of his customer stops only when the customer firmly indicates that his services are no longer desired. In this regard, Hass recalls with considerable pride his dealings with the Fishers:

"The Fishers came into the store very focused and self-assured. They were bent on buying the sofa displayed in our store window. I told them that I would be happy to sell them the piece but offered to show them a number of other sofas in different styles and price ranges. They took me up on my offer but ended up buying their original pick. When the Fishers left the store, they expressed gratitude to me for taking out the time to expand their options even though they came in with a set idea to order a specific item."

Another aspect of Hass' paternalism is his attitude toward the disclosure of *material defects*. These are chips, discolorations, and other defects objectionable to the extent that a customer would surely return the article to the store upon discovery. Hass will always point out such defects up front in his sales presentation. To ensure that knowledge of material defects does not slip by him, Hass arrives early every day to inspect the furniture in the showroom. He can always be heard on the telephone adjuring the manufacturer to carefully inspect the furniture before shipping out customer orders. Why all this meticulous scrutiny and worry about material defects? In Hass' own words: "Not to do so violates the basic trust my customer places in me. Moreover, consider the practicality of the matter. Discovery of undisclosed material defects will leave the customer in an outrage as to why I did not point them out in my sales presentation. The customer will undoubtedly demand a refund. What a mess! Imagine the loss of goodwill to Alpha."

Hass' paternalism has its limits, however. A case in point is how Hass markets the second-hand restored furniture in the store. To the untrained eye, those pieces can easily pass as newly manufactured. But Hass will never let his customers in on the secret. In Hass' words:

"Rest assured, we don't overcharge on these items—the customer pays no more than she would if she had bought the same item from a store that specializes in restored second-hand furniture. Maybe I delude the customer into thinking the item is new, but she leaves the store feeling that she got a bargain. The customer is happy, Alpha generates goodwill, and my own reputation is enhanced. It's definitely a win-win situation!

"Imagine what would happen if I disclosed up front that the item was a restored second-hand piece. Just say 'second-hand' and the customer conjures up an image of an ancient piece of wood that will soon decay or crack. Before you know it, the customer either walks away or begins to engage in aggressive bargaining."

Hass employs similar reasoning in excusing himself from disclosing insignificant flaws, such as scratches and nicks, in the furniture he sells. To disclose these imperfections is to invite the customer to engage in aggressive bargaining to lower the price. Nondisclosure of insignificant defects does not, in the mind of Hass, violate the basic trust the customer places in him. Moreover, as Hass put it:

"Consider the practicality of the matter. The customer may never discover the insignificant defect. Suppose she does. She may not be particular about it, and even if she is, she may resign herself to the possibility that the scratch first developed after she took possession of the furniture. In the worst scenario, the customer complains and demands a price adjustment. In that eventuality, I listen very sympathetically, and, if necessary, I offer to shave off a few dollars from the next installment payment. This will quickly restore any lost goodwill."

Another limitation of Hass' paternalism is that he will never express moral reservations to a customer regarding a purchase the customer is ready to make. In this regard, Hass recalls with a snicker the following incident:

"Ilan and Shalhevet Spiegel came into the showroom very focused and self-assured. They were determined to buy an exquisite dining room set. As I walked the couple through the showroom and showed them what I could order for them from our catalogs, the couple opened up to me. They were 'furniture fanatics,' obsessed with a need to replace their dining room set every three years with a new one 10 percent more expensive than their previous set. But the Spiegels were people of very limited means, struggling to make ends meet for basic necessities. I was convinced that the purchase of an exquisite dining room set, and for that matter the purchase of even an ordinary set, was for them a downright imprudent act.

"But my job is only to *protect my customer from an uninformed decision.* Once I'm convinced that all the facts are on the ground, I leave the customer to his own devices. I'm not here to make moral judgments! To boot, I could get fired for talking a customer out of making a purchase."

One final limitation Hass' paternalism took was in respect to comparison shopping. If he is aware that the competition offers a lower-priced alternative, he feels no compulsion to disclose this to the customer. In Hass' words:

"Comparison shopping is the customer's responsibility. If the consumer chooses not to engage in comparison shopping, it is at his own risk. If protecting the interest of my customer comes into conflict with my own best interests, my own interests come first. This is certainly the case here. Sending a customer to the competition is one sure way to get fired."

Limited Paternalism and Halakhah

Sheldon Hass' limited paternalism has many nuances. In this section we will examine it from the perspective of Halakhah. Let us begin with Hass' attitude toward his disclosure obligation.

The Disclosure Obligation

Hass' notion that his responsibility is to disclose only material defects but does not extend to nonmaterial defects would find halakhic disfavor. Halakhah requires a salesperson to disclose both categories of defects. But the rationale behind the disclosure requirements for each of these categories of defects is not the same. In respect to material defects, the disclosure requirement, as Hass' instincts told him, is rooted in a duty not to betray the basic trust the customer places in him. An examination of the details of the law bears this out.

Discovery of an undisclosed material defect allows the customer to cancel the original transaction.[1] Such a discovery makes the original deal an agreement entered into by error (*mekah ta'ut*).[2] Because this law was enacted to benefit the customer, he has a right, if he so demands, to keep the article without any adjustment. The salesperson must accede to this demand even if the price of the article has gone up since the original deal was struck.[3] To be sure, the customer need not accept the salesperson's offer to keep the original deal intact and only to downwardly adjust the price on the basis of the discovery of the defect.[4]

Taken together, the above provisions regarding the consequences of nondisclosure of a significant defect can be understood as penalties the sages imposed on the salesperson for engaging in fraudulent conduct. But examination of several other provisions of the law pertaining to material defect points to an understanding of nondisclosure of this type of defect as amounting to betraying the basic trust the customer places in the salesperson.

1. In the instance where the customer discovers an undisclosed material defect, Halakhah empowers the salesperson to reject the *customer's offer* to keep the deal intact and make a price adjustment.[5]

2. Given the presumption that the customer intended to acquire merchandise free of any material defect,[6] discovery of such a defect should allow the customer to void the original deal even if it turns out that he received fair value for the price he actually paid.

Now, if the remedy against a significant defect is nothing more than penalties imposed on a salesperson who engaged in fraud, the latter two laws are not readily understandable. What these laws point to is that entering into a sales situation creates a *presumption* that the customer relies on the salesperson to protect him against the self-harmful conduct of buying defective merchandise. If the salesperson is not willing to provide this protection, a presumption is immediately created that the customer does not want to deal with the salesperson altogether. Discovery of a material defect, therefore, makes it as if the transaction never took place. Because the customer's desire to finesse or revise the original transaction flies in the face of this operative presumption, the customer's proposal for a price adjustment has no legal force. Similarly, the absence of price fraud in the instance of the discovery of a material defect should not work to revive a transaction that Halakhah now regards as never having taken place.

Disclosure of Nonmaterial Defects

Halakhah's disclosure requirement for the salesperson, according to R. Isaac b. Sheshet Perfet (Spain, 1326–1408), extends to nonmaterial defects as well.[7] To be sure, discovery of this type of defect does not automatically empower the customer to cancel the original deal. But consider that the presence of this type of defect depreciates the value of the merchandise from what the customer thought it was worth at the time he entered into the deal. Now, if the customer was overcharged, the salesperson exploited the ignorance of the customer and was guilty of price fraud (*ona'ah*).[8] The details of this law will be discussed below.

Another scenario for the nonmaterial defect case occurs when the seller charges no more than the actual fair-market value of the article. Because the seller's nondisclosure exploits the customer's ignorance, the customer goes away from the deal with a false sense of bargain. Such conduct violates the prohibition against creating a false impression (*geneivat da'at*). The prototype here is Samuel's case involving the sale to a non-Jew of meat originating from an organically defective animal (*nebelah*). Duping the customer into believing he is getting a bargain by misrepresenting the meat as originating from a healthy animal constitutes *geneivat da'at*.[9] While price fraud may not be involved, as the non-Jew is charged a fair price for what he actually receives, the transaction is, nonetheless, prohibited, since it leaves the customer with a feeling of obligation to the storekeeper which is undeserved.[10]

Hass' practice of passing on restored second-hand furniture as new is specifically prohibited by the Mishnah.[11] While Hass charges a fair market price for what the customer actually receives, the practice generates a false sense of bargain. Rather than being a win-win situation, as Hass claims, the practice violates *geneivat da'at* law.

What the law of *geneivat da'at* does is to significantly expand the salesperson's disclosure obligation beyond what he must say so as not to violate the basic trust placed in him. This expanded responsibility consists of a requirement not to dash the reasonable expectations of his customer, even when it pertains to revealing the limitations of the product at hand.

The principle stated above can be derived from an analysis of the wine-barrel hospitality case discussed at Hullin 94a.

Here we are told that a host (H) should not delude his guest (G) into believing that he has acted toward him with magnanimous hospitality when in fact he has not done so. Opening a barrel of wine in honor of someone usually constitutes a gesture of magnanimous hospitality, as the wine remaining in the barrel may deteriorate as a result of its exposure to the air.[12] The magnanimity of the gesture is considerably reduced, however, when H happens to have sold the barrel of wine to a retailer just prior to the arrival of G. (A price adjustment will, of course, be made with the retailer.)

What constitutes proper conduct for H in these circumstances is a matter of dispute between Rashi and Tosafot. In Rashi's view, H is prohibited from telling G that he is opening the barrel especially for him. Since G will reasonably assume that the barrel was not sold prior to his arrival, H's declaration will generate for himself an undeserved sense of indebtedness.[13] But if G is operating under that assumption he will just as assuredly be misled even if H says nothing while pouring out the wine for him. For this reason Tosafot disagrees with Rashi, requiring H to disabuse G of his erroneous assumption and inform him that the barrel was sold prior to his arrival. Such disclosure will leave no doubt in G's mind that H's hospitality gesture entailed no particular expense.[14]

Rashi's position here is puzzling. To be sure, there is nothing inherent in H's opening of the barrel that directly communicates to G that he is the recipient of generous hospitality. But given the reasonableness of G's assumption that the barrel was not sold prior to his arrival, H's action generates a false impression of magnanimity. H should therefore be obliged to set G straight.

Perhaps the key to understanding Rashi's position is that the case at hand takes place in a social setting. Gestures of friendship, according to talmudic dictum, must be made openly and not in a manner that might result in the recipient's not connecting the friend with the gift: one who bestows a gift on a friend is obligated to inform him of it.[15] Underling this rule of etiquette is the rabbis' conviction that open gestures of friendship promote pleasant and harmonious interpersonal relations.[16]

Let us assume that this rule of etiquette is operative for both parties in the wine-barrel hospitality case. Now, if H intends to bestow a generous gesture of hospitality on G, proper protocol requires him to forthrightly tell G that the barrel is being opened in his honor, rather than rely on G's reaching the same conclusion on his own based on the reasonable assumption that the barrel was not sold prior to his arrival. H's silence in the face of his having made an apparently magnanimous gesture should itself shake G's assumption that the opening of the barrel entailed considerable expense for H.

One could argue that if G is a reasonable person, he should interpret H's silence as a gracious way of telling him that no particular expense was involved in the hospitality gesture. Openly informing G runs the risk of offending him, as he might infer from the revelation that the barrel would certainly not have been opened for him if an expense had been involved. Depending upon H's exact words, his tone and voice inflection, G might find additional reason to take offense, concluding, for example, that H regards him as unworthy of a magnanimous gesture of hospitality. Hence, drawing attention to the lack of expense involved by a gracious silence represents the most diplomatic approach to resolving an awkward situation. The situation is a good application of the talmudic dictum *milla be'sela mashtuka b'trein* ("a word is worth a sela, silence two selas"; Megillah 18a).

The foregoing discussion leads to an understanding of the dispute between Rashi and Tosafot. In Rashi's view, H is saddled only by a responsibility to clarify his intent. The silence with which he performs an apparently magnanimous gesture communicates to G that the gesture did not entail any particular expense. Given the awkwardness of the situation, silence is the most gracious way to make G understand this. Tosafot, on the other hand, regards H's silence as an inadequate means of undeceiving G of his erroneous impression. There are several reasons for this. One is that a false impression cannot be undone unless the force that attempts to remove it is at least as strong as the force that created it. Since the false impression was created by H's action, H's silence, notwithstanding its communicative power, cannot remove it. Only an explicit statement will accomplish this. Another reason is the consideration that the false impression here is not merely a conceptual error. It relates to personal worth, as it involves G's sense of H's regard for him. Since G wants to believe that H holds him in high regard, cognitive dissonance may set in and prevent him from recognizing the message inherent in H's silence.[17] Nothing less than an explicit statement is required here.

This understanding makes Rashi's position tenable only for a social setting. This is so because it is *etiquette* which gives silence its communicative power. In a commercial setting, Rashi could very well be in agreement with Tosafot. Indeed, Rashi explicitly espouses the position that silence is not an adequate disabusing mechanism in a commercial setting. Rashi avers this position in connection with the formula the rabbis of the Talmud devised to inform townspeople that the day's supply of meat was not kosher. A public announcement to this effect served a double purpose. First, it informed the Gentile patrons that the meat for the day was not kosher and hence averted for the Jewish proprietors a violation of *geneivat da'at*. In addition, it alerted the Jews of the town not to purchase meat from a Gentile supplier on that day. The formula the rabbis chose for making this announcement was "Meat for the army has fallen into our hands" (*nafla bisra l'bnei heila*).[18] In the absence of the *nafla bisra* proclamation, a Jew, according to Rashi, may not sell non-kosher meat to a Gentile under the presumption that it is kosher (*be'hezkat kesheirah*). Since the Gentile reasonably assumes that the meat is kosher, the butcher's silence dupes the customer into thinking he is buying kosher meat.[19]

Proceeding from this analysis, if the customer reasonably expects the product at hand to have a certain feature and in fact it does not have it, the salesperson is obligated to disclose this to the customer. Failure to do so violates for the seller the *geneivat da'at* interdict. This is so because the seller's disclosure obligation consists not only of a duty not to mislead in an affirmative manner but also of a requirement to disabuse the customer of his reasonable misperception about the product at hand.

Further support for this thesis can be derived from a point in *geneivat da'at* law expounded in the Jerusalem Talmud at Makkot 2:6. The case entails the following elements: A is well versed in one tractate of the Talmud, but the townspeople mistakenly think he is proficient in two tractates and accord him the honor due someone who is proficient in two tractates. The Jerusalem Talmud rules that A is obligated to disabuse the townspeople of their mistaken impression of him. This ruling apparently contradicts the rule, elucidated at Hullin 94a, that an individual is exempt from correcting a mistaken impression that is rooted in self-deception. Ready reconciliation of the two texts follows from the reasonable-man hypothesis. One aspect of this principle is that A may not accept B's offer of something when B's offer reasonably stems from a mistaken impression he has of A. Notwithstanding that A did nothing to affirmatively create this false impression, he bears a responsibility to disabuse B of the misperception he has of him. This applies, however, only when B's misperception of him is reasonable. If this is not the case, A bears no disabusing responsibility, as B is guilty of self-deception. Now, since the various tractates of the Talmud, especially those in the same order,[20] are interconnected, complement each other, and overlap somewhat, proficiency in one tractate can easily be mistaken for proficiency in two tractates. Accordingly, a talmudic scholar must disabuse the townspeople of their inaccurate assessment of him. Similarly, the seller's disclosure obligation consists not only of a duty not to mislead in an affirmative manner but also of a requirement to disabuse the customer of his reasonable misperceptions about the product at hand.

The Seller's Reasonable Expectations

It follows from the discussion so far that Halakhah rejects *caveat emptor* ("let the buyer beware") as the operative moral ethic of the marketplace. One should not, however, conclude that Halakhah excuses the consumer from any information-gathering responsibility and gives him protection even if he conducts himself mindlessly in a transaction. Elsewhere in this volume we have dealt with this issue as it relates to market conduct in general.[21] At this junction, we will expand on this issue as it relates specifically to easing the salesperson's disclosure obligation.

One indication that Halakhah imposes a measure of responsibility on the customer in a personal sale setting is that the salesperson is relieved of a responsibility to point out to the customer any visibly evident flaws in the merchandise at hand. Since the customer presumably picks up on the visibly obvious flaws, going forward and consummating the transaction signals his willingness to accept the merchandise with the imperfections.[22]

The more demanding Halakhah is on the customer in regard to his responsibility to pick up on defects of the product at hand, the less precise will be the demands it places on the salesperson to point out these defects. Halakhah's criterion of deception, therefore, depends on the balance it calls on between the reasonable expectations of the salesperson and the reasonable expectations of the customer. In this regard a dispute recorded in the modern responsa literature is relevant. The case deals with the practice of butchers of soaking liver in blood. Since the practice gives the impression that the liver derives from a freshly slaughtered animal, the conduct might constitute deceptive representation of the liver. R. Mosheh Feinstein (New York, 1895–1986) permits the practice and contrasts it to the sales practice of soaking meat in water which the Talmud prohibits as deceptive. The difference between the two cases is clear: Soaking meat in water creates the impression as a *definite matter* that the meat is of a better quality than it actually is. Because the practice *deceives* consumers it is prohibited. On the other hand, soaking liver in blood creates only a doubt in the mind of the consumer as to what the status of the liver is. Since liver that was not derived from a freshly slaughtered animal may naturally take on the appearance of the liver at hand, the onus is on the consumer to inquire of the butcher as to the status of the liver at hand. Given that the onus of inquiry is on the customer, the butcher bears no responsibility to volunteer the status of the liver. If the customer makes no inquiry, his lack of solicitation can be understood in either of two ways. One possibility is that he is not meticulous in the above matter. Alternatively, the customer does desire fresh liver, but because he is negligent in his duty to inquire, is guilty of self-deception.[23]

Sharply disputing R. Feinstein's view, R. Yehoshua Baumol (New York, 1880–1948) regards the practice of soaking liver in blood as a deceptive sales tactic. In his view, conduct that creates doubt in the mind of the consumer regarding the quality of the product being sold constitutes deceptive representation.[24]

Eliciting the Customer's Particular Needs

In the opening vignette we find Hass offering to expand options for the Fishers even though the couple signals to him that they have made up their mind to purchase the sofa in the store window. While Hass' approach may make sense from a business standpoint, he bears no ethical duty to do this.

Evidencing that Halakhah does not inherently impose the role of counselor on the salesperson in his dealings with customers is the following case recorded in the codes. The essential elements are the following:

S sells an ox to B, but does not inform him that the ox is vicious (*naghan*). Because the ox is a menace to society, it must be destroyed and may not be used for plowing.[25] When the transaction is completed, B discovers that the ox is a *naghan*. B's intention all along was to purchase an ox for plowing, but he was silent on this point in his negotiations with S. B sues for a refund on the grounds that most customers purchase oxen for plowing and not for butchering. Because majority practice does not decide in a monetary matter,[26] B will not prevail on the basis of the above argument. What B needs to demonstrate is that the circumstances of his transaction with S manifests that S was aware of his plowing intent. One way of proving this is to refer to the purchasing price. Specifically, suppose the fair market value of an ox suitable for plowing is higher than the corresponding value of the same ox when it is suitable only for butchering. Here, the higher price B agreed to pay should have clearly communicated to S his plowing intent.

Another way for B to validate his claim is to point to the circumstance that he is a long-standing customer of S and has established a track record that his practice is to purchase oxen for plowing. Notwithstanding that B was silent in the present transaction regarding his plowing intent, S should have reasonably understood this intent by assuming B would follow his normal pattern.[27]

The legal treatment of the *naghan* case is apparently astonishing. To be sure, majority practice does not decide in a monetary matter. This principle should, however, say no more than that B's claim to overturn the original transaction based on S's nondisclosure is rejected. But since the *majority* purchase an ox for the purpose of plowing, how can S knowingly sell B a *naghan* without first eliciting from B that his intent is to buy the ox for consumption. What follows is that Halakhah does not *inherently* conceptualize the role of a salesperson as a counselor.

R. Yom Tov Lipmann b. Nathan ha-Levi Heller's (Moravia, 1579–1654) comment on the *naghan* case amounts to an advocacy of the above principle. Why the transaction is not overturned is explained by R. Heller as stemming from the proposition that the *onus* is on B to inform S of his plowing intent.[28] R. Heller's point is generalizable into the assertion that Halakhah imposes on S the responsibility of being a counselor only when B relies on his judgment or when S takes this role upon himself by making a recommendation to B. But when B asks S for a specific item, S bears no responsibility to probe B's intended use of the item to ensure that B's best interests will be served by the purchase. Here, S's duty is merely to disclose to B any defects the product may have. Recall that the *naghan* case refers to the instance where the *price* of the ox is the same when its *only* use is consumption and when it can also be used for plowing. Given the absence of a price difference, *naghan* status cannot be *objectively* regarded as a defect. A duty for S to disclose the *naghan* status of his animal cannot be identified.

Let us return to the opening vignette. Given that Alpha furniture can accommodate a large range of shoppers with varying budgets and tastes, it would be unethical for Hass to push a particular selection on a customer without first ascertaining the customer's budget and taste in furniture. Such conduct constitutes the proffering of ill-suited advice and violates for Hass the interdict against proffering ill-suited advice (*lifnei iver lo titen mikh'shol*, Leviticus 19:14).[29]

Let us change the scenario a bit. Instead of selling furniture, suppose Hass is selling securities. Which portfolio is right for the Fishers will depend on such factors as their investment goals, their time horizon, and the degree of their risk aversion. To push a specific portfolio on them without first eliciting their investment goals and constraints would, of course, violate *lifnei iver*. But suppose the Fishers come to Hass very focused and tell him that they want to invest, say, in a mutual fund that specializes in energy stocks. Is this case comparable to the scenario where the Fishers come to Alpha and tell Hass they want to buy the sofa in the store window? Under New York Stock Exchange rule 405, member firms must "use due diligence to learn the facts relative to every customer."[30] Operating under this rule, brokerage houses typically ascertain a prospect's net worth, income, and investment goals before taking on the account.[31] Rule 405 amounts to a judgment by society that the average man is presumed ignorant regarding securities even when the initiation of the investment comes from the customer himself. This rule compares well with the Halakhah's attitude that the seller's disclosure obligation is geared to whatever the relevant consumer's reasonable expectations are.

Now, if the broker views rule 405 merely as a mechanism to protect himself from litigation by a client who is disappointed with the performance of his investment, then the duty "to use due diligence" will be discharged in a perfunctory manner. The goal will merely be to get the required paper on file.

From a halakhic perspective, rule 405 should be viewed as society's judgment that risk is an inherent *defect* of a financial product. Because how risk is perceived depends on such factors as the client's net worth, income, time horizon, and risk aversion, the broker must elicit this information from the client before taking on his account.

Letting the Customer Do Himself In

Recall the scene in the opening vignette where Hass allows the Spiegels to go through with their order for an exquisite dining room set even though he has become convinced in dealing with them that they are "furniture fanatics" and the installment payments will deprive them of necessities. From a halakhic perspective, several moral principles are relevant here.

Lifnei Iver and the Passive Case

According to R. Mordecai Yaakov Breisch (Switzerland, 1895–1977), the prohibition against proffering someone ill-suited advice extends even to passive counseling. In his view, if A is in a position to provide B with timely information that would avert harm for him but fails to do so, A violates *lifnei iver*.[32] The application of R. Breisch's ruling apparently requires Hass to voice his reservations to the couple and perhaps even requires him to refuse to take their order. Several mitigating factors can, however, be identified here. We take it as a given that in respect to the prohibition of proffering ill-suited advice, Halakhah does not treat the passive case more stringently than the active case. Consider the following scenario in relation to the active case: With the *intent* of proffering *ill-suited advice*, B offers an *unsolicited* recommendation to A to enter into a particular investment. In the past A never sought out B's advice, and in any case he does not regard B's opinion as something to take seriously, let alone to rely on. Before encountering B, A had already made up his mind to engage in the investment B spoke of. As matters turned out, the investment failed. Because A never took B's recommendation as *advice* when he went forward with the investment, B has not violated *lifnei iver*, notwithstanding his evil intent.

Hass' encounter with the Spiegels involves the selfsame elements. Consider that before the Spiegels even stepped into Alpha they had already made up their mind to order an exquisite dining room set. Naturally, the Spiegels are interested to see what Alpha has on display and desire to pump Hass for any useful information he might have. But they do not view Hass as a potential counselor and are not interested in asking his *opinion* on anything, even as a courtesy. Because Hass does not play the role of potential counselor for the Spiegels, his silence should not be viewed as passive counsel to them to enter into the deal. This judgment is bolstered by the consideration that Hass has no new information to offer the Spiegels to convince them not to enter the deal. The Spiegels are fully aware of the deprivation consequences of their decision to order the exquisite set. What Hass has to say is only to *moralize* the Spiegels' conduct as imprudent. In all probability Hass' protest will be of no avail and might even cause a scene in the store.

Lo Ta'amod al Dam Rei'akha

Another religious imperative to consider in evaluating whether or not Hass has a duty to protest or even withdraw from his transaction with the Spiegels is the biblical injunction of "Do not stand idly by the blood of your neighbor" (*lo ta'amod al dam rei'akha*, Leviticus 19:16). While the verse speaks of the prohibition of a bystander's remaining idle in a life-threatening situation, Sifra extends the interdict to the prohibition of withholding testimony in a monetary matter.[33] Basing himself on Sifra, R. Israel Meir ha-Kohen Kagan (Poland, 1838–1933) understands the monetary application of the *lo ta'amod* interdict in broad terms: A's failure to supply B with timely information that would avert a financial loss for B is a violation of the *lo ta'amod* interdict.[34] Does the *lo ta'amod* interdict apply even when the disclosure is against the financial interests of the informer? No. Evidencing this is a point in law in connection with the mitzvah of restoring lost property (*hashavat avedah*). This mitzvah consists of both a positive and a negative duty. The positive duty is set out at Deuteronomy 22:13, and the negative duty consists of *lo ta'amod*.[35] Now, consider that an individual is not required to engage in the task of *hashavat avedah* when it would be at the expense of restoring his own property or losing time on his job. This exemption is exegetically derived from the verse "save when there shall be no needy among you" (*efes ki lo yehiyeh bekha evyon*, Deuteronomy 15:4).[36] The word *efes* is interpreted to mean "end" or "prevent," with the meaning being: "Be careful not to engage in conduct that might result in causing poverty for you."[37]

From the preceding analysis it follows that the obligation, should the opportunity arise, to take action to avert a loss for a fellow is by no means absolute. A's perception that his provision of timely information to B would be to his own detriment exempts him from the obligation.

Financial Ruination and the Duty of the Salesperson

Finally, let us consider the merits of Hass' argument that confessing his reservation to the Spiegels runs the risk of jeopardizing his job. He raises the same issue in regard to disclosing price comparisons to his customer. Hass' argument has merit.

Relevant to the issue at hand is the ruling of R. Mosheh Sofer (Hungary, 1762–1839) regarding the dictum that an individual is not required to spend more than one-fifth of his wealth in order to fulfill a mitzvah. R. Mosheh Isserles (Poland, 1525 or 1530–1572) contends that the one-fifth rule does not apply in respect to a negative commandment. Avoidance of the infringement of a negative commandment requires an individual, if necessary, to go to any expense.[38] Disputing R. Isserles' view, R. Sofer extends the one-fifth rule to a negative commandment as well. To be sure, the leniency applies only if the negative commandment would be violated passively (*shev veal ta'aseh*). Avoidance of the violation of a negative commandment in an active manner requires an individual, if necessary, to go to any expense.[39]

Following R. Sofer's line, Halakhah would countenance Hass' passively violating various prohibitions if he perceived that avoiding these infractions would threaten his job security. Such an assessment apparently meets the one-fifth rule. The passivity condition is met when Hass does not actively encourage the Spiegels to enter into the deal. In the instance where the problem is Alpha's pricing policy, the passivity condition is met when Hass plays no role in formulating the pricing policy.

While the threat of job loss gives Hass license to passively violate Halakhah, remaining employed at Alpha on a permanent basis is very problematic. This is so because any resentment or disappointment customers suffer on account of Alpha's business policies will surely be directed at no one other than Hass, the salesperson they dealt with. To be sure, Hass' personal conduct satisfies the letter of the law, but in his professional life he will not be a positive force for promoting harmony in society.[40] Moreover, the ideal is to choose a lifestyle that will afford opportunities to display virtue and integrity in an objectively verifiable manner.[41] Because Hass works in a moral minefield, customer resentment against Alpha works to overshadow his virtue and even make it go unnoticed. By remaining at Alpha, Hass severely limits his potential to exert a positive influence on the moral climate of society.

The Salesperson's Disclosure Obligation and the *Ona'ah Interdict*

Let us now turn to a consideration of Hass' insistence that he is under no obligation to advise a customer that the merchandise he seeks is available elsewhere at a lower price. Hass' conduct here may run into violation of the law of *ona'ah* (price fraud).

The law of *ona'ah* prohibits an individual from concluding a transaction at a price that is more favorable to himself than the competitive norm.[42] A transaction involving *ona'ah* is regarded as a form of theft.[43] Depending on how widely the price of the subject transaction departs from the competitive norm, the injured party may have recourse to void or adjust the transaction. Provided the price discrepancy is assessed to be within the margin of error,[44] the plaintiff's right to void the transaction is recognized when the difference between the sale price and the competitive norm is more than one-sixth.[45] When the differential was exactly one-sixth, neither of the parties may subsequently void the transaction on account of the price discrepancy. The plaintiff is, however, entitled to full restitution of the *ona'ah* involved.[46] Finally, third-degree *ona'ah* occurs when the sale price differs from the market price by less than one-sixth. Here, the transaction not only remains binding, but in addition, the complainant has no legal claim to the price differential.[47] In the latter instance, however, the plaintiff's claim would be denied only when the transaction involved a product that is nonstandardized in nature. Should the case involve a homogeneous product, the plaintiff's claim for the differential is honored.[48]

Does the law of *ona'ah* require Hass to reveal to his customers *any and all* information he has regarding lower-priced opportunities elsewhere in the marketplace? Or does the law of *ona'ah* operate on much more narrow parameters? Resolution of this question requires an investigation of the rationale behind the law of *ona'ah*.

Ona'ah and Opportunity Cost

There are several ways to rationalize the rule that a transaction can be overturned or its price terms modified on the basis of the availability of a better opportunity for the plaintiff when the deal was entered into. One possibility is that the claim is essentially a plea of *ignorance* of market conditions by the plaintiff. Specifically, had he only been aware of the better opportunity, he would have availed himself of it. This understanding makes the *ona'ah* claim the plaintiff's protest that the transaction at hand entailed an *actual* loss for him in the form of a forgone opportunity. Economists call the loss of this forgone opportunity an opportunity cost. Since Halakhah does not expect a market participant to transact in the marketplace with perfect knowledge, legitimacy is given to the *ona'ah* claim. Absent this presumption of ignorance, the *ona'ah* claim would be thrown out.

The above approach must, however, be refined. Certainty that the plaintiff was aware of the market norm at the time he entered into the transaction at hand does not *automatically* vitiate his subsequent *ona'ah* claim. The Talmud, at Bava Mezia 51a, specifically deals with such a case. The particulars are as follows: S was selling a parcel of silk ribbons for six zuz. B knew that they were worth only five and was convinced that he could bargain down the price to five and a half. But concluding the transaction at five and a half would reduce the *ona'ah* involved to third-degree, and he would have no recourse to recover the half-zuz overpayment. Instead, B decided against bargaining with S and paid his asking price of six zuz. Immediately upon completing the deal, B informed S that he was launching a second-degree *ona'ah* claim against him. Making such a declaration immediately after the deal was concluded indicates that B was aware of the *ona'ah* all along. Nonetheless, B does not lose his *ona'ah* rights, as his conduct manifested a strategy to first secure possession of the ribbons and only then to launch an *ona'ah* claim. B's conduct clearly shows that he did not waive his rights in this matter.[49]

Another possible rationale for the *ona'ah* claim is that Halakhah regards the price that was reasonably within the plaintiff's reach as the fair value of the article at hand. What *ona'ah* does, therefore, is to *define* the competitive norm. Market participants are *entitled* to trade the article at hand on the basis of its competitive norm. Unless the plaintiff conducts himself in a manner that demonstrates that he has waived his rights in the matter, his *ona'ah* claim remains intact.

Now, if Halakhah held market participants to a responsibility to engage in market search before striking a deal, then an *ona'ah* claim would have no basis. The implication to be drawn from making the competitive norm an *entitlement* of traders is that Halakhah *releases* market participants to a certain degree of a responsibility to engage in market search. Thus, deliberately transacting to one's advantage at an *ona'ah* price exploits the ignorance of one's opposite number and deprives him of his entitlement. To be sure, Halakhah does not legitimize the *mindless* consumer. Consider that if the price discrepancy involved goes beyond the margin of error, the *ona'ah* claim is not honored. What this shows is that Halakhah fully expects market participants to have at least an approximate notion of market conditions when striking a deal. What are we, then, to make of a transaction concluded on price terms that exceed reasonable misjudgment of value? The only plausible interpretation is that the underlying intention of the parties involved was not to trade the article at hand but rather just to use it as a *vehicle* to effect a voluntary gift transfer.[50]

Support for this formulation of the *ona'ah* claim can be seen from the fact that Halakhah regards the *ona'ah* offense as a form of theft. If the *ona'ah* claim is no more than the plaintiff's protest that the transaction at hand incurred an opportunity cost for him, the issue is only whether the original transaction was entered into by error (*mekah ta'ut*) or should be adjusted. Calling the offense involved a form of theft indicates that the defendant's *ona'ah* offense has violated the plaintiff's legitimate right to trade the commodity at hand on the basis of its competitive norm.

Further support that *ona'ah* should be viewed as a right to trade on the basis of the competitive norm is the analysis of third-degree *ona'ah* by R. Asher b. Jehiel (Germany 1250–1327). Noting the absence of any provision for legal redress in third-degree *ona'ah* cases, R. Asher speculates whether it might be permissible, in the first instance, to contract into third-degree *ona'ah*. Pivotal to the resolution of this question, in R. Asher's view, is the definition of market price. Is market price to be understood as a single value, or is it to be defined as the range of deviations of less than one-sixth from the price of the disputed transaction? Adopting the latter view leads to the conclusion that third-degree *ona'ah* is not fraud at all. Subscription to the former view leads, however, to the conclusion that knowledge of the market norm prohibits either party from contracting into a price agreement that is even slightly more favorable to himself than the norm. The absence of legal redress for third-degree *ona'ah* would then be explained by the presumption that when the degree of *ona'ah* involved is of such a relatively small amount, the plaintiff waives his claim to restitution. This presumption follows from our inability to fix the value of the article sold. While some experts would insist that *ona'ah* took place, others would just as vehemently deny it. Since the experts are divided as to whether *ona'ah* occurred, and, if it did, by how much, we may safely presume that the victim of this possible price fraud waives his rights to restitution.

Though offering no definitive resolution of the dilemma, R. Asher urged the following guideline for third-degree *ona'ah* cases. Cognizant of the prevailing norm, an individual should not contract into a price agreement that is even slightly more favorable to himself than this value. On the other hand, in the event an individual falls victim to third-degree *ona'ah*, he should accept his loss graciously and express no complaint.[51]

What can be extrapolated from R. Asher's analysis is that the validity of an *ona'ah* claim is always based on the assessment of experts. Because experts are divided in a third-degree *ona'ah* case as to whether price fraud took place, the *ona'ah* claim is uncollectible. But in first- and second-degree *ona'ah*, expert testimony establishes that the price of the transaction at hand was at variance with what the article is *objectively* worth. *Ona'ah* is hence a right to trade a commodity based on its competitive norm.

First-Degree *Ona'ah*

Within the framework of the above conceptualization of the *ona'ah* claim, the market opportunities reasonably accessible to both the buyer and seller at the time they strike their deal define the competitive norm for the transaction at hand. This formulation of market norm explains why the sages found it necessary to establish the category of first-degree *ona'ah*. Would it not have sufficed for the sages to declare that *ona'ah* amounting to one-sixth or more calls for the differential to be returned to the victim? Perhaps the answer is that calling for the offender to simply return the price differential does not *fully* capture the opportunities reasonable accessible to the buyer and seller, respectively, when the *ona'ah* involved is greater than one-sixth.

Several opinions cited in the Jerusalem Talmud take this approach. The specific issue addressed is why the *buyer* (B) has the right to overturn the transaction when the degree of *ona'ah* is more than one-sixth. A number of opinions advanced in answering this question are consistent with the opportunity cost thesis.[52]

1. B's right to overturn first-degree *ona'ah*, according to R. Zeira, is based on the argument that this approach works best to quiet the ridicule directed at B for demonstrating that he is naive in commercial matters.

2. Another approach is offered by an anonymous authority: Credibility is given to B's contention that his original intention was to purchase an expensive item that would confer status on him. Because the item at hand turns out to be not a status symbol but just an ordinary item that is terribly overpriced, calling for the price differential to be returned effectively frustrates B's original intention of obtaining a status item. Hence, allowing B to realize his original objective calls for the first-degree *ona'ah* transaction to become null and void.[53]

The aforementioned approaches can easily supply a rationale for why the *seller* can insist on voiding the transaction when the *ona'ah* involved is first-degree. While the transferability of R. Zeira's rationale to the case at hand is straightforward, application of the anonymous opinion to the seller's rights in first-degree *ona'ah* requires some extrapolation. Applying the underlying logic of this view to the case at hand produces the following argument: Sympathy is found with the seller's complaint that he does not want to acquire a reputation as a deep discount seller. Validating the first-degree *ona'ah* sale and only requiring a return of the price differential sets up the seller for fierce customer negotiation for discounts. With the aim of minimizing reputational harm of this sort, the sages call for first-degree *ona'ah* to be voided, rather than requiring only a return of the price differential.

Circumstances Where *Ona'ah* Does Not Apply

The reasonably accessible price rationale for the *ona'ah* claim points to a number of scenarios where Hass is relieved of any obligation to inform customers of the availability of a lower-priced alternative elsewhere. Let us proceed to describe these scenarios.

The Superior-Product Case

Furniture stores essentially fall into either of two categories. One set of stores, of which Alpha is a prime example, features an elaborate showroom displaying a variety of individual pieces as well as ensembles, such as kitchen, dining room, and bedroom sets. These stores also feature salesmen who provide creative ideas for ensembles, advice on how to arrange financing, and expertise on the proper care and maintenance of the furniture. Another set of stores features none of the amenities of the display stores. Instead, customers are provided with catalogs that display photographs of furniture. These stores will order the furniture from the manufacturer for their customers.

Suppose a customer of Alpha launches an *ona'ah* claim against the company based on the availability of the same furniture item at a catalog store at a lower price. Since Alpha offers the item in question together with the display feature and the services of expert salespeople, Alpha clearly offers a *superior* product and is entitled to charge more than the catalog stores. Alpha and the catalog stores are located in differentiated markets, and therefore it is invalid to use the catalog stores for comparison purposes in an *ona'ah claim*. Alpha can only be held responsible to be in line with the pricing of other display stores. Given that the *ona'ah* claim based on the price at the catalog store is rejected, Hass bears no obligation to inform customers that catalog stores are *charging less* for the same piece of furniture.

The thesis that superiority separates a product from the competition as far as the *ona'ah* claim is concerned follows directly from R. Asher b. Jehiel's analysis of third-degree *ona'ah*. Recall that what stands at the basis of the plaintiff's waiving his rights here is the presumed division among experts as to whether the transaction disadvantaged the plaintiff. Differences among experts would, however, not be expected to emerge when the subject product contains all the features of competing products and displays, in addition, a distinctive characteristic. Differentiation here clearly separates the subject product from the competition and confers an element of monopoly status upon the seller. Monopoly status, in turn, vitiates the *ona'ah* claim.

One may well argue that in the context of the modern product market no two competing products are identical. Differentiation today has advanced considerably beyond the level of the physical properties of the product to include such factors as proximity to the consumer, convenience of hours, complementarities of consumption, product display, and service level. All market purchases involve some tradeoff of offsetting advantages and disadvantages, and thus the law of *ona'ah* should have wide operational significance within the framework of the modern product market. Relating the argument for defining a product market in broad terms to the furniture market leads to the proposition that the showroom and catalog stores should be lumped together in a single product market. While the showroom store offers differentiation in the form of product display, the catalog store may offer the convenience of proximity to the consumer.

The preceding argument is not entirely valid. Differentiation, as it appears to this writer, works to erode the distinctiveness of a competing brand only when a basis exists for presuming that consumers value the differentiation involved. Pointing clearly in this direction is the determining role R. Asher assigns to the agreement or disagreement of experts in adjudicating *ona'ah* cases. Clearly, cost differences among sellers play no direct role in judging the merits of an *ona'ah* claim. What does matter is the legitimacy of the presumption that consumers want to spend extra money for the differentiation involved. Following this line, proximity to the consumer would not be regarded as an offsetting advantage for the catalog store in the furniture market. Since the furniture market is not a local, neighborhood market, proximity of the seller to the consumer cannot be said to generate a presumption that consumers are willing to spend extra money to acquire this advantage. In respect to the consumer non-durable market, proximity, within limits, especially in the inclement-weather season, may be regarded by consumers as an advantage to which they attach a price significance. Scientific surveys could prove very helpful in determining which aspects of differentiation consumers are willing to pay extra money for. Such information would naturally add a measure of refinement to the preceding analysis.

The Separated Marketplace Case

Given that the competitive norm is defined as the prices reasonably accessible to buyer and seller at the time they strike their deal, the *ona'ah* claim should be valid only if the better deal is available in the same marketplace where the actual purchase is made. But if accessing the better opportunity entails a *clear-cut time cost* for the plaintiff, then the better opportunity should be regarded as being located in a *separate* marketplace. Because this better opportunity would not *reasonably* have been considered by the plaintiff when he entered into the disputed transaction, his right to trade on the competitive norm does not extend to this opportunity. Thus the plaintiff's *ona'ah* claim is rejected.

The principle that marketplace separation should invalidate an *ona'ah* claim can be derived from the rule that governs the liquidation procedure for property dedicated to the Sanctuary. The rule states that the sale of such property for the benefit of the Sanctuary must be conducted both in the locale (*mekomah*) where the dedication was made and in the time period (*ubesha'ato*) when the dedication was made (*ein le-hekdesh ela mekomah ubesha'ato*).[54] The *mekomah ubesha'ato* rule, according to Nahmanides (Spain, 1194–1270)[55] and R. Yom Tov Ishbili (Spain, ca. 1250–1330),[56] applies not only to the Sanctuary but to monetary matters generally. Explicitly positing the *mekomah ubesha'ato* rule in connection with the law of *ona'ah* is R. Abraham David Wahrmann (Ukraine, ca. 1771–1840).[57]

Proceeding from the above analysis is that Hass is under no obligation to reveal to a customer the availability of a lower-priced opportunity when that opportunity is available outside the local marketplace.

The Discount-Price Case

Another issue for consideration is whether Hass is obligated to inform customers of lower-priced opportunities in the form of discount sales. The following mishnaic-talmudic text is relevant to this issue:

> [R. Judah says] He may not lower the price of his goods below the market price. But the sages say: He is remembered for good.[58]

> What is the reason for the sages? Because he lowers the market price (*mirvah letar'a*).[59]

Halakhah takes the view of the sages as normative.[60] But the commentators differ as to how far the price-cutting privilege goes.

One school of thought, led by R. Meir b. Isaac Eisenstadt (Poland, 1670–1744), understands the price-cutter (A) of the Mishnah to be a retail grain dealer. A's price-cutting is legitimate, according to R. Eisenstadt et al., only because it results in the reduction of the market price of essential commodities, i.e., grain.[61] The scenario whereby this result obtains is described by R. Solomon b. Isaac (Rashi, France, 1040–1105) in his commentary ad loc.: A's price-cutting makes hoarders of grain believe that the market price of grain is on the way down. This leads them to dump their supplies on the market, with the result that the market price of grain goes down.[62] Suppose the commodity at hand was not grain but beer. Here, avers R. Eisenstadt, A's price-cutting will assuredly not set into motion market forces that will push down the market price of grain. This assertion is reinforced in situations where the economy operates under government price controls. When A's price-cutting will not set into motion market forces that will push down the price of grain, A's conduct is regarded as an unfair competitive tactic.[63]

Sharply disputing the above view, R. Shelomoh Kluger (Ukraine, 1785–1869) avers that the sages legitimize price-cutting even when it does not set into motion market forces that will drive down the price of grain. Moreover, the tactic is legitimate even when the conduct does not force rival sellers to match the price cut. A close reading of Rashi's remarks referred to earlier, clearly demonstrates that his scenario involving a retail grain dealer is offered only as constituting the circumstances where the sages would heap praise on the price- cutter. But price-cutting is fundamentally a legitimate competitive tactic, even when it has no effect on either lowering the price of grain or lowering the price rival sellers charge for the commodity at hand.[64]

Proceeding from R. Shelomoh Kluger's interpretation of the sages is that under certain conditions Halakhah would find no objection to a non-uniform price structure for a particular commodity. This occurs when aggregate demand exceeds aggregate supply at the lower price the price-cutter (A) sets. Here, the effect of the price cut is merely to redistribute aggregate demand in favor of A but not to force rival sellers to match the price cut.

In the foregoing scenario, A should lose any right to lodge an *ona'ah* claim. This is so because *deliberate* price-cutting communicates a desire on the part of A to gain customers at the *expense* of the higher-priced rivals. Moreover, when the price cut is communicated in advertisements, giving validity to A's *ona'ah* claim amounts to nothing less than giving approval to a deceptive advertising technique.

If an *ona'ah* claim is invalid for a deliberate price-cutter, then, rival sellers should be under no obligation to inform customers of the lower-priced opportunity A offers. This is so because the law of fair competition requires rival sellers only to *tolerate* A's price cut, but does not go so far as to require them to *effectively send* customers to him.

This conclusion is reinforced by the fact that Halakhah adopts the reasonable-man standard. Given that it is common knowledge that discount, clearance, and even loss-leader sales are a feature of the modern marketplace, it is the duty of the reasonable man to inform himself of this phenomenon. If the consumer chooses not to investigate the marketplace for bargains when he is in the market for a particular item, his neglect to do so is at his own risk.

Limited Paternalism in the Secular Business Ethics Literature

Several commentators in the secular literature on business ethics have addressed the issue of paternalism in the context of personal sales situations. Professors James M. Ebejer and Michael J. Morden propose that the sales situation imposes a duty of *limited paternalism* on the salesperson vis-à-vis his customer. Carrying out this duty requires the salesperson to identify the customer's needs. He must also disclose to the customer all relevant information regarding his product or service without hiding crucial stipulations in small print.

The limited paternalism obligation, in Ebejer and Morden's view, is grounded in the presumption that the customer relies on the salesperson for his superior knowledge. Because of this reliance, the salesperson is obligated to protect the customer against an uninformed decision that could be detrimental. Since the customer cannot be presumed to rely on the salesperson in respect to expertise that is not sale-specific, the salesperson bears no responsibility to protect the customer against an uninformed decision in these matters. Therefore, informing the customer in respect to price comparisons with rival sellers is not the salesperson's responsibility.[65]

Another view of the appropriate ethic is advanced by Professor George Brockway. He is in basic agreement with Ebejer and Morden that the salesperson's duty vis-à-vis his customer in a personal sale situation is limited paternalism. But in contrast to these commentators, who ground the salesperson's duty in the customer's reliance upon his expertise, Brockway grounds the duty in the trust and dependency the customer vests in the salesperson. The limited paternalism duty concretely translates into an obligation not to knowingly allow the customer to make a self-harmful decision. Brockway refers to this as the *non-maleficence* principle.

Brockway agrees that the salesperson is not required to provide his customer with comparative price information. In Brockway's thinking, the salesperson is relieved of this duty simply because the customer never vested him with trust and dependency in respect to this matter.

The moral ethics of limited paternalism makes the salesperson, to a certain extent, "his buyer's keeper."[66]

In his critique of Ebejer and Morden, Professor Kerry S. Walters demonstrates that subscription to the *limited* paternalism ethic leads to the peculiar claim that an agent's hands are clean if he conforms to the formal prescriptions of a role-specific obligation, even when he allows something to be done that runs counter to his personal moral convictions. To illustrate: Suppose A believes tobacco is a harmful product. Nonetheless, on the basis of the limited paternalism principle, A should be allowed to sell tobacco products to B, provided only that he informs B of the medical risks involved. Similarly, suppose A is a seller of a very expensive luxury product. In his sales interaction with B, A becomes convinced that if B buys the product, he will, in consequence, be depriving himself of basic necessities. Here again, on the basis of the limited paternalism principle, A washes his hands of the matter by simply confessing his reservations to B. Both these conclusions are, for Walters, morally unacceptable. This is so because the salesperson, like anyone else, has certain ethical obligations that extend beyond role-specific or professional ones. Because role-specific duties should never preempt the private individual's sense of personal responsibility, limited paternalism as a sales ethic is only a necessary but not a sufficient condition.

Walters offers, however, one caveat. Operating in ethically compartmentalized spheres of responsibility is not always morally unacceptable. To illustrate, suppose A sells apples that are treated with alar. Because the evidence suggesting that alar may be carcinogenic is inconclusive, it would not be unethical for A to refrain from using alar-treated apples in his private life, yet sell these apples to others, provided he makes buyers aware of the available evidence. Since A's decision to refrain from using alar-treated apples is not an uncontestable ethical judgment but, rather, an appraisal about which reasonable people can reasonably disagree, the use of the limited paternalism ethic is here morally acceptable.[67]

Secular and Halakhic Views of Limited Paternalism Compared

In comparing the halakhic perspective with the various secular business ethics approaches, a number of similarities and differences stand out.

On the similarity side, Halakhah comes down hard on the seller in respect to his disclosure obligation. The disclosure obligation is designed to protect the customer against fraud, but also to ensure a fair price as well as to protect the customer from a false sense of bargain.

There can be no doubt that the disclosure obligation is grounded in the customer's trust of the salesperson rather than in the customer's reliance on the salesperson's expertise. This can be seen from the fact that the plaintiff's rights emerging from the seller's failure to make disclosures are not diminished if the buyer is a businessman in the same line. This point is explicitly recorded in the codes in relation to the plaintiff's rights in an *ona'ah claim*.[68]

In contrast to the secular approaches, Halakhah imposes some degree of responsibility on the salesperson to protect the customer against his ignorance regarding price comparisons.

In respect to eliciting the customer's particular needs, Halakhah does not regard the role of salesperson as inherently shouldering this responsibility. Nonetheless, if the product or service of the salesperson comes in different varieties, the salesperson may not push on the customer a specific variety of his product without first eliciting the particular needs and objectives of the customer. Otherwise, the salesperson would be in violation of *lifnei iver*. A stricter standard, however, obtains for the securities industry. Because this industry operates under a due-diligence rule, the salesperson must treat risk as an inherent defect of his product. Accordingly, Halakhah's disclosure obligation applies here in full force even when the customer initiates a request for a particular financial product. Carrying out his disclosure obligation requires the salesperson to elicit the customer's investment objectives, time horizons, and degree of aversion to risk. Only then will the customer be capable of making an informed decision regarding the financial product he has requested.

Finally, let us examine from the perspective of Halakhah Walters' contention that role-specific duties should never preempt the private individual's sense of responsibility. This ethical principle, as will be recalled, can be applied to a number of scenarios. The halakhic treatment of the bulk of Walters' scenarios will be addressed elsewhere in this volume.[69] Here, we will consider only the scenario where the salesperson is convinced that the purchase at hand would be financially imprudent for the customer. For Halakhah the key here is whether the customer came into the store well focused with a particular request or with the aim of availing herself of the counsel of the salesperson. If the customer signals that she is not interested in the counseling service of the salesperson, then the latter cannot be said to be guilty of *passively* violating *lifnei iver* by allowing the customer to go forward with the purchase. The obligation of the salesperson here is merely in the area of disclosure.

Problem 1

Kloperman's car is operating very noisily. His instinct tells him that the problem is with the car's muffler and tailpipe. Kloperman brings his car into Rubie Indigo's auto repair shop and instructs Rubie to replace the car's muffler and exhaust pipes. Rubie takes down Kloperman's number and tells him that he will call when the job is done. "Expect a call in about a week," Rubie tells him.

After examining the car, Rubie discovers that the excessive noise is due to a hole in the tailpipe, and not to a faulty muffler system.

In former times, when Rubie was corrupt, he would have seized the moment to engage in veiled misconduct. To this end, he would have repaired the hole, removed the old muffler system, and then spray-painted and rein-stalled it. Kloperman would have been charged a hefty bill for a new muffler system. But Rubie is reformed and this option is unthinkable. As he sees matters, Rubie feels he has three options:

1. He can, following Kloperman's instructions, replace the muffler and exhaust pipe at a relatively high price.

2. Without consulting Kloperman, Rubie can take matters in his own hands and make a paternalistic decision for Kloperman that he does not need a new muffler system and proceed to repair the hole in the tailpipe. When Kloperman returns, Rubie will inform him what he did and say, "I was happy to save you an unnecessary expense."

3. Rubie can call Kloperman and tell him: "After examining your car I discovered that the noise problem was due to a hole in the tailpipe. If I repair the hole the noise problem will end. Do you still want me to replace your muffler system?"[70]

From the standpoint of Halakhah, which of the above options should Rubie pursue?

Problem 2

Rubie Indigo owns and runs a restaurant in Paris. For the convenience of his patrons, two menus are placed on each table. One menu lists all the dishes in French and quotes prices in francs. The other menu lists all the dishes in English and quotes prices in dollars. For each dish across the board, prices are higher in the English version of the menu.

Evaluate the ethics of Rubie's practice.

Problem 3

Professor Lance Wineman's excitement at winning a one-year fellowship from the J. B. Say Foundation was considerably deflated when he realized that the award would leave him without medical insurance coverage for the year. Wineman faced this prospect because the terms of his fellowship required him to take a leave of absence from his teaching post at Brickmire College. For the duration of his fellowship, Wineman would be off Brickmire's payroll, receiving neither salary nor benefits. The Foundation was willing to pay the salary he would have earned at Brickmire for the year of the fellowship, but not the benefit package. When Wineman inquired at Brickmire's benefit office, he was told that he had the option of remaining on the college's Blue Lance Health Insurance plan if he would continue to pay the premiums out of his own pocket. Wineman hit the roof when he learned that the premium would amount to $4,000 for the year. Confident that he could do better with a private health insurance company, Wineman stumbled into the offices of Red Spear Health Insurance Company, located just outside the Brickmire campus. One of the company's agents, Rubie Indigo, listened sympathetically to Wineman's tale of woe. Because Brickmire provided medical insurance free of charge to all faculty who were teaching, Wineman wanted to resume his coverage at Brickmire as soon as he finished his fellowship. Wineman made this point specifically to Rubie, punctuating to him that he only wanted to take out a one-year policy with Red Spear. At this juncture Wineman spouted out his sum-total knowledge of what his Blue Lance policy consisted of: "I have a $600 deductible, a 20 percent coinsurance, and a primary-doctor referral clause, can you get me the same policy for less than $4,000?" As a beaming Wineman looked on, Indigo came up with what he claimed was Red Spear's equivalent policy for only $2,500.

An excited Wineman was ready to sign up for the Red Spear policy, but Indigo knew that the policy might entail a problem for Wineman. If Wineman developed a serious medical problem during the year of his fellowship, he exposed himself to the risk that neither Blue Lance nor Red Spear would insure him in the future. Let us see why. Recall that Red Spear writes Wineman only a one-year policy. The policy Indigo has in mind is a one-year termination policy. Renewal of the policy is entirely at the discretion of Red Spear. If the company decides that Wineman is uninsurable when he finishes his fellowship, then it has every right to refuse to insure him. In a similar vein, let us not lose sight of the fact that Wineman left Blue Lance voluntarily. Blue Lance would therefore have every right to reject his reapplication by invoking the preexisting-condition clause.[71]

From the perspective of Halakhah, does Rubie Indigo have a responsibility to advise Wineman of his potential problem before he lets him sign up for the Red Spear policy?

Suppose the Red Spear policy Indigo is showing Wineman consists of ten clauses entailing various features and limitations. Is it ethical for Indigo to highlight only some of these clauses in the presentation to Wineman, and to say, "Before you sign on, please read the policy prospectus"? Should we regard this approach as throwing Wineman off and deluding him into thinking that the other clauses are not important and therefore that he need not read the prospectus?

Problem 4

Imagine yourself as head of a radiology department in a corporate-owned hospital. The institution has been in the red for five years, and before that management chose not to replace imaging equipment for financial reasons. Your CT, mammography, and ultrasound units are now outdated. As a result, you believe the quality of your patient care to be seriously compromised.

What do you do? Make the best of a bad situation and try to ignore the problem, or inform patients and referring physicians that you consider the care you provide to be substandard?[72]

1. Maimonides (Egypt, 1135–1204), *Yad*, Mekhirah 15:5; R. Jacob b. Asher (Germany, 1270–1343), *Tur*, Hoshen Mishpat 232:6; R. Joseph Caro (Israel, 1488–1575) *Shulhan Arukh*, Hoshen Mishpat 232:6; R. Jehiel Michel Epstein (Belarus, 1829–1908), *Arukh ha-Shulhan*, Hoshen Mishpat 232:7.

2. R. Yom Tov Vidal of Tolosa (Spain, 14th cent.), *Maggid Mishneh* at *Yad*, op. cit. 15:4.

3. *Ar.haSh.*, op. cit. 232:6.

4. *Yad*, op. cit. 15:4; *Tur*, op. cit. 232:4; *Sh.Ar.*, op. cit. 232:4; *Ar.haSh.*, op. cit. 232:6.

5. *Yad*, op. cit. 15:4; *Tur*, op. cit. 232:4; *Sh.Ar.*, op. cit. 232:4; *Ar.haSh.*, op. cit. 232:6.

6. *Yad*, op. cit. 15:6; *Tur*, op. cit. 232:7; *Sh.Ar.*, op. cit. 232:7.

7. R. Isaac b. Sheshet Perfet, *Responsa Ribash* 403; *Ar.haSh.*, op. cit. 228:3.

8. R. Yaakov Yeshayahu Bloi (Israel, 1929–), *Pithei Hoshen*, Hilkhot Genevah ve-Ona'ah 12:1 n.2 and 12:4.

9. Hullin 94a.

10. R. Joshua b. Alexander ha-Kohen Falk (Poland, 1555–1614), Sma to *Sh.Ar.*, op. cit. 228 n. 7; *Ar.haSh.*, op. cit. 228:3.

11. Mishnah, Bava Mezia 4:12; Rif, ad loc., *Yad*, op. cit. 18:2; R. Asher b. Jehiel (Germany, 1250–1327), Rosh, Bava Mezia 4:24; *Tur*, op. cit. 228:9; *Sh.Ar.*, op. cit. 228:9; *Ar.haSh.*, op. cit. 228:5.

12. R. Solomon b. Isaac (France, 1040–1105), Rashi, Hullin 94a.

13. Ibid.

14. Tosafot to ibid.

15. Bezah 16a.

16. Rashi to ibid.

17. Illustrating the phenomenon of cognitive dissonance is Kassarjian and Cohen's study of the effect the Surgeon General's Report had on smokers' attitudes and behavior. The findings showed that 36.5 percent of the surveyed smokers did not believe that the report had established a linkage between smoking and cancer. Moreover, the figure among heavy smokers was 41 percent, suggesting that the more committed one is to a product, the greater the dissonance and the less likely one is to admit the product's adverse effect. Study cited in Richard L. Oliver, "An Interpretation of the Attitudinal and Behavioral Effects of Puffery," *Journal of Consumer Affairs* 13, no. 1, (March 1979): 827.

18. Hullin 94a.

19. Rashi at Hullin 94a. See, however, R. Gershom b. Judah Me'Or ha-Golah (Hullin 94a), who follows Rashi's line in his understanding of the wine-barrel case but interprets it as referring to a *commercial* setting.

20. The Mishnah is divided into six orders (*sedarim*): (1) Zeraim ("seeds"), (2) Mo'ed

("festivals"), (3) Nashim ("women"), 4) Nezikin ("damages"), (5) Kodashim ("holy things"), and (6) Toharot ("purities"). The various tractates of the Babylonian Talmud fit into these orders, but Kodashim and Toharot are not found in the Jerusalem Talmud.

21. Please turn to pp. 40–41 of this volume.

22. R. Binyamin Rabinovits-Teomim, Hukkat Mishpat 16:1, be'urim 2, n. 2.

23. R. Mosheh Feinstein, *Iggerot Mosheh*, Yoreh De'ah 1:30–31.

24. R. Yehoshua Baumol, *Responsa Emek Halakhah* 2:4–6.

25. Sma to *Sh.Ar.*, op. cit. 232, n. 57.

26. Samuel, Bava Batra 92b; Rif, ad loc., Rosh, Bava Batra 6:2; *Tur*, op. cit. 232:23; *Sh.Ar.*, op. cit. 232:23; *Ar.haSh.*, op. cit. 232:36. A variant on the case dealt with in the text obtains when B performs a symbolic act (*kinyan*) on the ox but does not hand over to S any part of the purchasing price. Upon discovering that the ox is vicious, B desires to cancel the transaction. See *Ar.haSh.*, loc. cit.

27. *Tur*, op. cit.; *Sh.Ar.*, op. cit.; *Ar.haSh.*, op. cit.

28. R. Yom Tov Lipmann G. Nathan ha-Levi Heller, *Filpula Harifta*, Rosh, Bava Batra 5, n. 2.

29. *Torat Kohanim* at Leviticus 19:14; *Yad*, Rozeah 12:14.

30. *New York Stock Exchange Guide* (New York: Commerce Clearing House, 1994), Constitution and Rules, vol. 2, par. 2405, rule 405.

31. Conversation with Alfred A. Freeman, CFA, vice-president of investments with Josephthal & Co. Inc. I am indebted to Rabbi Freeman for locating the New York Stock Exchange rule cited in the preceding footnote.

32. R. Mordecai Yaakov Breisch, *Helkat Ya'akov* 3:136.

33. Sifra at Leviticus 19:16, ot 41.

34. R. Israel Meir ha-Kohen Kagan, *Hafez Hayyim, Be'er Mayim Hayyim*, Hilkhot Issurei Rekhilut 9:1.

35. See Sanhedrin 73a.

36. Mishnah, Bava Mezia 2:13; Rif, Bava Mezia 33a; *Yad*, Gezelah 12:1; Rosh, Bava Mezia 2:30; *Tur*, op. cit. 264:1; *Sh.Ar.*, op. cit. 264:1; *Ar.haSh.*, op. cit. 264:1.

37. R. Judah, Bava Mezia 33a, and Rashi ad loc.; *Ar.haSh.*, loc. cit.

38. R. Mosheh Isserles (Poland, 1525 or 1530–1572), Rema, *Sh.Ar.*, Orah Hayyim 656:1. See also *Sedai Hemed*, vol. 9, pp. 7, 64.

39. R. Mosheh Sofer, *Responsa Hatam Sofer*, Hoshen Mishpat 177 and his gloss at *Sh.Ar.* Orah Hayyim 656:1.

For an extended discussion of the one-fifth rule as it pertains to the disclosure of professional confidences, see Alfred S. Cohen, "Privacy: A Jewish Perspective," *Journal of Halakhah and Contemporary Society* 1, no. 1 (Spring 1981): 81–102. For an opposing view in respect to this issue, see Mosheh ha-Levi Spero, "Halakhic Definitions of Confidentiality in the Psychotherapeutic Encounter: Theory and Practice," *Tradition* 20, no. 4 (Winter 1982): 313–14, fn. 73.

For support of Rabbi Cohen's position, see R. Hanokh Agus (Poland, 1860–1940), *Marheshet* 1:43; and R. Eliezer Yehudah Waldenberg (Israel, contemp.), *Responsa Ziz Eliezer* 19:1.

The one-fifth rule does not validate passively violating Halakhah when the issue is danger to human life. See R. Israel Meir ha-Kohen Kagan, *Ahavat Hesed* 2:20, n. 2. See, however, *Ziz Eliezer* ad loc.

40. Please turn to pp. 310–11 of this volume.

41. Please turn to pp. 24–27 of this volume.

42. Baraita, Bava Mezia 51a; Rif, ad loc.; *Yad*, op. cit. 12:1; Rosh, Bava Mezia 4:17; *Tur*, op. cit. 227:1; *Sh.Ar.*, op. cit. 227:1; *Ar.haSh.*, op. cit. 227:1.

43. Bava Mezia 61a; *Tur*, op. cit. 227:1; Sma, *Sh.Ar.*, Hoshen Mishpat 227, n. 1.

44. Bava Batra 78a and Rashi ad loc.; Rif, ad loc.; *Yad*, op. cit. 27:5; Rosh, Bava Batra 5:7; *Tur*, op. cit. 220:5; *Sh.Ar.*, op. cit. 220:8; *Ar.haSh.*, op. cit. 220:7.

45. Bava Mezia 50b; Rif, ad loc.; *Yad*, op. cit. 12:4; Rosh, Bava Mezia 4:15; *Tur*, op. cit. 227:6; *Sh.Ar.*, op. cit. 227:4; *Ar.haSh.*, op. cit. 227:3.

46. Bava Mezia 50b; Rif, ad loc.; *Yad*, op. cit. 12:2; Rosh, op. cit. 4:15; *Tur*, op. cit. 227:3; *Sh.Ar.*, op. cit. 227:2; *Ar.haSh.* loc. cit.

47. Bava Mezia 50b; Rif, ad loc.; *Yad*, op. cit. 12:3; *Tur*, op. cit. 227:4; *Sh.Ar.*, loc. cit.; *Ar.haSh.*, loc. cit.

48. *Ar.haSh.*, op. cit. 227:7.

49. Rema, *Sh.Ar.*, op. cit. 227:7.

R. Joel Sirkes (Bah at *Tur*, op. cit. 227, n. 9) understands the talmudic case as referring to the instance where B did not conclude the deal until he had first declared in the presence of witnesses his intention to launch a second-degree *ona'ah* claim against S. Here, B's conduct clearly demonstrates that he does not waive his *ona'ah* rights in the matter.

Bah disputes Rema and takes the position that plaintiff loses his *ona'ah* rights in Rema's case.

50. Bava Batra 78a and Rashi ad loc.; Rif, ad loc.; *Yad*, op. cit. 27:5; Rosh, Bava Batra 5:7; *Tur*, op. cit. 220:5; *Sh.Ar.,* op. cit. 220:8; *Ar.haSh.*, op. cit. 220:7.

51. Rosh, Bava Mezia 4:20.

52. See, however, R. Yohanan's opinion at Jerusalem Talmud, Bava Mezia 13b.

53. Jerusalem Talmud, loc. cit.

54. Mishnah, Erkhin 6:5.

55. Nahmanides (Spain, 1194–1270), Ramban, Kiddushin 12a.

56. R. Yom Tov Ishbili (Spain, ca. 1250–1330), Ritva, Kiddushin 12a.

57. R. Abraham David Wahrmann, *Kesef ha-Kedoshim* at *Sh.Ar.*, op. cit. 227:9.

58. Mishnah, Bava Mezia 4:12.

59. Bava Mezia 60a–60b.

60. *Yad*, Mekhirah 18:4; *Tur*, op. cit. 228:18; *Sh.Ar.*, op. cit. 228:18; *Ar.haSh.*, op. cit. 228:18.

61. R. Meir b. Isaac Eisenstadt, *Panim Me'irot* 1:78; *Ar. haSh.*, loc. cit.; R. Judah Leib Graubart (Russia and Canada, 1861–1937), *Havalim ba-Neimim* 2:113.

62. Rashi, Bava Mezia 60b.

63. *Panim Me'irot*, loc. cit.; see also *Ar.haSh.*, loc. cit.

64. R. Shelomoh Kluger, *Hokhmat Shelomoh* at *Sh.Ar.*, op. cit. 228:18.

65. James M. Ebejer and Michael J. Morden, "Paternalism in the Marketplace: Should a Salesman Be His Buyer's Keeper?" *Journal of Business Ethics* 7 (1988): 337–39.

66. George Brockway, "Limited Paternalism and the Salesperson: A Reconsideration," *Journal of Business Ethics* 12 (1993): 275–79.

67. Kerry S. Walters, "Limited Paternalism and the Pontius Pilate Plight," *Journal of Business Ethics* 8 (1989): 955–62.

68. *Tanna Kamma*, Mishnah, Bava Mezia 4:4; *Yad,* op. cit. 12:8; *Tur*, op. cit. 227:14; *Ar.haSh.*, op. cit. 227:15.

69. Please turn to pp. 387–88 of this volume.

70. Adapted from Walters, "Limited Paternalism," p. 956.

71. Adapted from Thomas I. Carson, "Ethical Issues in Sales: Two Case Studies," *Journal of Business Ethics* 17 (1998): 725–28.

72. Peter I. Ogle, "Business Ethics Can Tarnish Medicine's Nobler Traditions," *Diagnostic Imaging*, February 1999, p. 7.

Make the Customer Like You: The Limits of Flattery

Harry Lev is a very successful auto salesman. He ascribes his good fortune to the personal bond he establishes with his customers. People, Harry explains, are generally averse to dealing with a stranger. To be receptive to a sales pitch, a prospect must first like the salesperson. But the customer will not like the salesperson unless the salesperson *likes him first.* Before he delivers his sales pitch, Harry attempts in various ways to make his prospect like him.

Typically, Harry begins by telling the prospect something about himself. This usually induces the prospect to reciprocate. Over the years, Harry has become quite adept at sizing up people very quickly. He usually can pick up on something in the personality, profession, or background of the prospect that he *genuinely* finds admirable or, at least, redeeming. Harry is sure to compliment or otherwise show the customer respect or appreciation for this attribute or quality. Only then does Harry proceed with his sales pitch.

Relatedly, experience has taught Harry that maintaining a cheerful countenance is an invaluable asset for a salesperson. Colleagues often observe Harry smiling while speaking to a customer on the telephone. According to Harry, doing this puts a *smile in his voice.*

To make a customer feel special, Harry will occasionally reveal a secret about the deal and urge the customer not to publicize it. Harry's favorite is to whisper to a prospect that the manufacturer's guarantee may well extend beyond what is explicitly mentioned in the warranty. In hushed tones, Harry goes on to explain that in the event a significant number of new-model cars report the same mechanical problem, the manufacturer may inform distributors that it will cover the cost of repair beyond the standard warranty. The problem is, he says, that neither manufacturers nor dealers publicize these *informal* warranties. But the Center for Auto Safety, an auto-complaint clearinghouse, monitors these matters and can deduce which components are likely to fall under informal warranties. When he finishes telling all this to the customer, Harry writes down the name and address of the clearing house on his business card and hands it over to the appreciative customer.[1] Harry concludes with a soft admonition not to publicize what he has revealed.

Harry invests much time and energy in acquiring esoteric information that people can use to their great advantage in everyday life experiences. Harry is sure to adroitly weave this valuable information into his pre–sales talk conversations with his customers. If air travel, for instance, comes up in the conversation, Harry, exuberantly citing chapter and verse of his authoritative source, will pontificate that for the 747 jet, rows 11–18 provide the smoothest ride.[2] Providing valuable tidbits, Harry feels, lowers the customer's resistance to sales talk, increasing the likelihood of a sale.

Committed to professional growth, Harry keeps abreast of the latest innovative sales techniques, especially those that are designed to make the customer like the salesperson. Recently, Harry added the following technique to his repertoire. With the aim of making customers not regard him as a stranger, Harry breaks up the sales meeting twice; once for a coffee break, and a second time to afford the customer(s) the liberty to think matters through in privacy. In Harry's own words, "Conducting business this way makes the customer feel that he has met with me not once, but three times. By the time I am ready to zero in on my final sales pitch, the customer no longer regards me as a stranger."[3]

Make the Customer Like You: A Halakhic Analysis

Making someone feel good about himself is certainly admirable. Such conduct fulfills the biblical precept to "love your neighbor as [you love] yourself" (Leviticus 19:18). By making his customer like him, Harry not only becomes a more productive salesperson, but he apparently transforms a business encounter into a mitzvah performance of "love your neighbor."

To be sure, fulfillment of "love your neighbor" in its ideal form obtains only when the conduct is driven by a desire to uplift one's fellow purely and solely for the sake of doing so. This level of performance of a mitzvah is called *lishmah* (lit. for its own sake). But in the case at hand, Harry's conduct is driven by an ulterior motive. Specifically, it is his expectation that "love your neighbor" conduct will pave the way to a sales commission. Nonetheless, Harry's ulterior motive does not empty his "love your neighbor" conduct of its mitzvah content; it only reduces its level of performance to what is called *shelo lishmah* (lit. not for its own sake). Pertinent here is the following talmudic dictum: "A man should always occupy himself with Torah and good deeds, even if it is not for their own sake; out of [doing good] with an ulterior motive there comes [doing good] for its own sake."[4] We should note that the legitimacy of Harry's artificially exuding a cheerful countenance need not resort to the *shelo lishmah* rationale. Rather, the conduct constitutes proper social etiquette. Its appropriateness finds expression in Shammai's dictum: ". . . and receive everyone with a cheerful face" (Avot 1:15).

As a sales tactic, making the customer feel good about himself is subject to a restriction. It enjoys validity only when the compliment or the appreciation the salesperson exudes is *sincere*. Should the sentiment expressed amount to nothing more than false praise (*hanuppah*), the conduct is prohibited. The condemnation of flattery by Maimonides (Egypt, 1135–1204) is instructive here: "It is forbidden to accustom oneself to smooth speech and flatteries. One must not say one thing and mean another. Inward and outward self should correspond; only what we have in mind, should we utter with the mouth."[5]

It should not be concluded, however, that engaging in false praise is absolutely forbidden as a sales tactic. The halakhic prohibition of falsehood is not absolute, and under certain conditions it is suspended. Examining these exceptions to the prohibition against falsehood, however, will demonstrate that their application to the area of sales practice is very limited. We begin with the talmudic text at Ketubbot 17a:

> Our rabbis taught: How does one dance before the bride? [i.e., what does one sing to or say to the bride?] Bet Shammai say: "The bride as she is." And Bet Hillel say: "Beautiful and gracious bride!" But Bet Shammai said to Bet Hillel: "If she was lame or blind, does one say to her, 'Beautiful and gracious bride,' even though the Torah said, *Keep thee far from a false matter* (Exodus 23:7)?" Said Bet Hillel to Bet Shammai: "According to your words, if a person makes a bad purchase in the market, should one praise it in his eyes or deprecate it? Surely one should praise it in his eyes." Therefore, the sages said: "Man's disposition should always be pleasant with people."

It follows from Bet Hillel's view, which Halakhah adopts as normative,[6] that the practice of engaging in false praise is legitimate in specific instances. Let us investigate the underlying rationale for Bet Hillel's view.

One rationale for Bet Hillel is offered by R. Yom Tov Ishbili (Spain, ca. 1250–1330). In his view, Bet Hillel espouses the principle of *darkhei shalom* (lit. ways of peace).[7] What this principle asserts is that falsehood is legitimate conduct when its purpose is to end conflict and/or to avert the outbreak of discord. Three illustrations of the principle are recorded at Yevamot 65b:

> R. Ile'a further stated in the name of R. Eleazar son of R. Shimon: One may modify a statement in the interest of peace; for it is said in Scripture, *your father gave us final instruction. He said, "This is what you must say to Joseph: Forgive the spiteful deed and the sin your brothers committed when they did evil to you"* (Genesis 50:16–17).
>
> R. Nathan said it is a commandment; for it is stated in Scripture, *and Samuel said: "How can I go? If Saul hears it, he will kill me"* (I Samuel 16:2). [In response to this, God advised Samuel to say that he came to *sacrifice to the Lord* (ibid.), though his mission, in fact, was to anoint David as King.]
>
> At the school of R. Ishmael it was taught: Great is the cause of peace, seeing that for its sake even the Holy One, blessed be He, modified a statement; for at first it is written, *my husband is old* (Genesis 18:12), while afterward it is written, [*God said to Abraham, Why did Sarah laugh and say, "Can I really have a child when*] *I am so old?"* (Genesis 18:12).

Take note that in the three illustrations cited above, *darkhei shalom* conduct is designed to accomplish much more than just the enhancement of the quality of interpersonal relations. Rather, it is designed either to end conflict or to avert the outbreak of discord. Specifically, Joseph's conduct after the death of his father (Jacob) conveyed to his brothers that he harbored a grudge against them for selling him into slavery.[8] Similarly, the cover God provides Samuel is given to avert the civil war that would inevitably have erupted if the true nature of Samuel's mission became known. Finally, God did not tell Abraham that Sarah had questioned his virility in order to spare Abraham the slight, thereby preserving domestic harmony for Abraham and Sarah.

The preceding analysis shows that *darkhei shalom* does not suspend the prohibition against falsehood unless its purpose is to end conflict or avert the eruption of discord. If the conduct is merely intended to enhance the quality of human relations, the prohibition against falsehood is not suspended. Now, if Bet Hillel's position falls under the rubric of *darkhei shalom* conduct, it must meet this test.

Let us take up the bridal-praise formula first. To see why Bet Hillel's formula works not only to raise the spirits of the newlywed couple but also to avert discord, we need only speculate on the state of affairs that would exist in the absence of the uniform formula. To begin, note that there is a rabbinical[9] precept to gladden the heart of a newlywed couple.[10] An essential feature of the precept apparently consists of complimenting the groom on the bride's beauty and grace.[11] Absent a uniform formula, there would be a great disparity in the treatment of newlywed couples. The compliment "beautiful and gracious bride" would hardly be heard at a wedding where the bride does not radiate these attributes. Proclaiming each and every bride beautiful and gracious, therefore, reduces or otherwise discourages invidious comparisons, averting envy and discord.

Let us now turn to the bad-purchase case. Within the framework of the *darkhei shalom* rationale, engaging in false praise should be legitimate only when the alternative of truth-telling does not better promote peace of mind for the vendee. This would be the case, for instance, when the vendee does not recall where he bought the articles. Since he has no recourse to undo or otherwise modify the transaction he entered into, telling the truth serves no useful purpose; it only makes the vendee feel foolish. False praise, on the other hand, helps the vendee make the best of his situation. Suppose, however, that the vendee does recall where the purchase was made and is a victim of an overcharge or the article has a defect. Here, false praise is decidedly against the interests of the vendee. Instead, he should be apprised of his mistake.

Without invoking the *darkhei shalom* rationale, both R. Samuel b. Joseph Strashun (Lithuania, 1794–1872)[12] and R. Israel Meir ha-Kohen Kagan (Poland, 1838–1933)[13] understand the bad-purchase case in the vein discussed above.

Another rationale for Bet Hillel is offered by R. Judah Loew b. Bezalel (Maharal, Worms, ca. 1525–1609) et al. Falsehood, in this view, applies only to mischaracterizing an objective reality. But in respect to aesthetic judgments, it is a matter of individual taste. Proclaiming every bride beautiful and gracious does not violate the prohibition against falsehood. To be sure, in specific instances the formula will run counter to popular sentiment. Nevertheless, the description presumably conforms with the bridegroom's feeling in the matter. If he did not find his prospective bride beautiful and charming, he presumably would not have married her. What constitutes beauty is a *judgmental* matter. Pronouncing the bride beautiful and gracious does not, therefore, amount to a mischaracterization of reality, notwithstanding majority opinion to the contrary. Similarly, approving the buyer's "unseemly" purchase does not amount to falsehood, as a sales transaction creates a presumption of buyer satisfaction.[14]

In Maharal's view, what the speaker intends to impart by uttering Hillel's formula is that the bride is beautiful and charming *in the eyes of the bridegroom*.

One could raise an objection. Notwithstanding the intentions of the speaker, the formula may generate a false impression to the bridegroom. Specifically, the bridegroom may take the remark to impart that the speaker *independently* shares the bridegroom's sentiment that his bride is beautiful and gracious. Maharal's rationale solves the issue of falsehood but apparently leaves open the difficulty that the formula creates the setting for violation of generating a false impression (*geneivat da'at*).

Maharal implicitly addresses this difficulty by expressing a preference for the bridal-praise formula that the Babylonian Talmud tells us was used in the land of Israel: "There is neither paint nor polish nor hair dying, and nevertheless she is graceful."[15] More than Bet Hillel's formula, this one makes it clear that the speaker is merely mouthing the sentiments of the bridegroom without necessarily agreeing.

Resolution of the difficulty perhaps lies in the recognition that *geneivat da'at* is not violated when the victim is guilty of self-deception.[16]

The self-deception caveat explains why Bet Hillel's formula does not inevitably result in violation of the *geneivat da'at* interdict. Since the sages established the same praise formula for each and every bride, the only *reasonable* meaning to put into the formula is the common-denominator meaning that *every bridegroom* can read into it. The compelling or reasonable reading of the formula is no more than a mouthing of the sentiments of the bridegroom. Reading anything more than this into the speaker's statement that "the bride is beautiful and gracious" makes the bridegroom guilty of self-deception.

Another rationale for Bet Hillel's position, espoused by R. Nethanel b.

Naphtali Zevi Weil (Germany 1687–1769), is based on the observation that "beautiful and gracious" can refer to a bride's *deeds* as well as to her physical appearance and personality. If the speaker regards some aspect of the bride's deeds as admirable, use of Bet Hillel's formula does not make him guilty of false praise even if she is generally regarded as neither physically beautiful nor as having a gracious personality. Under the presumption that something can be found about the bride's deeds that is redeeming,[17] proclaiming the bride to be beautiful and gracious should not constitute false praise in the unbeautiful-bride case, even if the bride is a stranger to the speaker.[18]

The difficulty raised earlier in connection with Maharal's rationale is equally compelling here. Specifically, use of an invariant praise formula inevitably results in instances where the bridegroom takes the compliment "beautiful and gracious" to refer to his bride's physical appearance or personality, when, in fact, the speaker is referring only to her deeds. R. Weil's rationale resolves the falsehood issue, but the *geneivat da'at* issue apparently remains.

To resolve the difficulty, we need only resort to the self-deception caveat, referred to earlier. In *everyday usage*, "beautiful and gracious" refers to physical appearance and personality traits. But by mandating the phrase "beautiful and gracious" as a *uniform* bridal praise formula, it is clear that the rabbis intended this phrase to fit *each and every bride*. The only meaning that makes this possible is to understand "beautiful and gracious" as referring to the bride's *deeds* rather than to her physical appearance or personality.

In the context of the rabbinically mandated praise formula, "beautiful and gracious" takes on a meaning different from everyday usage. Given the knowledge that the compliment "beautiful and gracious" is directed at *each and every bride*, the bridegroom should not reasonably read into the compliment anything more than what the rabbis intended these words to denote. If the bridegroom takes the compliment as referring to his bride's physical appearance or personality, but the speaker referred only to her deeds, the bridegroom is guilty of self-deception. Thus the use of Bet Hillel's formula does not violate *geneivat da'at*.

It may be concluded from the foregoing discussion that Halakhah affords some latitude to engage in false praise. The application to the world of commerce, however, is very limited.

Recall that *darkhei shalom* does not become an operative factor in a commercial context until the transaction is already complete. Thus, engaging in insincere flattery of a customer as a means of inducing him to be receptive to a sales pitch is an unacceptable sales practice. Likewise unethical is the practice of exuding feigned enthusiasm for the product in order to induce a sale. To be sure, exaggerations relating to the performance domain may misrepresent the product in a material way and entail outright fraud.

Once the transaction is complete, buyer (B) satisfaction with the product may be presumed. Since B at this juncture is effectively stuck with his purchase, it is ethical for A to offer him reassurance that he has made a fine purchase. A's false praise here is legitimate even if it was volunteered and was not solicited by B.

If *darkhei shalom* is what validates false praise in the bad-purchase case, then it should apparently make no difference whether the person offering the false praise is a third party or the salesperson. But this is not so. If A is the salesperson in the transaction at hand, the false praise must not go beyond reassuring the customer that he has received full value for his money. Inveigling the customer into believing that he has obtained a bargain when in fact this is not the case generates a false sense of indebtedness on the part of the customer. This would be a violation of the prohibition against creating a false impression (*geneivat da'at*). It is analogous to the talmudic case involving the sale to a non-Jew of meat originating from an organically defective animal. Duping the customer into believing he is getting a bargain by misrepresenting the meat as originating from a healthy animal constitutes *geneivat da'at*.[19] While price fraud may not be involved, as the non-Jew is charged a fair price for what he actually receives, the transaction is, nonetheless, prohibited, since it leaves the customer with a feeling of obligation to the storekeeper that is undeserved.[20]

Creating a false sense of bargain is a prohibited sales technique, whether it is used as a means of closing the deal or foisted on the customer only after the deal is completed.

Recall that Maharal validates false praise in the bad-purchase case because it presumably expresses the sentiments of the buyer. The license for false praise amounts, therefore, to nothing more than affirming respect for the purchaser's judgment. Going beyond this violates the *geneivat da'at* interdict.

Problem

Harry Lev is an antique and oil painting dealer. Very much eager to obtain customer referrals, Lev does not want a customer to walk away from a *done deal* with any lingering doubts. Accordingly, if Lev picks up any bad vibrations after the deal is struck, he will typically say the following: "Mr. customer, have no regrets about your purchase. If you had not bought the item, many others would have snapped it up. I'll tell you a secret, if you had not bought it, I would have bought it *myself.*"

Evaluate the halakhic ethics of Lev's practice.

1. Center for Auto Safety, 2001 S Street, N.W., Washington, D.C. 20009, tel. 202-328-7700.

2. *The Book of Inside Information* (Greenwich, Conn.: Boardroom Classics, 1995), p. 369.

3. James W. Pickens, *The Art of Closing Any Deal* (New York: Warner Books, 1991), pp. 109–11.

4. Pesahim 50b.

5. Maimonides, *Yad*, De'ot 2:6.

6. R. Jacob b. Asher (Germany, 1270–1343), *Tur*, Even ha-Ezer 65:l; R. Joseph Caro (Israel, 1488–1575), *Shulhan Arukh*, Even ha-Ezer 65:1; R. Jehiel Michel Epstein (Belarus, 1829–1908), Even ha-Ezer 65:1.

7. R. Yom Tov Ishbili, Ritva, Ketubbot 16b.

8. Genesis Rabbah 100:8.

9. *Yad*, Avel 14:1.

10. *Tur*, op. cit. 65:1; *Sh.Ar.*, op. cit. 65:1; *Ar.haSh.*, op. cit. 65:1.

11. Ibid. and Rav Ashi, Berakhot 6b.

12. R. Samuel b. Joseph Strashun, Rashash, Ketubbot 17a.

13. R. Israel Meir ha-Kohen Kagen, *Hilkhot Issurei Rekhilut K'lal* 9:12.

14. Maharal, Ketubbot 17a.

15. Ketubbot 17a.

16. Hullin 94a.

17. Cf. Eruvim 19a.

18. R. Nethanel b. Naphtali Levi Weil, *Korban Netanel* at Rosh, Ketubbot 2:2, n. 4.

19. Samuel at Hullin 94a.

20. *Ar.haSh.*, op. cit. 228:3.

4. Pricing Policies

Trading on Superior and Insider Information

Voluntary exchange is often predicated upon asymmetrical information on the part of the parties to the transaction. Without the informational advantage, the transaction would presumably have been concluded on terms less favorable to the party possessing the superior information.

Our purpose in the following series of cases will be to investigate the ethics of trading on superior information as treated in Jewish law.

Trading on superior information classifies itself into two categories of cases. In the first category, the only moral issue involves the ethics of not sharing the superior information with one's opposite number. In the second category, the moral dilemma expands because the trade entails misappropriation of the superior information and/or the violation of some other ethical norm. As a means of distinguishing the two kinds of cases, we refer to the former category as trading on superior information and the latter as trading on insider information.

The Mineral Rights Case

Beginning in 1957, Texas Gulf Sulphur (TGS) conducted exploratory activities on its property located on the Canadian Shield in eastern Canada. After aerial geophysical surveys discovered numerous anomalies, i.e., unusual variations in the conductivity of rocks, it was decided that it would be very promising to conduct a diamond-core drilling operation for further evaluation. Analysis of the core of the initial hole indicated a remarkable mineral ore strike. The discovery convinced TGS that it was desirable to acquire the mineral rights of the surrounding property owners. To facilitate these acquisitions, the president of TGS instructed the exploration group to keep the results of the drilling operation confidential and undisclosed even to the other officers, directors, and employees of TGS. In addition, the hole was concealed and a barren core was intentionally drilled off the anomaly. Having taken these measures, TGS proceeded with its land-acquisition program.[1]

The government found nothing objectionable in the secrecy TGS employed in acquiring mineral rights to the surrounding properties. This was apparently common practice in the mining industry.[2]

The Mineral Rights Case and Halakhah

The most salient feature of the transaction described in the preceding section is that TGS entered into the negotiations with superior knowledge. Does TGS' informational advantage make the transaction at hand inherently unfair? No. Recall that the disclosure obligation is geared to the reasonable expectations of one's opposite number.[3] Consider that in the case at hand the relationship between the parties involved is decidedly *adversarial*. By bidding, say, $7,500 for the property, TGS is communicating to the landowner that the property is worth *more* than $7,500 to the company. Because the transaction is by nature adversarial, the onus is on the landowner to conduct geological tests to determine whether TGS' bid is fair. If the landowner is willing to accept the bid without making an investment to determine the mineralization of the property, he is at his own risk. To insist that TGS surrender the results of its geological tests at the negotiation session is to make the landowner into a TGS partner instead of a seller of land to the company.

Before the negotiation, TGS took action to conceal any trace of its geological test. It did so by moving its drill rig away from the original core site and concealed the location by filling the hole with saplings. The company went on to drill a second hole off the anomaly to produce a barren core.[4] TGS' evasive actions should not be viewed as a *geneivat da'at* (creating a false impression) violation against the landowner.[5] Consider that the superior information TGS comes into the negotiation with is an advantage the company itself created by means of its investment. The company should therefore be within its right to protect its investment from free-riding.

Relatedly, suppose TGS is anxious that direct and open contact with the landowners will tip off its mineral find. Accordingly, TGS sets up a subsidiary corporation, ASL, to approach the landowners with a bid. ASL presents itself as a land-acquisition company. Is this tactic unethical? No. Consider that the transaction at hand is not governed by any competitive norm. Instead, the negotiation itself will determine the price of the parcels of land. What TGS accomplishes with this stratagem is to capture a larger gain for owning the land than would be possible had the company entered the negotiations without masquerading its true identity. But let us not forget that the parties in the negotiations are in an *adversarial* relationship. The onus is on the landowners to grill ASL with queries such as: Do you know of any investments made in our land to determine its mineralization? Are you a principal or an agent? Are you an independent company or a subsidiary of some other company? ASL can refuse to answer these questions. But if it does answer them, it must do so in a forthright manner. If the landowners fail to pursue these inquiries, it is at their own risk.

Umdana and TGS' Land-Acquisition Negotiation

In evaluating the halakhic validity of TGS' land-acquisition negotiation, let us bring into the analysis the principle of *umdana* (inferential fact determination).

Umdana retroactively voids a transaction when it is evident that if certain information had been known at the time of negotiation, the transaction would not have been entered into. Illustrating *umdana* is the following talmudic case, recorded at Ketubbot 97a: During a time of dearth in Nehardea, people sold their houses in order to raise cash to buy grain. However, at the time the sale of the houses were being effected, ships carrying grain were waiting in the bay for the high waters to subside. The arrival of new grain supplies would naturally have depressed grain prices and obviated the need of the people to sell their mansions to raise cash. Had the Nehardeans only known of the impending arrival of the grain ships, they surely would not have sold their houses. On the basis of *umdana*, R. Nahman ruled that the sales of the houses were retroactively void. Likewise, *umdana* should retroactively render null and void the TGS mineral rights contracts. Had the surrounding property owners only shared the secret of TGS' mineral strike, they certainly would not have agreed to the terms of the TGS offer.

Despite the affinity between the two cases, *umdana* cannot work to vitiate the TGS mineral rights contracts. We offer the following three rationales to support this assertion:

1. According to R. Abraham David Wahrmann (Ukraine, ca. 1771–1840), *umdana*, as an independent legal principle, works to void a transaction only when the presumption leads to the assertion that had the plaintiff only been equipped with the informational advantage, he would have *walked* away from the transaction.

This requirement is satisfied in the talmudic case at Ketubbot 97a. Circumstances made it evident that the Nehardeans were interested in selling their houses *only as a means of raising cash to pay the soaring price of grain*. Had the typical Nehardean only known that new grain supplies were on the way at the time he was negotiating the sale of his house, he surely would have walked away from the negotiations.[6]

This is not the case, however, in the mineral rights transaction. Here there is no evidence that TGS' bid to the landowners coincided with a landowner's need to raise cash to finance some pressing need. Quite to the contrary, there was every indication that the landowners were interested in TGS' bid on its own merits and as an end in itself. Accordingly, what the landowners would have done had they shared the secret of the mineral find is purely speculative. They might have held out for a higher bid or perhaps even walked away from the transaction. One thing is, however, certain. There is no basis to assert that had the landowners known the secret they would *presumably* have walked away from the deal.

2. As Tosafot points out, *umdana* is an *ex ante* rather than an *ex post facto* calculation. Dissatisfaction with the outcome of a transaction does not work to void it unless it is evident that the disaffected party would not have agreed to incur the *risk* of the unfavorable event.[7] To illustrate, suppose B buys an ox from S explicitly for the purpose of slaughtering it. Upon completion of the sale, B slaughters the ox and discovers that it is *trefa* (organically defective) and hence forbidden to be consumed. Halakhah rules that unless physical evidence can be found in the carcass that indicates that the animal was already a *trefa* at the time the sale was completed, B has no recourse to cancel the transaction.[8] But why doesn't *umdana* work to cancel the transaction? Is it not self-evident that no one would purchase an ox for butchering if it turned out to be a *trefa*? The answer, posits Tosafot, is that it is equally self-evident that a vendee *ex ante* would incur the *risk* that the animal he is buying might turn out to be a *trefa*.

In the talmudic case, *umdana* works to produce an *ex ante* presumption that the Nehardeans would not have been interested in selling their houses if they had only known of the impending arrival of new grain supplies.[9] An *ex ante* case for *umdana* cannot be made in the mineral rights case, however. While it is self-evident on an *ex post facto* basis that the surrounding property owners would have held out for a higher price for their mineral rights if they had shared the secret of TGS' mineral strike, this proposition is certainly not evident on an *ex ante* basis, as the seller of a property right assuredly incurs the risk that the price of his asset might increase in value at some time after he sells it.

3. R. Mosheh Sofer (Hungary, 1762–1839), in his analysis of the parameters of *umdana*, distinguishes between instances where the *umdana* relates to the article of the transfer and instances where it relates to the *circumstances* of either the buyer or seller. Only in the latter category of cases, according to R. Sofer, does *umdana* work to vitiate a transaction. Once a transaction is completed, *umdana* rooted in the buyer's disappointment with his purchase cannot work to vitiate the transaction. Doing so is tantamount to negating the concept of ownership transfer. Preserving the integrity of the concept of ownership

transfer forces the attitude that once a symbolic act (*kinyan*) effects ownership transfer, what happens subsequently to the article of transfer is no longer the concern of the seller.[10]

Similarly, once a transaction is completed, *umdana* rooted in the seller's regret, due to price appreciation, for having made the sale cannot work to cancel the transaction. Doing so is tantamount to negating the concept of ownership transfer. In consequence, *umdana* is not operative in the mineral rights case. Since *umdana* relates, not to the circumstances of buyer or seller but rather to the value of the article of transfer, it cannot be invoked to vitiate the transaction.

Cicero's Moral Dilemma

More than 2,000 years ago the Roman statesman Cicero presented the following moral dilemma:

> A merchant brings grain from Alexandria to Rhodes, where famine conditions prevail. While current market conditions allow the merchant to sell his grain at a very favorable price, he knows that several other ships laden with grain are on their way to Rhodes. If the Rhodians learn of the imminent arrival of the ships, the demand and hence the market price for the merchant's grain will fall. Is he to report the fact to the Rhodians, or is he to keep his own counsel and sell his own stock at the highest market price?[11]

In evaluating this moral dilemma, the most salient feature is that the commodity at hand is grain. Grain is a standardized commodity that usually sells at an identifiable price. From the perspective of Halakhah, therefore, the most fundamental issue here is whether the law of *ona'ah* (price fraud)[12] constrains the pricing policy of the Alexandrian merchant. Recall, however, that *ona'ah* is a right to transact at the market norm.[13] Given the famine conditions in Rhodes, the Alexandrian merchant enjoyed a monopoly position at the time of the grain sale. Since the Rhodians did not have a lower-priced alternative at the time, the law of *ona'ah* does not call for any adjustment of the transaction.

Another consideration here is that grain is an essential commodity. By dint of a talmudic ordinance, vendors dealing in commodities essential to human life (*hayyei nefesh*) were restricted to a 20 percent profit rate limit. Elsewhere in this volume we have discussed the particulars of this ordinance. Recall that the ordinance should not be equated with a price-fixing edict. No intention to interfere with the natural market forces of supply and demand was meant. Instead, vendors of foodstuffs were permitted to sell at the market price. The practical significance of the ordinance was to prohibit sellers from collusively restricting supply for the purpose of raising their profit margin above the 20 percent level. Included in the edict was a prohibition preventing monopolists from artificially raising market price by holding back supply.[14]

This understanding of the talmudic foodstuffs ordinance has an implication for Cicero's moral dilemma. Consider that famine conditions produce natural market forces that raise price dramatically above its ordinary level. By *withholding supply*, the Rhodian merchant can catapult his profits above what he could realize if he offered his entire stock of grain for sale. Artificially pushing up price in this manner is, however, proscribed by the talmudic foodstuffs ordinance.

Cicero's Moral Dilemma and the Inelastic Demand Case

While a complaint of overcharge is not given validity when the reference price is anything but the current market norm, an exception to the rule can be identified: "It has been taught, R. Judah b. Batera [mid-1st. cent.] said: The sale of a horse, sword, and buckler on [the field of] battle is not subject to *ona'ah*, because one's very life is dependent upon them."[15]

Given the life-threatening environment of the battlefield, the vendee would pay, if he had to, *any* sum to acquire the implements of war. Economists describe a desperate need of this sort with the phrase "perfectly inelastic demand." Consider, too, that the buyer, for all intents and purposes, will not hazard to investigate market alternatives during a raging battle. The vendor therefore enjoys a monopoly position here.

Since the vendee's demand for a horse or weapon in the battlefield zone is perfectly inelastic, he certainly receives subjective equivalence for whatever price he agrees to pay for these articles. This is the reasoning of R. Judah b. Batera. Whether his ruling represents mainstream talmudic thought is a matter of dispute among the early decisors. R. Hai ben Sherira of Pumbedita (Babylonia, 939–1038)[16] and R. Isaac ben Jacob Alfasi of Algeria (1012–1103)[17] rule that R. Judah b. Batera's opinion represents a minority view and should therefore be rejected. R. Hananel b. Hushi'el, an eleventh-century North African decisor, however, rules in accordance with R. Judah b. Batera.[18]

The acceptability of R. Judah ben Batera's opinion, according to R. Moses ha-Kohen of Lunel, a thirteenth-century French decisor, hinges heavily upon the validity of assimilating his battlefield case with the fugitive-ferryman case discussed at Bava Kamma 115a. Here, the Talmud relates that if an absconding criminal agrees to pay a ferryman an above-market price to provide him with conveyance across a river, he is entitled to recoup from the ferryman the differential involved.[19]

The point of similarity between the two cases is that in both instances the buyer's interest in the product involved is price-inelastic; i.e., he would agree, for all intents and purposes, to pay any price the seller insists on. In the ferry-man-fugitive case, since the conveyance averts the fugitive's imminent capture, the latter certainly receives subjective equivalence in his transaction with the ferryman. Nonetheless, if his fugitive status were removed, his demand for the conveyance would properly be described as price-elastic, and he would pre-sumably not value the service above market price. With his price-inelastic demand reflecting transitory subjective value, the fugitive is entitled to recoup from the ferryman any amount he paid him above the competitive norm. Similarly, remove the condition of war and the vendee would presumably not agree to pay the asking price at hand for the implements of war.

Though R. Moses ha-Kohen advances no specifics to explain why this assimilation should be rejected, two points of dissimilarity stand out. First, whereas the demand-inducing factor in the battlefield case affects all market demanders equally, causing the aggregate demand schedule for implements of war to shift upward, no such upward shift in demand occurs in the fugitive-fer-ryman case. The demand-inducing factor uniquely affects the fugitive's subjec-tive evaluation of the ferryman's services, leaving everyone else's demand for the service unaffected. Second, whereas a competitive norm exists for the ser-vices of the ferryman at the time the fugitive struck his bargain, no *competitive norm* exists at the time an individual buys implements of war on a battlefield. While the commercial market for horses and weapons is normally subject to a competitive norm, the marketplace for these articles completely collapses with-in the framework of the battlefield zone. The economic environment that pre-vails in such a scene effectively precludes the emergence of a competitive price for these articles. Resource mobility and knowledge of market alternatives are conspicuously absent here, as the movement of market participants is severely restricted. With economic activity characteristically unorganized and sporadic, the market for these articles becomes minutely fragmented. Within this frame-work, price is determined by the individual bargains buyers and sellers reach. Since the *buyer's bid determines value here*, his *ona'ah* claim should be denied, notwithstanding the circumstantial nature of his demand in this case.

What proceeds clearly from the school of thought that accepts the analogy between the fugitive-ferryman case and the battlefield case is the general prin-ciple that exercise of monopoly power, when the relevant aggregate demand schedule is perfectly inelastic, is ethically immoral.

Selling at whatever price the market will bear when the relevant demand the monopolist faces is price-elastic, however, presents no moral issue in Jewish law. This is evident from the long-standing sanction given to the communal practice of auctioning the privilege of performing a public ceremonial function of a religious character to the highest bidder.[20] With the ceremonial honor put up for sale unavailable elsewhere, the competitive bidding among the auction participants *determines* value. Hence, no moral issue is raised here. Capitalizing on "site value,"[21] auctioning a rare painting, and selling the patent rights of a new invention to the highest bidder provide other examples of monopoly pricing under conditions of elastic demand.

Let us apply the preceding analysis to Cicero's moral dilemma. What was the merchant's assessment when he arrived at Rhodes? Did he think the Rhodians were near starvation and facing certain death if they did not acquire grain immediately? If so, the Rhodians would have no time to wait for the arrival of the grain ships that were on their way. This makes the Rhodian's demand for the Alexandrian's grain price-inelastic. Consequently, the Alexandrian merchant suffers no loss in potential profit by sharing the secret with the Rhodians that grain ships are on the way. Cicero's dilemma dealt with the instance where the Rhodians had not yet harbored a price-inelastic demand for the Alexandrian's grain.

At this juncture, let us introduce a variant into Cicero's moral dilemma. Suppose the Alexandrian merchant comes with the knowledge that the grain ships behind him will take, say, at least three days to arrive. If the Rhodians don't get new provisions considerably before that time, they will all starve to death. Without the knowledge of how desperate their situation really is, some Rhodians might opt to pass up the opportunity to purchase grain from the Alexandrian and wait for the next grain shipment to arrive. Since keeping the information to himself fails to warn the Rhodians of a life-threatening situation, the Alexandrian is duty bound to share his information with them. But revealing the secret will at the same time push the Rhodian demand for his grain to the point of being perfectly inelastic in respect to price. Given that it is unethical for a seller to exploit a buyer's life-threatening situation to earn additional windfall profits on a sale, the Alexandrian may not exploit the market value of his informational advantage. Instead, the Alexandrian's price is limited to what the market will bear now without the knowledge that his grain is the Rhodians' only hope for survival.

Rothschild's London Exchange Coup

On June 19, 1815, Napoleon went down to defeat in the battle of Waterloo at the hands of Lord Wellington. The Rothschild network of couriers, which was in all respects a private news-gathering agency, brought news of the British victory to Nathan Rothschild in London many hours before anyone else in the city learned the news. For days the London Exchange had strained its ears. If Napoleon won, English consoles were bound to drop. If he lost, the enemy empire would collapse and consoles rise. Equipped with the scoop of the British victory, Nathan Rothschild entered the trading pit in the London Exchange. His name was already such that a single substantial move on his part sufficed to bear or bull an issue. Instead of sinking his worth in consoles, as another man in his position would surely have done, Rothschild sold consoles. Rothschild's substantial trade triggered panic-selling of British consoles. After the consoles had plummeted in value, Rothschild proceeded to buy a giant parcel of consoles "for a song." News soon reached the London Exchange of Wellington's victory. British consoles soared in price. Rothschild then sold his consoles and made a fortune.[22]

One salient point in evaluating the ethics of Rothschild's conduct is the consideration that the informational advantage here was the product of Rothschild's investment in a private news-gathering agency. To be sure, Rothschild cannot be said to have had a property right in the news of Wellington's victory, as the news was the property of the public domain. But did Rothschild enjoy a right to protect his investment against free-riding? For argument's sake, let us assume that Rothschild would have suffered no loss if his trade had been copied by other investors. Hence, concealing the news of Wellington's victory by selling consoles effectively denied fellow investors the opportunity to profit from the news, while all along entailing no loss for Rothschild. Such conduct should be prohibited by dint of the interdict not to act in the manner of the inhabitants of Sodom. This interdict is violated when A refuses to allow B to infringe upon his right even though such infringement generates no loss for him and at the same time affords B the opportunity to secure a benefit or avoid a loss.[23]

Rothschild's conduct, however, can be defended on the basis of the comment by R. Mordecai b. Hillel (Germany, 1240–1298) et al. on the following talmudic dictum pertaining to squatters: Unless the apartment involved was up for rent, Halakhah denies the landlord's claim for rent against the squatter.[24] Commenting on this law, R. Mordecai b. Hillel et al. posit that while the rent claim for having occupied the apartment is denied, the landlord is within his rights to deny the squatter's request to live in the apartment gratis. Since the landlord could theoretically rent the apartment, notwithstanding that at present he opts not to, denying the squatter's request to live in the apartment gratis is legitimate.[25]

Applying R. Mordecai b. Hillel's ruling to the case in question frees the Rothschild trade of a Sodomitic element. Given the commercial value of Rothschild's superior information, it is legitimate to protect his investment against free-riding.

The assumption that free-riding entails no loss for Rothschild is in all probability invalid. Investment profits depend critically upon timing. What profit Rothschild will actually realize from the scoop depends upon the price at which he sells the consoles. To gain maximal advantage from the commercial value of his superior information, he would have to sell the consoles at a price that, at the very least, reflects the British victory at Waterloo. The longer Rothschild can manage to keep his scoop a secret, the more likely the actual news of Wellington's victory will result in a run-up in the price of British consoles. Since the news of the victory is a surprise event for the marketplace, the price of consoles at that time provides a gauge of the value of consoles that factors in the British victory. But if Rothschild's superior information leaks, then the firm news of the British victory will, in all probability, not cause any run-up in the price of consoles, as this information will have already been discounted by the market. Hence, investor copying of the Rothschild trade may effectively deprive the financier of the advantage of a surprise event, which would be very helpful in deciding the timing of the sale of his consoles. Without this edge, Rothschild suffers the prospect that a wave of sudden selling may depress the price of consoles before he gets around to liquidating his own position.

Proceeding from the right to protect an investment from free-riding is the right to employ diversionary tactics for the purpose of keeping the public off balance in respect to the informational advantage. Selling consoles on the knowledge of Wellington's victory is a diversionary tactic that is at once costly and daring. Several scenarios are possible. In one scenario, Rothschild's substantial selling does not trigger panic selling and the tactic manages only to throw the public off in regard to Wellington's victory. By shortening the time span between his own entry as a buyer of consoles and the arrival of the report of Wellington's victory, Rothschild increases the probability that the actual report will be a surprise event. Should the tactic trigger panic selling, as circumstances proved to be the case, Rothschild would be conferred with the additional bonanza of the opportunity to purchase a huge parcel of consoles "for a song."

Characterizing the selling of consoles on the knowledge of Wellington's victory as sending a false signal to the market is valid only on the assumption that traders have a legitimate right to share gratis in Rothschild's superior information. Since Halakhah recognizes no such right, Rothschild cannot be said to be guilty of *geneivat da'at* conduct.

In the context of the modern investment stratagem of arbitrage, Rothschild's conduct can be defended on even more fundamental grounds. Arbitrage entails the purchase and sale of the same or related commodities in order to profit from price discrepancies. To illustrate, suppose the current price of gold and silver is $375 and $5 an ounce respectively. This represents a 75:1 spread in the price ratio. A expects this spread to narrow considerably. Speculating on his intuition, he purchases 100 contracts of silver in the London Metals Exchange. Later that same day, A sells short 100 contracts of gold on the New York Commodity Exchange. To be sure, the prices of precious metals, including gold and silver, usually rise and fall in tandem. But, if the spread between the price of gold and silver narrows, as A expects, the strategy will pay off in a net profit regardless of the direction taken by the price of precious metals. Two scenarios are possible: If the price of gold and silver rises, the profit generated by the liquidation of the long position on silver will more than offset the loss incurred on the closing out of the short position on gold. If, on the other hand, the prices of gold and silver fall, the profit earned on the liquidation of the short position on gold will more than offset the loss incurred in closing out the long position on silver.

The prevalence of arbitrage activity puts to question the reasonableness of inferring a trader's opinion of price direction on the basis of a particular trade he makes. Any such inference is entirely at the risk of the one who makes it.

Trading on Insider Information

We begin our discussion of insider trading with a brief overview of legislation against this practice in the United States. We will then present a number of landmark court decisions in this area, and evaluate them from a halakhic standpoint.

The Securities and Exchange Act of 1934

Congress enacted the Securities and Exchange Act of 1934 in response to certain unethical trading practices that had contributed to the stock market crash of 1929. The act was designed primarily as a mechanism to regulate sales and purchases of securities, and to protect investors against manipulation and deception in the stock market.

Under section 10(b), the Securities and Exchange Commission was vested with general regulatory powers over securities transactions. The SEC was given express authority to prescribe rules necessary and appropriate in the public interest to prohibit any manipulative or deceptive device utilized by any person in relation to securities transactions.

In 1942, the SEC utilized the rule-making power granted by section 10(b) to promulgate rule 10b5. This rule proscribed making "affirmative misrepresentations, half-truths or omissions in connection with a purchase or sale of securities."[26]

SEC v. Texas Gulf Sulphur Co.

Texas Gulf Sulphur (TGS), as will be recalled, made a significant mineral discovery on property it owned near Timmins, Ontario, and ceased drilling for several months so that it could acquire land around the site. During this period, company officers, employees, and tippees purchased stock in the open market without disclosing the potentially significant discovery to the investing public. After rumors of the discovery were given prominent attention in the press, TGS issued a press release stating that the rumors were exaggerated. Over the next four days, company officers, employees, and tippees made further purchases of stock before TGS finally disclosed to the investing public that the company had in fact made a significant mineral discovery.[27]

In *SEC v. Texas Gulf Sulphur* (1968), the court found the TGS officials guilty of violating rule 10b5. In deciding against the defendants, the court interpreted the rule as requiring anyone in possession of material insider information to either disclose it or abstain from trading in the securities concerned. The rule, according to the court, is based in principle on the justifiable expectation of the securities marketplace that all investors trading on impersonal exchanges should have equal access to material information.[28]

The Equal-Access Doctrine and Halakhah

From the perspective of Halakhah the equal-access doctrine is an inadequate basis for overturning an insider trade. Let us not forget that the transaction at hand is a stock transfer conducted in the impersonal financial markets. The entire transaction is predicated on variant and possibly even *opposite* expectations: S buys because he is convinced that the price of the asset will rise. B sells because he believes the opposite. Alternatively, S may be in basic agreement with B but nonetheless is convinced that other assets will rise in value more. Given the variant and even opposite beliefs that underlie a stock share transfer, entry into this marketplace is accompanied by an advisory to the reasonable man that he should *research all the publicly accessible information on which his trade will be made.* Ignoring this warning in whole or in part is at his own risk. Accordingly, if S can show that B was in all likelihood not aware of publicly available reasons not to buy the asset in question, B has no basis to overturn the trade. What victimized B was not his ignorance of the insider information but his failure to investigate *publicly* available information.

Becoming *fully* informed of the publicly available data pertinent to an investment requires a considerable investment in time, energy, and financial resources. The less fully informed an investor is in respect to publicly available data, the weaker is the equal-access theory in making the case for overturning transactions involving insider trading.

While the equal-access doctrine is not a compelling force in the argument to overturn transactions involving insider trading, this equity benchmark provides a vital economic argument for the government to disallow publicly traded firms from allowing their members to engage in insider trading. This issue will be discussed later in this volume.

The Misappropriation Theory and Halakhah

In evaluating the TGS insider trading case, the most salient feature on which to focus is an identification of the property right in the information. We will refer to this approach as the misappropriation theory.

Standing as the most basic issue here is whether TGS has a property right in the report of the mineral find, separate and distinct from its property right in the mineral discovery itself. The discovery was brought to light, of course, by the labor services of both TGS employees and outside consultants. But the output we are dealing with here is *information*, which is something intangible. In Halakhah a property right can be acquired only in something tangible (*davor sheyesh bo mammash*).[29] In this regard tangibility is defined as something that has height, width, and depth.[30]

The tangibility condition can, however, be met here by means of appropriate contract design. Instead of a *quid pro quo* arrangement, calling for the employee to confer title to specific information to TGS in exchange for compensation, the contract would call for the employee to commit himself to engage in specific tasks for TGS, including the production and provision of reports. The selfsame approach was proposed by R. David b. Solomon ibn Abi Zimra (Israel, 1479–1573) in finding the legal underpinning of an agreement between a householder and a dyer. Instead of viewing the agreement as calling for the dyer to confer the householder with title to the dye, this decisor understood the obligation of the dyer to consist of a *commitment* to dye the householder's garment. Since a personal commitment is bound up in the physical being of the obligator, the tangibility requirement is met.[31]

Another saving factor here is the recognition Halakhah gives to prevailing business practice in respect to the nature of property rights that can be acquired. If prevailing business practice gives recognition to the acquisition of something that is intangible, Halakhah too would recognize the practice.[32]

Applying the above approaches to the case at hand provides a ready legal underpinning for TGS' acquisition of the mineral ore reports. But what principle prohibits the employee from divulging the information to anyone other than the employer? Confidentiality here, as it appears to this writer, proceeds from the very nature of the labor agreement. Once a labor agreement is struck, the output of the worker is automatically the legal property of the employer. This principle is expressed in the talmudic dictum *yad po'el keyad baal ha-bayit*, i.e., the hand of the worker is like the hand of the employer (Bava Mezia 10a). In a market economy, *yad po'el* translates into the worker's obligation to hand over the entire *value* of his output to his employer. Given that the *value* of the mineral report to TGS is considerably diminished if its confidentiality is breached, *yad po'el* prohibits the employee from divulging its contents to any-one but his employer in the proper chain of command.

The confidentiality requirement implicit in a labor contract where the obligation of the worker consists of providing information can be reinforced by the insertion of an explicit secrecy clause. Since intangibility is not a legal impediment when it comes to making a personal commitment operative, the secrecy clause is halakhically binding. The confidentiality objective can also be explicitly achieved by binding the employee with an oath of secrecy.

Given the pivotal role knowledge of the report plays in TGS' negotiations with neighboring property owners, the informational advantage is a commod-ity having market value.

Adding substantially to this value is the protection secular law affords the mineral ore report as a trade secret.[33]

In a milestone case, *Carpenter v. United States*, the Supreme Court of the United States ruled that a *company's confidential information qualifies as prop-erty to which the company has a right of exclusive use.*[34]

At this juncture it is appropriate to ask exactly who owns the property rights in the mineral ore report. Is it the corporation as a separate legal entity? Is it the shareholders who are the policymakers of the firm? Or do *all* shareholders on a pro-rata basis own the rights to the mineral ore report? In Halakhah, authorities dispute who should be regarded as the *owner* of a publicly traded company. Let us take note that a significant school of thought identifies the owners as the shareholders who are the policymakers as well as the shareholders who have sig-nificant holdings in the company. Insignificant shareholders who are not poli-cymakers are not regarded as owners.[35] This dispute relates to the issue of assigning *responsibility for the policies of the firm*. Here the key factor is who *con-trols* the assets of the business. But in the case at hand, the issue is who *enjoys the right to make personal use of the assets of the firm*. As a publicly traded company, all investors, including those who are policymakers, agree in advance that they are only *residual claimants* of the assets of the firm. No one, therefore, enjoys the right to expropriate an asset of the firm for *personal use* or *profit* without prop-er authorization. All disputants should, therefore, agree that the property right in the mineral ore report is vested in *all* the shareholders of TGS, with no one having the right to expropriate it for personal gain.

Given the proprietary interest the shareholders have in the mineral ore report, trading on the nonpublic knowledge of this report amounts to exploiting another's property for commercial gain. Recall that R. Yose prohibits such conduct and calls for the disgorgement of the profits earned.[36]

Chiarella v. United States

Chiarella was a "mark-up man" for a financial printer, Pandick Press. The clients of Pandick Press were corporations involved in acquiring target companies through mergers and takeovers. Because of the need for secrecy involved in such acquisitions, names were omitted from the documents until the final printing. However, Chiarella was able to deduce the names of the target corporations and used the information to purchase stocks in the targets prior to the takeover announcements. Once the announcements of the takeovers were made, he sold the stock at a substantial profit.[37]

The government brought a criminal action against Chiarella, and the district court found that he had violated Section 10(b) of the 1934 Securities and Exchange Act and SEC rule 10b5. The Second Circuit Court of Appeals affirmed the conviction.[38]

On appeal, the Supreme Court reversed the convictions. Holding that mere possession of material nonpublic information does not give rise to a duty to disclose before trading, the court explicitly rejected the "parity of information" theory espoused in *SEC v. Texas Gulf Sulfur*. According to the *Chiarella* majority, in order for there to be a duty to disclose, there must exist a relationship of trust and confidence between the parties to a transaction. Since Chiarella was not an agent, fiduciary, or one in whom the sellers had placed their trust and confidence at the time of the transaction, he was under no obligation to disclose his knowledge of the impending takeover prior to the transactions. Hence his trading activities were held not to be in violation of the securities fraud law.[39]

The *Chiarella* court's rejection of the parity of information theory is, as the previous discussion indicated, in accord with Halakhah. Its overturn of Chiarella's conviction, however, is at odds with R. Yose's dictum. Analysis of the details of the case readily points to the presence of all the elements needed to trigger a disgorgement requirement for Chiarella. The information Chiarella made use of to trade on was the property right of the acquiring companies that hired Pandick Press. Chiarella had no right to trade on the confidential information, as such conduct directly violated his terms of employment with Pandick Press. Trading on the confidential information carries with it the dan-

ger of alerting the marketplace to the identity of the target company. Any subsequent run-up in the price of the target company's shares resulting from the
leak increases, for the acquiring companies, the cost of achieving control of the
target. Chiarella's trading entails a possible loss for the acquiring companies.
Moreover, Chiarella's breach of confidentiality inflicts damage in the form of
reputational harm to his employer, Pandick Press.

It follows from this analysis that Halakhah, far from exonerating Chiarella,
would treat him very harshly. By dint of R. Yose's dictum, Chiarella would be
required to give up the profits he earned on the insider trading and hand them
over to the acquiring companies.

Moreover, Pandick Press may have a legitimate damage suit against
Chiarella. Relevant in assessing this claim is the following case dealt with by R.
Solomon Leib Tabak (Hungary, 1832–1908): While employed by E, W picks up
E's trade secret. W reveals the trade secret to C. Equipped with the trade secret,
C goes into competition with E. E sues W for loss in earnings resulting from C's
competition. In his evaluation of the claim, R. Tabak lays down the principle
that an employee is responsible for causing his employer a loss in earnings even
when the link between the worker's action and the damage is indirect (*gerame*).
For W to be held liable, however, the following conditions must be met: (1) The
confidentiality clause must be stipulated before E gives the trade secret to W;
(2) It must be evident that E relies on W not to reveal the secret, as would be
the case when it is known that another party is in readiness to use the trade
secret in competition with E; (3) The monetary loss relates directly to the job
for which W was hired.[40]

Let us relate R. Tabak's criteria to the case at hand. The confidentiality condition is easily met, as Chiarella's contract prohibited him from trading on
insider information. Since the viability of a financial printer hinges on the confidentiality element, it is evident that Pandick Press relied on Chiarella to maintain secrecy. Satisfaction of the third condition obtains when the acquiring
companies either sue Pandick Press to recover fees and/or cancel outstanding
contracts with it on account of Chiarella's insider trading.

We should note that R. Tabak's criteria pertain only in respect to the issue
of the employee's responsibility for the monetary loss he indirectly causes his
employer. Irrespective of whether each and every element of R. Tabak's liability criterion obtains, an employee is prohibited from taking action that might
even indirectly cause the employer a monetary loss.[41]

United States v. O'Hagan

James Herman O'Hagan allegedly learned in 1988 that Grand Met PLC, a
client of his law firm, Dorsey and Whitney, planned to launch a tender offer for

the Pillsbury Company. O'Hagan began purchasing call options for Pillsbury stock, as well as shares of the stock. Following Dorsey and Whitney's withdrawal from the representation, Grand Met publicly announced its tender offer. The price of Pillsbury stock rose dramatically, and O'Hagan sold his call options and stock at a profit of more than $4.3 million.

An SEC investigation culminated in a fifty-seven-count indictment alleging that O'Hagan defrauded his law firm and his client, Grand Met, by misappropriating for his own trading purposes material, nonpublic information regarding the tender offer. A jury convicted O'Hagan on all counts, and he was sentenced to prison. The Eighth Circuit reversed all of the convictions, holding that securities law liability may not be grounded on the misappropriation theory.

On June 25, 1997, the Supreme Court, in a six to three decision, reversed the Eighth Circuit and affirmed the validity of the SEC's litigation-constructed misappropriation theory of Rule 10b-5 liability.

In advancing the misappropriation theory, the court ruled that *a company's confidential information qualifies as property to which the company has a right of exclusive use.* Accordingly, the undisclosed misappropriation of such information constitutes fraud akin to embezzlement.

Consider that the information O'Hagan misappropriated had value only in the trading of Pillsbury stock and stock options. Because O'Hagan's misappropriation was not complete until he used the information to trade in Pillsbury in stock and stock options, his conduct constituted fraud in securities trading and not just a breach of his duty of loyalty to his employer. Moreover, O'Hagan made use of a deceptive device. His deception consisted of his failure to disclose his personal trading to Grand Met and Dorsey, in breach of his duty to do so.

While the decision extended the reach of rule 10b to corporate *outsiders* who breached a duty to the source of the information, the court identified a case where the rule would not apply. This exception occurs when the fiduciary discloses to the source that he plans to trade on the nonpublic information. Here, because there is no deceptive device, the fiduciary-turned-trader does not violate rule 10b-5.[42]

United States v. O'Hagan and Halakhah

The Supreme Court's adoption of the misappropriation theory in its treatment of insider trading cases is in general conformity with the halakhic approach to the issue. But Halakhah would not agree that disclosing to the source that he plans to trade on the nonpublic information frees the fiduciary of violation of the law. Without explicit permission from the source to trade, the fiduciary remains bound by R. Yose's dictum not to do business with someone else's asset. Along these lines, Halakhah's treatment of tippee liability would be much more stringent than the guidepost that proceeds from *O'Hagan*. The reader is referred to the discussion of this point in the next section.

Dirks vs. SEC

Dirks was an investment analyst and officer of Delafield Childs, Inc., a registered broker dealer specializing in providing financial analysis of insurance company securities to institutional investors. Secrist, a former officer of Equity Funding Corporation of America (EFCA), an insurance holding company, contacted Dirks and informed him that EFCA's assets were vastly overstated as a result of massive fraud within the corporation. Secrist told Dirks that EFCA was selling partnerships in nonexistent real estate and creating fictitious insurance policies and records.

Dirks conducted a program of extensive research and investigation in response to Secrist's accusations. Dirks' efforts finally paid off when he managed to coax some former company officials to admit to doctoring the company's insurance records or having been aware of such improprieties.

Although Dirks did not personally trade on the information he developed, he passed on the damaging facts to both his own clients and other investors. These tippees profited handsomely from the revelations. Specifically, owners of large blocks of EFCA stocks sold in advance of the precipitous price drop brought on by public disclosure of the fraud. Other traders sold short or purchased put options in order to further profit from the knowledge of the debacle at EFCA.[43]

Invoking the parity of information doctrine, the SEC censured Dirks for selectively disclosing the insider information he had obtained about EFCA.[44] On the basis of this doctrine, any person who knows or should know that the information he possesses is insider information is bound either to publicly disclose that information or to abstain from both personally trading on it and from tipping others.[45]

On appeal, the Supreme Court overturned the SEC censure of Dirks. In rejecting the SEC judgment, the court insisted that the disclosure-or-abstain rule cannot be invoked when its operation would exert an inhibiting influence on the role of market analysts. Holding Dirks culpable for his behavior would discourage other analysts from conducting similar investigations in the future. One way to encourage investigations to ferret out fraud is to afford Dirks and others like him a property right in their disclosures, thereby permitting them to reap the profits of their labor.[46]

The Dirks Case and Halakhah

One fundamental issue the Dirks case raises is that the conduct of both Secrist and Dirks violated the prohibition against talebearing.[47] Talebearing occurs when A makes a damaging, albeit *true* report about B's misconduct to C. Two varieties of this misconduct have been identified by the sages. If C is merely a third party in respect to a true but damaging report, then A's talebearing is called *lashon ha-ra*. Should C be the victim or intended victim of B's wrongdoing, then A's talebearing is called *rekhilut*.

If A's motive in making his report is to avert some loss or damage for C, then making the report may be permissible. But certain very stringent conditions must be met. Elsewhere in this volume we have detailed these restrictions.[48] Let us use these criteria to evaluate the ethics of Secrist's and Dirks' conduct. For purposes of exposition, we assume that a society governed by Halakhah would create an agency akin to the SEC to regulate the financial markets. Accordingly, we shall regard the SEC as the Bet Din of the financial markets.

In pursuing his objective to expose fraud at EFCA, Secrist may have acted properly up to the point of contact with Dirks. Proper handling of the scandal would have required Secrist, in his initial step, to directly confront the wrongdoers. In the event confrontation fails to make the wrongdoers come forward and confess their guilt, Secrist's next step would be to present his allegations to the top management of EFCA. Should management prove unwilling to investigate his charges, Secrist would be obligated to present his allegations directly to the SEC.

By enlisting Dirks' help instead of going directly to the SEC, Secrist acted improperly. Secrist's motive was revenge against his former employers. He disclosed the damaging information to Dirks in the hope that the latter would disseminate the information to his clients, who, in turn, would unload their holdings of EFCA shares on the market. The precipitous decline of EFCA shares that would accompany the substantial selling would, in turn, put pressure on the SEC to launch an investigation into the affairs of EFCA.[49] Alerting the authorities to the scandal in this manner effectively protects a select group of shareholders from loss at the expense of the investing public. Since it is the avoidance of loss for the investing public that legitimizes Secrist's revelations, sharing the information with someone who will inevitably disclose the information on a selective basis violates *rekhilut*.

We now turn to Dirks' conduct. From the standpoint of Halakhah, the only legitimate role for him is to exert pressure on EFCA's management and/or the SEC to investigate the allegations. Since the entire investing public is entitled to the damaging information, disclosing it exclusively to his clients amounts to advising them to defraud the investing public. Such conduct by Dirks violates both the *rekhilut* and the *lifnei iver* prohibitions.

Because selective disclosure here entails violations of various biblical pro-hibitions, Halakhah, in opposition to the *Dirks* court, would not afford Dirks a property right in his discovery. But suppose Dirks acts properly and hands over the information he developed to the SEC. Is he entitled to any compensation for his efforts? No. Dirks' disclosure assuredly averted financial disaster for the public. But the actual beneficiaries of his efforts cannot be identified. Hence, even if we presume that those who would have otherwise bought EFCA shares would give Dirks a reward for his information, Dirks has no way to collect his reward. Mandating the SEC to give Dirks a reward for the information he devel-oped, however, is certainly within the legislative prerogative of a society gov-erned by Halakhah.

Tippee Liability and American Law

The *Dirks* court enunciated the parameters for tippee liability in insider trading cases. In setting forth its criterion in this matter, the court affirmed the principle that mere possession of nonpublic material information does not give rise to a duty to disclose or abstain. This duty can be created only by a fiducia-ry relationship. Accordingly, a duty for a non-insider to disclose or abstain can only come about by way of inheriting this duty from the insider. The tippee does not inherit the duty to disclose or abstain from the insider unless a two-pronged test is met. First, the tippee must determine that the tipper has breached a fiduciary duty by improperly disclosing the nonpublic information to him. Whether or not disclosure is a breach of duty depends upon the tipper's purpose in making the disclosure. If it personally benefits the tipper, either directly or indirectly, the disclosure is improper. Examples of direct or indirect personal benefits include financial gain, reputational gain that will translate into future earnings, and the dissemination of confidential information to a trading relative or friend as a gift. Tippee liability, however, is *not* established by merely showing the tipper's breach of duty. The second prong of the test requires that the tippee either knew or should have known that there had been a breach.[50]

The test for determining tippee liability was applied in the case of *Securities and Exchange Commission v. Switzer*.[51] In this case University of Oklahoma football coach Barry Switzer overheard, while sunbathing at a secondary school track meet, a conversation between G. Platt, president of Texas International Co. (TIC), and his wife that divulged material nonpublic information relating to a major forthcoming event at TIC. In the overheard conversation, Platt revealed to his wife that TIC was planning to liquidate its subsidiary, Phoenix. The disclosure included the planned date of the public announcement. This information was likely to affect the investment decision of a reasonably prudent investor because the pro-rata value of Phoenix assets could reasonably be expected to exceed the market price of its stock at the time of the public announcement. Switzer and some of his friends bought shares in the company based on what he had overheard.[52]

The *Switzer* court applied the two-pronged *Dirks* test to determine whether a tippee acquired a fiduciary duty. Specifically, the court required a showing, first, that an insider breached a fiduciary duty to the shareholders by disclosing insider information, and second, that the tippee knew or should have known there had been a breach. The court found that Platt did not breach a fiduciary duty, and therefore Switzer did not acquire or assume a fiduciary duty. It determined that Platt had no intention to communicate the information to Switzer, and that Switzer inadvertently overheard the conversation. Because Switzer did not acquire a fiduciary duty, any information he passed to other defendants did not constitute insider trading.[53]

Furthermore, the court stated that even if the plaintiff (the SEC) had satisfied the first prong of the *Dirks* test, it failed to satisfy the second prong. Specifically, the court found that the "defendants did not know nor did they have reason to know, that the information disseminated by a corporate insider was for an improper purpose."[54]

Tippee Liability and Halakhah

Several variants of tippee involvement in insider trading cases can be identified. In one class of cases, analogous to the TGS insider trading case, the informational advantage is the property of the shareholders. Trading on the information, as discussed earlier, amounts to doing business with someone else's asset. Given the above rationale, disgorgement should be called for whether the trader was an insider or a tippee outsider. Being unaware that the information was confidential should not be an extenuating factor, as the tippee had no right to trade on the information.

Taking advantage of an insider on his offer to sell material nonpublic information entails the additional violation for the tippee of abetting a transgressor which is an aspect of the *lifnei iver* interdict.

Another type of insider trading falls into the category of cases analogous to the *Dirks* case. The salient feature here is that the informational advantage is not a property right but consists of an accusation of fraud. For expositional

convenience, our analysis of the halakhic perspective of this strain of tippee liability in insider trading cases will refer to the *Dirks* case, discussed above.

Given that an accusation of fraud made outside the Bet Din amounts to
lashon ha-ra, Dirks and his tippees are prohibited from accepting the allegations as fact or even as possibly true. Acting upon Secrist's information by selling EFCA stock short or buying put options on that company's stock manifests,
on the part of the tippees, a conviction that the price of EFCA shares will
decline, and hence amounts to giving credence or plausibility to the *lashon ha-
ra*.

While it is forbidden to give credence to *lashon ha-ra*, an individual is, nevertheless, permitted to be cautious on the basis of what he has heard and take
action to avoid damage or financial loss. The legitimacy of adopting a guarded
policy in respect to *lashon ha-ra*, however, should not work to permit the tippee
to unload his portfolio of EFCA shares. Such conduct would be analogous to
selling merchandise that one suspects might be defective. A sale of this kind
exploits the ignorance of one's opposite number and is therefore prohibited.

Since public disclosure of the *lashon ha-ra* is not an option open to the
tippee shareholder, the tippee will effectively be stuck with his EFCA holdings.
Trading in EFCA shares would be suspended while the company is under official investigation. If the charges proved true, liquidation of the company would
be ordered. If the charges, on the other hand, turned out not to be substantiat-
ed, trading in the shares would resume.

Final judgment regarding the ethics for the tippee in selling off his EFCA
shares must, however, take into account the degree to which the *lashon ha-ra*
has permeated the investment community. As a preliminary matter, we note
that every transaction in the secondary financial markets is predicated on the
basis of contrary expectations. Accordingly, a participant in these markets can
be fully expected to realize that an exchange of information with his opposite
number may well make him change his mind about going through with the
transaction.

From the contrary-expectation feature of the secondary financial markets,
it follows that once the rumor of fraud at EFCA becomes known to the financial community, the burden of both discovering and interpreting the import of
the information should fall on the buyer. Selling EFCA shares under these conditions cannot be said to amount to exploiting the ignorance of an unsuspecting public.

What, however, is the criterion that decides when information passes from
the category of being confidential to the category of being accessible to the
investing public? Two factors are crucial here.

1. The tippee's source should be someone whose information is second-
hand. Obtaining the information from someone who has no direct knowledge

of the fraud indicates that broadcast of the rumor is beyond the stage of selective and controlled dissemination and has entered the phase of being circulated in a spontaneous and uncontrolled manner.

2. A price decline in EFCA shares occurs either just prior to or subsequent to the tippee's exposure to the rumor. Absent other developments, the tippee should have the right to ascribe the drop in price to the rumor of fraudulent practices at EFCA. Selling off EFCA shares in this investment climate cannot, therefore, be characterized as exploiting an unsuspecting investment public. Quite to the contrary, the burden of discovering the rumor should fall squarely on the prospective buyer of EFCA stock.

When the two mitigating factors described above combine together, a strong case can be made for allowing the tippee to unload his holdings of EFCA shares.

1. *SEC v. Texas Gulf Sulphur Co.*, 258 F. Supp. 269–71 (S.D. N.Y. 1966).

2. Ibid., p. 271.

3. For the development of this point, please turn to pp. 35–45 of this volume.

4. *SEC v. Texas Gulf Sulphur Co.*, 258 F. Supp. 271 (S.D. N.Y. 1966).

5. Samuel, Hullin 94a; R. Isaac b. Jacob Alfasi (Algeria, 1012–1103), Rif, ad loc.; Maimonides (Egypt, 1135–1204), *Yad*, Genevah 18:3; R. Asher b. Jehiel (Germany, 1250–1327), Rosh, Hullin, 7:18; R. Jacob b. Asher (Germany, 1270–1343), *Tur*, Hoshen Mishpat 228:6; R. Joseph Caro (Israel, 1488–1575), *Shulhan Arukh*, Hoshen Mishpat 228:1; R. Jehiel Michel Epstein (Belarus, 1829–1908), *Arukh ha-Shulhan*, Hoshen Mishpat 228:3.

6. R. Abraham David Wahrmann, *Kesef ha-Kedoshim*, Sh.Ar., Hoshen Mishpat 227:9.

7. Tosafot, Ketubbot 47b.

8. Hullin 51a; Rif, ad loc.; *Yad*, Mekhirah 15:6; Rosh, Hullin 3:34; *Tur*, op. cit. 232:11; Sh.Ar., op. cit. 232:1; Ar.haSh., op. cit. 232:17.

9. Tosafot, Ketubbot 47b.

10. R. Mosheh Sofer, *Responsa Hatam Sofer*, Hoshen Mishpat 70.

11. Cicero, *De Officiis*, bk. III, chap. iii (W. Miller trans., 1968). For an analysis of Cicero's case as it relates to the ethics of insider trading, see Gary Lawson, "The Ethics of Insider Trading," *Harvard Journal of Law and Public Policy* 2, no. 3 (Summer, 1988): 737–83.

12. Baraita, Bava Mezia 51a; Rif, ad loc.; *Yad*, op. cit. 12:1; Rosh, Bava Mezia 4:17; *Tur*, op. cit., 227:1; Sh.Ar., op. cit. 227:1; Ar.haSh., op. cit. 228:1.

13. For the development of this point, please turn to pp. 127–31 of this volume.

14. Please turn to pp. 225–26 of this book.

15. Bava Mezia 58b.

16. R. Hai b. Sherira, *Ketab-al Shira wa-al*, translated into Hebrew by R. Isaac al Bargelone, *Sefer ha-Mikkah ve-ha-Mimkar* (Venice, 1602).

17. Rif, Bava Mezia 58b.

18. Rabbenu Hannanel (11th cent.), Bava Mezia 58b.

19. R. Moses ha-Kohen of Lunel, quoted in *Shittah M'kubbetzet*, Bava Mezia 58b.

20. R. Meir Eisenstadt (Austria, 1670–1744), *Panim Me'irot* 11:25; see R. Ezra Basri, *Dinei Mamonot*, vol. 2 (Jerusalem: Sucath David, 1976), p. 172.

21. Real estate transactions are not subject to the full scope of *ona'ah* regulation. This exclusion proceeds from exegetical interpretation of the biblical source of *ona'ah*, "And if

thou sell unto thy neighbor or acquire aught of thy neighbor's hand" (Leviticus 25:14). Something that is acquired (by being passed) from hand to hand (is subject to *ona'ah* regulation), thus excluding land, which is not movable (see Bava Mezia 56b). Nahmanides (commentary at Leviticus 25:14) points out that insofar as a biblical interdict against *ona'ah* is mentioned explicitly in connection with real estate transactions, the exemption noted above must be taken to refer exclusively to the restitution procedure normally provided for in *ona'ah* cases. Hence, real estate transactions are subject to the prohibition against *ona'ah*, though not to its prescribed restitution procedure.

It follows as a corollary from our analysis of the ethics of monopoly pricing that the interdict is violated only when the real estate transaction involves an authentic opportunity cost; i.e., property of the same general characteristics was available in the marketplace at a price above or below the transaction price at hand. No moral issue, however, is involved regarding the price differential attributed to site value.

22. Frederic Morton, *The Rothschilds: A Family Portrait* (New York: Atheneum, 1962), pp. 48–50.

23. For an overview of the prohibition against acting in the manner of the inhabitants of Sodom, see Aaron Levine, *Economics and Jewish Law,* (Hoboken, N.J.: Ktav, 1987), pp. 36–41.

24. Bava Kamma 21a.

25. Mordecai, Bava Kamma 2:16; R. Joseph Habiba (Spain, early 15th cent.), commentary on Rif, Bava Kamma 21a; R. Mosheh Isserles (Poland, 1525 or 1530–1572), Rema, *Sh.Ar.*, op. cit. 363:6; *Ar.haSh.*, op. cit. 363:16. Other authorities vest the landlord with the right to object to the squatter's presence even when he could not theoretically rent out the apartment; see R. Abraham Hirsch b. Jacob Eisenstadt (Poland, 1813–1868), *Pithei Teshuvah* to *Sh.Ar.*, op. cit. 363, n. 3.

26. 17 Code of Federal Regulations 10b; 17 CFR 240.10b5.

27. *SEC v. Texas Gulf Sulphur Co.*, 401 F.2d 833, 843, 847 (2d Cir. 1968).

28. Ibid at 848.

29. *Yad,* op. cit. 22:13, and R. Yom Tov Vidal of Tolosa (Spain, 14th cent.), *Maggid Mishneh,* ad loc.; *Tur,* op. cit. 212:1; *Sh.Ar.*, op. cit. 212:1; *Ar.haSh.*, op. cit. 212:1.

30. R. Hai Gaon (Babylonia, 938–1038), *Sefer ha-Mikkah ve-ha-Mimkar*, sha'ar 2.

31. R. David b. Solomon ibn Abi Zimra (Radvaz), quoted by R. Moses b. Joseph Trani (Israel, 1500–1580), *Responsa Mabit* 132. For an opposing view, see *Ar.haSh.*, op. cit. 212:2.

32. *Ar.haSh.*, op. cit. 212:3.

33. Nicholas Wolfson, "Trade Secrets and Secret Trading," *San Diego Law Review* 25, no. 95 (1988): 110.

34. *Carpenter v. United States*, 484 U.S. 19 (1987), at 25–27.

35. See Barry Bressler, "Ethical Investment: The Responsibility of Ownership in Jewish Law," and Michael J. Broyde and Steven H. Resnicoff, "Jewish Law and the Corporate Paradign" in *Jewish Business Ethics: The Firm and Its Stakeholders*, ed. Aaron Levine and Moses L. Pava (Northvale, N.J.: Jason Aronson, 1999), forthcoming. See also Michael J. Broyde and Steven H. Resnicoff, "Jewish Law and Modern Business Structures: The Corporate Paradigm," *Wayne Law Review* 43, no. 4 (Fall 1997): 1792–1800.

36. Please turn to pp. 72–74 of this volume.

37. 445 U.S. 222, 224 (1980).

38. 588 F. 2d 1358 (2d Cir. 1978), rev'd, 445 U.S. 222 (1980).

39. 445 U.S. at 231–35.

40. R. Solomon Leib Tabak, *Responsa Erekh Shai* 183:1.

41. *Pithe Hoshen, Hilkhot Sekhirut*, pp. 163–64.

42. *United States v. O'Hagan*, no. 96842 (Slip Opinion).

43. 681 F. 2d 842 at 829–31; 463 U.S. 646 at 648–49.

44. 681 F. 2d at 829.

45. 463 U.S. at 651.

46. Ibid. at 65859.

47. Leviticus 19:16.

48. Please turn to pp. 283–84 of this volume.

49. *Dirks v. SEC*, 463 U.S. 646, 669 (1982).

50. 463 U.S. 646, 655–62.

51. *SEC v. Switzer*, 590 F. Supp. 756 (W.D. Okla. 1984).

52. 590 F. Supp. 756, 761–64.

53. Ibid at 764–67.

54. Ibid at 766.

Insider Trading and Public Policy

The economic literature has produced several arguments in favor of the government's adopting a laissez-faire policy toward insider trading. If this proposal was adopted, companies would be free, on an individual basis, to decide whether to permit insider trading by their employees.

To begin, let us identify the type of an insider trading case that Halakhah might permit under voluntary agreement by the affected parties. Suppose Grand Met PLC and Dorsey and Whitney had given O'Hagan explicit permission to trade in Pillsbury shares. Recall that Halakhah rejects the parity of information doctrine as it applies to trading on the impersonal financial markets. Since O'Hagan's trade did not entail misappropriation, and the financial markets are not entitled to disclosure of his informational advantage, Halakhah would perhaps have no objection to the trade. But suppose O'Hagan merely informs Grand Met and Dorsey and Whitney that he plans to trade in Pillsbury stocks, but they do not give him permission to do so. Here, legislation may not legalize O'Hagan's action, as his conduct would entail the prohibition of misappropriation.

Recall that Dirks' conduct violated the prohibitions of tortfeasing, talebearing, and offering ill-suited advice. Legislation to legalize Dirks' actions would also not find sanction in Halakhah.

The upshot of this analysis is that the issue of laissez-faire legislation in Halakhah covers a much more limited ambit of cases than those who proposed this idea had in mind.

We will now present the case for laissez-faire along with the arguments the literature has advanced in favor of it. We will next demonstrate that the case against laissez-faire can be stated in theological terms. Halakhah's opposition to the laissez-faire approach will then have been demonstrated.

The Economic Case for Legalizing Insider Trading

One facet of the economic case for legalizing insider trading is the thesis that insider trading is an indispensable method of compensating entrepreneurs. What makes this compensation scheme attractive is that it allows managers to profit from their efforts on behalf of the firm without having to negotiate with owners. When managers believe that their entrepreneurial activities will enhance the value of the firm, they can invest in the company's shares at their discretion. Having acquired an interest in the future course of the share price, managers will concentrate their efforts on behalf of the company to ensure that their programs will succeed and the resulting enhanced performance be disclosed.[1]

One major objection that the above compensation scheme faces is that insider trading does not reward efficient managers as such. Rather, it rewards the *possessors* of confidential information, whether or not favorable to the corporation's prospects.

Moreover, such a plan gives insiders as much of an incentive to destroy a company as to revolutionize it, or to reduce earnings as much as to increase them. One can imagine cases where managers would have an incentive to accelerate the demise of their firm. Managers would have an incentive to manipulate the disclosure of information about the firm in a manner calculated to produce sharp, if temporary, spurts in the price of the firm's stock. Their energies would be deflected from managing the firm so as to maximize its present worth to managing publicity about the firm so as to maximize the volatility of its stock.[2]

It is inconsistent to claim that such market forces as concern for one's reputation are sufficient to deter insiders from exploiting bad news, and at the same time, deny to such factors the power to motivate good entrepreneurial performance.[3]

Judge Frank H. Easterbrook's analysis of the adverse-selection problem sheds light on why conflict of interest can be expected to become widespread under a rule permitting insider trading. Let us suppose that firm A allows its executives to engage in insider trading, but firm B contractually forbids such conduct. Given the absence of government involvement in the enforcement against insider trading, B will find it very costly to enforce its prohibition. Most important, it will be very costly to detect an insider's trades because he can hide his trading activity. Specifically, the insider can buy stock in street names or through nominees, or he can route orders through a chain of brokers to make tracing difficult—the list of evasive devices is long.

About the only thing a firm can do by itself to reduce the costs of enforcing compliance with a no-trading pledge is to prohibit all ownership of stock by its employees. This drastic response could not interdict managers' passing of tips to friends and family or secretly trading through nominees. If a ban were enforceable, however, its costs might far exceed those of insider trading, as stock ownership is very useful in aligning managers' incentives with those of other shareholders.

Whenever a firm writes a contract it either does not plan to or cannot enforce, it will face a serious problem of adverse selection. Accordingly, dishonest executives will find employment with B especially attractive. Since they will get their salaries and also be able to engage in insider trading, they will be overcompensated. To avoid overcompensating the dishonest executives, B will be forced to reduce salaries across the board. As a result, the honest executives—those who do not trade on insider information—will be underpaid and will leave. To increase the quality of its managers, B will have no recourse but to rescind its "voluntary prohibition" of insider trading.[4]

Price Efficiency

Another facet of the economic case for legalizing insider trading is the price-efficiency argument. This argument stresses the importance to the economy of directing financial capital to those places where society values it most. Stock prices are considered to be at their true values when they reflect as accurately as possible the prospects of the corporate issuers. If a firm's value is underrepresented by its share price because, for example, the firm has strategic reasons for not divulging information about a valuable discovery, a marketing strategy, or an expansion or acquisition plan, then it will be more costly than it would otherwise be for that firm to raise capital in the equity market. The firm, therefore, will not engage in the optimal amount of investing, and resources will not flow to those uses that society values most highly.

Advocates for legalizing insider trading believe that trading on insider information moves share prices toward their true value more quickly than if insider trading were banned.[5]

The thesis that insider trading promotes efficiency in the capital markets faces, however, several difficulties.

One difficulty is that illegal insider trading has not been shown empirically to have any significant effect on share prices. A recent study examined increases in the stock prices of target firms in 172 successful tender offers over a three-week period before their announcement. The study found that by one day prior to the announcement, the average stock had appreciated to 38.8 percent of its price one day after the tender offer was announced. It was, however, shown that a significant portion of the run-up could be explained by three legally available influences on pre-bid trading: media speculation, the bidder's foothold acquisition in the target, and whether the bid was friendly or hostile. Thus, a large portion of the run-up could be explained by factors other than illegal insider trading.[6]

Another criticism of the price-efficiency rationale for insider trading is that permitting insider trading may delay or distort the transmission of valuable information to the market. This would occur if insiders at lower echelons of management concealed information from their superiors in order to avoid the danger of an early price run-up that would diminish their gains and leave them with too little time to arrange financing of their trades. It might also occur if members of the firm deliberately released false information in order to take advantage of profits available from resulting price swings.

Finally, legalizing insider trading is not the most efficient means of promoting correct pricing in the capital markets. The latter goal could be achieved instantaneously by adopting a disclosure rule requiring full disclosure by the company of material nonpublic information. There will, of course, be situations in which immediate full disclosure is undesirable, as, for example, in the TGS case discussed above. In these instances, however, there is no reason to believe that insider trading leads to an optimal price adjustment path for company shares.[7]

Transaction Costs

Another consideration in evaluating the thesis that insider trading promotes efficiency in the capital markets is an analysis of the transaction costs that arise from insider trading. A rule permitting insider trading can be expected to put into motion two opposing forces affecting transaction costs. On the debit side, it can be expected to cause an adverse-selection problem for the specialist. By maintaining an inventory of various stocks, the specialist provides continuous trading opportunities for investors. In a legal environment that permits insider trading, the specialist faces the risk that his opposite number may be an insider. Given the increased risk factor, the specialist can be expected to reduce his bid price and/or increase his ask price. Thus a rule permitting insider trading increases for the specialist the spread between his bid and ask prices. The result for firms is that the cost of using the market for financing rises, thereby altering the proportions of the funds they choose to derive from debt and equity.

Counteracting somewhat this negative effect on transaction costs is that a rule permitting insider trading reduces duplicative information gathering in the marketplace. This follows from the proposition that the presence of insiders in the market exerts a disincentive for outsiders to engage in information gathering. Since gains from changes in market value associated with new information will be captured by insiders before outsiders, outsiders will be discouraged from engaging in information gathering. Thus insider trading reduces the overall amount of money that society spends to achieve an adjustment in share prices because it reduces the cost to society of duplicative information gathering by outsiders.[8]

In his treatment of the economics of insider trading, Professor Mark Klock demonstrates that legal commentators have overlooked a tremendous volume of economic literature that is less conservative (and arguably more realistic) than the usual law and economics literature. This overlooked economic literature supports prohibitions on insider trading as a matter of economic efficiency.

Klock presents the argument to support prohibitions on insider trading as follows: If insider trading is permitted, insiders will have an advantage over outsiders and will make above-average returns. Because the insiders' advantage is unfair, outsiders will respond by lowering their investments in securities. The cost of capital for firms will rise. Because the markets for physical capital and securities are linked, there will be a net decline in aggregate investment, resulting in lower levels of gross national output over time. In short, there will be less aggregate wealth to be shared among insiders and outsiders.[9]

The upshot of Klock's analysis is that the economic case for legalizing insider trading is unconvincing.

Imitatio Dei and Economic Public Policy

In this section we will demonstrate that many of the arguments against legalizing insider trading can be put in theological terms. Let us begin with the concept of *imitatio Dei*.

In Judaism, the guidepost for interpersonal conduct is the duty to emulate God's attribute of mercy. This behavioral norm is called *imitatio Dei* ("imitation of God"). In this section, we will develop the thesis that *imitatio Dei* is also the guidepost for economic public policy in a society governed by Halakhah. We begin with an exposition of what this behavioral imperative denotes for interpersonal conduct.

After the Lord your God shall you walk (Deuteronomy 13:5) [R. Hama b. Hanina asks:] Is it then possible to "walk after" the Divine Presence? Has not Scripture already said, *for the Lord your God is a devouring fire* (Deuteronomy 4:24)? But it means, walk after the attributes of the Holy One. Even as He clothes the naked [clothing Adam and Eve with the garments of skins (Genesis 3:21)], so must you provide clothes for the naked. The Holy One visited the sick [appearing to Abraham after his circumcision (Genesis 18:1)]; so must you visit the sick. The Holy One consoled the bereaved [blessing Isaac after Abraham's death (Genesis 25:11)]; so must you console the bereaved. The Holy One buried the dead [interring Moses (Deuteronomy 34:6)]; so must you bury the dead.[10]

To walk in all His ways (Deuteronomy 10:12) These are the "ways of the Lord": as it is written, *The Lord, the Lord, God, merciful and gracious, long-suffering and abundant in goodness and truth, keeping mercy unto the thousandth generation, forgiving iniquity and transgression and sin* (Exodus 34:6-7).[11]

And it shall come to pass that whosoever shall call on the Name of the Lord shall be saved (Joel 3:5). Is it possible, then, for a man to be called by the name of Holy One? But this means: Just as He is called "merciful and gracious" . . . so must you be merciful and gracious, and give of your gifts freely to all; just as the Holy One is called "righteous" . . . so must you be righteous. The Holy One is called "loving" . . . so must you be loving. That is why it is said, *And it shall come to pass that whoever shall be called by the name of the Lord shall be delivered* (Joel 3:5). And it also is said, *Everyone that is called by My name, and whom I created for My glory, I formed him, yea I made him (Isaiah 43:3).* And it also is said, *The Lord has made everything for His own purpose.*[12]

At the outset, let us take note that Maimonides (Egypt, 1135–1204) counts the duty of *imitatio Dei* as one of the 613 precepts.[13] The significance of this, as Professor Yizhak Twersky pointed out, is to make *imitatio Dei* not just a theological concept but also a halakhic imperative.[14]

R. Naftali Zevi Yehudah Berlin (Russia, 1817–1893) derives the selfsame point from the proof-texts cited above at Isaiah 43:7 and Proverbs 16:4. These texts make *imitatio Dei* not merely a matter of nobility of spirit but a God-given duty, its practice being the very goal of creation.[15]

As a behavioral imperative, *imitatio Dei* extends beyond a duty to emulate those attributes of God's mercy explicitly enumerated at Exodus 34:67. By the exegesis of Joel 3:5, a duty to emulate God in every manifestation of His mercy is established.[16]

In R. Joseph B. Soloveitchik's thinking, *imitatio Dei* both imposes specific conduct and sets a standard for character. Deuteronomy 13:5 directs man to engage in *imitatio Dei* conduct. Joel 3:5, however, sets a standard for human *character*. Not only should man's conduct be God-like, but he must nurture a God-like character, becoming worthy of being called by the names of God. Engaging in God-like actions naturally and with no sense of burden demonstrates a God-like character.[17]

The Social Component of *Imitatio Dei*

While the source texts cited above all relate to *imitatio Dei* in connection with interpersonal conduct, this duty, according to Maimonides, applies to the ruler as well as to private citizens. What this behavioral imperative implies for the ruler is that his rewards and punishments should not be based on the passion of the moment, but rather on a careful consideration of equity with the aim of promoting social welfare. Since the sovereign must perforce be involved in the administration of justice, *imitatio Dei* requires him to mete out punishment in the same manner that God metes out punishment.[18] As a private citizen, however, man is only bidden to emulate God's attributes of mercy. Emulating attributes of God relating to punishment is strictly forbidden.[19]

Supporting the proposition that the *imitatio Dei* concept has a social component is Abba Saul's exegesis of the verse *Zeh E-li ve-anvehu* ("This is my God and I will glorify Him," Exodus 15:2). Abba Saul understands *ve-anvehu* to consist of two words, *ve-ani ve-hu* (lit. "and I and Him"), with the import being: "I will be like Him; just as He is *rahum* (merciful) and *hanun* (gracious), so too will I be merciful and gracious" (Shabbat 133b).

In light of the *imitatio Dei* lesson derived from Deuteronomy 10:12, Abba Saul's exegesis appears superfluous. Closer examination of the dictum reveals, however, that Abba Saul adds a social component to the *imitatio Dei* principle. This follows from the consideration that the circumstance that inspired the Jewish people to proclaim *zeh E-li ve-anvehu* was the miracle of the splitting of the Red Sea. No one was singled out to experience the miracle. Quite to the contrary, God wrought this miracle for the Jewish people in its entirety. In contrast to the manna, whose benefit manifested itself on different levels according to individual merit,[20] the miracle at the Red Sea blanketed the Jewish people as a whole,[21] making no distinctions between the deserving and the undeserving.[22] Here, Abba Saul advances *imitatio Dei* beyond interpersonal relations, making it man's duty to incorporate God's attributes of mercy into the community's social fabric and legal environment.

Imitatio Dei and the Moral Climate of Society

One aspect of God's mercy is the weakening of the power of the evil inclination that He effects for those who strive for moral betterment. Expressing this dimension of God's mercy is Resh Lakish's dictum: ". . . if one wishes to defile himself [with sin] the door is merely *opened* for him; but if one comes to purify himself, he is *assisted*."[23] Divine assistance is not triggered only by great human initiatives. An unexceptional act of spiritual striving also merits divine assistance, and so too, perhaps, does an unarticulated spiritual search. Evidencing this is the talmudic dictum that the Almighty demands only that we present to Him an opening of repentance no bigger than the eye of a needle. If we can manage this, then God promises us that He will respond by widening the opening so that even wagons and carriages can pass through.[24]

The immense degree of compassion inherent in God's assistance in our battle against the evil inclination is expressed by Resh Lakish in the following dictum:

> The evil inclination renews its powerful attack on man every day, and tries to kill him, as it says: *the wicked one watches for the righteous and seeks*

to execute him (Psalms 37:32). Were it not for God's assistance, no man could survive the onslaught, as it says: *But God will not forsake him to his power, nor let him be condemned in his judgment* (Psalms 37:33).[25]

The seductive power of the evil inclination is greatest when man is thrust into a setting involving either a conflict of interest or an opportunity to engage in hidden misconduct. It is here that cunning and shrewdness can often camouflage deceitful and fraudulent conduct and at the same time enable the perpetrator to avoid both legal consequences and social outrage.

To be spared the challenge of a test of piety is regarded in Jewish religious doctrine as ideal. Witness both the warning of the sages not to deliberately enter into a situation that will engulf us in a test of piety[26] and the plea we make to God in our daily prayers not to thrust us into a test of piety.[27]

As private citizens we are very limited in what we can do to assist our fellow man in his battle against the evil inclination. But *imitatio Dei* is a mandate for government too, and government can accomplish much in this area. The government's duty here, as it appears to this writer, is to ensure that society's legal environment minimizes settings for hidden misconduct. On this point the reader is referred to the case study in this volume called "Rubie Indigo's Adventures into Veiled Misconduct."

Lifnei Iver and Government Legislation

Another aspect of the government's responsibility for the moral climate is the prohibition against the enactment of laws that inherently generate settings for invisible misconduct. An analysis of Rav's dictum, recorded at Bava Mezia 75b, bears out this prohibition:

> Said R. Judah in the name of Rav: Whoever has money and lends it without witnesses violates the prohibition of *Do not place a stumbling block before the blind* (*lifnei iver lo titan mikshal*, Leviticus 19:14). Resh Lakish said: He brings a curse upon himself, as it is written, *Let the lying lips be put to silence, which speak grievous things proudly and contemptuously against the righteous* (Psalms 31:19).

When a loan transaction takes place without the formality of witnesses, the borrower can eliminate his debt by denying that the transaction took place. This being so, lending money without witnesses is prohibited. To do otherwise, explains R. Solomon b. Isaac (Rashi, France, 1040–1105), would effectively *tempt* the debtor to repudiate his lawful debt, and hence the lender will be in violation of the *lifnei iver* interdict.[28]

Picking up on Rashi's remarks, R. Joel Sirkes (Poland, 1561–1650) and R. Joshua b. Alexander ha-Kohen Falk (Poland, 1555–1614) understand Rav's dictum to be rooted in the concern that the debtor will *willfully* repudiate a debt that he knows is a lawful one.

In the event the debtor is a *talmid hakham* (rabbinical scholar), the above concern does not exist. Therefore, lending money to a *talmid hakham* without the formality of witnesses does not violate the *lifnei iver* interdict. The latter action is, nonetheless, prohibited by Resh Lakish's dictum. The concern here is that the *talmid hakham*'s preoccupation with his studies might cause him to forget his indebtedness and consequently lead him to deny the creditor's claim. Given the *talmid hakham*'s stature, his denials will find credence and the public will curse the lender.[29]

Disputing the foregoing opinions, R. Abraham b. Moses di Boton (Greece, 1545–1588) and R. Jacob Moses Lorberbaum (Poland, 1760–1832) understand Rav's dictum to be rooted in the concern that the debtor might forget the loan and consequently deny the debt, all along convinced that the creditor's claim is false. This rationale applies whether or not the debtor is a *talmid hakham*.[30]

In defending his position that the concern for willful repudiation cannot stand at the basis of Rav's dictum, R. Boton invokes the talmudic principle that exhortations are never directed at those who are predisposed to *willfully* violate them (*atu b'reshie askinan*). The basis of the application of the *lifnei iver* interdict to the making of an unwitnessed loan must therefore be the concern that the debtor might come to forget his obligation and consequently be led to deny it.[31]

A narrower understanding of *atu b'reshie askinan*, however, follows from Rashi et al. Given the inherent futility of exhorting the willfully evil who do not care if their misconduct is discovered, the Torah never ascribes this character trait to the subjects of its exhortation. This is what is meant by the talmudic phrase *atu b'reshie askinan*. The Torah does, however, direct its exhortation to the willfully evil who want to avoid social disapproval by covering up their misconduct. Witness that the phrase *ve-yareta me'Elohekha* ("and you shall fear your God") is employed by the Torah specifically in connection with those of its prohibitions that man convinces himself he can violate without detection.[32]

Supporting the narrow interpretation of *atu b'reshie askinan* is the connection the Talmud makes between this phrase and the *veyareta me'Elohekha* exhortation employed in relation to the duty to give deference to a *talmid hakham* by standing up as he approaches.[33] Invoking *atu b'reshie askinan*, the Talmud rejects the possibility that *veyareta me'Elohekha* adjures against closing our eyes and pretending that the *talmid hakham* is not in our presence. Rather, *veyareta me'Elohekha* forewarns against closing our eyes *just before* the *talmid hakham* arrives. Here, the willful sinner might be tempted to show the *talmid hakham* disrespect and yet imagine that by claiming that he simply did not notice his presence he will escape social outrage for the misconduct. Thus, the Torah forewarns that the Almighty knows man's true circumstances and true intentions.[34]

Proceeding from this conceptualization of *atu b'reshie askinan* is the following refinement of Rav's dictum: Lending money without the formality of witnesses is prohibited because such action generates for the debtor a setting for *veiled misconduct*. Since denying the debt outright brands the debtor an ingrate, there is no concern that the debtor will adopt this tactic. Such a *brazen* approach is unthinkable by dint of the principle of *atu b'reshie askinan*. Rather, the concern is that the unwitnessed transaction will lead the debtor to shrewdly evade payment by pleading *ignorance* of the indebtedness.[35] By taking an oath affirming his ignorance of the debt, the defendant avoids the stigma of being branded an ingrate and at the same time escapes payment.[36]

We see an application of Rav's dictum in the prohibition of the government in a Jewish society enacting a law that inherently generates settings for invisible misconduct.

Legislation in the Moral Sphere: Practical Implications

Imitatio Dei makes government the guardian of the moral climate of society. What *imitatio Dei* denotes for government in respect to specific economic issues is, however, somewhat problematic. The difficulty arises out of the consideration that implementing any particular rule of conduct is at the expense of the moral climate that would have been fostered under an alternative rule. In consequence, keen economic analysis to determine the opportunity cost of alternative courses of action is required. Moreover, God's mercy is designed for man's *ultimate* good.[37] Hence, *imitatio Dei* disallows the confinement of economic policymaking to a short-run analysis. The long-term consequences of alternative courses of action must be evaluated. Given the limitations of extrapolating the direct and indirect consequences of a particular policy, the onus of persuasion facing those who propose change is imposing.

Notwithstanding these difficulties, *imitatio Dei* offers direction for economic public policy. Elsewhere we have dealt with this topic at length.[38] The proposition relevant for the issue at hand is that legislation should not be initiated to alter the distribution of property rights when such a change would inherently create conflict of interest and veiled-misconduct situations.

Legalizing insider trading does violence to the *imitatio Dei* ideal. By opening the door for compensation schemes that allow employees to trade on insider information, deregulation creates opportunities for managers to profit from their own sloth, ineptness, and/or destructive behavior. This drives a wedge between the interests of the managers and the interests of the shareholders.

Left to its own devices, the private sector, as indicated, would be bedeviled with difficulties in enforcing the insider trading prohibitions. Thus, in a society governed by Halakhah, the government's mission to suffuse the legal environment with *imitatio Dei* conduct requires that it play a vigorous role in enforcing the ban on insider trading.

In an effort to rectify the ineffectiveness of the enforcement remedies available to the SEC for insider-trading violations, Congress enacted the Insider Trading Sanctions Act of 1984 (ITSA). Congress designed the ITSA to impose a severe monetary civil penalty as the primary means of deterring future violations of insider trading. Under this legislation, the SEC has the authority to seek, and the courts have the power to impose, up to a maximum penalty of treble damages on insider-trading violations subject to the act.[39]

In 1988, Congress passed the Insider Trading and Securities Fraud Enforcement Act (ITSFEA). This act significantly increased the maximum criminal penalties for insider-trading offenses.[40] One provision of ITSFEA empowered the SEC to award bounty payments to persons who furnish information leading to the imposition of civil penalties for insider trading. Without being subject to judicial review, the SEC was empowered with broad discretion concerning the bounty payments.[41]

These recent congressional enactments in the area of insider trading, as the thrust of the preceding discussion indicates, would be very much applauded by Halakhah.

Problem

I. M. Frier has devised a clever scheme to test the honesty of his employees. Frier leaves an open envelope at the foot of the coffee table located in the company lounge. The envelope is stamped and addressed to his grandson, Ivan. Frier's name and address appear just below the flap of the envelope. Inside the envelope is a birthday card. Inside the card there is mention of a $200 "enclosed" gift which is to be used toward the purchase of a bicycle. In reality, the envelope contains three $100 bills. The bills are crisp, new ones that are stuck together. To ascertain which employee picks up the envelope, Frier installs a surveillance camera in an inconspicuous spot on the ceiling of the lounge. In order not to intrude on his employees, the camera is trained exclusively on the envelope that Frier seeks to protect against theft.

If it becomes evident that an employee has pocketed the money, Frier confronts the employee with the incriminating film and warns that any further indiscretion would result in an immediate firing. Since the employee is overwhelmed with gratitude at not being fired on the spot, Frier's scene works wonders in dramatically increasing the culprit employee's work ethic and productivity.

On the other hand, if the employee returns or mails the birthday card but pockets the extra $100, Frier fires the employee on the spot, proclaiming: "The worst thing is a crook who masquerades himself as a good Samaritan."

From the standpoint of Halakhah, evaluate Frier's conduct. To answer this question, you will need to study material elsewhere in this volume in addition to the preceding case study.

1. Henry Mann, *Insider Trading and the Stock Market* (New York: Free Press, 1966), pp. 138–45.

2. Richard A. Posner, *Economic Analysis of Law*, 5th ed. (New York: Aspen Law and Business, 1998), pp. 459–60.

3. Saul Levmore, "In Defense of the Regulation of Insider Trading," *Harvard Journal of Law and Public Policy* 11, no. 1 (Winter, 1998): 10–45.

4. Frank H. Easterbrook, "Insider Trading as an Agency Problem," in *Principles and Agents: The Structure of Business*, ed., John W. Platt and Richard J. Zeckhauser (Boston: Harvard Business School Press, 1985), p. 914.

5. Henry Mann, "Insider Trading and the Law Professors," *Vanderbilt Law Review* 23 (1970), 56–56.

6. Office of the Chief Economist, Securities and Exchange Commission, "Stock Trading Before the Announcement of Tender Offers: Insider Trading or Market Anticipation?" pp. 3, 324.

7. Iman Anabtawi, "Toward a Definition of Insider Trading," *Stanford Law Review* 41 (January 1989): 39–46.

8. Ibid., pp. 39–69.

9. Mark Klock, "Mainstream Economics and the Case for Prohibiting Inside Trading," *Georgia State University Law Review* 10 (1994): 297.

10. Sotah 14a.

11. Sifrei, Deuteronomy 10:12.

12. Ibid.

13. Maimonides, *Sefer ha-Mitzvot*, mitzvat aseh, no. 8; *Yad*, De'ot 1:6.

14. R. Yizhak Twersky, "On Law and Ethics in the *Mishneh Torah*: A Case Study of *Hilkhot Megillah* II:17," *Tradition* 24, no. 2 (Winter 1989): 14–23. See also Lawrence Kaplan, "*Hilkhot Megillah* 2:17 Revisited: A Halakhic Analysis," *Tradition* 26, no. 1 (Fall 1991): 14–21.

15. R. Naftali Zevi Yehudah Berlin, *Emek Neziv*, Sifrei at Deuteronomy 10:2, piska 13.

16. Ibid.

17. R. Joseph B. Soloveitchik, *Shiurim le-Zekher Abba Mori*, vol. 2 (Jerusalem, 1986), pp. 170–1.

18. Maimonides, *Guide of the Perplexed*, trans. S. Pines (Chicago: University of Chicago Press, 1963), chap. 54, pp. 12–67.

19. For the development of this point, see R. Norman Lamm, "Notes on the Concept of *Imitatio Dei*," in *Rabbi Joseph H. Lookstein Memorial Volume*, ed. R. Leo Landman (New York: Ktav, 1980), pp. 227–29.

20. Yoma 75a.

21. Mekhilta at Exodus 15:2.

22. Exodus Rabbah 21:7 and R. Samuel Jaffe b. Isaac Ashkenazi (Turkey, 16th cent.), *Yefeh To'ar*, Exodus Rabbah, ad loc.; R. Jacob Culi (Turkey, ca. 1685–1732), *Me-Am Lo'ez*, Exodus 14:19.

23. Yoma 38b.

24. Song of Songs Rabbah 5:2.

25. Kiddushin 30b.

26. Sanhedrin 107a.

27. Berakhot 60b.

28. Rashi at Bava Mezia 75b.

29. R. Joel Sirkes, Bah to Tur, Hoshen Mishpat 70, n. 1; R. Joshua b. Alexander ha-Kohen Falk, *Perishah* to *Tur*, Hoshen Mishpat 70, n. 1.

30. R. Abraham b. Moses di Boton, *Lehem Mishneh* to *Yad*, Malveh 2:7; R. Jacob Moses Lorberbaum, *Netivot ha-Mishpat* 70, n. 1.

31. *Lehem Mishneh*, loc. cit.

32. Rashi, at Leviticus 19:14. The Torah makes use of the phrase "And you shall fear your God" in connection with the following moral imperatives: (1) the prohibition against offering ill-suited advice (Leviticus 19:14); (2) the duty to bestow honor upon a talmudic scholar (Leviticus 19:32); (3) the injunction against causing someone needless mental anguish (Leviticus 25:36); (4) the interdict against charging interest (Leviticus 25:36); and (5) the prohibition against working an Israelite bondman oppressively (Leviticus 25:43).

33. Leviticus 19:32, Kiddushin 32b.

34. Kiddushin 32b–33a.

35. In the event the defendant admits the indebtedness but pleads ignorance of whether the debt was repaid, the plaintiff is entitled to recover his claim in full. See Mishnah, Bava Kamma 10:7; Rif, ad loc.; *Yad*, To'en ve-Nitan 1:9; Rosh, Bava Kamma 10:32; *Tur*, Hoshen Mishpat 75:9; *Shulhan Arukh*, Hoshen Mishpat 75:9; *Arukh ha-Shulhan*, Hoshen Mishpat 75:1314.

36. In defending his interpretation of Rav's dictum, R. Boton adduces a *reductio ad absurdum* argument: If the dictum is rooted in concern about the willful denial of a lawful debt, then by force of the *lifnei iver* interdict, even a properly witnessed loan should be prohibited. This follows from the fact that Jewish law does not require a debt to be repaid with the formality of witnesses (see Ketubbot 18a). Consequently, even if the loan was entered into by means of witnesses, the debtor could escape payment by denying the obligation.

The difficulty is, however, resolved with the recognition that a witnessed loan transaction does not generate a setting of hidden misconduct for the debtor. In the latter instance, a plea of ignorance will not be sufficient to allow the debtor to escape liability (see *Shulhan Arukh*, Hoshen Mishpat 75:12). Here, the debtor can escape payment only by claiming outright that he paid off the debt. Provided that the debt was not entered into by means of *kinyan*, taking an oath that he repaid the debt enables the debtor to evade responsibility (see Hoshen Mishpat 70:1.). Since a witnessed loan transaction does not generate a situation wherein the debtor can escape responsibility by engaging in hidden misconduct, the making of the loan cannot entail violation of the *lifnei iver* interdict.

37. Deuteronomy 8:16.

38. Aaron Levine, *Economic Public Policy and Jewish Law* (Hoboken, N.J., Ktav, 1993).

39. Insider Trading Sanction Act of 1984, Pub. L. No. 98376, 98 Stat. 1264 (1984).

40. Pub. L. no. 100704, 102 Stat. 4677 (1988).

41. Sec. 3 (a) (2), 21A(e), 102 Stat. at 4679.

Price Matching at the Electronics Emporium

Price matching is a marketing stratagem employed by such retail sellers as appliance and electronics dealers. Typically, the store employing the policy challenges its customers to search local newspapers and find an ad for the same item (i.e., same make and model) they have purchased. If the item is advertised elsewhere at a lower price, even if the ad appears as much as a month after the purchase, presentation of the ad along with proof of purchase entitles the customer to the difference in price.

Matthew Zole, owner-manager of Electronics Emporium, a large electronics store, was planning to introduce a price-matching program of the genre described above. But before he could implement it, his attention was drawn to a marketing study by Leo J. Shapiro and Associates. The study found that offering to match a competitor's price made a store seem more attractive to as many as two out of three customers.[1] Zole was immediately struck by the enigma of why price matching was not attractive to *all* customers. Drawing upon his training as an economics major in college, Zole ventured to solve the oddity with the aid of the concept of opportunity cost. Price matching, he reasoned, makes a customer work hard to collect on the store's promise of a rebate. Specifically, a customer must comb newspaper ads for as long as a month and then return to the store of purchase with receipt in hand. If the *maximum anticipated* saving resulting from all this bother is no more than, say, $30 on a $600 item, the toil and effort is, for many, simply not worth it. For price matching to be maximally appealing, the customer must believe that the store making the offer is in fact the lowest-priced outlet, and therefore there is no need to check out the competition. The more appealing price matching is to the customer, the more profitable it will be for the store that makes the offer.

Enamored by the power of his own economic analysis, Zole was determined to take price matching upscale. To implement his idea, Zole took out full-page ads in the local newspapers. In the ads, Electronics Emporium proclaimed itself to be the lowest-priced electronics store in the city. To give the claim instant credibility, selected items were advertised at prices that Zole felt certain either beat or trounced the competition. Finally, a price-matching offer appeared at the conclusion of the message.

Zole fully realized that to sustain the credibility of his low-price claim, both competitor prices and market intelligence would have to be monitored much more closely than was his practice in the past. Scanning newspaper ads and picking up information on the mindset of competitors from declared comparison shoppers would simply not suffice. Toward the end of monitoring the competition much more closely, Zole hired Rubie Indigo as a secret comparison shopper.[2] His job was to pose as a customer at competing outlets and elicit as much price-related information as possible without arousing suspicion. Indigo was not to actually make a purchase unless doing so was a necessary means to deflect discovery of the true purpose behind his inquiries.

Electronics Emporium's price-matching program proved a huge success. Three months into the program, sales increased substantially. In addition, very few customers made demands for rebates on the basis of the price-matching program.

At this juncture, Zole felt that a change in strategy was in order. Electronics Emporium had achieved a solid reputation as the lowest-priced electronics dealer in the city. This reputation would surely continue on *momentum alone* for a while. Dispensing with the services of a secret comparison shopper was therefore indicated. Zole continued to claim in media advertising that Electronics Emporium was the lowest-priced electronics dealer. This claim, along with a description of its price-matching policy, was also prominently displayed in the front window of its store.

Zole felt certain that the new stratagem would surely result in an increase in the incidence of customer demands for rebates. But any increase in rebates paid out, reasoned Zole, would be swamped by the savings effected by dropping Indigo from the payroll.

Zole understood that an increase in customer demand for rebates would signal a weakening of Electronics Emporium's reputation as the lowest-priced seller. Accordingly, Zole resolved to monitor customer rebate data on a weekly basis. In the event that the data indicated that Electronics Emporium's reputation as the lowest-priced seller was weakening, Zole was resigned to have a cost-benefit analysis decide whether efforts to beef up its reputation should be undertaken.

Price Matching at ShopSmart

Emboldened by the success of his price-matching program, Zole introduced a variant of the policy at Electronics Emporium's subsidiary, the ShopSmart supermarket chain. The plan called for the chain to print on its shopping bags the slogan: "We will not be undersold." The same slogan appeared in huge letters on the storefront along with an advisory that customers should consult management for the details of the store's price-matching promise. Interested customers were handed a flier in which they were told that the offer was valid only for a purchase of twenty-five or more items. If a customer could find some other chain that was currently charging less for the whole set of goods taken together, and supplied proof of her purchases at ShopSmart, she would be entitled to the price difference. In addition, the offer was valid only for identically branded items.

Price Matching and the Law of *Ona'ah*

One is immediately struck by the affinity between the rights a price-matching program confers on the customer and the rights a customer *automatically* enjoys under the law of *ona'ah* (price fraud). The reader is referred to the case study entitled "Sheldon Hass' Brand of Limited Paternalism" for a detailed discussion of the laws of *ona'ah*. An identity between the customer's rights under price matching and *ona'ah* should, of course, not be assumed. From the perspective of Halakhah, a price-matching program should not be designed to deprive the customer of a right he would otherwise enjoy under the law of *ona'ah*. Relatedly, the protection *ona'ah* confers to the customer has its limits. Price matching, therefore, has much room to expand the rights of the customer. Let us set Zole's price-matching programs against the laws of *ona'ah* with the aim of assessing to what extent the programs expanded or deprived the customer's *ona'ah* rights.

Let us begin with the objectionable aspects of the programs:

1. By limiting its price-matching program to the instance where the customer purchased twenty-five items or more, the program denies the *ona'ah* rights of the customer whose purchases fall short of this amount.

2. Recall that Halakhah establishes three separate categories of the offense. In first-degree *ona'ah*, the price discrepancy between the subject transaction and the competitive norm is more than one-sixth. Here, plaintiff's right to void the transaction is recognized. In second-degree *ona'ah*, the differential involved is exactly one-sixth. Neither party is entitled to subsequently void the transaction on account of the *ona'ah* involved, but the plaintiff is entitled to full restitution of the *ona'ah*. Finally, third-degree *ona'ah* occurs when the sale price differs from the market price by less than one-sixth. The transaction not only remains binding, but in addition, the complainant has no legal claim to the price differential. In the latter instance, however, the plaintiff's claim is denied only when the transaction involved a product that is nonstandardized in nature. Should the case involve a homogeneous product, the plaintiff's claim for the differential is honored.

Because Halakhah establishes three categories of offenses in relation to *ona'ah*, it is inappropriate to lump together all the items of purchase in considering the merits of the *ona'ah* claim. To see why, consider the following case: Suppose three items in the bundle of twenty-five involved second-degree *ona'ah* against ShopSmart, with the total claim amounting to $3. Let us also suppose that the other twenty-three items were all cheaper at ShopSmart, but involved only third-degree *ona'ah* relative to competing store B, with the difference in price also amounting to $3. Under the price-matching plan, the customer is not entitled to any rebate. But the law of *ona'ah* would entitle the customer to a $3 claim against ShopSmart.

Similarly, suppose one or more of the items of purchase entailed first-degree *ona'ah*. The law of *ona'ah* would entitle the customer to a refund. But price matching at ShopSmart does not provide for this option. The selfsame objection holds for Electronics Emporium's price-matching offer.

3. Another objection to treating the various items of purchase as a single unit is that it imposes an *artificial* cost on the customer who wants to exercise his *ona'ah* rights in respect to a particular item. Accordingly, even if the lumping requirement for the particular circumstance at hand does not impose additional *monetary* losses in relation to the law of *ona'ah*, the plan still imposes extra costs on the customer in the form of toil and effort, and hence emasculates the customer's *ona'ah* rights.

Mandated Price Matching and *Ona'ah*

We now turn to the issue of whether the law of *ona'ah* works to *mandate* a price-matching policy for a firm operating in a competitive marketplace. Arguing against such a requirement is the recognition that the availability of an item at a particular price does not always make a higher-priced seller of the same item in violation of *ona'ah*. The taxonomy of cases provided below illustrates situations where the price difference between sellers does not make for an *ona'ah* violation for the higher-priced seller.

1. By making good on its guarantee regardless of how large the price difference is between itself and the lower-priced outlet, price matching goes beyond the customer's rights in an *ona'ah* proceeding. This is so because an *ona'ah* claim is recognized only when the price discrepancy involved falls within the margin of error. Individuals freely entering into a market transaction are presumed to have an approximate notion of the value of the article involved. What are we, then, to make of a transaction concluded on price terms that exceed reasonable misjudgment of value? The only plausible interpretation is that the underlying intention of the parties involved was not to trade the article at hand but rather just to use the transaction as a *vehicle* to effect a voluntary gift transfer.[3]

2. Price-matching guarantees often relate to competitors located outside the marketplace area of the store making the offer. Food Lion, a grocery chain located in North Carolina, for instance, makes the claim that its prices are the

lowest in the entire state. But such far-flung guarantees go beyond the *ona'ah* rights of the customer. From the standpoint of *ona'ah*, marketplace separation insulates a seller from the *ona'ah* claim of his competitor's customer base.

3. Price-matching guarantees typically relate to the availability of an *identical-brand item* elsewhere at a lower price. But suppose the firm making the guarantee offers its customers every amenity its rival offers *plus* some advantage that the competitor does not offer. This circumstance characterizes the firm making the offer as a *higher-grade* seller as compared to its rival. From the standpoint of *ona'ah*, a *higher-grade* seller is entitled to charge a higher price for an identical item available at the *lower-grade* seller. To illustrate, suppose Electronics Emporium charges a higher price for a brand-name camera than its competitor, ElectroGadget. Examination of the respective merchandise-return policies of the two firms reveals, however, a major difference. Electronics Emporium buys back merchandise a customer returns for the same price the customer paid for it, provided the item is returned within thirty days of purchase.[4] ElectroGadget, however, buys back a returned item only if it is brought back to the store within two days of purchase. In addition, no cash refund is given. Instead, the customer is given a credit slip which can be used toward the purchase of any other item in the store. In relation to ElectroGadget, Electronics Emporium should be characterized as a *higher-grade* seller. The higher price it charges for the same standardized item should therefore not be regarded as an infraction of *ona'ah*.

4. Under a price-matching guarantee, a customer may well be able to collect a promised rebate even when the lower price of a competing outlet represented a discount sale below the prevailing norm. In sharp contrast, *ona'ah* claims are adjudicated on the basis of the price the item commands in the marketplace rather than on the basis of the price it was actually sold at.

The halakhic sources for the aforementioned instances where the law of *ona'ah* does not apply were taken up in the chapter entitled "Sheldon Hass' Brand of Limited Paternalism."

The Thirty-Day Challenge and *Ona'ah*

Price-matching guarantees, as mentioned earlier, often extend over a thirty-day period. This feature of the policy, in all probability, confers the customer with rights beyond what the law of *ona'ah* entitles him to, as can be seen by recognizing that the sages set a time limit for an *ona'ah* claim.

In the instance where the customer is victimized, lapse of sufficient time to allow him the opportunity to show his purchase to an expert assessor forfeits for him any legal recourse against *ona'ah*.[5] This time span, as R. Solomon b.

Isaac (Rashi; France, 1040–1105) points out, provides the complainant with sufficient time to ascertain whether or not his purchase involved *ona'ah*. Silence beyond this interval is, therefore, taken as an implicit waiver of his legal claims against *ona'ah*.[6]

The buyer's silence beyond the legal limit is not construed as an implicit waiver, however, when the article is purchased on credit. Here, the buyer may defend his prolonged silence on the ground that he had not yet made payment and thus had not yet investigated whether the purchase involved *ona'ah*. Nonetheless, once the customer makes use of the article bought on credit, his extended rights in respect to *ona'ah* are no longer recognized.[7]

Consider, too, that if a customer lodges an *ona'ah* claim based on the lower price that now prevails under changed market conditions, it is rejected.[8] Moreover, Halakhah regards market conditions as inherently unstable, and price, therefore, as subject to frequent change. Consequently, if buyer and seller dispute whether the comparison price represents changed market conditions, the burden of proof is on the party who claims that market conditions did not change.[9]

Regarding market price as subject to frequent change naturally works to impair the customer's ability to collect on his *ona'ah* claim. The thirty-day challenge, in all probability, confers the customer with rights beyond what the law of *ona'ah* entitles him to.

The upshot of the above discussion is that Halakhah does not require a vendor to announce a price-matching policy in advance of the sale of his goods. Price matching guarantees, in their typical form, generally confer a customer with far greater rights than those which *ona'ah* entitles him to. This is especially so in respect to the thirty-day challenge that often is a feature of price-matching guarantees. Moreover, Halakhah confers a vendor with some degree of latitude in deliberately charging above the price other firms are charging for the identical item. Notwithstanding the generally expanded rights the customer enjoys under price matching, this policy should not be designed in a manner that deprives the buyer of a right he would otherwise have under the law of *ona'ah*.

Secret Comparison Shopping and *Ona'at Devarim*

As a means of sustaining the credibility of his claim that Electronics Emporium was the lowest-priced electronics store in the city, Zole hired Rubie Indigo as a secret comparison shopper. Since Indigo's intent was to price electronics and gather intelligence rather than to make a purchase, his conduct amounts to pricing an article with no intent to buy. Such conduct is specifical-

ly cited in the Mishnah[10] as an application of the prohibition of causing someone needless mental anguish (*ona'at devarim*).[11] One could, however, raise an
objection here. Perhaps Indigo does not violate *ona'at devarim*. Consider that
Indigo never enters a store with a *closed mind* in respect to making a purchase.
If he feels that his identity as a professional comparison shopper is in danger of
being exposed, he will assuredly make a purchase as a means of quieting the
suspicions of the salesperson. Indigo's conduct should, therefore, be no worse
than that of a consumer who is comparison shopping. Provided the consumer
engages in comparison shopping in an open-minded manner, the dashed
expectations of a particular salesperson need not concern him.[12] Analogously,
since Indigo is prepared to make a purchase if exposure of his identity is threatened, he should not be responsible for the dashed expectations of a salesperson.

The comparison, however, is flawed. *Good faith* is what separates the two
cases. Because he makes use of the salesperson's time in good faith, the sincere
comparison shopper does not violate *ona'at devarim*. In sharp contrast, Indigo
deliberately abuses the salesperson's time and should, therefore, be responsible
for the salesperson's dashed expectations when his inquiries do not culminate
in a sale.

Given that Indigo's job description inevitably puts him in violation of
ona'at devarim, his job is illegitimate from a halakhic perspective. Accordingly,
Indigo's conduct is not free of ethical taint even when his inquiries culminate
in a purchase. Consider that the motivation behind his purchase is to quiet suspicion that he is a professional comparison shopper. The purchase for Indigo is
but a duping device designed to restore his good standing as a serious customer.
What the ploy accomplishes is to allow Indigo to continue in his charade.
Because the purchase allows Indigo to continue in his illegitimate job, the purchase violates the prohibition against creating a false impression.[13]

Electronics Emporium's Lowest-Price Claim and Halakhah

Matthew Zole, as will be recalled, was bent on building a reputation for
Electronics Emporium as the lowest-priced retail seller of electronics in the city.
Toward this end Zole launched a price-matching policy that he combined with
advertising selected items for prices which he knew would either beat or
trounce the competition. By not relying on the price-matching policy alone as
the basis of the low-price claim, Zole took appropriate measures to ensure that
the claim would not be an empty one.

The ethical concern Zole demonstrated here was, however, absent in the
approach he took to *sustain* the claim's credibility. Since Indigo's work as a professional shopper violates the *ona'at devarim* interdict, hiring him for this pur-

pose places Zole in the category of one who *instigates* evil (*meisit*). Instigating someone to sin is prohibited by the Torah in connection with idolatry (Deuteronomy 13:7–12). In the opinion of R. Jacob b. Joseph Reicher (Austria, d. 1733) and others, the prohibition extends to the instigation of any sin.[14]

Another moral pitfall for Zole occurs when he drops Indigo but does not at the same time discontinue the claim that Electronics Emporium is the lowest-priced electronics store in the city. Since Zole, at this juncture, is not prepared to do anything to validate the lowest-price claim, it amounts to an empty, and hence false claim.

Price Matching at ShopSmart and *Geneivat Da'at*

Price matching at ShopSmart may entail violation of the *geneivat da'at* interdict. The issue here is that the firm gives much more prominence to its promise not to be undersold than to the details of its price-matching program. This imbalance is evident everywhere the firm communicates its policy. In the store's front window a huge sign announcing "We will not be undersold" appears. To be sure, the same sign announces that the store has a price-matching policy. But no details are offered. For specifics the customer is advised to consult management. Inside the store the slogan "We will not be undersold" is printed in bold letters on the shopping bags. The flier providing the details of the price-matching plan is not strategically placed at the checkout counters. Instead, it is made available to customers *only* upon request.

We must recognize that the imbalance described above has the capacity to deceive and/or confuse. Anyone who fails to pick up the flier may find himself left with any number of erroneous impressions. One possibility for error is that the customer might understand ShopSmart as claiming that it is the lowest-priced seller in the local area. Another possibility is that the price-matching intent will be understood, but on terms much more generous than the actuality.

Given the imbalance in promotion between what ShopSmart promises and the restrictions it puts on its promises, the company's price-matching program dashes the reasonable expectation of its customers. Thus price matching at ShopSmart violates *geneivat da'at* law.

In an analogous case, the FTC in 1984 took action against the Thompson Medical Company. In this case the FTC determined that the company had conveyed the false impression that its product, Aspercreme, was an aspirin rub, when, in fact, the product had no aspirin content. Among other complaints, the FTC felt that the company's disclaimer, which appeared at the conclusion of its ads, was far too inadequate to counter the false impression conveyed by both the advertising copy and the name of the product.[15]

Problem 1

Rubie Indigo was planning to buy his *kallah*, Shalhevet, a diamond ring. Very concerned that he should not appear unsophisticated in this matter, Rubie set out to visit a diamond dealer. Feigning interest in purchasing a stone, Rubie pumped the dealer for as much information as he could get about the four-c's (color, cut, clarity, and carat). Equipped with his new sophistication, Rubie was now ready to take Shalhevet to Tiffany and select a ring. At Tiffany's Rubie dazzled the sales personnel, to say nothing of Shalhevet, with his knowledge of the esoterica of the four-c's. Just as Shalhevet seemed ready to select a two-carat, pear-shaped D ring, she surprised everyone by saying to the salesperson, "Thank you for your wonderful service, let us think about it." Outside the store, Shalhevet told Rubie, "I really love the pear-shaped ring. My parents know Greg, a diamond dealer, who said that he could get me any ring I pick out at 5 percent less. Let's buy the ring from Greg."

From the standpoint of Halakhah, what ethical principles do Rubie, Shalhevet, and Greg violate?

Problem 2

Walter Klugman was on his way to work in the morning. As he neared Sol's 24-hour convenience store along the route to the D-train, Klugman remembered that he had two letters in his vest pocket that he wanted to mail as soon as possible. "Perhaps Sol sells postage stamps and I can put the stamps on the letters and drop then in the mailbox near the subway station." Sol did indeed sell postage stamps; but to Klugman's chagrin, the price was 45 cents for a 32-cent stamp. Begrudgingly, Klugman bought the stamps but felt outraged that Sol had the brazen gall to charge a price higher than the post office charges for the same stamp. "Sol's pricing policy entails *ona'ah*," Klugman muttered to himself. "I'll take up the matter with my rabbi this Sabbath."

When Klugman returned from work that night he was overcome with a tremendous thirst and had a craving for a Dr. Pepper. In his desperation, Klugman located a vending machine on the platform of his local subway station which carried Dr. Pepper. The price for the 12-ounce can was $1.50. As Klugman guzzled down his Dr. Pepper, he felt his second episode of outrage for the day! "Why, this same can goes for 90 cents at Sol's." Another problem for the rabbi to solve.

Critically evaluate the halakhic merit of Klugman's two incidents of outrage.

1. Quoted in Francine Schwadel, "Who Wins With Price Matching Plans?" *Wall Street Journal*, March 16, 1989.

2. Indigo should more properly be described as a professional snooper or spy. But Zole preferred the more elegant term of secret comparison shopper.

3. Bava Batra 78a and R. Samuel b. Meir (France, ca. 1080–1174), Rashbam, ad loc.; R. Isaac b. Jacob Alfasi (Algeria, 1013–1103), Rif, ad loc.; Maimonides (Egypt 1135–1204), *Yad*, Mekhirah 27:5; R. Asher b. Jehiel (Germany, 1240–1327), Rosh, Bava Batra 5:7; R. Jacob b. Asher (Germany, 1270–1343), *Tur*, Hoshen Mishpat 220:5; R. Joseph Caro (Israel, 1488–1575), *Shulhan Arukh*, Hoshen Mishpat 220:8; R. Jehiel Michel Epstein (Belarus, 1829–1908), *Arukh ha-Shulhan*, Hoshen Mishpat 220:7.

4. In designing its returns policy, a business must be careful not to violate the rabbinical extensions of the prohibition against interest (*ribbit*) called *avak ribbit* (lit. the dust of *ribbit*). Violation of *avak ribbit* obtains when the business offers to void the original sale if the customer returns the merchandise within a given time period. Because this policy renders the original transaction *retroactively* null and void, the money the customer paid must now be viewed as a *loan* to the business. Since the customer not only gets back his money but gets free use of merchandise for the time period he held it, the business returns to the customer something more than his money and hence violates *avak ribbit*. The problem can easily be overcome by designing the returns policy in terms of a *buy back* rather than in terms of *voiding* the original sale. For a discussion of this point, see R. Yisroel Reisman, *The Laws of Ribbis* (New York: Mesorah, 1995), pp. 41–42.

5. Bava Mezia 49b; Rif, ad loc., *Yad*, op. cit. 12:5; Rosh, op. cit. 4:15; *Tur*, op. cit. 227:15; *Sh.Ar.*, op. cit. 227:7; *Ar.haSh.*, op. cit. 227:8.

6. Rashi, Bava Mezia 49b.

7. *Ar.haSh.*, op. cit. 227:10. For the time limitation Halakhah sets for the seller in respect to an *ona'ah* claim, see *Sh.Ar.*, op. cit. 227:11.

8. R. Asher b. Jehiel, *Responsa Rosh* 102:4; *Tur*, op. cit. 227:1; *Sh.Ar.*, op. cit. 227:9; *Ar.haSh.*, op. cit. 227:12.

9. R. Mordecai b. Hillel (Germany, ca. 1240–1298), *Mordecai*, Ketubbot 7:206; Rema, *Sh.Ar.*, op. cit. 227:9; *Ar.haSh.*, op. cit. 227:12.

10. Mishnah, Bava Mezia 4:10.

11. Rif, Bava Mezia 4:10; Rosh, op. cit. 4:22; *Tur*, op. cit. 228:3; *Sh.Ar.*, op. cit. 228:4; *Ar.haSh.*, op. cit. 228:2.

12. Rashi at Leviticus 25:17; R. Judah, Bava Mezia 58b and Rashi ad loc.; R. Menahem b. Solomon Meiri (France, ca. 1249–1306), *Beit ha-Behirah*, Bava Mezia 58b).

13. For the legal sources of this prohibition, see p. 35 of this volume.

14. R. Jacob b. Joseph Reischer, *Responsa Shevut Yaakov* 3:168; R. Mosheh Feinstein, *Iggerot Mosheh*, Orah Hayyim 1:99. See, however, R. Meir Dan Plotzki (Czechoslovakia, 1867–1928), *Klei Hemdah*, Re'eh, sec. 4. For a broader discussion of the *meisit* prohibition, please turn to pp. 375-—76 of this volume.

15. *In re Thompson Medical Co., Inc.*, 103 FTC 648 (1984).

Scalping at the Nosson Scharf Concert

Sidney Pirsam works professionally as an agent for Jewish entertainers, specializing in bar mitzvah and wedding bookings. Constantly searching for new talent, Pirsam discovered the biggest star of his career at the wedding celebration of his nephew, Zelig. At this affair, Nosson Scharf, a friend of the groom, was prevailed upon to entertain the guests with a few original songs. So mesmerizing was Nosson's performance that the guests temporarily forgot that they were attending a wedding. Quick to assess Scharf's commercial potential, Pirsam had the young man signed up before the evening was over. It took no more than a few successful bookings for Pirsam to become convinced that Nosson Scharf had electrifying appeal. He was therefore prepared to make a substantial investment in the young man. It consisted of sponsoring a Nosson Scharf concert at the 8,000-seat Music Emporium. In order for the concert to be held, the place would have to be booked three months in advance of the production. Pirsam decided to price the tickets at $15 a piece. His calculations indicated that 5,000 tickets would have to be sold to reach the break-even point.

In this, his first venture into the promotion end of the music business, Pirsam left no stone unturned in his quest to ensure the financial success of the event. Immediately after signing his contract with the Music Emporium, Pirsam aggressively booked Nosson for any event he could muster up. Three weeks before the concert, however, Pirsam abruptly reversed course, declining all offers. In his mind, this stratagem would produce the optimum blend of admiration and yearning for Nosson's talents, which he felt would translate into a stampede for tickets as the concert drew near. In addition, beginning two weeks before the concert, Pirsam took out full-page promotional ads in the local newspapers. Finally, Pirsam sold a block of 1,000 tickets to Mevasser, a local ticket broker, at a 20 percent discount.

Beyond Pirsam's wildest expectations, the Nosson Scharf concert took off in ballistic fashion. Ten days before the concert, the smashing pace of ticket sales made it evident that Madison Square Garden would have been a more appropriate setting for the concert. Pirsam, accordingly, initiated a policy of limiting tickets to one per customer. Once the policy went into effect, huge lines of 500 or more people became the norm for the remaining days of the ticket sales. To be sure, some of them were there to purchase tickets for other events scheduled in the weeks ahead at the Music Emporium. But the very substantial presence of Nosson Scharf enthusiasts could not be mistaken. Indeed, as a means of both guaranteeing themselves a ticket and minimizing waiting time during their work schedules, some fanatical fans camped out at the ticket booth many hours before it opened.

As soon as Mevasser got wind of Pirsam's one ticket per customer policy, he raised his price to $40 per ticket. Another effect of the policy was to spring into action another player. Glick, a local speculator, hired the Indigo brothers, Cyrus and Rubie, to stand on line again and again to purchase tickets from the box office. (In street parlance people who do this are called diggers.)

On the day of the concert, both the box office and Mevasser were sold out. Tickets were nevertheless available through Glick's agents. Strategically locating themselves in the vicinity of the Music Emporium, Glick's scalpers hawked the concert tickets to every passerby. The price charged was on an individual customer basis. Rumor had it that some patrons paid as much as $600 to get into the concert that evening.

Price Scalping and *Ona'ah*

In assessing the halakhic attitude toward the price policies faced by patrons of the Nosson Scharf concert, the most basic issue is the ethics of a seller's raising the price as a means of taking advantage of the customers' heightened interest in the product. Directly bearing on this issue are the laws of *ona'ah* (price fraud).

Recall that the law of *ona'ah* gives a market participant the right to trade a commodity on the basis of its competitive norm.[1] But if the lower-priced reference price does not reflect the competitive norm that *prevailed* when the disputed transaction was entered into, the *ona'ah* claim is thrown out.[2] The basic issue here, therefore, is: What was the competitive norm when Mevasser raised his price to $40 a ticket? If the box office price of $15 a ticket was still regarded as the competitive norm at that time, then Mevasser's pricing policy is in violation of the law of *ona'ah*. But consider that it was Pirsam's policy of restricting tickets to one per customer that triggered Mevasser to raise his price to $40 per ticket. As soon as Pirsam introduced this policy, the $15 box office price should no longer be regarded as the competitive norm. Why? Because such a policy communicates a belief that demand exceeds supply at the $15 price. Otherwise, why the need for restrictions on the number of tickets one can buy? Since the $15 price is not a market clearing price, Pirsam just as easily could have increased the ticket price as a means of eliminating the disequilibrium situation. Instead, he chose to maintain the $15 price and allow queuing to determine who would get the available tickets. Indeed, as a means of securing the public's goodwill, promoters will often hold back on the price they charge for their most popular productions. Pirsam's $15 price should therefore be regarded as a *discount* from the market clearing price. Accordingly, Mevasser should be free to charge what he feels the market clearing price is.

Reinforcing the assertion that the $15 price becomes a disequilibrium price as soon as the one ticket per customer policy is put into play are the following considerations. First, from the time the concert tickets were put up for sale up to the time the restrictive policy was instituted, Nosson Scharf performed in a number of engagements. Second, over this same period, Pirsam heavily advertised the Music Emporium concert. Both these factors work not only to make *more* people amenable to purchasing the concert tickets at the $15 price, but also to increase the maximum price people would be willing to pay to attend the concert.[3] Ironically, Pirsam's frantic efforts to *increase* ticket sales had the effect of making the $15 price a disequilibrium price.

Since Pirsam's $15 price must be viewed as a *discount* from the market price, the law of *ona'ah* in no way requires Mevasser to match the $15 price. Instead, Mevasser is free to set the price at whatever level he feels the market will bear.

Ticket Scalping on the Day of the Concert

We now move to an evaluation of the ethics of ticket scalping on the day of the concert. Recall that on the day of the concert both the box office and Mevasser were sold out. Since Glick enjoys a monopoly position on the day of the concert, anyone who purchases a ticket from one of his agents on that day cannot claim that the purchase entailed an opportunity cost. In the context of exploiting a monopoly position, negotiating a price on an individual customer basis is no less ethical than setting a uniform price for all customers. In the economic literature, the former pricing policy is referred to as first-degree price discrimination. Its goal is to discover the maximum price each customer would be willing to pay for the good at hand and charge the customer that price. In the short run price discrimination may very well reap for the monopolist seller a greater profit than would be the case under a uniform pricing policy. Given, however, the reasonable assumption that non-confidentiality is the norm for the marketplace, price discrimination usually breeds resentment among customers. Each customer either knows or imagines that he paid a higher price than someone else for the same item. Any seller who is interested in cultivating the goodwill of his customers will therefore usually adopt a non-discriminatory pricing policy. Mevasser, as will be recalled, also temporarily enjoyed a monopoly position in the ticket sales for the Nosson Scharf concert. Instead of charging $40 a ticket on a non-discriminatory basis, he just as easily could have negotiated a price for each customer individually. Mevasser's concern for his good standing as a legitimate ticket broker, however, led him to opt for the former policy.

Glick's Operation and *Hassagat Gevul*

To be sure, Glick's initiation of a first-degree price discrimination policy on the day of the concert does not violate *ona'ah*. But his enterprise constitutes unfair competition (*hassagat gevul*). Consider that it is Pirsam's toil and effort that both sets up the concert and promotes it. Glick springs into action only after it is evident that the $15 box office price is a *disequilibrium* price. The cue here is Pirsam's initiative of one ticket per customer. Thus Glick's employment of diggers as a means of diverting customer demand to himself and away from the box office amounts to expropriating someone else's toil and effort for commercial gain, and is, therefore, an unfair competitive tactic. Elsewhere in this volume we discuss the source of this prohibition.[4]

A variation of the above case occurs when a box office customer (A) decides not to attend the concert and sells the ticket to someone else at a profit. Since A's purchase was not part of a scheme to *divert* ticket sales to another seller, there should be nothing objectionable about this windfall.

Violating the Seller's Preference and the Conduct of the Indigo Brothers

Another objection to Glick's operation is that the conduct of the Indigo brothers in getting on line again and again violates Pirsam's explicit policy of one ticket per customer. From the perspective of Halakhah, the basic issue here is whether Pirsam's stipulation is binding on ticket purchasers. Generally, a condition laid down by the seller at the time the transaction is entered into is binding on the buyer only if the consequences of alternative actions are made explicit to the buyer at that time. This is called the *tenai kaful*, or the double-condition requirement.[5] In the case at hand, satisfaction of *tenai kaful* requires the seller to stipulate that in the event the customer makes a second purchase, the sale is canceled.

To be sure, the *tenai kaful* condition is dropped in some instances. This occurs when the intent of the stipulator is objectively evident. Illustrating this point is the following real estate transaction: S sells his land to B. In the course of the negotiation, S mentions to B that he is selling his land because he plans to settle in Israel. Should S cancel his plan to settle in Israel, the sales transaction with B becomes void. Notwithstanding the absence of the *tenai kaful* condition, it is objectively evident that S intended to sell his land only in the eventuality that he would emigrate.[6]

The one ticket per customer policy apparently falls into the rubric of cases in which the *tenai kaful* condition is dispensed with. One fundamental consideration here is that the initiation of the policy, in itself, reflects a conviction on

Pirsam's part that demand exceeds supply at the $15 box office price. Reading into Pirsam's mindset a desire to cancel any ticket sale that entails infraction of his rule is not unreasonable, as voiding the sale entails no risk of loss for him. Moreover, it is not a matter of indifference for Pirsam if customers maneuver to violate his rule. Every additional ticket a customer manages to obtain is a likely candidate for scalping. The more a customer pays for a ticket, the less money he is likely to spend on souvenirs and concession items at the concert. Finally, infraction of the rule is likely to result in damage to Pirsam's reputation. Consider that Glick's ticket inventory derives from the box office supply. This will lead some customers to take the presence of scalpers as evidence of Pirsam's laxity in enforcing his rule. Others might go one step further and accuse Pirsam of secretly colluding with Glick and sharing in the profits of exploitation.

The aforementioned leads to the proposition that Pirsam's policy is binding on customers. This gives the inadvertent ticket sales to the Indigo brothers the character of a transaction concluded in error (*mekah ta'ut*). The Indigo brothers' machinations to obtain tickets in the face of the policy amounts to snatching away tickets from a protesting clerk while leaving the admission price at the ticket window. Such action is a form of extortion called *hamas*.[7]

Ticket Scalping and Secular Law

In the United States, state law regulates ticket scalping at places of public entertainment. Wide variations can be found. Louisiana, for instance, requires only that the ticket price be clearly printed on the ticket. But at least eighteen states attempt to ban ticket scalping entirely. The trend is clearly in the direction of more ticket scalping regulation.[8]

Illustrating a legislative approach to ticket scalping is New York State's regulation of this phenomenon. One provision of the law requires that the admission price be printed on the face of each ticket. The maximum premium the ticket can be resold for must also be printed on the face of each ticket. In 1994, this premium was not to exceed $2 plus lawful taxes. In addition, everyone in the business of reselling public entertainment tickets must be licensed by the state. To cover the eventuality that the licensed firm might be assessed a fine for violating the state's regulations in this area, the licensed firm is required to post a $1,000 bond with the state. Finally, a stiff penalty is imposed on those caught scalping within 1,000 feet of the site of the entertainment event. The penalties apply only to a place of entertainment which has a seating capacity in excess of 5,000 persons. In addition, the penalty does not apply to the resale of tickets from a licensed location, regardless of its proximity to the site of the entertainment event. Finally, the penalty was not meant for the individual who purchases the ticket for personal use and decides later to resell it for a profit.[9]

Conflict Between *Dina d'Malkhuta* and Halakhah

The provision of the New York State law that calls for a maximum premium for ticket brokers is inconsistent with the unregulated stance Halakhah takes here.

Recall that in the realm of *civil law*, talmudic decisors dispute the question of how much authority is given to the secular law of the land (*dina d'malkhuta*) in litigation between Jews when it is in conflict with Halakhah. Representing the view that gives *dina d'malkhuta* the widest authority is R. Mosheh Isserles (Poland, 1525 or 1530–1572). In his view, *dina d'malkhuta* prevails, with few exceptions, even when it is in conflict with Halakhah. But this is on the condition that the particular law operates in the public's benefit.[10] Limiting the premium a broker may charge in reselling entertainment tickets, however, may work against the public's interest. Such a constraint can only serve as a *disincentive* to put one's capital at risk in financing an entertainment event. Instead of reflecting the public's best interest, legislation requiring maximum premiums may merely reflect the successful lobbying of promoters. Given the important role ticket brokers play in ensuring the viability of large-scale entertainment events, maximum premiums may ironically work against the best *long-term* interests of the promoters themselves.

Adopting a much more narrow scope for *dina d'malkhuta* is R. Shabbetai b. Meir ha-Kohen (Poland, 1621–1662). In his view, *dina d'malkhuta* prevails in a litigation between Jews only when the non-Jewish law does not contradict Torah law, or in a case when the practical application of Torah law is not clear. Following R. Shabbetai b. Meir ha-Kohen's line, R. Abraham Isaiah Karelitz (Israel, 1878–1952) disputes the notion that there is anything missing from Halakhah. A halakhic position can be extrapolated for any issue. If *dina d'malkhuta* contradicts Halakhah, even if the Halakhah was derived by means of extrapolation, the law of the land must be set aside.[11] The import of these latter views is to put to question whether *dina d'malkhuta* supersedes Halakhah here.

In the opinion of this writer, *dina d'malkhuta* prevails in the matter at hand. What is critical in this judgment is the recognition that New York State law does not merely require that *promoters* print the maximum resale premium on the face of their tickets. Such an approach would amount to state *imposition* of a requirement on ticket brokers. Instead, the law calls for *brokers* to be licensed by the state and to post bond. There is no circumventing the licensing procedure. Doing so undermines the state's legitimate right, recognized by Halakhah, to deter fraud and prevent misrepresentation. The conditions that go along with the granting of a license, namely, the maximum premium constraint and the posting of a bond, place every applicant in the position of *agreeing in advance* to conduct business in accordance with state rules. Accordingly, the ticket broker is bound by the maximum premium rule even if market conditions allow for an increase in price.

The proposition that the maximum premium rule should be operative also follows from the formulation of the *dina d'malkhuta* principle by R. Isaac Schmelkes (Poland, 1818–1906). In a case dealing with the right to reissue a Torah work for commercial gain, R. Schmelkes finds no halakhic objection, but nevertheless prohibits it because it violates *dina d'malkhuta*. Since the consequence of making the law of the land supersede Halakhah here results only in a foregone opportunity to earn a profit rather than an actual loss, *dina d'malkhuta* prevails.[12] Similarly, in the case at hand, adhering to the maximum premium rule results in no actual loss for the ticket broker, but only in a foregone opportunity to earn a profit. *Dina d'malkhuta* should therefore prevail.

Problem

From the perspective of Halakhah, comment on the ethics of each of the following pricing policies:[13]

1. A hardware store has been selling snow shovels for $15. The morning after a major snowstorm, the store raises the price to $20.

2. A grocery store has several months' supply of peanut butter in stock on the shelves and in its storeroom. The owner hears that the wholesale price of peanut butter has increased and immediately raises the price on the current stock of peanut butter.

3. A severe shortage of Red Delicious apples has developed in a community, and none of the grocery stores or produce markets has any of this type of apple on its shelves. Other varieties of apples are plentiful in all of the stores. One grocer receives a single shipment of Red Delicious apples at the regular wholesale cost and raises the retail price of Red Delicious apples by 25 percent over the regular price.

4. A grocery chain has stores in many communities. Most of them face competition from other groceries. In one community the chain has no competition. Although its costs and volume of sales are the same there as elsewhere, the chain sets prices that average 5 percent higher than in other communities.

5. A landlord rents out a small house. When the lease is due for renewal, the landlord learns that the tenant has taken a job very close to the house and is, therefore, unlikely to move. The landlord raises the rent $40 per month more than he had been planning to do.

6. A store has been sold out of the popular Cabbage Patch dolls for a

month. A week before the big holiday season, a single doll is discovered in a storeroom. The managers know that many customers would like to buy the doll. They announce over the store's public address system that the doll will be sold by auction to the customer who offers to pay the most.

1. Please turn to pp. 127–31 of this volume.

2. Please turn to pp. 133–35, 196 of this volume.

3. In the parlance of economic theory, Pirsam's investments work not only to *shift* the demand curve outward but also to reduce the elasticity of the original demand curve.

4. Please turn to pp. 72–74 of this volume.

5. For the *tenai kaful* condition, see Maimonides (Egypt, 1135–1204), *Yad*, Ishut 6:17; R. Asher b. Jehiel (Germany, 1250–1327), Rosh, Gittin 6:9; R. Jacob b. Asher (Germany, 1270–1343), *Tur*, Even ha-Ezer 38:2; R. Joseph Caro (Israel, 1488–1575), *Shulhan Arukh*, Even ha-Ezer 38:2; R. Jehiel Michel Epstein (Belarus, 1829–1908), *Sh.Ar.*, Even ha-Ezer 38:267.

6. R. Isaac, quoted in Tosafot, Kiddushin 49b, s.v. *devarim*.

7. See R. Jacob Moses Lorberbaum (Poland, 1760–1832), *Netivot ha-Mishpat, Sh.Ar.*, Hoshen Mishpat 205, n. 1.

8. "Ticket Scalping: Free Market Mirage," *American Journal of Criminal Law* 19, no. 35 (1991): 6–12.

9. Arts and Cultural Affairs, Sections 25.07, 25.08, 25.09, 25.22, 25.23, 25.15, 25.29, 25.35.

10. Please turn to pp. 43–4 of this volume.

11. Ibid.

12. R. Isaac Schmelkes, *Beit Yizhak*, Yoreh De'ah 2:75, pt. 5.

13. The scenarios were selected almost verbatim from Daniel Kahneman, Jack L. Knetsch, and Richard Thaler, "Fairness as a Constraint on Profit Seeking: Entitlements in the Market," *American Economic Review* 76, no. 4 (1986): 728–41.

The authors' interest was to investigate how community standards of fairness on the setting of prices and wages influence the behavior of firms. Toward the end, randomly selected residents of Toronto and Vancouver were asked to rate a number of pricing policies, including the scenarios quoted in the text, on the basis of their perceptions of fairness. The results of the survey were as follows (N represents the number of respondents):

1. (N = 107) Acceptable 18 percent   Unfair 82 percent
2. (N = 147) Acceptable 21 percent   Unfair 79 percent
3. (N = 102) Acceptable 37 percent   Unfair 63 percent
4. (N = 101) Acceptable 24 percent   Unfair 76 percent
5. (N = 157) Acceptable 9 percent   Unfair 91 percent
6. (N = 101) Acceptable 26 percent   Unfair 74 percent

The Risk Averter

In both his personal life and business affairs, Zelig Parnes is a risk averter. As Parnes puts it, "When confronted with risk, take on for yourself as little as possible, and shift onto your opposite number as much as possible."

Let us first take a glimpse at how Parnes operates his medical equipment–leasing business. The one-year deal Parnes offered Dr. Noam Kantor for leasing an X-ray machine provides a typical example:

1. The leasing fee was set at $200 a month.

2. Payment was due on the first of each month. A penalty clause called for a 5 percent surcharge on any outstanding balance.

3. In addition to the leasing fee, Dr. Kantor was made responsible for the depreciation or wear and tear of the machine during the leasing period. This translated into an additional $10 a month.

4. At the expiration of the lease, on March 1, 2000, Dr. Kantor would be given the option to buy the X-ray machine for $6,000. The actual cost at the time would, however, be reduced to only $3,600, as Kantor would be given credit for the $2,400 in monthly leasing fees he had paid up to that point.

5. If, over the leasing period, the X-ray machine was stolen, lost, or destroyed, even on account of unforeseen and unavoidable circumstances, Dr. Kantor would be responsible. For the purpose of figuring out liability in these eventualities, the reference price was set at the $6,000 option-to-purchase price. Depending on when the loss occurs, a variable percentage of the reference price would be used to determine liability.

6. Dr. Kantor would be held responsible for depreciation in the market value of the X-ray machine from the beginning to the end of the leasing period. In talmudic parlance this is called *aharayut zula*. This would occur, for instance, if new technology that was developed during the leasing period rendered X-ray machines less valuable as a diagnostic tool. For the purpose of determining liability here, the current market value of the machine was agreed to be $5,600.

At the expiration of the leasing period, Kantor met with Parnes and expressed an interest in exercising his option to buy the X-ray machine:

"I would love to buy the machine now. But I have a cash-flow problem. Instead, let's discuss terms for another one-year lease."

"Wait a minute, Dr. Kantor," Parnes countered, "If your heart is set on buying the machine, let's see if we can work this out. Perhaps one of your patients has given you a promissory note. I'll buy it at a discount."

It so happened that Sidney Karnes, one of Dr. Kantor's patients, had given him a promissory note in payment for medical services. The note had a face value of $3,650; it was payable to the bearer, and its due date was June 1, 2000.

Absorbing all these details, Parnes exclaimed that he would gladly take the note as full payment for the X-ray machine. All Kantor had to do was endorse the promissory note and hand it over to him. One catch, however! Parnes insisted that Kantor should be responsible for the entire $3,650 face value of the note in the event Karnes defaulted. Because he knew Karnes well and trusted him implicitly, Kantor readily agreed to this stipulation.

As Kantor handed over the endorsed promissory note, Parnes was beaming.

"Dr. Kantor," he said, "I'm glad to help you out in your cash-flow problem. I do this type of favor all the time. Why, just the other day, Leon Spitz, one of my partners, asked me to cash a $500 post-dated check he had received from his brother-in-law. I said, `Sure! I'll give you $450 cash for the check.' I told Leon to endorse the check and deposit it in our joint business account. We then made a record of the transaction; duly noting that $500 of my funds was mingled in our joint business account. The record also included the provision that in case the check bounced, Leon would make good on it."

If Kantor needed any proof that what Parnes did for him was the type of favor he did all the time, it came immediately after the two concluded their business. At that juncture, Aytan Kramer, a close friend of Parnes, burst on the scene. Kramer implored Parnes to lend him his credit card. Parnes was obliging.

"Here's my Master Card. Spend on it as much as you like. Just remember, you're also responsible for any interest payments that accrue on the card for the purchases you make."

Parnes' Leasing Agreement and Halakhah

We now turn to a halakhic analysis of the terms of Parnes' leasing arrangement.

Preliminarily, let us note that transactions between Jews[1] are regulated against *ribbit* (interest charges).[2] The prohibition is violated on a biblical level in the context of a loan transaction for which the interest payment is *kezuzah* (lit. prearranged). The sages expanded the ambit of the *ribbit* interdict. Included in their extensions are applications to a variety of commercial transactions. Rabbinical extensions of the *ribbit* interdict are called *avak ribbit* (lit. dust of *ribbit*).[3]

One application of *avak ribbit* is to leasing agreements of a specific variety. The key element here is responsibility for the loss or damage to the article of rental in the event of unavoidable circumstances. This is called *aharayut 'onsin*. Ordinarily, the responsibility of the lessee extends only to being responsible in the event of theft or the disappearance of the article of rental (*genevah va-avedah*).[4] Leasing agreements that impose *aharayut 'onsin* on the lessee may violate *avak ribbit* law. This obtains when the article of rental is assessed at the outset of the agreement and the lessee's reimbursement liability in the event *'onsin* is set equal to that value.[5] Since reimbursement is set equal to the value the article of rental had at the outset of the agreement, the agreement resembles a loan arrangement and the leasing fee has the appearance of a *ribbit* payment.[6]

Assumption by the lessor of *aharayut 'onsin* does not automatically free a leasing agreement of *avak ribbit*, irrespective of how it is structured. The following talmudic text is relevant here:

> Rav Hama used to rent out [Tyrian] zuz coins for a fee of one peshita [a coin worth one-eighth of a Tyrian zuz] per day. [He was careful to specify that the coins were being *rented*, not lent, Rashi.] [Eventually], Rav Hama's money was depleted [i.e., he lost all his money, as a punishment for violating the prohibition of *ribbit*]. He had reasoned [that renting out money for a fee is permitted, because] why is it any different [than renting out an article such as] a spade? [If one is permitted to rent out a spade for a fee, one should also be permitted to rent out coins for a fee.] But this is not so. [As regards] a spade, it itself is returned (*hadra b'einah*) [to its owner when the rental period expires]. And [furthermore], its depreciation [through wear and tear] is recognizable (*yadia pehateh*). [Therefore, the owner is allowed to take a rental fee. In contrast, regarding] coins, they themselves are not returned [to the original owner when the rental period expires]. And [furthermore, even if the original coins are returned intact], they [suffer] no recognizable depreciation. [Therefore the owner is not allowed to charge a fee for renting them out. Any fee that he charges constitutes *ribbit*.][7]

Commentators have advanced various interpretations of this text.[8] Tosafot's interpretation is regarded as normative.[9] In Tosafot's view, Rav Hama accepted *aharayut 'onsin* upon himself. Because the lessee was relieved of *aharayut 'onsin*, Rav Hama felt that charging him for the use of the coin was not *ribbit*. Rav Hama was, however, mistaken. Conspicuously absent from his transaction were both *hadra b'einah* and *yadia pehateh*. Notwithstanding that Rav Hama accepted *aharayut 'onsin*, at least one of these features must be present if violation of *avak ribbit* is to be avoided.

Commenting on Tosafot's view, R. Israel b. Petahiah Isserlein (Germany, 1290–1460) posits that if the lessor accepted both *aharayut genevah va-avedah* and *aharayut 'onsin*, the leasing agreement becomes free of *avak ribbit* violation. Specifically, when the level of responsibility indicated above is assumed by the lessor, both the *hadra b'einah* and *yadia pehateh* conditions can be dispensed with.[10]

The preceding discussion provides a model for a leasing agreement that avoids *avak ribbit* violation. Parnes' leasing agreement does not fit this model. What is most striking is that Parnes imposed every conceivable risk associated with the transaction on Dr. Kantor. To be free of *avak ribbit*, Parnes should assume responsibility for *genevah va-avedah* and *'onsin*. Once this level of responsibility is assumed by Parnes, he is free to impose *aharayut zula* on Kantor and charge him for the estimated wear and tear the X-ray machine undergoes over the leasing period. In addition, Parnes may stipulate a leasing fee.

In his analysis of a hire-purchase agreement riddled with *avak ribbit* violations, R. Yizhak Ya'akov Weisz (Israel, 1902–1989) called for the lessor to assume responsibility for *genevah va-avedah* and *'onsin*, but he permitted the lessor to insure against *genevah va-avedah*. The cost of the insurance premium could then be passed on to the lessee in the form of a higher leasing fee.[11]

Another way Parnes can shift some risk on to Kantor is to make use of the following concept recorded by R. Jacob b. Asher (Germany, 1270–1232):[12] Kantor's liability in the event of *'ones* is set at the value the X-ray machine has at the time of breakage. Since the lease is no longer operative at the time of breakage, this approach effectively frees Kantor of *aharayut 'onsin* for the entire leasing period. Given that the X-ray machine depreciates, the legitimacy of charging Kantor a leasing fee for the use of the machine is established. Imposing *aharayut zula* on Kantor for the leasing period would, however, confer a *ribbit* character to the leasing fee. Accordingly, Parnes must assume *aharayut zula* for the entire leasing period.

The Late-Fee Clause and *Ha'aramat Ribbit*

Let us now turn to a consideration of the late-fee provision of the leasing agreement. Recall that it took the form of a 5 percent surcharge on any outstanding balance. The halakhic validity of this clause can be put to question on the basis of an aspect of *ribbit* law called *ha-aramat ribbit* (circumvention of *ribbit* law). The originator of this prohibition was R. Solomon b. Abraham Adret (Spain, ca. 1235–1310). Out of concern that parties to a loan transaction might evade the *ribbit* prohibition by setting up a penalty clause if the principal was not paid on time, the sages, according to R. Adret, prohibited a penalty clause.[13]

While R. Adret's stringency is adopted in respect to loan transactions,[14] the use of penalty clauses in credit sales is permitted.[15] Accordingly, a lease may call for a penalty if rental payments are not made on time.[16] Likewise, if a sales transaction called for the purchasing price to be paid in installments, a separate late fee may be charged for each installment.[17]

One caveat should, however, be noted. A late fee is legitimate only when it is a one-time payment. If the late fee is structured to increase with time as long as the debt is outstanding, the penalty clause is prohibited. In the latter instance, the penalty clause works to compensate the seller for waiting for his payment, rather than as just a disincentive to prevent late payments. The latter form of penalty clause is prohibited.[18]

It follows that Parnes' penalty clause violated *ribbit* law. By calling for a 5 percent surcharge on any outstanding balance, the clause works to *increase* the penalty over time.

For Parnes' penalty clause to have legitimacy, it must be changed to a one-time penalty fee operative for each installment period. Recall that the lease's option to purchase agreement opens two courses of action for Kantor. If he chooses to exercise the purchase option, the monthly payments turn out to be monthly installments on a purchase. Attaching a one-time penalty for lateness to each installment of a purchasing price is legitimate. Alternatively, Kantor may choose not to exercise his option. Under this scenario, the monthly payments become leasing fees. Here, again, it is legitimate to charge a one-time penalty for delay in the payment of each of the monthly leasing fees.

One final note. The penalty clause must be entered into in a manner that counteracts *asmakhta*. Elsewhere in this volume we deal with this issue in a different context.[19] This discussion can easily be applied to the issue at hand.

The Option to Purchase and *Avak Ribbit* Law

Let us now turn to an analysis of the option to purchase aspect of the Parnes-Kantor agreement.

Note that Parnes makes no explicit offer to sell the X-ray machine on a cash basis. But an interest charge is surely concealed in the $6,000 asking price. Consider, Parnes is willing to accept installment payments amounting to $6,000 stretched out over a year as payment for the X-ray machine. Given the time value of money, Parnes would presumably accept less than $6,000 as the up-front cash price of the X-ray machine.

The issue at hand is a special form of *ribbit* violation called *zad ehad de-ribbit* (lit. interest contingent on one side of a transaction). Specifically, the agreement between the parties allows for two alternative courses, only one of which involves *ribbit*. Whether *ribbit* is violated depends on which course of action the parties choose.[20] This pertains to the case at hand. Recall that the agreement is

a leasing-purchase option arrangement. If Kantor opts not to exercise his purchase option, the monthly payments he makes will be nothing more than leasing fees. No violation of *ribbit* will be involved. It is only if Kantor opts to buy
the X-ray machine that the monthly payments become *installment payments*
and the concealed interest charges become an issue.

Decisors dispute whether *zad ehad de-ribbit* is an aspect of *avak ribbit* or
whether it violates *ribbit* law on a Torah level, called *ribbit kezuzah*.[21] Since the
problem arises here in the context of a sales transaction, all disputants would
agree that the issue at hand is only *avak ribbit*.

In evaluating the halakhic validity of Parnes' purchase option deal, let us
take note that an interest charge in a credit sale is not always prohibited. If the
following three conditions are met, there is no objection to the practice: (1) the
seller may not explicitly quote a lower price for a cash deal and a higher price
for a credit sale;[22] (2) the article at hand must not sell in the cash market at a
set price;[23] and (3) the credit price should not exceed this reference cash price
by more than a nominal amount;[24] an increase of more than 20 percent is
regarded as more than nominal and is therefore prohibited.[25]

Parnes' option purchase deal can be tailored to fit into the above guideposts. First, let us note that Parnes' X-ray machines are neither current-year
models nor brand-new. Because the value of the machines must be assessed on
an individual basis, the price of the machine is not well defined in the cash market. Once the value of a machine in the current period is determined, Parnes
should not mark up the price for the credit sale by more than 20 percent.
Finally, Parnes should not quote a cash price for the X-ray machines.

The Sale of a Promissory Note and *Ribbit* Law

We now turn to an analysis of the *ribbit* problem connected with the sale of
promissory notes.[26] In his treatment of the sale of promissory notes,
Maimonides (Egypt, 1135–1204) avers that this transaction is akin to a *ribbit*
contract, but is, nevertheless, permissible. To see the affinity to *ribbit*, consider
what the purchaser of the note accomplishes: B borrows $1,000 from L and
writes a promissory note obligating himself to pay L $1,000 in two months. P
then purchases the note at a discount price of $900 from L. At the end of two
months B makes a $1,000 payment, not to the original lender, L, but instead to
P. What P accomplishes with the transaction is to advance L $900 and collect
$1,000 from B two months later. Notwithstanding the affinity of P's gain to *rib-
bit*, the gain is permissible because what the Torah prohibits is only *ribbit* that
passes from borrower (B) to lender (L). Since B did not borrow money from P,
there is no objection to B's making the $1,000 payment to P.[27]

To ensure that the sale of a promissory note does not entail violation of *ribbit* law, P must assume responsibility if B defaults.[28] Without the assumption of this responsibility, the sales transaction, according to R. David b. Samuel ha-Levi (Poland, 1586–1667), is not recognized as having taken place. What makes one an owner of debt, in his view, is the assumption of loss in the event of the debtor's default.[29] Without the assumption of this responsibility, P's capital transfer will be regarded as a loan to L, with the promissory note serving as collateral for the transaction. Consequently P is entitled to no more than the $900 he advanced L.

It follows as a corollary from this rationale that if L guarantees the *entire face value* of the promissory loan and not just the price P pays for it, the transaction violates *ribbit* law on a Torah level. This is, indeed, the view of some authorities.[30]

P's assumption of responsibility for loss in the event of B's default is what makes the sales transaction valid. Once the transfer of the promissory note is legally accomplished, P is, however, protected against fraud. Accordingly, if it turns out that the promissory note is a forgery or L has already collected the debt, P is entitled to a refund of his $900 purchasing price.[31]

From the preceding analysis, it can be seen that Parnes' acceptance of Kantor's third-party-issued promissory note as payment for the X-ray machine amounts to a *ribbit* agreement between them. This is so because Parnes' insistence that Kantor guarantee the note makes the sale of the note halakhically invalid. Instead, what takes place is a loan transaction between Parnes and Kantor. The loan amounts to Parnes' $3,600 asking price for his X-ray machine, with the $3,650 promissory note serving as collateral for this loan. Since Kantor guarantees the $3,650 face value of the promissory note, he effectively is agreeing to return $3,650 to Parnes when he only received $3,600 from him. The transaction violates *ribbit* law, possibly even on the level of Torah law, as discussed earlier.

Cashing a Check at a Discount

We now turn to the *ribbit* problem connected with cashing a check issued by a third party at a discount. Most basic to the issue at hand is how secular law treats checks.

In his treatment of the topic from the standpoint of Israeli society, R. Yaakov Yeshayahu Bloi (Israel, 1929–) avers that a checking account held in an Israeli bank does not assume the status of a bailment for the depositor. Rather, once a bank creates a checking account for a customer, the deposit becomes a *debt* owed by the bank to the customer. This follows from the fact that the bank has the authority to lend out the money in the checking accounts it creates. Consequently, what A does when he writes a check to B is to assign the debt the bank owes him to B. In B's hands, the check is no different from a promissory note. Now, suppose A writes a check to B in the amount of $100, and C is willing to cash the check in the amount of $90. Provided C accepts responsibility in the event the check proves uncollectible, the practice should not be objectionable.[32]

In his analysis of the topic, Rabbi J. David Bleich demonstrates that in the United States the writing of a check by A to B is nothing more than a *directive* to the bank to make payment to B. The check does not, however, constitute A's assignment of the debt the bank owes him to B. This is evidenced by the fact that A enjoys the legal right to issue a stop-payment order after he issues the check to B. Another proof is what happens if A issues checks and then dies before they are cashed. Here the law allows the bank to honor A's checks within a ten-day period following his death. Nonetheless, any person claiming an interest in the account, e.g., a creditor, may order the bank to stop payment and thereby prevent the bank from honoring the check even during the ten-day period.

The upshot is that when A writes a check to B, the check in no way constitutes an *irrevocable* assignment of A's claim against the bank to B.[33]

In R. Bleich's opinion, R. Bloi's position is incorrect even in respect to checks drawn in Israel. To be sure, in Israeli law the issuance of a stop-payment order is, in most circumstances, a penal offense. But even in Israel, once a stop-payment order is issued, the bank no longer has the obligation and authority to render payment on the check.

Moreover, the holder of a check cannot force the bank upon which it is drawn to honor the check and to issue the funds against which it is drawn. If, for any reason, the bank refuses to honor the check, the holder's only recourse is against the drawer or any prior endorser.[34]

In his treatment of the *ribbit* problem involved in the cashing of checks at a discount, R. Yisroel Reisman includes an extensive analysis of secular banking laws. He concludes that there is a major difference between Israeli and European law, on the one hand, and American law, on the other. Checks drawn on Israeli and European banks should take on the status of promissory notes, but checks drawn on American banks are merely instruments of collection and therefore cannot be sold at a discount without violating *ribbit* law.[35]

Thus Parnes' check-cashing arrangement with Spitz violates *ribbit* law. Given that a bank's debt to a depositor is not reassigned when a depositor writes a check against his deposit, the check Spitz presents to Parnes must be viewed as collateral in a loan arrangement between them. In exchange for Parnes' $450 advance, Spitz gives Parnes the $500 check. Since Spitz guarantees the face value of the check, the loan transaction violates *ribbit* on the level of Torah law.

Making Use of Someone Else's Credit Card and *Ribbit* Law

Let us now turn to a halakhic consideration of Parnes' dealings with Aytan Kramer. As a Master Card holder, Parnes is entitled to draw upon the line of credit the company, Interbank Card Association, agreed to extend him. The agreement between the company and Master Card holders calls for a thirty-day grace period when the customer is not charged interest for card purchases. For outstanding balances beyond the thirty-day grace period the customer is charged interest. Since the interest payment is not a one-time late fee, but rather a charge that increases over time as long as the outstanding balance remains, the finance charges are decidedly *ribbit* payments. But *ribbit* is a prohibited arrangement only in transactions among Jews, and Interbank Card Association is a non-Jewish company. Thus there is no halakhic problem for Parnes to be a Master Card holder.

By charging his purchases against Parnes' Master Card, Kramer draws upon Parnes' credit line with Interbank Card Association. Kramer's use of the card causes the company to extend a loan to Parnes. *The loan is decidedly to the cardholder and not to the user of the card.* When Parnes hands over his credit card to Kramer, he is *using the card as a vehicle to make a personal loan to Kramer* in the amount of his purchases. Parnes' stipulation that Kramer will be responsible for any finance charges that accrue because of his use of the card amounts, therefore, to a stipulation that Kramer is responsible to return to him a larger sum than he borrowed. The stipulation violates *ribbit* law. The prohibition involved here, however, is *zad ehad de-ribbit*. This is so because the arrangement allows for two courses of action. If Kramer pays back the loan within the thirty-day grace period, no finance charges will be involved. Finance charges will only come into play if Kramer delays his debt payment to Parnes beyond the thirty-day grace period.

In his treatment of the *ribbit* problem involved in using someone else's credit card, R. Avrohom Mosheh Lewanoni (New York, contemp.) prohibits the borrower of the card (B) from paying the finance charges even directly to the credit card company. This is so because the finance charges are not B's responsibility but the obligation of the cardholder (A). B's payment of the finance charges would amount to paying these charges on behalf of A. B's payment must accordingly be viewed as a *ribbit* payment to A for the loan he extended him.[36]

A variant case is discussed by R. Lewanoni: Suppose B promises A that he will reimburse him for any charges he runs up on his credit card *within the thir-*

ty-day grace period. B fails to keep his word, and in consequence A is saddled with the finance charges that accrue because of B's purchases. Here, it may be permissible for B to pay the finance charges. Payment of these charges does not amount to *ribbit* but is compensation for the damages A suffers because B did not keep his word to pay back the charges against the card within the thirty-day grace period. R. Lewanoni reaches no definitive conclusion on this matter. He notes, however, that if A had already paid the finance charges, there is no objection against B later compensating A by sending him a small gift.[37] Certain guideposts must, however, be observed here in light of the prohibition the sages imposed on a borrower voluntarily sending even a small gift to his creditor after paying his debt. This prohibition is called *ribbit me'uheret* (lit. delayed interest payment).[38] The prohibition applies, however, only when the debtor explicitly informs his creditor that the gift is an expression of gratitude for the loan he extended him. If the gift is small, and it is not evident that it was sent in gratitude for the loan, there is, however, no objection to it.[39]

1. The prohibition of *ribbit* on both a biblical and a rabbinical level does not apply when either of the parties to the transaction is a non-Jew (cf. *Yad*, Malveh 5:1).

In the instance when a non-Jew conferred favors and demonstrated kindness to a Jew in the past, the recipient of the kindnesses should return the favor to the non-Jew in the form of offering the latter an interest-free loan in time of need. See R. Solomon Eger (Germany, 1786–1852), *Gilyan Maharsha, Sh.Ar.,* Yoreh De'ah 159:1.

2. Exodus 22:24; Leviticus 25:36; Deuteronomy 23:20; R. Joseph Caro (Israel, 1488–1575) *Shulhan Arukh,* Yoreh De'ah 159–77.

3. *Sh.Ar.,* op. cit. 161.

4. R. Judah, Baraita, Bava Mezia 80b; R. Isaac b. Jacob Alfasi (Algeria, 1012–1103), Rif, ad loc.; Maimonides (Egypt, 1135–1204), *Yad,* Sekhirut 1:2; R. Asher b. Jehiel (Germany 1250–1327), Rosh, Bava Mezia 6:17; R. Jacob b. Asher (Germany 1270–1343), *Tur,* Hoshen Mishpat 307:1; *Sh.Ar.,* op. cit 307:1; R. Jehiel Michel Epstein (Belarus, 1829–1908), *Arukh ha-Shulhan,* Hoshen Mishpat 307:1.

5. Rav Kahana and Rav Assi, Bava Mezia 69b; Rosh, Bava Mezia 5:49; *Tur,* Yoreh De'ah 176; R. Joshua ha-Kohen Falk (Poland, 1555–1614), *Derishah, Tur,* loc. cit., n. 2; R. Mosheh Isserles (Poland, 1525 or 1530–1572), Rema, *Sh.Ar.,* op. cit. 176:3; R. Shabbetai b. Meir ha-Kohen (Poland, 1621–1661), *Siftei Kohen, Sh.Ar.,* op. cit. 176, n. 4; R. Abraham Danzig (Prague, 1748–1820), *Hokhmat Adam* 136:7.

6. R. Joseph Habiba (Spain, early 15th cent.) at Rif, Bava Mezia 69b; *Tur,* loc. cit.; *Hokhmat Adam,* loc. cit.

Another school of thought, led by R. Solomon b. Abraham Adret (Spain, ca. 1235–1310), quoted in *Shittah Mekubbezet,* Bava Mezia 69b, finds nothing objectionable in a lessee's accepting upon himself *aharayut 'onsin* set at the value the article of rental had at the outset of the agreement. Preliminarily, let us note that by dint of Torah law a paid bailee (*shomer sakhar*) is obligated only for *aharayut genevah va-avedah.* Nonetheless, a stipulation by the *shomer sakhar* to accept *aharayut 'onsin* is fully valid and does not transform the arrangement from a bailment into a loan. Consider that the legal status of a lessee in respect to responsibility in the event of a loss or damage to the article of rental is the same as a *shomer sakhar.* Acceptance of *aharayut 'onsin* by the lessee should likewise not transform the agreement from a lease into a loan. Fixing liability in the event of *'ones* to the value the article of rental had at the outset of the agreement should also not work to impart a loan character to the agreement. This is so because in the event that no mishap occurs, the lessee returns the article of rental with no depreciation charge. Because the lessee can escape the depreciation charge, he does not resemble a debtor, who must always restore the entire value of the loan he received. R. Caro follows R. Adret's line (*Sh.Ar.*, op. cit. 176:3). But R. Shneur Zalman of Liadi (Russia, 1745–1813), *Shulhan Arukh of the Rav*, Hilkhot Ribbit, n. 35, posits that R. Jacob's position, cited in the text, is the preferred view.

7. Bava Mezia 69b.

8. Three schools of thought can be identified: (1) R. Solomon b. Isaac (France, 1040–1105), Rashi, Bava Mezia 69b, posits that a leasing agreement is not free of *ribbit* violation unless both the *hadra b'einah* and *yadia pehateh* factors are present. (2) In the opinion of R. Yehudah b. Natan (France, 11th–12th cent.), quoted in Tosafot ad loc., the controlling factor in freeing a leasing agreement of a *ribbit* problem is the *hadra b'einah* factor. Once *hadra b'einah* is present, the absence of *yadia pehateh* will not impart a *ribbit* character to the leasing agreement. In R. Yehudah's version of the R. Hama incident, the phrase *veyadia pehateh* does not appear. (3) In the view of Tosafot (loc. cit.), the presence of either *hadra b'einah* or *yadia pehateh* frees a rental agreement of the *ribbit* problem.

9. Tosafot, Bava Mezia 69b; R. Solomon b. Abraham Adret (Spain, ca. 1235–1310), quoted in *Shittah Mekubbezet*, Bava Mezia 69b; R. Yom Tov Ishbili (Spain, ca. 1250–1330), Ritva, Bava Mezia 69b; Rosh, Bava Mezia 5:46; *Sh.Ar.*, op. cit. 176:1; *Hokhmat Adam* 136:5.

10. R. Israel b. Pethahiah Isserlein, *Terumat ha-Deshen* 302; Rema, *Sh.Ar.*, op. cit. 176:1. For a variant view, see R. Elijah b. Solomon Zalman (Vilna 1720–1797), *Bi'ur ha-Gra*, *Sh.Ar.*, op. cit., n. 2.

11. R. Yizhak Yaakov Weisz (Jerusalem, 1902–1989), *Responsa Minhat Yizhak* 4:20.

12. *Tur*, op. cit. 176:2.

13. *Responsa Rashba* 1:651.

14. *Sh.Ar.*, op. cit. 177:14; *Hokhmat Adam* 132:13. In the context of a loan transaction, the sages approved several leniencies in respect to *ha'aramat ribbit*; see Rema, *Sh.Ar.*, loc. cit., and *Hokhmat Adam,* loc. cit.

15. *Sh.Ar.*, op. cit. 177:18; *Siftei Kohen* to *Sh.Ar.*, loc. cit., n. 38; *Hokhmat Adam,* loc. cit.

16. R. Avrohom Mosheh Lewanoni, *Mishnat Ribbit* 11:8.

17. Ibid. 11, n. 11.

18. *Sh.Ar.*, op. cit. 177:16 and Rema loc. cit.; *Hokhmat Adam* 132:14.

19. Please turn to pp. 271–4 of this volume.

20. Cf. Megillah 27b, Bava Mezia 65b.

21. R. David b. Samuel ha-Levi (Poland, 1586–1667), Taz, *Sh.Ar.*, op. cit. 174, n. 1, rules that *zad ehad de-ribbit* is *ribbit kezuzah*. *Siftei Kohen*, *Sh.Ar.*, op. cit. 172, n. 29, however, regards *zad ehad de-ribbit* as *avak ribbit*.

22. Mishnah, Bava Mezia 5:2; Rif, ad loc.; *Yad*, Malveh 8:1; Rosh, Bava Mezia 5:21–22; *Tur*, op. cit. 173:1; *Sh.Ar.*, op. cit. 173:1; *Hokhmat Adam* 139:1.

23. *Tur*, op. cit. 173:1; *Sh.Ar.*, op. cit. 176:1; *Hokhmat Adam* 139:2.

24. *Tur*, loc. cit. *Sh.Ar.*, loc. cit.; *Hokhmat Adam* 139:3.

25. R. Jacob Moses Lorberbaum (Poland, 1760–1832), *Havvat Da'at*, *Sh.Ar.*, op. cit. 173, hiddushim, n. 4.

26. Many decisors hold that the sale of a promissory note is not halakhically recognized unless a proper *kinyan* (symbolic act) is performed. For a discussion of this issue, see R. Yisroel Reisman, *The Law of Ribbis* (Brooklyn, N.Y.: Mesorah, 1995), pp. 211–12.

27. *Yad*, Malveh 5:14.

28. *Tur*, op. cit. 173:4; *Sh.Ar.*, op. cit. 173:4; *Hokhmat Adam* 139:8.

29. Taz, *Sh.Ar.*, op. cit., n. 3.

30. R. Joseph b. Moses Trani (Israel, 1500–1580), *Responsa Maharit*, Yoreh De'ah 39. Another opinion in this matter is expressed by R. Shmuel ha-Sardi (Spain, ca. 1190–ca. 1256), *Sefer ha-Terumot* 4:13. In his view, guaranteeing the face value of the note for the buyer only violates *avak ribbit* law.

In searching for a rationale for R. Shmuel ha-Sardi's view, let us take note that Nahmanides (Spain, 1194–1270), quoted in *Maggid Mishneh, Yad*, loc. cit., offers a different explanation of why the discount sale of a promissory note without transferring the risk of default to the buyer violates *ribbit* law. The practice is objectionable because the buyer thereby makes capital available to the seller of the note on terms that are "close to profit and far from loss." Making capital available to someone on such terms violates *avak ribbit* law. R. Shmuel ha-Sardi could very well agree with Nahmanides' rationale. Within this rationale, the discount sale of a promissory note is legally recognized even when the risk of default on the part of the debtor is not transferred to the buyer. With the sale valid irrespective that the risk of default was not transferred to the buyer, there is no difference whether the seller guarantees the face value of the note or just the purchasing price. In both instances what is violated is the rabbinical prohibition of making capital available to someone on terms "near to profit and far from loss."

31. *Tur*, op. cit. 173:4; *Sh.Ar.*, op. cit. 173:4; *Hokhmat Adam* 139:8.

32. R. Yaakov Yeshayahu Bloi, *Berit Yehudah* 15:17, nn. 38–39.

33. Rabbi J. David Bleich, *Contemporary Halakhic Problems*, vol. 4 (Hoboken, N.J.: Ktav, 1995), p. 546.

34. Ibid., p. 567.

35. Reisman, *Laws of Ribbis*, pp. 229–33.

36. *Mishnat Ribbit* 17:7.

37. Ibid. 17, n. 11.

38. Rabban Gamliel, Mishnah, Bava Mezia 5:10; Rif, ad loc.; *Yad*, op. cit. 5:11; Rosh, Bava Mezia 5:79; *Tur*, op. cit. 160:6; *Sh.Ar.*, op. cit. 160:6; *Hokhmat Adam* 131:8.

39. Rema, *Sh.Ar.*, op. cit. 160:6.

The Pricing of Pharmaceuticals

In recent years, pharmaceutical companies have been under attack for their pricing policies. Within the framework of the current unregulated price environment, drug companies have consistently demonstrated their willingness to charge for life's necessities whatever the market will bear. To cite but a few examples:

Ceradose, a drug used to treat Gaucher's disease, costs an average of $300,000 per year. A single dose of Genentech's tissue plasminogen activator, a genetically engineered drug for treating heart attacks, costs $2,200.[1]

Looking beyond the astronomical prices of individual drugs, a report prepared by a United States Senate Committee found that pharmaceutical price inflation was six times that of the general rate of inflation for the period 1980–1992. Not surprisingly, the same report found that profit margins for pharmaceutical companies were four times those of the average Fortune 500 company.[2]

Critics call for price regulation of the drug industry. In rebuttal the industry insists that its potential for high profits is necessary to attract the capital needed to do research and development on new drugs. Without a constant stream of new, patentable products, brand-name companies would eventually go out of business.

The Pricing of Pharmaceuticals and Halakhah

In his *Torat ha-Adam*, Nahmanides (Spain, 1194–1270) clearly enunciates a prohibition against earning windfall profits in the sale of pharmaceuticals. In making the moral case against the practice, Nahmanides begins with the dictum that providing medication to someone in need is an aspect of the mitzvah of restoring lost property to its rightful owner (*hashavat avedah*). Specifically, making the medication available restores a sick person to himself (*hashavat gufo*). Since the taking of a fee for the performance of a mitzvah is generally prohibited, restriction on the pricing policy for a seller of drugs follows. Accordingly, should S be in possession of herbs which B needs for medication, it is unethical for S to take advantage of B's need and hike up their price more than warranted (*yoter min ha-ra'uy*). The practice is unethical *whether the herbs are available elsewhere or not.*

The restrictions Halakhah place on S's pricing policy go beyond ethical guideposts. Since it is B's desperation that makes him agree to the excessive price, the stipulation is not legally binding. B escapes the extra payment by merely claiming that his stipulation was made in jest (*mashteh ani bakh*). This holds whether the herbs were available elsewhere or not.[3]

In the sale of medications, Nahmanides entitles the seller to only their *damim* (lit. value). What exactly Nahmanides means by this phrase can be seen from the conceptual linkage he makes between the price constraint a seller of medication is subject to and the price constraint a doctor is subject to. In respect to the latter, Nahmanides posits that a physician is entitled to no more than compensation for lost earnings and a fee for his toil and effort. It is, however, unethical for a physician to charge a fee for offering a diagnosis or a treatment program.[4]

Nahmanides' guideposts for medical fees provide a basis to extrapolate Halakhah's view on price regulation in the pharmaceutical industry. Before a formulation can be arrived at, however, it must be noted that Nahmanides' analysis evidently deals with a part-time physician who earns his livelihood primarily outside the medical profession. What level of earning is a doctor entitled to if he devotes himself full-time to the medical profession? Resolution of this issue will provide the guidepost for price constraint for the monopolist pharmaceutical dealer.

Addressing himself to the issue of medical fees, R. Hayyim David ha-Levi (Israel, 1924—98) draws a parallel from the compensation full-time teachers of Torah are entitled to. Teaching Torah is a mitzvah. As such, the teacher is entitled only to compensation for lost earnings. But if an individual forsakes the pursuit of a livelihood and devotes himself full-time to Torah teaching, R. Asher b. Jehiel (Germany, ca. 1250–1327, Bekhorot 4:5) entitles him to a salary. In a similar vein, the Talmud (Ketubbot 105a) records that the civil judges of Jerusalem were compensated with ninety-nine maneh out of Temple funds. Since assuming the judicial role is an aspect of teaching Torah, compensation should obtain only when an individual abandons his work to take on a case. R. Isaac of Dampierre (1120–1200, Tosafot ad loc.) justifies the judges' salaries on the ground that they made themselves available on a standby basis and the community was therefore bound to support them.

R. Hayyim David ha-Levi equates a medical practitioner with a teacher of Torah. Accordingly, if a doctor devotes himself full-time to his profession, he is entitled to a salary. Given both the high social standing of the doctor and the likelihood that he could command relatively high earnings outside the medical profession, R. Hayyim David ha-Levi finds no moral issue with very comfortable salaries for members of the medical profession.[5]

R. Hayyim David ha-Levi's thesis requires further clarification. The legitimacy of a full-time doctor earning a salary rests on the talmudic dictum that the civil judges of Jerusalem were given ninety-nine maneh for their salary.[6] R. Hayyim David ha-Levi regards salary as calculated to equal what these judges could earn elsewhere. Economists call this alternative compensation opportunity-cost earnings. This assumption can, however, be questioned. In rationalizing this payment, Tosafot merely states that the prohibition of accepting payment for the mitzvah of teaching Torah is *inoperative* when the individual devotes himself full-time to his profession. In respect to the salary of judges, the Talmud comments (Ketubbot 105a) that in the event it proved inadequate, e.g., the judge's family increased in size, the stipend was increased. The ninety-nine maneh was calculated to provide an *adequate* support level and was not an opportunity-cost payment.

In his treatment of medical fees, R. Shelomoh Zalman Auerbach posits that a full-time doctor is entitled to an opportunity-cost payment. Opportunity cost should be based, in his view, only on *current* alternative employment opportunities, such as a job in medical research. Opportunity cost should not, however, be calculated on the basis of what the doctor could now earn had he not trained himself for the medical profession.[7]

The guideposts decisors have formulated for medical fees for full-time physicians should equally apply for price regulation of the monopolist pharmaceutical dealer. What is indicated is that the vendor of medications is entitled to no more than opportunity-cost earnings.

Attitude of Halakhah Toward Windfall Profits in Essential Goods

Reinforcing the assertion that Halakhah rejects a free market approach to the pricing of pharmaceuticals is the general attitude it takes regarding windfall profits in respect to items essential to a minimum standard of living.

Talmudic sages expressed a deep concern that commodities essential to life should be available in the marketplace at the lowest possible price. Toward this end, the sages engaged in a variety of efforts designed to reduce windfall profits of sellers. These measures ranged from jawboning, policies designed to depress the demand side of the marketplace, and, in the case of essential foodstuffs, a one-sixth profit rate constraint. These interventions are briefly described below.

An instance of the use of the jawboning technique as a means of lowering the price of a ritual item is recorded at Sukkah 34b. Here we are told that Samuel warned the sellers of *hadassim*, the myrtle twigs constituting one of the Four Species used in the ritual for the festival of Sukkot, not to raise the price of undamaged branches or he would publicize that clipped *hadassim* were also acceptable. Samuel, in fact, held that clipped *hadassim* were acceptable. Promulgating this leniency would have shifted the demand curve for undamaged *hadassim* downward and hence *forced* a price reduction on the sellers. Why Samuel opted for the weaker measure of merely bluffing the sellers is explained by Tosafot ad loc. as stemming from the circumstances that use of undamaged *hadassim* constitutes an enhancement of the mitzvah (*hiddur mitzvah*). Samuel's policy was designed to achieve a dual objective. On the one hand, he wanted to encourage lower prices for a ritual item. But on the other hand, he did not want to discourage the purchase of undamaged *hadassim* because their use constitutes *hiddur mitzvah*. Striking a balance between the two objectives led him to merely bluff the sellers rather than promulgate his lenient ruling.

Samuel is once again found taking up the cause of consumers in his fight against price gouging by vendors of earthenware pots. Following the rabbinic view that the use of earthenware pots in which *hamez* (leavened food) was cooked before Passover was prohibited after the holiday, the people customarily bought new earthenware pots after Passover. Capitalizing on this surge of demand, the vendors raised the prices of their pots. Disturbed by the price hike, Samuel threatened the vendors that unless they reduced the price of their wares to the pre-Passover level, he would issue a ruling that the old pots could be used after Passover. The only thing that stopped him from actually issuing such a ruling was that the price gouging took place in an area under the jurisdiction of Rav, and Samuel did not want to undermine the authority of his colleague, who took a stringent view on the status of *hamez* that was held over during the Passover holiday.[8]

A still more drastic intervention designed to affect the demand side of the marketplace is recorded at Mishnah Keritot 1:7.

> It once happened in Jerusalem that the price of a pair of doves [the sacrificial requirement for a woman who gave birth to allow her to partake of sacrificial meat] rose to a gold dinar. Said R. Shimon b. Gamaliel, by this Sanctuary, I shall not go to sleep tonight before they cost but a [silver] dinar! Then he entered the Bet Din and taught: If a woman had five certain births or five certain issues, she need only bring one offering, and may then partake of sacrificial flesh, and she is not bound to bring the other [offerings]. Thereupon the price of a pair of birds stood at a quarter of a [silver] dinar each.

What R. Shimon b. Gamliel did, according to R. Solomon b. Isaac (Rashi, France, 1040–1105), was to temporarily change the law. Relying on the principle "For it is time to act for God, they have voided Your Torah" (Psalms 119:126), R. Shimon b. Gamliel believed that the very high price of birds would lead women to neglect their sacrificial requirements and go on to eat holy meat (*kodeshim*) in a state of impurity.[9]

A less drastic interpretation of R. Shimon b. Gamliel's action is offered by Tosafot. In this view, R. Shimon b. Gamliel did not abolish entirely the law that each birth or even doubtful birth required a separate sacrifice in the form of a pair of doves. What R. Shimon b. Gamliel permitted was that one pair of doves would allow a woman who had multiple births to immediately partake of *kodeshim*; the other sacrifices would remain as an obligation but could be brought at a later time, when the price of birds went down.[10]

Finally, we take note of the view of R. Hayyim Berlin (Russia, 1832–1913). In his understanding, R. Shimon b. Gamliel's ruling entailed no change of law whatsoever. What the sage did was merely to promulgate that the law of multiple sacrifices applied only to a woman of comfortable means. As for a poor woman, even after having multiple births a single set of birds would suffice to allow her to eat *kodeshim*. In the event this woman becomes wealthy, the remaining sacrifices would, however, become obligatory upon her. R. Berlin derives this leniency by observing that the multiple-sacrifices rule derives from the verse "*This law* applies whether a woman gives birth to a boy or a girl" (Leviticus 36:7). This verse appears immediately after the Torah's description of the sacrificial requirements of the woman of comfortable means, and it is only then (Leviticus 36:8) that the Torah addresses the sacrificial requirements of the poor woman. Hence the multiple-sacrifice rule does not apply to a woman who was poor at the time of her births. R. Berlin's interpretation makes R. Shimon b. Gamliel's intervention a matter of *eliminating ignorance* of the law, which worked to lower prices in the marketplace.[11]

We now turn to the Talmud's essential foodstuffs ordinance. This edict set a one-sixth profit rate limit for this sector.[12]

How the ancient ordinance worked in practice is a matter of dispute. Nevertheless, the following description, we believe, represents mainstream thought on its operational significance.

1. The ordinance did not interfere with natural market forces of supply and demand. Thus it did not entail price fixing; instead vendors of foodstuffs were permitted to sell at the market price.[13]

If the foodstuffs ordinance allows market forces free rein, then its practical significance is merely to prohibit sellers from collusively restricting supply for the purpose of raising their profit margin above the one-sixth level. The ordinance restricts both cartelization and restraint of trade practices by the monopoly firm in the essential foodstuffs industry. *Tacit* collusion in the form of holding back supply from the marketplace also has the effect of raising price. This form of collusion, which is designed to raise profit margins above the one-sixth level, may very well have also been prohibited by the talmudic ordinance.

2. The foodstuffs ordinance called for the appointment of market commissioners by the Jewish court (Bet Din) to monitor the regulated sector.[14] If the ordinance was not intended to countermand market conditions, then the role

of market officials must only have been to enforce the competitive norm. Without this monitoring, ignorance of market conditions could have resulted in transactions concluded in divergence from the competitive norm.

To be sure, judicial redress is often open to victims of price divergence of this sort in the form of an *ona'ah* (price fraud) claim. But the *ona'ah* claim is at best an *ex post facto* remedy. Legal technicalities often make it difficult for a complainant to legally recover losses on account of *ona'ah*. Moreover, many instances of *ona'ah* go undetected by the victim. Out of concern for the subsistence needs of the masses, the sages added another layer of protection in the foodstuffs sector. Price commissioners were assigned to enforce market price and prevent instances of *ona'ah*.

3. Another critical issue is whether an allowance for the implicit labor costs of the owner is included in the cost base against which the one-sixth profit rate constraint is calculated. The widely held view is that if the owner provides his labor services on a continuous basis, i.e., a retailer, an allowance for the labor services is included in the base.[15] Presumably the return is limited to the competitive rate for the type of work performed.

The failure to make provision for implicit wages for the owner when his labor services are not extended on a continuous basis, i.e., a wholesaler, was probably due to a conviction on the part of the framers of the ordinance that wholesalers provided no useful social service.[16]

In enacting the foodstuffs ordinance, the sages, according to R. Joshua b. Alexander ha-Kohen Falk (Poland, 1555–1614), relied on the biblical injunction "And let your brother live with you" (Leviticus 15:36).[17] R. Falk's comment makes the edict a mandate to sellers of essential foodstuffs to forgo some part of their potential profit so as to allow consumers to obtain subsistence without undue hardship.

Assessing the Laissez-faire Argument

In this section we will evaluate the laissez-faire approach to the pricing of pharmaceuticals from a halakhic perspective.

One feature of the pharmaceutical industry is the substantial costs it incurs in research and development expenditures for new drugs. Consider that the vast majority of compounds screened for medicinal potential never even make it to human testing, let alone to market. Moreover, drug products must pass the U.S. Food and Drug Administration's reviews for safety and efficiency before they can be sold. Without the freedom for drug companies to raise prices as they please, new drug development would be crippled.[18]

On the face of it Halakhah would find sympathy with the above argument against price regulation. Public policy discourse must consider the long-term consequences of alternative courses of action. Should a particular policy offer the likely prospect of adversely affecting certain desirable objectives, the policy should be rejected. Evidencing Halakhah's concern for the long run in designing public policy is the following episode in the life of R. Huna, recorded at Ta'anit 20b:

> On the eve of every Shabbat [Friday] he [R. Huna] would send a messenger to the market, and any vegetables that the [market] gardeners had left over he bought up and had them thrown into the river. Should he not, rather, have had these distributed to the poor? [He was afraid] lest they would then at times be led to rely upon him. [In that case, why should] he take the trouble to buy them at all? This would lead [the gardeners] to do wrong in the future [by not providing an adequate supply].

As this passage shows, R. Huna understood the importance of economic incentives in ensuring the long-run viability of economic activity. Since he felt that the availability of an adequate supply of vegetables for the honor of the Sabbath was a desirable outcome, he took pains to craft his subsidy to this industry in a manner that would ensure its long-run viability.

We take it as a given that Halakhah would regard it as desirable to encourage the development of new drugs that alleviate suffering and promote longevity. Given the huge research-and-development expenditures necessary to bring forth these drugs, price regulation should apparently be rejected.

Bolstering the case for laissez-faire is the consideration that Halakhah displays a delicate sensitivity not to upset the economic incentives in the medical field. This can be seen from a point in the law dealing with the prohibition of either demanding or offering a fee for work rendered on the Sabbath (*sekhar shabbat*).[19] Out of concern that the *sekhar shabbat* prohibition might cause a physician to hesitate in responding to a call for assistance on the Sabbath, the sages suspended the *sekhar shabbat* interdict in connection with medical fees.[20] On similar grounds the sages refrained from proclaiming that physicians taking *sekhar shabbat* would see no "sign of blessing" from the fee. Such a harsh pronouncement would surely have deterred physicians from demanding *sekhar shabbat*, but would at the same time have removed the economic incentive for them to respond to a call for assistance on the Sabbath.[21]

What emerges from the above analysis is that Halakhah will not interfere with the physician's economic incentives even in the face of a patient's call for assistance. Interference with economic incentives in the health-related field should certainly be a concern in the absence of the moral force of a patient's cry for help. Adopting a laissez-faire attitude toward the pricing of pharmaceuticals is therefore indicated.

The merits of this argument should, however, be considered in the light of Professor Richard R. Nelson's useful distinction between basic and applied research.

Basic research refers to human activity directed toward the discovery of facts and data observed in reproducible experiments. It also refers to the discovery of theories or relationships between facts. Applied research, on the other hand, is defined as human activity directed toward the creation of new and improved practical products and processes.[22] In the drug industry, basic research takes the form of the screening of compounds for potential activity against target diseases. It also includes the conducting of animal tests and preliminary human tests.

Since basic research entails a general foray into the unknown, only monopoly firms, with huge resources at their disposal, can be expected to undertake this investment. But here only if the government imposes no restrictions on the firm's pricing policy, allowing it to anticipate huge rewards on its risk taking. The other alternative is for government to finance basic research.

Once basic research has come up with some promising data or theory, the profit motive will drive the holder of the information to develop it further toward practical ends.[23]

In the United States, the lion's share of basic research in the health-related area is conducted not by the drug companies but by the federal government. Historically, the federal government has footed more than half the annual bill for health-related research. Three-quarters of this federally sponsored research comes from the National Institutes of Health (NIH).

Private industry is involved in R & D in the drug area mostly on the applied level. This occurs in several ways. First, if a compound looks promising enough, the NIH invites private companies to bid for the right to bring the drug to market. In addition, since the mid-1980s, the NIH has also negotiated formal research-and-development agreements with private partners. These private firms participate in NIH basic research projects in exchange for an option to negotiate an exclusive license for any commercial product that may result.[24]

Given the profit constraints Halakhah imposes on the pharmaceutical firm, basic research in the health-related field becomes a pure public good. A pure public good is a good that is a preferred item in people's budgets, but paradoxically will not be produced because of the absence of the profit motive. Government taxation is the only means of ensuring that the good will, in fact, be produced. This is the case for the issue at hand. Basic research is by its very nature an unfocused, general foray into the unknown, with no practical objective in mind. Moreover, society will not optimally benefit from this activity unless the findings of the research are *shared*. The profit motive to engage in this activity is therefore conspicuously absent. Yet an adequate and ongoing financial commitment to basic research in the health-related field will assuredly produce discoveries that will enhance the quality of life for everyone. Thus investment in basic research in the health-related area is a preferred item in everyone's budget, provided assurances are given of widespread participation which, in turn, guarantees adequate funding at minimum individual cost. Without government taxation there is no assurance that society's preferred expenditures on basic research in the health-related area will actually take place. No coercion is involved here, as the role of government is merely to actualize a demand for a preferred item in everyone's budget.

The pure public good phenomenon finds halakhic recognition in the power given to the Jewish community to tax its residents to construct a town wall.[25] In respect to this levy, even majority opposition cannot legally block the project.[26]

The rationale behind the town-wall levy is the presumption that all the permanent residents of the town regard security measures as a preferred item in their budgets. What the tax does, therefore, is to eliminate the free-rider motive in respect to an undertaking everyone desires.[27]

Given the pure public good character of basic research in the health-related area, taxation to ensure the viability of this endeavor is, from the perspective of Halakhah, a legitimate function of government.

Basic Research and *Dei Mahsoro*

Government taxation to support basic research in the health-related field proceeds also from society's duty to attend to the needs of the poor. This obligation is formulated by the Torah in the form of *dei mahsoro* (lit. sufficient for his needs).[28] Alleviating for the poor the physical and mental anguish of sickness fits squarely into this obligation. Halakhah gives expenditures for this purpose the highest ranking in charitable giving.[29]

Consider that basic research is the building block in developing cures and treatments for devastating diseases. A steady and adequate expenditure in this direction coupled with guarantees of free access for the poor works to significantly improve the quality of life of the poor over time.

Elsewhere, we have developed the thesis that Judaism's antipoverty obligation is a dual system, consisting of both private and public components.[30] Because basic research, as discussed earlier, takes on the character of a pure public good, reliance on voluntarism, in all likelihood, will not adequately finance this activity. First, without guarantees that the poor will be given free access to the fruits of basic research in the health-related area, society will not treat this expenditure as part of its charity obligation. Moreover, even if people regarded basic research in the health-related area as a charity obligation, the expenditure would rate a low priority. This is so because relieving misery here and now takes precedence over expenditures on basic research that works only to relieve the misery of the poor in *future* times. Another reason for neglect is that expenditures on basic research offers the prospect of producing useful findings only when the activity is conducted on a steady and large-scale basis. This may make people reluctant to contribute unless they are assured of widespread participation. Finally, reliance on voluntarism here would undoubtedly shortchange research on diseases that only affect a tiny percentage of the population.

In consequence, the commitment to relieve the misery of the poor over time requires the public sector to act *here and now* as a proxy for the future. It does so by taxing society for basic research in the health-related area with the aim of assuring a steady and adequate expenditure for this purpose.

By ensuring a steady and adequate flow of research and development, government taxation effectively shifts the risk associated with this expenditure from private industry to society at large. Under this arrangement, private industry enters the drug-development field only when profit considerations motivate it to do so. Since private industry enters the health-related field on the level of applied research, the argument that the potential for high profits must exist to ensure the development of new drugs is considerably undermined.

Public funding of basic research carries with it a regulatory responsibility for government in the pricing of drugs. One aspect of this responsibility is to ensure that the pricing policies of firms making use of government-sponsored research should afford them no more than opportunity-cost earnings. Another responsibility is to ensure that the poor are guaranteed free access to the drugs.

Patent Protection and the Pharmaceutical Industry

One feature of the pharmaceutical industry is that innovative drugs qualify for patent protection. Under the law the holder of the patent is entitled to exclusive marketing rights for a seventeen-year period. At the expiration of this time, the patent-holder retains exclusive use of its brand-name, but competing companies are free to copy the drug and seek approval from the FDA for its sale. Drugs competing with the brand-name drugs are called generic drugs.[31]

This arrangement appears to restrict competition and therefore to contribute to higher drug prices. Economic theory, however, takes a generally favorable view of patents. Without the prospect of monopoly protection, an inventor might despair of ever profiting from years devoted to an endless search for new products and processes. Patent law provides a necessary incentive to engage in innovative activity.[32] Applied to the pharmaceutical industry, patent rights are a necessary incentive to foster the development of new drugs.

Patent protection law finds its parallel in Halakhah. R. Mosheh Sofer's (Hungary, 1762–1839) analysis of an 1820 infringement case involving the Rodelheim *Mahzor* (High Holiday prayer book) bears directly on the issue of patent rights for innovative drugs.

Wolf Heidenheim, the publisher of the *mahzor*, had secured a rabbinical ban against republication by other persons for a period of twenty-five years. Shortly afterward, a publisher in Dyhernfurth proceeded to issue the Rodelheim *Mahzor*. Rabbis took opposing views, but the majority upheld Heidenheim's right to the protection of his work.

After defending Heidenheim on the basis of the rabbinical notices against republication printed in the *mahzor*, R. Sofer found an even more basic reason to restrain the publisher in Dyhernfurth. Heidenheim had not reprinted an extant edition of the *mahzor* from the public domain; rather, he had produced an improved edition of the *mahzor*, complete with revisions, annotations, and a German translation of the Hebrew text. Since the Rodelheim *Mahzor* entailed considerable innovation on the part of Heidenheim, its re-issuance by the firm in Dyhernfurth amounted to no less than appropriating someone else's toil and effort for the purpose of commercial advantage.

R. Sofer found the action of the second publisher analogous to the understanding of the talmudic dictum recorded at Bava Batra 21b that was expounded by R. Meir b. Samuel (France, ca. 1060–ca. 1155): "Fishing nets must be kept away from a fish the full length of the fish's swim. And how much is this? Rabbah son of R. Huna [d. 322] says: a parasang."

R. Meir understands the dictum as referring to a situation where A, in hopes of attracting large numbers of fish to the vicinity, casts a net containing a dead fish. B must not cast his net in the same vicinity because interloping action of this sort is regarded as a form of robbery. Since it is A's initiative that attracts the swarms of fish, B's interloping action effectively appropriates A's toil and effort for the purpose of commercial advantage.[33] Likewise, R. Sofer posits, the publisher in Dyhernfurth must be prevented from reaping commercial advantage from the reissuing of the Rodelheim *Mahzor*. The second publisher's action amounts to appropriation of Heidenheim's toil and effort for commercial gain.

Basing himself on the fisherman case, R. Sofer issued a ban against publishers reprinting the Rodelheim prayer book for a period of twenty-five years. The rationale for the twenty-five years was that it would take Heidenheim this much time, entailing multiple printings, to recoup his investment at a fair return.[34]

It follows from R. Sofer's ruling that the discoverer of a new drug would be entitled to a monopoly privilege for a period of time so that he could recoup his investment at a fair return. Copying and commercializing his discovery before such time amounts to expropriating someone else's toil and effort for commercial gain. Thus secular society's patent approach to protecting innovative drugs is very much consonant with Halakhah.

We should note, however, that making medicine available to someone in need, as discussed earlier, is a mitzvah activity. As such, the provider is entitled only to opportunity-cost earnings. One implication of this is that the discoverer of a new drug is not automatically entitled to an exclusive privilege to market it. To illustrate: Machliss discovers a breakthrough drug effective in the treatment of advanced stages of lung cancer. The government sets a $3 per pill price, which amounts to the cost of the recommended daily dosage. The price is geared to afford Machliss opportunity-cost earnings. It is based on the assumption that Machliss will sell out his entire annual full-capacity production of one million pills. But at $3 per pill, annual market demand will exceed one hundred million pills. Machliss has no interest in devoting his time, effort, and resources to expand his capacity. Nonetheless, he has no objection to making his trade secret available to others, provided they agree to a production quota and a royalty fee. Machliss' demands are unreasonable and therefore must be rejected. It is society's duty to make the cancer drug as widely available as possible. Moreover, Machliss is entitled to earn from his mitzvah activity no more than opportunity-cost earnings. Accordingly, *hassagat gevul* law works only to protect Machliss' opportunity-cost earnings but not to guarantee him earnings above this level.

We take note that the commercial value of a new drug depends on such factors as the number of people who stand to benefit from its discovery, the income distribution among the affected group, and the cost of producing the drug. The opportunity-cost earnings of the manufacturer of the drug, on the other hand, are determined by the minimum payments necessary to induce the resources involved to put out their work effort. These two values can and do diverge. Divergence between them is especially likely when the government assumes the function of sponsoring basic research and thus the pharmaceutical firms are not involved in a high- risk effort.

Developing a drug and bringing it to market, as discussed earlier, is a mitz-vah activity. As such, the firm involved is entitled only to opportunity-cost earnings. This consideration argues for building in some amount of flexibility in formulating patent rights as they apply to the health-related field. Specifically, if the commercial value of the drug is assessed to be very large rel-ative to the opportunity cost of the manufacturer, conferring less than a seven-teen-year patent may be in order.

Halakhic Guideposts and Drug Pricing

The guideposts Halakhah calls for in the structuring of the pharmaceutical industry foster lower drug prices. We offer the following two case studies, involving the drugs Ergamisol and Clorazil, to illustrate this point.

Ergamisol

Approximately thirty years ago, Johnson & Johnson introduced Levamisole, a drug used to deworm sheep. Under the sponsorship of the National Cancer Institute, and with free pills provided by Johnson & Johnson, Dr. Charles Moertel of the Mayo Comprehensive Cancer Center tested Levamisole in combination with a staple chemotherapy drug called 5-fluo-rouracil as a treatment for cancer. The combination proved effective in patients with advanced (stage C) colon cancer. It reduced recurrence of the disease by 40 percent and cut deaths by a third.

Based on Dr. Moertel's research, the FDA quickly approved levamisole for human use. In 1990, the Janssen division of Johnson & Johnson introduced the drug under the brand-name Ergamisol. At the same time, the animal version was licensed for manufacture by American Cyanamid Co. A tremendous price differential existed between Ergamisol and the older veterinary version of the drug. Ergamisol cost $1,250 to $1,500 for a year's supply. The cost for treating sheep was as low as $14.95.

The price discrepancy caused quite a stir. At the annual meeting of the American Society for Clinical Oncology in May 1992, Dr. Moertel blasted Johnson & Johnson for its unconscionable pricing of the drug. In August 1992, a consumer filed suit against Janssen. He claimed that he had been forced to pay "an outrageous, unconscionable, and extortionate price for a life-saving drug" that was sold at a fraction of the cost for treating sheep.[35]

From the standpoint of Halakhah, the basic issue here is that the govern-ment sponsored the research that proved Levamisole effective in treating human colon cancer. As such, it was unconscionable for the government to give Janssen carte blanche in its pricing policy. Instead, it should have imposed cost-plus pricing on it. If, in fact, as Johnson & Johnson claimed, the company engaged in costly research over decades to determine whether Levamisole could be used to treat humans, then these costs would legitimately be taken into account in arriving at a price.

The neglect of the government to set and enforce guideposts for the pricing of Ergamisol does not mean that the purchaser of this drug is without recourse against Johnson & Johnson. Given that the difference between Ergamisol and Levamisole is essentially *in name only*, the greater than one-sixth difference in price between the two drugs should allow the purchaser of Ergamisol to void the sale and get his money back. Ordinarily, an enormous difference in price between the subject and the comparison good signals that the transaction was concluded on price terms that exceed reasonable misjudgment. Accordingly, the only plausible interpretation is that the underlying intention of the parties involved was not to trade the article at hand but to use it as a *vehicle* to effect a voluntary gift transfer.[36] Given that Johnson & Johnson withheld the information that Levamisole is a colon cancer drug, the plaintiff's *ona'ah* claim should remain intact, notwithstanding the enormous difference in price between Ergamisol and Levamisole. Far from signaling an intent to make a voluntary transfer to Johnson & Johnson, the overcharge reflects the successful duping conduct of the seller. The plaintiff's *ona'ah* claim hence remains intact.

Clozaril

In 1990, Sandoz Pharmaceuticals Corp. got FDA approval to market its drug Clozaril, used to teat schizophrenia. The company's initial pricing of the drug made its annual cost to a user come to $8,944. One feature of the marketing of this drug was a *mandatory* and expensive blood-monitoring system designed to detect a side effect that could otherwise be fatal to as many as 2 percent of patients. Without its proprietary system, Sandoz claimed, some patients would die and the drug would inevitably be pulled from the market.

The blood monitoring was the more expensive part of the package, and because of it, critics claimed, few would be able to afford the drug. Medicaid officials, the Veterans Administration, and others mounted an unsuccessful campaign to force Sandoz to uncouple the drug from the blood-testing program. The VA, for instance, claimed it could do the blood work for $1.86.[37]

In order to facilitate analysis of this case from a halakhic standpoint, let us assume that the basic research for Clorazil was financed by society as a whole. Within this framework, Sandoz is entitled to no more than cost-plus pricing for its drug. Moreover, with the aim of reducing costs, it would be the duty of government to investigate the feasibility of uncoupling the drug from the blood-testing program. Finally, the government would require Sandoz to make its drug available to the poor free of charge. If the incidence of schizophrenia is mainly or even disproportionately among the poor, the latter requirement would assuredly make Clorazil unprofitable. In this instance, Sandoz would qualify for a government subsidy. The rationale for this subsidy is that to relieve the misery of the poor is both an individual and a societal obligation. If neither the profit motive nor voluntarism offers any prospect of relieving a particular form of misery, then it is the duty of government to tax society for this purpose.

1. Baruch A. Brody, *Ethical Issues in Drug Testing, Approval and Pricing* (New York: Oxford University Press, 1995), p. 230.

2. *Earning a Failing Grade: A Report Card on 1992 Drug Manufacturer Price Inflation*, Staff of Senate Special Commission on Aging, 103 Cong., 1st Sess., p. 3, n. 2.

3. Nahmanides, *Torat ha-Adam*, Inyan ha-Sakanah, pp. 44–45. Nahmanides' ruling is adopted by R. Jacob b. Asher (Spain, 1270–1340), *Tur*, Yoreh De'ah 336:3; R. Joseph Caro (Israel, 1448–1575), *Shulhan Arukh*, Yoreh De'ah, 336:4; R. Jehiel Michel Epstein (Belarus, 1829–1908), *Arukh ha-Shulhan*, Yoreh De'ah 336:34.

4. Nahmanides, op. cit.; *Tur*, op. cit.; *Sh.Ar.*, op. cit.; *Ar. haSh.*; op. cit. 336:4.

5. R. Hayyim David ha-Levi, "Tashlum Sekhar ha-Rofeh ba-Halakhah," *Shevilin*, Kislev 5737 (1977), pp. 22–29.

6. Daniel Sperber, *Roman Palestine*, 2nd ed. (Ramat Gan, Bar-Ilan University Press, 1991), pp. 35–37, 241, n. 8., posits that the ninety-nine maneh was a daily stipend.

7. R. Shelomoh Zalman Auerbach, quoted by A. S. Abraham in *Nishmat Avraham*, Hilkhot Bikkur Holim, p. 234

8. Pesahim 30a.

9. Rashi, at Mishnah Keritot 1:7.

10. Tosafot, Bava Batra 166a.

11. R. Hayyim Berlin, quoted by R. Naftali Yehudah Zevi Berlin, *Harhev Davar*, Leviticus 23, ot alef.

12. Bava Batra 90a; R. Isaac b. Jacob Alfasi (Algeria, 1013–1103), Rif, ad loc.; Maimonides (Egypt, 1135–1204), *Yad*, Mekhirah 14:1; R. Asher b. Jehiel (Germany, 1250–1327), Rosh, Bava Batra 5:2; *Tur*, Hoshen Mishpat 231:27; *Sh.Ar.*, Hoshen Mishpat 231:20; *Ar.haSh.*, Hoshen Mishpat 231:20.

13. *Tur*, op. cit.; *Sh.Ar.*, op. cit.; *Ar.haSh.*, op. cit. Maimonides (op. cit.), however, identifies the foodstuffs ordinance with a price-fixing obligation on the part of the Jewish court.

14. Ibid.

15. R. Menahem b. Solomon Meiri (France, ca. 1249–1306), *Beit ha-Behirah*, Bava Mezia 40b; Rosh, Bava Mezia 3:16; *Tur*, Hoshen Mishpat 231 and comment of *Perisha*, n. 26. R. Joel Sirkes (Poland, 1561–1650), however, interpreting Maimonides' position on this matter, posits that the one-sixth profit rate is the return the owner receives for his labor services (Bah to *Tur*, loc. cit., n. 26).

16. For support for this thesis, see, *Ar.haSh.*, op. cit. 231:23.

17. R. Joshua ha-Kohen Falk (Poland, 1555–1614), *Sefer Me'irat Einayim, Sh.Ar.*, Hoshen Mishpat 231, no. 43.

18. "Do We Pay Too Much for Prescription Drugs?" *Consumer Reports* 58, no. 10 (October 1993): 669.

19. Tosefta, Shabbat 18:16; *Yad.*, Shabbat 6:25; *Tur*, Orah Hayyim 306:5; *Sh.Ar.*, Orah

Hayyim 306:4; *Ar.haSh.*, Orah Hayyim 306:9.

20. R. Hayyim Isaac Algazi (Turkey, 18th cent.), *Derekh Ez ha-Hayyim*, responsum 2; R. Hayyim Modai (Turkey, 1700–1784), *Hayyim L'Olam*, p. 130; R. Yehoshua Neuwirth, *Shmirat Shabbat ki-Hilkhata*, p. 164, n. 135.

21. *Hayyim L'Olam*, loc. cit.

22. Richard R. Nelson, "The Simple Economics of Basic Scientific Research," *Journal of Political Economy*, vol. 67, no. 3, June 1959, p. 299.

23. Ibid., pp. 302, 305.

24. "Do We Pay Too Much for Prescription Drugs?" p. 670.

25. Mishnah, Bava Batra 1:4; Rif., ad loc.; *Yad*, Shekhenim 6:1; Rosh, Bava Batra 1:22; *Tur*, Hoshen Mishpat 163:1; *Sh.Ar.*, Hoshen Mishpat 163:1; *Ar.haSh.*, Hoshen Mishpat 163:1.

26. R. Mosheh Isserles (Poland, 1525 or 1530–1572) Rema, *Sh.Ar.*, op. cit. 163:1; *Ar.haSh.*, op. cit. 163:1.

27. For the development of this thesis, see Aaron Levine, *Free Enterprise and Jewish Law: Aspects of Jewish Business Ethics* (New York: Ktav, 1980), pp. 136–47.

28. Deuteronomy 15:8; Ketubbot 67b; Rif, ad loc.; *Yad*, Mattenot Aniyyim 7:3; Rosh, Ketubbot 6:8; *Tur*, Yoreh De'ah 250:1; *Sh.Ar.*, Yoreh De'ah 250:1; *Ar.haSh.*, Yoreh De'ah 250:13.

29. *Sh.Ar.*, op. cit. 249:16.

30. Aaron Levine, *Economics and Jewish Law: Halakhic Perspectives* (Hoboken, N.J.: Ktav, 1987), pp. 113–33.

31. "Do We Pay Too Much for Prescription Drugs?" pp. 671–72.

32. Paul A. Samuelson and William Nordhaus, *Economics*, 15th ed. (New York, McGraw-Hill, 1995), p. 155.

33. R. Meir b. Samuel, quoted in Tosafot, Kiddushin 59a.

34. R. Mosheh Sofer, *Responsa Hatam Sofer*, Hoshen Mishpat 79. See also Hoshen Mishpat 41 and 6:57.

35. Philip Kotler and Gary Armstrong, *Principles of Marketing*, 6th ed. (Englewood Cliffs, N.J.,: Prentice-Hall, 1994), p. 388.

36. For the rules of *ona'ah* pertinent to the Ergamisol case, please turn to pp. 193–6 of this volume.

37. N. Craig Smith and John A. Quelch, *Ethics in Marketing*, (Homewood, Ill.: Irwin, 1993), pp. 441–45.

5. Labor Relations

The Mean Boss

Any casual observer of I. M. Frier's greeting card operation would reasonably conclude that the executive deliberately organized his workplace to insure *inaccessibility* for himself. Consider, for instance, Frier's use of caller I.D. If the incoming number indicates that the caller is someone he does not wish to speak to, such as a creditor, Frier typically plays the answering machine message. This message informs the listener that Frier is not available and invites the caller to leave a message.

Frier's policy is to see no one in his office without an appointment. If someone drops in without an appointment, he is typically told that Frier is in a conference or is otherwise unavailable and cannot be interrupted. Charity collectors are singled out for particularly harsh treatment. On the theory that another fundraiser advised the present collector to come, Frier is determined to find out the name of the person who abused his generosity. Pity the culprit! For the unauthorized use of his name, the fundraiser will suffer a sharp rebuke and a reduction in next year's donation.

Another of Frier's practices is not to allow appointments to go ahead of schedule. Accordingly, if someone arrives early and requests an early start, Frier will have the receptionist say: "Mr. Frier is not ready to see you." Frier generally blocks early starts of appointments even when he is not busy with something else at the time. When the person with the appointment is an employee, Frier will often *deliberately* delay the start of the meeting. Typifying Frier's attitude and conduct here is his colorful recollection of a meeting with Leonard Sugarman, the company's resident poet. Sugarman writes the prose as well as the dialogue between the cartoon characters that appear in the company's greeting cards:

"Sugarman made a 3 p.m. appointment with me. He wanted a private office and a laptop computer. Because Sugarman was a stickler for punctuality, he arrived in the reception area a full ten minutes ahead of schedule. When my secretary buzzed the intercom to alert me of Sugarman's arrival, I ambled out of my office just to become visible to him. But, I didn't greet him, and it goes without saying that I made no gesture to him to start our meeting ahead of time. Just at 3 p.m., as I had prearranged, my grandson, Ivan, popped into my office. I kept Ivan in the office for at least fifteen minutes before I signaled the receptionist to let Sugarman in. I knew that my conduct enraged Sugarman. I could hear him cursing me under his breath: 'Frier does this only to remind me that *he* is the boss and because he is the boss and I'm the employee, I must tolerate his demeaning conduct.' Believe me, the cursing is not all that bad! It serves as a venting device and when the emotional release is over, Sugarman, I'm convinced, was catapulted to a mindset of levelheaded, honest self-appraisal. Instead of succumbing to the temptation to assert his dignity and independence by quitting on the spot, Sugarman began to balance his expected prospects against the opportunity cost of quitting. In short, the poet became an economist! By the time Sugarman entered my office, his original agenda quickly dissipated and he became downright servile. In no time, he began to request a critique of his work and was eager for me to tell him how he could improve his job performance."

What makes Frier's labor relations all the more appalling is his glaring one-sidedness. Standing in sharp relief with the layers of inaccessibility he creates for himself are the demands he places on his workers in respect to face time and the busywork he imposes on them.

In respect to face time, Frier takes no prisoners. His rules call for employees to check in and leave by punching a timeclock. In addition, workers are expected to give an account for any time they are missing from their workstations. For any time missed, an employee will have his pay docked, and no excuses are countenanced.

There is nothing that makes Frier more furious than sloth and idleness in the workplace. It should come as no surprise that near the top in the hierarchy of "capital crimes" for an employee is to be caught playing a video game on the computer during business hours. If Frier notices that an employee has nothing to do, he is quick to give him some busywork. Frier's treatment of his administrative assistant, Claudia Weinstock, provides a case in point. For Claudia there is no such thing as being "in between" assignments. As soon as Frier feels that a lull is approaching in Claudia's workflow, he will assign her busywork. Typically, he asks her to check up on delinquent customer accounts. He does so in full knowledge that the customer's check has already been received or that the accounts have been handed over to a collection agency. Frier imagines that Claudia will not catch on that she has been assigned busywork. This is so because Frier alone decides when to turn a delinquent account over to a collection agency, and in addition it is his practice to grab all envelopes that appear to contain payments before Claudia has a chance to look at the mail. If Claudia complains because she gets flak from a customer for calling about a bill already paid, or because she has picked up on the redundancy of her task, Frier responds by saying, "Oh, my! *This time* you're right."

Claudia's busy work also sometimes includes proofreading of the prose and cartoon-character dialogue produced for the company's cards. On occasion Frier can be seen agonizing over which materials he should select to put on the greeting cards. "Let me see each design in its edited, polished form," he snaps, "then I will decide." Because some of Claudia's proofreading work will be done on material the company ultimately will not use, Frier is convinced that he can push proofreading on her that is, in actuality, busy work. Accordingly, when a lull develops in Claudia's workflow, Frier assign her proofreading on material he knows in advance will not be used on the company's greeting cards. Frier thinks that Claudia will never catch on that her assignment is busy work. He is wrong. Claudia is adept in picking up subtle changes in Frier's mood. The vibrations she picks up from him when the material he gives her has a chance of passing muster are not the same as the vibrations she picks up when the work he hands her is only busy work. Because she has no concrete basis for complaining when busy work of this type is given to her, she does not complain and instead suffers silently.

Frier is a somewhat paradoxical figure. In business, he is hard-nosed and by nature suspicious, displaying a gruff and distant demeanor. But as a family man he is the very personification of the mushy messages his greeting card company grinds out. Frier took his children into the business. His latest project is to introduce his eight-year-old grandson, Ivan, to the family business. During summer vacation and school holidays, Frier spares no opportunity to bring young Ivan to the office so that he can observe first-hand how the business works. As grandfather Frier put it: "Training in the school of hard knocks is just as important, if not more important, than book learning at school."

Making Oneself Inaccessible and Halakhah

The vignette in the preceding section raises a number of moral issues. One issue is the extent of an individual's right to deny someone access to himself.

Recall that R. Shelomoh Zalman Auerbach invoked the principle of *darkhei shalom* to allow a householder to indirectly inform an unexpected caller that he was not home.[1] Application of the rule here provides legitimization for some of Frier's designs to avoid accessibility. There is, however, no excuse for his gruff manner. If Frier does not wish to speak to or see a particular person, the denial should be sweetened as much as possible, even with the aid of a "white lie," if necessary.

Let us take note that the right to deny people access to oneself is not absolute. Frier's treatment of creditors provides a case in point. Refusing to make payment on the claim of a legitimate creditor when one has the resources to do so runs afoul of the biblical prohibition of "Do not [unjustly] withhold (*lo ta'ashok*) that which is due your neighbor" (Leviticus 19:13). The prohibition is violated on a biblical level when the debtor uses strong-arm techniques to refuse payment when the creditor presents his claim.[2] Pushing off the creditor by telling him to return some other time (*leikh va-shuv*) violates *lo ta'ashok* on a rabbinical level.[3] Specifically, the conduct violates King Solomon's admonition: "Do not say to your fellow, Go and return, and tomorrow I will give,' though you have it with you'" (Proverbs 3:28).[4]

Frier's treatment of charity collectors is particularly appalling. While he is within his rights to refuse to see charity collectors at his place of business, his notion that a charity collector has no right to make a patron's name available to another fundraiser is mistaken. R. Mosheh Feinstein (New York, 1895–1986) deals with this issue in his responsa. What is at issue, according to R. Feinstein, is whether King Solomon's admonition, "He who blesses his friend in a loud voice early every morning, it shall be considered a curse for him" (Proverbs 27:14), applies here. Specifically, is there concern that spreading the word of A's charitable giving might lead to a scenario wherein many collectors converge upon him, and because he is embarrassed to refuse the solicitations, he will end up giving beyond his means. Rejecting this concern, R. Feinstein limits King Solomon's admonition to matters of hospitality and to revealing the information to "unsavory" people. In respect to a solicitation for charity, however, nothing is wrong in spreading the word that A is a prospective donor. In the event A is besieged by charity collectors, he will not be embarrassed to refuse to respond beyond the ordinary donation.

Suppose, however, that the solicitor is a well-known Torah sage and the target donor (A) is a wealthy man. A will certainly feel pressure to contribute what he otherwise would not. But nothing improper has occurred. Consider that an individual is obligated to donate one-tenth (*ma'aser*) of his income to charity, and in all likelihood A has not yet fulfilled his obligation. Consider also that verbal, as opposed to physical, coercion is permissible in connection with the charity obligation. Consequently, if the Torah sage shames A into contributing to the charitable cause at hand, a mitzvah (positive spiritual duty) and not anything improper has resulted. Moreover, since it is a mitzvah, on the level of an optional duty, to donate as much as 20 percent of one's income to charity, the same judgment would be in order if the sage's solicitation pushes A into the 20 percent charity level. If A has already donated to charity on the 20 percent level, he will not be embarrassed to excuse himself, irrespective of who the solicitor is.[5]

Let us now turn to Frier's practice of denying a request to start an appointment early. Recall R. Auerbach's proposition that an individual is not obligated to see anyone against his will. But consider that Frier has already agreed to see A. If A arrives early and requests an early start, and Frier is not busy with anything else at the time, Frier should accede to the request. Since accommodating A entails no monetary cost for Frier, the duty of *gemilut hasadim* (i.e., to perform deeds of kindness) requires Frier to accede to the request for the early appointment.[6] This requirement holds whether A is rich or poor.[7]

Finally, let us turn to Frier's practice of deliberately delaying the start of a meeting scheduled with an employee. His practice here is objectionable on several grounds. For one, delaying the start of a meeting throws the appointee's schedule off. This can result in inconvenience, mental anguish, and even financial loss. Since the delay is deliberate, the mental anguish the employee suffers is Frier's responsibility and should therefore be regarded as *needless* mental anguish.[8] Making Frier liable for the employee's loss is, however, another matter. This issue is dealt with elsewhere in this volume.[9]

Another troublesome aspect of Frier's conduct is his demeaning attitude toward his employees. Frier feels that he has the right to *underline* their state of dependency. Such conduct is prohibited, as can be derived from Rav's dictum at Bava Mezia 10a:

> A worker can withdraw from his employment even in the middle of the day, for the children of Israel are servants unto Me (Leviticus 25:42). In effect, God says, "They are My servants, and not servants to other servants!"

To see why Rav's dictum prohibits Frier's conduct, let us probe into the rationale behind the dictum. According to R. Yom Tov Ishbili (Spain, ca. 1250–1330), the retraction right is conferred to ensure that a worker not be bound to his employer against his will. Without the retraction right, the labor contract is akin to servitude. Following this line, R. Ishbili goes on to say that the retraction right is conferred only to a worker who contracts to work at specific hours (*po'el*). Absent the retraction right, obligating oneself to work at specific hours is akin to servitude. But the retraction right is not conferred to a worker who is paid for finished work and does not obligate himself to work at specific hours (*kabbelan*). Because the *kabbelan*'s undertaking carries with it the liberty to withhold work at any specific time, the sages did not give him the right of retraction.[10]

R. Ishbili's exposition requires clarification. Conferring the *po'el* with a retraction right, in R. Ishbili's thinking, is what frees the labor agreement from being akin to servitude. But consider that the *po'el* labor agreement only generates a commitment by the employee to undertake the employer's assignment but not a lien by the employer on the person of the *po'el*.[11] Hence the *po'el* contract is *inherently not akin to servitude*. That is why there is no objection to the *po'el*'s voluntarily agreeing to a no-retraction clause. This clause does not violate "They are My servants, and not servants to other servants."[12] Why then is it necessary to confer the *po'el* with a retraction right? This difficulty leads to the proposition that the retraction right is rooted in a *psychological* need of the worker. Because he obligates himself to work at specific hours, the agreement naturally makes him feel he is losing his independence. This feeling is not rooted in the *legal* status that becomes operative as a result of the agreement, but is purely psychological in nature. Giving the *po'el* a retraction right removes the psychological burden of loss of independence.

It follows from this analysis that the Torah's definition of servitude in connection with the prohibition of "They are My servants and not servants to other servants" does not simply relate to the legal realm but consists of a psychological element as well. If the Torah is concerned that a *po'el* should not psychologically feel that his labor contract entails a state of dependency, then, *a fortiori*, the employer should not *underline* the *po'el*'s state of dependency.

If Rav's dictum can be understood to prohibit an employer from *underlining* his workers' dependency status, then such misconduct becomes an aspect of needless mental anguish and thus violates the *ona'at devarim* interdict.

Proceeding from the above analysis is a clear-cut prohibition against deliberately delaying a meeting with an employee. Such conduct displays a callous disregard for the worker. Frier effectively communicates to his employee that *because I'm your boss you will have to tolerate disrespectful treatment*. Frier's assertion that he demeans his employee as a means of ascertaining the level of the worker's job satisfaction should not work to legitimize the conduct.

Most troublesome of all is Frier's project of bringing his grandson, Ivan, to his office to observe first-hand the inner workings of the family greeting card business. Observing his grandfather in action will assuredly train Ivan in the skills of becoming inaccessible, but it will prove a disaster in respect to moral education. But suppose Frier cleans up his operation. Pitfalls still remain. Recall that the mission of parents and teachers is to inculcate children to use every opportunity in life to make a positive statement about truth and integrity.[13] Exposing a child to a work environment that constantly makes use of "permissible lies" not only fails in this mission, but habituates a child to lie as well.

Face Time, Busywork, and Halakhah

Let us now turn to a consideration of Frier's conduct in respect to face time and busywork.

Frier's strict rules regarding face time are not inconsistent with the duty Halakhah imposes on the worker not to be idle on the employer's time.[14] A worker who idles on his employer's time forfeits the wages he would have earned for this time period.[15]

Maimonides (Egypt, 1135–1204) records the prohibition against idling on the employer's time with the following ruling:

> Just as the employer is enjoined not to deprive the poor worker of his hire or to withhold it from him when it is due, so is the worker enjoined not to deprive the employer of the benefit of his work by idling away his time, a little here and a little there, thus wasting the whole day deceitfully. Indeed the worker must be very punctual in the matter of time, seeing that the sages were so solicitous in this matter that they exempted the worker from saying the four benedictions of the [after-meal] grace.
>
> The worker must work with all his power, seeing that the just Jacob said, *And you know that I served your father with all my strength* (Genesis 31:6), and that he received his reward therefore in this world too, as it is said, *And the man increased exceedingly* (Genesis 30:43).[16]

While an employer has the legal right to set strict rules against idling on company time for his employees, what is his ethical duty in response to an employee's request for a flexible time schedule? To illustrate: Suppose Claudia approaches Frier and explains to him that a nine-to-five schedule is incompatible with her personal lifestyle and her family responsibilities. Changing her work schedule to a ten-to-six routine would save her much expense and aggravation. Alternatively, Claudia proposes a ten-to-four schedule and promises to make up the time by taking work home. Suppose, also, that Frier will suffer no loss in productivity if he accedes to Claudia's request. Since the benefit Claudia seeks entails no loss for Frier, it should be categorized as *zeh neheneh ve-zeh lo haser* (this one benefits and the other one loses nothing). The sages regard denying a benefit when it costs one nothing as reflecting the character trait of the people of Sodom. In some instances, a Bet Din (Jewish court) will even coerce (*kofin*) an individual not to act in the manner of the Sodomites.[17]

The contention that Frier suffers no loss by acceding to Claudia's request, however, is questionable. First, if Frier himself maintains a nine-to-five schedule, accommodating her proposed ten-to-six schedule requires him to either change his own schedule or keep the office open longer. Since acceding to Claudia's request entails a loss for Frier, the *zeh neheneh* principle does not apply.

Moreover, accommodating Claudia's request to take work home may also entail a loss for Frier. Acceding to the request would set the stage for similar requests by other employees. But not all work assignments can be done at home just as easily as at the office. Consider, too, the disputes that would arise as to what is a reasonable amount of time to allot for an *unsupervised* assignment. Acceding to requests for alternative work schedules on a selective basis can only foster dissension and jealousy in the workforce, and thus reduce its morale and efficiency.

Moreover, consider that production is, by its very nature, a team effort. Face-to-face interaction among members of the team fosters creativity, team spirit, and motivation. Every request for special work-schedule arrangements reduces the face-to-face interactions among the team members and at some point may reduce the team's efficiency.

The upshot of the preceding analysis is that acceding to requests for special work schedules may reduce the team's efficiency. The *zeh neheneh* principle, therefore, is not an operative norm here.

Another aspect of the worker's duty to his boss is energetic application to the task at hand. Proceeding from the requirement of energetic exertion is the prohibition of the employee's working at night while under contract during the day.[18] Similarly, a worker may not refuse to use his wages to provide himself with minimum nourishment, even if the money saved is used to support his family.[19] By the same token, a schoolteacher may not stay up late at night or rise very early.[20] In all these instances, the conduct is prohibited because it reduces the worker's productivity while performing his contracted work.

Once it is recognized that the worker owes his boss not only time on the job but energetic performance of the job, the employer should enjoy the liberty to take measures to ensure that result. Suppose the employer regards idleness in the workplace as contagious. He fears that the idleness of even a single worker will drag down the work ethic he wants to foster for his business. Assigning busywork when a lull in the workflow develops should, therefore, be legitimate. However, an examination of the prohibition against ordering a Hebrew servant (*eved ivri*) to do work that is either degrading or useless (*perekh* work) puts to question the legitimacy of using busywork as a means to foster productivity. Addressing the parameters of this prohibition, *Torat Kohanim* interprets *perekh* to mean: "You are not to tell him to warm a cup that is not wanted at all, or say to him, 'Cool this cup' when you do not need it, or 'Go on hoeing' under this tree until I come."[22] *Torat Kohanim* understands the prohibition against *perekh* as applying only to the *eved ivri* but not to a hired worker. Notwithstanding this legal permissibility, posits R. Aaron ha-Levi (Spain, 1235–1300), pious conduct (*middat hasidut*) requires an individual to refrain from assigning a worker *perekh* work.[23]

R. Meir b. Barukh (Germany, ca. 1215–1293) expresses a different view. He holds that the prohibition against *perekh* work applies with equal force vis-à-vis a worker. Any amenity the Torah gives an *eved ivri* is, *a fortiori*, conferred on a *po'el*. This is so because entering into the status of *eved ivri* violates for the individual the admonition of "They are My servants, and not servants to other servants." Accordingly, any amenity the Torah confers on an *eved ivri* it must also confer on the po'el, who violated no prohibition by entering into his labor contract.[24]

The prohibition against assigning *perekh* work is formulated in the Torah in blanket terms, with no consideration for the motive behind the assignment. This indicates that the assignment of busywork to an employee is morally wrong even when fostering productivity is what motivates the employer. Such conduct, in the thinking of R. Aaron ha-Levi, falls short of pious conduct, and in the view of R. Meir b. Barukh rises to the level of prohibited conduct.

Instead of reflecting a desire to promote a work ethic, the assignment of busy work may bespeak mean-spiritedness on the part of the employer. Specifically, the employer's attitude may be that since he is paying the worker for his time, the worker is not entitled to any respite from exertion even if he has no work to give him. Alternatively, the employer may view busywork as a vehicle to feel a sense of power to dominate or control another human being. For the latter two scenarios, the assignment of busywork amounts to denying the worker a benefit in the form of a respite from exertion when allowing the worker this benefit costs the employer nothing. Because the latter two scenarios are clear-cut applications of the principle of *zeh neheneh*, all disputants should agree that the conduct is morally wrong.

Another consideration in evaluating the ethics of assigning busywork is the feeling of anguish the worker experiences when he is convinced, or even suspects, that the work he is assigned is busywork. When a worker makes this judgment, he surely feels that the employer is assaulting his dignity and rubbing in his status of dependency. If the busywork is rooted in the employer's desire to promote a work ethic, the worker's mental anguish should not be categorized as needless mental anguish. But if busywork is the employer's tool for demonstrating to the worker the power he has over him, or reflects a begrudging attitude about allowing the worker a respite from exertion, even if it costs the employer nothing, then the assignment should be regarded as causing the worker needless mental anguish. In the absence of a profit motive, the assignment of busywork when the employee suspects or is convinced that it is busywork puts the employer in the position of violating the prohibition of causing someone needless mental anguish (*ona'at devarim*).[25] The infraction of the prohibition against *ona'at devarim* here is on top of the violation of the prohibition against assigning *perekh* work.

The upshot of the preceding analysis is to put into question Frier's policy of assigning busywork to his employees. If his motive is to foster a strong work ethic in his place of business, his conduct is nevertheless objectionable. At the very least, his conduct here falls short of the *middat hasidut* behavioral standard. To be sure, his conduct, according to R. Meir b. Barukh, rises to the level of transgressing the prohibition against assigning *perekh* work.

A much harsher judgment against Frier must be made if his assignment of busywork is not rooted in a profit motive but instead reflects a begrudging attitude toward allowing his employees a respite or a desire to demonstrate the power he has over them. Here, in addition to falling short of the behavioral standard set by the *perekh* interdict, Frier violates the principle of *zeh neheneh* and transgresses the interdict against *ona'at devarim*.

Problem

Sue Shellenbarger, a former bureau chief of the *Wall Street Journal*, delivers a salvo against the practice of imposing face-time demands on employees. In her opinion, the managerial obsession with face time is the number-one enemy of employees trying to juggle personal and family needs with jobs. Moreover, in her opinion, face time doesn't work well as a management tool unless you happen to be running an assembly line. It values visibility over results, rewarding people who spend a long time doing work that others may do more quickly.

Shellenbarger sympathizes greatly with the face-time underground: the legions who daily find clever ways around their bosses' face-time demands and live to tell about it. Here are some of the strategies she lists:

Before leaving the office, put a fresh, steaming cup of coffee on your desk. People will assume you are coming right back.

Hang around at the office until the last supervisor leaves—then go.

Arrive early and let them see you, your car, and your office up and running, and then leave for the morning.

Go in on Saturday and stay for a few hours. You don't need to do any work, just make sure someone sees you.

If you leave early, call back in and ask someone to look something up in your office. They'll assume you're at an out-of-office meeting.

If you must make personal calls, always have a pad in front of you. Write on it frequently, and speak firmly. The rest of the office will think you're negotiating.

Leave personal belongings (coat, jacket, etc.) in your office to give the impression that you're coming back.[26]

1. Please turn to pp. 19–20 of this volume.

2. Maimonides (Egypt, 1135–1204), *Yad, Gezelah* 1:4; R. Jacob b. Asher (Spain, 1270–1340), *Tur*, Hoshen Mishpat 359:8; R. Joseph Caro (Israel, 1488–1575), *Shulhan Arukh*, Hoshen Mishpat 359:9; R. Jehiel Michel Epstein (Belarus, 1829–1908), *Arukh ha-Shulhan*, Hoshen Mishpat 359:7.

3. *Yad, Sekhirut* 11:5; *Ar.haSh.*, op. cit. 97:3.

4. Bava Mezia 110b; R. Isaac Alfasi (Algeria, 1013–1103), Rif, ad loc.; *Yad*, op. cit.; R, Asher b. Jehiel (Germany ca. 1250–1327), Rosh, Bava Mezia 9:43; *Tur*, op. cit. 97:6, 339:8; *Sh.Ar.*, op. cit. 97:3, 339:8; *Ar.haSh.*, op. cit. 97:3, 339:10.

5. R. Mosheh Feinstein, *Iggerot Mosheh*, Yoreh De'ah 3:95.

6. Mishnah Pe'ah 1:1 and commentary of R. Ovadiah Yarei Bertinoro (Italy, ca. 1344–1505), ad loc.

7. See R. Zalman Nehemia Goldberg, "Ba-Hiyyuvei Gemilut Hesed," in *Yad REM le-Zehker Eliezer Meir Lipschitz* (Jerusalem, 1975), pp. 97–111.

8. Leviticus 25:17. The prohibition is violated even when it is the offender's *failure to take action* that causes the needless mental anguish for the victim. On this point, see discussion at pp. 307–08 of this volume.

9. Please turn to pp. 270–71; 274–77 of this volume.

10. R. Yom Tov Ishbili (Seville, ca. 1250–1330), Ritva, Bava Mezia 76b.

11. In his analysis of the nature of the claim an employer has on the *po'el* as a result of the labor contract, R. Mosheh Feinstein (*Iggerot Mosheh*, Hoshen Mishpat 1:81) identifies three approaches: (1) R. Aryeh Loeb b. Joseph ha-Kohen Heller (Poland, 1745—1813) (*Kezot ha-Hoshen, Sh.Ar.*, Hoshen Mishpat 333, n. 5) regards the claim as taking the form of a lien on the person of the *po'el*. (2) Tosafot (Kiddushin 17a, s.v. *halla*) explicitly rejects this approach and instead, in R. Feinstein's view, conceptualizes the labor contract as generating reciprocal claims for the parties involved. Specifically, the employer has a claim on the *po'el* that the agreed-upon assignment should be done, and the *po'el* has a claim on the employer to provide the work and compensate him upon completion of the job. (3) R. Jacob Moses Lorberbaum (Poland, 1760–1832, *Netivot ha-Mishpat, Sh.Ar.*, op. cit. 333, n. 6) regards the labor contact as generating only *self-requirements* for the parties, but with no reciprocal claims proceeding as a result of the *po'el* contract. R. Feinstein regards the third view as normative. For an extensive discussion of the view of the rishonim on this issue, see R. Menahem Shelomoh Levi, *Me-Shel Soferim Hilkhot Sekhirut Po'elim*, pp. 18–21.

12. R. Ishmael b. Abraham Isaac ha-Kohen (Italy, 1723–1811), *Responsa Zera Emet*, vol. 2, Yoreh De'ah 97.

13. For a discussion of this point, please turn to pp. 24–27 of this volume.

14. *Yad*, op. cit. 13:7; *Tur*, op. cit. 337:20; *Sh.Ar.*, op. cit. 337:20; *Ar.haSh.*, op. cit. 337:26.

15. Shillem Warhaftig, *Dinei Avodah ba-Mishpat ha-Ivri*, vol. 1 (Jerusalem: Moreshet, 1968), p. 324.

16. *Yad*, op. cit. 13:7.

17. For a discussion of the principle of *zeh neheneh*, please turn to pp. 337–48 of this volume.

18. Tosefta, Bava Mezia 8:2; Jerusalem Talmud, Demai 8:3; Rif, Bava Mezia 90b; *Yad*, op. cit. 13:6; Rosh, Bava Mezia 7:3; *Tur*, op. cit. 337:19; *Sh.Ar.*, op. cit. 337:19; *Ar.haSh.*, op. cit. 337:25.

19. Jerusalem Talmud, Demai, loc. cit; Rif, loc. cit; *Sh.Ar.*, loc. cit.; *Ar.haSh.*, loc. cit.

20. R. Mordecai b. Hillel (Germany, ca. 1240–ca. 1298), Bava Mezia 6:343.

21. *Yad*, loc. cit.; *Tur*, loc. cit.; *Sh.Ar.*, loc. cit.; *Ar.haSh.*, loc. cit.

22. *Torat Kohanim* at Leviticus 25:43.

23. R. Aaron ha-Levi, *Sefer ha-Hinnukh* 346.

24. R. Meir b. Barukh, *Responsa Maharam of Rothenburg* (Prague ed.), 4:85.

25. For a discussion of *ona'at devarim*, please turn to pp. 306–8 of this volume.

26. Sue Shellenbarger, "How to Look Like a Workaholic While Still Having a Life," *Wall Street Journal*, December 28, 1994, p. B1.

Layoffs at Rechev

Rechev is a multi-product firm located in the Appalachian Mountains area. One aspect of its operations consists of the manufacture of delivery vehicles made to order for regional motor express companies. For this particular line the production system entails the following: Rechev orders chassis from the big auto companies in Detroit and then modifies them to receive a particular body. The average production cycle is four weeks per vehicle, requiring about 175 working hours.

The viability of Rechev's truck-body business depends on both its ability to generate delivery truck orders as well as the availability of chassis at its plant to meet these orders. In 1980, Rechev's chassis supply was interrupted by the slowdown of the auto industry. On July 1, Rheinholt Suss, Rechev's CEO, had firm information that no deliveries would be made to the plant for at least three months. Production could continue for another month by making use of the current inventory of chassis, but by August 1, widespread layoffs would have to be implemented. Suss' humanitarian impulse urged him to immediately share the devastating news he had just received from Detroit with the work force. Advance notice would afford the affected workers an early start in their search for new employment. Suss' empathetic attitude toward the workers quickly dissipated as his attention turned toward the costs advance notice would entail for Rechev. While Suss could not come up with any *tangible costs*, his imagination ran wild in identifying *hypothetical costs*. For one, job search would be a *full-time* pursuit for the many workers who lived near the plant, where few, if any, alternative employment opportunities existed. As a result, advance notice of the layoffs could be expected to generate a rash of absenteeism on the part of the workers slated for layoffs. Production schedules would consequently not be met, and Rechev's reputation would suffer. Similarly, advance notice would probably adversely affect productivity, as demoralized workers could not be expected to approach their assigned tasks with much diligence or zeal. Finally, the prospect of interacting with disgruntled workers on a daily basis for an entire month was so unsettling for Suss that this factor alone just about clinched his decision not to give any advance notice regarding the impending layoffs.

Convinced that he was acting in the best interest of the firm, Suss sprung the layoff notice on twenty truck-body assembly line workers at the conclusion of the August 1 work day. In a prepared statement which he read to the entire group, Suss announced that the company had decided to discontinue its delivery vehicle line. The layoffs would be effective immediately.

Layoffs at Rechev and Secular Law

From the perspective of secular law, the most salient feature to focus on in evaluating the ethics of the layoffs at Rechev is that the affected workers were hired for an indefinite period. Hence the *employment-at-will* doctrine is operative here. This traditional common-law rule provides that, in the absence of a contract, either the employer or the employee can terminate the relationship at any time, for any reason or no reason.[1]

During the 1980s, legislation and court rulings in over forty states made revolutionary changes in the at-will doctrine.[2] The exception most relevant to the issue at hand is embodied in the rulings of Massachusetts and California courts that every contract contains an implied covenant of good faith and fair dealing. Under this doctrine, any discharge without good cause, such as incompetence, corruption, or habitual tardiness, is actionable.[3] To date, however, the courts have not extended application of the implied covenant of good faith and fair dealing to a requirement that an employee-at-will is entitled to notice. Thus secular law would find no fault with the no-notice treatment the workers at Rechev received.

Layoffs at Rechev and Halakhah

We now turn to an analysis of the ethics of the layoffs at Rechev from the perspective of Halakhah.

Let us begin with the employment-at-will doctrine. From the perspective of Halakhah, this doctrine presents two separate issues. The first relates to the circumstance where the job in question is still open. The issue here is whether the original occupant has a legal or moral claim to keep the job ahead of other applicants. We have dealt with this question elsewhere.[4] The second issue relates to the notice requirement. Since normative Halakhah rules that the employee-at-will has no legal claim for tenure, the issue will come up both in the instance when the job in question was eliminated as well as in the instance where the job remains open. We will proceed to demonstrate that the employee-at-will is entitled to notice. This requirement proceeds from both contract and tort law.

The Notice Requirement and Contract Law

In Halakhah, the requirement to give an employee-at-will notice is a matter of contract law. The extent of this requirement is a matter of dispute. Three views have been advanced. The most lenient opinion here is espoused by R. Malchiel Tenenbaum (Poland, d. 1910). In his view, the wage period is what defines and determines what the hiring period is. To illustrate: E hires W. The agreement calls for W to be paid on a monthly basis. Given the monthly pay-roll, the agreement is understood to require E to retain W for at least a month. Once the employment tie continues into the next payroll cycle, E must retain W at least until the end of the second payroll cycle. Notwithstanding the sudden-ness of the discharge, there is no moral objection against terminating an employee-at-will at the end of a payroll cycle.[5]

A second opinion in the matter of notice for an employee-at-will is expressed by R. Abraham Isaiah Karelitz (Israel, 1878–1953). In his treatment of this matter, we find him in essential agreement with R. Tenenbaum. He offers, however, several caveats: (1) Since it is uncommon for a job seeker today to hire himself out for less than thirty days, the minimum length of a labor contract is thirty days, even if the payroll cycle called for by the agreement is an interval less than this. The analogy is that a leasing agreement made for an indefinite time is regarded as being operative for thirty days. (2) If there is a local custom regarding the length of the notice given to an employee-at-will, it is halakhical-ly recognized and should be operative. (3) Within the payroll-cycle criterion, termination with no notice is illegal when finding new employment requires job search. Here, the amount of time needed to find new employment should be factored into the calculation of what the hiring period is. The amount of time needed for job hunting should be determined by a Bet Din (Jewish court) on a case-to-case basis.[6]

A third view on the notice requirement was advanced by a Tel Aviv Bet Din. In a far-reaching decision the Bet Din took the notice requirement a step fur-ther. In its opinion, a thirty-day notice is always required. The court arrived at its decision by drawing an analogy to the case of a leasing arrangement entered into for an indefinite period. Here, by dint of a talmudic ordinance, neither the landlord nor the tenant may terminate the agreement without a thirty-day notice. To be sure, the rationale for entitling the tenant to a thirty-day notice is the concern that sudden eviction might leave him without a roof over his head. Since sudden termination would not, in the usual circumstance, leave the affected worker without a roof over his head, extending the talmudic ordinance to entitle a discharged worker with a right for a thirty-day notice would not be valid. But consider that the talmudic ordinance entitles the landlord to the same right to a thirty-day notice. Here, the concern is only that the landlord should not suffer an interruption of his rental income. Since the talmudic ordinance for the right of a thirty-day notice was given to both the landlord and the ten-ant, a right to receive notice should follow for an employee hired for an indefi-nite term.[7]

The thrust of the preceding discussion indicates that the requirement of notice for an employee-at-will is for Halakhah a matter of contract law. Views vary as to the extent of this obligation. In calling for a notice requirement,

Halakhah's concept of fair dealing goes beyond the parallel secular law doctrine in this matter.

The Notice Requirement and Tort Law

The requirement to give an employee-at-will notice also follows from the following ruling of R. Joseph Caro (Israel, 1488–1575) et al., which relates to a point in tort law: By means of verbal consent E hires W. Before the work is scheduled to begin, E retracts. What is E's obligation to W ? If W can secure alternative employment for the time period E originally hired him for, W has no monetary claim against E. Nonetheless, if securing the new job entails considerable toil and effort, W will have legitimate grievance against E for causing him inconvenience. W's grievance rises to the level of a monetary claim when, in consequence of E's retraction, he is shut out of employment. To be valid, still another condition must be satisfied. This is the requirement of alternative offers at the same time W entered into his verbal agreement with E. The latter condition is, however, dropped in the instance where B was already on E's job when the latter's retraction took place.[8]

In consideration that in consequence of E's retraction W ends up not working but spending the day in idleness, W is not entitled to the entire forgone earnings he suffers as a result of E's retraction. Instead, W is entitled only to the portion of his wage he would settle for if he was given the option of spending the day in leisure.[9] The discounted wage, called *ke-po'el bateil* (lit. [the wages] of an idle worker), according to R. David b. Samuel ha-Levi (Poland, 1586–1667), is equal to one-half the wage rate.[10]

Several caveats should be noted. First, E bears responsibility for W's losses in the circumstances described above only when he was *negligent* in not informing W in a timely fashion that the work would not be available. But if unavoidable and unforeseen circumstances brought on E's retraction, then E bears no responsibility for W's loss.[11] Moreover, if W should have known in timely fashion that the work would not be available, E bears no responsibility for W's loss.[12]

Let us take note that W's compensation claim is an application of the principle that under certain conditions E is responsible for the loss he causes W even when the loss involved was not inflicted directly by either E's person or property. The classes of cases falling under this rubric are called *garmi* (lit. causing someone indirect damage).[13]

Disputing R. Joseph Caro, R. Meir b. Barukh (Germany, ca. 1215–1293) frees the employer from any compensation responsibility in the above cases. Consider that the loss here is not an actual monetary loss but only a forgone earning. Now, if E forces W into an enclosed area and locks him in, thereby preventing W from hiring himself out, E's action takes on the character of a tort-feasor (*adam ha-mazik*), and he bears responsibility to W for his forgone earnings. But E's role here in depriving W of his earnings consists of *hiring* him. Because W fully expects to do work for E, he does not hire himself out for that day to someone else. The causative link between E's action and W's loss is sufficiently direct to raise the issue of culpability for E. But since E does not inflict harm to W with his body, E's action is not classified as *adam ha-mazik* but as *garmi*. Only *adam ha-mazik* bears responsibility for all five categories of damage, including responsibility for the victim's forgone earnings (*shevet*). *Garmi*, however, bears responsibility only for out-of-pocket losses sustained by the victim (*nezek*).[14]

R. Meir b. Barukh's position finds an advocate in the person of R. Aryeh Loeb b. Joseph ha-Kohen Heller (Kezot, Poland, 1745–1813).[15] Kezot, however, casts doubt as to the authenticity of R. Meir b. Barukh's view. In another version of his view, we find R. Meir coming down hard on the reneging employer. To validate his claim, the disappointed worker need only demonstrate that he was shut out of employment as a result of the retraction. Demonstrating that alternative offers were available to him at the time the verbal agreement was entered into is, however, not necessary.[16] In this reading, R. Meir follows Tosafot,[17] who go even further than R. Caro in protecting the rights of the worker.[18]

Let us apply this discussion to the layoffs at Rechev. Absent any new arrangements between Rechev and its workers, the original verbal agreement between them serves as the basis of their employment relationship now and in the future. The original verbal agreement is never *automatically* canceled, even as successive payroll cycles wind down. Since the original verbal agreement remained intact until the moment Suss announced the layoffs, the affected workers were entitled to *timely* notice. This holds true whether the layoff announcement occurred in the middle or at the end of a wage period. But the notice at Rechev did not afford the affected workers any opportunity to search for new employment before the discharges became effective. Consider also that there was no excuse for delaying the notice other than Suss' preoccupation with petty selfish concerns. Irrespective of whether the affected workers can prove a monetary claim against Rechev, the discharge notice Suss issued should be classified as *garmi*.

Once the *garmi* character of a discharge notice is recognized, it becomes incumbent upon the employer to take action to prevent it. This is so because *garmi* is actionable in Jewish law. This means that if a Bet Din becomes aware that A has committed a *garmi* action, it will enjoin A to remove his potential harm immediately. Rather than deal with the *garmi* action only after it has inflicted damage or loss, the Bet Din will take action to prevent the harm.

This principle is illustrated by the restrictions the sages imposed on property owners not to use their property in a manner that would potentially inflict a detriment on a neighbor. One such restriction is the prohibition for A to place his ladder within four cubits of a neighbor's (B's) dovecote. The concern here is that while A is placing his ladder against his own wall, a marten might jump onto the ladder and from the ladder spring into the dovecote.[19] Although there is usually no marten waiting to jump onto a ladder as one places it near a dovecote, it is nevertheless forbidden to place the ladder near the dovecote due to the possibility that such direct damage might occur.[20]

What emerges from the ladder-dovecote case is that an action with *garmi* potential is enjoinable. Specifically, rather than deal with the *threatening* action only after it has inflicted damage or loss, the Bet Din will take action to prevent the harm. Analogously, if Suss had consulted a Bet Din as to whether he should share the *decision* about the layoffs with the workers, the Bet Din would have ordered him to *immediately* inform the workers affected by the decision. The only leeway here is the consideration that as a matter of strict law an employee hired for an indefinite term is entitled only to a thirty-day notice. Accordingly, should the decision to implement the layoffs occur more than thirty days before the effective date, the employer need give no more than a thirty-day notice.

Plant Closings and Notice

The judgment that an employee hired for an indefinite period is entitled only to a thirty-day notice must be reserved. Consider that the rationale behind this rule is that thirty days is sufficient for the worker to find new employment without interruption. Under ordinary conditions this may be so. But layoff or discharge may at times be very traumatic. One qualifying instance is the closing of a plant. If the company is the only significant employer in the area, the closing of the plant may signal the economic ruination of the entire local economy. With the local community no longer viable, displaced workers along with many other local residents will be driven to relocate elsewhere. Mass layoffs, even when the company is not the only significant employer in the community, may be symptomatic of an industry-wide decline. Reentry into the labor market may require the displaced workers to undergo significant retraining.

Halakhic sensitivity to the problem of displacement finds a parallel in the notice requirement for a tenant who leases an apartment for an indefinite period. Recall that the usual notice requirement is thirty days. But in recognition that apartment hunting is a much more onerous task in the winter season (from Sukkot to Pesah) than in the summer season (from Pesah to Sukkot), the rule was laid down that a landlord forfeits his right to evict a tenant in the winter unless the tenant is given a full thirty-day notice of eviction *before* the winter season begins. In recognition that a housing shortage usually exists in a big city, the notice requirement for a tenant who has an indefinite lease in a large city is always twelve months, regardless of whether the landlord seeks eviction in summer or winter.[21]

Halakhic sensitivity to the deprivation effects that eviction engenders can also be seen in the expanded notice rights Halakhah grants in connection with commercial leases entered into for an indefinite period. In recognition that storekeepers usually extend credit to their customers for a year, the landlord must give at least a year's notice. Shorter notice would subject the storekeeper to losses, as customers would come by to pay their debts and not find him in his accustomed place. Conferring the storekeeper with a one-year-notice right allows him to smoothly collect old debts as well as inform customers of his new location.[22]

In recognition that dyers and bakers usually extend credit to their customers over a three-year period, the Talmud extends the notice requirements for these commercial leases to three years.[23]

To be sure, specific application of the talmudic rules for notice to the modern scene is problematic. But Halakhah's sympathy to the deprivation effects of eviction for the tenant should provide a solid philosophical underpinning for legislation that addresses the issue of appropriate notice for the employee-at-will who requires retraining and/or relocation before he can hope to be reabsorbed in the labor market. The appropriateness of such legislation is heightened in consideration that discharge without sufficient notice takes on a *garmi* character.

Let us now turn to a consideration of the Worker Adjustment and Retraining Notification Act (WARN) and Halakhah's attitude toward it.

Worker Adjustment and Retraining Notification Act

Legislated in 1988, WARN requires employers with more than a hundred employees to give workers a sixty-day warning if they intend to close a facility with fifty full-time employees or lay off one-third of the work force at a site for more than six months.

Employers covered under the act face various actions for violating WARN's notice requirement. The most important of these is the requirement to provide each affected employee with back pay for each day of violation.[24]

The legislative history of the statute indicates that WARN was enacted in response to the congressional finding that worker displacements, which were materializing as a consequence of plant closings and massive layoffs, had become a problem of national scope. Congressional proponents of the bill pointed to studies showing that the millions of American families affected by these closings and layoffs had suffered great financial losses as well as a diminu-tion of mental and physical health. Furthermore, researchers had found that unemployment placed serious strains upon the families of displaced workers.[25]

Given the *garmi* character of discharge with insufficient notice, Halakhah would be in general sympathy with the WARN legislation.

Business-Circumstance Exceptions to WARN Liability

The WARN legislation recognizes certain exceptions to its advance-notice requirements. These are: (1) the faltering-business exception, and (2) the unforeseeable-business-circumstance exception.

1. In the first case, WARN relaxes the requirement of sixty days' notice when, at the point notice is required, the employer was actively seeking capital or business that, if obtained, would have avoided or postponed the shutdown. The exception further requires that the employer, reasonably and in good faith, believes that giving the requisite notice would have precluded the company from obtaining the needed business or capital. Even with a faltering business, the employer must give as much notice as is practicable, together with an expla-nation of the reasons for giving less than sixty days' notice.

2. WARN also relaxes the requirement of sixty days' notice when the clos-ing or mass layoff is caused by business circumstances that were not reasonably foreseeable as of the time that notice would have been required. Providing a qualifying circumstance is the company's sudden loss of a major customer.[26]

From the standpoint of Halakhah, both exceptions described above appear to be valid. In the faltering-business case, the good-faith judgment of the employer is that not giving notice is the best way of avoiding or at least delay-ing job loss. Non-notification, therefore, cannot be regarded as *garmi* conduct on the part of the employer. Moreover, if the economic viability of the compa-ny is at stake, the employee's right to either continued employment or notice does not take precedence over the employer's right to continue to derive a liveli-hood from his own company. An analogous case occurs in connection with a residential lease entered into for an indefinite period of time. Recall that Halakhah imposes stringent notice requirements on the landlord. Halakhah's sensitivity to the dislocation effects the tenant will suffer as a result of not receiving proper notice becomes secondary, however, in the instance when the landlord's own residence collapses and he is in need of new living quarters. Here, to accommodate for his own living quarters, the landlord may demand that the tenant vacate the apartment immediately.[27] What the law says is that the landlord's right to take up residence in his own apartment supersedes the tenant's right to continue to rent the apartment. Similarly, when the right of the owner to continue to derive a livelihood from his company is in conflict with the right of his employee to either continued employment or notice, the economic interests of the employer prevail.

Halakhic Basis for WARN

The appropriateness of enacting WARN legislation for a society committed to Halakhah proceeds from the insight of Nahmanides (Spain, 1194–1270) into an aspect of the duty to conduct oneself *lifnim mi-shurat ha-din* (lit. beyond the letter of the law). One source for this obligation is the verse: "And you shall do what is fair and good in the eyes of the Eternal" (Deuteronomy 6:18). Commenting on this verse, Nahmanides avers:

> At first he [Moses] stated that you are to keep His statutes and His testimonies which He [God] commanded you, and now he is stating that even where He has not commanded you, give thought, as well, to do what is good and right in His eyes, for He loves the good and the right. Now this is a great principle, *for it is impossible to mention in the Torah all aspects of man's conduct with his neighbors and friends, and all his various transactions, and the ordinances of all societies and countries.* But since He mentioned many of them, such as *You shall not be a gossipmonger among your people* (Leviticus 19:16); *You shall not take revenge, and you shall not bear a grudge against the members of your people"* (Leviticus 19:18); *You shall not stand aside while your fellow's blood is shed* (Leviticus 19:16); *You shall not curse the deaf* (Leviticus 19:15); *In the presence of an old person shall you rise* (Leviticus 19:32), and the like, He reverted to state in a general way that, in all matters, one should do what is good and right, including even compromise and going beyond the requirements of the law.[28]

Nahmanides' contention that "You shall do what is fair and good" obligates us to apply halakhic prescriptions to contexts the Torah did not deal with has much relevancy for the issue at hand. The labor market in the time of the Talmud featured much less sophisticated skills and was much more homogenous compared to the labor market today. The rules of notice prescribed for this ancient labor market cannot be applied in a blanket way to the modern labor market. What constitutes appropriate notice and fair treatment for a worker traumatized by the layoff imposed on him must, therefore, be determined by resorting to halakhic analogues. WARN legislation is solidly rooted in Nahmanides' understanding of the duty to "do what is fair and good in the eyes of the Eternal."

Other Halakhic Considerations

In assessing the halakhic layoff policy at Rechev, two other considerations are in order: the concepts of *minhag* and the duty to conduct oneself *lifnim mi-shurat ha-din* . Let us take up each of these in turn.

Minhag and the Labor Contract

In labor relations, *minhag* (prevailing practice) creates a contractual obligation when the explicit arrangements did not cover the issue at hand. To illustrate: By dint of Halakhah, the working hours of a *po'el* (per diem worker) begin at sunrise and end at nightfall. Suppose the labor contract was silent on the issue of hours but local practice was for a shorter work day than Halakhah calls for. Here, *minhag* prevails over Halakhah.[29]

Recall that R. Karelitz invoked *minhag* as a legal basis for an employee-at-will's right to notification. *Minhag* may also work to entitle a discharged worker to other perquisites. In a 1955 case, a rabbinical court in Haifa entitled a discharged employee to severance. The ruling was based on the judgment that the practice of severance had become sufficiently widespread and defined so as to make it an implied contractual requirement.[30]

Lifnim mi-shurat ha-din and the Layoffs at Rechev

Another principle in Halakhah that creates responsibilities for Rechev toward its discharged workers is the duty to conduct oneself *lifnim mi-shurat ha-din* (lit. beyond the letter of the law). One aspect of this responsibility, dealt with earlier, is the duty for the firm to be aware that it has obligations in contexts not explicitly covered by Halakhah. To arrive at what these obligations are, halakhic analogues must be resorted to.

Another aspect of *lifnim mi-shurat ha-din* conduct obtains in the context where one's halakhic duty is well defined. Here, *lifnim mi-shurat ha-din* may push an individual to display greater responsibility or generosity than the strict letter of the law requires. This latter obligation is derived from the verse "And make them know the way wherein they must go, and the deed that they must do" (Exodus 18:20). In this passage *deed* refers to strict law, and *that they must do* refers to *lifnim mi-shurat ha-din*.[31] In the opinion of R. Isaac of Corbeil (France, d. 1280), Exodus 18:20 is the main source of the *lifnim mi-shurat ha-din* obligation.[32]

Our purpose here will be to draw out the duties that proceed from Exodus 18:20, with particular emphasis on the case study at hand.

We begin with the extent of the *lifnim mi-shurat ha-din* obligation. Tosafot (France, 12th–14th cent.) offer an operational guideline.[33] Sorting out the various talmudic cases dealing with the *lifnim mi-shurat ha-din* concept, they divide the cases into three separate categories.

The first category deals with cases where Halakhah prescribes a general behavioral norm for a particular circumstance, but exempts certain people from this norm. Here, *lifnim mi-shurat ha-din* requires the person exempted to waive his privileged status and conform to the general legal norm, even if he would incur a monetary loss by doing so.

Illustrating the above rule is R. Hiyya's behavior in a currency-validation case, discussed at Bava Kamma 99b. The following background information will clarify the point at issue. In talmudic times, merchants were sometimes offered for payment coins that they were uncertain would circulate in the marketplace. Moneychangers were approached for advice on such questions. Determining whether a particular coin would be accepted as a medium of exchange was regarded by the sages as a very precise art. Only an authoritative expert, i.e., one who needed no further instruction in the art, was really qualified to make such judgments. Consequently, moneychangers who had not attained authoritative status were responsible for replacing coins they erroneously determined would circulate.[34] To be sure, the authoritative expert, too, was responsible for his error, in the event he stipulated a fee for his service.[35] While his judgment cannot be viewed as a form of negligence, the fee arrangement makes it clear that the client relied on his judgment. Since the damage resulted directly from relying on the expert's advice, his action is regarded as a form of *garmi*.[36]

Against this background, the Talmud relates that R. Hiyya, who was an authoritative moneychanger, once erroneously advised a woman gratis that the coin she was offered would circulate. Upon learning his mistake, R. Hiyya, acting *lifnim mi-shurat ha-din*, chose to reimburse the woman for her loss. Since a professional non-expert moneychanger was usually liable in this case, R. Hiyya waived the special privilege proceeding from his status as an authoritative moneychanger, even though in so doing he incurred a monetary loss.[37]

Lifnim mi-shurat ha-din conduct of a less demanding nature is expected of man when Halakhah generally exempts everyone from a certain duty but waiving the privilege and performing the duty does not generate a monetary loss for the exempted party. An illustration is the case in which Samuel's father restored lost donkeys to their owner (Bava Mezia 24b). By the strict letter of the law, the finder of a lost animal must make a public announcement of his find. If the animal is capable of working to earn its keep, the finder is not obligated to hold it more than twelve months even if the owner has not made a claim. After this period, the finder may sell the animal and hold the proceeds for the owner. Acting *lifnim mi-shurat ha-din*, Samuel's father held the donkeys for more than twelve months until they were claimed.[38] Since holding on to the donkeys instead of selling them involved no monetary loss for Samuel's father, the *lifnim mi-shurat ha-din* mandate required him to hold on to them until they were claimed.[39]

When the legal right consists of a damage claim against an employee, *lifnim mi-shurat ha-din* conduct, according to Tosafot, does not require the employer to waive his claim. Another moral principle of special piety, as discussed in the following talmudic text at Bava Mezia 83a, may, however, at least recommend that he do so:

> Some porters broke a barrel of wine belonging to Rabbah b. Bar Hannan. Thereupon he seized their garments; so they went and complained to Rav. "Return their garments to them," he ordered. "Is that the law?" he inquired. "Yes," he rejoined, "*that you shall walk in the way of good men* (Proverbs 2:20)." Their garments having been returned, they observed, "We are poor men, have worked all day, and are hungry. Are we to get nothing?" "Go and pay them," he ordered. "Is that the law?" he asked. "Yes," he rejoined, "*and keep the path of the righteous* (Proverbs 2:20)."

Under the assumption that the wine barrels were broken through the negligence of the porters,[40] Rabbah b. Bar Hannan had a legitimate damage claim against them. While the behavioral expectation to act *lifnim mi-shurat ha-din* did not require Rabbah b. Bar Hannan to forgo his damage claim, Rav urged him to do so on the basis of the moral principle "that you shall walk in the way of good men." Upon learning that the porters were indigent, Rav even urged Rabbah b. Bar Hannan to pay them their wages on the basis of the ethical imperative "and keep the path of the righteous."[41] These ethical teachings evidently demand of man an even more generous and selfless nature than the *lifnim mi-shurat ha-din* imperative.

In the understanding of R. Joseph Hayyim b. Elijah al-Hakkam (Iraq, 1834–1909), the higher moral standard proceeding from Proverbs 2:20 is directed only to society's ethical elite.[42]

While Tosafot understand the ethical principles proceeding from the verse in Proverbs as constituting a moral principle distinct from the *lifnim mi-shurat ha-din* behavioral expectation, R. Solomon b. Isaac (Rashi, France, 1040–1105) and others regard these teachings as forming an integral part of it.[43]

The dispute between Rashi and Tosafot points up a major difference in opinion as to how far the duty of *lifnim mi-shurat ha-din* goes. This gap is

somewhat narrowed by R. Mosheh Feinstein's (New York, 1895–1986) understanding of the Rabbah b. Bar Hannan incident discussed above. R. Feinstein's
thesis begins with an explanation of how the duty to forgo a damage claim can
be read into "that you shall walk in the way of good men" (Proverbs 2:20). His
answer: A good person will not press his debtor to pay up when he knows that
the latter has no ability to do so. Such conduct violates the biblical prohibition:
"When you lend money to My people, to the poor man among you, *do not press
him for repayment*" (Exodus 22:24). Relying on the talmudic presumption that
a poor person is not likely to become a person of means, Rav ordered Rabbah
b. Bar Hannan to forgive his damage claim against the poor workers. Given the
unlikelihood that the poor workers would ever be able to make good on this
debt, forgiving the debt amounts to no more than relieving them of a psychological burden. Once Rabbah b. Bar Hannan canceled the workers' debt to him,
Rav felt that the workers were due their wages not merely as a matter of charity but as a matter of legal entitlement.[44]

It follows from R. Feinstein's analysis that Rashi is in basic agreement with
Tosafot: *Lifnim mi-shurat ha-din* conduct generally makes a claim only on the
toil and effort of an individual. If the sought-after benefit entails a financial
outlay, *lifnim mi-shurat ha-din* does not, as a general matter, require it.

Another dimension of the operational significance of the *lifnim mi-shurat
ha-din* concept concerns the question of whether Halakhah empowers the
Jewish court to *force* an individual to give up his legal rights and act in accordance with this legal principle.

Espousing judicial coercion in such cases, R. Mordecai b. Hillel (Germany,
1240–1298) validates the practice only if the individual who is asked to give up
his legal rights is a man of wealth.[45] Following the above line, R. Joel Sirkes
(Poland, 1561–1640) validates the practice even when the legal right involved is
a damage claim against an employee, similar to the talmudic porter case.[46]

Another school of thought, led by R. Hananel b. Hushi'el (North Africa,
11th cent.) does not legitimize the use of judicial coercion to force a party to a
lawsuit to act *lifnim mi-shurat ha-din*. The judicial role, according to this school
of thought, is confined to informing the party of what *lifnim mi-shurat ha-din*
conduct consists.[47]

Let us now apply the discussion to labor relations.

In a case dealing with the discharge of a worker from a religious institution,
a Haifa Bet Din took the position that the practice of giving severance pay was
not at that time sufficiently widespread and defined for *minhag* to be invoked
as a basis to fix a judgment against the defendant. Instead, the court noted the
long tenure of the employee and the circumstance that he was a poor man.
Accordingly, the court urged the institution to conduct itself *lifnim mi-shurat*

ha-din and provide the worker with a specific sum as severance. In addition, the court felt that the institution should be concerned with the former employee's future and help him find another job.[48]

Ha-A'nakah and the Severance Pay Requirement

Another approach in making the moral case for severance pay is advanced by R. Aaron ha-Levi (Spain, 1235–1300). In his view, precedent for this obligation can be found in the *ha-a'nakah* (severance gift) requirement the Torah prescribes for the indentured Hebrew (*eved ivri*) when he is set free upon completion of his six-year term. Addressing the master, the Torah writes: "And when you let him go free from you, you shall not let him go empty. You shall furnish him liberally of your flock and of your threshing floor and of your wine press; of that which the Lord your God has blessed you, shall you give to him" (Deuteronomy 15:12–14).

To be sure, the institution of *eved ivri* is today obsolete; nevertheless, the concept of *ha-a'nakah* remains intact as a moral force. In this connection R. Aaron ha-Levi writes:

> Nevertheless, even at this time, *let the wise one listen and add wisdom* (Proverbs 1:5). Should [he] hire one from among the children of Israel, and he works for him for a long time, or even a brief while, when he leaves him, let [the employer] give *ha-a'nakah* from that which the Lord has blessed him.[49]

Rechev and Socially Responsible Industrial Relations

The foregoing discussion has demonstrated that Rechev bears a legal responsibility to inform the affected workers of their impending layoffs. The extent of this obligation from a legal perspective is a matter of dispute. But a moral case can be made to notify the affected workers as soon as the layoff decision is made. Failure to provide the workers with timely notice exposes the firm to possible monetary judgment. Moreover, from a moral standpoint, Rechev is obligated both to help the laid-off workers find new employment and to provide them with severance pay.

Adoption of a halakhic layoff policy should not be forced on Rechev as a result of litigation. Rather, the guidepost a Bet Din would offer in respect to layoff policy should be part of Rechev's industrial relations policy in the first place.

The treatment of workers called for by Halakhah in its layoff policy may very well sacrifice both short- and long-term profits. Halakhah's layoff policy can therefore be viewed as a call upon the firm to engage in socially responsible behavior. Once the halakhic layoff policy is an integral aspect of the firm's operations, however, it makes good business sense to seek out the least-cost means of achieving the goals inherent in this policy. No different from other business policies, giving attention to this issue on a systematic and long-term planning basis rather than an ad hoc basis promotes the least-cost objective in the long run.

Illustrating an innovative idea in layoff policy that is consistent with halakhic goals is the approach of Rhino Foods to this issue. Rhino Foods is a maker of specialty desserts in Burlington, Vermont. Faced with the prospect of significant layoffs in 1993, the company saved jobs by lending its employees to neighboring businesses. The other firms paid the salaries of the "borrowed" employees while Rhino continued funding the employer's share of their health insurance and workers' compensation. All the employees retained their seniority at Rhino and continued to accrue whatever profit sharing they were due.[50]

1. For a discussion of the employment-at-will doctrine, see Joseph L. Frascona et al., *Business Law and the Legal Environment: Test and Cases*, 4th ed. (Boston: Allyn & Bacon, 1991), pp. 35–46.

2. Ibid.

3. Jethro K. Lieberman and George J. Siedel, *Business Law and the Environment* (Fort Worth: Dryden Press, 1992), p. 1175.

4. Aaron Levine, "Performance Appraisal and Halakhah," in *Hazon Nahum*, ed. Yaakov Elman and Jeffrey S. Gurock (New York: Michael Scharf Publication Trust of Yeshiva University, 1997), pp. 619–26.

5. R. Malchiel Tenenbaum, *Divrei Malkhi'el*, Hoshen Mishpat 3:51.

6. R. Abraham Isaiah Karelitz (Israel, 1878–1953), Hazon Ish, Bava Kamma 23.

7. *Piskei Din Rabbaniyim* 3:282–83.

8. R. Jacob b. Asher (Germany, 1270–1343), *Tur*, Hoshen Mishpat 333:12; R. Joseph Caro, *Shulhan Arukh*, Hoshen Mishpat 333:12; R. Jehiel Michel Epstein (Belarus, 1829–1908), *Arukh ha-Shulhan*, Hoshen Mishpat 333:13.

9. Ibid.

10. R. David b. Samuel ha-Levi, *Turei Zahav* on *Sh.Ar.*, op. cit. 333:1.

11. *Sh.Ar.*, op. cit. 333:2; *Ar.ha.Sh.*, op. cit. 333:4.

12. *Ar.haSh.*, op. cit. 333:4.

13. R. Joshua b. Alexander ha-Kohen Falk (Poland, 1555–1614), Sma at *Sh.Ar.*, op. cit. n. 8. See, however, R. Jacob Moses Lorberbaum (Poland, 1760–1832), *Nitivot ha-Mishpat* at *Sh.Ar.*, op. cit., n. 3.

14. R. Meir b. Barukh (Germany, 1215–1293), *Responsa Maharam* (Prague ed.), 821.

15. R. Aryeh Loeb b. Joseph ha-Kohen, *Kezot ha-Hoshen*, *Sh.Ar.*, op. cit. 333, n. 2.

16. R. Meir b. Barukh, quoted by R. Mordecai b. Hillel ha-Kohen (Germany, 1240–1298), Mordecai, Bava Mezia 6:342.

17. Tosafot, Bava Mezia 76b, s.v. *ain*.

18. *Kezot ha-Hoshen*, loc. cit. , n. 3.

19. Bava Batra 22b.

20. Nahmanides (Spain, 1194–1270), Ramban, Bava Batra 22b.

21. Mishnah, Bava Mezia, 101b; R. Isaac b. Jacob Alfasi (Algeria, 1013–1103), Rif, ad loc.; R. Asher b. Jehiel (Germany, 1250–1327), Rosh, Bava Mezia 8:24; Maimonides (Egypt,

1135–1204), *Yad*, Sekhirut 6:7; *Tur*, op. cit. 312:8; *Sh.Ar.*, op. cit. 312:6; *Ar.haSh.*, op. cit. 312:15.

22. Mishnah, Bava Mezia 8:6 and R. Solomon b. Isaac (France, 1040–1105), Rashi, ad loc. s.v. *u-ba-hanuyot*; Rif, ad loc.; Rosh, op. cit.; *Yad*, op. cit.; *Tur*, op. cit.; *Sh.Ar.*, op. cit.; *Ar.haSh.*, op. cit. 312:16.

23. Rabban Shimon b. Gamliel, Mishnah, Bava Mezia 8:6; Rif, ad loc.; Rosh op. cit.; *Tur*, op. cit.; R. Mosheh Isserles (Poland, 1525 or 1530–1572), Rema, *Sh.Ar.*, op. cit. 312:6; *Ar.haSh.*, op. cit.

24. Mark E. Roszkowski, *Business Law: Principles, Cases, and Policy*, 3rd ed. (New York, Harper Collins., 1992), pp. 115–78.

25. 134 Cong. Rec. S8875.

26. Roszkowski, *Business Law*.

27. Bava Mezia 101b; Rif, ad loc.; Rosh, Bava Mezia 8:24; *Yad*, op. cit. 6:9; *Sh.Ar.*, op. cit 312:11; *Ar.haSh.*, op. cit. 312:20.

28. Nahmanides at Deuteronomy 6:18.

29. Mishnah, Bava Mezia 7:1; Rif, ad loc.; *Yad*, op. cit. 9:1; Rosh, Bava Mezia 7:1; *Tur*, op. cit. 331:1; *Sh.Ar.*, op. cit. 331:1; *Ar.haSh.*, op. cit. 331:16.

30. *Piskei Din shel Battei ha-Din ha-Rabbaniyim be-Yisrael*, 1:330–31.

31. Bava Kamma 100a.

32. R. Isaac of Corbeil, Semah, 49.

33. Tosafot, Bava Mezia 24b, s.v. *lifnim*.

34. R. Pappa, Bava Kamma 99b; Rif, ad loc.; *Yad*, op. cit. 10:5; Rosh, Bava Kamma 9:16; *Tur*, op. cit. 306:10; *Sh.Ar.*, op. cit. 306:6; *Ar.haSh.*, op. cit. 306:13. Some of the above authorities (R. Isaac Alfasi, Maimonides, R. Joseph Caro, and R. Epstein) hold that the non-expert moneychanger is not liable for his erroneous free advice unless it is evident to the court that the inquirer relied upon his judgment. R. Asher b. Jehiel and *Tur*, however, hold the non-expert liable even if this condition is not met. R. Mosheh Isserles (Rema, *Sh.Ar.*, loc. cit) rules in accordance with R. Asher b. Jehiel.

35. Rif, loc. cit., *Yad*, loc. cit., Rosh, loc. cit; *Tur*, loc. cit.; *Sh.Ar.*, loc. cit.; *Ar.haSh.*, loc. cit.

36. *Ar.haSh.*, loc. cit. *Garmi* is a talmudic term used to describe tortious damage caused indirectly by the tortfeasor's person. For a discussion of the various damages that fall under the rubric of *garmi*, see *Encyclopedia Talmudit*, vol. 6, pp. 461–97.

37. Tosafot, Bava Mezia 24b.

38. Rashi, Bava Mezia 24b, however, understands Samuel's father to have found the donkeys more than twelve months after their owner reported them lost. By the strict letter of the law, Samuel's father was not obligated to return the donkeys, as constructive abandonment on the part of the owner could safely be presumed after such a prolonged period of loss. Acting *lifnim mi-shurat ha-din*, Samuel's father restored the donkeys to their owner.

39. Tosafot, Bava Mezia 24b, s.v. *lifnim*.

40. Most commentaries (Rashi s.v. *shekula'i*, Bava Mezia 83a, Tosafot, Bava Mezia 24b, and *Tur*, Hoshen Mishpat 304:1 on the interpretation of Beit Yosef ad loc.) interpret the incident as referring to the circumstances where the barrels were broken through the negligence of the porters. R. Samuel Eliezer b. Judah ha-Levi Edels (Poland, 1555–1631, Maharsha, ad loc.), however, understands Rabbah b. Bar Hannan to have instructed the porters to transport the barrels over an incline. The porters could therefore not be held responsible for the subsequent breakage. Rav wryly indicated this to Rabbah b. Bar Hannan by quoting to him the verse "that you shall walk in the way of good men." A play on the word *way* was meant. Since Rabbah b. Bar Hannan instructed the porters to transport the barrels over an incline instead

of a *good way* (i.e., a smooth and even road), the porters cannot be held responsible for the breakage.

41. Tosafot, Bava Mezia 24b.

42. R. Joseph Hayyim b. Elijah al-Hakkam, *Ben Yehoyada*, Bava Mezia 83a. See also R. Eliezer Yehudah Waldenberg (Israel, contemp.), *Responsa Ziz Eliezer* 8:3, ot 8.

43. Rashi, Bava Mezia 83a, s.v. *ba-derekh*; *Tur*, loc. cit., R. Joel Sirkes (Poland, 1561–1640), Bah, *Tur*, op. cit. 304:1; R. Menahem Mendel Krochmal (Moravia, 1600–1661), *Responsa Zemah Zedek* 89; R. Mosheh Teitelbaum (Hungary, 1759–1841), *Responsa Heshiv Mosheh*, Yoreh De'ah 48.

44. R. Mosheh Feinstein, *Iggerot Mosheh*, Hoshen Mishpat 1:60.

45. R. Mordecai b. Hillel, Mordecai, Bava Mezia 2:257.

46. Bah, *Tur*, op. cit. 12, n. 4.

47. R. Hananel b. Hushei'el, Bava Mezia 24b; Rosh, Bava Mezia 2:7; R. Yom Tov Ishbili (Spain 1270–1321), Ritva, Bava Mezia 24b; R. Joseph Caro, *Beit Yosef, Tur*, op. cit. 12:6; R. Shabbetai b. Meir ha-Kohen, Siftei Kohen, *Sh.Ar.* Hoshen Mishpat 259, n. 3; *Ar.haSh.*, op. cit. 304:11.

48. *Piskei Din shel Battei ha-Din ha-Rabbaniyim* 3, p. 95.

49. R. Aaron ha-Levi (Spain, 1235–1300), *Sefer ha-Hinnukh* 481.

50. R. Maynard, "A Creative Alternative to Company Downsizing," *Nation's Business* 82 (January 1994): 10.

Adlers v. Frank and Other Missed Appointments

Rabbi Lester Kleinberg was a very punctilious man in respect to his appointments. It was this trait that made him decide to pass up public transportation in favor of a car service to make his dental appointment at 9:30 a.m. In the rabbi's view, public transportation was unreliable. The extra cost of using a car service was a worthwhile price to pay to avoid the anxiety of the public transportation alternative.

To make sure that he would not be late for appointments, Kleinberg always factored in an additional ten minutes above the call-out and estimated travel time. Figuring that the actual travel time to his dentist, Dr. William Shain, was no more than ten minutes, Kleinberg called Kingsway at 9:00 a.m. and firmly told the dispatcher, "I have an appointment. You must pick me up within ten minutes." The reassuring voice of the dispatcher responded, "Car Fifteen will be over within ten minutes." Well, it was fourteen minutes from the time Kleinberg placed his call to Kingsway, and Car 15 had not yet arrived. Kleinberg fumbled for his keys and stormed into his home to call Kingsway about the delay. Before he could make the call, a congregant called with an urgent question that required Kleinberg's full and immediate attention. It was not until 9:26 that Kleinberg got off the phone. Fuming that Kingsway was a full sixteen minutes late, Kleinberg gave up on Kingsway and instead decided to call Reliable Car Service. To his surprise, Reliable said that a car would be over "right away." Fearing that he would miss the rendezvous with Reliable, Kleinberg ran to meet the car in front of his house. In his haste, he failed to call Kingsway and cancel. Reliable pulled up at Kleinberg's doorstep at 9:29. As fate would have it, at that very moment Car 15 finally arrived. The Kingsway driver demanded that Kleinberg cancel Reliable and give his company the business. If this was not acceptable, Kleinberg owed his company $5 for the call-out. Kleinberg rebuffed this demand, and all along was irate because the conversation with the driver was eating up precious time. As he sped away in the Reliable vehicle, he opened his window and shouted, "You were late and therefore *automatically* canceled."

Kleinberg arrived at Dr. Shain's office at 9:41. Whereupon the receptionist informed him that because he had not called in that he would be late, his appointment slot had been given to someone else. Just as the frustrated rabbi turned to the door, the receptionist sympathetically called out:

"Rabbi, I'm sorry, but we'll have to bill you $25 for missing your appointment. Read your appointment card, it says very plainly: 'If your appointment is not canceled twenty-four hours before its scheduled time, you will be billed $25 for a no show.'

"Dr. Shain sends you his best regards. He asked me to mail you this envelope. I guess I can give it to you personally."

On the ride home on the D-train, Rabbi Kleinberg opened the envelope the receptionist had handed him. The envelope contained an article that described a $130,000 damage suit a couple had lodged against a rabbi for allegedly being an hour and a half late to perform their wedding ceremony (*Adlers v. Frank*). The rabbi's tardiness, according to the plaintiffs, had led to a chain reaction of calamities: an inflated liquor bill as bored guests took to drink; vicious gossip that the marriage might be off; for the bride, a long wait in a stifling room as she awaited, in frustration, her "grand entrance"; and finally, for the groom, the reemergence of an old back injury.[1]

A note from Dr. William Shain was attached to the article, it read:

Dear Rabbi Kleinberg:

Don't feel too bad about the $25 fee. I'm going easy on you!

With best wishes,
> Dr. William (Bill) Shain

The preceding vignette raises a number of ethical issues. Let us begin with Rabbi Kleinberg's interactions with Kingsway Car Service.

Recall that the rabbi made it clear to Kingsway that he had an appointment and required a car within ten minutes. This stipulation should free Kleinberg of any financial obligation to Kingsway if the car arrived late. Two scenarios present themselves:

1. The dispatcher knows that it is impossible for Car 15 to arrive within ten minutes. He makes this representation anyway only to forestall Rabbi Kleinberg from calling another car service. Since the dispatcher's representation is a blatant lie (*sheker*), the original verbal agreement between Kleinberg and Kingsway must be regarded as an arrangement entered into by means of error (*mekah ta'ut*). Consequently, Kleinberg bears no obligation to Kingsway when the ten-minute waiting period expires.

2. But suppose the dispatcher made his representation in good faith, and what brought on the delay was an unavoidable circumstance, such as a traffic accident. Here, too, Rabbi Kleinberg bears no responsibility to Kingsway when the ten-minute waiting period expires. This is so because the rabbi's stipulation makes it clear that if the car does not arrive on time, the company's service is no longer desired. The case at hand is analogous to the talmudic case where A hires B to deliver a flute for a wedding ceremony. If the flute will not arrive in time for the ceremony, the delivery becomes useless. The work is therefore categorized as *davar ha-avud* ([work if not done immediately] entails a loss).[2]

Similarly in the case at hand, by setting a time limit for Kingsway, Kleinberg signals that beyond this window the services of the company are no longer desired.

Now, if E hires W for *davar ha-avud* and W quits or disappears in the middle of the job, E is, of course, entitled to hire a substitute (S) to complete the job. What E's obligation to W is depends on the reason the latter quit or disappeared. If W's failure to perform was due to unavoidable circumstances, such as sickness, W is entitled to the stipulated wage for the time he actually worked. But if the quitting or disappearance was due to negligence or the desire to get a higher wage, then E has no obligation whatsoever to W. In the latter instance, the differential payment E makes to S above what he originally stipulated with W may be charged to W. E may charge this differential cost to W even to the point where W would lose the entire wage he was slated to receive.[3]

In the case at hand, Kingsway should be regarded as having disappeared in the middle of a *davar ha-avud* job. This is so because the job begins with the call-out and Kingsway's lateness is equivalent to disappearing in the middle of the job. If the lateness was due to an unavoidable circumstance ('*ones*), then Kingsway is entitled to its basic call out-fee. Kingsway bears the burden of proving '*ones*. Absent such proof, Rabbi Kleinberg bears no compensation responsibility, even as Car 15 pulls up in front of his house.

It follows from this analysis that the Kingsway driver acted improperly when he arrived at Kleinberg's home. Given that Kingsway took on a *davar ha-avud* assignment, the verbal agreement between Kingsway and Kleinberg was canceled as soon as Kleinberg's ten-minute time frame elapsed. With the car service order legitimately canceled, the driver had no right to demand that Rabbi Kleinberg cancel Reliable and give the business at hand to Kingsway or else pay Kingsway a call-out fee.

In the talmudic *davar ha-avud* case, another tactic is available to the disappointed employer (E). This tactic consists of cajoling the reneging employee (W) to stay on the job by offering him a raise. If the tactic succeeds, E bears no responsibility to make good on his promise for a raise. Moreover, if W demands the extra fee up front, the differential pay is recoverable in a Bet Din (Jewish court). This tactic is referred to as *mat'an* (lit. he deceives them).[4]

Application of the *mat'an* principle to the case at hand apparently allows Rabbi Kleinberg to call up Kingsway at the expiration of the time limit he set and offer them a *premium* above their usual rate to rush a car to him. If the tactic succeeds, Rabbi Kleinberg bears responsibility only for the ordinary rate and not for the differential above the rate he offered.

Application of *mat'an* to the case at hand, however, is problematic. *Mat'an* is legitimate only if the worker's retraction was improper and not due to '*ones*.[5] The rationale behind this distinction is the recognition that bluffing is ordinarily morally objectionable. It becomes permissible only as a means of *counter-acting* unethical conduct.[6] If the worker retracts on account of *'ones*, Halakhah will not sanction bluffing as a means to induce him to complete the job. Now, Rabbi Kleinberg does not know for certain why Car 15 did not make his deadline. If the reason is unavoidable and unforeseen circumstances, then Rabbi Kleinberg has no halakhic sanction to make use of the bluffing tactic with Kingsway as a means to get to his appointment.

Rabbi Kleinberg can, perhaps, be criticized for not calling Kingsway to cancel before he picked up the phone to call Reliable. If Kingsway runs its operation by means of a two-way radio, Kleinberg's call would be of value to the company, as the dispatcher could immediately divert Car 15 to another call. Hillel's aphorism "What is hateful to you, do not to your neighbor"[7] surely recommends this courtesy. Likewise, the mitzvah to promote harmony and goodwill in our interpersonal relations also informs this conduct.[8] Let us not lose sight, however, that Kleinberg is involved in a *davar ha-avud* situation whether or not Kingsway was negligent in failing to meet his time limit. Kleinberg therefore has the right to set up alternative arrangements to make his appointment. There can be no doubt that Kleinberg has a right to make his priority the setting up of these arrangements. It is only when these arrangements are set in motion that informing Kingsway of the cancellation comes into play.

At this juncture, let us consider the possibility that the aforementioned religious imperatives require Kingsway to arrange with each customer that in the event of unforeseeable delay the company will call back the customer and inform him. The duty to conduct oneself *lifnim mi-shurat ha-din* (beyond the letter of the law)[9] apparently also requires Kingsway to implement this policy. Consider, however, that the aforementioned religious principles are not operative as a matter of strict requirement when implementation of the said policy entails more than a trifling expense for the company.[10] This is the case here. Kingsway may well assess that implementing the policy will entail an opportunity cost considerably above the cost of the calls to customers informing them about the delay. For one, if the unforeseen delay coincides with a period of time when the volume of incoming calls is heavy, a lot of pressure will be put on the dispatcher to juggle between handling incoming calls with patience and courtesy and at the same time making good on the company's promise to call back on delays in a timely manner. Given the added pressure the policy brings on, deterioration of the quality of Kingsway's service may result.

Moreover, suppose Kingsway is the only car service company in the local area that promises to call customers in the event of an unforeseen delay. Operating under this policy may result in undeserved reputation loss for Kingsway. Consider the following scenario: C calls Kingsway and tells the dispatcher (D) that he has an appointment and the car must arrive within fifteen minutes. D assures C that Car 15 will arrive within fifteen minutes, and if any hitches develop, the company will call him *before* the fifteen-minute period ends. Fifteen minutes pass and Car 15 has still not arrived. Because C relies on D's promise, he believes that Car 15 will arrive momentarily and, therefore, waits another seven minutes before finally taking matters into his own hands and calling Kingsway about the delay. When C calls, he is informed that, indeed, unforeseen circumstances have caused Car 15 to be delayed, but it will arrive within five minutes. C is irate. He feels that D knew all along that Car 15 would not arrive on time and made use of a false promise as a means of locking him into Kingsway's service. As far as C is concerned, Kingsway is both unreliable and dishonest, and this is what he will tell anyone who asks for a reference on Kingsway. In actuality, D was planning to call C about the delay but got sidetracked by incoming calls and lost the window of opportunity to inform C of the delay in a timely fashion. Objectively, Kingsway's car service is no less reliable than the other car services in the neighborhood, and in addition, this company makes an honest effort to avert unnecessary aggravation for its customers, but since every instance of failure will be *magnified* by the public, Kingsway will not gain goodwill from its policy.

The upshot of this analysis is that a policy of promising a customer to call him back in the event of an unforeseen delay may boomerang against the best financial interests of Kingsway. Therefore Kingsway does not have an ethical duty to implement this policy.

Liability for Missing an Appointment

We turn now to an analysis of whether Kleinberg incurs liability if he misses his appointment with the dentist. In evaluating this issue we will consider a number of legal theories each of which may provide a basis for fixing Kleinberg's liability.

Labor Law

Kleinberg's appointment with Shain amounts to a verbal agreement between the parties that each will show up at the dental office at the designated time. Kleinberg's failure to show at the designated time makes the case at hand analogous to the following talmudic case: By means of verbal agreement, E hires W to perform a specific task. The task is slated to begin, say, on Monday morning. When W arrives at the work scene, before he actually starts the task at hand, E retracts. W's travel to the work site is regarded halakhically as if the work had begun. If W cannot find alternative employment for Monday morning in consequence of E's retraction, E must make good on W's loss. In consideration that in consequence of E's retraction W spends his day in idleness rather than in work, W is entitled only to the wages of an idle worker (*kepo'el bateil*).[11] Citing a number of authorities, R. David ha-Levi (Poland, 1586–1667) regards this sum to be equal to one-half the stipulated wage.[12]

On the basis of labor law, Dr. Shain is entitled to compensation only if a substitute for Rabbi Kleinberg's appointment slot cannot be found at the time of the rabbi's no-show. If it is Dr. Shain's practice to overbook, Kleinberg's empty appointment slot can easily be filled and Shain suffers no loss as a result of Kleinberg's no-show.

At this juncture let us take note that in the talmudic case cited above, E bears no compensation responsibility to W if E's retraction was forced on him by unavoidable and unforeseen circumstances.[13] Since Kleinberg's no-show was not due to negligence on his part, but rather was forced on him by '*ones*, Kleinberg bears no compensation responsibility to Shain for his no-show even if Shain could not replace Kleinberg's appointment slot with another patient.

Charging the $25 Fee and *Asmakhta*

While labor law frees Rabbi Kleinberg of any obligation to compensate Dr. Shain for the loss he suffers, Kleinberg should apparently be obligated to pay the $25 no-show fee. Recall that Rabbi Kleinberg agreed to this condition in advance of his appointment. But let us consider the possibility that Kleinberg's agreement to the fee may fall short of Halakhah's standard of a binding commitment. For an obligation to become legally binding, two critical tests must be met. First, the commitment must be made with deliberate and perfect intent (*gemirat da'at*). Second, the commitment must generate reliance (*semikhat da'at*) on the part of the party to whom it was made.[14] Both these related conditions may be absent in a transaction which projects the finalization of an obligation into the future, becoming operative only upon the fulfillment of a specific condition. A transaction containing these elements is referred to in the talmudic literature as *asmakhta*. With the obligation becoming operative only when a condition is fulfilled, the person obligating himself may very well rely on the probability that the condition will not be fulfilled, and thus that he will not become obligated. Because the presumption of perfect intent was lacking, the presumption that the commitment generated reliance is equally lacking.

A transaction characterized as *asmakhta* does not confer title.[15] With the *asmakhta* transaction regarded as invalid *ab initio*, a transfer made subsequent to the fulfillment of the conditions is characteristically involuntary and hence a form of robbery.[16]

In the final analysis, the halakhic validity of the no-show fee hinges on whether it satisfies the various criteria for an *asmakhta* undertaking proposed by rishonim.[17] In what follows we will present these criteria and apply the no-show fee to them.

One school of thought, led by R. Solomon b. Isaac (Rashi, France, 1040–1105), takes the position that *asmakhta* obtains when A makes a conditional obligation to B but can escape it altogether because he partially controls the triggering condition that makes the obligation operative. Let us illustrate this principle with a case discussed in the Talmud (Bava Mezia 73b and Tosafot ad loc.): A agrees to buy current vintage wine for B at the low-price Belshafet marketplace. Furthermore, A stipulates that in the event he misses the window of opportunity to buy the wine while it is still cheap, he will make good to B the price differential involved. Now, if A acts quickly, he can obtain the wine at the low price. If, on the other hand, A is negligent and tarries, he will miss the window of opportunity and will be liable to B to make good on the difference in price. Since A relies on himself (*toleh be-da'at azmo*) to act quickly and avoid liability to B, he lacks firm resolve to make payment to B when it turns out that he missed the window of opportunity and faces the higher price.

A variation of the above case occurs when it is entirely within the control of the obligor to prevent the triggering condition. Illustrating this is the tenant farmer's (A's) stipulation to his landlord (B) that in the event he does not cultivate the field, he will make good on B's loss of a crop. Consider that whether the price of seed is high or low, it is still within A's power to cultivate his field and avoid paying B for a lost crop. Because A realizes that he has no one to blame but himself if he ends up being liable to B, A resolves firmly to meet his obligation if it becomes operative. Here, A's stipulation does not take on the character of *asmakhta* unless he specifies a sum to indemnify B that is clearly in excess of his forgone income.

At the other extreme stands the case where the obligor has absolutely no control over the triggering mechanism. Illustrating this case is a wager in a game of chance. Since each player realizes that he has no control over the outcome of the game, each player fully and firmly resolves to turn over the pot to the winner.[18]

Application of Rashi's criteria to the no-show fee renders this clause in the agreement null and void. This is so because it is not entirely within Kleinberg's power to avoid the $25 no-show fee. Specifically, he avoids the fee only if he gives twenty-four hours notice. Because Kleinberg imagines that if reason to cancel the appointment develops, it will become apparent to him more than twenty-four hours before the appointment, he lacks firm resolve to pay the no-show fee when the reason to cancel develops only within twenty-four hours of the appointment. Kleinberg's agreement to pay the no-show fee, therefore, falls into the *toleh be-da'at azmo* criterion and should be classified as *asmakhta*.

Disputing Rashi's criterion, R. Jacob Tam (France, ca. 1100–1171) regards the salient feature of *asmakhta* to consist of the circumstance where it is evident that both parties desire the completion of the underlying agreement, and the conditional commitment is given merely as an assurance of good faith.[19]

R. Tam's formulation of *asmakhta* is clearly satisfied in the no-show fee case. Both Dr. Shain and Rabbi Kleinberg desire that the dental appointment should take place as scheduled. As a matter of good faith, Rabbi Kleinberg agrees to pay a $25 fee in the event of a no-show on his part.

R. Solomon b. Abraham Adret (Spain, ca. 1235–1310) advances still another criterion as to what constitutes *asmakhta*. Formulating an undertaking in terms of a penalty, in R. Adret's view, is what makes a conditional commitment an *asmakhta*.[20]

Application of R. Adret's criterion to the issue at hand frees the no-show fee of an *asmakhta* character only when the *fee* cannot be regarded as a penalty. If the $25 fee is half or less than half of the fee the doctor would collect if the appointment is kept, the fee would qualify as *kepo'el bateil* and hence reflect no more than the doctor's actual losses. But suppose, Kleinberg's appointment slot is easily filled or that Kleinberg's no-show was due to `ones. Since Halakhah absolves Kleinberg of any responsibility in the latter two instances, the call for a $25 no-show fee must be viewed as a *penalty* and therefore takes on an *asmakhta* character.

The broadest conceptualization of *asmakhta* is that of Maimonides (Egypt, 1135–1204). Any conditional obligation is in his view an *asmakhta*.[21] Application of Maimonides' criterion to the no-show fee renders this clause null and void.

Asmakhta can be counteracted by means of incorporating the phrase *me-akhshav* (lit. from now) into the agreement between the parties. The logic of this concept is that had A not *unreservedly* committed himself to the condition, he would not have conferred B with title or ownership from the time of the stipulation.[22]

The exact form *me-akhshav* takes is a matter of dispute among the rishonim. Three views can be identified:

1. Maimonides et al. take the view that *me-akhshav* counteracts *asmakhta* only when A accompanies this phrase with a symbolic act that legally binds him to the agreement at hand. This is known as the *kanu mi-yado* (lit. acquired from his hand) condition.[23] The symbolic act is usually executed by means of *kinyan sudar* (lit. the acquisition of the handkerchief): A acquires B's handkerchief and

thereby undertakes the obligation involved.[24] (As a matter of custom, A returns the handkerchief to B after acquiring possession of it.)

2. *Asmakhta*, according to R. Solomon b. Abraham Adret (Spain, ca. 1235–1310), is counteracted either by *me-akhshav* or by *kanu mi-yado*. Both conditions, however, are not required.[25]

3. Another school of thought, led by R. Jacob Tam (France, ca. 1100–1171), regards *asmakhta* as being counteracted only when both *me-akhshav* and *kanu mi-yado* are done in the presence of an authoritative Jewish court (Bet Din Hashuv).[26]

The upshot of the above analysis is that counteracting *asmakhta* is no small matter. Printing an advisory of a no-show fee on an appointment card will certainly not suffice. Though the rules of *asmakhta* do not apply to contracts that are binding by secular law,[27] a policy advisement printed on an appointment card is by no means a contract. To be binding, the patient must explicitly bind himself to pay the fee by means of the phrase "from now." In addition, the undertaking must be made by means of *kinyan* (symbolic act).

The Use of the No-Show Fee Advisement as a Bluff

In the opening vignette we find Dr. Shain trying to collect on the no-show fee. In a variant, Dr. Shain uses the advisory only as a bluff. Out of fear that open discussion of the no-show fee will antagonize his patients, Dr. Shain confines mention of this policy to an advisement he prints on his appointment cards. Dr. Shain has no intention to bill or accept payment for a no-show, but feels that the advisement serves to deter the ethically lackadaisical. These people harbor the attitude that appointments made with him are only *tentative* in the first place.

Notwithstanding that Dr. Shain's intention is to direct his advisory to the ethically lackadaisical, the appointment card is handed to every patient and hence the message is communicated to all. Recall that collecting on a no-show fee often violates Halakhah. Because the language of the advisory allows for no exceptions, issuance of the card creates the impression that Dr. Shain is prepared to flaunt Halakhah in chasing after the no-show fee. To be sure, bluffing the ethically lackadaisical should provide an instance of application of *mat'an*, discussed above. But if the bluff, at the same time, generates the impression that Dr. Shain is prepared to flaunt Halakhah, the tactic should be prohibited. Thus handing the advisory to all patients is halakhically unacceptable. Targeting the advisory to patients guilty of no-shows without notice in the past, however, should, be permissible.

Adlers v. Frank

We now turn to an analysis of *Adlers v. Frank* from the perspective of Halakhah. In evaluating the merits of the case, let us consider several legal theories that could possibly form a basis for the Adlers' claim.

Labor Law

By agreeing to perform the marriage ceremony of the couple at a designated place and at a designated time, Rabbi Frank enters into a verbal labor agreement with the couple. Because a marriage celebration consists of events and rituals that are scheduled in a prescribed order and at appropriate intervals, tardiness on the part of the officiant will often generate indirect losses for the couple and certainly will cause considerable mental anguish. The job of officiant at a marriage celebration should therefore be categorized as *davar ha-avud*. Now, if Rabbi Frank had been hired to engage in a manufacturing process, and as a result of his negligent tardiness in arriving at the work site, the industrial materials spoiled, there would be a basis to hold him responsible for the employer's loss.[28] But consider that the tardiness of the rabbi *per se* in the case at hand entails no direct financial loss for the couple. If the couple suffers losses here it is only because the tardiness of the rabbi *triggers* events and actions that have untoward consequences for the couple. To be sure, the job of officiant should be categorized as *davar ha-avud*, but since the tardiness *per se* does not part-and-parcel entail a financial loss, the case falls into the category of non-financial loss (*davar ha-avud she-eino shel mamon*). In the latter case, no assessment is made against the worker to make good on the employer's loss.[29]

The upshot is that labor law provides no basis to validate the Adlers' claim against the rabbi. Moreover, if Rabbi Frank's tardiness was not due to negligence on his part but instead was the result of unavoidable and unforeseen circumstances, he bears no blame for the untoward consequences the Adlers suffered.

Adlers v. Frank and the Law of Garmi

In this section we will evaluate the Adlers' claim against Frank in light of tort law. Specifically, we will examine whether the law of *garmi* (liability for indirect action) can be invoked here as a basis to validate the Adlers' claim against Rabbi Frank. Let us consider the following case:

R throws O's utensil from the top of a roof. Under the roof lie cushions that shield the utensil from damage. Before the utensil reaches the cushions, R himself removes the cushions, and in consequence O's utensil breaks. R bears no financial liability to O.[30]

In rationalizing why R escapes liability, R. Asher b. Jehiel (Germany, ca. 1250–1327) invokes three independent exculpating factors for *garmi* cases.

1. R's action of removing the cushions is not a culpable action. To qualify as *garmi*, the tortfeasor must commit a tortious act (*ma-a'sse hezek*) on either the person or property of the victim.

2. To be liable the tortfeasor's action must fit into the category of *bari hezeka* (lit. certain to cause damage). Because cushions were under the utensil when R threw it from the roof, R's action fails the *bari hezeka* standard, and therefore he bears no compensation liability.

3. To bear financial responsibility, the tortfeasor's action must in and of itself produce bodily or property damage to the victim. If the harm proceeds merely as a lagged effect of the tortfeasor's action, the latter bears no financial responsibility in the matter. This requirement is called the *miyyad* (lit. immediately) condition. It is for this reason, independently, that R bears no responsibility for the breakage of O's utensil. This is so because the utensil does not break until it actually reaches the ground. Since R's removal of the cushion does not in and of itself break the utensil, the *miyyad* condition fails.[31]

Let us apply R. Asher's conditions for *garmi* liability to the case at hand. All three standards fail here.

The most basic issue is that Rabbi Frank did not commit a tortious act (*ma-a'sse hezek*) on either the person or property of the Adlers. Instead, what triggered the chain of calamities was the rabbi's *tardiness*.

The *bari hezeka* standard fails in the case at hand. Frank's tardiness cannot be said to inevitably cause the guests to take to drink and engage in gossip. Likewise, his tardiness cannot be said to have foreseeably caused the reemergence of the groom's old back injury. Finally, if the bride had not made the *decision* to stay put, she would not have suffered from the effects of a stifling room.

The *miyyad* condition also fails. Consider that it is not the *tardiness* of the rabbi *per se* that produces the aggravation and losses for the Adlers. Instead, the rabbi's tardiness *triggers* events and actions that produce a chain reaction of calamities for the victims. Hence the *miyyad* condition fails.

In his treatment of *garmi* liability, Nahmanides (Spain, 1194–1270) mentions only the *bari hezeka* condition. *Bari hezeka* obtains, in his view, when A's conduct will *inevitably and without outside assistance* cause harm to B's person or property.[32]

Clearly, *Adlers v. Frank* fails to meet Nahmanides' criterion for *garmi* liability.

In his treatment of *garmi*, R. Menahem b. Solomon Meiri (France, ca. 1249–1306) defines *garmi* in terms of the tortfeasor's intention to inflict harm or damage that is accomplished without outside facilitation.[33] R. Menahem b. Solomon Meiri's criterion for *garmi* clearly also fails for the case at hand.

While the thrust of the discussion thus far has been that *garmi* will not provide an underpinning for the Adlers' claim against Frank, there is a variant of *garmi* that may be relevant here. This is the ruling of R. Mosheh Isserles (Poland, 1525 or 1530–1572) in connection with a broken out-of-town court appointment. Here, R. Isserles rules that the stood-up party is entitled to recover his travel expenses.[34] The rationale behind this ruling, according to R. Meir b. Isaac Auerbach (Jerusalem, 1815–1878), is that since A had legitimate expectation that B would show up for the court appearance, we can regard it as if B *instructed* A to incur the necessary travel expense. B's failure to show up, therefore, makes him responsible for A's expenditures.[35]

Application of this ruling to the case at hand once again comes up short of meeting the *garmi* liability condition. To be sure, the Adlers had every right to expect the rabbi to arrive on time, but the expectation does not amount to an implicit instruction on the part of the rabbi that in the event of his tardiness the guests should overindulge in liquor and engage in gossip. Likewise, the rabbi gave no implicit instruction that in the event of his tardiness the bride should remain cooped up in a stifling room.

Moreover, in the couple's suit against Rabbi Frank there appears to be an element of harassment. Not everything that went wrong at the wedding can be dumped on the rabbi. The gossip the guests engaged in provides a case in point. Since the couple knew that the only reason the ceremony was being postponed was because the officiant had not yet arrived, the couple should have seen to it that an announcement to this effect was made. The announcement would have prevented the gossip. Moreover, if two events occur in succession, there is no basis for concluding that the preceding event *caused* the succeeding event. Logicians call this the *post hoc ergo propter hoc* ("After this, therefore necessarily because of this") fallacy. If Rabbi Frank had arrived on time and the groom's back injury had occurred subsequent to his arrival, can anyone imagine for a moment that the Adlers would have fallen into the *post hoc* fallacy and blamed the rabbi for the groom's back injury? So why blame the rabbi when the back injury occurs subsequent to the time when he *should have been* at the affair? Doing so represents an egregious form of the *post hoc* fallacy.

One final point on *Adlers v. Frank*. The rabbi's tardiness undeniably caused the couple much aggravation. It would therefore be the gracious thing for him to waive his fee as the officiant. Such a gesture would be especially appropriate if the rabbi's tardiness was not entirely due to unavoidable and unforeseen circumstances.

1. David Margolick, "At the Bar," *New York Times*, July 27, 1990, p. B5.

2. Mishnah, Bava Mezia 6:1.

3. R. Asher b. Jehiel (Germany, 1250–1327), Rosh, Bava Mezia 6:6; Maimonides (Egypt, 1135–1204), *Yad*, Sekhirut 9:4; R. Jacob b. Asher (Germany, 1270–1343), *Tur*, Hoshen Mishpat 333:3; R. Joseph Caro (Israel, 1488–1575), *Shulhan Arukh*, Hoshen Mishpat 333:5; R. Jehiel Michel Epstein (Belarus, 1829–1908), *Arukh ha-Shulhan*, Hoshen Mishpat 333:18–20.

4. Rosh, op. cit., *Yad*, op cit.; *Tur*, op. cit. *Sh.Ar.*, op. cit; *Ar.haSh.*, op. cit. 333:19.

5. Ibid.

6. For the development of this point, please turn to pp. 329–30 of this volume.

7. Shabbat 31a.

8. The mitzvah referred to in the text is "Seek peace and pursue it" (Psalms 34:15). For a discussion of the ramifications of this mitzvah as it pertains to labor relations, see pp. 310–1 of this volume.

9. Please turn to pp. 258–62 of this volume.

10. Please turn to pp. 259-62, 312-14 of this volume.

11. *Sh.Ar.*, op. cit. 333:1; *Ar.haSh.*, op. cit. 333:13.

12. R. David b. Samuel ha-Levi (Poland, 1586–1667), *Turei Zahav*, *Sh.Ar.*, op. cit 333:1.

13. *Sh.Ar.*, op. cit.; *Ar.haSh.*, op. cit. 333:4.

14. For a discussion of the talmudic and rishonic sources dealing with the *gemirat da'at* and the *semikhat da'at* conditions, see Shalom Albeck, *Dinei Mamanot be-Talmud* (Tel Aviv: Dvir, 1976), pp. 112–43.

15. Bava Batra 168a; Rif, ad loc.; *Yad*, Mekhirah 11:5; Rosh, Bava Batra, 10:19; *Tur*, op. cit 207:12; *Sh.Ar.*, op. cit. 207:9–13; *Ar.haSh.*, op. cit. 207:22–53.

16. R. Solomon b. Isaac (France, 1040–1105), Rashi, Sanhedrin 24b, s.v. *lo*.

17. The term rishonim designates scholars who were active in the period from the eleventh to the middle of the fifteenth century.

18. Rashi, Sanhedrin 24b on the interpretation of Tosafot, ad loc.; Tosafot, Bava Mezia 73b–74a; Nahmanides (Spain, 1194–1270), Ramban, Bava Batra 168a; R. Mosheh Isserles (Poland, 1525 or 1530–1572), Rema, *Sh.Ar.*, op. cit. 207:13.

19. R. Jacob Tam (France, ca. 1100–1171), quoted in Tosafot, Bava Metzia 74a, s.v. *hai*, and in Tosafot, Sanhedrin 25a, s.v. *khol*.

20. R. Solomon b. Abraham Adret (Spain, ca. 1235–1310), Rashba, quoted in *Shitah Mekubbetzet*, Bava Batra 168a.

21. *Yad*, Mekhirah 11:2.

22. Ibid. 11:7.

23. Ibid.; *Tur*, op. cit. 207:1314; *Sh.Ar.*, op. cit. 207:14.

24. R. Joshua b. Alexander ha-Kohen Falk (Poland, 1555–1614), Sema, *Sh.Ar.*, op. cit. 207, n. 38.

25. R. Solomon b. Abraham Adret, *Responsa Rashba* 3:60.

26. R. Jacob Tam, quoted in Tosafot, Bava Mezia 66a, s.v. *u-Minyumi*; R. Nissim b. Reuben Gerondi (Spain, 1310–1375), Ran, Nedarim 27b, s.v. *ve-hu*; Rosh, Bava Mezia 5:29; R. Mordecai b. Hillel ha-Kohen (Germany, 1240–1298), Mordecai, Bava Mezia 5:321. This school of thought is quoted in Rema, *Sh.Ar.*, op. cit. 207:14.

Rishonim have advanced various opinions as what constitutes a Bet Din Hashuv. Three individuals who have expertise on the laws of *asmakhta* satisfy the criterion of Bet Din Hashuv, according to R. Asher b. Jehiel (*Responsa Rosh*, k'lal 72, n. 5). R. Mordecai b. Hillel, however, defines Bet Din Hashuv as the most distinguished local court (Mordecai, Bava Batra 5:323). Finally, R. Yom Tov Vidal of Tolosa (Spain, 14th cent.) regards a publicly appointed judge, even if not ordained, as meeting the definition of Bet Din Hashuv (*Maggid Mishneh*, *Yad*, Mekhirah 11:13).

Still another mechanism for counteracting *asmakhta* exists. Because it is of no practical value for Dr. Shain, no mention of it was made in the text. The procedure consists of the following: A reinforces his conditional commitment by performing a symbolic act (i.e., *kinyan sudar*) in the presence of Bet Din (*kanu be-Bet Din*). In addition to the symbolic act, A must entrust to this court the rights he has in the property he wishes to transfer conditionally to B. What the latter accomplishes is to make the court rather than A the principal who confers title to B in the event the obligating condition is triggered. (See *Yad*, op. cit. 11:13–14.)

27. *Ar.haSh.*, op. cit. 201:3.

28. Rema, op. cit. 333:6.

29. Ibid.

30. Rosh, Bava Batra 2:17.

31. Ibid.

32. Ramban, Bava Batra, *Dinei de-Garmi*.

33. R. Menahem b. Solomon Meiri (France, 1294–1366), *Beit ha-Behirah*, Bava Kamma, 55b.

34. Rema, *Sh.Ar.*, op. cit. 14:5.

35. R. Meir b. Isaac Auerbach (Jerusalem, 1815–1878), *Imrei Binah 2, Dinei Dayannim*.

Teacher Evaluation at Brickmire College

Lance Wineman is an assistant professor of economics at Brickmire College, a small liberal arts college in the Northeast. The college has a long tradition of stressing effective teaching in making its personnel decisions. It was this tradition that rang in Wineman's mind over and over again when he received a call from his dean, Dr. Donald Blackstone, to arrange an appointment with him. At the meeting Blackstone laid out for Wineman his scores on the student evaluation-of-teaching questionnaire that his office had administered the previous semester. This form is reproduced as Figure 1.

With a concerned and somber face, Blackstone pointed out to Wineman that he had scored a mediocre 3.8 on the questionnaire. The only bright spot was his score of 4.8 for item 1. Blackstone was very curious about the discrepancy between Wineman's smashing 4.8 for item 1 and his overall mediocre score. Wineman had a good explanation but felt it would be best not to share it with Blackstone.[1]

While Wineman sat brooding, Blackstone pulled out a student publication called the *Asymmetric Information Fixer*. This publication provided students with *intelligence reports* on professors and courses. It had published the evaluation results for the past five years, systematizing the data by presenting them in ranked and comparative form. Basing themselves on the five-year data bank as well as on the written comments of the respondents, student leaders had produced profiles of the professors and of the courses they taught. Every attempt at fairness was made. Minority opinion was duly incorporated or at least noted in constructing the profiles. In respect to Wineman the publication wrote, among other things:

> Dr. Wineman may very well prepare his lessons, but his students go away with the distinct impression that his lectures are entirely extemporaneous. This impression is bolstered by the observation that Wineman never comes into class with index cards or notes. . . . Wineman too often goes on tangents, which has the effect of turning off many students and leaving others in a state of confusion.
>
> While a minority of the students describe him as gentle, quiet and scholarly, most students regard him as boring[2] and uninspiring; and as one of this group put it . . . "he is as dynamic as a dead Liberace."

As the unflattering words of the *authoritative* profile sank in, Wineman found himself being led to the door by the dean. The dean's parting words were: "Journeymen come here and go . . . *tenure* is the *prize* reserved for those who demonstrate *excellence* in teaching."

Figure 1. Student Evaluation

Instructor:_____Semester_____
Course_____Code_____

ANSWER ON A SCALE FROM 1 TO 5

1 = Strongly disagree 2 = Disagree 3 = Neutral 4 = Agree 5 = Strongly agree

1. Course objectives were clearly stated	[1] [2] [3] [4] [5]
2. Course requirements were clearly stated	[1] [2] [3] [4] [5]
3. Instructor was well prepared for each class	[1] [2] [3] [4] [5]
4. Lectures were well organized	[1] [2] [3] [4] [5]
5. Instructor presented subject matter clearly	[1] [2] [3] [4] [5]
6. Instructor seemed enthusiastic about subject matter	[1] [2] [3] [4] [5]
7. Instructor was helpful when students had difficulty	[1] [2] [3] [4] [5]
8. Instructor encouraged student questions and participation in class	[1] [2] [3] [4] [5]
9. Instructor encouraged students to think critically	[1] [2] [3] [4] [5]
10. Instructor demonstrated mastery of subject matter	[1] [2] [3] [4] [5]
11. Instructor made helpful comments on papers/exams	[1] [2] [3] [4] [5]
12. Instructor assigned grades fairly and impartially	[1] [2] [3] [4] [5]
13. Instructor was available for consultation	[1] [2] [3] [4] [5]
14. I learned a great deal in the course	[1] [2] [3] [4] [5]
15. I would take this instructor again	[1] [2] [3] [4] [5]

ANSWER THE NEXT TWO QUESTIONS ON A SCALE FROM 1 (POOR) TO 5 (EXCELLENT)

16. Overall evaluation of the course	[1] [2] [3] [4] [5]
17. Overall evaluation of the instructor	[1] [2] [3] [4] [5]

USE THE REVERSE SIDE FOR ADDITIONAL COMMENTS AND SUGGESTIONS

The basic issue raised by this vignette is what constitutes the proper channel and mode of expression for students to communicate their judgments regarding the teaching effectiveness of their professors. We will proceed to address this issue in general terms and then go on to critique the procedure at Brickmire.

As consumers of educational services, students should have every right to voice complaints about the quality of the service they are receiving. Ingrained in student culture, however, is the notion that communicating criticism openly and directly to the professor is ineffective and possibly counterproductive. This is so because criticisms and complaints may very well offend the professor. In consequence, the student may suffer bias in the way the professor grades his or her paper and in the degree of enthusiasm the professor shows for the student in writing letters of recommendation. To be effective, student complaints against faculty must be addressed to the administration and in anonymous form.

Filling out an evaluation form at the completion of a course appears, therefore, to be an appropriate mode of expression for students. But suppose a certain complaint is unrepresentative of class opinion. Overcoming this problem apparently calls for the administration to make the questionnaires a requirement rather than something optional. This approach ensures that the results will be statistically significant, appropriately discounting extreme opinions. In addition, this approach allows the administration to place faculty performance in the perspective of relative rankings.

Evaluation Questionnaires and the Interdict Against *Lashon ha-Ra*

From the perspective of Halakhah, directing a complaint against one's teacher to the administration of the school may run afoul of various biblical prohibitions. If the complaint is baseless, the report constitutes slander (*mozi shem ra*).[3] But even if the complaint is valid, the report may violate the biblical prohibition against talebearing: "You shall not go about as a talebearer among your people" (Leviticus 19:16). Depending upon the circumstances, talebearing may involve the violation of a total of thirty-one pentateuchal positive commandments and prohibitions.[4]

Maimonides formulates the prohibition against talebearing as follows: "There is a much more serious sin than [gossip], which is also included in this prohibition (Leviticus 19:6): *lashon ha-ra*, i.e., relating *deprecating* facts about a fellow, even if they are true."[5]

A student's critical comment to an administrator regarding his professor's teaching ability or effectiveness can do various kinds of reputational harm to the professor. Hence such comments fall squarely into the ambit of *lashon ha-ra*.

In his classic work on the prohibition against talebearing, R. Israel Meir ha-Kohen Kagan (Hafez Hayyim, Poland, 1838–1933) provides a number of examples of cases of *lashon ha-ra* that generate reputational damage. One example, involving a rabbinical scholar (*talmid hakham*) as the target of the evil talk, is very much akin to the case at hand: S's report to L that R (a rabbinical scholar) is an ineffective communicator and/or has only a limited knowledge of Halakhah is *lashon ha-ra*. Such talk deprecates R's reputation. In the event R occupies a religious-educational position, the *lashon ha-ra* entails the additional sin of an action designed to deprive R of his livelihood.[6]

One cannot summarily judge that a student criticism of faculty directed to the university administration constitutes *lashon ha-ra*, however, without considering the *motivation* behind the report. S's damaging report to L regarding V is not automatically *lashon ha-ra* unless S's motivation is to ridicule or denigrate V. If S's motive in making the report is to secure for himself or someone else a rightful entitlement, then the report should not be *automatically* characterized as outright *lashon ha-ra*. Hafez Hayyim derives this principle from Sifra's understanding of the biblical injunction "Do not stand idly by the blood of your neighbor" (*lo ta'amod al dam rei'kha*, Leviticus 19:16). While the verse prohibits a bystander from remaining idle in a life-threatening situation, Sifra extends the interdict to a prohibition against withholding testimony in a monetary matter. Basing himself on Sifra, Hafez Hayyim understands the monetary application of the *lo ta'amod* interdict in broad terms: A's failure to supply B with timely information that would avert a financial loss for B is a violation of the *lo ta'amod* interdict.[7]

By extension, with the aim of recovering his loss or at least avoiding aggravation or loss in the future, A may relate the offense B committed against him to someone who has the potential to reform or influence B.[8]

To be sure, *lo ta'amod* does not suspend the interdict against *lashon ha-ra* in a blanket manner. To be free of the *lashon ha-ra* interdict, a number of conditions must be satisfied. We will proceed to enumerate these conditions and relate them to the issue at hand:

1. The complainant (A) must be *certain* that the damage or grievance committed against him by B constitutes a violation of his rights. Making an invalid complaint against B to C amounts to *mozi shem ra*.

2. Unless A is certain that B will not accept his complaint, A must seek satisfaction by first approaching B directly.

3. The damaging report must be known to A first-hand. If the objectionable conduct is not known to A first-hand, Hafez Hayyim is unresolved as to whether disclosure should be made. In any event, A may not present his report as fact, but may merely disclose what he has heard and advise the concerned party to exercise caution on the basis of the information.

4. Since exaggeration is falsehood, A must exercise caution not to magnify or embellish the offense he is reporting.

5. If A fears that his report will result in B's suffering penalties more severe that what is due him by dint of Halakhah, the disclosure should not be made.

6. In reporting against B, A's actions should be entirely motivated by a desire to secure what is rightfully his and/or to show zealousness for truth and justice. If the motivation behind the revelation is, however, a long-standing grudge against the offender or a desire to ridicule or degrade him for his present misdeed, the disclosure should not be made.

7. If A's legitimate objectives can be achieved by other means, *lashon ha-ra* should not be resorted to. Similarly, in seeking a remedy against B, A must make every effort to see to it that B's degradation is minimized. Indeed, unless his objective would be compromised, A must *minimize* B's offense in his report to C.[9]

Conditions 2 and 6 are apparently readily satisfied in relation to student-evaluation questionnaires. But meeting the remaining five conditions is somewhat problematic. Let us begin by examining the various biases Wineman was subject to.

For one, faculty culture has it that students don't take kindly to tough graders. By Brickmire's standards, Wineman is a tough grader.

In addition, there are only a few economics majors at Brickmire. Wineman's classes were heavily populated with students who took his course either to satisfy the college's social science requirement or to satisfy requirements in the accountancy program. The upshot is that very few students took Wineman out of pure choice.[10]

Another bias Wineman suffered from was that students judged his teaching ability by the amount of learning they achieved in his courses. But a teacher's task is only to facilitate student achievement, not to guarantee results no matter how little effort the students make. Instead of asking students how much they learned in Wineman's class (item 14 of Fig. 1), the evaluation should ask students how well Wineman taught the course. Indeed, Professor Michael Scriven, an expert on teacher evaluation, proposes that this substitution should be made in the questionnaire.[11] Making the substitution does not, however, remove the bias entirely. Some students will always blame an unsatisfactory educational experience on their professor. This was certainly the case in Wineman's situation. Of the students who gave Wineman a lackluster rating, Norman Abramowitz's profile is typical. Abramowitz found it difficult to follow Wineman's lectures and felt the professor was especially bad at presenting graphical material. Blaming Wineman for his inferior educational experience is perhaps not warranted. Abramowitz may himself be at fault. Consider that

Abramowitz never comes to class prepared with the assigned reading from the textbook; nor is he much of a note taker. Abramowitz's most difficult moments came when he missed the previous class and found that he lacked essential background material to make sense out of the lecture. In these floundering moments, Abramowitz would mumble to himself, "If Wineman had only a modicum of pedagogical skill and/or some *sensitivity* for his students, I would not be totally lost now."

Let us continue this exercise of probing the minds of Wineman's students in order to discover additional complaints against him. We will leave it to the reader to decide whether the complaints are valid.

Some of the students took the course even less seriously than Abramowitz and company. Typical of this group was Stuart Katz. While sharing the work ethic of the Abramowitz group in all essentials, what set Katz apart was his spotty attendance. Since Wineman made attendance a requirement, Katz made it a point to make an "appearance" in every class, and not to fail to sign the attendance sheet. Needless to say, Katz experienced some episodes of blackout during examinations. In these profoundly empty and trying moments, Katz's thoughts turned toward Wineman: "If he had only made his lectures more interesting and dynamic, I would have taken the course much more seriously and might have even been inspired to read the text. But Wineman didn't put much energy into his lectures, why . . . he never even came to class with index cards."

Let us now turn to the bright and hardworking students in Wineman's class, namely, Friedman, Klein, and Becker. All three attended class regularly, did their assignments, and took excellent notes. Though all agreed that Wineman demonstrated mastery of the subject matter (Fig. 1, item 10), this group also had significant complaints. Friedman, for one, felt that Wineman spent far too much class time accommodating the needs of the weaker students. If someone wanted a concept repeated or to be filled in on material that had been dealt with in a previous class, the proper place and time for this was the professor's office during office hours. Encouraging a clearly excessive number of "stupid questions" left precious little time for Wineman to elucidate the really difficult material and to challenge the critical thinking of his students. In some instances, Friedman felt, silly questions and comments had the effect of interfering with the flow and continuity of the professor's presentation. If Wineman had any *organizational ability*, he would take charge and make sure that class time was spent *efficiently*. These considerations led Friedman to rate Wineman a 3 on items 4, 5, and 9.

Though somewhat more tolerant than Friedman in respect to Wineman's practice of accommodating the needs of weaker students on class time, Klein had his share of gripes. What disturbed him to no end was that Wineman never even gave so much as a hint on how examination questions would break down in relative emphasis between text and class notes. Though grapevine intelligence had it that Wineman always emphasized class notes, Klein's threshold for tolerating risk was very low, and he did not want to rely on historical data.

Another matter of disturbance for Klein was that the notation employed in the text differed considerably from the notation Wineman used in class. The difference, in Klein's opinion, reflected both lack of preparation by Wineman and a *disdain* for the productive use of student time. These attitudes, combined with Klein's moderate agreement with Friedman's concerns, led him to rate Wineman: 2(2); 3(3); 4(3); 5(4); 9(2).

The brightest and hardest worker in the class was Becker. His preparations reached a peak near examination time. It was in those intense moments that Becker unearthed esoteric discrepancies or apparent minor contradictions between the class notes and the text. The timing of these discoveries obviated any possibility for Becker to confront Wineman for clarification. These experiences, combined with the notation problem mentioned earlier, made Becker come down harshly on Wineman. Among Becker's scores on the questionnaire, the following items received a 3: 3, 5, 7, 9, 10, 12, and 13.

We should note that while some students described Wineman as thorough and scholarly in the classroom and warm and gentle in his interaction with students, the consensus was that he was not dynamic and certainly lacked charisma. It is not surprising, therefore, to find that he was mostly rated either 1 or 2 on item 6.

What the aforementioned demonstrates is that bias and exaggeration of various forms enter into student ratings of teaching effectiveness. Bias and exaggeration make for inaccurate and hence false judgments on teaching effectiveness, whether it relates only to a determination of competency or to a determination of superior service. If evaluation questionnaires are used for summary purposes, they may entail infractions of *mozi shem ra* and hence violate Hafez Hayyim's fifth condition.

Publishing the Evaluation Results

Brickmire's policy of making the evaluation results available to a student publication violates the guideposts described above.

Publishing the questionnaire results in the *Asymmetric Information Fixer* does not simply make information more conveniently accessible to those in legitimate need; it also makes it readily available to individuals whose need for the data is only a matter of curiosity and entertainment. Because the prohibition against *lashon ha-ra* is not suspended in the absence of the need factor, the *Asymmetric Information Fixer* is guilty of disseminating *lashon ha-ra*.

One feature of the publication's format was that it ranked the entire faculty of the college on the basis of both overall performance and the individual items on the questionnaire. Presenting the evaluative data in this fashion injects a new element of *lashon ha-ra* in respect to faculty who score below par in their overall rating and possibly even in respect to faculty who score above par in their overall rating. To illustrate, suppose it is agreed that an overall score of less than 3 constitutes a poor performance. Public disclosure that A's score was below 3 communicates that he or she is an ineffective teacher, and hence the disclosure constitutes *lashon ha-ra*. Disclosing A's below-par score together with the scores of his (her) colleagues rubs in A's humiliation more deeply, thereby compounding the sin of *lashon ha-ra*. Now, suppose it is agreed that an overall score of 3.5 is a respectable score. Disclosing B's score of 3.5 together with the comparative data signals that other professors are superior to B, but does not degrade him. Relevant here is the ruling by R. Hayyim Hezekiah Medini (Russia, 1832–1904) that voicing an opinion that A is a greater talmudic scholar than B does not amount to degrading B and is therefore a permissible.[12] The rationale behind this ruling is apparently that the opinion expressed should be viewed as a superiority claim. Since the speaker implicitly concedes that B is also a scholar, the statement in no way *degrades* B. The *Asymmetric Information Fixer*'s report of comparative rankings in respect to each of the individual items, however, complicates matters. B's overall score of 3.5 communicates that he is an effective teacher. But a score below 3.5 on any of the items on the questionnaire communicates a definite *flaw* in his teaching skills. Thus comparative data have the effect of rubbing in B's humiliation in respect to a particular flaw and consequently inject an additional component of *lashon ha-ra* in respect to the report on B.

Another problem with publishing comparative data is that the practice violates the rabbinical extension of *lashon ha-ra*, called *avak* (lit. dust) *lashon ha-ra*. The interdict entails a prohibition against making conversation that incites *lashon ha-ra*. Accordingly, A should not praise B to someone (C) who is known to dislike B. Such praise will only serve to provoke C to knock B down from his pedestal so as to demonstrate that the praise is unwarranted. Similarly, A should not praise B excessively even to B's friend (D). Excessive praise will only provoke D to point out that B really has a fault of some kind.[13] Indeed, A himself might be moved to *qualify* his effusive praise by pointing out that B does have a certain fault.[14] In his treatment of this interdict, Hafez Hayyim prohibits A from *publicly* praising B, even if the praise is moderate. Since people have both admirers and detractors, public praise of B is bound to incite one of his detractors to knock B down and point out a fault he has.[15]

Publication of the relative ranking of faculty in evaluation questionnaires violates *avak lashon ha-ra* because the information will arouse *debate* about the validity of the results.

To give students a feel for the consistency of a professor's teaching performance, the *Asymmetric Information Fixer* publishes faculty evaluation data for five-year periods. This practice is halakhically objectionable. At once, it repeats the *lashon ha-ra* of previous years and disseminates it again. The practice may even add a new dimension of *lashon ha-ra*. This occurs when the professor's overall or specific-item performance is satisfactory for the current year, but is revealed to have been below par for one or more of the previous five years. To be sure, the professor's record shows improvement, but the references to his past are painful reminders of failure. *Reminding* someone of his past misdeeds is cited in the Mishnah as a specific example of the prohibition of causing someone needless mental anguish (*ona'at devarim*).[16] If B's words to A cause the latter needless anguish, the prohibition against *lashon ha-ra* prohibits B from making the same communication to C.[17] Thus, publishing the past failure of professors violates the interdict against *lashon ha-ra*.

By providing its readers with faculty profiles based on the statistical data and student comments that appeared on the form, the *Asymmetric Information Fixer* again compounds the sin of *lashon ha-ra*. Profiles make the *lashon ha-ra* inherent in the statistical presentation more *concrete* and *detailed*. In addition, notwithstanding the policy to take full account of minority opinion, the subjectivism and interpretation involved in drawing up portraits introduces additional distortions.

Ironically, the policy of presenting *balanced* profiles of faculty ensures that the publication will violate *lashon ha-ra* even in respect to faculty that the *Asymmetric Information Fixer* clearly intends to present as excellent teachers. This is so because minority opinion will work itself into the profile either by modifying praise or by *noting* criticism in respect to specific items on the questionnaire.

Perhaps the most disturbing aspect of the student publication's approach is its use of "put down" humor in describing Wineman: ". . . as dynamic as a dead Liberace." For one, this description illustrates how a profile can distort the available data rather that highlight it. Note that none of the items on the questionnaire asked the students to rate Wineman on the quality of dynamism. The item on the questionnaire that comes closest to this trait is question 6, which asked students to rate Wineman on whether he seemed *enthusiastic* about the subject matter. Suppose all the students gave Wineman the lowest-possible rating on this item. But if students understood enthusiasm in the sense of excitement and passion, Wineman could easily accommodate student needs by only slightly modifying his conduct. For starters, Wineman should react with excitement and appreciation when students demonstrate penetrating insights or ask sharp questions in class. At the junction in the course when Wineman demonstrates that economic theory has predictive value, he should punctuate the lesson with redemptive fervor. Another opportunity for passion is to comment on pending legislation in Congress. Taking out a few moments to laud the work of this year's Nobel laureate would go a long way in demonstrating passion for scholarship in his field. Finally, Wineman should pepper both his lectures and his interaction with students with an occasional smile and/or chuckle.

Given the meaning people ordinarily attach to the word *enthusiasm*, the "dead Liberace" comment is out of order. Two possibilities present themselves. One is that the comment reflects an exercise in idiosyncratic gymnastics on the part of the student who made the comment: enthusiasm was equated with dynamism and then stretched to mean flamboyant dress and histrionic lecture style. Alternatively, the comments manifests an implicit introduction by the student of *a criterion for effective teaching not covered in the questionnaire, namely, showmanship and/or charisma.* Along with this new criterion came the judgment that Wineman was pitifully lacking in it. By incorporating the "dead Liberace" comment in its profile of Wineman, the *Asymmetric Information Fixer* endorsed the student's thinking. Since the comment either perverts the intent of question 6 or implicitly introduces an unauthorized criterion of effective teaching, the publication is guilty of maligning (*mozi shem ra*) Wineman's reputation as a teacher.

Recall that the essence of *lashon ha-ra* is defined as degrading or deriding an individual. Once the *Asymmetric Information Fixer* describes faculty in derisive terms, its publication of evaluative information on faculty must be viewed as *lashon ha-ra*, notwithstanding any constructive benefits that ensue from it.

Student Evaluations as a Feedback Device and Investigative Tool

While the use of questionnaires for summary purposes must be rejected, this evaluative tool, under controlled conditions, has several legitimate purposes.

One legitimate purpose is that it can serve as an efficient feedback device to enhance teaching effectiveness. Students who feel that voicing complaints directly to faculty is futile or even counterproductive must have a mechanism to deliver negative feedback. At the same time, faculty have a need to determine whether criticism received is representative of the group. By enlisting the anonymous participation of all the students, the questionnaire establishes an efficient feedback pipeline between faculty and students.

Another legitimate purpose of such questionnaires is to serve as an investigative tool for administration to determine whether the educational process is working in the classroom. The case for using a questionnaire for this purpose begins with the recognition that the dean of a college or principal of a school functions halakhically as the steward (*apotropos*) of the students.[18] Carrying out his stewardship role requires the dean to solicit student input to ascertain whether the educational process is working in the various courses. Requesting the members of each class to fill out questionnaires represents a convenient and efficient means to begin this task.

The purpose, of course, is to identify courses where the educational process is apparently not working. Toward this end, the initial focus of the dean's office should be on an overall rating of the educational experience and learning process. To properly evaluate the significance of the overall score, a *red-flag* number must be determined. The later is a rating that indicates the educational process is probably not working. It could, for argument's sake, be a rating below the mean score of all faculty on this item. Suppose the red-flag number is 3. A rating of 3 signals a need for the administration to *investigate* why the learning process is apparently not working in the particular course.

The use of evaluation questionnaires as an investigative tool with the feature of consultative intervention does not violate faculty rights. As educational consumers, students have every right to voice complaints against faculty to the dean when they believe that to do so directly to faculty would either be futile or counterproductive. Suppose there is no questionnaire in place at Brickmire and a student comes to Blackstone to complain about Wineman. Blackstone must not brush the student aside out of concern that what he is hearing is bona fide *lashon ha-ra*. Quite to the contrary. In situations like this, Hafez Hayyim recommends that the listener encourage the complainant to vent his or her emotions and to detail every particular of the grievance. A patient and sympathetic hearing of the complaint oftentimes allows the listener to weed out exaggerations and distortions, and serve the role of *peacemaker* between complainant and offender.[19] Depending on the nature and frequency of student complaints in respect to a particular faculty member, the dean will exercise judgment in deciding when consultation with faculty is necessary. Absent any formal student evaluation system, complaints against faculty must *assuredly* be addressed. Setting up a *formal* system that calls for intervention in the red-flag case does not, therefore, violate any faculty prerogatives.

Halakhic Controls on Evaluation Questionnaires

Notwithstanding its legitimate goals, a questionnaire is not acceptable as an evaluation tool if its operation inevitably entails violations of Halakhah. Since infraction of *lashon ha-ra* and related prohibitions is a major concern here, controls must be instituted so as to avoid infractions of these prohibitions. Specific attention must be given to avoiding the pitfalls of speaking, listening to, and disseminating *lashon ha-ra*. In this section we will identify the relevant halakhic concerns and then proceed to describe the mechanics of the questionnaire.

The Questionnaire's Design

The most fundamental concern is that the *design* of the instrument itself should be sound. Content items should be free of ambiguity and capture the components of effective teaching. In this regard, researchers have noted that unless the evaluation questionnaire is constructed with the aid of professionals, its results will be unreliable.[20] In halakhic terms, the inclusion of irrelevant items and/or ambiguity in what the item says inevitably produces invalid criticisms and inaccurate responses by the students. This, in turn, results in unfair judgments of faculty in respect to various components of teaching effectiveness. Periodic refinement of the evaluative tool in consultation with current research is therefore an essential component of the halakhic system.

Illustrating the above concern is item 14 of the questionnaire (see Fig. 1). Recall Scriven's point that a questionnaire should never ask variations of the question "How much did you learn from this class?" Instead, it should be "How well do you think the instructor taught the class?"

Another illustration is the identification some students and the *Asymmetric Information Fixer* made between enthusiasm (item 6) and dynamism.

Avoiding Unnecessary Degradation

Notwithstanding that the questionnaire's goals are worthy, the system must operate to eliminate *unnecessary* degradation of faculty. Toward this end, items 16 and 17 (see Fig. 1) suggest themselves for revision. Instead of asking students to provide an overall rating of the instructor and the course, the two items should be consolidated into a single rating of the overall *educational experience* and *learning process* of the course. Let us designate the new item 16*.

The rationale for this change is the Torah's prohibition against causing someone needless mental anguish. This translates into an obligation to mitigate, if possible, someone's pain or degradation. The blame for a negative educational experience cannot always be fixed on the professor. For one, the fault may lie in the student's work ethic, attitude, or motivation. Factors outside the control of both professor and student could also be responsible. Examples of these factors include a heterogeneous class in respect to academic ability, an excessively large class size, and the failure of the department to either establish a prerequisite for the course or to ensure that the material covered in the course material does not overlap with that of other courses. A poor rating on item 15 denigrates the professor. A poor rating on 16* does the same, but there is a difference. A poor rating on 16* is *broad* enough to allow for the possibility of mitigating circumstance to account for the negative experience. A poor rating on 15, on the other hand, *blots* out this consideration entirely.

Replacing 15 and 16 with 16* ensures that the initial communications of students to the dean relate to the educational experience and the learning process in the classroom rather than the more narrow issues of teaching ability, faculty effort, and effectiveness. What a red-flag rating *directly* communicates to the dean is not that the professor is *inept* but rather that the educational process is not working in the class and that remedial action is warranted.

Eligibility to Participate in Evaluation

Let us now turn to the issue of eligibility. A thorny issue is raised here regarding the question of whether students whose attendance in the course involved is spotty should be eligible to participate in the evaluation. What constitutes excessive absence for purposes of participating in an evaluation is debatable. For argument's sake, let us define excessive absence as meaning one-fourth of the term's lectures. Since the student's rating here is based on insufficient observations, and, perhaps, on second-hand opinion as well, the report will almost inevitably entail *mozi shem ra* and related prohibitions. Recall, however, that in the face of B's legitimate need, Hafez Hayyim permits A to disclose information to B even when its source is second-hand. In this instance, A need only inform B that the information he is providing is second-hand and should therefore not be taken as fact. As educational consumers, irregular class attendees are no less entitled to seek effective teaching both for themselves and for their fellow students. The goals of including irregular attendees in the evaluation and avoiding violation of Halakhah can be reconciled by printing the questionnaires in two colors, say, red and white. In the class session designated for the filling out of questionnaires, irregular attendees would be given red forms and those who have met the attendance requirements would be given white forms. This way, irregular attendees will have their say, but the information they provide will be treated by the dean as second-hand.

The above system is, however, halakhically unacceptable. For one, recall that the disclosure of second-hand *lashon ha-ra* must be accompanied with a caution that the report is not fact. If the informer fears that his report will indeed be taken as fact without investigation, the disclosure should not be made. The upshot here is that the delivery of second-hand *lashon ha-ra* should ideally serve no more than as a *catalyst* for B to launch his own investigation, which, in turn, will be based on first-hand reports. It follows that if B is known to be in the process of gathering first-hand reports to help him make a decision, A should not make a disclosure. This is the case at hand. Brickmire has in place a student evaluation system that provides the dean with a flow of first-hand information in respect to how the educational process is working in the class-room. With a first-hand information pipeline in place, no one has the right to offer information that is based on a combination of shaky first-hand impressions and second-hand sources. Consider, too, the possibility that excessively absent students base their reports, in part, on impressions they gather from non-current students. This makes the reports of the excessively absent students not only second-hand *mozi shem ra*, but also, to some extent, irrelevant.

One final point. Empowering excessively absent students with the ballot may incite *lashon ha-ra* and hence run afoul of *avak lashon ha-ra*. This is so because with an *official* first-hand information pipeline in place, regular attendees have no halakhic right to share their critical insights of the course and the professor with those whose first-hand knowledge is shaky. If excessively absent students are denied the ballot, there is no incentive for them to pry critical information from regular attendees and other sources. On the other hand, allowing excessively absent students to participate in the evaluation of teachers proliferates *lashon ha-ra* communications among students. Thus, conferring excessively absent students with the right to participate in the evaluation violates *avak lashon ha-ra*.

One might argue that it is undesirable to exclude excessively absent students from participating in the evaluation of teachers. Consider the possibility that the reason students stay away from a certain professor's course is because attending the lectures is a waste of time. If the dean's pipeline admits only first-hand information, how will the administration become aware of these attitudes? This concern can be accommodated by comparing the class roster to the number of questionnaire responses. If a significant discrepancy exists between these numbers, investigation by the dean is warranted.

Student Access to the Evaluation

Another issue is the appropriateness of providing students with access to the results of the teacher evaluations. As consumers of educational services, students have every right to make inquiries with fellow students regarding the teaching effectiveness of professors they plan to take. Given this right of inquiry, the questionnaire results should be made available to students. Indeed, making the results available to students may very well work to minimize infractions of *lashon ha-ra* and related prohibitions on campus. This is so because inquiries go on whether the evaluation results are available to students or not. If students are denied the results, how many of them would be careful to ferret out biases and avoid all the pitfalls of *lashon ha-ra*? Making the evaluations available to students obviates the need to seek references on a one-to-one basis and, in addition, ensures that students will be making program decisions based on relatively more accurate information than otherwise.

But since it is immediate need that legitimizes making the evaluation results available to students, the information provided must be both limited and controlled. For one, students who require information to make decisions regarding their programs have no need to know the evaluation scores of professors they have no plans to take. Relatedly, there is no need for students to have a relative ranking for the *entire faculty by name*. Accordingly, evaluation-result requests by students should be honored only on a discrete, course-by-course basis. In order to discourage discussion and dissection of the data, the results should be provided in a setting where students cannot congregate. Finally, controls should be instituted to ensure that the information is released only to current students and is not photocopied or removed from the place where it is provided.

Be'appei Telata

Arguing for broader public dissemination of student evaluation results is Rabbah b. R. Huna's dictum: "Disparaging remarks made in the presence of three persons do not constitute *lashon ha-ra*" (*kol milta d'mit'amri be'appei telata let bah mi'shum lishna bisha*, hereafter *be'appei telata*).[21] What *be'appei telata* apparently conveys is that once disparaging remarks are in the public domain, there is no prohibition against further disseminating the report. Applying this leniency to the case at hand allows Brickmire to publish whatever evaluation information it makes available to students. Rishonic understanding of *be'appei telata*, as Hafez Hayyim points out, imparts such a narrow meaning to this dictum that it hardly becomes a basis for leniency in *lashon ha-ra*.[22] How these views apply to the case at hand will now be examined.

Let us begin with the understanding of *be'appei telata* propounded by R. Solomon b. Isaac (Rashi, France, 1040–1105). In his view, the dictum does not refer to a report that is *lashon ha-ra*, but rather to private information. Ordinarily, if A relates information about himself to B, without explicit permission to reveal it to others, B must treat the information confidentially. But if A relates information about himself to a group of three, the confidentially rule no longer obtains, as we presume that A will not object if any member of the group passes on the information. If the information A relates to the group is *lashon ha-ra*, none of them may pass it on to others.[23] Rashi's understanding of the dictum makes the leniency irrelevant for the issue at hand.

Another understanding of *be'appei telata* is advanced by R. Samuel b. Meir (Rashbam, France, ca. 1080–1174). In his view, *be'appei telata* refers to an instance involving talebearing (*rekhilut*). Ordinarily, it is prohibited for I to inform V that S made disparaging remarks about him (V). Doing so entails the prohibition of *rekhilut*. But suppose I heard the disparaging report in the company of two other persons, D and E. Here, I is under no halakhic restraint against passing on the disparaging remarks to V, the rationale being that the situation makes it certain that V will eventually get wind of the disparaging remarks about him. Since it is only a matter of time before V picks up the remarks, I may pass on the disparaging remarks to V immediately upon hearing them.[24] Note that Rashbam's understanding of *be'appei telata* provides no basis for S to deliver his disparaging report in the first place. Quite to the contrary, as Hafez Hayyim points out, delivering a disparaging report about V in the presence of three people degrades him more than if the same report was related only to one person. The more degradation V suffers on account of S's *lashon ha-ra*, the more severe S's sin becomes.[25]

Applying Rashbam's understanding of *be'appei telata* to the case at hand apparently allows a student to inform a professor that his rating on the evaluation was poor. But causing someone needless mental anguish (*ona'at devarim*) is prohibited. In Rashbam's case, I's report gives V *accelerated knowledge* of the disparaging comments, which affords him early opportunity to plan appropriate measures to counteract the disparaging report. But what useful purpose would it serve for a student to inform a professor that he made a poor showing on the evaluation. Since the professor is privy to the results of the evaluation before the student gets access to the information, making the report only serves to rub in the anguish the professor feels on account of the poor results. Thus, the student making the disparaging report is in violation of the *ona'at devarim* interdict.

Another understanding of *be'appei telata* is provided by Tosafot. In Tosafot's view, the dispensation is for the one who delivers the original report. But the case does not speak of a report that is outright *lashon ha-ra*. Here *be'appei telata* worsens the sin rather than mitigates it. Instead, the dictum deals with an instance of *avak lashon ha-ra*. To illustrate: A inquires of B where to find a cooking fire in the neighborhood. B refers A to C, and adds that cooking is continually going on in C's house. B's comment is *avak lashon ha-ra*. This is so because A can read into it that C continually indulges himself. Because a derogatory intent can be read into the comment, B should not make the remark even when no degradation is intended, as would be the case when C has a large household or is very hospitable to strangers. If B intends no degradation, however, he may make this *avak lashon ha-ra* comment to a group of three. The rationale here being that making the comment to three is tantamount to making the comment directly to C's face. Since B would presumably not insult C to his face, making an *avak lashon ha-ra* comment about him to a group of three indicates that no denigration of C is intended.[26] Tosafot's understanding of Rabbah b. Huna's dictum as referring to *avak lashon ha-ra* makes it irrelevant to the issue at hand.

Finally, let us take note of what Maimonides says. In his view, *be'appei telata* conveys the principle that once *lashon ha-ra* has been spoken to a group of three, the disparaging report is regarded as being known to everyone. Consequently, any member of the original group may reveal the disparaging report. Maimonides adds, however, an important caveat. What is permissible is only to share the report with someone who makes a request for the information. No one may take the initiative and *deliberately* publicize *lashon ha-ra*.[27]

Proceeding from Maimonides' understanding of *be'appei telata* is the permissibility for a student to respond to a request to share any teacher-evaluation information he has. Posting evaluation results in the lobby of one of the college buildings or publishing them in the school newspaper, however, is clearly prohibited.

Administration of the Evaluation

Let us now move to the administration of the questionnaire and the handling of the results. In administering the questionnaire, students should be asked to fill out their responses in three different segments. Part I records student responses to the individual items on the questionnaire (items 1–15); Part II records student responses to item 16*; Part III records any supplemental written comments the students may have to offer. These comments may be conveyed anonymously. Part III should be returned immediately to the professor. Parts I and II should be sent to the dean's office. With the aim of completing the feedback process for the professor, a copy of Parts I and II should be made and forwarded to the instructor.

A series of *self-appraisal* items for the professor should be prepared based on the evaluation questions, and he should fill them out at the same time that the students are filling out the questionnaires. The professor's response on the self-appraisal form should be forwarded to the dean's office together with Parts I and II of the evaluation.

The initial focus of the dean's office should only be on Part II, consisting of the students' overall rating of the educational experience and the learning process. A red-flag rating, as explained earlier, signals a need for the administration to *investigate* why the learning process is apparently not working in the particular course. At this juncture, the dean should study student responses on the individual items of Part I along with the corresponding responses of the professor on the self-appraisal form. The dean should then meet with the faculty member in order to devise a plan for improving the learning experience. At the meeting, the instructor should share with the dean the written comments by the students that comprise Part III of the evaluation.

Teacher Evaluations and Self-Appraisals

The rejection of student evaluations of teachers as a measure of teaching effectiveness requires further clarification. The evaluation's chief flaw is that decisions should not be made with an inherently biased instrument. But there is one case when this would not be so, and this is the instance where the faculty member's self-appraisal rating corresponds closely with student ratings of him. What the correspondence says is that the faculty member does not regard the collective student judgment of him as biased or unfair. Accordingly, the evaluation scores should be admissible evidence of teaching effectiveness when the self-appraisal matches the scores. The focus here, however, is misguided because this policy leaves faculty who fail the matching test with no alternative means of demonstrating teaching merit. Thus the flip side of accepting evaluations in the matching case is that a faculty member's claims of merit are always rejected when his evaluation scores fall below a certain level.

Toward a Halakhic Measure of Teaching Effectiveness

In this section we will describe a faculty personnel policy based on halakhic principles.

Let us first take up the issue of faculty termination. Elsewhere in this volume, we have demonstrated that Halakhah requires an organization to set up its labor relations with a performance-appraisal system. The essential elements of the system consist of goal setting, performance appraisal, feedback, and opportunity to correct negative feedback.[28] Application of this model to the case at hand makes the student evaluation of teachers the feedback mechanism for faculty at Brickmire. A red-flag rating requires, as discussed earlier, consultative intervention by the dean. What should emerge from this consultation is a *definitive remedial plan* for the faculty member to make the educational process work. Failure of consultative efforts to raise the faculty member's subsequent evaluation score above the red-flag level indicates that the remedial plan was not successfully implemented. At this juncture, the dean should launch a first-hand investigation to determine whether the faculty member implemented the elements of the remedial plan. Should the investigation confirm the negative indication of the failing evaluation score, grounds for discharging the faculty member have been established. Note that the role a failing evaluation plays in discharging a faculty member is merely to *launch* an investigation as to whether the remedial plan was successfully implemented. It is the *outcome* of the investigation that leads to the discharge of the faculty member.

At this juncture let us note that feedback can improve teaching effectiveness for *all* faculty along the entire continuum of competency. Research, however, has shown that student evaluations without consultation intervention are not likely to lead to improved teaching. With the aim of promoting effective teaching, colleges should integrate consultative services for faculty with their student-evaluation programs. The service would help faculty interpret criticism and devise a plan of action for improvement. Because faculty will not avail themselves of this system if they perceive it as punitive, the support system should ideally be independent of both administration and peers.[29]

If such a system is adopted, its use should be made mandatory for faculty who score a red-flag rating.

Student Evaluations and Teaching Merit

The use of student evaluations to determine teaching merit is very limited and not at all practical. A uniform policy of offering to renew faculty contracts on the basis of a passing evaluation avoids violation of *lashon ha-ra*, but is a disaster in respect to promoting teaching excellence. Moreover, promoting teaching excellence requires that some rewards, such as merit pay and tenure, be limited to faculty who demonstrate superior teaching skills and not be conferred for mediocrity. Relying on student evaluations to distinguish between superior and good is halakhically unacceptable because bias taints the data and makes them inaccurate.

In order to judge teaching merit, Brickmire must come up with an evaluative system that both accurately measures teaching effectiveness and is halakhically sound. Peer review provides an alternative to student evaluations as a method of judging teaching effectiveness. In the following section we will discuss peer review from the standpoint of Halakhah. We will then proceed to demonstrate that student evaluations can assume a role within the framework of an evaluative system that employs peer review.

Peer Review

Peer review consists of classroom visits and an evaluation of the teacher's professional dossier.

Research has roundly criticized the use of peer ratings based on visitation for summary purposes. They are unreliable because of the small number of observations, judgments based on political considerations or friendships, and over-reliance on style preferences that have little to do with the objectives of teaching.[30]

Peer review also examines a teacher's professional dossier for evidence of teaching merit. In describing this component of peer review, we will follow Professor French-Lazovik's treatment of this topic.

One important task the evaluators should address is the quality of the professor's instructional material. To demonstrate merit here, the professor should provide such materials as course outlines, reading lists, texts used, handouts, problem sets, and assignments for each course he or she teaches. The task for evaluators is to consider such questions as whether these materials are current, whether they represent the best work in the field, and whether they represent superficial or thorough coverage of course content.

Another issue peers should consider is what kinds of intellectual tasks the professor set for the students, and how the students performed. The material should include such items as copies of graded examinations, examples of research papers, and examples of teachers' feedback to students on written work.

Still another issue for evaluators is the commitment of the faculty member to achieve excellence in teaching. The dossier should include changes the professor made on the basis of student feedback.

Finally, professors should give evidence that they are knowledgeable and current in their fields as well as committed to the teaching mission of their department or university.[31]

Peer review casts evaluators in the role of judges. Elsewhere in this work we have demonstrated that Halakhah recognizes that subtle forms of bias taint the integrity of the judicial decision-making process.[32] Thus, from a halakhic standpoint, the concerns raised earlier regarding the biases involved in peer visits to classrooms apply to the peer review process in general. Indeed, one could put to question the entire process on the basis of the dictum that "every craftsman hates his fellow craftsman" (*kol uman sonei benei ummanuto*).[33] On the basis of this dictum, Hafez Hayyim warns against making inquiries about a craftsman from his competitor.[34] The report is bound to be riddled with falsehoods, inaccuracies, and distortions. The bias issue, however, is not insurmountable. This is so because Halakhah rules that an individual who is other-wise disqualified to serve as judge can act in this capacity provided the litigants in the case agree.[35] Applying this principle to the case at hand allows Brickmire to set up a peer review system as its basis for evaluating teaching merit. All that is needed is that each faculty member should be apprised of the system before signing an employment agreement.

In any case, however, blatant bias must be eliminated. Illustrating blatant bias is the failure of Brickmire to mandate that the peer review committee use uniform standards and procedures for each teaching-merit case. The require-ment to eliminate blatant bias follows from several considerations. One is that the agreement of an appointee (A) to the peer review concept is not tanta-mount to an agreement to subject himself to blatant forms of bias. Moreover, even if the blatant form of bias is specified up front, agreement to it may very well fail the legal test of what constitutes *resolve* and therefore render the agree-ment non binding in respect to the clause dealing with blatant bias. (An agree-ment that fails to meet the test of resolve is called *asmakhta*.)[36] To illustrate, suppose Brickmire empowers the peer review committee to adopt on, an indi-vidual case basis, whatever standards and procedures it feels are appropriate. A agrees to this clause only because he imagines that when his own teaching merit is up for evaluation, the committee will adopt for his case standards and proce-dures that he will regard as fair. Since A believes that the circumstances that would lead him to object to the discretionary-power clause will never happen, A's agreement to the clause fails the legal test of resolve and renders the agree-ment non binding in respect to this clause.

Moreover, the principle expressed in the verse "Her ways are ways of pleas-antness" (*derakheha darkhei no'am*, Proverbs 3:17) requires Brickmire to set up all its rules and procedures in a manner that would foster harmonious relations within its organization. A failure to eliminate blatant bias in the peer review process would do great disservice to this principle.[37]

The Role of Student Evaluations in the Framework of a Peer Review

Recall that student evaluation scores in the matching case are not admissi-ble as evidence of teaching merit because that would leave faculty who fail the matching test with no alternative means of demonstrating teaching merit. This is no longer so when there is a peer review system. Once a peer review system is in place, faculty should have the option of demonstrating teaching merit through the peer review process or by demonstrating a correspondence between their self-appraisal and student evaluation scores.

It remains to be clarified whether Brickmire can adopt the student ques-tionnaire as its tool for evaluating teaching merit and make use of peer review only on an ad hoc basis, at the request of faculty. From the standpoint of Halakhah, this policy is unacceptable. Giving the questionnaire prominence over peer review communicates the message that the questionnaire is reliable for determining teaching merit, and that peer review is resorted to only as special favor to faculty when the questionnaire fails to deliver for them. What is appropriate, therefore, is to install both systems at Brickmire. At the juncture when summary decisions regarding teaching merit are made, faculty should be given the choice of which instrument they would like to be used to demonstrate their teaching merit.

Conclusion

As a feedback device for faculty and as an investigative tool for administration, student evaluations of teachers should occupy a prominent place in higher education. Notwithstanding their worthy goals, such evaluations must operate in a manner that minimizes the degradation of faculty members. Toward this end, students should be given only limited access to evaluation results under controlled conditions. Publication of evaluation results, historical scores, and comparative and summary profiles of faculty should be prohibited.

Because the students' ratings of their teachers are subject to various biases, evaluation results may not be directly used for summary purposes. Nonetheless, administration must follow up red-flag ratings by consulting with faculty members who score poorly. The purpose of the consultation is to produce a remedial plan of action. A policy that calls for discharge if a passing evaluation rating is not achieved subsequent to the consultative efforts is in consonance with Halakhah. What discharges the faculty member is not reliance on the evaluation as evidence of incompetence, but rather the teacher's failure to successfully implement the remedial plan.

Since the distinction between good and excellent entails a precise judgment, student evaluations are not reliable for this type of judgment. To evaluate teaching merit, a college must put in place a peer review system. Once a peer review system is in place, student evaluations can assume a place in demonstrating teaching merit. Specifically, student evaluations are admissible as evidence of teaching effectiveness if the professor's score is higher than or closely corresponds to his self-appraisal scores.

1. If you're curious about the explanation, read this note: Wineman was convinced that the difference between scoring a 1 and a 5 on item 1 of the questionnaire was all a matter of a little creative thinking. On the first day of class, (all) professors announce the objective of the course to their students. But this takes up only a few minutes and is done in a very nonchalant manner. Because the course objective is not highlighted when it is first mentioned and is not repeated again, most students will be hard put to remember what the professor said

about the course objective. Consequently, when students fill out the questionnaire at the end of the semester, honestly compels them to grade their professor poorly on item 1.

Realizing the foolhardiness of the above approach to the course objective, Wineman set out to hit a homerun on this item. On the first day of his Economic Principles I course, Wineman makes it a point to *highlight* course objective. He begins by informing his students that the course objective for Economic Principles I is, like everything else in economics, a matter of raging debate. One school of thought believes that the purpose of the introductory course is to broaden the appeal of the discipline as much as possible by demonstrating that it sheds light on the concerns of everyday life. This orientation translates into a course content that stresses institutional history and arrangements and statistical data, with discussions centering on organized labor, government regulation of business, taxes, health care, and environmental economics. Another school of thought, however, feels that the objective of the introductory course should be to provide a solid foundation for an understanding of economic theory.

At this juncture Wineman plays up to the egos of his students by telling them that they are very fortunate to be enrolled in an elite institution of higher learning. Upholding the high standards of the college requires him to do no less than to take a rigorous approach to the course. The course will, therefore, feature the development of an econometric model along with detailed discussions of monetary and fiscal policy. Wineman makes it a point to repeat a shorter version of his talk at strategic points during the semester when attendance is almost perfect, namely, at review sessions and examination sessions.

Wineman's sparkling score of 4.8 on item 1 surely vindicates his strategic thinking on this matter!

2. Professor Wineman may well be on the boring side as a lecturer, but he sure puts in an energetic effort to inject an element of humor into his final exams. Sample this opening question on his Intro Micro exam:

1. How many economists does it take to change a light bulb?

(a) Two, i.e., one to *assume* a ladder, and another to change the bulb.

(b) 100, i.e., 99 to hold everything else constant (*ceterius paribus*) and one to change the bulb.

(c) None, i.e., if the light bulb needed to be changed, market forces would have *automatically* taken care of it.

(d) All of the above are possible answers, depending on your sense of humor.

(e) None of the above; economics is a very serious, dry discipline that allows no room for a sense of humor.

(Now that you have gotten question 1 right, go on to the rest of the exam with confidence and a big smile!)

3. The biblical source for the prohibition against slander is disputed at Ketubbot 46a: R. Eleazar derives the warning from the verse "You shall not go about as a talebearer among your people" (Leviticus 19:16). R. Natan derives the admonishment from the verse "When you go out as a camp against your enemies, you must avoid everything evil" (Deuteronomy 23:10).

4. R. Israel Meir ha-Kohen Kagan (Poland, 1828–1933), *Hafez Hayyim*, Lavin 117, Essin 114.

5. Maimonides, *Yad*, De'ot 7:2.

6. *Hafez Hayyim*, op. cit., Hilkhot Issurei Lashon ha-Ra 5:4.

7. Ibid., Hilkhot Issurei Rekhilut 9:1, *Be'er Mayim Hayyim* 1.

8. *Hafez Hayyim*, Hilkhot Lashon ha-Ra 10:13, *Be'er Mayim Hayyim* 34.

9. *Hafez Hayyim*, Hilkhot Issurei Lashon ha-Ra 10:117, Hilkhot Rekhilut 9:1–15.

10. Statistical studies are inconclusive on the issues of whether student ratings correlate positively with grades and negatively with a course that is a requirement. See Lawrence M. Aleamoni, "Student Ratings of Instruction," in *Handbook of Teacher Evaluation*, ed. Jason Millman (Beverly Hills, Calif. Sage, 1981), pp. 11–45.

11. Michael Scriven, "Summative Teacher Evaluation," in *Handbook of Teacher Evaluation*, p. 250.

12. R. Hayyim Hezekiah Medini, *Sedei Hemed*, vol. 4, k'lal 86, p. 524.

13. Erkhin 16a; R. Isaac b. Jacob Alfasi (Algeria, 1013–1103), Rif, Shabbat, 14a; *Yad*, De'ot 7:4; *Hafez Hayyim*, Hilkhot Issurei Lashon ha-Ra 9:1.

14. R. Solomon b. Isaac (France, 1040–1105), Rashi, Erkhin 16a.

15. *Hafez Hayyim*, op. cit. 9:2.

16. Mishnah, Bava Mezia 4:10.

17. *Hafez Hayyim*, op. cit. 4:1, and *Be'er Mayim Hayyim*, n. 1.

18. Yonason Rosenblum, *Reb Yaakov: The Life and Times of Rabbi Yaakov Kamenetsky* (Brooklyn, N.Y., Mesorah, 1993) p. 150.

19. *Hafez Hayyim*, Hilkhot Issurei Lashon ha-Ra 6:4.

20. Aleamoni, "Student Ratings of Instruction," p. 113.

21. Bava Batra 39a.

22. *Hafez Hayyim*, op. cit. 2:1; *Be'er Mayim Hayyim* ad loc.

23. Rashi, Erkhin 16a; *Be'er Mayim Hayyim*, ad loc., 2, n. 3.

24. Rashbam, Bava Batra 39a.

25. *Be'er Mayim Hayyim*, loc. cit., n. 1.

26. Tosafot, Erkhin 16a; *Be'er Mayim Hayyim*, loc. cit., n. 2.

27. Maimonides, *Yad*, De'ot 7:2; *Be'er Mayim Hayyim*, loc. cit. 2, note 3.

28. Please turn to pp. 305–18 of this volume.

29. Scriven, "Summative Teacher Evaluation," p. 247.

30. Ibid., pp. 251–252.

31. Grace French-Lazovik, "Documentary Evidence in the Evaluation of Teaching," in *Handbook of Teacher Evaluation*, ed. Jason Millman (Beverly Hills, Calif., Sage Publications, 1981), pp. 73–89.

32. Please turn to p. 6 of this volume.

33. Midrash Tanhuma, Genesis 8.

34. *Hafez Hayyim*, op. cit. *Haggahot ha-Mehaber* 4:11.

35. R. Jehiel Michel Epstein (Belarus, 1829–1908), *Arukh ha-Shulhan*, Hoshen Mishpat 7:10.

36. Bava Batra 168a; Rif, ad loc.; *Yad*, Mekhirah 11; Rosh, Bava Batra 10:19; R. Jacob ben Asher (Germany, 1270–1343), *Tur*, Hoshen Mishpat 207:12; R. Joseph Caro (Israel, 1488–1575), *Shulhan Arukh*, Hoshen Mishpat 207:9-13; R. Jehiel Michel Epstein (Belarus, 1829–1908), *Arukh ha-Shulhan*, Hoshen Mishpat 207:22-53. For an extended treatment of the *asmakhta* principle, see Aaron Levine, *Economics and Jewish Law* (Hoboken: Ktav, 1987), pp. 194–200.

37. Mishnah Gittin 5:8, Gittin 59b; for an extended treatment of the *darkhei shalom* principle, and especially its role in the interpretation of scriptural rules and rabbinical enactments, see Aaron Kirschenbaum, *Equity in Jewish Law* (Hoboken, N.J.: Ktav, 1991) pp. 151–83. See also Aaron Levine, *Economic Public Policy and Jewish Law* (Hoboken, N.J.: Ktav, 1993) pp. 10–12, 61–62.

The Firing of Claudia Weinstock

On February 18, 1997, Claudia Weinstock was hired by I. M. Frier, CEO of the Frier Greeting Card Company, as his administrative assistant. She was hired for an indefinite period of time without a formal contract. At Claudia's job interview, just before he made a firm offer to her, Frier remarked: "From looking at your resume it appears that you can handle whatever assignments I have in mind to give you. Please know that most of the work you will be doing is routine. But don't worry, life here will never be dull! Moreover, as my administrative assistant some of the glamour that is attached to my job as CEO will rub off on you. I welcome your candid opinions on the policy issues we'll be working on together."

Claudia had been on the job no more than fourteen months when, on April 17, 1998, Frier called her into his office at the end of the workday and shocked her with the following revelation:

"I regret to inform you that you are *terminated*, effective immediately. Of course you'll get one-month severance. I have reached this decision based on the following:

"One. Claudia, your computer skills are poor. You simply don't have the database capabilities we require here. And this is a big disappointment because you came to us with some database capability. So why didn't you put in the time and effort to adjust to our needs?

"Two. You were late an hour or more on four different occasions. I know you made up the time, and I appreciate your integrity on this. But if you're not here, I have to answer the telephone. You know how much I *disdain* answering the telephone myself.[1]

"Three. I've received a number of complaints from customers that you are not cheerful and sometimes even grumpy and discourteous when dealing with them in telephone conversations.

"Four. Most troublesome of all, Claudia, is that you have an *attitude* problem. Every time I give you *routine* work to do, such as photocopying, I can *almost* hear you mumble under your breath, `Boss, do it yourself.'"

As Frier's harsh words sank in, Claudia burst out into hysterical tears and sobbing. When she gained a bit of composure, she blurted out: "All true, but I could have corrected everything if you had only discussed the situation with me."

As Claudia made her way to the door, she gathered up enough courage to say the following to Frier: "If I have an attitude problem, it's mostly your fault. You promised me that I could voice my opinion on policy matters. Well, two months after I began work, you held that big board meeting. You called it the 'vision thing.' At the meeting, the agenda item was whether we should go with the cartoon characters and the humor or stick with the traditional mushy material. I had a definite opinion on this, but I couldn't get a word in edgewise."[2]

Taken aback by Claudia's tirade, Frier felt compelled to have the last word.

"I can't believe what I'm hearing! You misunderstood my promise. Sure, I'm interested in your input when my ideas are in the formative stages of development. But once I make up my mind on something and am prepared to present it to the board, I expect *total loyalty* from you, and not, of all things, *opposition at a board meeting.*"

The above scene describes a workplace riddled with dashed expectations and grievances. Much of this aggravation could have been avoided if Frier had only set up his labor relations by means of a performance-appraisal system.

Performance appraisal is the systematic observation and evaluation of work-related behavior. What follows is a description of the basic elements of a performance-appraisal system. We will then proceed to demonstrate that Halakhah requires an employer to set up such a system in his workplace.

Performance Appraisal

A performance-appraisal system consists of three elements: goal setting, performance assessment, and feedback.[3] We will use the preceding case study to describe how these three elements work.

At the outset, Frier should have made it clear to Claudia what he expected of her. Expectations should be formulated in terms of specific objectives and, when possible, quantifiable goals. This procedure is referred to as management by objective (MBO). An essential feature of this system is the participation of the subordinate in the setting of the goals.

Recall that when Frier hired Claudia, he told her that on the basis of her resume he felt confident she could handle what he had in mind for her. MBO would reject this approach out of hand. Instead, Frier should have provided Claudia with *an enumeration and description* of the duties he planned to assign her. Had Frier only done his homework, he would have picked up on the fact that Claudia's computer literacy did not extend to a facility for the type of database his company used. If Frier wanted to hire Claudia anyway, he should have entered negotiations with her to come up with a plan that would enable her to upgrade her skills within a reasonable time frame without disrupting the workflow of the office.

At the job interview, Frier should have shared with Claudia his conviction that in the greeting card business a large dosage of cheerfulness is a prerequisite for an efficient work environment. Once the philosophical spadework was laid,

Frier should have told Claudia that he *expected* her to contribute positively to the creation of this ideal environment. To dramatize the importance of cheerfulness in the operation of the company, Frier should have introduced Claudia to Leonard Sugerman, the company's resident poet. One look at Sugerman would have convinced Claudia that even slight stress could easily dissipate the sensitive poet's inspirational energy. As matters turned out, Claudia was not even aware that the company had a resident poet until she was well into her second month at the greeting card company.

At the outset, Frier should have laid down his attitude about lateness and makeup work.

Finally, Frier should have laid out for Claudia his ground rules on "independent thinking" by employees. By setting forth these parameters in advance, Frier would have spared Claudia the devastation she suffered on that fateful day when the "vision thing" was debated at the company's board meeting.

Performance Appraisals and Halakhah

In extrapolating Halakhah's attitude toward performance appraisals, we need only recognize that the workplace is a natural setting for dashed expectations. Employees who are either denied or passed over for promotion, merit increases, selection for management training, or transfer to a different department, will often experience dashed expectations. This holds even more so for those who are handed layoff or discharge notices. Without a satisfactory performance-appraisal system in place, the occurrence of dashed expectations would increase considerably. For one, if expectations are not clearly laid out at the outset, a meeting of the minds will often fail to occur and dashed expectations become inevitable. Moreover, without performance appraisal, what will prevent an employer from making personnel decisions based on current expectations rather than on how well the employee met the expectations set for him or her at the beginning of the decision period. Finally, when several people are competing for organizational rewards, personnel decisions may be viewed as unfair by those who lose out when the decision is not made with the benefit of a satisfactory performance-appraisal system.

Causing one's fellow needless mental anguish is prohibited by the Torah by dint of the *ona'at devarim* interdict.[4] A nuance of this prohibition that is relevant to the case at hand entails the prohibition of pricing an article that one has no intention of buying.[5] What is objectionable here, according to R. Menahem b. Solomon Meiri (France, 1249–1316), is that pricing an article creates an anticipation on the part of the seller that he will make a sale. This anticipation is dashed when the inquirer decides not to pursue the matter further. While the prospective buyer need not concern himself with the disappointment a vendor may experience should his *serious* price inquiry not result in his making a purchase, pricing an article he has no intention of buying causes the vendor *needless* distress and therefore is prohibited.[6]

Arranging labor relations with the basic elements of a performance-appraisal system constitutes a serious effort on the part of the employer to eliminate needless mental anguish in the workplace. If, despite the implementation of this system, personnel decisions cause employees to experience dashed expectations, the employer cannot be held morally responsible for their disappointments. But what if personnel decisions are made without the benefit of a performance-appraisal system? To the extent that these decisions are perceived by the employees as either arbitrary or inconsistent, the resulting mental anguish they experience should be the responsibility of the employer. Any amount of dashed expectations that could have been avoided had a performance appraisal system been in place should be characterized as needless mental anguish and the responsibility of the employer.

In large organizations, personnel decisions are typically not made by top management. Instead, they are made by supervisors and/or middle-level management. Suppose the organization has no performance-appraisal system in place. Personnel decisions will inevitably result in needless mental anguish. But who violates the *ona'at devarim* interdict? Is it only the supervisor and middle-level manager who make and hand down personnel decisions? What about top management and the owners of the company? Does the failure to institute performance appraisal put them in violation of the *ona'at devarim* interdict? Resolution of this question revolves around the issue of whether *ona'at devarim* is violated even when one inflicts needless mental anguish by means of inaction. Several sources address this issue. One is the following text at Mekhilta Exodus 180:22:

> Said R. Shimon to R. Ishmael: Master! I cannot for the life of me understand what I have done to deserve execution. Whereupon R. Ishmael replied: Have you ever kept a man who came to you for a lawsuit or consultation waiting until you had a drink, put on your shoes and cloak? The Torah stated: *If afflict you afflicted* (Exodus 22:22)—whether a grievous affliction or a trivial one. He answered him: You have consoled me, O master.

It follows from this text that R. Shimon violated *ona'at devarim* by his inaction or passivity. Specifically, by not immediately giving his attention to an anxiety-ridden person, he effectively prolonged that person's state of anxiety, thereby violating *ona'at devarim*.

Another relevant source is the ruling of R. Judah b. Samuel he-Hasid (Germany, ca. 1150–1217) that A should not let himself be seen by B if B's predicament is such that B would be embarrassed to be seen. Illustrating this is the instance when A observes B soliciting charity from C. If A does not quickly move away, B will soon become aware of A's presence[7] and will be embarrassed. To avoid embarrassment for B, A must quickly move away to make sure B will not become aware of his presence. The prohibition R. Judah b. Samuel he-Hasid refers to, according to R. Joseph D. Epstein, is *ona'at devarim*.[8] Here, again, is an illustration of *ona'at devarim* violated by means of inaction or passivity.

Proceeding from the principle that *ona'at devarim* is violated even by means of passivity is the requirement for the owners of a company to arrange labor relations by means of a performance-appraisal system. This is so because their failure to do so will inevitably result in needless mental anguish for their employees.

Lo Tisnah et Ahikha

The halakhic principle of *lo tisnah et akhiha* (do not hate your brother) also points to the implementation of at least some aspects of a performance-appraisal system. This is based on R. Hayyim Ibn Attar's (Jerusalem, 1696–1743) understanding of Leviticus 19:17: "Do not hate your brother in your heart, you must [instead] admonish him, and [in consequence] you will no longer ascribe to him sin." What the Torah adjures here, according to R. Hayyim, is that A should not withhold from expressing to B a complaint he harbors against him. Instead, A should openly confront B with the complaint. Doing so holds the prospect that A will no longer harbor his grievance against B. This is so because, in response to the complaint, B will either satisfactorily excuse his conduct or make amends and correct the objectionable conduct in question.[9]

R. Hayyim's understanding of Leviticus 19:17 finds ready application to labor relations. Applied to the employer, the verse enjoins him not to withhold from an employee a complaint he has against him. Instead, the employer must provide his worker with negative feedback. The purpose of the negative feedback is, however, to give the employee a chance to correct the complaint and/or improve his performance.

The application of *lo tisnah et ahikha* to labor relations requires further clarification in light of the criterion Halakhah adopts for lawful termination of an employee. This criterion consists of unrecoverable loss (*pseida d'lo hadra*).[10]

Illustrating unrecoverable loss is the case of the professional arborist who ruins the saplings he was hired to tend. His failure to plant saplings in accordance with professional standards reduces the proprietor's crop yield from what it could have been had the job been done properly. While the incompetent arborist is held culpable for the saplings he ruins, the potential loss in productivity is speculative and therefore not subject to collection. Since part of the proprietor's loss cannot be recovered, the arborist's malfeasance is regarded as generating an unrecoverable loss.[11]

Decisors dispute whether worker malfeasance in the form of unrecoverable loss warrants summary dismissal. Maimonides (Egypt, 1135–1204) et al. entitle an employer to dismiss without warning a worker guilty of this conduct.[12] R. Abraham b. David of Posquières (France, 1125–1198) and others, however, would not subject a worker to discharge unless he is guilty of three incidents of generating irretrievable loss or is guilty of this conduct after having been warned against it.[13]

Let us now relate the *lo tisnah* requirement to this rishonic dispute. Maimonides' view entitles the employer to dismiss the worker summarily in the irretrievable-loss case. Hence the requirement to warn the worker before dismissal on the basis of *lo tisna* does not apply in that case. But if the loss involved is recoverable, then *lo tisna* should entitle the worker to a warning before he is subject to dismissal.

Indeed, in the recoverable-loss case, one authority entitles the employer with a dismissal right only after three separate warnings are issued to the worker.[14]

The application of *lo tisna* to even the irretrievable-loss case follows, however, from R. Abraham b. David's view. To be sure, three incidents of causing the employer irretrievable loss brand the employee as incompetent and allow the employer to fire him. But the moral force of *lo tisna* disallows the employer from being *indifferent* to the worker's plight. Instead, *lo tisna* requires negative feedback in the form of a warning to the worker. This requirement gives the worker a chance to improve and avoid being fired.

The gap between these two schools of thought is somewhat narrowed by R. Yom Tom Vidal of Tolosa (Spain, 14th cent.). In his understanding of Maimonides, summary dismissal applies only for an employee hired by the community. If an employee is hired privately, summary dismissal is not operative.[15] Presumably, in the latter case, dismissal does not become an option unless the worker establishes a pattern of incompetence (*hazakah*) or a warning is issued to him. By dint of *lo tisna* the requirement to deliver negative feedback after the first incident is, as discussed above, a matter of moral force.

What emerges clearly from the above analyses is that Halakhah is against the *critical-incident* approach to performance appraisal. Under this approach, a supervisor observes employee behavior and documents incidents of negative performance. Instead of providing the employee with negative feedback, the supervisor continues to record negative incidents until a case for dismissal can be made. In the opening vignette Frier made use of this method in arriving at his decision to fire Claudia. Because this method does not provide the employee with an opportunity to correct complaints against him (her), it violates Halakhah.

Another implication of the application of *lo tisna* to labor relations is that the employer should introduce a grievance procedure in the workplace. Out of fear that job security and organizational rewards are jeopardized by confronting supervisors with complaints, subordinates naturally withhold criticism and complaints against the company. Unless management takes the initiative here, complaints against company policy and criticism of management will likely remain mostly suppressed. By encouraging honest, open, and respectful communications, a grievance procedure works to reduce employee discord and engenders higher fulfillment of Leviticus 19:17.

In addition, to the foregoing, several other moral principles obligate an employer to institute performance appraisal in the workplace.

Bakesh Shalom

Interpreting the verse "seek peace [*bakesh shalom*] and pursue it" (Psalms 34:15), Midrash Tanhuma comments:

> The Torah does not command [us] to *pursue* the mitzvot, but rather, *If you come across a bird's nest . . . you must first chase away the mother, and only then may you take the young* (Deuteronomy 22:6–7); *If you come across your enemy's donkey going astray, bring it back to him* (Exodus 23:4); *If you see the donkey of someone you hate lying under its load . . . you must make every effort to help him* [unload it] (Exodus 23:5). In all these cases, if they [these situations] come to your hand, you are commanded to carry out what the Torah requires, but you are not enjoined to actively discover these mitzvah opportunities. But in respect to peace, *seek peace and pursue it*: seek out peace in your place, and pursue it in another place. And this is what Israel did, even though the Almighty told them: *"Now set out and cross the Arnon Brook. See, I have given over Sihon, the Amorite king of Heshbon, and his land into your hands. Begin the occupation! Provoke him into war!"* (Deuteronomy 2:24), [Nevertheless, Israel] pursued peace, as it says: *"Israel sent emissaries to Sihon, king of the Amorites, with the following message: Let us pass through your land. We will not turn aside to the fields and vineyards . . ."* (Numbers 21:21–22).

Note that the biblical source of the mitzvah to promote peace, according to R. Isaac of Corbeil (France, d. 1280), is the verse: "You must love your neighbor as [you love] yourself" (Leviticus 19:18).[16] Now, if the mitzvah to promote peace is rooted in Leviticus 19:18, then *bakesh shalom* speaks not only of an obligation to promote peace among strangers, but *a fortiori* of an obligation to take the initiative in promoting peace and harmony in one's interpersonal relations. The selfsame *a fortiori* reasoning can be applied to Mekhilta's teaching: If *bakesh shalom* is understood as a mandate to seek peace with our enemies, i.e., Sihon, then *a fortiori* it should be understood as a mandate to *foster* peace and harmony in our interpersonal relations.

As a means of promoting good labor relations as well as reducing discord in his labor force, *bakesh shalom* urges an employer to institute performance appraisal in the workplace.

Imitatio Dei

The individual's duty to take the initiative in promoting peace and harmony in his interpersonal relations also emerges from the mitzvah to emulate God's attributes of mercy in our interpersonal conduct.[17] Referred to as *imitatio Dei*, this duty extends beyond emulating the thirteen attributes of God's mercy explicitly enumerated at Exodus 34:6-7. Rather, *imitatio Dei* applies to every manifestation of God's mercy.[18]

Maimonides counts *imitatio Dei* as one of the 613 precepts.[19] The significance of this, as Professor Yizhak Twersky pointed out, is to make *imitatio Dei* not just a theological concept, but a halakhic imperative.[20]

One manifestation of God's mercy is *shalom* (peace).[21] A nuance of this attribute that relates to the employer's performance-appraisal requirement is the mercy God shows us in preventing the outbreak of discord. In this regard, R. Shimon b. Halafta observes that in the first five days of creation, God created an equal number of things for the heaven and the earth.

> On the sixth day, when He came to create man, He said: "If I create man as one of the upper elements of the universe, the upper elements will outnumber the lower by one created object, and if I create him as one of the lower created objects, the lower will outnumber the upper by one created object." What did He do? He created man of the upper as well as of the lower beings; this is proved by what is written: *The Lord God formed man of the dust of the ground* (Genesis 2:7), i.e., out of the lower parts of creation; *And He breathed into his nostrils the breath of life* (ibid.), i.e., out of the upper spheres.[22]

Imitatio Dei, in the form of emulating God's attribute of *shalom*, urges an employer to arrange his labor relations by means of a performance-appraisal system because doing so minimizes discord in the workplace.

The Prohibition Against *Lashon ha-Ra*

Recall that Frier invoked customer complaints as a factor that justified firing Claudia. From the perspective of Halakhah, accepting a customer's complaint against Claudia at face value and taking action against her on the basis of the complaint is prohibited. For one, the customer's complaint may be riddled with exaggeration and inaccuracy, and for all we know, might even be a fabrication. If so, the customer would be guilty of maligning Claudia (*mozi shem ra*). Moreover, even if we assume that the complaint is valid, if Frier accepts it at face value without first *confronting* Claudia and investigating its merits, he would violate the interdict against accepting *lashon ha-ra*.[23]

Without a performance-appraisal system in effect, the laws of *lashon ha-ra* may very well work to frustrate an employer from achieving the performance standard he desires. To illustrate, suppose Frier receives several complaints against Claudia, and Claudia denies each and every one. What Frier then faces is the customer's word against Claudia's word. Since each complaint must be considered as a separate and independent event, firing Claudia based on the *number* of complaints received amounts to giving credence to *lashon ha-ra* and is therefore prohibited conduct. But dealing with complaints makes Frier miserable. A miserable Frier, in turn, drags down the efficiency of the workplace, especially adversely impacting on the productivity of Sugarman, the company's delicate resident poet. Claudia's complaint-riddled performance, therefore, frustrates the emergence of the cheerful, tension-free work environment Frier so desperately desires.

Setting up a performance-appraisal system is the answer. Specifically, at the very outset, Frier should tell Claudia that she is expected to contribute *positively* to a cheerful and tension-free work environment. Receiving three non-trivial complaints against her by three different customers over the span of a year will be taken as evidence that she is not living up to this expectation.

Personal and Monetary Obligations

Various moral principles urge an employer to set up a performance-appraisal system in his workplace. What, however, are the personal and monetary implications of this obligation?

One aspect of the halakhic underpinnings of a performance- appraisal system is represented by the *ona'at devarim* and *lo tisna* interdicts. These interdicts are negative commandments of the Torah. As such, both carry an obligation to incur a loss, if necessary, in order to avoid violating them.

The extent of the financial obligation to avoid violation of a negative commandment of the Torah is a matter of dispute. In the view of R. Mosheh Isserles (Poland, 1525 or 1530–1572), the obligation extends, if necessary, to losing one's entire net worth.[24] Disputing R. Isserles, R. Mosheh Sofer (Hungary, 1762–1839) argues that this stringency obtains only when the negative commandment will be violated in an active manner. When the negative commandment will be violated only in a passive manner, the loss one must incur, if necessary, to avoid violation is up to one-fifth of one's net worth.[25]

Arranging labor relations without a performance-appraisal system will inevitably result in needless mental anguish for the employees and violate for the employer his obligation to provide his workers with negative feedback. To avoid violating *ona'at devarim* and *lo tisna*, the employer is required to incur the necessary expense to set up a basic performance-appraisal system in the workplace.

Another aspect of the halakhic underpinning of a performance-appraisal system is represented by the *bakesh shalom* and *imitatio Dei* principles. These precepts are aspects of the duty to promote the well-being of our fellow (*gemilut hasadim*).[26] When one is confronted with a *hesed* opportunity, the situation may warrant a response in the form of personal attention and/or financial outlay. In respect to toil and effort, Halakhah sets no upper limit on what is expected of an individual in fulfilling a *hesed* opportunity. But as far as financial outlay is concerned, the sages established an upper limit consisting of one-fifth of net worth.[27]

This rule, according to R. Zalman Nehemia Goldberg, applies only when the object of the *hesed* is a poor person. When this is not the case, the rule is modified. In respect to the toil-and-effort component of the mitzvah, it makes no difference whether the target of the *hesed* is poor or not. Accordingly, suppose a rich man is sick: the mitzvah of *bikkur holim* (visiting the sick) requires people to visit him, with no limits placed on this duty in respect to time expended. But there is no obligation to either incur an expense or sustain a loss in connection with attending the needs of those who are not poor. The paradigm here is the mitzvah of restoring lost property to its rightful owner (*hashavat avedah*).[28] The finder is exempt from fulfilling this mitzvah if doing so would entail an expenditure or require him to incur an opportunity cost in the form of forgone earnings.[29] This exemption applies across the board, with few exceptions,[30] to any mitzvah falling within the category of *gemilut hasadim*.[31]

Thus the duty of *gemilut hasadim* urges an employer to devote time and energy to setting up a performance-appraisal system in his workplace. Given the proactive nature of *bakesh shalom* and *imitatio Dei*, this system must be set up at the outset of labor relations rather than in reaction to a workplace that is riddled with discord. Moreover, the proactive nature of these precepts urges an employer to give attention to this matter even outside the workday. But these precepts do not technically require an employer to incur an expense or even an opportunity cost in implementing ideas that would reduce discord in the workplace. One caveat should, however, be noted. R. Judah derives the financial exemption mentioned earlier in connection with *hashavat avedah* from the verse "save when there shall be no needy among you" (*efes ki lo yehiyeh bekha evyon*, Deuteronomy 15:4). The word *efes* is interpreted to mean "end" or "prevent," with the meaning being: "Be careful not to engage in conduct that will drive you to poverty." Commenting on this exemption, R. Judah avers that one who is meticulous about invoking it will himself (as divine punishment) be driven to poverty.[32]

R. Judah's dictum, in the understanding of R. Jehiel Michel Epstein (Belarus, 1829–1908), makes it improper to invoke the exemption when the contemplated loss is not clear-cut. Here, the duty to act beyond the letter of the law (*lifnim mi-shurat ha-din*) requires the passerby to take up the mitzvah.[33] R. Epstein's formulation supports the moral case for urging an employer to arrange labor relations with a performance-appraisal system. Because this system offers the prospect of improving worker morale and productivity, the initial expense should be viewed as an *investment* expenditure rather than as a purely altruistic *hesed* outlay.

The cost of implementing a performance-appraisal system might very well be given to economies of scale. This means that the larger the labor force involved, the lower the per worker cost of implementing the system.

Viewing performance appraisal as an investment outlay given to economies of scale makes a compelling moral case for a large firm to incur the necessary expense of implementing such a system.

All this demonstrates that a duty to set up a performance-appraisal system in the workplace proceeds from the *ona'at devarim* and *lo tisna* interdicts. Moreover, the moral case for instituting this system is reinforced by the *bakesh shalom* and *imitatio Dei* imperatives.

Improving the Basic Performance-Appraisal System

Research in the field of human resources management has brought to light various ways of improving the basic performance-appraisal system described above. Our purpose here will be to relate these research findings to Halakhah.

Self- Assessment

The performance-appraisal system we described earlier is an authoritative model. It casts the supervisor in the role of judge. This model is consistent with the traditional theory that efficiency is achieved by imposing management control over workers' behavior.

Recent research, as Professor Herbert H. Meyer points out, rejects the control approach of management. Few people like a dictatorial boss, and workers do not like having their dependent status accentuated. Instead of the authoritarian model, appraisal reviews between manager and subordinate should be based on the subordinate's self-review. Self-review has several advantages. First, because the employee is not forced into a dependent role, his dignity and self-respect are enhanced. Second, it puts the manager in the role of counselor, not judge. Third, it is more likely to elicit employee commitment to any development plans or goals formulated in the discussion; subordinates are more likely to develop a feeling of ownership in plans and goals that they help to create. Finally, discussions based on subordinates' reviews of their own performance are likely to be more satisfying to both parties and more productive than the more traditional manager-to-subordinate review.

Self-review will, of course, suffer from a self-serving bias on the part of the employee. But this leniency error, in Meyer's view, can be minimized by orienting the self-analysis toward self-development rather than appraisal for administrative purposes.[34]

In their treatment of performance appraisal, Professors Terry L. Leap and Michael D. Crino cite the following cutting-edge system employed by Digital Equipment Corporation. Evaluation begins with self-appraisal. Specifically, the employee is asked to provide each member of his work group with a statement of personal accomplishments and training over the past year. The chairperson of this group collects the reactions of work group members to this statement and forwards them to the ratee. The ratee is then asked to write a performance-appraisal document incorporating the coworker's input. This document is provided to the members of the appraisal committee. After the committee members have had an opportunity to review the document, the entire committee, including the ratee, meet to discuss it. If it is decided that the document needs to be revised, the ratee is asked to revise it, and another meeting is scheduled. When the committee accepts the document, a performance rating is determined and goals for the next performance-appraisal period are set.[35]

Digital Corporation's highly participatory approach to performance evaluation apparently overcomes the leniency error inherent in self-appraisal.

From a Torah perspective, the self-appraisal approach to performance assessment, described above, should find favor. By dint of the *bakesh shalom* and *imitatio Dei* imperatives, it is an employer's duty to foster a harmonious relationship with his employees. To achieve this objective, the employer must move somewhat away from a *strictly* authoritative relationship with his employees and instead exhibit a self-diminutive character trait in his dealings with them. The following nuances of the *bakesh shalom* and *imitatio Dei* imperatives bear this out.

In connection with *bakesh shalom*, the Talmud remarks that there is no one more meek than one who pursues peace.[36] What this dictum imparts is that the person who seeks to promote harmonious relations should possess the quality of selfdiminution.

The same principle emerges from the *imitatio Dei* imperative. Specifically, regarding the potion prescribed for the suspected adulteress (*sotah*), the Torah requires that a parchment inscribed with certain biblical verses is to be dissolved in a solution and the *sotah* be made to drink it. These verses contain God's name. Noting this procedure, R. Ishmael remarks: "Great is peace, for even the Great Name, written though it be in sanctity, did the Holy One, blessed be He, say that it may be blotted out in water, for the purpose of making peace between husband and wife."

Using this manifestation of God's mercy as his model, R. Meir engaged in *imitatio Dei* conduct. The elements of the story are as follows: R. Meir used to deliver discourses on Sabbath evenings. Once the discourse lasted a long time. A certain woman, who had attended the lecture, returned home and found that her husband was angry with her for being so late. The husband swore that he would not let her enter the house until she had spat in the face of the preacher. Several weeks later, the woman's neighbors prevailed upon her to attend R. Meir's lecture with them. Upon seeing them, R. Meir, by means of the Holy Spirit, perceived what had happened. He set out to reunite the woman and her husband. Claiming that he had an eye defect, R. Meir maneuvered so that the woman at his request spit in his face seven times to effect a cure. R. Meir then told the woman: "Go tell your husband: You told me to do it once, and I spat seven times." When R. Meir's disciples asked whether abusing the Torah for this purpose was permissible, R. Meir, citing R. Ishmael's dictum, told them that had engaged in *imitatio Dei* conduct.[37]

What these nuances of *bakesh shalom* and *imitatio Dei* imply for the employer is that he should set up his workplace so that subordinates perceive supervisors as counselors rather than as judges. Using subordinate self-appraisals as the basis for developing skills and nurturing a longterm relationship with the firm are also indicated.

Progress Reviews and Positive Feedback

Researchers have concluded that performance-appraisal feedback should not be confined to one formal, periodic interview to discuss the results of a formal appraisal. Instead, feedback should be a continuous process in the form of a progress review of the goals agreed upon by the subordinate. If the manager has a problem with a subordinate's performance, he should help the employee by coaching him or her on the skills or behavior that will bring good ratings at review time.

Another finding is that positive reinforcement is very important for employee morale and productivity. Without praise, employees assume that the manager is only going to pay attention to them when there are problems.[38]

In regard to positive reinforcement, Gibson cites the example of the Zytec Corporation. If a Zytec employee conducts a meeting that is particularly effective, anyone who attended the meeting can send the employee a memo congratulating him on a job well done. This reinforcement memo, called a "Zystroke," is produced in triplicate. The second copy is for the person who wrote the memo, and the third copy goes to the immediate boss of the individual who was sent the congratulatory note.

This approach is not unique to Zytec. Most firms with total quality management (TQM) programs have procedures for allowing personnel to praise one other.

Moreover, in some companies, memos and thank-you notes are being supplemented by other forms, such as stars that are worn on the collar. For every ten special notes thanking someone for doing a job well, the individual is given a small star, and for every ten small stars, the individual receives a larger star. Over a year's time, an individual can earn two to three large stars, which become part of the person's working garb and are an immediate indication that this individual has been cited by co-workers and supervisors as an excellent performer.[39]

What is salient here from the halakhic standpoint is that arranging labor relations with both continuous and positive feedback goes beyond the objective of eliminating unnecessary discord in the workplace. Avoiding violation of *ona'at devarim* does not require implementation of these ideas, but since they work to enhance interpersonal relations in the workplace, *bakesh shalom* and *imitatio Dei* urge their incorporation into a performance-appraisal system.

Positive feedback recommends itself from another standpoint. This feature in a performance-appraisal system is consistent with the moral responsibility in Judaism of *hakkarat ha-tov* (gratitude).[40]

One caveat should, however, be noted. Implementing these features may entail a major restructuring of the firm and not just an adjustment in the modus operandi of labor-management relations. This would be the case, for instance, when the owner of the business assumes many different functions. Because the employer spreads himself out thin, he naturally does not establish a close working relationship with his employees. Urging the firm to arrange labor relations with both continuous and positive feedback requires a major restructuring expense. Because *bakesh shalom* and *imitatio Dei* require only the expenditure of time and effort but not the incurring of an expense or opportunity cost, a duty to implement these features cannot be identified.

Problem

It was a full two years after her termination from the I. M. Frier Greeting Card Company and Claudia Weinstock was still out of a job. Suspecting that her former boss, I. M. Frier, was bad-mouthing her, Claudia set out to prove that her intuition was correct and get him to stop. Toward this end she enlisted the services of a company called Know the Source (KTS). The company promised Claudia that it would induce Frier to write a job-performance appraisal of her without letting on that it was Claudia herself who had commissioned the inquiry and enjoyed the property rights to the report.

A critical feature of KTS' method of operation was the use of shell companies. A shell company is a company that conducts no business whatsoever and exists in name only. KTS owned licenses to conduct business under one hundred different names.

When Claudia told KTS that it was Frier's practice to make use of a telephone answering machine as a monitoring device for incoming calls, KTS knew that the selection of the right shell company would be critical to its success. Claudia selected the name Stakeholder Variety Shops. In her words:

"Frier will imagine the store wants to arrange to carry his greeting cards. Whenever Frier imagines that calling back will generate business for him, he will even call back long-distance."

In the next phase, Avery Green of KTS connected with Frier and the following conversation took place:

Green: I'm Avery Green of Stakeholders Variety Shops. We have here an application for employment from a Claudia Weinstock. Her resume lists you as her most recent employer. Would you kindly provide us with a candid appraisal of her work?

Frier: I never give references over the phone. If you send me an official request for the appraisal on your firm's letterhead, I'll reply. I also require a signed statement from Claudia that she waives her right to be privy to my appraisal.

After receiving the official letter of request along with Claudia's waiver, Frier fired off the following letter:

Dear Mr. Green:

Claudia Weinstock worked for us for approximately a year. She turned out to be a disaster.

(1) Claudia's computer skills were poor.

(2) She was very presumptuous, often interfering with her superior's prerogatives.

(3) Claudia had a severe attitude problem and many customers complained about her demeanor.

(4) Claudia was both chronically late and absent from her work.

As soon as Claudia received Frier's letter, she made up her mind to sue him for both wrongful discharge and defamation of character.[41]

From a halakhic perspective, analyze the ethics of the conduct of KTS and Claudia. Would your judgment of the ethics of the matter change in a scenario where Frier is willing to send the appraisal without a waiver from Claudia?

1. Frier's obsession about making himself inaccessible is documented in this volume. The interested reader is referred to the case study called "The Mean Boss."

2. Claudia's idea was to go with the cartoon characters but to conclude the message with: "With all my love and an *unlimited* gift certificate at the store of your choice." (Note: no actual gift certificate is included in the greeting card message.)

3. For descriptions of performance-appraisal systems, see H. J. Bernardin and R. W. Beatty, *Performance Appraisal: Assessing Human Behavior at Work* (Boston: Kent, 1984).

4. Leviticus 25:17; Mishnah, Bava Mezia 4:10.

5. Mishnah, Bava Mezia, loc. cit.; R. Isaac b. Jacob Alfasi (Algeria, 1012–1103), Rif, Bava Mezia 58b; R. Asher b. Jehiel (Germany, 1250–1327), Rosh, Bava Mezia 4:22; R. Jacob b. Asher (Germany, 1270–1343), *Tur*, Hoshen Mishpat 228:3; R. Joseph Caro (Israel, 1488–1575), *Shulhan Arukh*, Hoshen Mishpat 228:4; R. Jehiel Michel Epstein (Belarus, 1829–1908), *Arukh ha-Shulhan*, Hoshen Mishpat 228:2.

6. R. Menahem b. Solomon Meiri (France, 1249–1316), *Bet ha-Behirah*, Bava Mezia 59a. Pricing an article with no intention to buy it is prohibited, according to R. Samuel b. Meir (ca. 1080–1174), Rashbam, Pesahim 114b, on account of the possible financial loss this behavior might cause the vendor. While the vendor is preoccupied with the insincere inquiry, serious customers may turn elsewhere.

7. R. Judah b. Samuel he-Hasid (Germany, ca. 1150–1217), *Sefer Hasidim*, 175.

8. R. Joseph D. Epstein, *Mizvat ha-Ezah* (New York: Torath Ha-Adam Institute, 1983), p. 305.

9. R. Hayyim Ibn Attar, *Ohr ha-Hayyim*, Leviticus 19:17.

10. Bava Mezia 109a; Rif, ad loc.; Maimonides (Egypt, 1130–1204), *Yad*, Sekhirut 10:7; Rosh, Bava Mezia 9:38; *Tur*, op. cit. 306:8; *Sh.Ar.*, op. cit. 306:8; *Ar.haSh.*, op. cit. 306:16.

11. Tosafot, Bava Batra 21b; R. Joshua b. Alexander ha-Kohen Falk (Poland, 1555–1614), *Derishah*, *Tur*, op. cit. 306, n. 12.

12. *Yad*, loc. cit., *Tur*, loc. cit., *Sh.Ar.*, loc. cit.

13. R. Abraham b. David of Posquières (France, 1125–1198), R. Solomon b. Abraham Adret (Spain, 1235–1310), R. Nissim b. Reuben Gerondi (Spain, 1310–1375), quoted by R. Joseph Habiba (Spain, early 15th cent.), *Nimmukei Yosef* on Rif, Bava Mezia 109a; R. Yom Tov Vidal of Tolosa (Spain, fl. 14th cent.), *Maggid Mishneh*, *Yad*, Sekhirut 10:7; *Ar.haSh.*, loc. cit.

14. *Nimmukei Yosef*, op. cit.

15. *Maggid Mishneh*, op. cit. For a different understanding of Maimonides, see R. Isser Zalman Meltzer (Russia, 1870–1953), *Even ha-Ezel*, *Yad*, Sekhirut 10:7.

16. R. Isaac of Corbeil (France, d. 1280), quoted by R. Aaron ha-Kohen of Lunel (France, 13th–14 cent.) in *Orhot Hayyim*, vol. 1, siman 5, ot 5.

17. Sotah 14a.

18. R. Naftali Zevi Yehudah Berlin (Russia, 1817–1893), *Emek Neziv*, Sifrei at Deuteronomy 10:2; piska 13.

19. Maimonides, *Sefer ha-Mitzvot*, mitzvat aseh, no. 8; *Yad*, De'ot 1:6.

20. R. Yizhak Twersky, "On Law and Ethics in the *Mishneh Torah*: A Case Study of *Hilkhot Megillah* II:17," *Tradition* 24 no. 2 (Winter 1989): 14–23.

21. Cf. Psalms 29:11; Sanhedrin 37a; Ukzin 3:11; Leviticus Rabbah 9:9; Deuteronomy Rabbah 5:12.

22. Genesis Rabbah 12:7.

23. See p. 302 n. 3 of this volume; Exodus 23:1 and R. Solomon b. Isaac, Rashi ad loc.

24. R. Mosheh Isserles, Rema, *Sh.Ar.*, Orah Hayyim 656:1.

25. R. Mosheh Sofer, *Responsa Hatam Sofer*, Hoshen Mishpat 177 and his gloss at *Sh.Ar.*, Orah Hayyim 656:1.

26. R. Yom Tov Lipmann b. Nathan ha-Levi Heller (Moravia, 1579–1654), *Tosafot Yom Tov*, Mishnah Pe'ah 1:1.

27. Jerusalem Talmud, Pe'ah 2a; commentary of R. Obadiah Bertinoro (Italy, ca. 1445–1505) to Mishnah Pe'ah 1:1.

28. Deuteronomy 22:13.

29. Mishnah, Bava Mezia 2:11; Rif, Bava Mezia 33a; *Yad*, Gezeilah ve-Avedah 12:1; Rosh, Bava Mezia 2:30; *Tur*, op. cit. 264:1; *Sh.Ar.*, op. cit. 264:1; *Ar.haSh*, op. cit. 264:1.

30. R. Goldberg notes two exceptions to this rule: (1) In connection with the mitzvah to honor one's parents, a son is not obligated to incur an expense in attending to the needs of his parents. Nonetheless, should attending to their needs entail an opportunity cost in the form of forgone earnings, he is required to incur this loss for the sake of the mitzvah. (2) A request by a *wealthy* Jew for an interest-free loan takes precedence over the opportunity to lend a non-Jew money with an obligation to pay interest.

31. R. Zalman Nehemia Goldberg, "Ba-Hiyyuvei Gemilut Hesed," in *Yad REM le-Zekker Eliezer Meir Lipschitz* (Jerusalem, 1975), pp. 97–111.

32. Bava Mezia 33a.

33. *Ar.haSh.*, loc. cit.

34. Herbert H. Meyer, "A Solution to the Performance Appraisal Feedback Enigma," *Academy of Management Executives* 5, no. 1 (1991): 68–76.

35. Terry L. Leap and Michael D. Crino, *Personnel/Human Resource Management*, 2nd ed. (New York: Macmillan, 1993), pp. 330–31.

36. Kallah Rabbati 3.

37. Jerusalem Talmud, Sotah 1:4.

38. Meyer, "Solution to the Performance Appraisal Feedback Enigma," pp. 71, 74.

39. Jane Whitney Gibson, *The Supervisory Challenge: Principles and Practices*, 2nd ed. (Englewood Cliffs, N.J.: Prentice-Hall, 1995), p. 216.

40. Cf. Genesis Rabbah 79:6; Exodus Rabbah 1:8, 9:10.

41. Adapted from Joan S. Lublin, "Company Checks Up on Bad-mouthing Bosses," *Wall Street Journal*, November 14, 1996, p. B1.

6. Consumer and Social Ethics in the Marketplace

Wolfgang's Telephone Answering Machine Message

The user of a telephone answering machine records a message in the device that will be heard by callers when no one picks up on incoming calls. Seymour Wolfgang, a philosophy professor at Brickmire College, recorded the following message for his telephone answering machine:

> Hello. You have reached Seymour Wolfgang. I am not available at this moment to take your call. Be assured that your call is very important to me. At the tone, please leave a message. I will get back to you as soon as possible.

When the novelty of using the new technology wore off, Wolfgang realized that he was not inclined to return phone calls to many of the people who left messages on his machine. Soon he found himself only selectively returning calls. The initial guilt Wolfgang felt about ignoring some messages quickly gave way to a serene confidence that he was under no moral obligation to return calls to people he had not specifically invited to call him. Wolfgang found no inconsistency between his recorded friendly promise to return calls as soon as possible and his discretionary conduct in carrying out the promise. As Wolfgang put it:

> Having my name in a telephone directory is not an invitation to the public to call me. Moreover, if the phone rings, I'm under no moral duty to answer it. If I do choose to answer the telephone, I'm under no moral duty to speak to the party at the other end of the line. Consequently, my promise to return calls should be understood as directed only to people I have specifically invited to call me.

In time, Wolfgang learned to use his telephone answering machine to monitor incoming calls. By allowing the telephone message to run until he had ascertained the identity of the caller, Wolfgang could decide which phone calls he wanted to pick up on. What a marvelous way to avoid wasting time in resisting the sales talks of telemarketers. Beyond this benefit, using the telephone answering machine as a monitoring device allowed Wolfgang to control the length of his telephone conversations. Providing a case in point are Professor Wolfgang's telephone conversations with Professor John Stark, his junior colleague at Brickmire College. Stark, who does work in the field of existentialism, frequently uses Wolfgang as a sounding board for his ideas. In the pre–answering machine era, a telephone call from Stark signaled a two-hour ordeal for Wolfgang. No more! Equipped with the answering machine, Wolfgang never picked up when he heard Stark at the other end of the line. Instead, Wolfgang returned the call to Stark's office in close proximity to the latter's 2:00 p.m. class. This ploy ensured that, on Stark's initiative, the conversation would end no later than 1:58 p.m. Depending on his mood, Wolfgang would place his call anywhere between 1:30 and 1:45 p.m. As he dialed Stark's number, Wolfgang would mumble under his breath: "I'm under no obligation to listen to Stark's nitwit ideas; whatever time I give him is generosity on my part."

In evaluating the ethics of Professor Wolfgang's conduct, both the limits of an individual's privacy right and the reasonable expectations of those who are exposed to the telephone message must be considered.

To simplify the investigation of these issues, assume that (1) the messages consist solely of the name and telephone number of the caller with no additional content;[1] and (2) the relationship between the caller and Wolfgang is such that Halakhah does not compel Wolfgang to return the call.[2]

Let us first take up the privacy issue. A ruling by R. Shelomoh Zalman Auerbach (Israel, 1910–1995) on the right of a householder to put off an unexpected visitor seems relevant here. As a preliminary matter, R. Auerbach notes that a householder is under no moral duty either to see an unexpected visitor or to divulge to him why it is inconvenient to see him. Given this right, the principle of *darkhei shalom* (the obligation to foster harmonious relations with one's fellow) permits (requires) the householder to either make his rebuff invisible or to sweeten it so that the visitor will not be offended. Because most people will interrupt whatever they are doing to see an important unexpected visitor, a visitor who is informed that the party he is seeking is unavailable might take this as a slight. Optimal promotion of *darkhei shalom*, according to R. Auerbach, allows a member of the household to inform the visitor that the person he seeks is not home.[3]

R. Auerbach's ruling has direct application to the case at hand. Wolfgang is under no moral duty either to speak on the telephone to people he did not invite to call him or to explain to them why he chooses not to speak to them. By logical extension, Wolfgang has every right to use his telephone answering machine to monitor incoming calls. This argument, however, only works to permit Wolfgang to record a message that he is either unavailable or not at home. To be sure, the message will at times speak an untruth. This would be the case, for example, when the message records that Wolfgang is not home when, in fact, he is standing next to the device, monitoring the call. But the untruth is spoken to avoid a strain with the caller. Hence *darkhei shalom* puts its seal of approval on the message. But *darkhei shalom* does not legitimize an insincere promise to return calls. Such a message only generates dashed expectations and fosters discord, rather than harmony.

We now turn to Wolfgang's contention that his promise to return calls should be understood as directed only to those people he has invited to call him. From the standpoint of Halakhah, Wolfgang's perspective is inverted. The determinative factor is not Wolfgang's intentions, but the understanding of those who are exposed to his recording. Undoubtedly, their opinions will differ. What counts is the opinion of the average or reasonable person in the group. If the average opinion among those exposed to the recording does not take Wolfgang's promise to call back to be directed to the caller at hand, but instead sees it merely as a promise to someone whose call Wolfgang has invited, then Wolfgang's recording is not morally objectionable. When this is not the case, revision of the recording is in order.

But how does Wolfgang determine what the reasonable man reads into his recording? Let us examine several scenarios.

Suppose Wolfgang's home telephone number is listed in the telephone directory. This circumstance makes his number accessible to the entire public. But only a small fraction of these people are likely to call him. Who are these people? His friends, relatives, colleagues, and students. What matters, therefore, in identifying Wolfgang's reasonable man is not the opinion of a representative sample of the entire telephone-using population, but rather the representative opinion of those who are likely to call him.

We take it as a given that Wolfgang's reasonable man does not take the professor's promise to return calls as entirely open-ended. The promise, for instance, is certainly not made to a crank caller who records his telephone number on Wolfgang's machine along with a vile message. Similarly, the promise is not made to the long-distance caller who conveniently omits an instruction to call back collect. To be sure, the aforementioned callers may very well expect to be called back on the basis of Wolfgang's recorded message. But such expectations are, for Wolfgang's reasonable man, outrageous, as only a totally open-ended reading of Wolfgang's recorded message would lead to such a conclusion.

Once we move beyond clear-cut instances that warrant no response, Wolfgang's selective returning of calls runs the risk of dashing the reasonable expectations of his callers and hence might violate the interdict against *ona'at devarim*.[4]

To legitimize use of the message described in the opening vignette, Wolfgang would first have to conduct a survey among his circle of friends, relatives, and associates. If it turns out that a representative sample of this group agrees with his contention that his promise to return calls is directed only to people whom he invites to call him, then use of the message would be legitimized. But if a substantial percentage of those surveyed, say 15 percent, holds Wolfgang to his promise to return calls, then the message violates the expectations of the reasonable man and therefore is unethical.[5]

If Wolfgang runs his answering machine message without first coming up with a validating survey, he will be guilty of making an insincere promise.[6] This is so because Wolfgang intends to return calls only on a selective basis, but his halakhic obligation may, in fact, go considerably beyond what he is prepared to do. Relying on self-assessment instead of halakhic guidance to determine what responsibilities one must assume as a result of making a promise puts to question the sincerity and integrity of the promise itself.

An objection may well be raised against the need for a validating survey. Why can't Wolfgang rely on his own intuition that his message will not generate needless mental anguish for the reasonable man? Recall that the sages devised a proclamation for people to announce that the day's supply of meat was not kosher in the form of the statement: "Meat for the army has fallen into our hands" (*nafla bisra lbnei heila*). The rabbis relied here on their intuition that this formulation would not deceive non-Jews into thinking that the meat was actually kosher.[7] The difference between the two cases is clear. Intuition is reliable only when the decision-maker faces the certainty of adverse consequences should circumstances prove he was in error. The prospect that an erroneous judgment will inflict punishment on the decision-maker works to thrust him into the realm of unbiased thinking. This was the case in the *nafla bisra* incident. If circumstances proved that the rabbis erred in their judgment and that *nafla bisra* misled non-Jews into believing that the meat they were buying was kosher, then the marketplace would become unsettled and the number of complaints against Jewish butchers would proliferate. In addition, the rabbis themselves would be accused of profaning God's name (*hillul haShem*). The knowledge that these frightening consequences follow on the heels of error objectifies the sages' thinking and enhances the reliability of their original assessment.

A different judgment must, however, be made for the case at hand. Suppose experience proves Wolfgang wrong in his assessment that his message does not generate dashed expectations. Will Wolfgang come to realize his error in judgment? Probably not. Among those who are chagrined by his practice of only selectively returning calls, many would regard it as either petty or beneath their dignity to bring the matter up. Others, such as junior colleagues and students, might, in addition, feel uncomfortable and/or intimidated about doing so. As for those who do complain, well . . . that's your unreasonable man! Since a trial run of the recorded message offers little prospect of punishing Wolfgang for an error in judgment, his self-assessment must be regarded as unreliable. If he wants to use the recording, he must first validate his intuition with a validating survey.

A variation of the above case occurs when Wolfgang's number is unlisted. Under this circumstance, his number may not be given to anyone else without his express permission. Doing so violates Jewish privacy law.[8] By holding an unpublished number, Wolfgang implicitly communicates an unwillingness to speak on the telephone to anyone to whom he has not given his number. Under these conditions, his promise to call back must be understood as directed to those he gave his number to and no one else. Accordingly, Wolfgang is under no moral duty to call back anyone to whom he did not give his number.

But what is Wolfgang's obligation to those to whom he gave his number? The case against only selectively returning calls here is compelling. When one's number is listed, handing it to someone signals no more than a willingness to save that person the toil and effort of finding out the number himself. It does not, however, signify as a definite matter an invitation to call. In sharp contrast, when one's number is unlisted and it cannot ethically be obtained by other means, handing it out to someone signifies an invitation to that person to call at his own discretion. If Wolfgang's promise is not to be reduced to a vapidity, his promise to call back must be directed to someone! A minimalist understanding of Wolfgang's promise requires him, therefore, to return the calls of people to whom he handed out his unlisted number.

Suppose a representative sample of those to whom Wolfgang gave his unlisted number reveals that they do not hold Wolfgang to his promise to return calls. Can the reasonable-man criteria be invoked here to free Wolfgang of an obligation to return calls on the basis of his message? No. This is so because Wolfgang's promise here is not directed to the reasonable man but to each and every caller, separately and personally. Thus the search for the reasonable man has no relevance for the above scenario.

Let us examine one final scenario. Suppose the telephone message described in the opening vignette is used by a business firm, say the Irwin Window Dressing Co. Is it ethical for Irwin to record this message for its customers and at the same time return calls only on a selective basis? Placing its number in the business directory should be viewed as Irwin's invitation to the public to call its office and make inquiries. To be sure, Irwin's invitation to call is not a personal one; it is directed to the public at large. Evaluation of the ethics of Irwin's intended policy should therefore turn on whether such a policy dashes the expectations of the reasonable man of the firm's customer base. Given the nature of its product line, its customer base may well be citywide in scope. To legitimize use of the message, Irwin would first have to conduct a survey of its customer base. If it turns out that a representative sample of its customer base agree that selective return of calls does not dash their expectations, the policy then becomes morally acceptable.

Postscript

After due consideration of the moral pitfalls inherent in his conduct of only selectively returning calls, Wolfgang decided to change his recorded message to the following:

Hello. You have reached Seymour Wolfgang. I am not available at this moment to take your call. At the tone, please leave a message. Be assured that whatever you say can and will be used to determine whether or not I will call you back.

I bet you thought Wolfgang had no sense of humor!

1. If the message communicated, for instance, an emergency situation that required immediate contact with Wolfgang, the mitzvah to confer one's fellow with acts of kindness (*gemilat hasadim*) would compel Wolfgang to return the call as soon as possible.

2. Illustrating this circumstance would be a call Wolfgang received from his father or mother. Here, the mitzvah to honor one's parents (*kibbud av ve-aim*) would compel Wolfgang to return the call as soon as possible.

3. R. Shelomoh Zalman Auerbach, quoted by R. Yaakov Fish, *Titan Emet leYaakov*, chap. 5, siman 24.

4. Leviticus 25:17. The Mishnah at Bava Mezia 4:10 enumerates a number of examples of conduct that violate the prohibition against causing someone needless mental anguish. The conduct described in the Mishnah most akin to the case at hand is the prohibition on pricing an article which one has no intention to buy. What is objectionable here, according to R. Menahem b. Solomon Meiri (France, 1249–1316), *Beit haBehirah*, Bava Mezia 59a, is that pricing an article creates an anticipation on the part of the seller that he will make a sale. This anticipation is dashed when the inquirer decides not to pursue the matter further.

Similarly, in the case at hand, if the typical caller expects Wolfgang to return his call on the basis of the recorded message, Wolfgang's failure to do so dashes the reasonable expectations of his callers and hence violates the *ona'at devarim* interdict.

5. For the development of this thesis, please turn to pp. 41–45 of this volume.

6. The prohibition against making an insincere promise is derived by Abaya (4th cent.) at Bava Mezia 49a in the following manner: In connection with the biblical prohibition against false weights and measures, the Torah writes: "Just (*zedek*) balances, just weights, a just ephah, and a just hin you shall have" (Leviticus 19:36). Since the hin is a measure of smaller

capacity than the ephah, its mention is apparently superfluous. If accuracy is required of a measure of a large capacity, it is certainly required in measures of small capacity. This apparent superfluity leads Abaya to connect *hin* with the Aramaic word for "yes," *hen*, giving the phrase the following interpretation: Be certain that your yes is *zedek* (sincere), and (by extension) be certain that your no is *zedek* (sincere). If an individual makes a commitment or an offer, he should fully intend to carry it out.

The duty to ensure that a commitment is made in a sincere manner is referred to as the *hin zedek* imperative.

7. Hullin 94b.

8. Yoma 4b.

Superthief's Advice on Home Security

In *Secrets of Superthief,* Jack Maclean, a former spectacularly successful burglar, contends that setting up an effective home security system is mostly a matter of daring imagination entailing little or no actual expense. Superthief's basic strategy for the homeowner is to play *mind games* with the would-be burglar. The objective of these mind games is to dupe the would-be intruder into believing that he is either ill-equipped to break into your home or that imminent danger awaits him if he does manage to gain entry.

Lauding Maclean's approach to deterring home burglary, Professor David Friedman, an economist, feels that Superthief's prescriptions are generalizable into an economic approach for dealing with conflict: To prevail in a conflict situation, it is not necessary to actually defeat the enemy or to make it impossible for him to defeat you. Instead, all that must be done is to make it *against the enemy's self-interest* to continue his objectionable conduct.

With slight variations, Superthief's program for home security is presented by Friedman as including the following ideas:

1. Place a large dog-feeding dish or a jumbo-sized rubber bone in the backyard. These objects will dupe the prowler into believing that there is a ferocious dog lurking about nearby. This sobering thought will assuredly keep him away from your property.

2. Make use of warning stickers that refer to imaginary alarm systems—imaginary not only in that you do not have them, but because nobody else has them either. Design the sticker, for instance, to warn the would-be intruder that your home is protected by a *laser* alarm system that features both active and passive defenses. To enhance the ominous effect of the message, disavow any liability to intruders on account of injuries sustained. Finally, to enhance the credibility of the ploy, be sure to credit the system to a *fictitious* company, and for good measure, provide an address as well (e.g., Laserlarm, Inc., Cupertino, CA).

A competent burglar may know how to deal with all the varieties of burglar alarms that really exist, but how can he know how to deal with one you fabricated while designing the sticker?

3. Tape a danger warning note to the backdoor of your home. The message could, for example, warn the addressee that the exterminators have come and the "back rooms" have not yet been aired. For good measure, add a P.S. that Saddam is sleeping in the kitchen.[1] Pragmatic inference will lead the prowler to identify Saddam with a vicious pit bull (can you imagine a poodle named Saddam?).[2]

Superthief's Advice and Halakhah

The common denominator behind Superthief's burglar-repelling ideas is the use of lies and false impressions to thwart the designs of the prowler. In light of the prohibitions against *sheker* (falsehood)[3] and *geneivat da'at* (creating a false impression),[4] these tactics can be put to question.

Several considerations point to the conclusion that the various tactics described above do not violate the *sheker* prohibition.

One mitigating factor is that the stratagems amount to nothing more than a bluff to counteract prohibited conduct on the part of the would-be intruder. An analogous case is the recourse Halakhah offers an employer who stands to suffer a *material* loss as a result of a work stoppage by his day-laborer (*po'el*). While the right of the *po'el* to withdraw without incurring penalty for the unfulfilled portion of his contract is generally recognized,[5] it is suspended when the employer would suffer a *material* loss if the work is not given immediate attention. Faced with the prospect of a work stoppage here, the employer may promise the recalcitrant worker a raise as an inducement to complete the work. Should the tactic succeed, the employer bears no responsibility to pay the differential[6] and is entitled to recover the extra wage in the event he paid it.[7]

Another consideration in respect to the *sheker* issue is that this prohibition is suspended when the falsehood is designed to promote peace and harmony. Use of the bluffing techniques described above works to avert a possible violent confrontation between the prowler and the homeowner and/or bystanders. This is so not only from pragmatic considerations but also from the standpoint of the legal environment the break-in creates. Breaking into someone's property brands the burglar a *rodef* (one who pursues another with the intent to kill him).[8] Though the burglar's original design is merely the theft of property, the presumption of resistance on the part of the proprietor forces the burglar to be prepared to eliminate him should he be discovered in the act.[9] Given the life-threatening danger the householder faces from the burglar, Halakhah confers him with a license to eliminate the burglar upon discovering him. Relatedly, the bystander is duty bound to extricate the proprietor from the life-threatening danger, even to the extent of eliminating the burglar if necessary.[10] Since a *state of war* theoretically exists between society and the burglar, bluffing stratagems employed to discourage the burglar from his designs prevents this state of war from coming into being.

The *geneivat da'at* issue for the case at hand can be dismissed on even more fundamental grounds. This interdict prohibits making use of false impressions to secure something that one is *otherwise not entitled to*. But the homeowner is certainly entitled to keep his property away from a thief! Making use of bluffing stratagems for the purpose of discouraging the thief from his designs secures for the proprietor nothing to which he is not fully entitled.

Supporting this formulation of the *geneivat da'at* interdict is the treatment in the responsa literature of the issue of whether an individual is permitted to sham a youthful appearance by dying his beard, for the purpose of enhancing his chances to secure employment. Addressing himself to this question, R. Mosheh Mordecai Epstein (Israel, 1866–1933) permits the conduct, provided that the employer's expectations of the employee's performance will be met. Realizing that productivity could decline sharply with advancing age, R. Epstein points out that, in the final analysis, the legitimacy of the conduct rests on the accuracy of the self-assessment of the job seeker.[11] Advancing a similar analysis, R. Eliezer Meir Preil (New Jersey, 1881–1934) arrives at the same conclusion.[12] Concurring with these rulings is R. Mosheh Feinstein (New York, 1895–1986).[13]

Proceeding from the above rulings is the permissibility of creating a false impression for the purpose of counteracting an unwarranted bias. To be sure, self-assessment plays a crucial role in making the judgment that absent the employer's *unwarranted* bias, the job applicant would have been hired. But self-assessment is very subjective. What this points to is that it is reliable only when the subjective element can be kept to a minimum. This would be the case when both the job title and the productivity expectations of the employer are well defined and the self-assessment relates to the ordinary, daily routine, as opposed to the hypothetical realm.[14]

The legitimacy of using the mind game technique to repel burglars is bolstered by the consideration that self-assessment plays no role in making the judgment that the bluffing ploys secure nothing for the homeowner that he is not otherwise entitled to.

Repelling Good as Well as Bad People

Another genre of mind game with the would-be burglar entails the use of a device that repels burglars but also frightens away innocents and hence discourages them from making legitimate contact with the homeowner. Illustrating such a device is the use of a soundtrack to broadcast the howling and barking sounds of a vicious dog. Such a device will not only repel thieves, but will discourage innocents from ringing the homeowner's front doorbell. This conduct violates R. Shimon b. Lakish's dictum: "Whoever raises a vicious dog in his house prevents kindness from coming into his house."[15]

Addressing himself to this dictum, R. Solomon b. Isaac (Rashi, France, 1040–1105) rationalizes it with the comment that "a wild dog will not let the poor approach one's door."[16] While R. Shimon b. Lakish's dictum refers to the prohibition on raising a vicious dog, the underlying logic of the interdict should extend it to broadcasting a soundtrack of the howls and barks of a vicious dog. In both instances, the poor will be driven away and the householder's home will become a place that withholds kindness.

On the basis of R. Shimon b. Lakish's dictum, it should also be prohibited for a householder to affix a BEWARE OF DOG sign on his front door. This prohibition holds whether or not there is an actual dog lurking inside. In both instances, the poor will be driven away and the householder's home will become a place that withholds kindness.

Free-Riding on the Reputation of an Established Firm

Free-riding on the name of a *real* home-security firm is a logical extension of Superthief's mind game technique. Toward this end, wire and tape the windows of your home without actually installing any burglar alarm system. For maximum deceptive impact, replicate as best you can the materials, colors, and shape of the devices a real company employs in installing its alarm system. Finally, display the name of the company selected, say, Mahteret company, along with its telephone number, in one of the front windows.

While the mind game technique for deterring home burglary represents a legitimate use of ruse in Halakhah, free-riding on the name of an established alarm company is prohibited conduct. Setting up a bogus alarm system under the Mahteret label could very well exert a ruinous impact on the business of this company. All it takes to unmask the charade is one successful burglary. When that happens, the company's reputation among homeowners will suffer. Moreover, burglars will find homes protected by the Mahteret label more inviting targets than those protected by competing companies. What the homeowner's ruse does is to tie the fortunes of Mahteret both to the delicate secrecy that underlies the deterrent effect of the bogus system and to the continuation of his good fortune in not being victimized by a successful break-in. Hence, setting up a bogus alarm system under the Mahteret label constitutes for the homeowner an actionable tort.

A variation of the above case is the issue of whether it is permissible to set up a bogus alarm *business* that operates under its own label. Most basic to resolving this issue is the recognition that without a marketplace of authentic alarm systems, the deterrent effect of a bogus alarm system would be entirely nil. Thus, setting up a bogus alarm business amounts to expropriating the toil and effort of established firms for commercial gain. Such action is a violation of Halakhah's prohibition against *hassagat gevul* (unfair encroachment into a competitor's business).[17]

Problem 1

Boris Klugman, an economics major at the men's division of Brickmire College, was enrolled in Professor Zelig Regenstein's intermediate microeconomics course. When Regenstein announced the date for the midterm exam, Klugman realized that it was on the same day as his sister's wedding in Detroit. With considerable trepidation, Klugman approached the professor for a make-up exam at some later date. To his surprise, Regenstein was extremely accommodating, quipping: "Don't worry, you can even stay for the *Sheva Berakhot*. I'll reschedule your exam a week later." Grapevine intelligence had it that over the last ten years Regenstein had established a pattern of composing makeup exams for the men's division based on a combination of questions from this year's and last year's women's division exams. Because Regenstein responded so warmly to his request for a makeup, Klugman felt more than a twinge of guilt when he arranged with Shalhavet, a counterpart at the women's division, to mail him the required micro exams at a Detroit address.

Well, when Klugman arrived for his makeup, he was shocked to find that the exam was *this year's men's division micro exam*. Because Klugman relied on grapevine intelligence, he had never bothered to try to pry exam questions from his classmates. As he muddled through the exam, Klugman felt both *stupid* and *betrayed* by Regenstein.

The next day, Klugman received a message to visit Professor Regenstein before class. To say the least, Klugman lived on a steady diet of tranquilizers up to the time of the meeting. As he entered Regenstein's office, the professor greeted him with a smile and said: "As I graded your exam it became evident to me that you had no advance knowledge of the questions. Otherwise, you would have done a lot better! You resisted the temptation to pry the questions from your classmates, even though I did not explicitly forbid you to do so. *Because I admire the trait of honesty*, I'm giving you a bonus of ten extra points. Let it be known that Regenstein rewards honesty!"

1. Evaluate the ethics of Regenstein's makeup policy. Was Regenstein guilty of *geneivat da'at* for switching exams with Klugman?

2. Is Klugman obligated to confess the truth regarding his "honesty"? Cite sources in your answer.

Problem 2

Cornelius Rothschild, a loan officer at the First National Tea Bank of Boston, recounts the following bizarre incident: One bright morning, a farmer by the name of Seymour Parsley, smoking a corn pipe and clad in a wide straw hat and overalls, approached his desk for a $200 loan. A quick check revealed that Parsley owned a $100,000 CD at the bank along with other substantial accounts. Needless to say, Rothschild decided to go along with the request and play it by the rules. The following exchange took place between Rothschild and Parsley:

Rothschild: Our interest rate is 17 percent. We're taking the $34 interest charge up front. In addition we require collateral.

Parsley: That's fine. I'll give you a $10,000 U.S. Savings Bond as collateral. But I need assurances that my Savings Bond will be safe with you.

Rothschild: Don't worry, we'll keep the $10,000 Savings Bond in our vault.

The same scenario repeated itself three years in a row. The fourth time around, Rothschild gathered up enough courage to blurt out:

"For the life of me, I can't figure out why a man that has substantial accounts with us and a $10,000 Savings Bond needs a $200 loan."

With a mischievous smile on his face, Parsley muttered in response:

"Can you think of a *cheaper* way to *rent* a safety deposit box?"

Did Seymour Parsley's conduct violate *geneivat da'at* law?

Problem 3

Because of the lead time necessary to prepare the graduation program, Brickmire College compiles its list of June degree recipients even before all the final grades are in for the spring semester. Moreover, the list is compiled before degree candidates are certified as having passed the Graduate Record Examination (GRE) in their majors. Getting a passing grade on the GRE is an exit requirement at Brickmire for all students. On the nonacademic side, the list of graduates is compiled before the bursar certifies that the degree candidate is not in arrears in tuition payment. Brickmire's procedure makes it possible for someone to be listed as a graduate but not be an *actual* June degree recipient.

Rubie Indigo was listed as a June B.A. degree recipient at Brickmire, but because of a deficiency he had, and was fully aware of, would not receive his degree in June. Rubie was "working on" correcting the deficiency and was planning to receive his degree as early as September and certainly not later than January. Before Rubie actually removes his deficiency, is it halakhically permissible for him to present himself as a the holder of a B.A. from Brickmire College? With the aim of forestalling a potential employer from contacting Brickmire to verify his graduation, is it halakhically permissible for Rubie to show his name on Brickmire's June graduation program to a job interviewer? In answering these questions, does it make a difference why Indigo will be denied a June degree?

Problem 4

This year the student senate at Brickmire College passed a resolution requiring faculty to put copies of their final examinations on permanent file in the dean's office. These old examinations would be made available to interested students.

At the faculty assembly, Dr. Lance Wineman, senior economics professor, spoke against the proposal.

"Mark my words," he said, "this is just the beginning. We're operating on a slippery slope. Next year the senate will require us to put both our midterms and quizzes on file. This process will culminate in a requirement to tape our classroom lectures and put the transcripts of these tapes on file, and I suspect that the latter requirement will be at faculty expense" (polite laughter).

"From an educational standpoint," he continued, "the proposal we have in front of us is a disaster. We all try to encourage our students to become intellectually curious. From my standpoint, progress in this direction is made when a student takes on an assignment without first asking himself, 'Will I be tested on this material?' The filing requirement sends a signal to our students, particularly to those of them who aspire only to make a grade in the B range, that mastery of the course is synonymous with mastery of the old test questions. If the proposal passes, I intend to make each new exam as different as possible from the old exams on file."

At Brickmire a student senate proposal becomes school policy unless it is vetoed by a two-thirds majority of the faculty assembly. Because those opposed to the measure could not muster the necessary two-thirds majority to accomplish the veto, the filing requirement became school policy.

Once the filing requirement has become school policy, are students legitimately entitled to expect that current examinations will resemble the old ones in some shape or form? Assuming that the expectation is reasonable, what percentage of the old questions, at least in general form, without repeating old numbers, must be incorporated in the current exam? In the policy environment of the filing requirement, is it ethical for Wineman to deliberately design his exams so that they will not resemble his old exams?

Problem 5

During a hostage situation in North Carolina's Central Prison, officials agreed to the demand of transfers for the hostage takers in exchange for release of the hostages. After the hostages were released, the state reneged. An aide to the governor stated, "If anyone is offended by the fact that these inmates may have been misled, that's just tough. You don't allow somebody to bargain his way out of prison; you don't reward a terrorist act."[18]

From the perspective of Halakhah, evaluate the ethics of the prison officials' handling of the hostage crisis. How would Kushta handle the hostage crisis?

1. In Friedman's text (see n. 2 below), the P.S. reads: "Rommel is in the bedroom."

2. David D. Friedman, *Price Theory* (Cincinnati: SouthWestern Publishing Co., 1986), pp. 45–57.

3. Exodus 23:7.

4. For the biblical source of the *geneivat da'at* interdict, please turn to p. 35 of this volume.

5. Bava Mezia 10a.

6. Bava Mezia 75b; R. Isaac b. Jacob Alfasi (Algeria, 1012–1103), Rif, ad loc.; Maimonides (Egypt, 1135–1204), *Yad*, Sekhirut 9:4; R. Jacob b. Asher (Germany, 1250–1327), *Tur*, Hoshen Mishpat 333:3; R. Joseph Caro (Israel, 1488–1575), *Shulhan Arukh*, Hoshen Mishpat 333:58; R. Jehiel Michel Epstein (Belarus, 1829–1908), *Arukh ha-Shulhan*, Hoshen Mishpat 333:18–22.

A halakhic basis for the use of the bluffing tactic to counteract clearly unethical conduct can be derived from the verse "With a pure person you act purely, and with a crooked person you act crookedly" (II Samuel 22:27). See the discussion of this verse at Megillah 13b. See also Ta'anit 25a and Yevamot 63a.

7. *Yad*, loc. cit., *Ar.haSh.*, op. cit. 333:19.

8. R. Mosheh Isserles (Poland, 1525–1572), Rema, *Sh.Ar.* 4, op. cit. 425:1.

9. Rava, Sanhedrin 72a; *Yad*, Genevah 9:9; *Ar.haSh.*; op. cit. 425:10.

10. Exodus 22:12; *Yad*, op. cit. 9:7; *Ar.haSh.*, op. cit. 425:10.

11. R. Mosheh Mordecai Epstein, *Responsa Levush Mordecai* 24.

12. R. Eliezer Meir Preil, *Ha-Me'Or* 1:267.

13. R. Mosheh Feinstein (New York, 1895–1986), *Iggerot Mosheh*, Yoreh De'ah 2:61.

14. For an elaboration of this point, see pp. 52–54 of this volume.

15. Shabbat 63a.

16. Rashi at Shabbat 63a ad loc.

17. For exposition of this principle, see pp. 72–74 of this volume.

18. *New York Times*, March 26, 1982. For an analysis of this case from the perspective of secular business ethics, see Francis V. Burke, Jr., "Lying During Crisis Negotiations: A Costly Means to Expedient Resolution," *Criminal Justice Ethics*, Winter–Spring 1995, pp. 49–62.

The Crest Hollow Affair

Kornfeld and Ziskind reside within several blocks of each other in the Flatbush section of Brooklyn. Members of different synagogues, they are socially only nodding acquaintances. Since their paths hardly ever cross, it was indeed a big surprise for Kornfeld to notice Ziskind amidst the crowd attending Torah Academy's annual dinner at the Crest Hollow in New Jersey. The guest of honor at the event was Aytan Kramer, a wealthy businessman with whom Kornfeld had some commercial ties. At $300 a plate the dinner was quite expensive. Adding to the expense was the circumstance that Kornfeld's wife, Zlota, had decided to go on a shopping spree that afternoon. With the family car unavailable for the evening, Kornfeld had to incur the additional expense of $65 to take a car service to the affair. Gleefully repeating to himself "I've just saved $65," Kornfeld waded through the crowd toward Ziskind with the intention of securing a ride back to Flatbush. After exchanging pleasantries with Ziskind, Kornfeld sheepishly asked him for a ride. To his chagrin, Ziskind did not spontaneously respond in the affirmative. Instead, only after an agonizing pause did the begrudging reply ring out in an annoyed tone: "Okay, but I'm leaving right after the main course. Be sure to meet me in the lobby by no later than 10:30 p.m."

Mindful of Ziskind's deadline, Kornfeld found himself nervously checking his watch every few minutes. While seated at his table, Kornfeld recalled that the yeshiva had chartered a bus for the convenience of the Flatbush invitees. "Surely, unoccupied seats will be available," he mused to himself. For a fleeting moment Kornfeld toyed with the notion of remaining at the affair to its conclusion and securing a "free ride" aboard the bus back to Flatbush. This option was, however, quickly quashed once Kornfeld began to ponder the opportunity cost of suffering through the after-dinner speeches. The arrival of a succulent steak at his place setting at 10:28 was not enough to sway Kornfeld to stay. Out of fear that he would miss his ride, Kornfeld jumped out of his seat and raced toward the lobby.

Ziskind never showed up at the appointed time. Until he finally turned up at 10:55, Kornfeld found himself alternating between pacing back and forth in the lobby and running back into the hall to make sure Ziskind had not left via a different exit.

On the trip back to Flatbush the icy silence between driver and passenger finally broke when Ziskind remarked, as the car approached the Washington Bridge, "Kornfeld, you are a man of good fortune; were it nor for meeting me here, you would have been out $65 for a car service—plus tolls." Taking this remark as a less than gentle hint to pay the $4 toll, Kornfeld began fumbling for his wallet. Before he got a chance to articulate a word, Ziskind had already stiffly acknowledged Kornfeld's gesture to pay the toll.

In the aftermath of the disillusionment and frustration he suffered at the Crest Hollow affair, Kornfeld absorbed a powerful lesson. In the future, before he went to a charity dinner, he would do the necessary homework. Several weeks before the affair, Kornfeld resolved, he would call the yeshiva and ascertain who was coming to the affair from Flatbush. Surely there would be someone whom he could ask for a ride without suffering the hassle he had experienced with Ziskind.

The Crest Hollow Affair and Halakhah

Before the ethics of asking Kornfeld to pay the tolls can be dealt with, the more fundamental issue of whether Ziskind is legally or at least morally bound to accede to Kornfeld's request for a ride must be addressed. Consider that Kornfeld's request entailed no expense or disadvantage for Ziskind. Kornfeld requested only a ride, leaving the time of departure to the convenience of Ziskind. Moreover, acceding to the request would not take Ziskind out of his way. Finally, since Ziskind was traveling alone, Kornfeld's presence would not invade any intended private conversations. Since Kornfeld's benefit entails no loss for Ziskind, the request should be categorized as *zeh neheneh ve-zeh lo haser* (this one benefits and the other loses nothing; hereafter *zeh neheneh*). Denying a fellow a benefit when it costs one nothing is regarded by the sages as reflecting the character trait of the people of Sodom.[1] In some instances, the Bet Din (a Jewish court) will coerce (*kofin*) an individual not to act in the manner of the Sodomites.[2]

Would a Bet Din *order* Ziskind to accede to Kornfeld's request for a ride? Perhaps not. The *kofin* principle has its limitations. In the opinion of one school of thought, led by Tosafot, *zeh neheneh* is only an *ex post* liability-exemption rule, but does not work to allow someone to affirmatively make use of another's property. A case in point is the squatter case discussed at Bava Kamma 21a: A settles on B's property without the latter's knowledge. The said property had not been put up for rent by B. When B discovers that A is squatting on his property, he makes a rental claim against A for the period of occupancy. Since A's action entails no loss for B, A bears no compensation responsibility for his period of occupancy. Nonetheless, having discovered A on his premises, B is allowed to evict him. B's right to do so obtains, according to Tosafot, even if he has no intent to either rent or use the property himself.[3]

Following Tosafot's line, R. Aaron ha-Levi (Spain, 1235–1300) avers that the *kofin* principle applies only when one does not use the other's property. To illustrate: Suppose A seeks to build on his own property opposite a neighbor's (B's) windows. B's objection that A's building will block his light is valid. But if A offers to build new windows for B, a continued objection by B would be Sodomitic, and the Bet Din will uphold A. R. Aaron ha-Levi continues:

> But to permit one to *affirmatively* make use of another's property, we do not apply *kofin*, and it would be impossible to rule otherwise, for if it was so ruled, there would be no end to the matter, and everyone would be attempting to coerce his neighbor in a like fashion. Thus, Rabbenu Asher and Ritva have ruled that in such circumstances we do not apply the *kofin* rule.[4]

Let us apply the above conceptualization of the *kofin* principle to the case at hand. To be sure, Kornfeld's request for a ride entails no expense or disadvantage for Ziskind; but the request entails allowing Kornfeld to make use of Ziskind's property. Thus Ziskind is apparently within his rights to refuse Kornfeld's request.

Rejection of the *kofin* principle here should, however, be reserved. Let us consider the rationale behind Tosafot's conceptualization of the *kofin* principle.

In his analysis of Tosafot's view, R. Shimon Shkop (Lithuania, 1860–1940) points out that ownership fundamentally manifests itself with the element of *control*. The squatter's plea confronts the owner, not only with a request to make use of the land gratis, but also with a demand that the owner relinquish his control of the said property for the period of occupancy. Since the great majority of people harbor a preference to retain control of their property, denying the squatter's request does not reflect a Sodomite character.[5]

Applying R. Shkop's rationale of Tosafot's view to the case at hand would call for Ziskind to accede to Kornfeld's request for a ride. Since Ziskind is not being asked to *relinquish control* over his car, but only to accept Kornfeld as a passenger along the planned route, denying the request amounts to Sodomite behavior.

Another school of thought, led by R. Mordecai b. Hillel (Germany, 1240–1298), conceptualizes the *kofin* principle more broadly. In this formulation, B's request to make affirmative use of A's property is not always illegitimate. The request is illegitimate only when A intends to use the property himself or has at least the *possibility* of renting it out to someone else, if he so desires, at the time the request is made. If A does not intend to use the property himself and, in addition, has no possibility of renting it out at the time the request is made, A's denial of B's request would be Sodomitic. Here, the Bet Din will direct A to allow B to make use of the property.[6]

Application of the above formulation to the case at hand should make it mandatory for Ziskind to accede to Kornfeld's request for a ride. Note that Ziskind had no intention of making use of the empty space in his car for storage or any other purpose at the time Kornfeld made his request for a ride. Consider also that Ziskind does not have a livery license to conduct a car service business, and therefore the opportunity to hire himself out as a car service at the time Kornfeld made his request was not open to him. Hence denying the request is Sodomitic on the basis of R. Mordecai b. Hillel's criterion. The Bet Din would order Ziskind to accept Kornfeld as a passenger along the route back to Flatbush without charge.

This judgment is reinforced by the consideration that Ziskind is not being asked to relinquish *control* of his car, but only to accept Kornfeld as a passenger along the planned route. Denying the request amounts to Sodomitic behavior.

The *Galei A-Da'ata* Caveat

Another consideration in the matter at hand is the following caveat Tosafot offer in respect to the *zeh neheneh* exemption: If an individual seeks a benefit free of charge, but demonstrates that he is prepared, if necessary, to incur an expense to acquire the benefit (*galei a-da'ata d'niha leh be-haza'a*; hereafter, *galei a-da'ata*), he forfeits thereby his *zeh neheneh* exemption.[7] R. Jacob b. Asher (Germany, 1270–1343) specifically applies this principle to the squatter case discussed above.[8]

Galei ada'ata is apparently operative in the Crest Hollow affair. Consider the following: Kornfeld arrived at the affair via a car service. By expending $65 for the trip, Kornfeld clearly demonstrated that he was prepared, if necessary, to incur a transportation expense in connection with attending the affair. Kornfeld's *galei ada'ata* should therefore vitiate the case for requiring Ziskind to give him a ride back to Flatbush.

A counteracting factor to consider, however, is that Kornfeld's *galei ada'ata* expressed itself in a rather weak fashion. Kornfeld made no explicit declaration to anyone that he would be prepared, if necessary, to pay for the trip back to Flatbush. Instead, Kornfeld's preparedness to do so was manifested only by virtue of his lifestyle, which consists of usually but not always paying for his transportation costs. Perhaps lifestyle is not a sufficiently strong indication to vitiate the *zeh neheneh* exemption.

Supportive of the above contention is the comment of R. Jehiel Michel Epstein (Belarus, 1829–1908) on the *galei ada'ata* principle as it pertains to the squatter case. In his view, *galei ada'ata* removes the *zeh neheneh* exemption only when the squatter's past history was to rent premises for his lodging. But when this is not the case, anything short of an explicit declaration to the owner that the rent would be paid results in the *zeh neheneh* exemption remaining intact.[9]

What emerges from R. Epstein's comment is that lifestyle in and of itself is not a strong enough indication to establish *galei ada'ata*. For this criterion to be met, there must be an explicit declaration of willingness to pay.

If we change the circumstances of the Crest Hollow affair just a bit, we can arrive at the conditions necessary to make the *galei ada'ata* principle operative. Let us assume that Kornfeld arranges for a car service to take him back to Flatbush. While waiting outside the hall for the car, he meets Ziskind. Anticipating that Ziskind will accede to his request for a ride, Kornfeld hurriedly runs to the nearby pay phone to cancel the car service. When Kornfeld makes his request for a ride, Ziskind is aware that he has just canceled his order for a car service. Since *galei ada'ata* is met here, denying Kornfeld's request for a *free* ride should not be regarded as Sodomitic.

Conferring legitimacy to Ziskind's denial of Kornfeld's request in the latter instance is, however, not clearcut. We take note that R. Jacob's application of the *galei ada'ata* caveat to the squatter case is disputed by R. Solomon b. Jehiel Luria (Ukraine, 1510–1594).[10] Following this line, R. David Tebele b. Moses (Belarus, 1792–1861) posits that *galei ada'ata* removes the *zeh neheneh* exemption only in cases analogous to the source case for this principle:

> If a man [A] has fields surrounding those of another [B] on three sides and fences the first, second, and third, the other [B] is not bound [to share the expenses]. R. Yose said, if he [A or B] takes upon himself the fourth, the whole cost [his share] devolves upon him [B].[11]

Various interpretations of the above case have been advanced by the talmudic commentaries. R. David Tebele's interpretation follows the line proposed by Rashi, who understands the fencing activity to refer to the inner fences that separate A's fields from B's.[12] The salient feature of the fencing case, in R. David Tebele's view, is that the construction project is inherently one of mutual benefit to the adjoining property owners. It protects A from B's visual trespass and protects B from A's visual trespass. Nevertheless, since private activities are not usually conducted in a field, credence is given to B's claim that he was not interested in securing privacy in his field. Consequently, B cannot be made to share in the expense of the fences A built. But if B builds the fourth fence himself, he is made to share in the expense of all four fences. By building the fourth fence, B, at the very least, communicates an interest in securing the benefit of privacy in his field. To be sure, B's action does not necessarily communicate a willingness to share in the expense of the four fences. But *galei ada'ata* in respect to securing the said benefit is sufficient to obligate B to share in the expense of the four fences. R. David Tebele's understanding of *galei ada'ata* puts him at odds with Tosafot, who regard *galei ada'ata* as vitiating a *zeh neheneh* claim only when it entails the communication of willingness to incur the necessary expenses.[13]

R. David Tebele rejects R. Jacob's application of *galei ada'ata* to the squatter case. *Galei ada'ata* vitiates the *zeh neheneh* claim only when the said benefit had already been produced by A for B but B could previously not be made to pay its value to him.[14] By extension, the circumstance that Kornfeld had ordered a car service to Flatbush before he asked Ziskind to give him a ride does not vitiate the *zeh neheneh* basis for requesting the free ride.

The Moral Imperative Against Sodomitic Behavior

As is demonstrated in the preceding sections, the parameters for judicial intervention in *zeh neheneh* cases are a matter of dispute. A Bet Din's refusal to order the defendant in a *zeh neheneh* case not to act in a Sodomitic manner does not in any way signal that the court finds the defendant's conduct morally acceptable. This is so because the court will not intervene in every private dispute. There will remain a slice of human conduct where condemnation and/or avoidance of Sodomitic conduct is left to self-regulation. Standing up for one's rights is morally acceptable, but *obsessively* insisting on one's rights to the point of creating excessive legal and psychological barriers between oneself and one's fellow man amounts to embracing a Sodomitic philosophy. Professor Aaron Kirschenbaum reads this attitude into the second authority quoted in the Mishnah at Avot 5:10.

> There are four types of people: . . . one who says, "What is mine is mine, and what is yours is yours," that person is of the common type, but some say such is a characteristic of the inhabitants of Sodom.

According to Professor Kirschenbaum, the second view in the Mishnah expresses the thought that obsessive preoccupation with private concerns can easily lead to a callous and even total neglect of the concerns of others. Such a mindset bespeaks a Sodomitic personality.[15]

Supporting Professor Kirschenbaum, in the opinion of the writer, is the following talmudic discussion regarding a Hebrew bondsman (*eved ivri*) who desires to remain with his master beyond his six-year term:

> *Because it has been good for him with you* (Deuteronomy 15:16). This teaches that your servant shall be "with you" in food and "with you" in

drink. That is, it should not be that you eat bread made of fine flour, and he eats bread made of inferior flour; that you drink aged wine, and he drinks new wine; that you sleep on soft mattresses, and he sleeps on straw. On account of this it was said: Anyone who buys a Jewish servant has virtually bought a master for himself.[16]

Explicating the contention that "anyone who buys a Jewish servant has virtually bought a *master* for himself," Tosafot, quoting the Jerusalem Talmud, aver that it refers to the following circumstance: The master has in his possession only one pillow. Taking the pillow for himself is unacceptable, as it violates the *equal* living standard requirement. Denying the pillow to both himself and the Hebrew bondsman is also objectionable, as it constitutes Sodomitic behavior. Because the master has no choice but to give the pillow to the servant, the master effectively is obligated to catapult his servant to a higher standard of living than he himself enjoys.[17]

Now, Tosafot's assertion that avoidance of Sodomitic conduct requires the master to hand over the pillow to the servant is astonishing. It flies in the face of all the opinions regarding the parameters of *kofin* cited above. Specifically, the *kofin* principle, according to Tosafot, does not legitimize a *zeh neheneh* request when it consists of *affirmative use* of someone's property. Moreover, since the master does not violate the equal- living standard requirement when he rents or sells the pillow to someone else, the *kofin* principle should not require him to surrender his only pillow to his servant. Note, however, that Tosafot does not here employ the expression *kofin*. Specifically, Tosafot does not say that the Bet Din will *order* the master to surrender his only pillow to his servant. Instead, Tosafot merely states that denying both himself and his servant the pillow *displays the attributes of a Sodomite*. What Tosafot is conveying here is merely that the duty not to act as a Sodomite is a *moral imperative*, whether or not all the technicalities are in place for the Bet Din to actually *order* the individual to desist from a particular objection or course of action.

One illustration of the difference between the *legal* imperative of *kofin* and the *moral* imperative of not to act in the Sodomitic manner is the *galei a-da'a-ta* case discussed earlier. If the issue is judicial intervention, the *galei ada'ata* factor works to vitiate the plaintiff's case for injunctive relief. But the circumstances of *galei a-da'ata* do not remove the *zeh neheneh* character of the plaintiff's request. Therefore it becomes a matter of moral duty for the defendant to accede to the petitioner's request, notwithstanding the *galei a-da'ata* factor.

The upshot of the above analysis is that a solid case can be made that the Bet Din would order Ziskind to accede to Kornfeld's request. Ziskind's duty here is even more compelling on moral grounds. Since Ziskind is duty bound to accept Kornfeld as a passenger without charge, it is unconscionable for him to ask Kornfeld to pay the tolls. Ziskind would have incurred the expense of the tolls in any case, and the presence of Kornfeld as a passenger adds nothing to his expense. Asking Kornfeld to pay the tolls amounts, therefore, to a blatant violation of the *zeh neheneh* no-compensation rule.

Ziskind's Begrudging Attitude

Another issue the Crest Hollow affair raises is Ziskind's begrudging attitude. Irrespective of whether the *kofin* principle compels Ziskind to accede to Kornfeld's request, conferring the favor carries with it the potential of fulfilling the mitzvah of "love your neighbor as (you love) yourself" (Leviticus 19:18). But if the benefactor does a kindness with a begrudging attitude, it jeopardizes the mitzvah element of his good deed.[18] In connection with the duty to give charity the Torah forewarns: "do not harden your heart or shut your hand against your needy brother" (Deuteronomy 14:7). On the basis of this verse, the rule is laid down that dispensing charity to the poor with an angry face forfeits for the benefactor his good deed.[19] Nonetheless, dispensing charity with a heavy heart minimally fulfills the charity obligation.[20] The difference here, according to R. Shabbetai b. Meir haKohen (Poland, 1621–1662), is whether the bad attitude remains hidden in the benefactor's heart or is communicated to the recipient. It is only in the latter instance that the bad attitude vitiates the mitzvah element of the good deed.[21]

Apparently basing itself on Deuteronomy 14:7,[22] Avot d'Rabbi Natan posits that the Torah regards a gift conferred with an angry face as if the benefactor gave the recipient nothing.[23] Presumably, R. Shabbetai b. Meir haKohen's caveat applies to this dictum as well. But it is often only a delicate line that separates the instances where the recipient's pain is the product of his own doing or imagination and where it is actually caused by the begrudging attitude of the benefactor. The mental anguish Kornfeld experienced in his interaction with Ziskind may very well be Ziskind's responsibility. To the extent this is so, Ziskind loses the mitzvah element of his good deed.

The Chartered Bus and Free-Rider Conduct

We now turn to the validity of Kornfeld's contention that in the event an unsold seat was available aboard the chartered bus, he was entitled to that seat free of charge.

Kornfeld's contention is erroneous. Consider these facts: Torah Academy had sent a notice to all Flatbush invitees that it was planning to arrange a chartered bus for them in connection with the Crest Hollow affair. The $25 price that the yeshiva set for a round-trip ticket, which amounted to a handsome subsidy to those who took the bus, made it obvious that it regarded the shuttle service as crucial to the financial success of the affair. Interested parties were urged to send in their reservations for the bus before a deadline set ten days before the affair. The project would be canceled, the letter went on to say, if sufficient subscriptions to the chartered bus failed to materialize before the deadline. When Kornfeld received this notice, he found the $25 price very appealing. But in the final analysis he decided to ignore the notice. One look at the bus schedule convinced him that the bus option would tie him down to the affair for several more hours than would be the case under alternative travel arrangements. Another negative for Kornfeld was the possible "low status" that might attach itself to dinner patrons who made use of the bus.[24]

The preceding description makes it plain that the chartered bus was a commercial project of the yeshiva. The round-trip occupancy of each seat was put up for sale at $25. In the terminology of the Talmud, each seat is *o'med liskhar* (up for rental). The *o'med liskhar* status of each seat does not change with the arrival of the deadline, as this element was introduced by the yeshiva only for the purpose of ensuring that it would not end up subsidizing a project for which there was little demand. Since the unsold seat was *o'med liskhar* at the moment Kornfeld made his request for a free ticket, he is no more entitled to a free ticket than he would be in respect to a free ride on a city bus.

At this juncture, consider several variations of the above scenario: Suppose Torah Academy withholds three tickets from sale which it reserves for its dean, Rabbi Samson, and his usual entourage of two students. It does this to increase Rabbi Samson's flexibility in respect to when he can leave the affair at Crest Hollow. If he gets caught up there later than anticipated, the chartered bus option will always be available to him. Suppose further that all remaining tickets were sold out, with the result that the yeshiva breaks even on the project. As matters turn out, Rabbi Samson availed himself of an earlier car ride. Given the circumstances that the three tickets were never up for sale, Kornfeld's request for a free ticket turns out to entail no loss for either the passengers or for Torah Academy.

Another scenario which apparently also meets the *lo haser* condition occurs when vacant seats open up as a result of ticketholders securing earlier car rides with friends they unexpectedly meet at the affair.

Torah Academy's motive in initiating the chartered bus project was to provide a goodwill gesture to its Flatbush invitees. Clearly, profit was not its objective. The high-priced dinner, i.e., $300 couvert, made Torah Academy amenable to subsidize the chartered bus, if necessary, so as to avoid even an innuendo that it was parlaying the transportation venture into a profit. Given these circumstances, one could argue that as soon as ticket sales reach the break-even point, the remaining unsold seats lose their character of *omdim liskhar*. Since the project becomes *lo haser* at this point in time, a request for a free ticket should apparently be honored.

The common denominator of the various scenarios discussed is that the person who makes the request for a free ticket was already on notice about the project by dint of the letter the yeshiva sent out. Giving legitimacy to the free-ticket request has the effect of inviting manipulative conduct on the part of the Flatbush invitees in the form of free-rider behavior. If unsold tickets become free tickets provided the request is made after the break-even point is reached, then those who want to buy tickets are encouraged to postpone expressing their interest in the project until after the registration period. This involves a no-risk strategy. If the break-even point is already realized, they get free tickets. If not, they pay for the tickets like everyone else. But, if this stratagem is widely adopted, the project will never get off the ground, as there will not be enough subscriptions before the deadline. Cooperative projects will never get off the ground unless free-rider conduct is banned.

Recognition of the destructive effect that free-rider conduct has on communal projects finds expression in the work of R. Meir b. Barukh of Rothenburg (Germany, ca. 1215–1293): Certain amenities were regarded by the sages as absolutely essential for the welfare of a town. These included the building of a wall to provide the townspeople with protection, water-supply projects, public road repairs, and a variety of projects of a religious character. To ensure that these projects would be undertaken, the sages ruled that the townspeople may coerce one other to financially participate in them.[25] In a responsum R. Meir offers a rationale for why coercion was called for in respect to these projects. If cooperative effort of a purely voluntary nature were relied upon, avers R. Meir, many would feign disinterest in the projects, relying on the collective efforts of others to finance them. Once the project is completed, the same people would demand the right to benefit from the project gratis on the basis of the *zeh neheneh* principle. Manipulative conduct of this sort inordinately delays the projects and hence endangers the town.[26]

Coercion will, of course, effectively forestall free-rider conduct. But the number of projects that the sages mandated on the Jewish community is relatively small. How then is free-rider conduct eliminated in connection with the preponderance of group enterprises where coercion is not authorized? Once the destructive effect of free-rider conduct is recognized, it is but a small step to propose that the *zeh neheneh* principle should be suspended in connection with any group project, even when the feature of coercion is absent. Explicitly taking this view is R. Yair Bacharach (Germany, 1638–1701). The specifics of the case are the following: For a number of years householders in town A customarily hired an expert shofar blower from a different town for the High Holiday services. It once happened that hostilities broke out in the surrounding area, with the result that the shofar blower demanded a hefty raise for his services. The wealthier elements of the town, consisting of six householders, proposed that an additional tax be levied on every household to cover the extra expense. The poorer elements, consisting of seven householders, balked at the proposal, claiming that they could not afford to pay any additional assessment to cover the raise. As a means of inducing the recalcitrant elements to join in the project, the sponsors threatened to exclude from the mitzvah of hearing the shofar all those who refused to pay their fair share of the expense. This would be accomplished by stipulating with the shofar blower that he perform the ritual only in the name of those who paid their fair share of the assessment.

In his ruling, R. Bacharach averred that coercion would be in order only when the additional assessment would not generate a deprivation effect on the majority of the townspeople. Here majority sponsorship forces everyone to financially participate on an ability-to-pay basis. However, when the additional assessment generates a deprivation effect on the majority of householders, those who refuse to join cannot be forced to participate. In the case at hand, the majority of the householders claimed that they could not afford the additional assessment. If their claim is true, the six sponsors cannot force the recalcitrant to participate.

R. Bacharach regards it as morally justifiable to deny access to the mitzvah to non sponsors. He rejects the claim that once the financing of the mitzvah project is complete, those who refused to join should be allowed free access to the mitzvah on the basis of the *zeh neheneh*. Invoking *zeh neheneh* here, he reasons, would encourage free-rider conduct and result in an unfair shifting of the burden of financing the mitzvah.

The legitimacy of excluding the non joiners in the shofar case, however, is not clearcut. It turns on whether the deprivation claim made by the non joiners is truthful. If it is, it would be morally objectionable to deny them access to the mitzvah when they are willing to strain their budgets to share in the expense of financing it. But if the deprivation claim is false, those who participate have every right to exclude the non joiners unless they agree to pay their fair share.[27]

Recognition of the destructive effects of free-rider conduct leads to the proposition that at the moment an individual declines to financially participate in a group project, he forfeits thereby any subsequent *zeh neheneh* claim to benefit from the project gratis. Otherwise, free-rider conduct would be encouraged. While the project at hand may very well suffer no loss whatsoever as a result of free-rider conduct, society will assuredly suffer a loss (*haser*) in the long run, in the form of wasted organizational effort and lost benefits from many worthwhile projects that never get off the ground. Since recognition of *zeh neheneh* here exerts a definitely pernicious long-term effect on society, suspension of the right in this case is indicated.

Supportive of the above thesis is the following ruling by R. Solomon b. Abraham Adret (Spain, ca. 1235–1310) in connection with the protection Jewish law affords against invasion of privacy (*hazek re'iyah*). The law prohibits A from installing a window facing B's courtyard because the latter would thereby be exposed to visual trespass.[28] Injunctive relief is given to B, according to R. Adret, even if the window merely poses a potential harm, as would occur when the window faces a ruin owned by B. Insofar as private activities are not customarily performed in a ruin, the window presents no immediate harm to B. Nonetheless, credence is given to B's claim that he plans to eventually renovate the ruin. Should A be allowed to maintain his window, B would suffer at once from A's visual penetration of his domain. B's petition to have the window walled up immediately is therefore acceded to. Given the predilection of most people to secure what is rightfully theirs with a minimum amount of litigation and nuisance, B's petition is not regarded as Sodomitic in character.[29]

It follows from R. Adret's analysis that the inevitability of future loss vitiates a claim of *zeh neheneh* even though the petition entails no loss for the respondent in the present circumstances. Similarly, conferring legitimacy to the *zeh neheneh* right when the petitioner has already declined to financially participate in the project will inevitably encourage free-rider conduct and hence generate losses in the future for this group as well as for society at large.

Application of this principle to the Crest Hollow affair leads to the proposition that Kornfeld should be denied a complimentary ticket on the bus. In the letter that accompanied its invitation to the affair, Torah Academy solicited Kornfeld to join the project. Kornfeld chose to ignore the letter. Giving legitimacy to his subsequent *zeh neheneh* request encourages free- rider conduct in the future and hence should be denied. If Kornfeld wants to ride back to Flatbush on the bus, the yeshiva has every right to charge him $12.50 for the trip.

Kornfeld's request should be denied, as well, from still another standpoint. Consider that Torah Academy's motive in sponsoring the chartered bus was to encourage attendance by providing an attractive service. The expenditure involved is inherently one that was undertaken both for the yeshiva's benefit and the benefit of the Flatbush invitees. To be sure, the benefit provided does not rise to the level of a monetary claim against the Flatbush invitees, as these people may claim alternative transportation plans. But as soon as someone demonstrates that he is pleased to make use of the service (*galei a-da'ata*), an obligation to compensate the yeshiva for the service provided should obtain.

Recall, however, Tosafot's lenient position in respect to the law of unjust enrichment: A's demonstration that he is pleased with the unsolicited expenditure B incurred on his behalf is not sufficient to generate a responsibility for A to compensate B. A is liable only when he demonstrates that he is willing to *spend money* to obtain the said benefit. In the Crest Hollow affair, Tosafot's strict criterion for liability also obtains. This is so because at the time Kornfeld made his entreaty for a complimentary ticket he had already ended his unsuccessful search for a free ride. Since the only viable option for Kornfeld at that time was to hire a car service, his request to board the bus amounts to a demonstration of willingness to pay for the ticket should his request for a free ride be denied.

Requesting a Car Ride to Crest Hollow

In our final point of investigation, we turn to the validity of Kornfeld's assumption that the *zeh neheneh* principle entitles him to a free car ride to the affair. Kornfeld's assumption is wrong. Conferring legitimacy to this attitude amounts to compelling B to confer A with a favor when A is himself in need of the same favor from B. Since the request entails a definite *haser*, rejecting it in the form presented is not Sodomitic. In the case at hand, reacting to Kornfeld's request for a free ride with the suggestion that he share in the travel expenses, including the tolls, should not be objectionable.

The judgment here is in sharp contrast to the one made earlier where Kornfeld hired a car service to get to the affair and asked Ziskind for a ride back to Flatbush. We take it as a given that Ziskind desires to drive his own car back to Flatbush. Leaving his car at Crest Hollow and taking a car service home is an option Ziskind will not even consider. Hence Kornfeld is not in a position to save Ziskind the expense involved in traveling back to Flatbush. But Ziskind is in a position to save this expense for Kornfeld. Since Kornfeld's request in no way increases the expense Ziskind would have in any case incurred in traveling back to Flatbush, denying the request for a free ride reflects a Sodomitic character.

Problem

Adam has a large library but lives in a small apartment and is very squeezed for space. During his frequent visits to Stephen's house, Adam notices that a certain closet in Stephen's spacious home is always empty. One day, Adam gathers up enough courage to ask Stephen to allow him to store some of his books in the empty closet. Is it *Sodomitic* on the part of Stephen to refuse?

1. Cf. Ketubbot 103a; Eruvin 49a; Bava Batra 59a, 168a.

2. For an extensive taxonomy of cases drawn from the rishonic and responsa literature where the Bet Din applies *kofin*, see Aaron Kirschenbaum, *Equity in Jewish Law* (Hoboken, N.J.: Ktav, 1991), pp. 185–236.

3. Tosafot, Bava Kamma 20b; R. Aaron ha-Levi, quoted by R. Joseph Habiba (Spain, early 15th cent.), *Nimmukei Yosef* at Rif, Bava Kamma 8b; see also R. Abraham Hirsch b. Jacob Eisenstadt (Poland, 1813–1868), *Pithei Teshuvah* to R. Joseph Caro (Israel, 1488–1575), *Shulhan Arukh*, Hoshen Mishpat 363, n. 3.

4. R. Aaron ha-Levi, loc. cit.

5. R. Shimon Shkop, *Hiddushei Rabbi Shimon Yehudah ha-Kohen*, Bava Kamma 19, pt. 3.

6. R. Mordecai b. Hillel, *Mordecai*, Bava Kamma 20b. Ruling in accordance with *Mordecai* are R. Moses Isserles (Poland, 1525 or 1530–1572), Rema, *Sh.Ar.*, op. cit. 363:6, and R. Jehiel Michel Epstein (Belarus, 1829–1908), *Arukh ha-Shulhan*, Hoshen Mishpat 363:16.

7. Tosafot, Bava Kamma 20b.

8. *Tur*, op. cit. 363:6.

9. *Ar.HaSh.*, op. cit. 363:19.

10. R. Solomon b. Jehiel Luria, *Yam shel Shelomoh*, Bava Kamma 2:16.

11. Mishnah, Bava Batra 1:3.

12. R. Solomon b. Isaac (France, 1040–1105), Rashi, commentary at Mishnah, Bava Batra 1:3.

13. In agreement with R. Tebele on this point is R. Meir Simhah haKohen (Latvia, 1843–1926), *Or Sameah*, Hilkhot Gezelah 3:9.

14. R. David Tebele b. Mosheh, *Nahalat David*, Bava Kamma 20b.

15. Kirschenbaum, *Equity in Jewish Law*, p. 189.

16. Kiddushin 20a.

17. Tosafot, Kiddushin 20a.

18. See Avot d'Rabbi Natan 13:4.

19. Maimonides (Egypt, 1135–1204), *Yad*, Mattenot Aniyyim 10:4; *Tur*, Yoreh De'ah 249:3; *Sh.Ar.*, Yoreh De'ah 249:3; *Ar.haSh.*, Yoreh De'ah 249:13.

20. *Yad*, op. cit. 10:14; *Tur*, op. cit. *Sh.Ar.*, op. cit. 249:13; *Ar.haSh.*, op. cit. 249:17.

21. R. Shabbetai b. Meir haKohen, *Siftei Kohen*, *Sh.Ar.*, op. cit. 249, n. 9.

22. See R. Elijah b. Solomon Zalman (Lithuania, 1720–1797), *Bi'ur haGra*, *Sh.Ar.*, op. cit. 249, n. 6.

23. Avot d'Rabbi Natan 13:4.

24. Kornfeld was wrong in assuming that low status would attach itself to riding the bus.

25. For sources and discussion regarding these mandated functions, see Aaron Levine, *Free Enterprise and Jewish Law: Aspects of Jewish Business Ethics* (New York: Ktav, 1980), pp. 136–60.

26. R. Meir b. Barukh, *Responsa Maharam* (Prague, 1608), 4:39.

27. R. Yair Bacharach, *Responsa Havvot Yair*, 186.

28. Bava Batra 59b; Rif, ad loc.; *Yad*, Shekhenim 5:6; Rosh, Bava Batra 3:75; *Tur*, Hoshen Mishpat 154:2; *Sh.Ar.*, Hoshen Mishpat 154:3; *Ar.haSh.*, Hoshen Mishpat 154:7.

29. R. Solomon b. Abraham Adret, *Responsa Rashba* 1144. R. Joseph Caro (*Sh.Ar.*, op. cit. 154:16), citing a large number of rishonim who follow R. Adret's view, regards this position as normative. For an opposing view, cited in *Sh.Ar.*, op. cit. see Rosh, Bava Batra 2:2.

Toys for Guns

ASL is a chain of electronics stores located in the Rover Hill section of Tremond, a township in the northwest. The company was originally organized as a partnership. But the good fortune of tremendous growth, combined with a desire to secure the advantage of perpetual life and limited liability, convinced the owners to reorganize the company as a corporation. The company can now best be described as a *closely held private corporation.* It has fifteen shareholders, with its CEO, I. M. Rainmaker, owning 20 percent of the outstanding shares.

Rainmaker believes that the pursuit of profit should not be ASL's only goal. Instead, the profit-maximization goal should be modified to accommodate a proactive social role. Toward this end, Rainmaker, without consulting fellow shareholders, launched a program to make a dent in the local crime rate. Working with the local police precinct, he inaugurated a "toys for guns" program. The program offered amnesty, along with a $100 voucher redeemable at Toys 'R Us, to anyone who turned in a weapon. Rainmaker committed $10,000 of corporate funds for the voucher certificates. At the same time, he believed that without an intensive educational and promotional effort, the program would not make a significant impact on the crime rate. Toward this end, he gave lectures on corporate time to local public schools and community groups, and arranged meetings with them. Rainmaker was very enthusiastic about "toys for guns." Fewer guns in dresser drawers should translate into fewer accidental shootings, fewer crimes of passion, and fewer guns stolen for later use in crime.

"Toys for guns" drew much favorable public attention. Ironically, several ASL shareholders were opposed to the program, feeling that "toys for guns" took the company far afield from its organizing purpose. At first, Rainmaker ignored the criticism, dismissing it as reflecting jealousy of all the media attention he was getting. But as the program gained momentum and Rainmaker set his sights on expanding it, he decided to present "toys for guns" formally to the shareholders for their approval.

In preparing for the shareholders meeting, Rainmaker decided that it would be politically unwise to present "toys for guns" as a venture into corporate social responsibility. Instead, he opted to package the project as a solid investment opportunity for ASL. At the meeting, Rainmaker addressed his fellow shareholders with the following remarks:

"I'm convinced that 'toys for guns' will put ASL on the commercial map. Media publicity for our company's social benefaction will incidentally draw attention to our products and services. This will do more for us than $100,000 worth of straight advertising! Moreover, it is not unreasonable to expect a bandwagon effect for the 'toys for guns' project in the form of other firms joining our effort. A real dent in the crime rate will be made. Increased neighborhood safety will generate many tangible benefits for us. Employee morale, for one, will be boosted. This will translate into increased productivity. The perception of a safer neighborhood will attract a whole new clientele into our stores. 'Toys for guns,' in short, is consistent with out *shared goal* of long-run profit maximization."

To his chagrin, Rainmaker encountered much opposition to his plan. Let us briefly take a look at the arguments shareholders opposed to the plan hurled at Rainmaker.

Some dissenters were convinced that only those who were least attached to their weapons would be attracted by the trade-in offer. Inherited guns and the spare weapons of criminals fall into this category. Those whose lifestyle requires them to carry guns, such as drug dealers and gang members, will not be induced by the offer to trade in their basic arsenal. The program, as one critic put it, "will at best only nibble at the edges of gun violence."

Critics with both a penchant for quoting authorities and a flare for economic analysis asserted that the gun buybacks, to be effective, would have to be coupled with a national ban on new sales of handguns. Otherwise, taking guns out of circulation in the face of constant market demand unwittingly subsidizes the gun industry.[1] Moreover, it would be naive to imagine that the gun-buyback program is exempt from normal market processes. Specifically, if the buyback price rises above the retail price for guns, the program could very well encourage gun thefts, with government serving, in effect, as a reliable fence.[2]

At this juncture, Melvin Friedman, Rainmaker's most vehement critic and chief rival to take control of the company, peered ominously at Rainmaker and with a good measure of sarcasm blurted out: "The only certain benefit of the project is the adulation and attention *you* are getting from the media."

Sensing that the tide was decidedly turning against Rainmaker, Nathan Schwartz, a close ally of Friedman's, chimed in with what many observers felt was the clinching argument against the project:

"Going through with this project is downright hypocrisy. 'Toys for guns' projects us as a do-good company with a big heart and a deep social conscience. But in truth we're not all that good. We're constantly hearing workers complain that our compensation package is below industry standards. Why, we're as much as three months behind in some of the accounts payable. And oh, yes, customer service could use a major improvement. Now, if we're going to throw around money for altruism, let us begin by putting our own house in order."

As the shareholders enthusiastically clapped in reaction to Schwartz's remarks, it became evident that the group was prepared to vote down "toys for guns."

Sensing imminent defeat, Rainmaker shocked the group by threatening to resign if "toys for guns" was voted down. Fearful that ASL would plunge into turmoil without the proven business acumen of Rainmaker, the group abruptly reversed course. "Toys for guns" was approved and was funded appropriately.

Corporate Social Responsibility in Secular Society

In implementing "toys for guns," ASL joined a phenomenon on the American scene called "corporate social responsibility." What it entails is the use of corporate wealth to engage in projects for the general good of society. This phenomenon finds its greatest frequency in the *public* corporate sector. Here are some illustrations of altruistic projects undertaken by public corporations.

1. Dow Chemical Company runs a multimillion-dollar project to educate the public about organ transplants and to encourage more organ donations. A notable aspect of the program is that it is unrelated to any of Dow's commercial interests.

2. Merck and Co. has given away millions of dollars worth of a drug to fight the world's leading cause of blindness.

3. Sixteen of the nation's largest corporations have opened their own private school for pupils aged two to nine in the Lowndale area of Chicago. The aim of the program is to show that children raised in poverty and in drug- and crime-plagued urban communities can learn as well as suburban children.[3]

The problem that corporate social programs present is that the diversion of corporate funds for these purposes conflicts with the presumptive shareholder desire to maximize profits.

Corporate altruism, according to Professor Milton Friedman, undermines the foundations of the capitalist system. This is so because the business corporation is not organized for an eleemosynary purpose, but rather to make as much money as possible for the shareholders within the limits set by law and ethical custom. Given the agency relationship between the executive and the shareholders, the executive is mandated to run the business with the aim of maximizing profits for the shareholders.

What makes the notion of corporate social responsibility subversive to capitalism is its introduction of a political mechanism into the marketplace. By means of self-selection or some form of appointment, the executive become simultaneously a legislator, executive, and jurist. He decides whom to tax, by how much, and for what purpose.

The political principle that underlines the political mechanism is *conformity*. This means that the individual has a say in what is being done but must conform if overruled. In sharp contrast, the political principle that underlies the market mechanism is *unanimity*. In an ideal free market resting on private property, no individual can coerce any other; all cooperation is voluntary. All parties to such cooperation benefit or they need not participate. By rescuing social responsibility from the corporate executive and putting it in the hands of individuals, we will be preventing coercion for purely *unselfish* reasons.

Friedman's final salvo against corporate social responsibility is that it is often totally futile. The executive is presumably an expert in running his company—in producing a product or selling it or financing it. But nothing about his selection makes him an expert in curing such systemic ills as inflation, environmental pollution, or hard-core unemployment. Will holding down the price of his product, for instance, reduce inflationary pressures? Or, by leaving more spending power in the hands of his customers, simply divert it elsewhere? Or, by forcing him to produce less because of the lower price, will it simply contribute to shortages?[4]

Friedman's critics feel that corporate social responsibility is compatible with the capitalist ethic. Professor Thomas Mulligan, for instance, points out that Friedman's model of the "lone ranger" executive is not typical in corporate America. Far more realistic is the consultative type, who undertakes corporate-responsible projects only after building the necessary consensus.[5]

Another flaw in Friedman's analysis is his conceptualization of corporate-responsible actions in the form of committing resources to combat society's systemic ills. This presentation ignores the reality that corporate social responsibility is more a matter of targeting projects that are do-able.[6]

Advocates of corporate social responsibility reject the notion that executives are merely agents of the shareholders. Consideration that the corporation is a legal person, separate and apart from its owners, has led some to conceptualize the corporation in terms of stakeholders. Stakeholders are groups and individuals who benefit from or are harmed by corporate actions. These include suppliers, customers, employers, stockholders, and the local community. Managers bear a fiduciary relationship to stakeholders. Their duty is to balance the multiple claims of conflicting stakeholders. The stakeholder theory does not give primacy to one stakeholder group over another, though there will surely be times when one group will benefit at the expense of the others.

In the traditional stockholder theory of the firm, the purpose of the firm is to maximize the welfare of the stockholders, subject to the constraints set by law and ethical custom. In the stakeholder theory of the firm, the purpose of the firm is to serve as a vehicle for coordinating stakeholder interests.[7]

"Toys for Guns" and Halakhah

From the perspective of Halakhah, the most fundamental issue the "toys for guns" vignette raises is whether Rainmaker enjoyed discretionary authority to engage in the project. Resolution of this issue turns on an identification of the legal relationship between shareholders and managers in respect to the wealth of a closely held corporation.

Bearing on this issue is a talmudic passage at Bava Mezia 104b that deals with *iska*. *Iska* is a special type of business partnership that Halakhah regulates. The distinctive feature of *iska* is that the financier (F) plays no operational or managerial role in the business enterprise. If the managing partner (MP) and the silent partner (F) have not stipulated the division of profits and losses, Halakhah calls for profits and losses to be divided equally. The portion of the capital for which MP assumes responsibility takes on the character of a loan (*milveh*), and the remaining portion takes on the character of a deposit (*pikkadon*). Commenting on the dual character of *iska*, the Talmud states:

> Now that we say that it is a semi-loan and a semi-trust, if he [the trader] wishes to drink beer therewith [i.e., for the loan part] he can do so. Rava said: [No.] It is therefore called *iska* [business] because he can say to him, "I gave it to you for trading, not for drinking beer."

Talmudic decisors regard Rava's position as normative.[8] Insofar as no *explicit* restriction was agreed to regarding the disposition of the *milveh* portion of the *iska*, Rava's position requires an explanation. Addressing himself to this issue, R. Solomon b. Isaac (France, 1040–1105) regards the restriction as proceeding from MP's implicit mandate to manage the *iska* in a manner that maximizes F's return on his investment. Because putting the *milveh* portion of the *iska* at risk in the venture effectively drives MP to be more diligent in his management of the enterprise, *the requirement to do so* is self-evident in the agreement.[9] In a similar vein, Tosafot (France and Germany, 12th–14th cent.) point out that the consequence of not investing the *milveh* in the venture is to immediately expose F's entire capital to risk of loss, with no additional capital to draw upon if needed. The implicit mandate to operate the *iska* to maximize F's gain, therefore, requires MP to invest the *milveh* portion of the *iska* in the venture.[10]

We should note that in respect to the *pikkadon* portion of the *iska*, a bailor-bailee (*mafkid-nifkad*) relationship exists between the financier and the active partner. MP's use of the funds in a manner that departs from F's mandate constitutes misappropriation (*shelihut yad*).[11]

It follows from this analysis that the manager of an *iska* arrangement is under a *fiduciary* duty to the financier. Implicit in this duty is a mandate to maximize profits for the financier. Moreover, the manager's authority is limited to the pursuit of profits. This can be seen from a point in the law of charity as it pertains to *iska* profits: Suppose it is customary for business partners to devote 10 percent of their *iska* profits to charity. The active partner, according to R. Mosheh Isserles (Poland, 1525 or 1530–1572), has no right to take it upon himself to donate 10 percent of the *iska* profits to charity. Instead, the financier is entitled to receive his full pre-tithing share of the profits and be given the opportunity to allocate his charitable funds in a manner of his own choosing.[12]

Proceeding clearly from R. Isserles' ruling is that even when a business entity operates under an implicit mandate to donate a specific percentage of its profits to charity, the *disposition* of the charitable funds is a matter of individual shareholder prerogative and does not fall under the purview of the business entity. How much more so does this judgment hold when the business entity operates without any understanding that a portion of its profits shall be devoted to charity.

Does this conceptualization of the role of the manager extend from *iska* to the modern business entity? Recall that the salient feature of *iska* is that the financier is a silent partner and has no say in the running of the business. The modern business entity that most resembles *iska* is the *limited partnership*. This arrangement consists of general and limited partners. The general partners manage the business and are personally liable for its debts. The limited partners contribute capital and share in profits and losses, but take no part in running the business and incur no liability with respect to partnership obligations beyond their contributions to capital.

Given that Halakhah severely circumscribes the discretion of the manager when the investor agrees in advance *to have no say* in the operation of the business enterprise, the same limited mandate should hold for the manager when the investors retain ultimate control in the decision-making. On the modern scene, the owners retain control when the business assumes the form of a single proprietorship, a partnership, or a closely held corporation. The halakhic conceptualization of the role of a manager of an *iska* should therefore apply equally to the manager within the above organizational structures.

The thesis of limited discretion for the manager requires further clarification. Suppose the manager encounters a business opportunity which his mandate does not explicitly cover. Does the manager enjoy discretion to decide what is in the best interest of the owner? Bearing on this issue is the following ruling by the seventeenth-century decisor R. Joseph Trani (Italy, 1568–1639):

Reuben consigned merchandise to Shimon, with the instruction to convey it to Egypt and sell it there. Reuben gave Shimon total discretion to
decide on price and terms of sale. The agreement also set compensation
for Shimon for a period of six months for his toil and effort. At the conclusion of the six-month period, Shimon was unsuccessful in finding customers for the merchandise. Seeing that the merchandise was beginning to
deteriorate, Shimon took it upon himself to sell it to a vizier on credit. The
vizier resided outside Egypt. Subsequent to making this deal, Shimon
agreed to sell his note on the vizier to Levi at a one-third discount. In turn,
Levi committed himself to collect the debt from the vizier and within
three months to make good to Shimon the pro-rated portion of the debt
due him. Toward his obligation to Shimon, Levi made an immediate payment of 1,000 *girsh*.

Shimon informed Reuben of his dealings. Reuben's response was, "What
you have done is done." Reuben also agreed to compensate Shimon for his
toil and effort for the additional time he had spent in Egypt.

As matters turned out, Levi reneged on the deal, insisting on the return
of his 1,000 *girsh*. Because Levi was a powerful individual, Shimon had no
choice but to comply. To meet Levi's demand, Shimon borrowed 1,000
girsh from Judah. Thereupon Shimon set out to the port to book passage
to the vizier and collect the debt from him. Shimon was, however, denied
passage on the boat. He then turned to Judah for help. Judah agreed to
book passage, collect the debt from the vizier, and keep for himself 1,000
girsh as payment for his loan. Judah was successful in collecting the debt.

At issue here is whether Shimon is entitled to any share of the profits realized from the sale of the goods to the vizier. Since Reuben apparently acqui-
esced after the fact to the deal Shimon had struck with Levi, Shimon should
take Levi's place in the deal as soon as the latter reneged. R. Trani ruled that
Shimon is not entitled to any share of the profits. His claim consists only of
compensation for toil and effort. Notwithstanding that Shimon acted in the
best interest of Reuben, selling the merchandise on credit to someone who
resides outside Egypt clearly exceeded Reuben's mandate. Reuben's subsequent
acquiescence to the deal does not retroactively change the mandate Shimon
must operate under. The matter at hand is analogous to the case recorded at
Bava Mezia 22a. Here we are told that Mari bar Isak's sharecropper took it upon
himself without authorization to honor a group of visiting rabbis with a platter of fruit. Mar Zutra refused to partake of the fruit even after Mari bar Isak
joined the group and proclaimed to the sharecropper that he should have
offered a better-quality fruit platter to the rabbis. Rather than taking his remark
as indicating genuine happiness that the sharecropper had offered the rabbis

fruit, Mar Zutra felt it was said out of embarrassment (*kesufa*) so as not to appear miserly to the rabbis. Here too, Reuben's acquiescence to what Shimon did manifests only a desire on his part to extricate himself from the arrangement in the best possible manner. Expressing approval after the fact does not change the circumstance that Shimon violated Reuben's mandate. The original arrangement, therefore, remains intact, and Reuben is not required to share any of the profits with Shimon.[13]

Several principles can be generalized from the preceding discussion. First, if F furnishes MP with capital for the purpose of investing it for him, a *mafkid-nifkad* relationship is thereby established between the partners in respect to the capital furnished. Moreover, MP's *nifkad* status places him under an implicit mandate to manage the funds with the aim of maximizing profits for F. Hence, committing corporate resources for altruistic projects constitutes *shelihut yad* on the part of the manager.

This demonstrates that Rainmaker enjoyed no discretionary authority to initiate the "toys for guns" project. As the CEO of a closely held corporation organized for a specific commercial purpose, Rainmaker's implicit mandate is to maximize shareholder value.

Given that "toys for guns" violates the shareholders mandate, Rainmaker has no right to devote corporate time to lectures and promotions of the "toys for guns" project. Such activity breaches his halakhic obligation not to idle on the employer's time.[14] By idling on the employer's time, he forfeits the wages he was slated to earn for that time period.[15]

The legal treatment of corporate altruism of the "toys for guns" genre reveals a large gap between secular law and Halakhah. Under the business judgment rule, secular law recognizes wide latitude for the executive and does not second guess his business decisions. Judicial review of either the bona fides or the reasonableness of a business management decision is quite narrow. As a practical matter, the business judgment defense is unlikely to fail in the absence of conflicts of interest, extraordinary amounts of profit forgone, or some other *affirmative* indication of bad faith.[16] Rainmaker's unilateral venture into corporate altruism would thus have no trouble meeting the business judgment rule.

From the standpoint of Halakhah, the ethics of Rainmaker's project turns on the issue of whether the expenditure should be regarded as corporate altruism masquerading as a business investment. If the shareholders regard the project as corporate altruism, then the expenditure constitutes *shelihut yad* on the part of Rainmaker. Given the latter possibility, moving the project along without consulting the shareholders is untenable. For the shareholders, the first order of business is to determine whether "toys for guns" is corporate altruism or a business investment. Should a majority decision decide that it falls into the category of corporate altruism, the item immediately moves off the firm's agenda. Validating the project requires a two-tier majority vote.

Business Social Responsibility and Halakhah

Denying the manager discretionary authority to engage in do-good projects for society at large should not be generalized into a contention that Halakhah denies that the firm owes any *altruistic* duties to its immediate stakeholders. Quite to the contrary. Halakhah *imposes* specific duties on the firm vis-à-vis its stakeholders. Because these duties go beyond the neoclassical, secular law and ethical custom threshold, they should rightfully be called altruistic duties. To illustrate: The requirements Halakhah imposes on the firm in respect to giving notice to an employee-at-will and protecting the privacy of customers go beyond secular law and ethical custom.[17]

The case for calling halakhic duties to stakeholders altruistic duties is made by the ethical imperative to conduct oneself *lifnim mi-shurat ha-din* (beyond the letter of the law). To see why, let us extrapolate the practical implications of this principle for a firm as it undergoes changes in its organizational structure.

Recall that ASL was originally organized as a partnership. In those early years, none of the partners were silent partners. Instead, all of them were active in the business and served as managers of the various stores. Consider the following scenario:

Melvin Friedman, one of the manager-partners of ASL, sells an electronic organizer to Lawrence Mishkin. Mishkin returns to the store after the expiration date of his warranty with the complaint that the data refuses to display on the screen. Mishkin asks Friedman to use his expertise to retrieve his data for him.

Since the defect occurred after the warranty expired, Friedman is under no *legal* obligation to accede to the request. But acceding to the request fulfills for Friedman an aspect of the mitzvah of *hashavat avedah* (restoration of lost property).[18] To be sure, Friedman is no more *obligated* than any other expert to help Mishkin. Consider, however, that Friedman sold the unit to Mishkin. Thus it becomes a matter of *lifnim mi-shurat ha-din* conduct for Friedman to exert himself for Mishkin and retrieve the data. Recall that *lifnim mi-shurat ha-din* conduct generally makes a claim only on an individual's time and effort but not on his financial resources.[19] Accordingly, if Mishkin shows up with his request when the store is teeming with customers, Friedman would be excused from immediately giving attention to his problem, as doing so might result in a loss of business. To fulfill his *lifnim mi-shurat ha-din* duty, Friedman should offer to look into Mishkin's problem within a specified period of time, say, a week. During this interval, Friedman should either attend to the problem during a lull in business or deal with the problem in off-business hours.

Let us now change the scenario. ASL is reorganized as a closely held private corporation. The shareholders remove themselves from the operation of the business and hire Rainmaker as CEO. Remembering that they devoted quite a chunk of time engaging in *lifnim mishurat* conduct when they were active in the operation of the business, they set out to *structure* the job of manager so as to eliminate *lifnim mi-shurat ha-din* conduct from the operation of the firm. Toward this end, Rainmaker hires Kaldor as manager and confers him with a job description that is *guaranteed* to fill up his day. In respect to customer service, Rainmaker instructs Kaldor that if the request is not covered by the warranty, it should be denied, albeit in a courteous fashion. Kaldor's contract calls for overtime pay if he works beyond normal business hours. Because this arrangement either makes *lifnim mi-shurat ha-din* conduct a dereliction of duty for Kaldor or triggers an obligation to pay him overtime, the plan effectively eliminates *lifnim mi-shurat ha-din* from the firm's operations.

The above arrangement violates Halakhah. The obligation to run a business in a *lifnim mi-shurat ha-din* fashion vis-à-vis its stakeholders squarely resides with the *owners*. It is the owners who must exert toil and effort in this regard. If the owners choose to remove themselves from the everyday operations of the business, they must designate surrogates to perform their duty for them, *even if this entails an expenditure on their part*. Setting up the business in a manner that eliminates the practice of *lifnim mi-shurat ha-din* is therefore unacceptable.

What follows is that a policy that routinely denies customer requests that do not fall into their *legal* entitlement violates *lifnim mi-shurat ha-din* law. Instead, accommodations with the customer should be made when it entails no cost for the firm. If acceding to the requests entails an out-of-pocket expense, this may, of course, be passed on to the customer. But the *lifnim mi-shurat ha-din* negotiation should not be converted into a *profit* opportunity for an additional service rendered. Moreover, to charge the manager with the above policy only when he is not busy with new business is unacceptable. Doing so makes *lifnim mi-shurat ha-din* an occasional or seasonal practice, when it should be a permanent and constant feature of business practice.

Halakhah and the Neoclassical Stakeholder Theory Debate

The analysis so far has identified significant differences between Halakhah, on the one hand, and the neoclassical and stakeholder theories, on the other, regarding the *normative* role of the manager of a business enterprise. In stakeholder theory, the shareholders are seen as but one of many stakeholders exerting a claim on the resources and policies of the firm. The fiduciary duty the managers owe the shareholders is not seen as automatically overriding other claims made on the firm. The theory provides neither a criterion for evaluating the merit of a stakeholder's claim on the firm nor a guidepost for mediating between competing claims. All this is apparently left to the discretion of the manager.[20] In sharp contrast, in the halakhic system, the fiduciary duty of the manager to the shareholder is overriding and translates into a profit-maximizing mandate for the manager. Moreover, the manager operates under a short leash, enjoying little discretion to use his own judgment to decide what is in the best interest of the shareholders. In respect to the profit-maximizing mandate, an affinity between Halakhah and the neoclassical school can be seen. But Halakhah breaks sharply with the neoclassical school's conceptualization of the firm's duties to its stakeholders. As the shareholders' agent, the manager must carry out their duties to the firm's stakeholders. What these duties are is not a matter of managerial discretion, but is determined by halakhic moral principles that translate into specific duties. The responsibility of the manager is to carry out these duties whether the shareholders specifically mandate them or not.

Corporate Altruism and Coercion

Let us now return to the "toys for guns" vignette. Recall that Rainmaker finally got approval for the project by resorting to high-pressure tactics in the form of threatening to resign as CEO.

Rainmaker's conduct here is morally objectionable. One issue his conduct raises is that it might constitute extortion. In developing this point, consider the classical case of *teluhu ve-zavin* (lit. he was [threatened] to be hanged and [because of this] sold), discussed at Bava Kamma 62a: B coerces S to sell him property he owns at its fair market value. Considering both the duress S is subject to and his receipt and acceptance of the cash representing the fair market value of the property, it is evident that he desires to transfer the article to B.[21] The sale, although immoral,[22] is nevertheless legally binding.[23] The Talmud adds that for it to be valid S must in the end declare, "I am willing" (*rozeh ani*).[24] Decisors regard S's acceptance of the purchasing price *without protest* as equivalent to declaring *rozeh ani*.[25] A variation of this case occurs when B snatches away S's article but leaves him with its fair market value. With the duress element absent here, S's acquiescence to the exchange does not become objectively evident unless S explicitly verbalizes his consent.[26]

Let us now move to another variant which has direct relevance to the case at hand. In this variant, A coerces B to make him a gift or sell his property below fair market value. This transaction, according to R. Jacob b. Asher and R. Joseph Caro, is invalid.[27] Both decisors define coercion in terms of either physical duress or monetary threats.[28]

Applying these latter two rulings to the case at hand renders Rainmaker's conduct extortion. Given the majority's initial opposition to the plan, the judgment holds even if the dissenters concede that the project will likely generate some benefits to the firm.

In opposition to the school of thought that regards monetary threats as a form of coercion, R. Joseph Colon would not invalidate a commercial transaction on this basis.[29] Rainmaker's conduct does not constitute extortion, therefore, according to R. Colon. Nonetheless, Rainmaker's use of pressure tactics to get his way may violate the prohibitions against coveting (*lo tit'avveh*) and lusting (*lo tahmod*). Elsewhere in this volume we discuss the particulars of these prohibitions.[30]

A saving factor here is that "toys for guns" is approved only if the shareholders formally vote in favor of it. This circumstance, as will be recalled, removes the *lo tahmod* prohibition, according to some authorities.

Another mitigating factor is that Rainmaker seeks the corporate funds not for his personal use but for the benefit of the corporation and of society at large. This circumstance should not, however, work to vitiate *lo tahmod* unless the shareholders are in agreement with Rainmaker that the project is an ingenious way of drawing attention to the firm's products and services, and disagree only about whether the expenditure is the optimal investment for the firm. Before investing in ASL, shareholders should have been aware that issues of business policy would at times be hotly contested and in the end decided by majority vote. If Rainmaker believes that "toys for guns," is in the best longterm interest of the firm, he has every right to fight for its approval, even to the extent of putting his job on the line.

But suppose the majority of the shareholders view "toys for guns" as purely corporate altruism and do not believe that the resulting publicity will draw any significant attention to their products or services. Then "toys for guns" is, for the majority of shareholders, a misplaced agenda item; it diverts profits for a non-business purpose and/or coopts the shareholders' personal prerogatives in respect to charity giving. In this context, threatening to resign as means of securing passage of the project puts Rainmaker at risk in respect to *lo tahmod*. That Rainmaker seeks the funds not for his personal use but for the benefit of the company and of society should not be a saving factor here. *Lo tahmod*, according to R. Bezalel Stern, is violated whether the acquirer seeks the article for himself or for someone else.[31]

Corporate Altruism and Misplaced Priorities

Recall Nathan Schwartz's clinching argument against "toys for guns": that the project represented hypocritical conduct. Schwartz's objection finds theological force in the dictum of R. Hayyim Ibn Attar (Israel, 1696–1743) on the verse "You shall not take the Name of God your God in vain" (Exodus 20:7). In R. Hayyim's view, the verse intimates a prohibition against conveying a false impression of piety. It indicates that an individual should not deceive people into believing that he is more scrupulously religious that he knows himself to be. Such conduct amounts to taking the name of God in vain.[32]

R. Hayyim's dictum finds ready application to the case at hand. Engaging in do-good projects for society at large, yet at the same time paying its workers wages below industry average and falling behind in paying its bills, projects an image of virtue and caring that is undeserved.

Relatedly, "toys for guns" is objectionable because it represents misplaced priorities on the part of ASL. Of critical importance here is the prohibition against false religious pride (*yohara*).[33]

In his exposition of the concept of *yohara*, R. Moshe Meiselman identifies it as occurring when an individual who is presumably not proficient in basic religious observance engages in a religious practice that is expected only of people of the highest level of piety. Illustrating this concept is the objection R. Mosheh Isserles raises against a woman wearing a tallit and reciting a blessing over it.[34] The objection begins by noting that even for a man, the mitzvah of *zizit* (wearing fringes) is not an absolute requirement. This is so because the mitzvah is triggered only if one chooses to wear a four-cornered garment. There is no obligation for a man to go out and buy a four-cornered garment so as to make the mitzvah incumbent upon himself. Nevertheless, men have taken it upon themselves to perform the mitzvah of *zizit*. The observance of this mitzvah is thus a matter of extra piety. For a woman, the obligation is even more remote, because she has the further option of wearing a four- cornered garment without placing *zizit* on it. Because tallit is a "doubly optional" mitzvah for a woman, wearing a tallit communicates that she is punctilious of even the highest forms of piety. Because this communication presumably belies the reality of the situation, this conduct constitutes *yohara*.

Yohara is basically objectionable, in R. Meiselman's view, because the motives of the individual are suspect. Had the individual's motives been pure, he would certainly have first become proficient in basic observance before leaping to conduct expected only of the religious elite. The fact that he has not done so brands the conduct as religious exhibitionism.[35]

Engaging in do-good projects for society at large, while paying its workers wages that are below the industry average and falling behind in paying its bills, evidences skewed priorities on the part of the firm. This can engender only cynicism among the underprivileged or mistreated parties, contaminating the moral climate of society. In response, media and insider pressure for the firm to set its own house straight before engaging in altruism for society at large is warranted.

Corporate Altruism and the Publicly Traded Company

Altruistic projects sponsored by publicly traded companies are quite common nowadays. Given the frequency of corporate altruism the practice should be viewed as enjoying the tacit consensus of the shareholders.

This argument, however, has limited applicability. Suppose shareholders launch a class-action suit against management for engaging in corporate altruism projects. Here, the tacit-consensus argument can be invoked to knock down the claim of misappropriation. Given the long history of the practice, corporate altruism does not dash the legitimate expectations of investors. Hence the plaintiff's claim of misappropriation is unproved. But long-standing practice does not make for *clear-cut shareholder approval.* Note that the salient feature of the public corporation is *diffusion* of ownership. Changing managerial policy requires a considerable expenditure of time and resources in the form of marshaling sufficient support for the change among fellow shareholders. Far from signaling shareholder approval, lack of protest against corporate do-good projects may reflect an attitude that given the tiny percentage[36] of the firm's resources involved, the effort to overhaul the practice is not worth it. Ironically, one concern might be that such a campaign would tarnish the image of the firm, projecting it as "mean-spirited." Removing do-good projects from the firm's agenda might leave the public in doubt as to whether the firm discharges its mandated duties to its stakeholders.

Recall that Halakhah requires a manager to operate under a clear-cut mandate. Seeking *ex post* approval for unauthorized action does not suffice. The survival of the corporate do-good phenomenon may very well provide a classical example of the operation of the talmudic *kesufa* principle referred to earlier.

In recent years, statutes in over half the states, as well as case law in Delaware, have authorized directors of public corporations to consider the interests of corporate stakeholders other than shareholders. These non-shareholder constituencies include employees, creditors, and local communities.[37] The import of this development is to give shareholders *advance* notice that a percentage of their investment dollars may very well be used for social welfare causes that will result in less than profit maximization for their share value.

To be sure, this development moves corporate structure in the direction of reducing shareholders' dashed expectations when the publicly traded company engages in altruistic projects. But this approach is far from optimal. To illustrate: suppose a publicly traded company (SD) devotes 1 percent of its net profits to altruistic projects over a number of years and suddenly changes the percentage to 2 percent. Does not the change in policy dash the legitimate expectations of shareholders? Similarly, suppose that SD sticks with the 1 percent allocation but increases its outlays for do-good projects for society at large and reduces its expenditures on *lifnim mi-shurat ha-din* conduct vis-à-vis its immediate stakeholders. This change in policy not only dashes shareholder and especially *stakeholder* expectations, but also introduces skewed priorities and hence violates *yohara*. Finally, suppose SD introduces a checkoff system whereby 5 percent of employee wages is earmarked for donation to a choice of three charities, say, the Red Cross, the American Cancer Association, and the United Way. Since this policy co-opts the employees' legitimate prerogative to donate to the charities of their own choice, Halakhah would find disfavor with it.

An approach more consistent with Halakhah would require all public corporations to deal with the issues of altruism in their charter of incorporation. Specifically, the percentage of net profits to be devoted to corporate altruism should be specified. How these funds will be allocated between do-good projects for society at large and *lifnim mi-shurat ha-din* conduct toward its immediate stakeholders should be designated. Finally, the charter should provide measures to ensure that neither skewed priorities nor the co-opting of employee prerogatives will be introduced.

1. Lawrence W. Sherman, professor at the University of Maryland and president of the Crime Control Institute, quoted in Erik Eckholm, "Add Gun Buybacks to the Public Wish List," *New York Times*, January 2, 1994, p. 3.

2. Philip J. Cook, professor of public policy at Duke University, quoted in ibid.

3. George A. Steiner and John F. Steiner, *Business, Government and Society* (New York: McGraw-Hill, 1991), pp. 117–19, 122.

4. Milton Friedman, "The Social Responsibility of Business Is to Increase Its Profits, *New York Times Magazine*, September 13, 1970, pp. 323, 122–28, 132–35.

5. Thomas Mulligan, "A Critique of Milton Friedman's Essay, 'The Social Responsibility of Business Is to Increase Its Profits,'" *Journal of Business Ethics* 5 (1986): 265-69.

6. Bill Shaw, "A Reply to Thomas Mulligan's Critique of Milton Friedman's Essay, 'The Social Responsibility of Business Is to Increase Its Profits,'" *Journal of Business Ethics* 7 (1988): 541.

7. William M. Evan and R. Edward Freeman, "A Stakeholder Theory of the Modern Corporation: Kantian Capitalism," in *Ethical Theory of Business*, ed. Tom L. Beauchamp and Norman Bowie, 3rd ed. (Englewood Cliffs, N.J.: Prentice-Hall, 1988), pp. 97–106.

8. Maimonides (Egypt, 1135–1204), *Yad*, Sheluhin veShutefin 7:4; R. Jacob b. Asher (Germany, 1270–1343), *Tur*, Yoreh De'ah 177:42; R. Joseph Caro (Israel, 1488–1575), *Shulhan Arukh*, Yoreh De'ah 177:30.

9. R. Solomon b. Isaac, Rashi, at Bava Mezia 104b, s.v. *l'hakhi*.

10. Tosafot, Bava Mezia 104b, s.v. *d'lo*.

11. R. Mosheh Isserles (Poland, 1525 or 1530–1572), Rema, *Shulhan Arukh*, Yoreh De'ah 177:5.

12. Ibid. 177:22.

13. R. Joseph Trani, *Maharit*, Hoshen Mishpat 112.

14. *Yad*, Sekhirut 13:7; *Tur*, Hoshen Mishpat 337:20; *Shulhan Arukh*, Hoshen Mishpat 337:26.

For various aspects of the productivity standard Halakhah sets for the worker, see Aaron Levine, *Economics and Jewish Law* (Hoboken, N.J.: Ktav, 1987), pp. 178–82.

15. See Shillem Warhaftig, *Dinei Avodah baMishpat haIvri* (Jerusalem: Moreshet, 1968), 1:324.

16. David L. Engel, "An Approach to Corporate Social Responsibility," *Stanford Law Review* 32, no. 1 (November 1979): 16.

17. Please turn to pp. 250–55; 68–71 of this volume.

18. Deuteronomy 22:1–3.

19. Please turn to pp. 258–62 of this volume.

20. See John R. Boatright, *Ethics and the Conduct of Business*, 2nd ed. (Upper Saddle River, N.J., Prentice-Hall, 1997), p. 363.

21. R. Samuel b. Meir, Rashbam, Bava Batra 48a.

A "fair market value" duress sale, according to R. Isaac Alfasi, on the interpretation of R. Abraham b. David of Posquières (quoted in *Beit Yosef, Tur*, op. cit. 205:1, and Rema, *Sh.Ar.*, op. cit. 205:1), is valid only when the buyer makes full payment at the time the transaction is entered into. Should the duress sale have been entered into by means of deed, the sale is invalid, despite its fair market value price.

22. The pressure tactics B uses to acquire S's property violates for B the *lo tahmod* interdict. See Ezra Basri, *Dinei Mamonot*, vol. 2 (Jerusalem: Sucath David, 1976), p. 70, n. 1.

23. R. Huna, Bava Kamma 62a; Rif, Bava Batra 48a; *Yad*, Mekhirah 10:1; Rosh, Bava Batra 3:51; *Tur*, op. cit. 205:1; *Sh.Ar.* op. cit. 205:1; R. Jehiel Michel Epstein (Belarus, 1829–1908), *Arukh ha-Shulhan*, Hoshen Mishpat 205:2.

24. Bava Kamma 62a.

25. R. Joseph Caro, *Beit Yosef, Tur*, op. cit.; Rema, *Sh.Ar.*, op. cit. n. 2; R. Eliyahu b. Solomon Zalman, Gra, *Sh.Ar.*, op. cit., n. 1.

26. R. Jacob Moses Lorberbaum (Poland, 1760–1832), *Netivot ha-Mishpat, Sh.Ar.*, op. cit. 205, n. 1.

27. *Tur*, op. cit.; *Sh.Ar.*, op. cit. 205:4.

28. *Tur*, op. cit.; *Sh.Ar.*, op. cit. 205:7.

29. R. Joseph Colon, *Responsa Maharik* 184, quoted in Rema, *Sh.Ar.*, op. cit. 205:7.

30. See pp. 96–98 of this volume.

31. R. Bezalel Stern, *Bezel ha-Hokhmah* 3:45.

32. R. Hayyim Ibn Attar, *Ohr ha-Hayyim* at Exodus 20:7.

33. Cf. Berakhot 17b, Pesahim 55b.

34. Rema, *Sh.Ar.*, Orah Hayyim 17:2.

35. Moshe Meiselman, *Jewish Women in Jewish Law* (New York: Ktav, 1978), pp. 152–54.

36. Few corporate contributions exceed 1 percent of pretax profits. Boatright, *Ethics and the Conduct of Business*, p. 348.

37. Eric W. Orts, "Beyond Shareholders: Interpreting Corporate Constituency Statutes," *George Washington Law Review* 61, no. 1 (November 1992): 16, 26–31.

Ethical Investment: The Case of Rawley Tobacco

E. Bradford Key is an account executive at the Wall Street firm of Eagle Bros., Inc. For Key, successful stock picking requires the investor to keep a sharp eye on changing price-earnings ratios in the stock market. It was this fundamental statistic that proved the decisive factor in making up Key's mind to take a big position in Rawley Tobacco stock and to strongly recommend the stock to his customers.

In the latter half of 1996, Rawley Tobacco stock was battered by a series of events both specific to the company and damaging to the tobacco industry. These events included a hefty jury award in a liability suit against the company, the increasing number of states that filed suit against the industry for reimbursement of Medicare costs, and the announcement that the Clinton administration planned to subject tobacco to regulation by the Food and Drug Administration.

The cumulative effect of these and other events pushed down Rawley Tobacco's stock valuation in October 1996 to about five times estimated 1997 operating profits, compared with eighteen times operating profits for Coca-Cola.

Key pitted Rawley Tobacco's relatively low price-earnings ratio against the company's bright prospects for growth in overseas markets where the regulatory environment is lax. Reflection upon this data made Key a confirmed tobacco bull. Sooner or later, he reasoned, Rawley Tobacco shareholders will do fine. The stock will not be permanently undervalued!

As Key cheerfully went about hawking the Rawley Tobacco investment to his clients, he was surprised to encounter resistance in the form of *moral* objections against the investment. The main concern was the overwhelming evidence that links smoking with many dreadful diseases. This finding should make the production and sale of cigarettes immoral and investment in tobacco companies unethical. To this objection, Key responded that his job was to identify good investment ideas and not to make moral judgments. Moreover, since health warnings were mandated, cigarette addiction should not be blamed on the tobacco companies. It was, however, pointed out that tobacco companies failed to provide consumers with health warnings in overseas markets where governments do not require them. Since people who smoke are at risk, tobacco companies should provide health warnings whether the government requires it or not. Key could not defend the ethics here, but insisted that the tobacco company's obligation is no more than to comply with the law of each country in which it operates. Because shareholders will otherwise lose out, socially responsible conduct should not voluntarily be assumed unless it is consistent with profit maximization.

At issue here are the criteria Halakhah adopts for determining whether an investment is ethical or not. The analysis entails both technical and philosophical (hashkafic) elements.

Technical Halakhah and Ethical Investing

Let us begin with the technical perspective. The most basic issue here is whether Halakhah establishes a clear-cut prohibition against smoking. Rabbis dispute this point. Those who prohibit smoking cite the overwhelming medical evidence that links smoking to various dreadful diseases. This evidence should make smoking a prohibited activity by dint of the biblical injunction: "Only take heed and watch yourself very carefully" (Deuteronomy 4:9).[1] Other rabbis take the evidence as only making smoking a very imprudent activity, but not making for a clear-cut prohibition against it. This is so because smoking does not expose an individual to an immediate danger and, in addition, the habit of smoking is reversible.[2]

Suppose we adopt the viewpoint that smoking entails a clear-cut prohibition. The production and sale of cigarettes, then, become a menacing threat to the public's health. By dint of the injunction "Do not stand idly by the blood of your neighbor" (lo ta'amod al dam rei'akha, Leviticus 19:16), we would be required to do whatever we could to extricate our fellow from the health danger of cigarette smoking. Admonishing smokers in respect to the dangers of smoking as well as lobbying the government to prohibit the production and sale of cigarettes represent appropriate actions. The extent to which Halakhah demands that one engage in anti–cigarette smoking activities will, of course, depend on one's position, circumstances, and expected effect. Nevertheless, because we are all *theoretically* obligated to extricate our fellow from the dangers of cigarette smoking, investing in Rawley Tobacco stock is unthinkable. It would amount to an implicit *approval* of the company's operations and hence make an *outright mockery* of the lo ta'amod obligation.

Suppose we adopt the viewpoint that Halakhah does not adopt a clear-cut prohibition against cigarette smoking. Adopting this viewpoint does not lead to the judgment that Rawley Tobacco is free of halakhic violation. Consider that Rawley Tobacco aggressively markets tobacco products internationally. Given the enormous health risk smoking entails, persuasive advertising amounts to offering the public ill-suited advice and hence violates the lifnei iver interdict.[3] Moreover, Rawley Tobacco fails to inform the public of the health risks smoking entails in those countries where health warnings are not required by law. Does this negative assessment lead to a prohibition on investing in Rawley Tobacco? Not necessarily. If Rawley Tobacco were a Jewish company, a Jew would be duty bound to reprove its policymakers and urge them to make the indicated changes.[4] To be sure, an assessment that reproof (*tokhahah*) would be of no avail might very well free an individual of this duty.[5] But Rawley Tobacco is not a Jewish company. As a matter of strict duty,[6] *tokhahah* does not apply to the conduct of a non-Jew.[7]

At this juncture, it is relevant to consider to what extent shareholders of a public corporation are responsible for the policies of the company. Some excellent recent work has been done on this issue.[8] One widely held view is that responsibility for policy applies only to shareholders whose stake in the firm is sufficiently large to force the directors to take their opinion into account. If the investor's stake in the company does not reach this level, the investor bears no moral responsibility for the sins of the firm.[9] It follows that a non-significant investment in Rawley Tobacco stock should be permissible.

Another issue to consider here is whether the investor in Rawley Tobacco stock should be regarded as *assisting* the company in carrying out its prohibited policies. Abetting or assisting someone in the commission of a sin violates the *lifnei iver* interdict.[10] The issue entails the question of investing in new equity shares as well as investing in the secondary market.

Let us first take up the issue of purchasing new equity shares. As a preliminary, note that Rawley Tobacco markets its new equity shares by eliciting the services of Golden, an underwriter. Golden guarantees a price on its securities and then sells them to the public. To be sure, Golden's underwriting activity makes it *temporarily* a significant shareholder of Rawley. But consider that Golden does not make a commitment to Rawley before it has its customers in the secondary market lined up. This circumstance should remove Golden from being halakhically regarded as a significant shareholder in Rawley and hence responsible for its prohibited policies.

Two scenarios present themselves. In one scenario Golden is the only investment banker willing to underwrite Rawley's new issue. Because Rawley cannot market its new equity shares without Golden, Golden should be regarded as a facilitator of Rawley's prohibited policies and hence in violation of *lifnei iver*.

Suppose, however, that if Golden does not underwrite Rawley, another investment banker, Bennet, would do so. This circumstance reduces the severity of the *lifnei iver* issue at hand to a rabbinical rather than a Torah level.[11] Consider further that as a non-Jewish company, Rawley Tobacco would hardly see itself as bound in any way by Halakhah. Since American law does not regard Rawley Tobacco's policies as illegal, the company would certainly deliberately ignore Halakhah, even if its officers were aware of the halakhic objections. Now, since Rawley Tobacco is presumably ready to violate Halakhah's dictates deliberately and can easily obtain capital from Bennet instead of from Golden, Golden is not regarded as a facilitator even on a rabbinical level.[12]

Let us now turn to the secondary financial market. Consider that A's purchase of Rawley Tobacco's shares in the secondary market does not furnish the company with any new capital. What happens is that A gives up his cash to B in exchange for B's Rawley Tobacco shares. Decidedly, the transaction does not furnish the company with new capital. Given the *indirect* role an investor in the secondary market plays in enabling Rawley Tobacco to carry out its prohibited policies, the investor's action should fall under the *lifnei de-lifnei* leniency. Under this leniency, an individual is not regarded as "placing a stumbling block before a blind man" if a supervening event (*lifnei de-lifnei*) is required before the untoward outcome occurs. Providing an illustration of this leniency is the permissibility of selling incense of the type used in idol worship to a non-Jew when the vendor knows that the incense will be resold to someone who will use it for idolatry. Since the first purchaser resells the incense, and thus does not use it for idolatry, the second purchaser's use of it only constitutes *lifnei de-lifnei* from the standpoint of the original seller and thus does not entail an infraction of the law for him.[13] Clearly, an investment in Rawley Tobacco shares purchased in the secondary financial market plays only a *lifnei de-lifnei* role in enabling Rawley Tobacco to carry out its prohibited policies. The investment should therefore be permitted.

The Conglomerate and Ethical Investment

Consider the following scenario: ASL is a conglomerate whose shares are publicly traded. The company controls three subsidiaries. Its main business, carried out by two of its subsidiaries, is chewing gum and detergents. Its third subsidiary is Rawley Tobacco. ASL issues new equity shares. In its prospectus, ASL describes its investment plan as consisting of the purchase of a new computer system. Halakhah should find no objection to our investment banker, Golden, underwriting the new issue even if no other underwriter is willing to do so. An analogous case was dealt with earlier in this volume. Recall that R. Feinstein permitted a caterer to rent his hall and provide food for a wedding feast even though it was certain that social dancing would take place at the affair. The rationale behind the permissible ruling was that making an object available to an individual cannot be regarded as abetting a transgression unless the article is used primarily for prohibited purposes. Should this not be the case, the recipient's subsequent use of the article for a prohibited purpose does not brand the one who makes it available an abettor of a transgression. Accordingly, since the catering hall is primarily rented for permissible purposes, i.e., the wedding ceremony and banquet, its rental should not be regarded as abetting transgressors. In R. Feinstein's view. the circumstance that the hall is rented primarily for permissible purposes is sufficient to remove the *lifnei iver* problem even in a setting where the issue is violation of this interdict on a biblical level.[14]

Let us apply R. Feinstein's ruling to the case at hand. Golden's purchase of ASL's new equity issue should be permissible even though it is a matter of certainty that the tobacco business will directly benefit from the new computer installation. Given that the main business of ASL is chewing gum and detergents, Golden's underwriting activities to specifically finance ASL's new computer system should not be viewed as abetting the company's tobacco business. What Golden is doing is essentially to hand over to ASL a permissible item, namely a computer system.

Marit Ayin

At this juncture it is appropriate to consider the issue of *marit ayin* (concern for appearance). R. Barry Bressler applies this general principle of Halakhah to the issue of ethical investment. In R. Bressler's view, the *marit ayin* principle requires investors to make sure that their financial involvement in a company do not give the impression that they either are responsible for or approve the objectionable policies of the company. An investment that draws public attention, according to R. Bressler, violates this caveat. He notes that a 5 percent stake in a public corporation triggers an SEC requirement of public disclosure of the holding. Therefore, a 5 percent stake in a public corporation makes an individual's financial involvement with the company a matter of public knowledge.[15]

Suppose Nathan Schwartz makes a 5 percent investment in ASL. If ownership of ASL shares is not widely diffused, Schwartz's 5 percent stake in the company will not compel policymakers to take his opinion into account. Halakhically, Nathan Schwartz will not be regarded as an owner of ASL and will technically not be responsible for its policies. But a 5 percent stake in a public company triggers an SEC disclosure obligation. Nathan Schwartz's ownership will become a matter of public knowledge, and will give the impression that he supports the polices of ASL, including the way it runs its Rawley Tobacco subsidiary. In consequence, increasing his stake in ASL to the 5 percent level should be prohibited on the basis of *marit ayin*.

In the opinion of this writer, *marit ayin* has limited relevancy to the issue of ethical investment. Its application should be confined to instances analogous to the conglomerate case just dealt with. The salient feature here is that the prospects of the firm's growth in sales and profits are not predicated on the violation of Halakhah. Making an insignificant but disclosure-triggering investment only gives the *appearance* that Nathan Schwartz approves the infractions involved. But suppose the case study is not ASL, but Rawley Tobacco as a separate entity. Here, the company's future prospects are entirely predicated upon the *continuation* of policies that violate Halakhah. In this case, making an investment in the company does not simply entail an *appearance* of approving of the prohibited policies; it amounts to *condoning* these policies. Consider that the regulatory environment in the United States today will work to force a shrinking domestic market for Rawley Tobacco in the future. The company's prospects for growth in sales and profits will be entirely dependent on its growth prospects in foreign markets. Success in the overseas markets depends, in turn, on Rawley Tobacco's continuing the policies of lax or no health warnings and heavy advertising directed at youth.

Hanuppah and Ethical Investment

Condoning the sin of evildoers violates the prohibition called *hanuppah* (prohibited flattery).[16] We take it as a given that the prohibition applies whether the evildoer is Jewish or non-Jewish. In his treatment of *hanuppah*, R. Jonah b. Abraham Gerondi (Spain, ca. 1200–1264) identifies nine different levels of severity in the violation of this prohibition. Several of the nuances are applicable to the case at hand. The most severe violation entails the circumstance where the evildoer's transgression is a matter of public knowledge. Declaring to the evildoer in the presence of onlookers that "you have done no wrong" constitutes *hanuppah*. In addition, the offender's conduct violates a particularly severe form of falsehood: "He who vindicates the wicked and condemns the righteous—both are an abomination to the Lord" (Proverbs 17:15).[17]

In his treatment of *hanuppah*, R. Eliezer b. Samuel (Alsace, ca. 1115–1198) expands the parameters of the interdict to include an observer's failure to protest the evil. In the opinion of this authority, *hanuppah* is violated when one acquiesces in the evil or fails to protest it, not because of fear of reprisals by the evildoer, but out of moral weakness.[18]

In applying the *hanuppah* prohibition to the Rawley Tobacco investment, one could argue that each shareholder, big or small, implicitly communicates to the makers of company policy: "Don't worry, *I will not protest your evil*. Because I am convinced that society's moral fiber is too weak to stop you, I wish to *profit* from your evil by investing in your company."

To be sure, the investment may very well manifest a libertarian philosophy on the part of shareholder that government should not involve itself in policing society's morals. In the latter instance, the *hanuppah* involved is of a more severe genre.

Notwithstanding the *implicit hanuppah* message the investment in Rawley Tobacco entails, let us not lose sight of the fact that *hanuppah* is a *social sin*. It is violated only in the context of a *personal* communication or interaction. Here there is no explicit communication, only an implicit one. If the shareholder is insignificant from the perspective of Rawley Tobacco, the policymakers pay no attention to what the investor is saying. The message comes from a *stock certificate* consisting of a faceless person with no actual articulation. Add to this that one of the major rationales behind the prohibition is that *hanuppah* encourages the sinner to continue his wicked ways.[19] Of course, the viability of Rawley Tobacco depends heavily on an active secondary financial market. But this argues no more than that the secondary financial market *as a whole or as an institution* serves to encourage Rawley Tobacco. The policymakers do not, however, take note of the participation of any *particular insignificant investor* (A) in the secondary market. Hence A's purchase of shares is a *non-event* as far as Rawley Tobacco's policymakers are concerned. Given the impersonal and insignificant manner in which Rawley Tobacco views A, his *hanuppah* communication to the policymakers should halakhically be regarded as if it were made to someone who is not listening.

The mitigating factors outlined above do not apply, however, when the shareholder (B) is significant from the perspective of Rawley Tobacco. Then his opinions will be taken into account by Rawley's policymakers. They will fully expect to contend with B and meet with him personally in a business context. In short, for the policymakers of Rawley Tobacco, B is a *real* person who delivers the encouraging message "you do no wrong."

Suppose for the moment that ownership of Rawley Tobacco shares is widely diffused and a 5 percent stake in the company is significant from the standpoint of Rawley's policymakers. Recall that a 5 percent stake in a publicly traded company triggers an SEC disclosure obligation. When all the above elements are in place, increasing one's stake in Rawley to 5 percent would violate *hanuppah* in its most severe form.

Let us note that investing in a public corporation takes place through a broker. This means that even an *insignificant* investor is implicitly declaring in the presence of onlookers that he or she does not regard the company's policies as evil. The investor also condones the company's activities when he tells his friends about his investment in Rawley Tobacco. To be sure, this declaration is not being made in a personal way to the policymakers of the company, but nevertheless the purchase entails this declaration to third parties. Condoning the sin of an offender while not in the offender's presence also violates *hanuppah*, albeit on a lesser level of severity than in the previous case.[20]

Philosophic Concerns and Ethical Investing

Let us now turn to the perspective of *hashkafah* (Jewish philosophy) on the issue of ethical investments. We begin with R. Joseph B. Soloveitchik's insight into the blessing God conferred on Adam the first: "Be fruitful and multiply and fill the earth and subdue it" (Genesis 1:28). R. Soloveitchik understands this blessing as a divine *mandate* to mankind to subdue the earth and master the environment (hereafter, *kibbush*). In R. Soloveitchik's thinking, the *kibbush* mandate amounts to a charge to man to self-actualize himself by realizing his God-like potential as a creative being.

Fulfillment of the mandate bids man to achieve dignity but along with it to attain a rarefied sense of responsibility.

Man achieves dignity when he reclaims himself from coexistence with nature, rising from a helpless existence to a powerful existence that is intelligent, planned, and majestic.

Coexistence with nature is undignified because man is incapable of discharging his responsibilities in a state of bondage. The more man masters nature, the freer he is to discharge his responsibilities. Therefore, dignity is not an end in itself. Without raising man's sense of responsibility, dignity has no value.[21]

Before the *kibbush* mandate can become operational as an evaluative criterion, the importance of the economic system in actuating the *kibbush* mandate must be noted.

The most fundamental point to be made here is that progress in subduing nature and mastering the environment cannot take place in an economic vacuum. Given the specialization and division of labor characteristic of modern society, production is impossible without the cooperative voluntary exchange of countless economic units. Professional services are the product of society's educational and research institutions. The financial underpinnings of these institutions, in turn, depend on the viability of commerce and industry. The import of these interlocking relations is to make the subduing of nature and the mastering of the environment the work of the economic system as a whole.

Moreover, dignity manifests itself in the degree of access one has to the available technical progress. This makes income the means of securing dignity. The higher the per capita income, the more widely accessible this technical progress will be. But the single most important factor in determining society's per capita income is labor productivity. Improvements in labor productivity, in turn, result from such factors as harder work, better training, more or better equipment, and innovative technology. Economic growth hence works to propel human dignity to greater and greater heights.

Recognition of the role the economic system plays in the dignity-responsibility formulation of the *kibbush* mandate makes the ordinary activities of earning a livelihood a fulfillment of this mandate. This is so because the income an economic actor earns provides him with a measure of command over society's technical progress, thereby contributing to his own self-dignity. In addition, participation in the economic system frees the individual from the shackles of dependency[22] and raises his sense of responsibility.

What emerges from the *kibbush* mandate is a criterion for evaluating the *inherent worthiness* of economic activity. If an economic activity contributes neither to advancing man's dignity nor to his sense of responsibility, it has no rationale for existence.

Illustrating a perversion of the *kibbush* mandate is the production and sale of cigarettes. This judgment is not predicated on the ability of Halakhah to establish a clear-cut prohibition against smoking. Suppose, for argument's sake, that a clear-cut prohibition cannot be established. Nonetheless, the causative links medical science has established between cigarette smoking and various dreadful diseases is undeniable. Far from advancing human dignity, the tobacco industry degrades human existence by causing disease, misery, and pain. Its very existence perverts the *kibbush* mandate.

Rawley Tobacco's core economic mission is to produce and sell cigarettes. While a technical halakhic case can be made for permitting investment in Rawley Tobacco, the investment would represent a clear-cut perversion of the *kibbush* mandate and therefore should not be made.

Who at Rawley violates the *kibbush* mandate? Certainly it is not only the policymakers but also those who are halakhically responsible for the policies. Significant shareholders of Rawley stock fall into the latter category. But consider that any investment in Rawley, whether significant or not, will be a force to reduce the investor's sense of responsibility for his fellow man. Why? Because it is events such as expanded sales and a loosening of the regulatory environment that drive Rawley stock up, and the converse of these events that drives the stock down. One buys the stock because he both anticipates and hopes for favorable events, and because he hopes against unfavorable events. Hence successful investing in Rawley is a force that works to corrupt one's morals and is usually accompanied by an increase in suffering in the world. Thus, even becoming an insignificant investor in Rawley violates the *kibbush* mandate.

Promoting Rawley Tobacco Stocks as an Investment

In the opening vignette we encountered E. Bradford Key promoting Rawley Tobacco Co. shares to his clients. Key's conduct is halakhically objectionable. The severity of his infraction depends on Halakhah's attitude toward smoking. Let us proceed to draw out the indicated implications.

If we adopt the viewpoint that smoking is a prohibited activity, Rawley Tobacco Co. should be shut down. Because investment in Rawley Tobacco amounts to making a mockery of the *lo ta'amod* interdict, investing in the company, even only a small amount, is prohibited conduct. Encouraging someone to invest in Rawley amounts, therefore, to encouraging sinful activity. An analogous case is dealt with by R. Aryeh Loeb b. Joseph ha-Kohen Heller (Kezot, Poland, 1745–1813?):

A hires two witnesses to give false testimony that B owes $100 to C. The witnesses testify in court and B pays $100 to C. Notwithstanding that A indirectly caused B a loss of $100, the Bet Din (Jewish court) will not order A to compensate B for his loss. The principle here is that credence is given to A's argument that the witnesses should never have obeyed his instructions to commit a sin: If you must choose between the words of the Master [i.e., God, who commands you not to sin] and the word of the disciple [A, who instructs you to sin], whose word should you obey? (*divrei ha-rav ve-divrei ha-talmid divrei mi shomin*).

This logic works only to disallow a Bet Din from issuing a judgment against A. But to fulfill his obligation to the Heavenly Court (*dinei shamayyim*), A should voluntarily compensate B for his loss.

Suppose that instead of *hiring* the false witnesses, A merely induces them to bear false testimony that B owes $100 to C. Here, A bears no obligation whatsoever to B, even in respect to *dinei shamayyim*. Nonetheless, there is no gainsaying that A's conduct played a role, albeit a very indirect one (*gorem de-gorem*) in causing the witnesses to sin. Hence A's conduct is immoral.[23] Several earlier rulings follow Kezot's line.[24]

Kezot's analysis has a direct bearing in evaluating Key's conduct. Pushing Rawley shares on his clients is morally wrong. Promoting Rawley stock induces his clients to sin by investing in the company. Moreover, Key's cumulative effort in pushing the Rawley shares contributes in some measure to the viability of the secondary financial market for Rawley and enhances the ability of the company to conduct its business.

Key's conduct may also violate the biblical injunction against *meisit* (inciting a fellow to sin). *Meisit* is mentioned in connection with the sin of idolatry. In this context it is a capital offense.[25] R. Jacob b. Joseph Reischer (Austria, d.

1733) and others extend the prohibition of *meisit* to all sins.[26] Before we apply the *meisit* prohibition to Key's conduct, let us note both a stringency and a caveat of this prohibition in connection with the sin of idolatry. As for the stringency, the essence of the prohibition is the *effort* expended to induce someone to commit idolatry. Consequently, the perpetrator of *meisit* violates the prohibition whether or not his efforts succeed. As for the caveat, the perpetrator of *meisit* does not violate the prohibition unless he assures the would-be inductee that he will join him in committing the proposed sin.[27]

Applying these parameters to Key's conduct makes him guilty of *meisit* conduct for pushing the Rawley investment on his clients, irrespective of whether they end up making the investment or not. To be sure, Key will not be guilty of *meisit* conduct unless he assures his customers that he himself is taking a position in Rawley stock.

Another objection to Key's promotion of Rawley stock is that it amounts to *hanuppah* conduct.

Suppose we take the viewpoint that smoking is not a prohibited activity. Rawley remains an evil company because its policies, as described earlier, violate Halakhah. Within the framework of this model, becoming a significant investor in Rawley makes the investor responsible for the company's prohibited policies. Pushing an investment of this type on a customer makes Key a *gorem de-gorem* in respect to the sin of the investor. In addition, Key violates the *meisit* and *hanuppah* interdicts.

Pushing even an insignificant investment of Rawley stock on his clients violates for Key the *hanuppah* interdict.

Consider that Key's professional reputation is enhanced when his recommendations perform well and suffers when his recommendations perform below par. Accordingly, whether or not Key takes a position in Rawley stock for himself, he will identify with the fortunes of the company. He will cheer on events that loosen the regulatory grip on Rawley and react with disappointment to events that tighten the regulatory grip on Rawley. Thus, promoting Rawley Tobacco stock does violence to the *kibbush* mandate.

Permissible Forms of Investing in Rawley

Several ways of investing in Rawley stock apparently meet the ethical standards we have discussed thus far. These include short selling and mutual fund investment. Let us take up each in turn.

Short Selling

In a short sale, the investor anticipates a decline in the price of the security at hand. Accordingly, he borrows the security and immediately sells it, anticipating that he will buy it back when the price declines and return it to the lender. If things work out as anticipated, the short seller will make money, because he will pay a lower price for the security than what he sold it for. Halakhah should find no objections to short selling Rawley Tobacco, even when it entails a significant investment. Let us see why. When the short sale is initiated, the investor (A) is merely *borrowing* someone else's (B's) shares and is therefore not their legal owner. This being the case, A is not responsible for Rawley's policies. To be sure, when A buys back the shares, he temporarily becomes a significant shareholder of Rawley. But the terms of the short sale require A to return the shares to B as soon as he buys the borrowed shares back. Because A's ownership in Rawley shares is so transient that he has no chance to control or influence the Rawley's policy, he should halakhically be regarded as no more an owner of Rawley than a permanent insignificant shareholder.

Consider that the short seller operates in the secondary financial market. Thus he does not take on the role of facilitator or abettor of Rawley's policies.

Finally, consider that the motivation behind the short sale is the anticipated decline in Rawley stock. Thus, in making the investment in Rawley, A is neither guilty of *hanuppah* nor in violation of the *kibbush* mandate.

Mutual Funds

A mutual fund company pools the resources of many small investors by selling them shares and using the proceeds to buy a diversified portfolio of securities. Such shares represent a proportionate ownership in the portfolio of securities held by the mutual fund. An investor in a mutual fund does not, however, acquire direct ownership of the securities the mutual fund company buys into. Instead, the price of the shares is merely *tied* to the assets of the fund.

Suppose a non-Jewish-owned mutual fund company, MF, has Rawley Tobacco shares in its portfolio. The Rawley shares constitute only an insignificant portion of a diversified portfolio of securities. Nathan Schwartz invests in MF. His investment in MF should find no halakhic objection. Let us see why.

Consider that Nathan Schwartz's investment in MF acquires for him no direct ownership of Rawley shares, and, in addition, that Schwartz has no say in MF's investment decisions. Schwartz, therefore, bears no responsibility for Rawley's policies, irrespective of the size of his investment in MF.

Relatedly, Schwartz's indirect ownership of Rawley stock confers him *lifnei-de-lifnei* status in relation to encouraging Rawley's policies.

Let us now move to the *hanuppah* issue. Recall that *hanuppah* is a social sin; it is not violated unless one communicates approval to the evildoer. By investing in MF, Schwartz acquires anonymity in respect to Rawley. As far as Rawley is concerned, Schwartz is nonexistent. Hence Schwartz's investment in MF communicates no message of approval to Rawley's policymakers. In respect to MF's managers, Schwartz's investment communicates implicitly only that he has confidence in their overall performance record, but says nothing regarding his approval of their individual stock selections.

Finally, let us take up the *kibbush* issue. To be in violation of the *kibbush* mandate, one must either be responsible for Rawley's policies or experience a reduced sense of responsibility on account of the investment. A mutual fund investor, as previously discussed, is neither a shareholder of Rawley nor responsible for its policies. Given MF's wide diversification of asset holdings, the performance of the Rawley investment in MF will not reduce Schwartz's sense of responsibility to his fellow man. But suppose that 3 percent of MF's assets are invested in Rawley shares. Other things equal, tobacco news will assuredly move MF's share price. Here, Schwartz will identify with Rawley's fortunes, and his ownership of MF violates the *kibbush* mandate. What this points to is an investigative responsibility for Schwartz. Before investing in a mutual fund, he should check out the asset holding of the company to ensure that its largest-percentage asset holdings are not in companies that violate the *kibbush* mandate.

Let us consider one final variation. Suppose Schwartz's investigation finds that on the basis of MF's latest report to shareholders, it has no large percentage investments in Rawley. He therefore goes ahead with the investment. In a subsequent report, Schwartz discovers that MF has increased its holdings of Rawley to a relatively high percentage of its asset holdings. Here, Schwartz should be under no obligation to liquidate his investment on the basis of MF's latest report. Since Schwartz violates no technical Halakhah by holding on to MF, he should bear no responsibility to incur a possible loss by switching to another investment.

Investment Ethics in the Secular Business Ethics Literature

The issue of investment ethics is discussed by several commentators in the pages of the *Journal of Business Ethics*. In this section we will survey this literature and proceed to contrast the perspective these commentators develop with the halakhic approach to this issue.

Let us first turn to the work of Professor William B. Irvine. He begins his analysis by invoking a popular investment ethics rule: don't invest in an evil company (hereafter, the "evil company principle"). Evil companies, Irvine tells us, come in two varieties. One variety is a *directly evil* company. This company commits wrongdoing in the very act of conducting its business. An illustration would be a company that uses slave labor to manufacture, say, pencils. Another variety of an evil company is the *indirectly evil* company. This company commits no wrongdoing in the creation of its product, but the nature of its product is such that it is an instrument of evil in the hand of users. Illustrating the second variety is a company that manufactures a poison whose only known use is to cause people to die horrible lingering deaths.

To be sure, a company can be both directly and indirectly evil. An example of this would be a company that uses slave labor to manufacture the poison described above.

Irvine is convinced that the evil company principle is flawed. In his opinion, one can easily imagine circumstances under which it would be morally permissible to buy the stock of a company that is, *at present*, extremely evil. Consider the following scenario: XYZ produces the deadly poison described above with slave labor. The president of the company becomes repentant and offers B the following deal: If B would agree to buy a certain amount of shares in XYZ, A promises, in return, to discontinue production of the poison and begin production of a new product that is beneficial to mankind. In addition, the company will no longer use slave labor, and a portion of B's investment will be used to compensate the former slaves for past injustices. Under these circumstances, it would be permissible, according to Irvine, for B to invest in the XYZ company.

The preceding analysis leads Irvine to conclude that what makes it wrong to invest in an evil company is the company's evil intentions for the future. But what moral principle explains the prohibition? Irvine's answer is the enablement principle. Three versions of this principle are offered: (1) it is morally wrong to do something that enables others to do wrong; (2) it is morally wrong to enable others to do wrong unless failure to do the thing in question will have even worse consequences; (3) it is morally wrong to do something that *one realizes* will enable others to do wrong.

The third version of the enablement principle distinguishes between cases of innocent enabling and cases of knowing enabling. Innocent enabling is illustrated with the following scenario: B buys shoes from S. S uses the cash to buy a gun which he uses to kill his wife. Because B could not reasonably have anticipated the tragic sequence of events, B is not regarded as an *enabler* of S's crime.

The enablement principle, in Irvine's thinking, makes it morally wrong for

A to make a significant investment in XYZ shares in the secondary financial market. To be sure, A's purchase does not infuse XYZ with new capital, but the transaction will, nonetheless, enhance XYZ's ability to conduct its business. This is so because a company's ability to issue new stock depends upon the willingness of investors to buy stock when it is no longer new. In particular, no underwriter will buy a company's new stock unless there are investors who will buy the stock from them in the secondary market. If investors systematically shun a company's old stock, the company will find it quite difficult to issue new stock. Conversely, the willingness of investors to buy a company's old stock makes it easier for the company to raise capital and hence makes it easier for the company to conduct its business.

Irvine stretches the enablement principle to make morally wrong even a small purchase of XYZ stock in the secondary financial market. Taken in isolation, A's insignificant purchase of XYZ stock will not affect the ability of the company to conduct its business. But the transaction should not be judged in isolation, but rather by its effect on the viability of the firm if many investors imitate A's action. Irvine calls this perspective the universalizability principle. Application of the universalizability principle renders a negative moral judgment on A's insignificant investment in XYZ shares.

One form of investment in XYZ to which the enablement principle would have no objection is the short sale of its stock. This is so because, other things equal, a short sale has the effect of increasing the supply of XYZ stock relative to demand. This puts downward pressure on the company's stock price. Downward pressure on the company's stock, in turn, hinders rather than enhances the company's ability to raise new capital. Because the short sale does not enhance the ability of the company to conduct business, there is no moral objection to this type of investment.[28]

Professor Robert Larmer provides a critique of William Irvine's work. At the outset, Larmer objects to the distinction Irvine draws between directly evil and indirectly evil companies. Consider that a company that manufactures a product must be taken as approving and encouraging the use of that product. Accordingly, if the sole or primary use of the product in question is immoral, then the manufacturer must be taken as approving and encouraging that use.

Larmer regards Irvine's rejection of the evil company principle as premature. This is so because what is morally undesirable is not the enabling of a company to do harm, but rather the enabling of a company *with evil intentions* to do harm. Far from supplanting or replacing the evil company principle, the enablement principle presupposes and requires it. There is, therefore, a strong case for accepting the evil company principle as basic and regarding the enablement principle as an extended or supplementary form of it.

Once it is recognized that the evil company principle remains intact, there is a moral objection to a small purchase of XYZ stock in the secondary financial market even without the aid of the universalizability principle. Specifically, what is wrong in A's investing in XYZ stock is not that the investment provides the company with resources whereby it can engage in wrongdoing, but rather that A's investment amounts to *condoning* the immoral conduct of the company. Because A's investment in XYZ shares amounts to condoning its policies, A's investment is immoral even if it is so insignificant as not to enable the company to conduct its business.[29]

Secular and Halakhic Ethics Compared

The Evil Company

Irvine defines the evil company with his examples of a company that produces pernicious poison and a company that produces pencils with slave labor. In either case the company generates a clear-cut and pernicious harm to one or more of its immediate stakeholders. In a civilized society, this company should be shut down! Several halakhic principles compel action, on various levels, to promote this objective. These are the *lo ta'amod* and *tokhahah* obligations, discussed earlier in this case study. To be sure, the extent to which Halakhah demands someone to engage in activities designed to shut down the evil company will depend on the person's position, circumstances, and expected impact. Nevertheless, because we are all *theoretically* obligated to protest and stop the danger that the evil company is generating, investing in the evil company is unthinkable. Such conduct amounts to an implicit *approval* of the company's operations and makes an *outright* mockery of our theoretical obligations to *shut down* the company.

I dare say that Irvine's example of an evil company provides a setting for engaging in a permissible bluffing stratagem. Let us use Irvine's own scenario to illustrate this. Suppose the president of the evil company, Mr. Big Evil, asks A to make an investment in his company and, in return, promises to shut down production of the poison and begin to produce a product beneficial to mankind. Since the evil company should be shut down and made to make restitution to society, Evil's demand for a bribe to shut down his company is brazenly immoral. Accordingly, there should be no moral issue for A to *feign* interest in the offer and all along maneuver to get the company to shut down without transferring any money to it. Toward this end, A could, for instance, agree to the deal but request two weeks to arrange financing and also insist that the deal is off unless Evil shuts down production and sale of the poison immediately.

Given that A's intention here is to stall until other forces come to bear to effect a permanent shutdown of the company, A's bluffing strategy is morally acceptable.

The search for a moral principle that prohibits even a small investment in the evil company, as described by Irvine, ends with the *lo ta'amod* and the *tokhahah* duties. These principles are much more fundamental than the enablement principle that Irvine invokes.

Investment in the evil company, as described by Irvine, amounts not only to *condoning* the conduct of the company but to making a *mockery* of one's *theoretical* duty to take action to shut down the company. Hence the *lo ta'amod* and *tokhahah* duties are more fundamental than the investment ethic Larmer invokes. To be sure, investing in the evil company violates the *kibbush* mandate and may run afoul of the prohibition against *hanuppah*. The aforementioned principles provide specific content for Larmer's notion that investing in the evil company amounts to *condoning* the company's evil conduct.

Rawley Tobacco, the fictional company described in this chapter, is an evil company of a different genre than the company described by Irvine. Its salient feature is that its policies comply with secular law but violate Halakhah. Recall that the specific assumptions we made for this case study led to the conclusion that the *lo ta'amod* and *tokhahah* duties are not operative. Thus the ethics of investing in Rawley revolves around a number of other criteria and moral principles. One important restraining factor is not to invest so heavily as to force the company's policymakers to take your opinion into account. A stake of this size makes you an owner of the company and hence responsible for its policies. Other principles that were brought into consideration were the *lifnei iver* principle, the *marit ayin* principle, the prohibition against *hanuppah*, and the *kibbush* mandate.

The Enablement Principle

The halakhic counterpart of Irvine's enablement principle is the *lifnei iver* interdict. For the purpose of comparing *lifnei iver* with its secular counterpart, we will use Rawley Tobacco as the example of the evil company rather than Irvine's XYZ corporation. As formulated by both Irvine and Larmer, the enablement principle is far broader in application than the *lifnei iver* interdict. Irvine and Larmer invoke the enablement principle to prohibit making a significant investment in evil company shares in the secondary financial market. By shoring up the enablement principle with the universalizability principle, Irvine finds a basis for prohibiting even the purchase of a small number of evil company shares in the secondary financial market. In sharp contrast, *lifnei iver* is not a prohibiting factor in the secondary financial market. Moreover, one can conjure up circumstances wherein even the purchase of new equity shares of an evil company is not proscribed by dint of *lifnei iver*. This occurs when the company is a conglomerate and only one of its entities is an evil company. Another mitigating factor that must be present is that another underwriter is willing to arrange the financing.

Avoiding the Greater Evil

At this juncture, let us consider Irvine's second version of the enablement principle from the perspective of Halakhah. Irvine's principle states: It is wrong to enable others to do wrong unless failure to do the thing in question will have even worse consequences.

The notion that it is morally acceptable to take action with the aim of minimizing a greater evil finds validity in respect to the *lifnei iver* interdict. In his survey of the rabbinic literature on this topic, Rabbi J. David Bleich cites a number of authorities who subscribe to this notion.[30] To cite but one example: R. Abraham Bornstein (Poland, 1839–1910) permits the sale of improperly slaughtered animals to a habitual sinner because the net effect is to prevent the more numerous transgressions incurred in eating meat of a non-kosher species.[31]

This principle is stretched to its limits by a contemporary Israeli decisor, R. Mosheh Sternbuch. In a responsum, R. Sternbuch addressed a query from a newly observant young man. The young man desired to invite his parents to Sabbath meals in hopeful anticipation that the Shabbat experience, over a period of time, would lead them to become observant. Because the parents customarily drove to their son's place, extending the invitation to them would in all likelihood involve the parents in forbidden travel on Shabbat.

In responding to this query, R. Sternbuch preliminarily points out that the interdict against facilitating a sin is not presented by the Torah in a manner that conveys an *absolute* prohibition. Instead, the Torah writes, "nor shall you place a *stumbling block* before the blind" (Leviticus 19:14). It can be inferred from the use of this phraseology that *lifnei iver* applies only in a situation where an act is designed to cause a harm in the form of a transgression. But if the conduct is designed to yield an ultimate benefit, it should not be regarded as a stumbling block. What is controlling here, in the thinking of R. Sternbuch, is the *intent* of the facilitator. If the facilitator's intention is spiritually beneficial, a *lifnei iver* character is not attached to the conduct.[32]

R. Bleich takes sharp issue with the analogies R. Sternbuch employs to reach this conclusion. Moreover, he demonstrates that the thrust in the rabbinic literature is to focus upon the net effect of action over inaction rather than upon benevolent intent.[33]

The preceding discussion has much relevancy for the Rawley Tobacco Co. case study. Consider the following scenario:

Aytan Kramer, a billionaire philanthropist, is imbued with a sense of mission to reduce the habit of smoking in society. Toward this end, Kramer plans to announce that he will acquire a substantial stake in Rawley and immediately embark upon a proxy fight to reform the company. For starters, his agenda will be to introduce health warnings on cigarette packages sold in overseas markets.

In evaluating the halakhic ethics of Kramer's investment, let us not forget that the significant stake Kramer takes in Rawley makes him responsible for the company's policies. But these policies will assuredly go on anyway, regardless of what Kramer does. Consider also that Kramer's intention in investing in Rawley is clearly benevolent, namely, to reform the company. On the basis of R. Sternbuch's criterion, there should be no objection to Kramer's plan of action. Moreover, consider that the publicity for Kramer's initial announcement and the subsequent proxy fights will surely convince some people to either stop or not begin the smoking habit. Hence Kramer's initiative will surely have a net beneficial effect.

Reinforcing this conclusion is a consideration of the probable impact of Kramer's socially responsible initiative on the price of Rawley shares. What is the relationship between corporate social responsibility and measures of financial performance? In a survey examining twenty-two research studies designed to examine this question, Professors Joshua Krausz and Moses L. Pava found that only a single study documented a negative association. Most studies showed either that social responsibility was positively related to financial performance or that there was no association. The authors concluded that there is virtually no evidence to suggest that social responsibility causes poor financial performance. Rather, on average, social responsibility may actually improve traditional financial performance.[34]

Kramer's bold plan to reform Rawley brings the Krausz-Pava doctrine to test in uncharted territory. The issuance of health warnings in overseas markets can work only to reduce the growth of sales in these markets. Thus Kramer's radical plan is *bearish* for Rawley shares and will probably spring short sellers into action. Because Kramer's plan works to reduce investor buying interest in Rawley shares, it fosters higher societal fulfillment of the *kibbush* mandate and at the same time reduces infractions of the *hanuppah* interdict.

The upshot of the above analysis is that Kramer's initiative will surely have a net beneficial effect. His investment plan should therefore be morally acceptable according to all authorities.

Directly and Indirectly Evil Companies

Recall Larmer's objection to the distinction Irvine drew between directly and indirectly evil companies: A company that manufactures a product must be taken as approving and encouraging the use of that product. Accordingly, if the sole or primary use of the product in question is immoral, then the manufacturer must be taken as approving and encouraging that use.

There can be no doubt that Halakhah would be in general agreement with Larmer's proposition. Consideration of the variety of circumstances the principle encompasses, however, calls for several refinements of the proposition. First, let us note that *lifnei iver* comes in two forms. One is the prohibition against facilitating sin by making a forbidden item *accessible* to a would-be sinner. Such conduct violates *lifnei iver* on a biblical level. Indirection here may remove the *lifnei iver* prohibition. Recall that it is permissible to sell incense of the type used in idol worship to a non-Jew when resale to idol worshipers is predicable. Since the first purchaser does not himself use the incense for idolatry, the second purchaser's use of it constitutes *lifnei de-lifnei* from the standpoint of the original seller and thus does not entail an infraction of the law for him.

The *lifnei de-lifnei* leniency is not an absolute rule. In some instances, *lifnei de-lifnei* is not a mitigating circumstance and the *lifnei iver* interdict remains intact, at least on a rabbinical level. This can be seen from Maimonides' (Egypt, 1135–1204) treatment of the prohibition on selling weapons to heathens and Jewish bandits:

> It is forbidden to sell a heathen arms of any kind, or to sharpen his weapons, or to sell him a knife or collars or fetters or chains of iron or bars of Indian steel, or [to sell him] bears or lions, or anything that may be a public danger. Shields may be sold to heathens, since they are solely defensive.
>
> Just as the sages forbade the direct sale of these things to a heathen, so did they forbid their sale to an Israelite who sells such things to a heathen. Weapons may, however, be sold to the local militia, since they protect the Israelite population.
>
> Whatever should not be sold to a heathen should not be sold to an Israelite brigand, for to do so is to support a transgressor and lead him astray.[35]

Maimonides' prohibition on selling weapons to a Jew who sells such things to a heathen is in apparent contradiction to the incense case referred to above. The difference between the two cases is clear-cut, however. In the incense case, the issue is confined to a determination of whether the seller (A) of the incense encouraged or facilitated the commission of sin. Since the idolater needs no encouragement, and A did not directly sell him the incense, A is guilty neither of encouraging the sin nor of directly assisting its commission. In the weapons case, the manufacturer has a duty to avert harm from his fellow. The circumstance that the manufacturer does not directly sell the weapon to a heathen works only to free him from being characterized as directly facilitating, assisting, or urging on any subsequent offense committed with the weapon. But by making the weapon *accessible* to the criminal, albeit not in a direct manner, the manufacturer has violated his duty to avert harm from his fellow. Hence *lifnei de-lifnei* is not a mitigating factor in the arms case.

Another form of *lifnei iver* violation consists of encouraging evildoers to sin. Provided this conduct is not accompanied by making a forbidden item accessible to the would-be sinner, the conduct cannot possibly violate pentateuchal law but instead violates rabbinical law. *Lifnei de-lifnei* should be a mitigating factor here. Illustrating this is one of the scenarios of the Rawley Tobacco case study. Let us assume that Halakhah does not establish any clear-cut prohibition against smoking and the problem with Rawley is its prohibited policies. Here, A's significant investment in Rawley in the secondary financial market should not violate *lifnei iver*. Given that A's investment has no effect whatsoever on either the formulation of Rawley policy or on making *cigarettes more accessible to consumers*, A's investment does not violate his duty to avert harm from his fellow. Since A's investment hands over cash not to the company but only to a fellow investor, A's action does not constitute *direct* encouragement of evildoers. Thus the search for a moral principle that would prohibit A from making a significant investment in Rawley in the secondary financial market cannot rely on the *lifnei iver* interdict. Support for prohibiting such conduct, however, may find a rationale in the prohibition against *hanuppah* and in the *kibbush* mandate.

At this juncture let us return to Maimonides' ruling in the arms-sales case. Maimonides' formulation of the restrictions that apply to the sale of arms makes it a prohibition to sell the arms only if the weapons will end up in the hands of those who will use them for crime. It is not immoral, however, to sell a weapon to a law-abiding citizen. Would Maimonides permit the sale of the lethal poison described by Irvine to a law-abiding citizen? No! The difference between the two cases in clear-cut. A weapon should not be characterized as an object whose *inherent* primary use is immoral. While a weapon is a tool for evil in the hands of a criminal, it is a means of legitimate self-defense in the hands of a law-abiding citizen. Accordingly, it is not immoral to sell a weapon to a law-abiding citizen. In sharp contrast, the *only* use of the poison described by Irvine is to commit murder or suicide. This characterization does not change depending on who buys the poison. Since the poison is *inherently* an instrument of evil, selling it to anyone amounts to a directly evil act.

At this juncture, let us address a variation of the above case, dealt with in the secular business ethics literature. The case, alluded to earlier in this volume, entails the ethics of selling tobacco products. Recall Walters's proposition that role-specific duties should never pre-empt the private individual's sense of personal responsibility. Accordingly, if A believes that tobacco products are harmful, it is unethical for him to sell them, notwithstanding that A issues an appropriate health warning before he concludes the sale.[36]

In extrapolating Halakhah's guideposts for the above case, perhaps the most fundamental point to be made is that A's subjective feeling in the matter is not the controlling factor in providing him with an ethical guidepost. Instead, A should seek out a ruling from a halakhic authority on the permissibility of smoking. If the ruling A gets is that smoking is absolutely prohibited, then it becomes unethical for A to sell tobacco products to B even if he issues an appropriate warning before he concludes the sale. Since B is prohibited from smoking, even though he can theoretically consume tobacco products in a manner that would not compromise his health, selling him tobacco products amounts to "strengthening the hand" of a transgressor. But suppose that the halakhic ruling A gets holds that smoking is only imprudent conduct but does not entail a clear-cut prohibition. Within this framework, it is not unethical for A to sell B tobacco products, provided A issues a proper health warning before concluding the sale. In countries where an appropriate health warning is already affixed to the tobacco-product package, A should be exempt from issuing any additional health warning. But in countries where the health warning is not required or is made in an inadequate manner, it would be unethical for A to sell B tobacco products before first apprising B of the health risks involved.

Moreover, let us not forget that tobacco is an impulse good.[37] An impulse good is a product the consumer would not make a special shopping trip to buy, but once in the store will pick up on impulse because it satisfies a strongly felt need. Sellers exploit the consumer's strongly felt need for an impulse good by strategically placing it near the checkout counter.[38] Because consumption of tobacco is imprudent, A is prohibited from engaging in any form of persuasion to induce someone to buy it. One form of persuasion is for A to strategically place tobacco products near the checkout counter in his retail outlet. Such conduct is prohibited.

Suppose the evidence regarding a product's effects is inconclusive, and reasonable people differ as to whether it is harmful. What are the ethical guideposts in selling such a product? Walters's case of alar-treated apples meets this description.[39] From the perspective of Halakhah, this is not a new category, but fits into the guideposts of the previous case. There is one proviso, however. Suppose the halakhic authority rules that on the basis of the available evidence, the product in question has a clean bill of health and there is no reason to exercise caution in not consuming it. Here, even if the seller personally decides to abstain from the product, he would be under no obligation to share his concerns with a customer. No health warning is required.

Selling an Item Used Primarily for a Permissible Purpose for a Prohibited Use

Let us consider one more scenario relating to the ethics of selling an item when the vendor knows that the article of sale will be used for a prohibited purpose. Suppose the article at hand is primarily used for a permissible purpose. Is the seller restrained from selling it if he knows the buyer at hand will use it for a prohibited purpose? This variant was dealt with earlier in the case study. Recall that R. Feinstein permitted a caterer to rent a hall and provide food for a wedding feast even though it was certain that social dancing would take place at the affair.

Let us consider a variant of the above case: Suppose B informs the salesperson (S) who is about to sell him a baseball bat that he plans to use it to beat up old ladies. May S go ahead with the sale? Is the circumstance that the baseball bat is primarily used for permissible purposes a mitigating factor? Or is the overriding consideration B's announced intention to use the bat for evil purposes? A fundamental issue here is whether S is obligated to take B's declaration of evil intent *seriously*. The rule Halakhah generally lays down is that a man lacks the legal capacity to make himself wicked by his own declaration (*ein adam meisim azmo rasha*).[40] Decisors have, however, construed this very narrowly. The understanding of the rule proffered by R. Solomon b. Abraham Adret (Spain, 1235–1310) is typical. According to R. Adret, the rule says only that A faces no legal consequences as a result of his admission. Specifically, on the basis of A's admission *alone*, the Bet Din will neither disqualify him to bear testimony nor impose a fine on him or order him to face corporal punishment.[41] Now, if *ein adam meisim* relates only to the issue of legal consequences, then S must take seriously B's declaration of evil intent. Since S is duty bound to avert harm from his fellow, it would be immoral for S to sell the baseball bat to B in the face of B's declaration of evil intent.

A related case is dealt with by R. Israel Meir ha-Kohen Kagan (Hafez Hayyim; Poland, 1838–1933): S informs L that he intends to inflict harm on V. The harm consists either of bodily injury, embarrassment, or financial damage.

Is L required to warn V of the harm he faces? Invoking the talmudic principle of "a man frequently threatens mischief and does not do it" (*avid inish de-gazim ve-la avid*, Shevuot 46a), Hafez Hayyim rules that L must warn V of S's threat only if S has already established a behavioral pattern of issuing threats and making good on them or, alternatively, if the circumstances indicate a strong likelihood that the threat will be carried out. However, when S's threat entails a danger to V's life, L must take it seriously and warn V. Here *avid inish de-gazim* does not apply. Moreover, perhaps *avid inish de-gazim* says no more than that S faces no legal penalties in consequence of his disclosure but that L must take S's threats against V seriously.[42]

Note that in Hafez Hayyim's discussion the issue revolves around whether the prohibition against speaking *rekhilut* (true but evil talk) is suspended for L in the face of the information L has about S's evil intentions against V.[43] In the case discussed earlier, the issue of *rekhilut* does not come up, as S reveals only his intention to use the baseball bat to beat up old ladies but does not identify who the victims might be. S's responsibility to refrain from selling the baseball bat to B, therefore, remains intact even if S communicates only a desire to intimidate old ladies to give him money but promises not to physically harm them.

1. The rabbinical authorities for this are cited in Fred Rosner, "Cigarette Smoking and Jewish Law," *Journal of Halachah and Contemporary Society* 4 (Fall 1982): 40–45.

2. This is the position taken by Rabbis S. Z. Auerbach and Ovadiah Yosef, quoted in A. S. Abraham, *Medical Halachah for Everyone* (Jerusalem and New York: Feldheim, 1980), p. 6. See also Rabbi J. David Bleich, "Survey of Recent Halkhic Periodic Literature," *Tradition* 16, no. 4 (Summer 1977): 121–23; 17, no. 3 (Summer 1978): 140–42.

3. Leviticus 19:14; *Torat Kohanim*, ad loc.; Maimonides (Egypt, 1135–1204), *Yad*, Rozeah 12:14.

4. Leviticus 19:17.

5. This is the view of R. Isaac b. Jacob Alfasi (Algeria, 1013–1103, Rif, Yevamot 65b, and Tosafot, Bava Batra 60b. R. Mosheh Isserles (Poland, 1525 or 1530–1571), Rema, *Sh.Ar.*, Orah Hayyim 608:2, however, regards the duty of *tokhahah* as remaining intact even when it will not be heeded.

6. Noting that God sent Jonah to Nineveh to rebuke the city of non-Jews, *Sefer Hasidim* (1124) posits that it is meritorious, even if not obligatory, to reprove non-Jews for wrongdoing.

7. R. Solomon b. Isaac, Rashi, Sanhedrin 75a; R. Shabbetai b. Meir ha-Kohen, *Siftei Kohen*, *Sh.Ar.*, Yoreh De'ah 151:6; R. Naftali Zevi Yehudah Berlin (Russia, 1817–1893), *Meshiv Davar* 2:31.

8. Please turn to p. 176, n. 35 of this volume.

9. Cf. R. Mosheh Feinstein (New York, 1895—1986), Resp. Iggerot Mosheh, Even ha-Ezer 1:7.

10. Leviticus 19:14; *Yad*, Rozeah 12:14.

11. R. Nissin b. Abraham Gerondi (Spain, 1310–1375), Ran, Avodah Zarah 6b. Tosafot (Hagigah 13a), however, take the view that if the sin is accessible to the violator without the

aid of A, A's facilitating action is entirely permissible, even on a rabbinical level. Both views are cited by R. Mosheh Isserles (Rema, *Sh.Ar.*, Yoreh De'ah 151:1), who rules in accordance with Tosafot, but recommends that pious people follow Ran's stringent position.

12. R. Shabbetai b. Meir ha-Kohen, *Siftei Kohen*, Yoreh De'ah 151:6, and comments by R. Ezekiel b. Judah ha-Levi Landau (Prague, 1713–1793), *Dagul me-Revavah* ad loc., on *Siftei Kohen*, loc. cit. The proposition that *lifnei iver* on a rabbinical level is suspended when the transgressor sins deliberately is advanced by R. Landau only in the instance where the transgressor is a Jew. When the transgressor is an non-Jew, R. Shabbetai ha-Kohen may well suspend the *lifnei iver* interdict even when the transgressor sins unwittingly.

13. Avodah Zarah 14a.

14. Please turn to pp. 49—51.

15. Barry Bressler, "Ethical Investment: The Responsibility of Ownership in Jewish Law," in *Jewish Business Ethics: The Firm and Its Stakeholders*, ed. Aaron Levine and Moses L. Pava (Northvale, N.J.: Jason Aronson, 1999), forthcoming.

16. The prohibition of *hanuppah* is based on Numbers 35:32. See Sifrei ad loc.

17. R. Jonah b. Abraham Gerondi, *Sha'arei Teshuvah*, sha'ar 3, 187.

18. R. Eliezer b. Samuel, *Yere'im* 55.

19. *Sha'arei Teshuvah*, loc. cit.

20. Ibid. 3:189.

21. R. Joseph B. Soloveitchik, *The Lonely Man of Faith* (New York: Doubleday, 1965), pp. 16–20.

22. For the sages' view that a state of human dependency is deplorable, see Shabbat 118a, Eruvin 18b, Pesahim 113a, Bezah 32b, Bava Batra 110a.

23. R. Aryeh Loeb b. Joseph ha-Kohen Heller, *Kezot* at *Shulhan Arukh*, Hoshen Mishpat 32, n. 1.

24. See R. Yair Hayyim b. Mosheh Samson Bacharach (Germany, 1638–1702), *Responsa Havvot Yair* 166; R. Zevi Hirsch b. Jacob Ashkenazi (Germany, 1660–1718), *Responsa Hakham Zevi* 139.

25. Deuteronomy 13:7–12.

26. R. Jacob b. Joseph Reicher, *Responsa Shevut Yaakov* 3:168; R. Mosheh Feinstein, *Iggerot Mosheh*, Orah Hayyim 1:99. See, however, R. Meir Dan Plotzki (Poland, 1867–1928), *Klei Hemdah*, Re'eh, sec. 4.

27. Maimonides (Egypt, 1135–1204) *Yad*, Avodat Kokhavim 5:1–2, and R. Joseph Caro (Israel, 1488–1575), *Kesef Mishneh*, ad loc.

28. William B. Irvine, "The Ethics of Investing," *Journal of Business Ethics* 6 (1987): 233–42.

29. Robert Larmer, "The Ethics of Investing: A Reply to William Irvine," *Journal of Business Ethics* 16 (1997): 397–400.

30. Rabbi J. David Bleich, *Contemporary Halakhic Problems,* vol. 4 (New York: Ktav, 1995), pp. 92–104.

31. R. Abraham Bornstein, *Responsa Avnei Nezer*, Yoreh De'ah 1:126. Note that the prohibition of eating meat from an improperly slaughtered animal (*nebelah*) comes in two forms. In one the animal is a kosher species and the slaughtering is done in a *technically* improper manner. The second obtains when the animal at hand is a non-kosher species. Here, even if the slaughtering is done in a technically proper manner, the dead animal has the status of a *nebelah*. Hence eating the meat of a non-kosher species violates more prohibitions than eating the meat of an improperly slaughtered kosher animal.

32. R. Mosheh Sternbuch, *Teshuvot ve-Hanhagot* 1:358.

33. Bleich, *Contemporary Halakhic Problems*, p. 98.

34. Joshua Krausz and Moses L. Pava, *Social Responsibility and Financial Performance: The*

Paradox of Social Cost (Westport, Conn., Quorum Press, 1995).

35. *Yad*, Rozeah 12:12–14.

36. Please turn to p. 136 of this volume.

37. Vince Staten, *Can You Trust a Tomato in January?* (New York: Simon & Schuster, 1993), p. 216.

38. Philip Kotler and Gary Armstrong, *Principles of Marketing*, 6th ed. (Englewood Cliffs, N.J.: Prentice-Hall, 1994), pp. 278–79.

39. Please turn to p. 136 of this volume.

40. Cf. Sanhedrin 9b.

41. R. Solomon b. Abraham Adret, *Responsa Rashba* 2:231. See also R. Solomon b. Simon Duran (North Africa, ca. 1400–1467), *Responsa Rashbash* 532; R. Hayyim Joseph David Azulai (Israel, 1724–1806), *Birkei Yosef*, Hoshen Mishpat 34, n. 33; R. Joseph Saul ha-Levi Nathanson (Poland, 1810–1875), *Responsa Sho'el u-Meshiv*, 1, pt. 2, no. 136.

42. R. Israel Meir ha-Kohen Kagan, *Hafez Hayyim*, Hilkhot Issurei Rekhilut 9:4 and *Be'er Mayim Hayyim*, n. 12.

43. For a discussion of the prohibition against *lashon ha-ra*, please turn to pp. 282–84, 286–89, 294–96 of this volume.

GLOSSARY OF ECONOMIC AND LEGAL TERMS

ADVERSE SELECTION. The problem created by asymmetric information *before* a transaction occurs: the people who are the most undesirable from the other party's point of view are the ones who are most likely to want to engage in the transaction.

APPLIED RESEARCH. Activity directed toward the creation of new and improved practical products and processes.

ARBITRAGE. The act of buying a currency or other commodity in one market and simultaneously selling it in another market at a higher price. Arbitrage is an important force in eliminating the price discrepancy, thereby making markets function more efficiently.

ASKED PRICE. Stock market term indicating the lowest price that will be taken by the holder of a security.

ASSET. A physical property or intangible right that has economic value.

ASYMMETRIC INFORMATION. The unequal knowledge that each party to a transaction has about the other party.

BID PRICE. Stock market term indicating the highest price someone is willing to pay for an issue.

BASIC RESEARCH. Activity directed toward the discovery of facts and data observed in reproductive experiments. It also refers to the discovery of theories or relationships between facts.

CARTEL. An agreement, often in writing, among manufacturers, dealers, etc., to restrict output of prices or to divide territories.

COGNITIVE DISSONANCE. The theory that people modify their beliefs to cope with or even deny reality rather than accept and adjust to it.

CONGLOMERATE. A union of two unrelated firms, as when a defense contractor joins a firm that produces bananas.

CONSUL. Abbreviation for "consolidated annuities." Funded government securities or stock which the government need not repay until it wishes. An investor in consuls can, however, sell them at prices reflecting the yield on comparable securities.

CONSUMER PRICE INDEX (CPI). A measure of inflation based on a market basket of goods and services purchased by urban households.

DISEQUILIBRIUM PRICE. A price which is inherently unstable. At the disequilibrium price, supply exceeds demand or demand exceeds supply.

ECONOMIES OF SCALE. The reduction in unit cost as one producer makes larger quantities of a product. Such reduction results from a decreasing marginal cost due to increasing specialization, use of capital equipment, and the benefit of quantity purchasing.

EFFICIENCY. Achieving maximum output value from a given set of inputs, or achieving the desired output with minimum cost of inputs.

ELASTIC DEMAND. Market demand that is relatively responsive to changes in the price of the subject product. How the firm's total revenue changes in consequence of either an increase or a decrease in its pricing of the subject product provides a measure of this responsiveness. If a cut in price increases the number of units demanded so much that the firm's total revenue increases, or if an increase in price reduces the number of units demanded so much that the firm's total revenue decreases, the demand is characterized as "price-elastic."

EMPLOYEE-AT-WILL. An employee hired for an indefinite period of time without a formal contract.

EQUILIBRIUM PRICE. The market price that clears the market. At equilibrium, the number of units suppliers want to offer is equal to the number of units demanders want to buy. Given the stability of supply and demand influences other than the price of the subject product, market price will tend toward the equilibrium price.

FIDUCIARY. A person or firm acting in a capacity of responsibility for the handling of funds for other persons or firms.

FREE RIDER. Anyone who receives benefits from a good or service without having to pay for them.

HUMAN CAPITAL. Capital in the form of various investments a worker has made (e.g., education, experience, skill development) that augment his productivity.

INELASTIC DEMAND. Market demand that is relatively unresponsive to changes in the price of the subject product. If the firm's total revenue changes in the same direction as its pricing change, the demand it faces for its product is characterized as "inelastic."

LAISSEZ-FAIRE. The philosophy that embraces the notion that a market system operates most efficiently when government minimizes its activity in the economy. According to this philosophy, governments should provide national defense and police protection, specify property rights, and enforce contracts drawn up between economic agents - and little or nothing else.

MONOPOLY. An industry in which there is only one supplier of a product for which there are no close substitutes.

MUTUAL FUND. An open-end investment company that offers to sell an unlimited amount of its shares to obtain funds to invest in corporation stock, bonds, or money market instruments. The company redeems its shares on demand at a price that reflects the value of its asset holdings.

OPPORTUNITY COST. The value of the best alternative sacrificed when taking an action.

OPTIONS. A privilege sold by one party to another which offers the buyer the right to buy (call) or sell (put) a security at an agreed-upon price during a specified period or on a specified date.

PRIMARY FINANCIAL MARKET. Market involving the creation and issuance of new securities, mortgages, and other claims to wealth. It is the market for initial sales of securities.

PROGRESSIVE TAX. A tax whose rate rises as income increases. Thus those with high incomes pay a greater percentage of their incomes as tax than do those with lower incomes.

PURE PUBLIC GOOD. Commodity or service whose benefits are not depleted by an additional user and for which it is generally difficult or impossible to exclude people from its benefits, even if they are unwilling to pay for it.

SECONDARY FINANCIAL MARKET. Market involving the transfer of existing securities from old investors to new investors. It is the market for already issued securities.

SELLING SHORT. The act of selling a security that is not owned. Securities belonging to someone else are borrowed and sold. When the short-seller covers, equivalent securities are bought back and restored to the original owner.

SHIFT OF THE DEMAND CURVE. An increase or decrease in the number of units of a particular product demanded at any hypothetical price charged, compared to a previous period. The shift is due to a change in the influence of factors other than the price of the subject product, such as a change in income, wealth, tastes, or the price of a complementary product.

SITE VALUE. Real estate market value attributed *solely* to the property's favorable location, as opposed to improvements undertaken by the owner.

SPECIALIST. An exchange member who acts as a broker in the execution of orders, and as a dealer by transacting for his own account. He maintains an orderly market in the limited securities with which he is involved, facilitating execution of odd-lot transactions (stock trades of less than 100 shares).

TORT. A private or civil wrong or injury, not involving a breach of contract.

TORTFEASOR. One who commits or is guilty of tort.

TRANSACTION COSTS. The time costs and other costs required to carry out market exchange.

GLOSSARY OF HALAKHIC AND
THEOLOGICAL TERMS

ADAM HA-MAZIK. Bodily harm or property damage committed by man by direct physical action.

AMORA, AMORAIM, AMORAIC. Designation of scholars who were active in the period from the completion of the *Mishnah* (ca. 200 C.E.) until the completion of the Babylonian and Jerusalem Talmuds (end of the 4th and 5th cent. respectively).

ANAN SAHADEI. Lit. "we are witnesses." Something of which the court is as certain as though it witnessed it.

ASMAKHTA. An agreement that either lacks the presumption of firm resolve on the part of the obligator or fails to generate a presumption of reliance on the part of the party to whom the commitment was made.

AVAK LASHON HA-RA. Lit. the "dust" of *evil talk*. Refers to speech that is not in and of itself *evil talk* but it provokes the listener to engage in *evil talk*. Such speech is prohibited by dint of rabbinical, as opposed to, pentateuchal law.

AVAK RIBBIT. Lit. "the dust of interest." Violations of Jewish law's prohibition against interest by virtue of rabbinical, as opposed to, pentateuchal, decree.

BARAITA. A teaching or a tradition of the *Tannaim* that was excluded from the *Mishnah* and incorporated in a later collection compiled by R. Hiyya and R. Oshaiah.

BET DIN. Jewish court of law.

DARKHEI NO'AM. Lit. "ways of pleasantness." The goal of achieving harmonious interpersonal relations.

DARKHEI SHALOM. Lit. "the ways of peace." Refers to the duty to end discord. Toward this end, the use of untruths is, under certain conditions, permitted.

DAVAR HA-AVUD. Circumstance that worker would cause a loss to his employer if he would not give immediate attention to the job at hand.

DEI MAHSORO. Lit. "sufficient for his need." Judaism's charity obligation, consisting of the duty, means permitting, to provide for the entire needs of the poor, both physical and psychological.

DINA D'MALKHUTA DINA. The halakhic rule that for disputes between Jews in civil matters, the law of the country is binding.

GARMI. Indirect damage that should have been foreseeable.

GEMILUT HASADIM. Lit. "the bestowal of loving kindness." The duty that encompasses the whole range of the responsibilities of sympathetic consideration toward one's fellow man.

GEMIRAT DA'AT. A firm resolve to conclude an agreement at hand.

GERAMA. Indirect damage that is too remote to have been foreseeable.

GENEIVAT DA'AT. Conduct designed to deceive or create a false impression.

HA-A'NAKAH. The gratuity that the master was enjoined to pay his Hebrew bond servant when he sets him free.

HA'ARAMAT RIBBIT. An arrangement for a payment by the borrower to his lender that is designed to evade the prohibition against *ribbit.*

HADAS, HADASSIM. Myrtle branch(es). One of the elements prescribed for the *mizvah* of the "four species."

HAKKARAT HATOV. Gratitude.

HALAKHAH. Jewish law.

HAMEZ. Any product made of or containing one of the five grains which are forbidden on Passover.

HANUPPAH. Insincere praise of a fellow; or flattery of the wicked.

HASSAGAT GEVUL. Lit. "removal of boundary." Trespass on economic, commercial and incorporeal rights.

HAYEI NEFESH. Food that is essential.

HAZAKAH. Conduct presumed to continue because it has already occurred three times.

HETTER ISKA. An elaborate form of the *iska* business partnership wherein conditions are attached with the design of protecting the financier from absorbing a loss on his principal and increasing the probability that he will realize a profit as well. These clauses are structured in such a manner that *ribbit* law is not violated.

HEZEK RE'IYAH. Visual penetration of privacy.

HIN ZEDEK. Lit. "a just *hin*" (dry measure). Refers to the duty to make commitments in good faith.

HINNUKH. Religious training.

IMITATIO DEI. Latin for "imitation of God." Judaism's behavioral imperative consisting of man's duty to emulate God's attributes of mercy in his interpersonal conduct.

ISKA. A form of business partnership consisting of an active partner and a financier who is a silent partner. In the absence of stipulation, half the capital transfer takes on the legal character of a loan, while the remaining half takes on the character of a pledge. The *iska* arrangement may violate *ribbit* law and is therefore subject to regulation.

KABBELAN. A pieceworker hired to perform a specific task, with no provisions regarding fixed hours.

KINYAN SUDAR. A legal form of acquisition of objects or confirmation of agreements, executed by the handing of a scarf (or any other article) by one of the contracting parties (or one of the witnesses to the agreement) to the other contracting party as a symbol that the object itself has been transferred or the obligation assumed.

LASHON HA-RA. Talebearing wherein A delivers a damaging but truthful report regarding B to C, with C being neither the object of B's mischief nor the intended target of his evil designs.

LIFNEI IVER. Lit. "in front of a blind person." Refers to (1) the prohibition not to cause those who are morally blind to stumble by giving them the means or preparing the way for them to sin; and (2) The prohibition against offering someone ill-suited advice.

LIFNIM MI-SHURAT HA-DIN. Beyond the letter of the law.

MARIT AYIN. Concern for appearances of wrong doing.

MEISIT. Inducing or enticing someone to sin.

MEKAH TA'UT. Mistaken transaction.

MILVEH. Loan.

MINHAG. Custom.

MISHNAH. Compiled and codified by R. Judah ha-Nasi in 200 C.E. It contains the essence of the Oral law as it had been handed down from the time of the Bible.

MIZVAH. A religious duty or a religious act.

MOZI SHEM RA. The utterance or spreading of a false statement harmful to another's character or reputation.

NEBELAH. A carcass of an animal that was not slaughtered according to the procedure prescribed by Halakhah.

ONA'AH. Price fraud involving selling above or below the competitive norm.

'ONES. Unavoidable circumstances.

ONA'AT DEVARIM. Conduct causing needless mental anguish to others.

PIKKADON. An object deposited with a custodian for safekeeping.

PO'EL. Day-laborer required to work at fixed hours.

PO'EL BATEIL. Idle or unemployed worker.

PSEIDA D'LO HADRA. Irretrievable loss.

REKHILUT. Talebearing wherein A delivers a damaging but truthful report regarding B to C, and C is either the object of B's mischief or the intended target of his evil designs.

RIBBIT. Prohibition against interest.

RIBBIT KEZUZAH. Prearranged interest payment.

RISHON, RISHONIC, RISHONIM. Designation of scholars who were active in the period from the eleventh to the middle of the fifteenth century.

RODEF. Lit. "a pursuer." In Jewish law, should an individual pursue another with the manifest intent to kill him, everybody is under a duty to rescue the victim, even by killing the pursuer, if no other means are available to induce the would-be murderer to desist. This general rule has been extended to cover the killing of a fetus endangering the life of the mother and the killing of a rapist caught before completion of his offense.

SANHEDRIN. Assembly of ordained scholars that functioned both as Supreme Court and Legislature before 70 C.E.

SEKHAR HITPASHRUT. Agreed-to sum of money.

SEKHAR TIRHAH. Remuneration for toil and effort.

SEKHAR SHABBAT. Compensation for work performed on the *Shabbat*.

SEMIKHAT DA'AT. Mental reliance. Without the presumption of mental reliance on the part of the principals to an agreement, the transaction lacks legal validity in Jewish law.

SHEKER. Falsehood.

SHELIHUT YAD. Misappropriation.

SHEVUAH HAMURAH. A severe oath, i.e., an oath imposed on an individual by dint of pentateuchal, as opposed to, rabbinic law. In cases requiring the pentateuchal oath, the deponent holds the Scroll of the Torah in his hand and swears by God. Before administering the oath, the court warns the deponent of the gravity of the oath and the inescapibility of Divine punishment for any false oath. In cases involving an oath administered by dint of rabbinic law, the former feature is absent and the latter is not required.

SHOFAR. Ram's horn sounded for memorial blowing on *Rosh Ha-Shanah* and other occasions.

SHOHAD. Bribery.

SODOMITIC. Exhibiting the character trait of a citizen of Sodom, i.e., denying a neighbor a benefit or privilege that involves no cost to oneself.

SOTAH. A woman whose behavior has established her as a suspected adulteress.

TALMID HAKHAM. Lit. "disciple of the wise." Scholar, student of the Torah.

TALMUD. The record of the discussions of scholars on the laws and teachings of the *Mishnah*. The Babylonian Talmud was codified ca. 500 C.E., the Palestinian Talmud ca. 400 C.E.

TANNA, TANNAIC, TANNAIM. Designation of scholars active in the period from the beginning of the common era up to 200 C.E. The period of the *Tannaim* spans six generations of scholars from Gamliel the Elder and his contemporaries to Judah ha-Nasi (the redactor of the *Mishnah*).

TENAI KAFUL. Lit. "double condition." A technicality of Jewish contract law that makes a conditional clause unenforceable unless the stipulations expressly spell out the consequences of both fulfillment and non fulfillment of the clause.

TOKHAHAH. Reproof.

TOSAFOT. Twelfth to fourteenth century French commentators of the Talmud.

TREFA. A person, animal or bird that has a flaw in one of its organs that will cause its death within twelve months.

UMDANA. Inferential fact finding.

YEZER HA-RA. Evil inclination in a person.

YOHARA. False religious pride.

ZUZ. A coin of the value of a *denarius*, six *ma'ah*, or twelve *dupondia*.

SUBJECT INDEX

NAME INDEX